The Old Meeting-house, Walpole, Suffolk.

An Inventory of

Nonconformist CHAPELS

and

MEETING-HOUSES

in Eastern England

Christopher Stell

Published by English Heritage at the National Monuments Record Centre, Great Western Village, Kemble Drive, Swindon SN2 2GZ

ISBN 1 873592 50 7
Product Code 50208

© English Heritage 2002

All illustrations (unless otherwise specified) are either © Crown copyright. NMR or © C.F. Stell.
Applications for the reproduction of illustrations, in the first instance, should be made to the National Monuments Record.

Crown copyright material is reproduced under licence from the Controller of Her Majesty's Stationery Office.

The Royal Commission on the Historical Monuments of England and English Heritage merged on 1 April 1999.

British Library Cataloguing in Publication Data
A CIP catalogue record for this book is available from the British Library.

All rights reserved
No part of this publication may be reproduced or transmitted in any form or by any means, electronic or mechanical, including photocopying, recording or any information storage and retrieval system without permission in writing from the publisher.

Brought to publication by Rachel Howard, René Rodgers and Robin Taylor, English Heritage
Edited by Susan Whimster
Page production by George Hammond
Indexed by Ann Hudson
Printed in England by Arkle Print Ltd

CONTENTS

	page
LIST OF ILLUSTRATIONS	vii
LIST OF PRINCIPAL MONUMENTS RECOMMENDED by the Royal Commission on the Historical Monuments of England as most worthy of preservation	xv
ACKNOWLEDGEMENTS	xvii
EDITORIAL NOTES and county boundary changes	xviii
PREFACE	xix
MAP showing county boundaries	xx
INVENTORY	
BEDFORDSHIRE	1
CAMBRIDGESHIRE AND THE ISLE OF ELY	26
ESSEX	47
GREATER LONDON	68
HERTFORDSHIRE	127
HUNTINGDON AND PETERBOROUGH	149
KENT	161
LINCOLNSHIRE	194
NORFOLK	229
SUFFOLK	278
SURREY	315
SUSSEX	329
ABBREVIATIONS and BIBLIOGRAPHICAL SOURCES	360
INDEX	363

LIST OF ILLUSTRATIONS

(illustrations are exterior photographs unless otherwise stated)

page

Map showing county boundaries — xx

BEDFORDSHIRE

- (2) Ampthill. Former Friends' meeting-house. Plan. — 2
- (8) Bedford. Bunyan Meeting-house. N front. — 3
- (9) Bedford. Howard Chapel. — 3
- (15) Blunham. Old Meeting-house. Sketch. — 4
- (17) Bolnhurst and Keysoe. Brook End Chapel.
    - Plan, sections and elevation. — 5
    - Exterior. — 6
    - Interior. — 6
- (18) Bolnhurst and Keysoe. Baptist chapel, Keysoe Row.
    - Plan and section. — 7
    - Exterior. — 7
- (20) Carlton and Chellington. Strict Baptist meeting-house, Carlton. Plan. — 8
    - Exterior. — 7
    - Interior. — 8
- (22) Clifton. Strict Baptist chapel. Exterior. — 9
    - Interior. — 9
- (23) Colmworth. Primitive Methodist chapel. Sketch. — 10
- (30) Eastcotts. Cotton End Chapel. — 10
- (35) Felmersham. Former Wesleyan chapel, Radwell. Sketch. — 11
- (39) Hockliffe. Hockliffe Chapel. Sketch. — 12
- (42) Houghton Regis. Baptist chapel. — 12
- (47) Leighton-Linslade. Friends' meeting-house, Leighton Buzzard. Plan. — 13
- (49) Luton. Union Chapel. — 14
- (51) Luton. Ebenezer Chapel. — 14
- (53) Luton. Congregational chapel, Stuart Street. — 15
- (65) Pertenhall. Former Moravian chapel. Plan. — 16
    - Exterior. — 16
    - Interior. — 17
- (67) Potton. The Old Meeting-house. — 18
- (73) Roxton. Roxton Chapel. Plan. — 19
    - Exterior. — 20
- (74) Sharnbrook. Former Strict Baptist chapel. — 20
- (81) Southill. Southill Chapel. Plan. — 22
    - Exterior. — 21
    - Interior. — 21
- (83) Stevington. Baptist meeting-house, West End.
    - Plan. — 23
    - Exterior. — 22
    - Interior. — 23
    - Clock. — 24
- (98) Wilshamstead. Wesleyan chapel. — 25

page

CAMBRIDGESHIRE and ISLE OF ELY

- (1) Barrington. Congregational chapel. — 27
- (2) Bassingbourn. Former Congregational chapel.
    - Plan. — 27
    - Exterior. — 28
- (7) Burwell. Former Congregational chapel.
    - Front. — 28
    - Rear. — 28
- (16) Cambridge. Emmanuel Church. — 30
- (20) Caxton, Baptist chapel. Sketch. — 31
- (23) Chatteris. Congregational chapel. — 32
- (33) Duxford. Congregational chapel. Restored front. — 33
- (34) Elsworth. Providence Chapel. Sketch. — 33
- (40) Fowlmere. Congregational chapel. — 34
- (42) Gamlingay. Baptist chapel (Old Meeting-house).
    - Plan. — 34
    - Exterior before *c*.1881. — 35
- (56) Isleham. Zoar Chapel. In 1953. — 36
- (58) Kingston. Congregational chapel. — 36
- (60) Linton. Congregational chapel. Exterior. — 37
    - Painting of former chapel. — 38
- (66) March. Congregational chapel. — 39
- (68) Melbourn. Old Meeting-house (Independent). Plan. — 39
    - Exterior. — 40
- (76) Soham. Baptist chapel. — 41
- (77) Soham. Congregational chapel. — 41
- (83) Swaffham Prior. Zoar Chapel. — 42
- (84) Swaffham Prior. Zion Chapel. — 42
- (97) Whittlesey. Zion Chapel. — 43
- (101) Wicken. Former Primitive Methodist chapel. Sketch. — 44
- (102) Willingham. The Old Baptist Chapel. Plan. — 44
    - Exterior. — 45
    - Interior. — 45
- (104) Willingham. Wesleyan chapel. — 46
- (107) Wisbech. Congregational chapel, Castle Square. Sketch. — 46

ESSEX

- (1) Abbess Beauchamp and Berners Roding. Former meeting-house, Abbess Roding.
    - Painting of front. — 48
- (9) Braintree and Bocking. Congregational chapel, Bocking End, Braintree.
    - Painting of exterior before 1818. — 49
    - Painting of exterior after 1818. — 49
- (17) Chelmsford. Former Friends' meeting-house. — 50

(27)	Colchester. Congregational chapel, Lion Walk. Exterior.	52	(42)	Camden. Former Wesleyan chapel, Prince of Wales Road.	79

(27) Colchester. Congregational chapel, Lion Walk.
  Exterior. 52
  Former Octagon Chapel. Side view and interior of model. 52
(28) Colchester. Former Congregational chapel, East Stockwell Street. 52
(33) Earls Colne. Friends' meeting-house. Section. 53
(39) Felsted. Former Friends' meeting-house, Bannister Green. 54
(40) Finchingfield. Congregational chapel. Sketch. 54
(41) Fordham. Former Countess of Huntingdon's chapel.
  Plan. 55
  Exterior. 55
(46) Great Bardfield. Friends' meeting-house. Sketch. 56
(61) Harlow. Baptist chapel, Potter Street. Plan. 57
  Exterior. 57
(70) Langham. Former Baptist chapel. Sketch. 58
(72) Layer Breton. Friends' meeting-house. 59
(73) Little Baddow. Congregational chapel. Plan. 59
  Exterior. 58
(81) Manningtree. Former Congregational chapel. 60
(82) Manningtree. Wesleyan chapel. 60
(88) Saffron Walden. Former General Baptist chapel.
  First chapel. 61
  Second chapel. 61
(91) Saffron Walden. Former Congregational chapel.
  Painting of former chapel, 1694. 62
(93) Southend-on-Sea. Congregational chapel, Nelson Street. 63
(99) Stebbing. Former Friends' meeting-house. Plan. 63
  Front. 64
  Sketch of date tablet. 63
(102) Terling. Congregational chapel. Plan. 65
  Front. 65
(104) Thaxted. Baptist chapel, Park Street. 66
(111) Tillingham. Peculiar People's chapel, South Street. 66
(119) Witham. Congregational chapel. 67
(121) Wivenhoe. Former Congregational chapel. 67

GREATER LONDON
(2) Barking. Baptist Tabernacle. 70
(9) Barnet. 'Free Church', Hampstead Garden Suburb. 70
(12) Barnet. Congregational chapel, Hendon. 71
(14) Barnet. Baptist chapel, Station Road, New Barnet. Sketch. 71
(22) Bexley. Trinity Chapel, Bexleyheath. 72
(25) Brent. Baptist chapel, Carlton Vale. 72
(27) Bromley. Congregational chapel, Penge.
  Exterior. 73
  Interior. 73
(29) Bromley. Former New Church, Anerley. 74
(31) Camden. Bloomsbury Baptist Chapel. Before 1913. 75
(35) Camden. Catholic Apostolic church, Gordon Square. 76
(36) Camden. Baptist chapel, Heath Street, Hampstead. 77
(39) Camden. Rosslyn Hill Chapel, Hampstead. 78
(41) Camden. Former Wesleyan chapel, Lady Margaret Road. 78

(42) Camden. Former Wesleyan chapel, Prince of Wales Road. 79
(45) Camden. Former West Street Chapel, Seven Dials. Sketch. 79
(47) Croydon. Strict Baptist chapel, Tamworth Road. 79
(59) Ealing. Baptist chapel, Castlebar Road, Haven Green. 80
(65) Enfield. Baker Street Chapel. 81
(66) Enfield. Congregational chapel, Chase Side. 81
(69) Enfield. Friends' meeting-house, Winchmore Hill. 82
(74) Greenwich. Former Congregational chapel, Greenwich Road. 82
(76) Greenwich. Former Wesleyan chapel, Calderwood Street, Woolwich. 83
(79) Hackney. Congregational chapel, Lower Clapton Road. Exterior. 83
  Interior. 84
(90) Hackney. Newington Green Meeting-house.
  Plan, 1859. 85
  Plan, 1970. 86
  Exterior before 1860. 86
  Exterior in 1945. 86
(91) Hackney. 'The Ark of the Covenant', Rookwood Road. 87
(105) Haringey. Former meeting-house, Southwood Lane, Highgate. Sketch. 89
(106) Haringey. Baptist chapel, Tottenham High Road. 89
(118) Haringey. Former Wesleyan 'Trinity Chapel', Wood Green. 90
(124) Harrow. Former Wesleyan chapel, Roxeth. 91
(127) Havering. Upminster Old Chapel. Sketch. 91
(132) Hillingdon. The Old Meeting-house, Uxbridge. Sketch. 92
(133) Hillingdon. Providence Chapel, Uxbridge. 93
(137) Hounslow. Congregational chapel, Boston Manor Road. In 1945. 94
(138) Hounslow. Congregational chapel, Hanworth Road. 94
(139) Hounslow. Friends' meeting-house, Quakers' Lane, Isleworth. Plan. 95
  Exterior. 95
(150) Islington. Former Congregational chapel, Upper Street. 96
(151) Islington. Union Chapel. Exterior. 98
  Interior. 97
(152) Islington. Former Congregational chapel, Offord Road. 98
(154) Islington. Woodbridge Chapel, Clerkenwell. Sketch. 99
(156) Islington. Former Northampton Tabernacle, Amwell Street. 99
(157) Islington. Wesley's Chapel, City Road. Exterior. 101
  Interior. 100
(162) Islington. Former New Church, Camden Road. 101
(171) Kensington and Chelsea. First Church of Christ Scientist, Sloane Terrace. 102
(174) Kensington and Chelsea. Moravian chapel, King's Road. 103

(181) Kingston upon Thames. Friends' meeting-house.
 Sketch. 105
(188) Lambeth. Trinity Chapel, Brixton. 105
(189) Lambeth. Christ Church, Westminster Bridge Road.
 Exterior. 107
 Interior before rebuilding. 106
(190) Lambeth. Stockwell New Chapel. Plan (after plans
 by John Ashdown, 1953–5). 108
(195) Lewisham. General Baptist meeting-house,
 Deptford Church Street.
 Plan, section and elevations. 109
(198) Lewisham. Presbyterian chapel, Brockley Road. 110
(206) Newham. Unitarian chapel, West Ham Lane. 111
(213) Richmond upon Thames. Bethlehem Chapel,
 Richmond. 112
(214) Richmond upon Thames. Congregational chapel,
 The Vineyard, Richmond. 112
(217) Southwark. Grove Chapel, Camberwell Grove. 113
(222) Southwark. Baptist chapel, Rye Lane, Peckham. 113
(223) Southwark. Metropolitan Tabernacle, Newington
 Butts. In 1911. 114
(225) Southwark. Former Unitarian chapel, Stamford
 Street. 115
(233) Tower Hamlets. Former Huguenot chapel,
 Fournier Street. 116
(239) Tower Hamlets. Former Presbyterian chapel,
 West Ferry Road. 117
(241) Tower Hamlets. St George's German Lutheran
 Church, Alie Street. 118
(249) Wandsworth. Friends' meeting-house, Wandsworth
 High Street. 119
(253) City of Westminster. Welsh Baptist chapel,
 Eastcastle Street. 120
(255) City of Westminster. Catholic Apostolic church,
 Maida Avenue. 121
(259) City of Westminster. Portland Chapel, St John's
 Wood Terrace. 122
(260) City of Westminster. Westminster Chapel,
 Buckingham Gate. Exterior before rebuilding
 of tower. 122
 Interior. 123
(261) City of Westminster. Former King's Weigh House
 Chapel, Duke Street. 124
(262) City of Westminster. Wesleyan chapel, Hinde Street. 125

HERTFORDSHIRE

(3) Aldbury. Baptist chapel. Sketch. 128
(9) Baldock. Former Friends' meeting-house. 128
(10) Baldock. Wesleyan chapel. Exterior. 129
 Interior. 129
(13) Berkhamsted Urban. General Baptist chapel,
 Berkhamsted. 129
(15) Bishop's Stortford. Congregational chapel, Exterior. 130
 Interior. 130
(18) Buntingford. Congregational chapel. 131
(21) Chorleywood. Baptist chapel, Hillside Road. 132
(22) Chorleywood. Former Primitive Methodist chapel. 132
(31) Hemel Hempstead. Box Lane Chapel, Boxmoor.
 Plan, sections and elevation. 134
 Interior. 135
(34) Hemel Hempstead. Salem Chapel, Two Waters.
 Sketch. 136
(35) Hemel Hempstead. Friends' meeting-house. Plan. 136
(37) Hertford. Congregational chapel, Cowbridge. 136
(38) Hertford. Friends' meeting-house. Plan and section. 138
 N front. 137
 Interior from SW. 137
(39) Hitchin. Baptist chapel, Tilehouse Street. 139
(45) Hoddesdon. Friends' meeting-house. 140
(48) Kings Langley. Zion Chapel. Sketch. 140
(49) King's Walden. Baptist chapel, Breachwood Green. 140
(60) Royston. Former Unitarian chapel, Upper King
 Street. 142
(61) St Albans. The Old Meeting-house, Lower Dagnall
 Street. Plan. 142
 Exterior in late 19th century. 142
 Exterior in 1994. 142
(62) St Albans. Baptist chapel, Upper Dagnall Street. 143
(64) St Albans. Independent Chapel, Spicer Street.
 Elevation. 144
(74) Tring Urban. Former General Baptist chapel,
 Frogmore Street, Tring. Sketch. 145
(76) Tring Urban. Strict Baptist chapel, Akeman Street. 145
(78) Tring Urban. Baptist chapel, New Mill. Painting. 146
(80) Ware. Old Independent Chapel, Church Street. 146
(81) Ware. Congregational chapel, High Street. 147
(85) Watford. 'Beechen Grove' Baptist chapel,
 Clarendon Road. 148

HUNTINGDON AND PETERBOROUGH

(2) Bluntisham. Former meeting-house. Painting. 150
(7) Earith. Former Wesleyan chapel. Sketch. 150
(8) Eaton Socon. Former Wesleyan chapel. 151
(13) Great Gidding. Particular Baptist chapel. Plan. 151
 S front. 152
 Interior before removal of fittings. 152
(16) Great Gransden. Providence Chapel. Plan. 153
 Exterior. 153
(18) Hail Weston. Former Baptist chapel. Plan. 154
 Interior. 154
(20) Houghton and Wyton. Houghton Chapel. 155
(24) Kimbolton. Former Moravian chapel. 155
(28) Peterborough. Former Congregational chapel,
 Priestgate. 156
(31) Peterborough. Wesleyan Methodist chapel,
 Werrington. Elevation. 156
(40) St Ives. Congregational 'Free Church'. Exterior
 with statue to Oliver Cromwell. 157
(41) St Ives. Former Friends' meeting-house. Plan and
 elevation. 158
(48) Somersham. Wesleyan chapel. 159
(49) Spaldwick. Union Chapel. 159
(51) Stilton. Former Wesleyan chapel. Sketch. 160
(60) Yelling. Baptist chapel. 160

KENT

(5)	Ashford. Congregational chapel.	162
(9)	Biddenden. Strict Baptist chapel, Bounds Cross. Sketch.	163
(12)	Boughton under Blean. Wesleyan chapel, Boughton Street.	163
(15)	Bredgar. Former Wesleyan chapel, Silver Street.	164
(18)	Broadstairs. St Mary's Chapel.	164
(24)	Canterbury. Strict Baptist chapel, Burgate Lane.	165
(26)	Canterbury. Wesleyan chapel, St Peter's Street.	
	Exterior.	166
	Interior (1942).	166
(28)	Chevening. General Baptist chapel, Bessels Green.	167
(29)	Chevening. Particular Baptist chapel, Bessels Green. Sketch.	168
(32)	Cranbrook. Former General Baptist chapel, High Street. From lithograph.	169
(33)	Cranbrook. Strict Baptist chapel, St David's Bridge.	169
(34)	Cranbrook. Providence Chapel, Stone Street.	
	Plan.	171
	Exterior.	170
(36)	Dartford. Zion Chapel. Sketch.	171
(37)	Dartford. Wesleyan chapel, Spital Street.	171
(38)	Deal. Former General Baptist chapel, High Street.	172
(42)	Dover. Adrian Street Chapel. Plan.	174
	Exterior.	173
	Interior.	173
(58)	Faversham. Wesleyan chapel, Preston Street.	176
(60)	Folkestone. Baptist chapel, St Michael's Street. Sketch.	176
(61)	Folkestone. Salem Chapel, Rendezvous Street.	176
(65)	Frittenden. Providence Chapel, Pound Hill.	177
(71)	Hartlip. Bible Christian chapel.	178
(72)	Hawkhurst. Baptist meeting-house.	178
(75)	Headcorn. General Baptist chapel.	179
(79)	Hernhill. Wesleyan chapel, Dargate. Sketch.	179
(88)	Maidstone. Earl Street Chapel. Plan.	180
	Exterior.	181
(97)	Margate. Wesleyan chapel, Birchington.	182
(101)	Ramsgate. Baptist chapel, Cavendish Street.	
	Exterior.	183
	Pulpit.	183
(105)	Rochester. Friends' meeting-house. Sketch.	184
(107)	Royal Tunbridge Wells. Former Presbyterian chapel, Little Mount Sion.	184
(109)	Royal Tunbridge Wells. Rehoboth Chapel, Chapel Place.	185
(110)	Royal Tunbridge Wells. Former Congregational chapel, Mount Pleasant Road.	185
(117)	Sandwich. The Old Meeting-house, Cornmarket.	186
(122)	Sheerness. Bethel Chapel, Bluetown.	187
(125)	Sittingbourne and Milton. Congregational chapel, Milton Regis.	188
(131)	Snodland. New Jerusalem Church.	188
(134)	Stone-cum-Ebony. Ebenezer Chapel, Stone.	189
(140)	Tenterden. The Old Meeting-house. Plan.	190
	Exterior.	191
	Interior.	191
(146)	Whitstable. Former Congregational chapel.	192
(150)	Wingham. Former Congregational chapel.	193

LINCOLNSHIRE

(4)	Alford. Wesleyan chapel, West Street.	195
(5)	Alkborough. Wesleyan chapel.	195
(13)	Bardney. Wesleyan chapel, Bardney Dairies.	196
(19)	Barrow upon Humber. Former Congregational chapel, Lords Lane.	196
(21)	Barton-upon-Humber. Former Congregational chapel, Chapel Street.	197
(28)	Bicker. Former Wesleyan chapel. Sketch.	197
(39)	Boston. Former Congregational chapel, Grove Street.	198
(43)	Boston. Former Universalist meeting-house, Chapel Row.	198
(44)	Boston. Spain Lane Chapel. Elevation.	199
	Gallery staircase.	199
(45)	Bourne. General Baptist chapel, West Street.	200
(46)	Bourne. Wesleyan chapel, Abbey Road.	200
(47)	Bourne. Baptist chapel, Dyke.	200
(49)	Brant Broughton and Stragglethorpe. Friends' meeting-house, Brant Broughton. Plan.	201
	Exterior.	201
(57)	Caistor. Former Congregational chapel.	202
(60)	Carrington. Wesleyan chapel, New Bolingbroke.	202
(66)	Cleethorpes. Primitive Methodist chapel, Grimsby Road.	203
(71)	Conisholme. Free Methodist chapel. Sketch.	203
(73)	Crowle. General Baptist chapel.	203
(86)	Epworth. Wesleyan chapel.	204
(92)	Friskney. Wesleyan chapel.	205
(93)	Friskney. Wesleyan chapel, Friskney Fen. Sketch.	205
(98)	Gainsborough. Friends' meeting-house. Rear.	206
(99)	Gainsborough. Former Methodist chapel, Little Church Lane.	206
(101)	Gedney. Former Friends' meeting-house. Sketch.	207
(104)	Glanford Brigg. Former Wesleyan chapel, Brigg.	207
(121)	Great Steeping. General Baptist meeting-house, Monksthorpe. Plan.	209
	Exterior.	209
	Monument to Joseph Harpam.	209
(124)	Haconby. 'Baptist and Primitive Methodist' chapel.	
	Exterior.	210
	Interior.	210
(135)	Heapham. Wesleyan chapel, Common Lane.	211
(148)	Horncastle. Former Baptist chapel.	212
(159)	Kirkstead. Abbey Chapel. Plan.	213
(170)	Lincoln. Friends' meeting-house, Park Street.	
	Plan.	215
	Drawing of interior in 1855, facing stand.	214
	Drawing of interior in 1855, facing gallery.	215
(177)	Louth. Wesleyan chapel, Eastgate.	216

(180)	Maltby le Marsh. Former General Baptist chapel. Sketch	217	(90)	Great Yarmouth. Former Congregational chapel, King Street.	243
	Interior.	217	(94)	Great Yarmouth. Primitive Methodist Temple, Priory Plain.	244
(184)	Market Rasen. Wesleyan chapel.	218	(96)	Guestwick. Guestwick Chapel.	
(189)	Messingham. Wesleyan chapel.	218		Plan, sections and elevation.	247
(194)	Moulton. Primitive Methodist chapel, Moulton Seas End.	218		Exterior.	245
				Interior.	245
(200)	North Scarle. Former Wesleyan chapel.	219	(109)	Holt. Free Methodist chapel.	246
(211)	Raithby. Methodist chapel.		(115)	Kenninghall. Former Baptist chapel.	248
	Exterior from stable yard.	221	(117)	King's Lynn. Stepney Chapel, Blackfriars Street.	249
	Upper doorway to chapel.	221	(119)	King's Lynn. Salem Chapel.	249
	Interior.	221	(120)	King's Lynn. Former Friends' meeting-house.	250
(217)	Sibsey. Primitive Methodist chapel, Northlands. Sketch.	220	(121)	King's Lynn. Primitive Methodist chapel, London Road.	250
(222)	Sleaford. Congregational chapel.	222	(124)	Little Snoring. Primitive Methodist chapel. Sketch.	250
(229)	South Killingholme. General Baptist chapel.	222	(125)	Little Walsingham. Wesleyan chapel.	251
(233)	Spalding. Friends' meeting-house.	223	(127)	Loddon. Wesleyan chapel.	251
(236)	Spilsby. Wesleyan chapel and manses.	224	(129)	Long Stratton. Congregational chapel.	252
(240)	Stamford. Former Wesleyan chapel, Barn Hill.	225	(130)	Long Stratton. Wesleyan chapel. Sketch.	252
(245)	Sutterton. Former General Baptist chapel.	225	(133)	Mattishall. Former Congregational meeting-house.	252
(254)	Tealby. Wesleyan chapel.	226	(134)	Mattishall. Congregational chapel. Monument to John Glover.	253
(268)	Wainfleet All Saints. Primitive Methodist chapel, Wainfleet Bank.	227	(135)	Mattishall. Former Friends' meeting-house.	253
(275)	Welton. Wesleyan chapel. Sketch.	227	(146)	North Lopham. Wesleyan chapel.	254
(285)	Woodhall Spa. Presbyterian chapel (Unitarian).	228	(149)	North Walsham. Friends' meeting-house. Plan.	255
				Exterior.	255
NORFOLK				Gallery seating.	256
(6)	Aylsham. Wesleyan Reform chapel.	230	(152)	Norwich. The Old Meeting-house. Plan.	258
(7)	Bacton. Baptist chapel. Sketch.	230		Exterior.	257
(13)	Beetley. Primitive Methodist chapel. Sketch.	231		Interior.	257
(19)	Briston. Independent chapel. Elevation.	231	(157)	Norwich. Friends' meeting-house, Upper Goat Lane.	259
(22)	Brooke. Baptist chapel, High Green.	232	(158)	Norwich. Friends' meeting-house, Gildencroft.	260
(27)	Buxton with Lammas. Former Friends' meeting-house. Elevation.	233	(159)	Norwich. The Octagon Chapel, Colegate. Plan.	260
(28)	Caister-on-Sea. Primitive Methodist chapel.	233		Exterior.	261
(29)	Carleton Rode. Baptist chapel.	233		Interior.	261
(34)	Claxton. Former Baptist chapel. Plan.	234	(167)	Oulton. Oulton Chapel.	
	Exterior	234		Plan, sections and elevation.	265
(41)	Cromer. Baptist meeting-house.	235		Exterior. Before restoration.	263
(42)	Denton. Congregational chapel.	237		Interior. Before restoration.	263
(46)	Diss. Former Park Fields Chapel, Park Road.	237	(168)	Overstrand. Wesleyan chapel.	264
(47)	Diss. Baptist chapel, Denmark Street.	236	(177)	Salhouse. Baptist chapel. Sketch.	266
(49)	Diss. Friends' meeting-house, Frenze Road.	236	(181)	Shelfanger. Former Baptist chapel.	266
(55)	Downham Market. Former Friends' meeting-house. Sketch.	238	(186)	Smallburgh. Former General Baptist chapel.	267
(60)	East Dereham. Former Congregational chapel, London Road.	238	(189)	South Creake. Former Independent chapel. From SE.	267
(63)	East Rudham. Former Primitive Methodist chapel.	239	(192)	South Lopham. Former Baptist chapel. Sketch.	268
(68)	Filby. Filby Chapel. Plan.	240	(202)	Swaffham. Wesleyan chapel.	269
(71)	Fleggburgh. Wesleyan chapel, Burgh St Margaret. Sketch.	240	(209)	Tharston. Hapton Chapel.	
(72)	Forncett. The Tabernacle. Plan and elevation.	240		Plan, sections and elevation.	271
(73)	Foulsham. Baptist chapel.	241		Exterior.	270
(81)	Gissing. Wesleyan chapel. Sketch.	241		Interior.	270
(89)	Great Yarmouth. Former Congregational chapel, Middlegate Street. Exterior.	242		Back wall (1967).	272
	Interior.	242	(214)	Thornham. Wesleyan chapel.	273

(217)	Tivetshall St Margaret. Friends' meeting-house. Elevation.	273	(131)	St Andrew, Ilketshall. Wesleyan chapel, Ilketshall St Andrew. Sketch.	305
(219)	Upwell. Baptist chapel.	274	(133)	Somersham. Strict Baptist chapel.	305
(225)	Wells-next-the-Sea. Former Wesleyan chapel.	274	(135)	Southwold. Former Wesleyan chapel, Mill Lane. Elevation.	305
(235)	Worstead. Baptist chapel, Meeting-house Hill.	275	(138)	Stoke Ash. Strict Baptist chapel.	306
(236)	Wortwell. Former Baptist chapel, Low Street.	276	(142)	Stradbroke. Baptist chapel.	306

SUFFOLK

(1)	Aldeburgh. Union Chapel. Sketch.	279	(143)	Sudbury. Baptist chapel.	307
(2)	Badingham. Badingham Chapel.	279	(149)	Walpole. The Old Meeting-house. Plan	309
(13)	Blythburgh. Primitive Methodist chapel.	280		Exterior, from east.	308
(23)	Bungay. Congregational chapel.	281		Pulpit.	308
(25)	Bury St Edmunds. Churchgate Street Chapel. Plan	283		NE end.	308
	Exterior. Before restoration.	282		Interior.	Frontispiece
	Interior. Before restoration.	282	(157)	Whepstead. Former Independent chapel.	310
(30)	Bury St Edmunds. Friends' meeting-house. Plan.	284	(158)	Wickhambrook. Congregational chapel.	311
	Exterior.	284	(166)	Woodbridge. Former Friends' meeting-house. Plan and sections.	312
(34)	Charsfield. Baptist chapel.	285		Exterior.	313
(39)	Cowlinge. Congregational chapel. Sketch.	285		Stairs to stand.	313
(44)	East Bergholt. Congregational chapel.	286	(168)	Wrentham. Congregational chapel. Plan.	314
(48)	Framlingham. The Old Meeting-house. Exterior.	287		Exterior.	313
	Dove above pulpit. Sketch.	287	(171)	Yoxford. Former Primitive Methodist chapel. Sketch.	314
(51)	Fressingfield. Strict Baptist chapel. Plan.	288			
	Exterior.	287			

SURREY

(52)	Friston. Strict Baptist chapel.	288	(1)	Albury. The Apostles' Chapel. Plan.	318
(55)	Great Finborough. Congregational chapel. Sketch.	289		Exterior.	316
(58)	Hadleigh. Baptist chapel.	289		Interior.	317
(62)	Halesworth. Congregational chapel.	290	(3)	Burstow. Baptist chapel, Outwood Common. Sketch.	319
(66)	Haverhill. Strict Baptist chapel, Camps Road.	291	(4)	Burstow. Strict Baptist chapel, Smallfield. Grave-boards.	319
(67)	Haverhill. The Old Independent Chapel, Hamlet Road.	292	(5)	Capel. Friends' meeting-house. Plan.	320
(73)	Horham. Strict Baptist chapel.	291	(6)	Charlwood. Providence Chapel.	320
(75)	Hundon. Congregational chapel. Sketch.	294	(10)	Dorking. Congregational chapel. Plan and elevation of 1719 meeting-house.	321
(76)	Ipswich. St Nicholas Street Meeting-house. Plan.	295	(17)	Epsom. 'Bugby's Chapel', Prospect Place.	322
	N front.	293	(19)	Esher. Friends' meeting-house.	322
	Interior.	293	(24)	Godalming. General Baptist chapel, Meadrow.	323
(78)	Ipswich. Former General Baptist chapel, St George's Street.	296	(27)	Godalming. Friends' meeting-house, Mill Lane. Plan.	324
(81)	Ipswich. 'Bethesda Chapel', Crown Street.	296		Exterior.	324
(82)	Ipswich. Brethren Meeting-room, High Street.	296	(31)	Guildford. Friends' meeting-house, Ward Street.	325
(83)	Ipswich. Former Congregational chapel, St Nicholas Street.	297	(33)	Haslemere. Congregational chapel.	325
(89)	Ipswich. Former Presbyterian chapel, Portman Road.	297	(34)	Hindhead and Churt. Congregational chapel, Hindhead.	325
(95)	Laxfield. Strict Baptist chapel.	298	(36)	Horley. Former General Baptist chapel, Horley Row.	326
(98)	Long Melford. Congregational chapel.	299	(52)	Stanwell. Congregational chapel, Poyle. Sketch.	327
(99)	Lowestoft. Congregational chapel, London Road North.	299	(53)	Tilford. Former chapel, Tilford House. Plan.	327
(104)	Melton. Former Primitive Methodist chapel. Relocation of chapel, 18 September 1861.	300		Exterior.	328
(111)	Mildenhall. Wesleyan chapel, High Street.	301	(54)	Weybridge. Congregational chapel, Queens Road	328
(127)	Rendham. Former Congregational chapel. Exterior.	303			

SUSSEX

	Interior.	303	(6)	Battle. Baptist chapel, Mount Street.	331
(128)	Rishangles. Strict Baptist chapel. NW front.	304	(9)	Billingshurst. General Baptist chapel. Plan.	331
	Communion pews, before removal in 1986.	304		Exterior.	331

(10)	Bosham. Congregational chapel.	332	(56) Horsham. General Baptist chapel. Plan.	345
(12)	Brighton. Former Presbyterian chapel, Union Street.	333	Exterior.	344
			Interior.	344
(15)	Brighton. New Road Chapel.	333	(58) Horsham. Friends' meeting-house. Sketch.	346
(23)	Catsfield. Former Wesleyan chapel.	334	(59) Hove. Baptist chapel, Holland Road.	346
(24)	Chichester. Former General Baptist chapel, Eastgate. Plan.	335	(61) Icklesham. Methodist chapel, Winchelsea.	346
			(62) Lewes. Former General Baptist meeting-house. Sketch.	347
	Exterior.	335		
	Interior.	335	(64) Lewes. Jireh Chapel. Plan.	349
(25)	Chichester. Former Presbyterian chapel, (Baffin's Hall), Baffins Lane. Plan.	337	Exterior, before alteration to forecourt.	348
			Interior.	348
	Exterior.	336	(65) Lewes. Friends' meeting-house.	350
(26)	Chichester. Providence Chapel, Chapel Street. Plan.	339	(67) Lewes. Westgate Chapel. Interior before 1913.	351
			(78) Northchapel. Former Dependents' chapel.	353
	Exterior.	338	(79) Northiam. General Baptist chapel.	353
	Interior.	338	(80) Northiam. Former Wesleyan chapel. Sketch.	353
(33)	Crawley. Friends' meeting-house, Ifield. Plan.	339	(86) Rye. Former Baptist chapel, Mermaid Street.	354
	Exterior.	340	(87) Rye. Former Independent chapel. Sketch.	354
(37)	Ditchling. General Baptist meeting-house. Plan.	341	(93) Steyning. Former Friends' meeting-house. Sketch.	355
	Exterior.	341	(95) Thakeham. Friends' meeting-house, 'Blue Idol'.	355
(38)	East Grinstead. Zion Chapel.	341	(97) Wadhurst. Rehoboth Chapel, Pell Green.	
(39)	Hadlow Down. Providence Chapel.	342	Exterior.	357
(47)	Hastings. Baptist chapel, Chapel Park Road, St Leonards.	342	Interior.	357
			(107) Withyham. Former Wesleyan chapel, Groombridge.	358
(51)	Heathfield. Calvinistic Independent chapel, Chapel Cross.	343	(108) Wivelsfield. Ote Hall Chapel.	358
			(109) Wivelsfield. Bethel Chapel. Sketch.	359
(54)	Herstmonceux. Congregational chapel. Elevation.	343	(112) Worthing. Former Wesleyan chapel, Bedford Row.	359

PRINCIPAL MONUMENTS

List of monuments described in this Inventory that were recommended by the Royal Commission on the Historical Monuments of England as being 'most worthy of preservation'. (For the complete list for England see the Forty-second Interim Report of that Commission, Command No. 9442, 1985).

Monument numbers, in brackets, are followed by page references.

Bedfordshire
  Carlton and Chellington. Strict Baptist meeting-house, Carlton. (20) 7.
  Clifton. Strict Baptist chapel. (22) 9.
  Pertenhall. Moravian chapel. [*Now demolished*]. (65) 16.
  Roxton. Roxton Chapel. (73) 19.
  Southill. Southill Chapel. (81) 21.
  Stevington. Baptist meeting-house. (83) 22.

Cambridgeshire and Isle of Ely
  Bassingbourn. Congregational chapel (URC). (2) 27.
  Cambridge. Emmanuel Church (URC). (16) 31.
  Linton. Congregational chapel (URC). (60) 36.
  Melbourn. Old Meeting-house (URC). (68) 39.

Essex
  Braintree and Bocking. Congregational chapel, Bocking End. (9) 48.
  Earls Colne. Friends' meeting-house. (33) 53.
  Felsted. Former Congregational chapel (URC). (38) 54.
  Harlow. Baptist chapel, Potter Street. (61) 57.
  Little Baddow. Congregational chapel (URC). (73) 58.
  Terling. Congregational chapel (URC). (102) 64.

Greater London
  Barnet. 'Free Church', Hampstead Garden Suburb. (9) 70.
  Camden. Catholic Apostolic church, Gordon Square. (35) 77.
  Enfield. Friends' meeting-house, Winchmore Hill. (69) 81.
  Hackney. Congregational chapel (URC), Lower Clapton Road. (79) 83.
  Hackney. Newington Green Meeting-house (Unitarian). (90) 85.
  Hackney. Church of the Good Shepherd, ('The Ark of the Covenant'), Rookwood Road. (91) 86.
  Hounslow. Friends' meeting-house, Isleworth. (139) 94.
  Islington. Union Chapel (Congregational). (151) 97.
  Islington. Wesley's Chapel, City Road (Methodist). (157) 99.
  City of Westminster. Catholic Apostolic church, Maida Avenue. (255) 121.
  City of Westminster. Westminster Chapel, Buckingham Gate (Congregational). (260) 123.
  City of Westminster. Former King's Weigh House Chapel, Duke Street. (261) 123.

Hertfordshire
  Baldock. Wesleyan chapel. (10) 128.
  Bishop's Stortford. Congregational chapel (URC). (15) 130.
  Braughing. Congregational chapel. (16) 131.
  Hertford. Friends' meeting-house. (38) 136.
  Hitchin. Baptist chapel, Tilehouse Street. (39) 138.
  Hoddesdon. Friends' meeting-house. (45) 140.

Huntingdon and Peterborough
  Great Gidding. Particular Baptist chapel. (13) 151.
  Great Gransden. Providence Chapel. (16) 153.

Kent
  Chevening. General Baptist chapel, Bessels Green (Unitarian). (28) 167.
  Cranbrook. Providence Chapel, Stone Street, (Strict Baptist). (34) 169.
  Dartford. Zion Chapel (Strict Baptist). (36) 170.
  Dover. Adrian Street Chapel (Unitarian). (42) 172.
  Ramsgate. Baptist chapel, Cavendish Street. (101) 183.
  Royal Tunbridge Wells. Former Congregational chapel, Mount Pleasant Road. (110) 185.
  Stone-cum-Ebony. Ebenezer Chapel, Stone. (134) 189.
  Tenterden. The Old Meeting-house (Unitarian). (140) 190.
  Wingham. Former Congregational chapel. (150) 192.

Lincolnshire
- Barrow upon Humber. Former Congregational chapel, Lords Lane. (19) 196.
- Boston. Spain Lane Chapel (Unitarian). (44) 199.
- Brant Broughton and Stragglethorpe. Friends' meeting-house, Brant Broughton. (49) 200.
- Great Steeping. General Baptist meeting-house, Monksthorpe. (121) 209.
- Lincoln. Former Congregational chapel, Newland (URC). (169) 215.
- Lincoln. Friends' meeting-house, Park Street. (170) 215.
- Raithby. Methodist chapel. (211) 220.
- South Killingholme. General Baptist chapel. (229) 222.

Norfolk
- Denton. Congregational chapel (URC). (42) 235.
- Diss. Friends' meeting-house, Frenze Road. (49) 236.
- Guestwick. Guestwick Chapel. (96) 244.
- Little Walsingham, Wesleyan chapel. (125) 250.
- North Walsham. Friends' meeting-house. (149) 254.
- Norwich. The Old Meeting-house (Congregational). (152) 256.
- Norwich. Friends' meeting-house, Upper Goat Lane. (157) 259.
- Norwich. The Octagon Chapel (Unitarian). (159) 260.
- Oulton. Oulton Chapel. (167) 262.

Suffolk
- Bury St Edmunds. Churchgate Street Chapel (Unitarian). (25) 281.
- Framlingham. The Old Meeting-house (Unitarian). (48) 287.
- Fressingfield. Strict Baptist chapel. (51) 287.
- Friston. Strict Baptist chapel. (52) 288.
- Halesworth. Congregational chapel (URC). (62) 289.
- Ipswich. St Nicholas Street Meeting-house (Unitarian). (76) 294.
- Ipswich. 'Bethesda Chapel' (Strict Baptist). (81) 296.
- Long Melford. Congregational chapel (URC). (98) 298.
- Walpole. The Old Meeting-house (Congregational). (149) 307.
- Whepstead. Former Independent chapel (Baptist). (157) 310.
- Wickhambrook. Congregational chapel (URC). (158) 310.
- Wrentham. Congregational chapel (URC). (168) 313.

Surrey
- Albury. The Apostles' Chapel (Catholic Apostolic). (1) 315.
- Charlwood. Providence Chapel. (6) 320.
- Esher. Friends' meeting-house. (19) 322.
- Godalming. Friends' meeting-house, Mill Lane. (27) 324.

Sussex
- Billingshurst. General Baptist chapel (Unitarian). (9) 331.
- Chichester. Former Presbyterian chapel, Baffins Lane. (25) 336.
- Chichester. Providence Chapel, Chapel Street (Calvinistic Independent). (26) 337.
- Crawley. Friends' meeting-house, Ifield. (33) 339.
- Heathfield. Calvinistic Independent chapel, Chapel Cross. (51) 343.
- Horsham. General Baptist chapel (Unitarian). (56) 344.
- Lewes. Jireh Chapel (Calvinistic Independent). (64) 347.
- Thakeham. Friends' meeting-house, 'Blue Idol'. (95) 355.
- Wadhurst. Rehoboth Chapel, Pell Green. (97) 356.

ACKNOWLEDGEMENTS

In preparing the fourth and concluding volume in this series the author has been greatly encouraged and materially assisted by many friends and colleagues whose patience has been sadly and sorely tried in awaiting its appearance. To all who have over many years urged the need to complete this series of Inventories, and without whose support success might not have been achieved, the author wishes to express his profound gratitude and obligation.

Particular thanks are due to all who supplied information which enabled the necessary fieldwork to be successfully undertaken or who furnished additional facts which might not otherwise have become available. Much advice and support was received in the early stages of the investigation from the late Mr H.G. Tibbutt whose publications on Bedfordshire chapels have been invaluable. The late Rev. F.A.J. Harding of St Albans made available his researches into nonconformity in that city. It is a great sadness to the writer that these and others such as the late Mr Godwin Arnold and Dr Richard Dufty, former Secretary of the Royal Commission on the Historical Monuments of England, whose early enthusiasm for and active interest in the subject played a major part in its inception and successful prosecution, have not survived to see its completion.

The writer is again especially indebted to Mr David Butler for generously making available the fruits of his own researches into Quaker Meeting-houses prior to their publication in 1999. The late Rev. William Leary kindly supplied information on Methodist chapels in Lincolnshire and Messrs Chris Pickford and Stephen Coleman of the Bedfordshire County Record Office generously helped with additional information on that county.

Grateful acknowledgement is also due to Mr Leonard J. Maquire for information on General Baptist chapels in the South-east, and to Pastor Ben Ramsbottom for advice on chapels of the Gospel Standard Baptists; also to Mr Mark Barnard whose excellent dissertation on Chapels and Meeting-houses in Suffolk has been most informative. Of the many persons who have assisted in innumerable ways further thanks are due to Mrs Jean Shelley for help on chapels in Surrey and Sussex, to Mrs Hilda Grieve for information on the work of James Fenton, and to other friends, members of the Chapels Society and other organizations with which the author is connected, whose interest and forbearance is hopefully now rewarded. Gratitude must also be expressed to many unnamed correspondents whose queries have often led to further research and whose observations have assisted in the elimination of errors which might easily have passed without notice.

To all ministers, church officers and others who over the years have, with little warning, willingly opened up their premises for inspection, particular thanks are due; without their co-operation the value of this survey would have been greatly diminished. Grateful acknowledgement is also made to the staff of Dr Williams's Library and its former librarian, Mr John Creasey, whose assistance has always been readily forthcoming.

To those former colleagues on the staff of the Royal Commission who in any way assisted in the work, and particularly to Dr Bridgett Jones for research, to Mrs Patricia Drummond who attempted with difficulty to maintain order within the Commission's files and to Mr Mike Seaforth who printed many of the photographs required for this volume, the writer is also much indebted.

C.F.S.

EDITORIAL NOTES

Denominational names used are generally those in use when the buildings were erected. Methodist chapels appear under the name of the original society where this could be ascertained. Presbyterian and Congregational chapels now used by the United Reformed Church are indicated in the text as (URC). No general attempt is made to distinguish the present grouping of continuing Congregational or Baptist congregations not involving a change in their principal designation; most of the latter, where not otherwise stated, will be found to be of Particular Baptist origin. Unitarian and Free Christian congregations appear under their proper historical appellations.

The name 'meeting-house' or 'chapel', although not generally given, should be assumed to be included as appropriate in the heading of each entry. The designation 'church', as increasingly applied indiscriminately to ecclesiastical structures, is generally avoided as incorrect and tending to ambiguity in the present context. 'Former' indicates that the building is now used by another stated denomination or for other purposes. Closure, change of use, or demolition is noted where this could reliably be determined. Much of the fieldwork was begun in the 1970s and, in view of the time which has passed since many of the records were made, further changes will inevitably be found to have taken place.

The measured drawings are reproduced to uniform scales of 12 feet to the inch (1:144) and 24 feet to the inch (1:288). Sequence hatching has been adopted throughout: the original or principal work is indicated in solid black, secondary work by cross-hatching and later minor additions by single-line hatching; where necessary this is more fully explained in the accompanying text. Dimensions are quoted in the text for most monuments built prior to 1800; these are internal unless otherwise stated, the length of the principal axis of the original pulpit or rostrum being given first.

Historical information concerning the origins and development of individual congregations necessarily derives in the main from published sources. The accuracy of these varies considerably and, although they have been used with caution, some errors may remain. Corrections or comments on any statement in this Inventory will be gratefully received.

Boundary Changes. The arrangement of the Inventory follows that of the three previously published volumes, being by historical county and civil parish; the names and boundaries are those obtaining immediately prior to local government reorganization in 1974. Boundary changes before this date which have affected the historical county structure but are nevertheless embodied in the Inventory were the addition of the Soke of Peterborough, formerly administered by Northamptonshire, to Huntingdonshire to form the short-lived county of Huntingdon and Peterborough; more sweeping have been the changes affecting the Home Counties, commencing with the formation of the County of London in 1888 from parts of Middlesex and adjoining counties, followed in 1965 by the incorporation of the remaining portion of Middlesex and further adjacent county districts to create the county of Greater London. Post-1974 county changes affecting the volume area are indicated on the map (p.xx) and in the Inventory in italics beside the individual parish names. These comprise: the inclusion of the northern parts of Lincolnshire within the new county of Humberside, since renamed as the administrative districts of North and North-East Lincolnshire; the conflation of Huntingdonshire and Peterborough with the county of Cambridgeshire and the Isle of Ely to form a new county of Cambridgeshire; a revision of the boundary between East and West Sussex (here treated as a single geographical county); and the transfer from Suffolk to Norfolk of a few parishes south of Great Yarmouth.

The detailed archive on which this published account is based will be available for consultation through the National Monuments Record. For more information please contact NMR Enquiry and Research Services, National Monuments Record Centre, Great Western Village, Kemble Drive, Swindon SN2 2GZ. Telephone 01793 414600.

Conversion Table
1 inch = 25.4 mm
1 foot (12 inches) = 304.8 mm
1 yard (3 feet) = 914.4 mm
1 mile (1760 yards) = 1.6 km

PREFACE

This fourth and final volume of the Inventory of Nonconformist Chapels and Meeting-houses covers an area from the English Channel to the Humber estuary. It embraces the Puritan strongholds of East Anglia where Continental influence and trade connections were strong, as well as long-neglected or poorly developed areas such as Lincolnshire where Methodism has left many evidences of a useful existence. But prominent within this volume is the presence of London, notable for the numerous congregations which once flourished within the City boundaries, but now more for the large chapels which housed their 19th-century successors.

The earliest meeting-houses to survive in Eastern England, as elsewhere in the country are those of the Quakers, of which the earliest, in Hertford, Hertfordshire (38), was built in 1670. In Lincolnshire the oldest Baptist chapel of 1701 is remotely situated at Monksthorpe (121). In the larger towns of East Anglia, Independent churches appeared even earlier. The Old Meeting in Norwich, Norfolk (152), which began in 1643, erected a meeting-house in 1693 which is of outstanding architectural interest having a façade of great Classical sophistication. Nor were such large buildings confined to towns, as is seen in the former chapels in Norfolk at Guestwick (96) and Oulton (167). A comparable building is Walpole Chapel in Suffolk (149), converted from a timber-framed house and enlarged *c*.1690, which illustrates the basic needs and simple worship of a rural congregation. Possibly the best-known chapels in Eastern England are St Nicholas Street, Ipswich, Suffolk (76), which Presbyterians built in 1700, and the chapel in Churchgate Street, Bury St Edmunds, Suffolk (25) of 1711.

The great variety in styles of building which may be seen throughout this region arose from the materials available. Useful building stone was to be had in north-west Bedfordshire and Huntingdonshire and good brick-earth in most of the eastern counties. Other materials were more locally used, such as clunch in Suffolk, flint throughout much of the South-East, and beach pebbles in coastal regions of East Anglia and elsewhere. Timber-framing continued in use in the South-East throughout the 18th and 19th centuries, often in small cheaply constructed weather-boarded chapels but also in larger buildings such as Jireh Chapel in Lewes, Sussex (64) where the outer cladding is partly in mathematical tiles.

A large number of diverse denominations appear in this part of England: besides the early Quakers and Baptists, both General and Particular, the Independents and Presbyterians, and later the Methodists in their various groupings, there were 'Culimites' in North Cambridgeshire, unfortunately leaving no physical presence, the 'Peculiar People' of Essex, some of whose small and simple chapels still remain, and the 'Cokelers', or Society of Dependents, of Sussex. More extensive were the Calvinistic Independent followers of William Huntington in Kent and Sussex who built notable chapels at Cranbrook and Lewes. At the opposite extreme of elaboration are the Catholic Apostolic Church with its Apostles' Chapel in Albury, Surrey (1) and the former Agapemonite church at Stamford Hill in London (91).

Particular attention has again been given to recording in detail all buildings dating from before 1800 but also to include as many later works as it has been possible to inspect, however briefly. The hope previously expressed that the continued threats to the more important chapels and meeting-houses might be restrained remains to be fulfilled. The destruction of the fittings at Great Gidding, Huntingdonshire (13) belatedly drew public attention to the problems of ecclesiastical exemption.

Small though significant numbers of chapels are now in the care of charitable trusts dedicated to their preservation: Oulton Chapel, Norfolk, is in the care of the Norfolk Historic Buildings Trust; Walpole Chapel, Suffolk, has been transferred to the Historic Chapels Trust; and Monksthorpe Chapel, Lincolnshire, is now administered by the National Trust. Where chapels have been converted into houses, as in numerous instances throughout this volume, the almost inevitable loss of fittings has destroyed much of their historical value and meaning even where they remain recognizable externally. Recording without preservation is no solution to the continued attrition of an important aspect of English national life. With due care many may yet fulfil the purpose for which they were built without losing their unique historical character.

CHRISTOPHER STELL

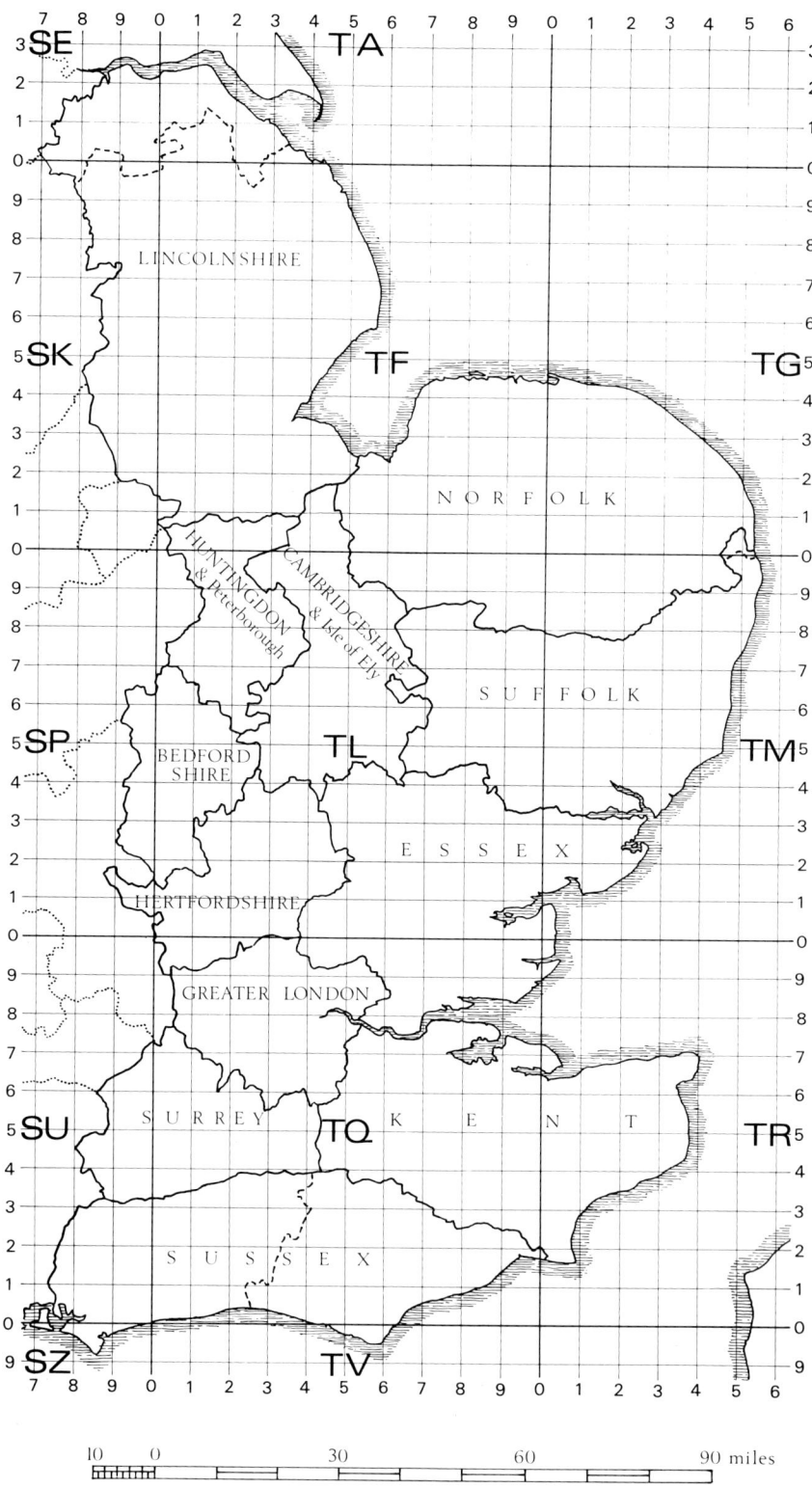

COUNTY BOUNDARIES. The boundaries of county areas within the present volume are indicated by continuous lines. Alterations resulting from the formation of the county of Humberside, the revision of the boundary between East and West Sussex and other minor changes within the volume area are shown by broken lines. © *Crown copyright. All rights reserved*

AN INVENTORY OF
NONCONFORMIST CHAPELS AND MEETING-HOUSES
IN EASTERN ENGLAND

BEDFORDSHIRE

The name of John Bunyan, the Bedfordshire tinker, which occupies a high place in English literature and in the history of English dissent, is particularly associated with his native county. The development of nonconformist congregations in the 17th century in the vicinity of Bedford was greatly influenced by his work, and the intermingling of Congregational and Baptist views, which was a feature of his teaching, is evident in the history of many of the churches referred to below; the case of the 'Bunyan Meeting' in Bedford (8) is particularly apposite, but several of the churches now designated 'Baptist' will be seen to have their roots in a more open form of Independency. The predominance of Baptist congregations greatly overshadows the fewer and generally later churches of a Congregational order, while the absence of any early Presbyterian meeting is notable.

The county has several 18th-century meeting-houses of interest: of these Stevington (83) of 1720–1 is the earliest, having the traditional wide frontage and pair of timber posts to support a double roof; this characteristic was repeated at Carlton (20) in 1760 and, more surprisingly, reappears early in the next century at Southill (81) of 1805. At Brook End, Keysoe (17), the chapel of 1741, now converted to a house, was more original in its design, particularly in the long brackets which help to support the ceiling. The other 18th-century Baptist chapels, at Blunham (15) and Maulden (61) of 1751, and Cranfield (24) of *c.*1773, have been much altered, as has the Congregational Howard Chapel in Bedford (9) of 1775, named after another famous resident of the county. The two principal Friends' meeting-houses, at Ampthill (2) of 1753, and Leighton Buzzard (47) of 1789, are small buildings, both enlarged, but the latter particularly is typical of the architecture of this society. The Moravians also appeared in Bedfordshire at an early stage and their Settlement in Bedford (10), developed from 1751, is thus of considerable historical importance, although the chapel itself has been rebuilt.

The early 19th century produced several monuments of note, the most remarkable being the now demolished Moravian chapel at Pertenhall (65) of 1827 and the thatched barn at Roxton (73), converted by the Congregationalist squire into a *chapelle ornée* of extraordinary external elaboration. A few urban chapels worthy of mention include Union Chapel, Luton (49) of 1839 in the Greek Doric style, the simpler Ebenezer Chapel (51) of 1853 in the same town, and the pedimented Wesleyan chapel in Biggleswade (13) of 1834, which contrasts with the plain functional manner of most of the other Methodist chapels in the region. The Wesleyan chapel in Chapel Street, Luton (56) of 1851–2 was a larger building of a type commonly found in towns but this together with other striking examples of later 19th-century design, at Houghton Regis (42) in the Lombardic style, and the Congregational chapel in Stuart Street, Luton (53) by John Tarring in the Decorated Gothic style, were demolished in the early 1970s. Two later Strict Baptist chapels of particular interest are at Clifton (22) of 1853, in which the original fittings remain complete, and at Sharnbrook (74), where the elevation of 1865 is a good example of the work of a local architect.

Apart from a few examples referred to above the county is not remarkable for any radical innovations in chapel design, the traditional elements familiar to local builders being adequate for the needs of a largely rural population. The majority of the buildings listed have brick walls, red brick throughout the 18th century but with yellow or gault brick introduced later. Stone rubble is used in the region to the NE of Bedford and some timber to the N and E, notably at Southill (81) but also in two chapels, Keysoe Row (18) and Roxton (73), which originated as barns and which are also exceptional in having thatched roofs; most roofs are tiled, with slate used as a replacement or in later work.

AMPTHILL

(1) UNION CHAPEL, Dunstable Street (TL 033378). A meeting-house fitted up in 1797 for the use of the Baptist minister of Maulden was replaced by the present brick chapel in 1822 and a separate church formed. The chapel, enlarged to the front in 1870, is of three bays with two tiers of round-arched windows; a Sunday-school was built alongside in 1893.

Bunker, S., *Seize the Day: A Bicentenary History of Ampthill Baptist Church* (1997). Peer, A.H., *A History of Ampthill Union Church* (1963).

(2) Former FRIENDS, Dunstable Street (TL 034378). A meeting was established in 1726 in a barn on the present site belonging to Christopher Bennell. This was replaced in 1753 by a new meeting-house costing £136 which was enlarged to the W in 1768 at a further cost of £74. Meetings ceased in 1880 and the building has since been used for a variety of charitable and social purposes.

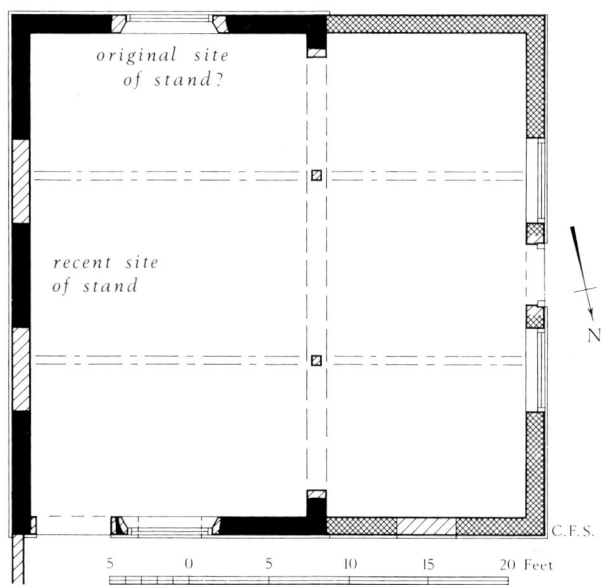

Former Friends' Meeting-house, AMPTHILL *Bedfordshire*

The meeting-house stands on the E side of the street concealed behind a single-storeyed cottage. The walls are of red brick and the roofs, which are in two parallel sections, are half-hipped and covered with tiles. The earliest portion, to the E (30¼ft by 17¼ft), is in Flemish bond with a plinth of English bond brickwork, a stepped cornice on the E side and platbands at eaves level to N and S. A doorway centrally at the N end has been replaced by a window, and two windows in the E wall overlooking the burial-ground have been blocked. The W enlargement (12½ft wide), entirely in English bond brickwork but otherwise matching the earlier work, had a doorway in the N wall; two windows in the W wall have quadrant-moulded brick heads but renewed frames, between them is a doorway, with moulded head and shaped brackets, inserted in the early 19th century. The interior, perhaps formerly divided by a partition, has a dado of vertical boarding rising at the E side behind the site of an early 19th-century stand. The roof, ceiled at collar level, has tie-beams and V-braces below the collars.

Fittings – *Inscriptions*: on bricks, include: in E wall 'MM:1753'; in original N wall, initials and date 1753; in W wall, reset: 'C.Bennel', 'In[ ] Bennell', 'Wm & Ruth Brown 7mo4 1753'. *Seating*: two benches are said to be now in the parish church next to the font.

Ampthill, Millbrook & Steppingley Magazine (September 1969). Butler (1999) 1–2.

(3) WESLEYAN, Dunstable Street (TL 034379). The chapel built in 1883 replaced an earlier one of 1813, the original date tablet from which is reset inside the present building. The former chapel, now demolished, stood in Chapel Lane (TL 033381); a burial-ground with several headstones and other monuments remains behind houses on the E side of the lane.

ASPLEY GUISE

(4) WESLEYAN, Mount Pleasant (SP 948359). Brick and slate, with rendered gabled front and round-arched windows: dated 1813. Later porch.

(5) Former PRIMITIVE METHODIST, Aspley Hill (SP 931355). Late 19th-century; gabled brick front of three tall round-arched bays with defaced inscription panel.

BARTON-LE-CLAY

(6) HOPE CHAPEL, Barton in the Clay (TL 083307). Strict Baptist, built 1830; brick and slate, gabled front, two blind round-arched windows and rebuilt porch. *Monument*: in front of chapel, William Thackray, 1863, first pastor.

Paul III (1958) 235–48.

(7) WESLEYAN, Barton in the Clay (TL 081308). Chapel of 1835 with rendered sides; re-fronted in red brick and stone in 1909.

BEDFORD

(8) BUNYAN MEETING-HOUSE, Mill Street (TL 052498). An Independent church formed in 1650 with John Gifford as pastor later met in the parish church of St John, to which Gifford was appointed rector in 1653. After Gifford's death in 1655 the services were frequently conducted by John Bunyan, who was ordained pastor 21 October 1671 and continued until his death in 1688. After c.1660 the church, which under Bunyan's influence came to disregard differences over baptismal practice, was obliged to meet elsewhere. The present site was acquired in 1672 and a barn fitted up for use which was replaced by a permanent meeting-house in 1707. The Old Meeting-house, as it came to be called, costing £400 and seating 700 persons, was a square timber-framed building with three parallel roofs supported by posts and with triple gables to N and S; the interior, partly refitted in 1769, had a pulpit against the E wall between tall windows, and galleries around three sides. Two ten-branch chandeliers given c.1770 by Samuel Whitbread M.P. remained until replaced by gas lighting in 1838, when one was given to the meeting at Cotton End (30) and the other to Shillington (78). When the meeting-house was demolished in 1849 the pulpit was given to Bunyan Meeting, Goldington, and a tablet inscribed 'Built 1707' was reset above a

Bunyan Meeting-house, Bedford. N front. (8)

doorway at No. 15 Cardington Road, Bedford. The church suffered two minor secessions in the late 18th century: in 1772 when the Independents objected to the pronounced Baptist emphasis of the minister, and in 1793 when Baptists objected to his less rigid successor.

The present meeting-house, designed by Wing and Jackson of Bedford and opened 20 February 1850, is of red brick with stone dressings in an early 18th-century style. It has two tiers of windows with rusticated surrounds after the manner of James Gibbs, the taller upper windows have round-arched heads. Giant pilasters divide the bays and support an entablature with modillion cornice and a pediment across the N front. A porch was added in 1876 and further rooms were built at the rear during the late 19th century. The interior was reseated in 1974.

Fittings – *Communion Table*: the original late 17th-century communion table, 12ft in length and supported on six turned legs, has been sawn into two sections, one 5ft long remaining in the meeting-house, the other in the church parlour. *Doors*: at main entrance, bronze, with scenes from *The Pilgrim's Progress*, by Frederick Thrupp, given 1876 by the Duke of Bedford. *Monuments*: in chapel at base of gallery stairs to Aleic [Alice] Hunnilove, 1688/9; also, reset on wall E of chapel, several wall monuments of the late 18th and early 19th century. *Miscellanea*: in Bunyan Museum behind chapel, many objects relating to John Bunyan, and other items including hexagonal pulpit from Zoar Chapel, Southwark (Greater London (224)).

CYB (1850) 197. Ivimey I (1811) 364ff.; II (1814) 13ff. Tibbutt, H.G., *Bunyan Meeting, Bedford, 1650–1950* (1950). Tibbutt, H.G. (ed.), 'The minutes of the first Independent Church (Now Bunyan Meeting) at Bedford 1656–1766', *Bedfordshire Historical Record Society* Vol. 55 (1976).

(9) HOWARD CHAPEL, Mill Street (TL 051498). Independent seceders from the Old Meeting gathered in a large warehouse 'at the bottom of the yard belonging to the Red Lion Inn, High Street', which was registered for worship 9 February 1773. The present chapel, formerly known as the Second or New Meeting, was renamed Howard Chapel in 1837 in honour of John Howard, the penal reformer, who was a principal supporter of the cause. The chapel was designed by Daniel Millard, joiner, of Bedford, and registered on 11 January 1775. The side walls of this building remain, of red brick with three bays of tall round-arched recesses enclosing two tiers of windows, the upper ones round-arched, the lower with segmental heads; the front was originally in a similar style, of three bays with a central pedimented doorcase, and the roof was pyramidal and surmounted by a ball finial. In 1849 the chapel was enlarged to the front in rendered brickwork with five bays of windows and a three-bay entrance portico. The interior (originally 41¾ft by 36ft) was refitted in 1866 under the supervision of John Usher, architect, of Bedford, who had earlier, in 1862, designed new school-rooms at the rear. In 1974 the chapel figured in an important legal decision concerning the operation of ecclesiastical exemption in cases of proposed demolition. (Gutted, derelict and roofless, 1996)

Howard Chapel, Bedford. (9)

Fittings (as in 1969) – *Chair*: in vestry, 'John Howard's chair, 1765', Windsor style. *Monuments*: wall monuments and headstones of the late 18th century and after, reset externally at E and W sides of chapel. *Table*: in vestry, circular, made from sounding board of 1775 pulpit removed 1823–4.

Tibbutt, H.G., *A History of Howard Congregational Church, Bedford* (1961).

(10) MORAVIAN SETTLEMENT, St Peter's Street (TL 052501). A request in 1738 from the Rev. Jacob Rogers, of St Paul's Church, for assistance from two Anglican but Moravian-inclined preachers of his acquaintance led to the commencement of separate meetings, for which a barn was registered in 1740. The society, recognized in 1742, was established in 1745 as the first Moravian congregation outside London. In 1751 the present site was acquired and a chapel built to which in 1757 was added, to the W a house for Single Sisters, and to the E a minister's house incorporating a Congregational Hall; a Single Brethren's House

had been built in 1751 in a detached position to the NE and later in the 18th century a house for the assistant ministers was added E of the minister's house.

The chapel, rebuilt in 1864 by James Horsford of Bedford, in an Italianate style in yellow brick with stone dressings and a slated roof has a pedimented S front of three bays with entrances in wings at the sides; it was enlarged in 1888 by an organ chamber at the N end. Flanking the chapel are the original Sisters' House and Manse, of two storeys and attics, the former of four bays with a tiled roof and dormer windows, the latter of three bays with a renewed tiled roof; the assistant minister's house to the E, of brick and slate in two storeys has a S front of six bays with a central gable and paired brackets to a wide cornice. The former Brethren's House, subsequently a Moravian Ladies' School and now part of Bedford School, is of brick and tile of three storeys with a front of seven bays. (Now jointly Moravian/URC)

The *burial-ground*, N of the chapel, opened in 1751, has many un-numbered rectangular markers of stone and slate, now loose, of the 18th century and later. *Organ*: in chapel, acquired 1832, rebuilt 1876, enlarged and re-fronted 1888, incorporates parts of an organ by Gerard Schmidt built 1715 as a town organ for St Paul's Church, Bedford. England (1888) refers to an angel on this case with a tablet behind inscribed 'The gift of Mr Francis Walker, alderman, and Mr John Russell, common councillor, 1736'.

England (1888) 36–40. Smith, W., *St Peter's Moravian Church, Bedford, 1745–1945* (1945). Welch, E. (ed.), 'The Bedford Moravian Church in the eighteenth century', *Bedfordshire Historical Record Society* Vol. 68 (1989).

(11) Former WESLEYAN, Bromham Road (TL 045501). The chapel of 1887 now in commercial use replaces 'Christ Church' built *c*.1836 for a congregation gathered by the Rev. Timothy Richard Matthews, chaplain of Bedford workhouse, and licensed for dissenters. *See also* Ravensden (68).

Page (1953) 25.

BIGGLESWADE

(12) PROVIDENCE CHAPEL, Back Lane (TL 192445). The Particular Baptist chapel built in 1843, probably for seceders from the Old Meeting-house in Foundry Lane (TL 196445) (1785, rebuilt *c*.1834, now demolished) has rendered walls and a slate roof; it was enlarged to the front in the later 19th century in gault brick with a gabled front of three bays with two tiers of sash windows.

(13) WESLEYAN, Shortmead Street (TL 189449). Gault brick with pedimented W front and rendered dressings, large tablet dated 1834. Three round-arched upper windows separated by pilasters, paired at ends, lower part covered by a wide late 19th-century porch. Interior has a continuous gallery on cast-iron columns. *Monuments*: in chapel (1) Elizabeth Harvey, of Hinxworth, Herts., 'she was honoured with the friendship of the Apostolic Wesley – the first Methodist chapel and preachers' house in this town were erected by her liberality: having become too small they were sold and the proceeds applied in aid of the present Chapel and Dwelling-house, A.D. 1834', signed 'Prior, Bedford'; (2) George Conquest, jnr., 1818, Mrs Elizabeth Conquest, 1819, and James Conquest, 1821. In burial-ground in front of chapel, many monuments of the mid 19th century and later.

BILLINGTON

(14) WESLEYAN (SP 941228). Brick and slate, rendered gabled front of three bays with round-arched openings and lunette with painted date 1838 (1851 census returns say 1835).

BLUNHAM

(15) OLD MEETING-HOUSE, High Street (TL 154514). The Baptist congregation originated in the mid 17th century and was initially in membership with the Old Meeting in Bedford, becoming autonomous in 1724. Meetings were held in a barn on the present site which was replaced by the existing building in 1751. In 1832 the meeting-house was greatly altered by raising the height of the walls, and the inside was partly refitted in the late 19th century. An internal baptistery was provided in 1856.

The walls are of red brick heightened and altered in yellow brick, and the pyramidal roof is covered with slates. The W front has two doorways with two windows between and three above, all with segmental-arched heads; the sides have two bays of windows, and two round-arched windows in the E wall flank the pulpit. A brick and tiled vestry projects to the N. On the front wall is a stone tablet with the initials TC, IH, and date 1751. The interior (34½ft by 37ft) has galleries around three sides, that to the W being the earliest, with some early 19th-century seating. The fielded-panelled front of the 18th-century pulpit remains in the vestry with a two-branch brass candle sconce of *c*.1800.

Fittings – *Monument*: reset externally on W wall, Hannah wife of Edward Sutton, 1795, *et al*. *Plate*: includes a pair of standing cups of 1725. *Table*: in vestibule, with two supports and bearers, of the early 19th century.

Page (1953) 18–20. *The Old Meeting Baptist Church, Blunham: Church Book 1724–1891* (Typescript, Bedfordshire County Record Office, 1976). Tibbutt, H.G., *The Old Meeting, Blunham* (1951).

THE OLD MEETING-HOUSE, BLUNHAM — CFS 1974

(16) PROVIDENCE CHAPEL (TL 152511) built 1843 for Strict Baptist seceders from the Old Meeting; brick and slate, entrance and two upper windows in gabled end wall, low front vestry, side wall blank.

BOLNHURST AND KEYSOE

(17) BROOK END CHAPEL, Keysoe Brook End (TL 073631). The Independent church formed in 1652 gradually became Baptist in the late 18th century but maintained a mixed membership until the following century. The first known pastor was John Donne, ejected

BOLNHURST AND KEYSOE *Bedfordshire*

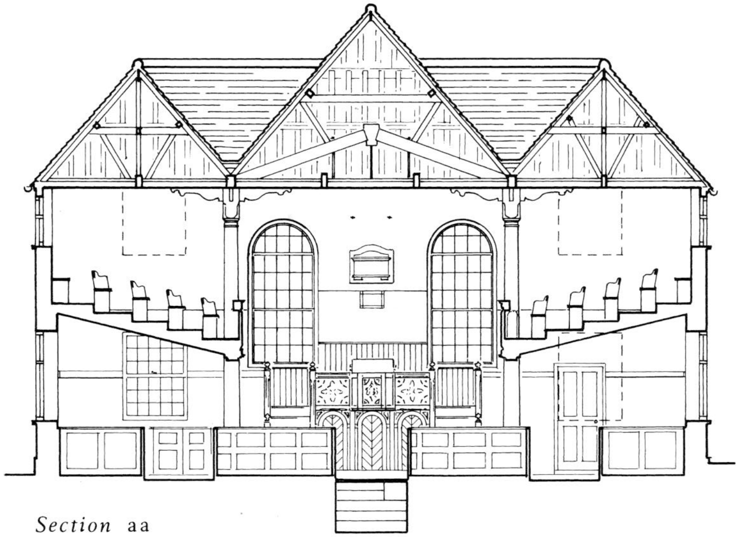

Brook End Chapel, Keysoe

Vestry

Front of Gallery

stove

Section aa

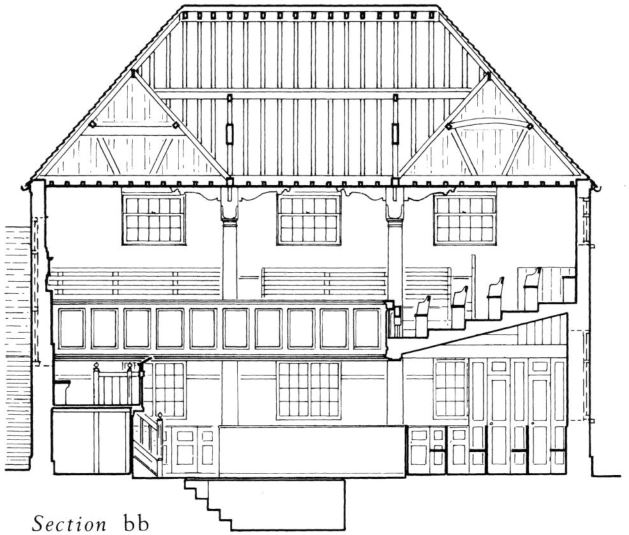

Section bb

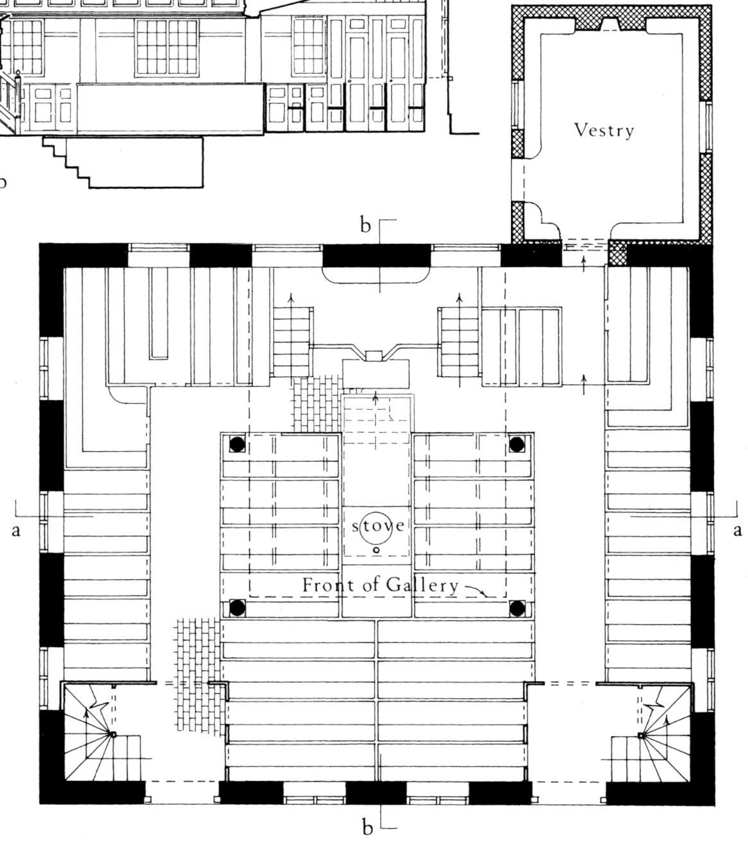

West Elevation

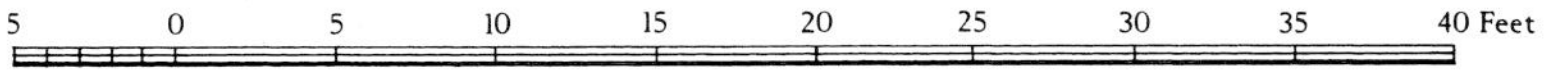

C.F.S.

BEDFORDSHIRE

Brook End Chapel, Keysoe Brook End.

minister of Pertenhall, who suffered imprisonment from 1688 with John Bunyan and others in the county gaol at Bedford.

The meeting-house built in 1741 has walls of red brick with a dentil brick eaves cornice and a hipped tiled roof of elaborate construction. The W wall, at right angles to the road, is of four bays with two segmental-arched doorways, two windows between and four small sash windows below the eaves; a painted tablet in moulded frame is inscribed 'BUILT | 1741'. The N and S walls are alike, of three bays with two tiers of windows; the E wall has two round-arched windows flanking the pulpit.

The interior (31¾ft by 39½ft) has four substantial timber columns supporting the roof structure and gallery fronts, with square bases, moulded capitals and long shaped brackets at the head. The fielded-panelled gallery fronts date from the 18th century, as do the box-pews to the lower floor, but the pulpit was replaced by a rostrum in the late 19th century. At the centre is a narrow table-pew with baptistery below. The roof comprises three parallel sections with valleys, supported by the four internal posts, closed at the ends by return roofs, the central section rises above the adjacent ridges. (The chapel was closed c.1978 and has since been converted to a house)

Tibbutt, H.G., *Keysoe Brook End and Keysoe Row Baptist Churches* (1959). Tibbutt, H.G., (ed.), 'Some early Nonconformist Church Books', *Bedfordshire Historical Record Society* Vol. 51 (1972) 19–22.

(18) BAPTIST, Keysoe Row (TL 085612). The chapel, registered in 1808 for a newly formed congregation, was built in the late 18th century as a small barn. The rendered walls, of timber-framed construction on a brick plinth, were extended to the S and re-fronted to the W in yellow brick in the later 19th century. The roof is half-hipped and thatched. The interior, refitted c.1872, is ceiled at collar level and has one original truss with braced tie-beam partly cut away and the ends supported by inserted octagonal posts. *Monuments*: in burial-ground (1) Joel Miles, 1825, 'The first Minister, sole proprietor and Founder of the *Baptist Meeting* Erected on this spot'; (2) Lydia widow of Joel Miles, 1828.

Tibbutt (1959) op. cit. above.

CARDINGTON

(19) WESLEYAN, Chapel End (TL 093482). Brick and slate, three-bay front with dentil brick cornice to pediment, two round-arched windows, later porch, and three square sash windows above; circular tablet dated 1823.

CARLTON AND CHELLINGTON

(20) STRICT BAPTIST, Carlton (SP 954553). An Independent congregation originating in the late 17th century was formed into a church in 1688 including some members previously attached to the meeting at Stevington. By 1703 the church discountenanced the practice of infant baptism while admitting a mixed membership, but by the time the present building was registered in 1760 the congregation was described as Particular Baptist.

The meeting-house has walls of coursed rubble and a hipped tiled roof in three principal sections with two valleys discharging

Baptist chapel, Keysoe Row. (18)

Strict Baptist meeting-house, Carlton. (20)

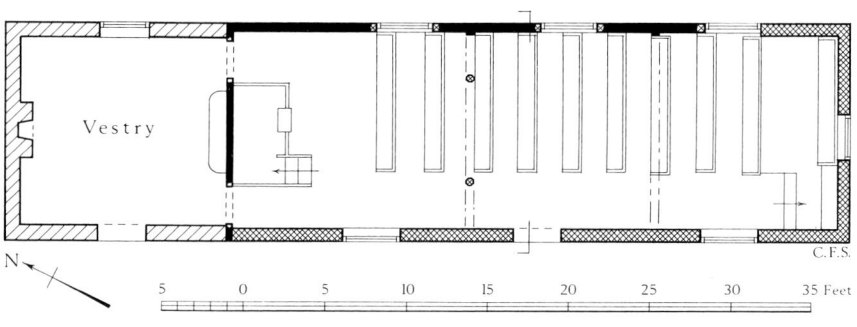
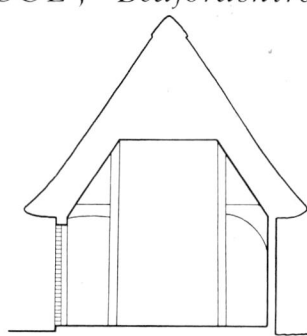

Baptist Chapel, Keysoe Row, BOLNHURST & KEYSOE, *Bedfordshire*

BEDFORDSHIRE

Strict Baptist meeting-house, Carlton. (20)

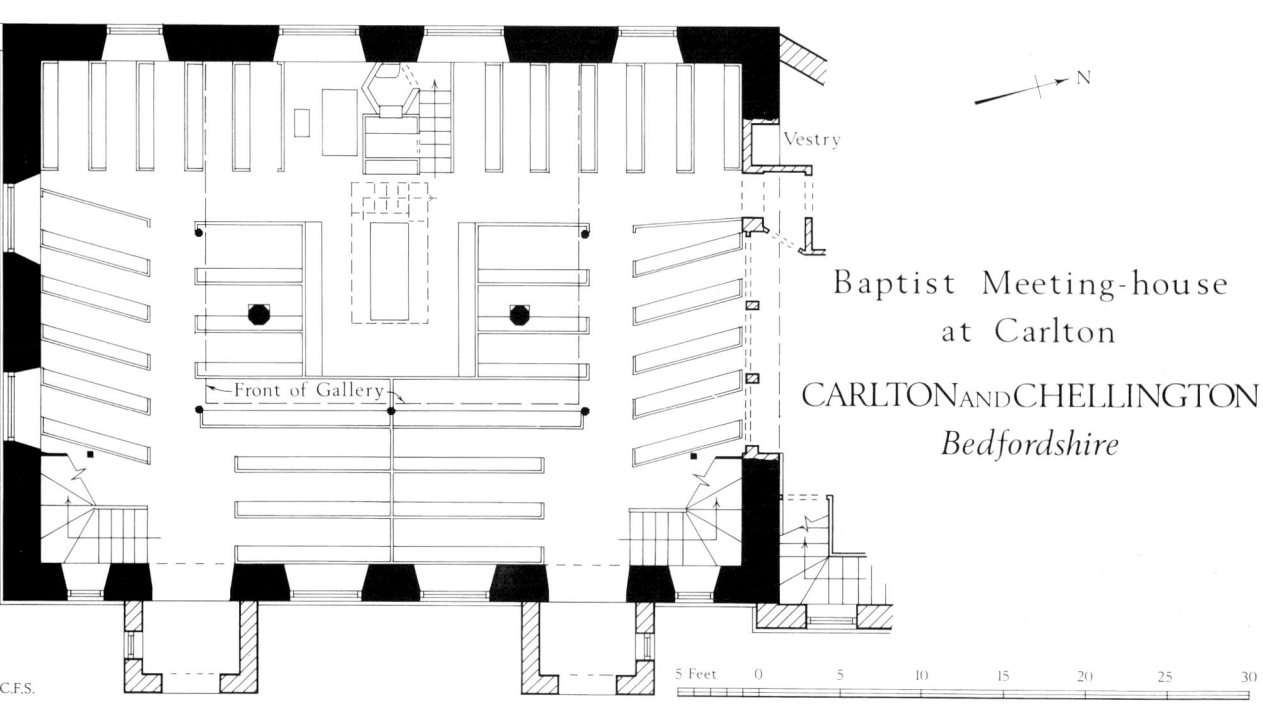

Baptist Meeting-house at Carlton

CARLTON AND CHELLINGTON
Bedfordshire

to the rear. The E front, of six bays with two tiers of windows, has two late 19th-century brick porches and a small tablet between the upper windows with the date of erection. In the W wall two wide windows with flat-arched heads flank the pulpit.

The interior (31½ft by 43¾ft) has two substantial octagonal posts supporting the centre of each valley beam and a gallery around three sides carried by smaller chamfered posts. The lower seating, renewed in the late 19th century, preserves the position of the central table-pew with baptistery below. The roof structure is entirely of oak, the trusses have tie-beams, collars, clasped purlins, and principal rafters uniform in depth with the common rafters. (Chapel occupied 1994 by an 'evangelical' church)

Fittings – *Clock*: on front of E gallery, signed 'E. Cavit, Bedford', of late 18th-century. *Communion Table*: oak, incorporating old material including stretcher carved with late 17th-century decoration. *Monuments* and *Floorslab*. *Monuments*: in chapel, on W wall (1) Rev. Thomas Hull, 1778, 25 years pastor, signed 'Jas. Andrews, Olney, fecit'; (2) Rev. Charles Vorley, 1837, 41 years pastor, signed 'Miller, Bedford', also headstone to same in burial-ground. *Floorslab*: (3) Hannah wife of Thomas Hull, 1770, and Mary their daughter [ ]. *Pulpit*: hexagonal with narrow panelled back-board, moulded sounding board, and Clerk's desk in front, 1760 (Clerk's desk removed before 1995). *Seating*: in gallery, unpainted softwood pews with shaped arm-rests and numbered doors. *Wallpaper*: on walls of vestry, monochrome pattern with scenes from Bunyan's *Pilgrim's Progress*, 19th-century.

Tibbutt, H.G. (ed.), 'Some early Nonconformist Church Books', *Bedfordshire Historical Record Society* Vol. 51 (1972) 45–60.

CHALGRAVE

(21) Former WESLEYAN, Tebworth (SP 992267). Red brick and slate, gabled front with octagonal corner buttresses and battlemented finials, three-bay sides with battlemented parapets, and SW porch with four-centred arched doorway and tablet dated 1842. The windows have square moulded labels and iron casements. Single gallery at entrance with original pulpit opposite. (Converted to secular use since 1992)

CLIFTON

(22) STRICT BAPTIST (TL 165388). Gault brick walls and hipped slate roof, built 1853; three-bay front with two tiers of round-arched windows and five-bay sides with segmental-arched sash

Strict Baptist chapel, Clifton. (22)

Strict Baptist chapel, Clifton. (22)

windows to three centre bays. Interior with galleries added 1863, paid for by an appeal in *The Little Gleaner* (November 1862), has a complete set of original fittings, with plain numbered pews of pitch pine, benches in end gallery, panelled pulpit on slender legs with Gothic tracery and table-pew in front with baptistery below. *Monuments*: in chapel (1) Septimus Sears, 1877, first pastor. In burial-ground (2) Joseph Sears, 1867, Catherine his wife, 1861, Septimus Sears, 1877, and Jane his widow, 1892.

COLMWORTH

(23) Former PRIMITIVE METHODIST, Chapel Lane (TL 103582). Combined cottage and preaching-room, dated 1866. Seating stepped up to right of entrance facing pulpit. (Now 'Colmworth Mission')

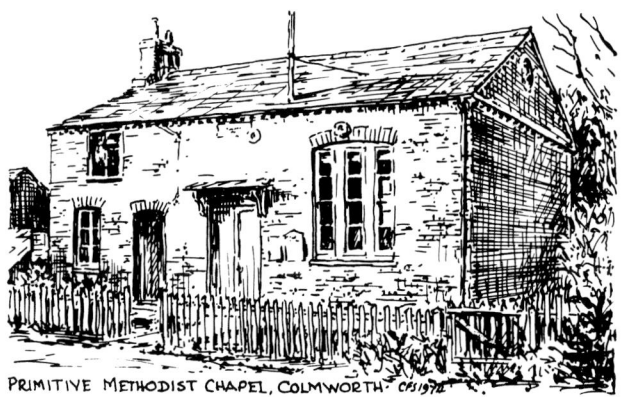

PRIMITIVE METHODIST CHAPEL, COLMWORTH

CRANFIELD

(24) BAPTIST (SP 961426). The church appears to have originated in the late 17th century as an Independent cause becoming Baptist by *c*.1700. The present chapel, although dated 1770 on a later inscription, was not registered until 1773; it was enlarged in 1820 and 1833 and further repaired in 1868 and later. The walls are of brick and the roof is slated. The E wall of *c*.1772 is of three bays with a central doorway between two windows with flat-arched heads of rubbed brick, and three small upper windows. The S and W walls, rebuilt in the early 19th century, have each two large round-arched windows with intersecting glazing bars; the S wall is gabled and has a tablet inserted in 1868. An early 19th-century vestry stands against the N wall. The interior (26ft by 26½ft) has an E gallery of the early 19th century, and a children's gallery above the N vestry, closed by later shutters. The burial-ground to the N was enlarged in 1858. (Chapel rebuilt or greatly altered 1973)

Tibbutt, H.G., *Cranfield Baptist Church, 1660–1960* (1961).

(25) WESLEYAN (SP 952419). Built 1839 with a broad front of three bays, extended by one bay to the right and new end entrance with lean-to porch built at opposite end. Date tablet reset.

DEAN AND SHELTON

(26) CONGREGATIONAL, Upper Dean (TL 048679). The chapel built in 1863 'at the sole cost of William Ackroyd Esq.' has walls of yellow brick with red-brick and stone dressings. The gabled front is divided into three bays by pilasters with carved Corinthian capitals and the side walls, of six bays, are similarly ornamented. (URC)

DUNSTABLE

(27) OLD BAPTIST CHAPEL, St Mary's Street (TL 018217). Baptists from Dunstable initially formed part of the 17th-century church meeting in and about Kensworth, Beds. (formerly Herts.), which divided into separate churches about 1688. The first meeting-house in St Mary's Street was built in 1708 and enlarged to double its size in 1807. The present chapel, which stands on the site of the former, was built in 1849. The walls are of yellow stock brick with red brick arches to the windows and the roof is slated. The NW front is gabled and has a central doorway with pilasters and a moulded cornice, two flanking windows and a blind round-arched recess above. The interior, refitted 1875–8, has a continuous gallery.

Monuments: in chapel on SW wall (1) Lawrence Chessher, 1819, minister, and Mary his wife, 1817; externally on NE wall (2) Mary Hudnal, of Tatternhoe, 1808. In burial-ground NW and NE late 18th-century headstones with winged cherubs' heads, inscriptions decayed.

Baker, R., *For the Generation Following: 1675–1975: A History of the Old Baptist Chapel, Dunstable* (1975).

(28) BAPTIST, West Street (TL 018219). A chapel was built in 1801 by a section of the church that formerly met at Thorn (41). The Dunstable members separated from the joint church in or about 1835 and rebuilt their chapel in 1847–8.

The chapel, by J. Clarke, has a three-bay front of red brick with pedimented centre, yellow brick quoins to the side bays and two tiers of windows, the upper ones round-arched, with an inner order of yellow brick. Some early 19th-century tombstones remain in front.

BM XL (1848) 427.

DUNTON

(29) Former BAPTIST, Chapel Street (TL 237442). Yellow gault brick with gabled front, upper windows added. Built *c*.1860. (Now a garage)

EASTCOTTS

(30) COTTON END CHAPEL (TL 085455). Meetings of Independents were held at Cotton End from the 17th century. In 1776 a church was established which has generally been regarded

Cotton End Chapel, Eastcotts. (30)

as Baptist, although for a long period in the 19th century it had a mixed congregation and a Congregational minister who also conducted a notable academy for ministerial students of his own denomination. The former meeting-house, registered in 1777, was 28ft square before being enlarged by 14ft in 1796 and subsequently further altered. It was replaced by the present chapel in 1836–7.

The chapel has walls of gault brick and a slate roof. The front, of three bays, with two tiers of round-arched windows and altered entrance, has a pediment with two large stone tablets, one dated 1836. The interior, partly refitted in the late 19th century, has a gallery around three sides with box-pews and benches with formerly open backs behind. A chandelier donated by Bunyan Meeting (8) in 1838 is unlocated.

Monuments: in chapel (1) Rev. William Kilpin, 1791; (2) Rev. John Holloway, 1831.

Tibbutt, H.G., *Cotton End Old Meeting, 1776–1962* (1963).

EATON BRAY

(31) PROVIDENCE CHAPEL (SP 975199). Strict Baptist, built 1835; red brick and slate with original sash windows on one side to the ground floor. The chapel was heightened and widened in 1851.

(32) WESLEYAN (SP 970212). Brick with rendered sides and hipped slate roof. An oval tablet reset inside the front vestibule is inscribed 'Built 1795, enlarged 1806, re-enlarged 1829' and on the front wall '… improved 1864'. Three-bay W front with corner pilasters, two doorways and two tiers of round-arched windows; three-bay sides with two tiers of windows, the upper ones arched. No 18th-century structure is recognizable and the interior (42ft by 28¾ft) with gallery around three sides was refitted *c*.1864. The seating comprises box-pews with stop-chamfered panelled doors and sides to the lower floor, and open pews with shaped ends to the gallery. Rostrum pulpit with open balustraded front and small railed communion area in front. *Monument*: in chapel, to James Battams, 1817, and Margaret his widow, 1839, recording a bequest of £200.

EGGINGTON

(33) Former WESLEYAN (SP 955252). Yellow brick and slate, built 1845, enlarged to the front and heightened 1867. S front of three bays with end pilasters and simple pediment; round-arched windows with cast-iron frames at sides. (Converted to house since *c*.1980)

ELSTOW

(34) BAPTIST (TL 050478). 'Bunyan Memorial Hall' of 1910 has a *window* of painted glass with fifteen scenes from *The Pilgrim's Progress*.

CYB (1911) 147.

FELMERSHAM

(35) Former WESLEYAN, Radwell (TL 005575). Rubble walls with red brick E front and slate roof, built 1807. Three-bay gabled front with round-arched central doorway and fanlight, two tiers of flat-arched sash windows and circular gable tablet with date of erection. Side walls each with a single sash window but with traces of other

FORMER WESLEYAN CHAPEL, RADWELL   CFS 1973

blocked windows in S wall. Rear wall has two large round-arched windows flanking the pulpit. The interior has an original E gallery with panelled front; the seating and pulpit (removed 1972) were renewed in the late 19th century. (Chapel demolished since 1973; site now occupied by a house incorporating the original circular date tablet)

Monuments: in chapel on N wall (1) Samuel Wright, 1814, and Mary his wife, 1813, stone tablet with moulded pediment and shaped apron; on S wall (2) Lucy wife of William Swannell, 1814, stone tablet with panelled cheeks, moulded pediment and apron; on W wall (3) Joseph Swannell, 1817, 'through whose pious zeal this Chapel was Erected'. In burial-ground W of chapel (4) Joseph Swannell, 1817, Mary wife of Joseph Swannell, jnr., 1817, and Joseph Worth infant son of Joseph and Catherine Swannell, 1841, panelled table-tomb with fluted corner pilasters in formerly railed enclosure.

Farrar, C.F., *The Ouse's Silent Tide* (1921) 50–2.

HARROLD

(36) CONGREGATIONAL (SP 948569). The first chapel, built in 1808, was replaced by the present building in 1836; this was enlarged to the front in 1863 by John Usher of Bedford. The pedimented S front is of yellow brick with red brick dressings and stone quoins. The E wall of red brick, dating from 1836, has been refenestrated as has the W wall, which is of rubble with brick dressings to the later windows. (URC)

Monuments: in chapel (1) John Mardling, 1811, 'through whose pious zeal this Chapel was erected …', and Hannah his widow, 1830; (2) Rev. George Bull Phillips, 1861, 33 years minister; (3) Rev. William Jones, 1886, more than 10 years pastor; in burial-ground to the W, acquired after 1836, (4) Benjamin Lever, 1849, and Letitia his widow, 1850.

CYB (1865) 301. Lay, H.C., *Harrold Congregational Church* (1959).

HAYNES

(37) WESLEYAN, Silver End Road (TL 100423). Chapel of gault brick with coloured brick decoration, rebuilt 1874. *Monuments*: in railed forecourt (1) Maria daughter of James and Maria Cole, 1840; (2) their children Charlotte, 1843, and Benjamin, 1843; (3) James Cole, 1853.

BEDFORDSHIRE

HEATH AND REACH

(38) BAPTIST (SP 926281). Small chapel of red brick and slate built 1822 as a preaching-station for Leighton Buzzard. Plain gabled front, interior refitted and lengthened. On outbuilding to W are several dated bricks including one inscribed 'JC 1822'.

Tibbutt, H.G., *The Baptists of Leighton Buzzard* (1963) 24–6.

HOCKLIFFE

(39) CONGREGATIONAL (SP 974266). Preaching, which was commenced by a minister from Woburn in a house registered in 1806, was transferred in 1809 to a barn, in which a gallery was built in 1812. The present chapel, on the SW side of Watling Street, was built in 1825 and a gallery inserted in 1834. The walls are of red brick and the roof is slated. The front is pedimented, of three bays with two stages of round-arched windows, the upper range blind until 1873, and a wide central doorway with fanlight. A lunette-shaped tablet in the pediment is inscribed 'HOCKLIFFE CHAPEL 1825'. Interior refitted in the late 19th century. (Derelict 2000)

Tibbutt, H.G., *Hockliffe and Eggington Congregational Church, 1809–1959* (1959).

HOUGHTON CONQUEST

(40) WESLEYAN, Rectory Lane (TL 044414). Yellow brick with three-bay gabled front divided by buttresses. Opened 1875.

HOUGHTON REGIS

(41) BAPTIST BURIAL-GROUND, Thorn (SP 999248). A new meeting-house, registered 10 July 1740, was built for a section of the church at Park Street, Luton (see (49)). The church at Thorn became autonomous in 1751 and after c.1801 met separately at Dunstable (28) and Houghton Regis (42). The meeting-house was subsequently demolished but its outline (about 18ft by 28ft) remains visible within a rectangular enclosure bounded by a ditch about 200 yards NW of Thorngreen Farm.

Monuments: (1) Sara[h] (Fowler) wife of Zaccheus Cole of Toddington, 1784, James Fowler her brother, 1784, son of John and Elizabeth Fowler of Old Park, and two infants, table-tomb with stone-panelled sides and square quarter balusters at the corners, signed 'Wing, Bedford'; (2) Sarah [ ] and John Bu[ ], table-tomb with brick sides and decayed capstone, early 19th-century; (3) wooden grave-board with square posts and rail,

Baptist chapel, Houghton Regis. (Demolished) (42)

mid 19th-century; also the following headstones (4) Rev.S[amuel?] [G...ns?], 1787, pastor, two cherubs' heads and floral decoration above oval inscription panel; (5) Elizabeth daughter of John and Elizabeth Fowler of Old Park, 1771; (6) Elizabeth wife of Philip Fowler, 1784; (7) headstone dated 1800; (8) Thomas Sutton Crow, son of Thomas and Ruth Crow, 1812; (9) Elizabeth wife of Philip Fowler jnr., 1795; (10) Sarah Harris, 1793; (11) Sarah Harris, 1790; (12) James, Charlotte and Ruth, children of George and Elizabeth Strange of Legrove, 1793, 1794, 1794; (13) Mrs Hannah Scroggs, 1834.

Brown, J. and Prothero, D., *The History of the Bedfordshire Union of Christians* (1946) 60. Fisher, J.S., *People of the Meeting House: Tales of a Church in Luton* (1975) 20–1.

(42) BAPTIST, Houghton Regis (TL 017237). Meetings began c.1760 in the house of Thomas Bunker, minister at Thorn (41). A 'temporary' meeting-house built in 1790 was replaced in 1803 using materials from Thorn but superseded c.1864 by a chapel of dark brick and stone in the Lombardic style with a prominent tower above the entrance. (Demolished 1972–3)

KNOTTING AND SOULDROP

(43) WESLEYAN, Souldrop (SP 984620). Small chapel dated 1912, of brick with wood-framed mullioned windows and enriched eaves cornices, in the domestic style of the period.

LANGFORD

(44) WESLEYAN, High Street (TL 186406). Gault brick front of three bays with pilasters; pediment altered. Opened 1862.

LEIGHTON-LINSLADE

(45) BAPTIST, Lake Street, Leighton Buzzard (SP 923249). A former General Baptist meeting-house appears to have been purchased privately for the use of a Particular Baptist church formed in 1775. This building was replaced c.1801 by a square chapel, about 32ft by 34ft, which was later enlarged; in 1864 it was superseded by the present chapel by J. Neale of Bristol. The walls are of brick with stone dressings in the Italian Romanesque style with a large wheel-window above the entrance. Adjacent on the N is a cottage of brick and tile, possibly concealing a timber frame of the late 17th century, enlarged to the front in yellow brick in the early 19th century for Sunday-school purposes; a brick is inscribed 'TT 1839'. *Monuments*: in chapel (1) Robert Hawkins, 1788, and Susanna his widow, 1807, 'who in her life time vested this Meeting-House and premises adjoining into the hands of six trustees for … Particular Baptists'; (2) Joseph James, 1791, first pastor; (3) Thomas Wake, 1828, pastor.

Rippon, J. *The Baptist Annual Register* IV (1801–2). Tibbutt, H.G., *The Baptists of Leighton Buzzard* (1963) 5–11.

(46) STRICT BAPTIST, New Road, Linslade (SP 914250). Red brick and slate, three-bay pedimented front with pointed-arched entrance and two tiers of sash windows with square labels; platband at upper cill level. A tablet in the pediment is inscribed 'BETHEL 1843'. Enlarged 1853.

Tibbutt (1963) op. cit. above, 29.

(47) FRIENDS, North Street, Leighton Buzzard (SP 922253). The house of Joseph Brooks was registered for Quakers on 20 July 1761, but a regular meeting was not settled until 1776. The present meeting-house, built in 1787 and registered on 15 April 1789, was enlarged to the N in 1812. It has brick walls and a hipped tiled roof. The E front with plinth and moulded eaves cornice is of dark glazed brickwork laid to header bond with red brick dressings. The original entrance between two wooden cross-framed windows has been reduced in width and a narrower doorcase with bracketed pediment added c.1812. The present entrance is covered by an open timber porch; to the N two sash windows light the principal room. The W wall, in an irregular mixture of English and Flemish bond brickwork, has been extended in lighter coloured brick and has three windows of the early 19th century. A cottage added against the N wall has been removed.

The interior (48¾ft by 18¾ft) is divided into two rooms by a partition with vertically sliding shutters; the smaller S room is subdivided by a modern partition. The stand against the N end comprises three tiers of seating with horizontally boarded backs and arm-rests with turned baluster supports.

Butler (1999) 4–5.

LITTLE STAUGHTON

(48) Site of BAPTIST (TL 109620). A Baptist meeting was commenced in 1751 but although in 1762 all Baptist services were transferred to Hail Weston (Hunts.(18)) minor meetings continued and a house was registered for Particular Baptists in 1766. Subsequently a meeting-house was built, registered for Protestant dissenters in 1786 and enlarged to the rear in 1793; this remained standing until 1944, when it was demolished as an alleged danger to aircraft from a nearby military airfield. The meeting-house (approximately 40ft square) had rendered walls, possibly on a timber frame, with a brick plinth and hipped tiled roofs. The W front of four bays had two adjacent entrances and two tiers of windows with renewed sashes. In the E wall were two round-arched windows between two tiers of plain sashes. A vestry projected on the N. The roof of the original building had a central flat or valley, the extension to the E had three separately hipped roofs with valleys discharging to the rear.

An extensive burial-ground remains around the site of the meeting-house on which is a flat slab commemorating the first pastor, the Rev. John Emery, 1799.

Page (1953) 10–12. Tibbutt, H.G., *Little Staughton Meeting* (1951).

LUTON

(49) UNION CHAPEL, Castle Street (TL 091210). Luton Baptists, originally a section of the Kensworth church, separated c.1690 and built a meeting-house in Park Street in 1698. This was replaced in

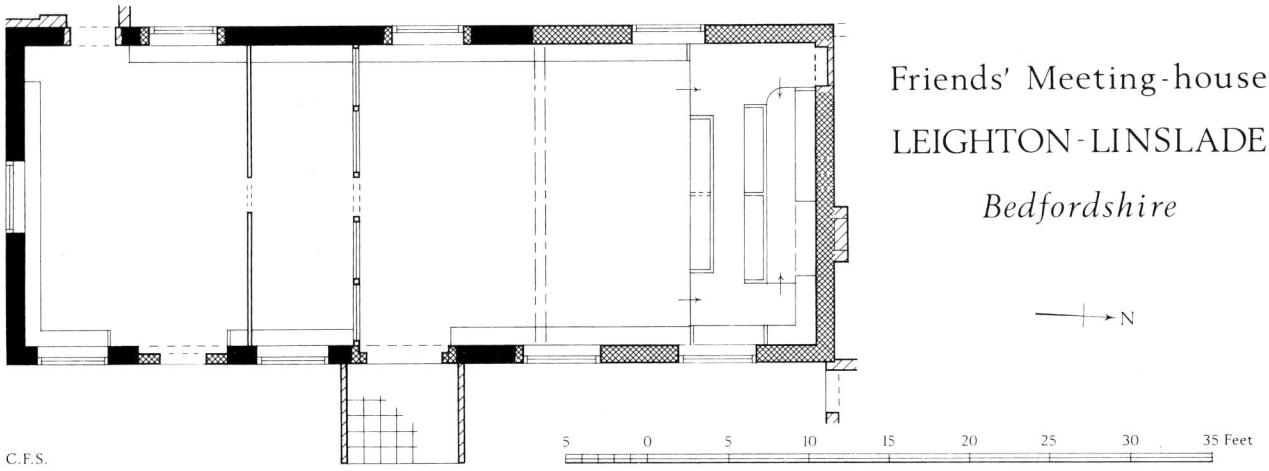

Friends' Meeting-house
LEIGHTON-LINSLADE
Bedfordshire

Union Chapel, Luton. (49)

Ebenezer Chapel, Luton. (51)

1815 by an octagonal chapel, itself replaced in 1867 and since rebuilt. A secession occurred in 1836–7 and the seceders bought 'part of Langley's Close, a meadow adjoining Langley Street' on which Union Chapel was built and registered in September 1839. The chapel was enlarged to the rear in 1844 and further premises built behind for the Sunday-school in 1892.

The chapel has rendered walls and a slate roof. The pedimented W front of three bays with two Doric columns *in antis* has two tiers of windows with battered jambs and a refashioned stepped approach to the central entrance. The side walls, originally of five bays, have tall round-arched recesses enclosing three tiers of windows. The interior has a continuous gallery and an upper W gallery with cast-iron front and plain backless benches; other fittings were renewed in the late 19th century. (Now in residential use following the union of three Baptist congregations; interior stripped *c.*1988)

Fisher, J.S., *People of the Meeting House: Tales of a Church in Luton* (1975).

(50) Former BAPTIST, Wellington Street (TL 089210). 'Ceylon Chapel', so named out of respect for a former minister of Park who served as a missionary on the island. The church originated in 1846 by a secession of members from Park Street and Union chapels and the chapel was built in 1849. This was extended and re-fronted *c.*1889 and a large Sunday-school erected in 1908. The original building, of brick, has tall pointed-arched windows in the side walls. The late 19th-century front, of brick with stone dressings, is of three bays with intermediate buttresses and pinnacles, the centre bay is gabled and has a traceried window of five lights above the entrance. The large Sunday-school behind the chapel is in the free Gothic style by George Baines and Son.

In 1975 this church united with those at Park Street and Union Chapel to form 'Luton Central Baptist Church'; Park Street Chapel was subsequently rebuilt for the combined congregation. (Ceylon Chapel was sold *c.*1985 and converted to offices)

B.Hbk (1911) 513. Fisher (1975) op. cit. above, 40, 49–50, 66.

(51) EBENEZER CHAPEL, Hastings Street (TL 089209). The Strict Baptist church meeting here originated in 1832 in a small chapel in Ebenezer Street, a narrow alley off Chapel Street, which survived until after 1945 but has since been demolished. The present chapel, built in 1853, is of brick with a rendered front wall of three bays with a pediment. There are two entrances at the front and round-arched windows throughout.

The interior retains a complete set of original fittings with a rear gallery facing a polygonal-fronted pulpit with arched back-board, three ranks of box-pews and two plaster ceiling roses.

Railings: in front of chapel, of cast iron, by Brown & Green Ltd, ironfounders, of Luton.

Paul III (1958) 208–15, illus. facing 216.

(52) BETHEL CHAPEL, Chapel Street (TL 090209). The second Strict Baptist church, which originated in 1873, built the first chapel on this site in 1877. That was replaced by the present building in 1906; this has a front of three bays with a shaped gable. A rear gallery has been extended forward in recent times.

Paul III (1958) 215–20. *The Times* 18 September 1993.

(53) CONGREGATIONAL, Stuart Street (TL 090211). The large and prominently sited chapel of 1865–6 by John Tarring is in the Decorated Gothic style. It comprises a nave with transepts and corner tower with spire. The walls are faced with polygonal masonry. The interior is galleried and has an organ apse above the vestry. (Demolished *c.*1971)

CYB (1866) 310; (1867) illus. facing 367.

(54) CONGREGATIONAL, Waldeck Road (TL 084229). The chapel intended to serve the new suburb of Bury Park was commenced in 1895 with the erection of a 'school-chapel', the present Sunday-school in Bury Park Road, to the designs of W.J. Pearson. To this was added in 1903 the chapel by George and R. Palmer Baines, which stands on a corner site and has a prominent tower with short spire. The Sunday-school was enlarged in 1916. (URC)

CYB (1897) 174; (1902) 145; (1903) 157–8.

(55) Former FRIENDS, Castle Street (TL 092211). The meeting-house built in 1799 to replace an earlier building of 1741, was enlarged in 1835. Brick walls with three round-arched windows in the SW wall. (Sold and demolished since c.1975)
  Butler (1999) 5–7.

(56) WESLEYAN, Chapel Street (TL 091211). Yellow brick with stone dressings, 1851–2 by W.W. Pocock. Five-bay front with two tiers of windows, the upper ones round-arched; three centre bays project and carry a raised pediment above three circular windows. (Demolished c.1980–2)

(57) PRIMITIVE METHODIST, High Town Road (TL 093218). The first chapel, built 1852, stands alongside its successor of 1897. The former, which was converted to a lecture hall and refenestrated, originally had a front of yellow brick with brown brick dressings; over all was a continuous entablature with terminal pilasters and a raised central pediment; there were six tall round-arched windows at the front and a double entrance below the central pair.

The later chapel, by J.D. and S.D. Mould of Manchester, has walls of purple brick with stone dressings. The front has a pedimented centre and paired arched entrances; flanking bays are brought forward and that to the left rises as a tower with a wooden upper stage and square dome with small cupola above.
  Kendall (1905) II: 353.

(58) Former PRIMITIVE METHODIST, Cardigan Street (TL 088215). Pedimented front of brick with wide round-arched surround to entrance between two tall windows. Built 1880. (Now converted to Hindu temple)
  Kendall (1905) II: 383.

(59) Former PRIMITIVE METHODIST, Castle Street (TL 091207). 'Mount Tabor' chapel, built 1897, now Luton Christian Fellowship, has a gabled front between buttresses rising to octagonal turrets and a window of four lights with plate tracery. A later hall adjoins to the right.
  Kendall (1905) II: 383.

MARSTON MORETAINE

(60) WESLEYAN, Little Shelton (SP 998426). The present chapel of 1858 with walls of red brick with yellow brick dressings and lancet windows stands alongside its plainer predecessor of 1813, now the Sunday-school. The former chapel, of brick with a slate roof now gabled but perhaps originally hipped, has a central segmental-arched doorway between round-arched windows. An oval tablet, reset inside, is inscribed 'The Methodist Chapel 1813'. *Monument*: in front of former chapel, Jane daughter of William and Jane Bennett, 1822.

MAULDEN

(61) BAPTIST (TL 047379). The church, which originated in the late 17th century, appears to have built a new meeting-house about 1751 which was considerably enlarged in the early 19th century and drastically altered in 1861. The present building, which may incorporate parts of the earlier structure, has been entirely encased in yellow brick with red brick dressings and given a hipped slate roof, all of 1861, but the proportions remain those of the former building. The front wall has two principal entrances and two tiers of round-arched windows in groups of two and three. The interior (32½ft by 53ft) has galleries around three sides with sliding shutters below both side galleries and above one of them. *Monuments*: many early 19th-century wall monuments remain in the chapel, including (1) Rev. Samuel Hobson, 1841, 33 years pastor; (2) Rev. William Coles, 1809. In burial-ground, headstones of late 18th and early 19th century reset against boundary walls, also wooden grave-boards including (3) James Savage, 1836.
  Peer, A.H., *A History of Ampthill Union Church* (1963) 14–24.

(62) PRIMITIVE METHODIST, The Brache (TL 052382). Gabled front of red brick with yellow brick dressings, dated 1860.

MELCHBOURNE AND YIELDEN

(63) WESLEYAN, Spring Lane, Yielden (TL 012670). Small chapel with red-brick gabled front and polychrome brick dressings. Arched date tablet of 1884 inscribed 'John Blunt architect'.

Congregational chapel, Stuart Street, Luton. (Demolished) (53)

MILTON ERNEST

(64) Former WESLEYAN (TL 018560). Small chapel of brick and slate, built 1839. Rendered pedimented front of three bays with simple pilasters, round-arched doorway with fanlight.

PERTENHALL

(65) Former MORAVIAN, Wood End (TL 091660). Meetings commenced in 1809 by John Henry Martyn, assistant curate and subsequently rector of Pertenhall, who lived in a house, Woodend, NW of the present chapel, resulted in the formation of a regular Moravian society and in his leaving the Church of England and eventually becoming a bishop of the Moravian Church. Prior to the erection of the chapel in 1827 services are believed to have been held in a garden building registered for worship in March 1823. Parts of its structure, possibly the roof timbers, were incorporated in the new building. A two-storeyed school-room was added to the SW in the mid 19th century. The chapel was closed before 1967.

Former Moravian chapel, Pertenhall. (Demolished) (65)

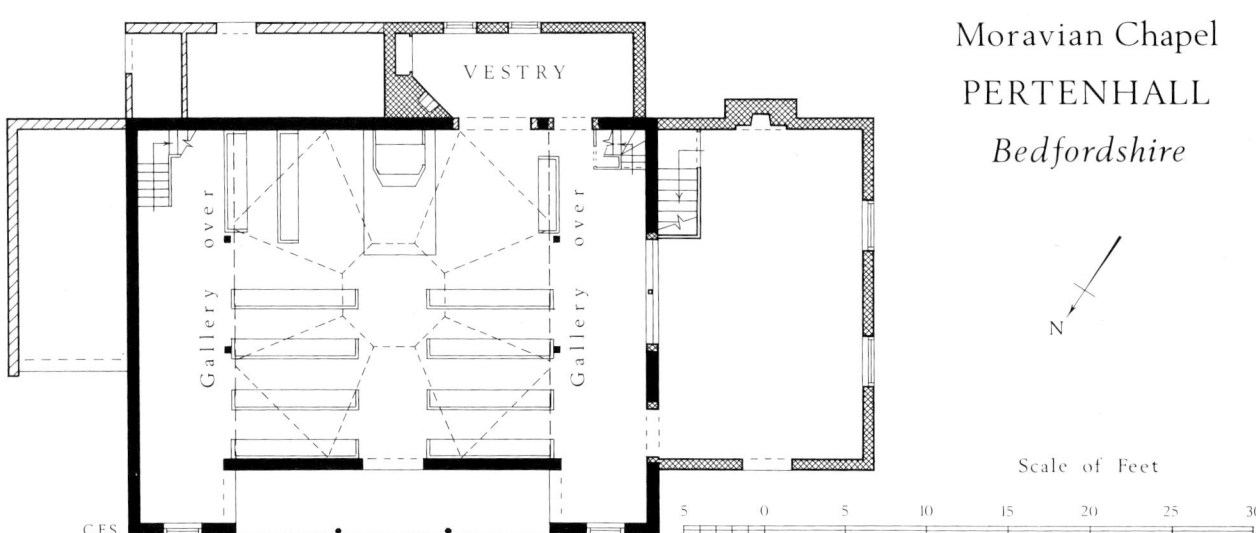

Moravian Chapel
PERTENHALL
Bedfordshire

Former Moravian chapel, Pertenhall. (Demolished)

The chapel is a small building standing at one end of a garden enclosure flanked on the NE by a range of cottages; the walls are of brick with a rendered timber-framed superstructure and the roof is slated. The body of the chapel is square, with narrow outshots against two sides which project at the front as gabled porches, each with a small circular window, and united by an open veranda covering a central entrance. The interior has a tiny gallery above each outshot; the plaster ceiling rises as a truncated octagonal dome below the square hipped roof to a square pyramidally roofed lantern, also reduced internally to an octagonal shape. (Chapel demolished since 1974 and replaced by garages; later school-room survives)

Fittings – *Inscription*: foundation stone at SW end of front wall, dated 17 April 1827. *Monuments*: in burial-ground behind chapel, flat rectangular tablets, many of slate, with dates from *c.*1830; also marble tablet to John King Martyn MA, 1849, bishop of the Brethren's Church, erected 1874.

England (1888) 38–9.

POTSGROVE

(66) Former WESLEYAN, Sheep Lane (SP 933305). Brick with three-bay gabled front and round-arched openings. Registered 1865. (Derelict 1978)

POTTON

(67) THE OLD MEETING-HOUSE, Horselow Street (TL 221493). A remarkable improvement in religious life in Potton between 1742 and 1762 recorded by John Wesley in his *Journal* (9 January 1762) may be attributed largely to the work of John Berridge, vicar of Everton from 1756. After 1758 several buildings were registered for nonconformists, including on 25 May 1761 'a Meeting in King Street for Baptists'. The present Baptist meeting-house, registered 1 May 1802 and described as 'newly erected', is a plain square building of brick with a pyramidal slated roof. The S front of three bays has two segmental-arched doorways with one window between and three recently altered windows above. The side walls have each two tiers of segmental-arched windows in three bays; a vestry projects to the E. The *burial-ground* was partly cleared *c.*1973 and several monuments destroyed; those remaining include one to William Tite, 1861, 25 years pastor of the Particular Baptist Church in Potton; loose and broken.

RAVENSDEN

(68) ZION CHAPEL (TL 067542). The Baptist congregation in Ravensden traces its origins to the work of the Rev. Timothy Richard Matthews, sometime curate of Colmworth and Bolnhurst, whose popular but eccentric preaching as chaplain to the House of Industry in Bedford led in 1834 to his removal to a new chapel built for him in Bromham Road, Bedford (11). In the same year he registered a building in Ravensden which he called 'The Episcopal Church', and after his death in 1845 some of his admirers collected money for the erection of Zion Chapel, opened in 1853. The chapel is a plain building of gault brick enlarged to the rear in 1863 and partly obscured by a cottage at the front.

Fittings – *Bugle*: brass, used by the Rev. T.R. Matthews at Bromham Road Chapel to attract public attention. *Communion Table*: in gallery, with thin turned legs, late 18th-century.

Fensome, L.C., *A Village Bethel* (*c.*1953).

The Old Meeting-house, Potton. (67)

RIDGMONT

(69) BAPTIST (SP 973358). Built in 1811 replacing an earlier meeting-house on the site, for a church formed 1701. Brick walls with gabled front, cement rendered in 1884.

(70) Former WESLEYAN (SP 977363). Red brick and slate with stone dressings, corner pinnacles and two-centred arched windows; gabled front with defaced tablet. Registered 1845.

RISELEY

(71) Former MORAVIAN (TL 044630). Services commenced in 1751 and John Cennick, the Moravian evangelist, preached here in the following year. A chapel built in 1759 was superseded by another on the present site in 1810. This was enlarged to the front and porches added in 1862 reusing two former front windows of three lights with intersecting glazing bars in the extended side walls.

The chapel has brick walls and a low gabled front with end porches and three round-arched windows between. (Now used as a small art gallery)

England (1888) 39, Pl. XVI.

(72) Site of BAPTIST (TL 043628). The former chapel, opened 1838 closed c.1945, on the corner of High Street and Keysoe Road, has been demolished. Two headstones remain, (1) James Curtis, 1840, and Naomi his widow 1875, with footstone; (2) Robert Bayes, 1868, and John William his infant son, 1858.

BM (December 1838) 552. Page (1953) 27.

ROXTON

(73) ROXTON CHAPEL (TL 152545). Occasional services which commenced in 1808 in a barn at one corner of Roxton Park with the support of the squire, Charles James Metcalfe, a member of the Independent church at St Neots, developed into regular meetings and a separate church was formed in 1822. The original late 18th-century barn, of three bays, which forms the body of the present chapel, was enlarged with wings to N and S and given a rustic appearance c.1825.

The chapel has rendered timber-framed walls and a thatched roof. The principal entrance is at the E end with minor entrances at the ends of the two wings, that to the S, which faces Roxton Hall, being treated as a bark-lined summer house. The windows

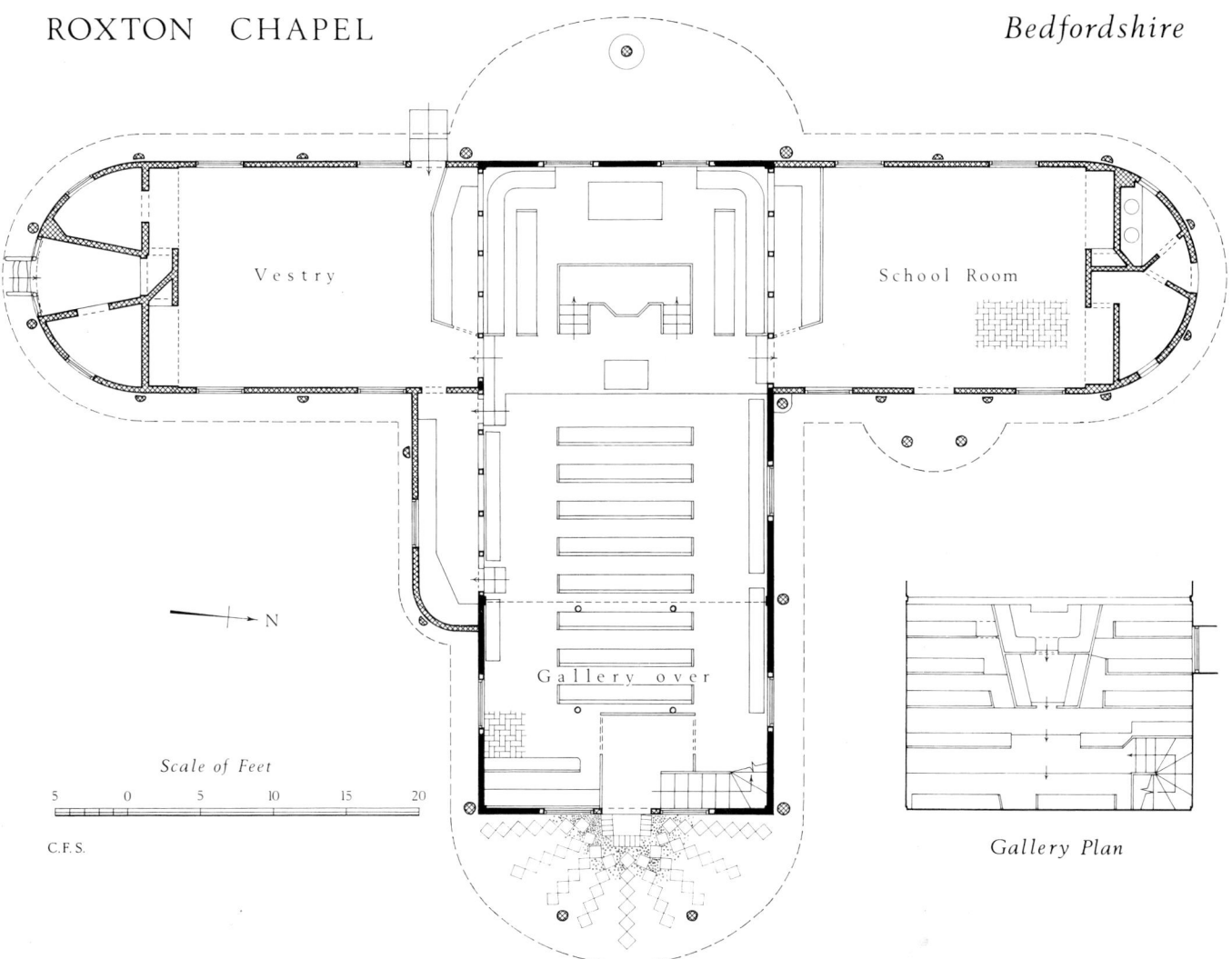

ROXTON CHAPEL — Bedfordshire

Gallery Plan

C.F.S.

Roxton Chapel. (73)

have ogee-arched heads of two principal lights. The walls are divided into bays by rustic pillars of tree trunks. The interior of the original building is ceiled at collar level and has a gallery at the E end with a central singers' pew. A private pew stands against the S wall with an open arcade of five ogee-arched bays to the chapel; similar arcades close the ends of the two wings behind which later screens enclose additional pews.

Fittings – *Clock*: on front of gallery, signed 'Clare, Bedford', of the mid 19th century. *Paving*: at E entrance, cobbles with radiating pattern of small square flagstones. *Pulpit*: in front of organ, rostrum incorporating early 19th-century panelling, formerly set against W wall. *Seating*: in chapel, plain open-backed benches.

Tibbutt, H.G., *Roxton Congregational Church, 1808–1958* (1958).

SHARNBROOK

(74) Former STRICT BAPTIST (SP 997596). The congregation formed into church order in 1719 rebuilt its meeting-house about 1786, registering it in 1790. The present chapel, erected in 1865 to the designs of John Usher, is of brick with rubble sides and a hipped slate roof. The SW front of three bays with a central pediment is of yellow brick with red and orange bricks in the window arches and a tiled frieze. The interior has an open timber roof, a gallery around three sides with cast-iron front and supporting columns, and varnished pitch-pine seating; behind the pulpit is a small tablet dated 1786.

Fittings – *Benefaction Tablet*: behind pulpit, recording a legacy of £200 from William Curtis. *Bootscraper*: of cast iron with lion's head on scraper bar *c*.1865. *Collecting Shovel*: wood, with short

Former Strict Baptist chapel, Sharnbrook. (74)

shaped handle and round-ended covered tray, late 18th-century. *Communion Table*: with two legs and ground bearers, corners cut and braces added, late 18th-century. *Monuments*: in chapel (1) James Ward of Souldrop, 1866; (2) Rev. Richard Emery, 1837, pastor nearly 5 years. *Plate*: pewter, includes a pair of two-handled cups and three plates.

Page (1953) 27–8.

(75) WESLEYAN, Park Lane (SP 996597). Red brick with stone dressings; dated 1911.

SHEFFORD

(76) BAPTIST (TL 143395). The chapel, built in 1825 in succession to a barn registered in 1814, has brick walls and a hipped slate roof. The front is covered by a later and altered porch with a large tablet reset above the entrance recording the date of erection. (Porch rebuilt, 1986). The interior, partly refitted, has an early 19th-century gallery at the S end with contemporary pews with shaped ends. *Clock*: on gallery front, signed 'Inskip, Shefford'. *Table*: in vestry, perhaps a former communion table, with two legs and ground bearers, early 19th-century.

Page (1953) 28–9.

(77) WESLEYAN, Ampthill Road (TL 141390). The chapel, built in 1912 on the site of an earlier building, is of brick with stone dressings in the free Gothic style, possibly by George Baines and Son. The front is gabled, with the parapet swept up at the apex, and flanked by corner turrets with bracketed cornices and iron finials. A mid 19th-century Sunday-school range lies behind. *Monuments*: (1) Thomas Inskip, 1859, and Harriet his wife, 1835, pedestal; also reset against boundary walls on E side, headstones and other monuments of the late 19th century.

SHILLINGTON

(78) CONGREGATIONAL (TL 125340). Union Chapel, opened 1841, is of yellow brick with a gabled front partly obscured by a utilitarian lean-to porch. Original box-pews remain but a chandelier donated by Bunyan Meeting, Bedford (8), can no longer be found.

EM NS XX (1842) 131–2.

(79) WESLEYAN, High Road (TL 127340). Gault brick with stone dressings, gabled front between octagonal corner buttresses. Built 1872, with adjacent Sunday-school of 1879.

(80) Former WESLEYAN, Pegsdon (TL 120303). Small brick chapel formerly with entrance in gabled front. Built 1841. (Now garage)

SOUTHILL

(81) SOUTHILL CHAPEL (TL 155421). The congregation originated as an Independent church formed in 1693 which gradually adopted Baptist principles after 1776 and became Strict Baptist in 1846. The chapel erected in 1805, probably on a new site but perhaps incorporating some older material, was repaired in 1847 and the roof rebuilt at or about that date. The walls are

Southill Chapel. (81)

Southill Chapel. (81)

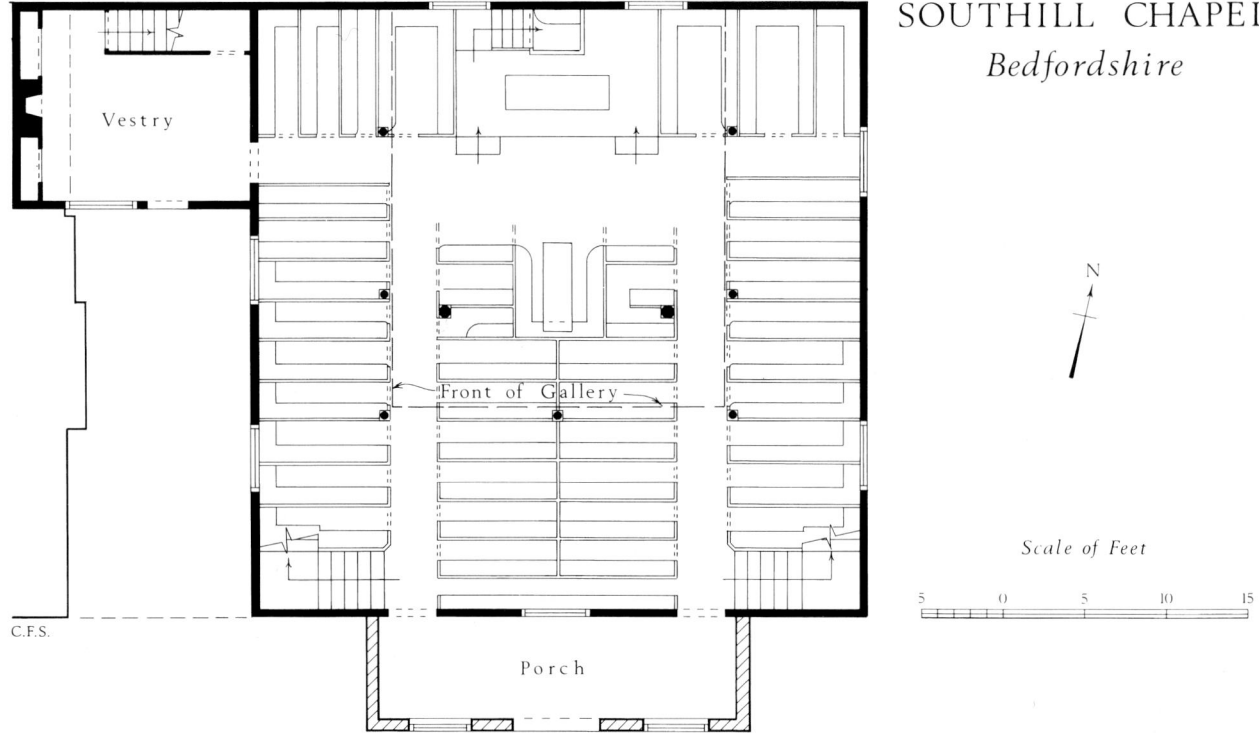

SOUTHILL CHAPEL
Bedfordshire

timber-framed and the roof is slated. The exterior is plain with sash windows and a later wide porch to the S covering the two original entrances. A vestry projects to the NW and has a school-room above, which continues above the gap between the chapel and the adjacent manse.

The interior ($37\frac{1}{2}$ ft square) retains most of its early 19th-century fittings. The roof is supported by two octagonal pillars of oak which carry the former valley beam. The floor is paved with bricks. A gallery around three sides is supported by turned wood columns and has a panelled front with applied mouldings. The upper school-room to the W has movable shutters opening into the body of the chapel.

Fittings – *Baptisteries*: originally under gallery near vestry door, new baptistery built below table-pew in 1847, subsequently resited under pulpit platform. *Collecting shovels*: each with enclosed box with single turned handle, of the late 19th century. *Clock*: on front of S gallery, 'Parliament clock' with shaped dial and chinoiserie ornament on pendulum case, signed 'James Pepper, Biggleswade', mid 18th-century. *Monuments*: in chapel (1) Ebenezer Barringer, 1850, and Wilkin Barringer, 1854; (2) Rev. Thomas Tay, 1842; (3) John Warburton, pastor, [1892]; (4) Rev. Edward Burton, 1817, signed 'B. Seager, Coventry, Sculpt.'. In porch (5) Rev. John Gamby, 1802, 'pastor of this church 15 years and 6 weeks', oval tablet. *Pulpit*: square with panelled front, c.1805. *Seating*: box-pews to lower floor and in gallery with unpainted panelled sides and painted numerals on doors; central table-pew, front removed; singers' pew with desk in cross gallery. *Stove*: 'tortoise stove', of late 19th-century (sold since 1969).

Paul III (1958) 53–92.

STANBRIDGE

(82) WESLEYAN (SP 965243). Red brick front of three bays with pilasters and pediment. Dated 1870. (Major alterations proposed 1972)

STEVINGTON

(83) BAPTIST, West End (SP 983537). The church, formed about 1655 apparently by Independents but becoming Baptist before the end of the 17th century, met from 1681 in Simon Peacocke's barn. The present meeting-house built in 1720–1 was extensively repaired in 1814, a vestry with school-room over was added in 1833, further repairs were carried out in 1855 and in 1891 a major

Baptist meeting-house, West End, Stevington. (83)

Baptist meeting-house, West End, Stevington. (83)

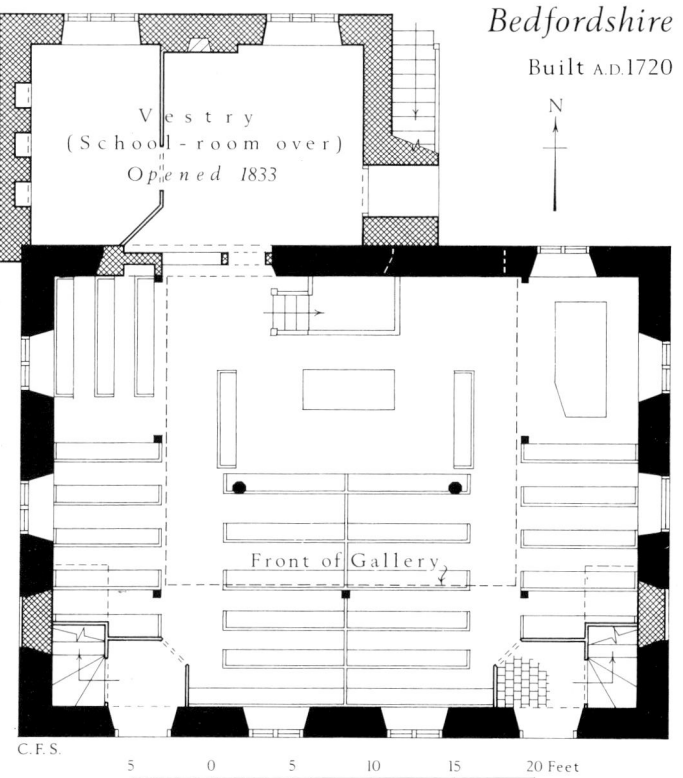

Baptist Meeting-house, STEVINGTON, *Bedfordshire*
Built A.D. 1720

programme of repair and refitting was undertaken. A baptistery built within the chapel yard in 1832 was replaced after 1894 by an internal baptistery.

The meeting-house has rubble walls and a tiled roof with central valley and double gables to each end wall; the doorways and windows have plain timber lintels. The S front has two entrances with a pair of cross-framed windows between and three windows of two principal lights above, all with wooden frames and leaded glazing. The vestry and Sunday-school projecting to the N are of rubble with a slate roof; to the E of the wing a wide upper window lights the pulpit.

The interior (27ft by 33ft) has two octagonal sectioned oak posts supporting the roof structure and a gallery around three sides with panelled front supported by chamfered posts. The seating and pulpit date from the late 19th century. The roof structure, of oak, comprises two trusses to each section of the main roof with tie-beams, struts below collars, and clasped purlins; there is no ridge; the principal and common rafters are of uniform depth.

Fittings – *Clock*: on front of S gallery, 'Parliament clock' with shaped dial, pendulum case decorated with painting of a horseman, signed 'Willm. Covington, Harrold', mid 18th-century. *Monuments*: in chapel (1) Rev. Joseph Such, 1831, 28 years pastor, oval tablet; (2) Mary wife of Rev. Joseph Such, 1805, oval tablet signed 'C. Drew, Bedford'; (3) Dinah widow of Rev. Joseph Such, 1857, signed 'Prior'; (4) John Haigh, 1850, 6½ years pastor; (5) Rev. J.C. Wooster, 1872, 6 years pastor. In vestry (6) Josiah, 1807, and Phebe, 1818, children of Joseph and Dinah Such; (7) Stephen son of Joseph and Dinah Such, 1831; (8) Susannah wife of Joseph Sheffield, 1798.

Tibbutt, H.G. (ed.), 'Some early Nonconformist Church Books', *Bedfordshire Historical Record Society* Vol. 51 (1972) 23–4.
Tibbutt, H.G., *Stevington Baptist Meeting, 1655–1955* (1955).

STOTFOLD

(84) Former BAPTIST, Rook Tree Lane (TL 222371). Built 1857 for church formed 1832, superseded 1967 by new chapel at The Green and converted to house. Brick with gabled front of three arched bays enclosing two tiers of windows.
BM XXV (1833) 132.

(85) Site of STRICT BAPTIST, Church Street (TL 219368). 'Rehoboth Chapel, 1841' replaced by pair of cottages, 1986, retaining date tablet.

(86) STRICT BAPTIST, Mill Lane (TL 222366). 'Hope Chapel, 1859', small, of grey brick.

TEMPSFORD

(87) WESLEYAN, Station Road (TL 167539). Gault brick with gabled front; flat-arched heads of red brick to two upper windows, porch and raking cornice added in the late 19th century. Small gable tablet inscribed 'EBENEZER 1804'. Rear gallery. *Monument*: on front wall, Rachel daughter of John and Elizabeth Browning, 1839.

THURLEIGH

(88) BAPTIST (TL 055585). The first chapel was built in 1827 and enlarged in 1841 and 1849. Its successor by F.T. Mercer, dated 1888, has a pedimented front with brick quoins and large arched window above the entrance. Galleried interior with contemporary fittings and Sunday-school gallery behind pulpit.
B.Hbk (1889) 383. *BM* XXXIII (1841) 572. Page (1953) 31–3.

TILSWORTH

(89) WESLEYAN (SP 981243). Rendered walls, three-bay gabled front with two tiers of round-arched windows. Dated 1862.

TODDINGTON

(90) BAPTIST, Station Road (TL 011290). The chapel of yellow brick with blue and red brick dressings was built in 1884, 'Rev. S.H. Akehurst architect'. It stands on the site of a chapel opened 1812 for a branch of the Independent Church at Hockcliffe. *Monuments*: in burial-ground (1) Richard Campion, 1845, *et al.*; (2) Thomas Willis, 1846, Alice his wife, 1845, *et al.*; (3) Ruth daughter of T[homas?] Willis, 1816; (4) Judith Fensom, George Willis and William Fensom, 1838, 1841, 1849.

Baptist meeting-house, West End, Stevington. Clock. (83)

Tibbutt, H.G., *Hockliffe and Eggington Congregational Church, 1809–1959* (1959) 6.

(91) WESLEYAN (TL 008287). Brown brick, gabled front with two round-arched windows. A circular tablet above the porch is dated 1846. Gable altered 1866.

Bourne, (ed.) (1993) 137–44.

TOTTERNHOE

(92) WESLEYAN, Castle Hill Road (SP 979219). Red brick and slate, gabled front with round-arched doorway with fanlight and similarly arched window above. Painted tablet in gable with date 1840; same date with name and initials on bricks around entrance. (Closed 1990, converted to house)

Bourne, (ed.) (1993) 145–53.

TURVEY

(93) CONGREGATIONAL (SP 944524). Brick and slate with gabled N front of three bays with two tiers of round-arched windows. Built 1828–9, altered and refitted 1894. Later Sunday-school above vestry to S with shuttered openings behind pulpit. *Monuments*: in chapel (1) Rev. Richard Cecil, 1863, first pastor. In burial-ground (2) Rev. Richard Cecil, 1863, table-tomb; (3) Mary wife of Joseph Paine, 1846; (4) Sarah Elizabeth wife of Nathaniel Godfrey, 1840; (5) John Abraham, 1849, *et al*.

(94) Former WESLEYAN (SP 942526). Rubble with brick dressings and slate roof; gabled front of three bays with central doorway and two tiers of windows, all with segmental-pointed arched heads. Circular tablet inscribed 'The Methodist Chapel, 1828'. Square ventilator and weather vane on roof, late 19th-century. (Converted to house)

WESTONING

(95) STRICT BAPTIST (TL 036328). 'Hope Chapel', built 1835 for a church existing from the late 18th century and formerly allied to the Old Meeting, Dunstable, has a plain broad front of brick with two tiers of sash windows and a slated roof. *Monuments*: Two wooden grave-boards in front of the chapel, one dated 1871.

In 1987–9 a much larger chapel was erected on an adjacent site, but the former building remains.

Grace (November 1993) 20–1. Paul III (1958) 220–34.

(96) WESLEYAN (TL 034325). Small chapel with rendered gabled front dated 1863; large porch built in front 1982.

Bourne, (ed.) (1993) 173–6.

WILDEN

(97) BAPTIST (TL 103551). Low building with gabled brick front, built 1846, enlarged 1862, for a church formed in 1806.

WILSHAMSTEAD

(98) WESLEYAN (TL 070437). Brick and slate, dated 1841. Pedimented front of yellow brick with central doorway in pilastered surround and two tiers of sash windows; side walls of red brick. Rear gallery. *Bootscrapers*: flanking entrance, of wrought iron with arched bases to standards. (Chapel demolished *c*.1971)

Wesleyan chapel, Wilshamstead. (Demolished) (98)

WOBURN

(99) Former CONGREGATIONAL, Duck Lane (SP 949330). Red brick with yellow brick dressings to tall round-arched windows, rendered pilasters and slated roof. Gabled NE front with two round-arched doorways; apsidal SW end. Built 1854 to replace chapel of 1804. (Demolition proposed 1986)

Barwell, W.M., *A Short History of the Woburn Congregational Church* (1899).

(100) Former WESLEYAN (SP 948330). Brick with three-bay gabled front and pointed-arched windows. (Derelict 1969)

WOOTTON

(101) BAPTIST (TL 009452). Rendered walls and hipped tiled roof; built 1836. Much altered and false gable added to front in late 19th century.

Page (1953) 33.

CAMBRIDGESHIRE AND ISLE OF ELY

(Cambridgeshire)

The early spread of nonconformity in Cambridgeshire is epitomized by three monuments in a private burial-ground in Oakington (71). The ministers, Francis Holcroft, Joseph Oddy and Henry Osland, two ejected from livings in the county and one the son of another, were responsible for laying the foundations of several churches whose origins, though not their present meeting-houses, date from the 17th century. Cambridge (15), Cottenham (26), Gamlingay (42), Linton (60), Melbourn (68) and Willingham (102) all had congregations of 17th-century origin. The earliest buildings now standing, although much altered or enlarged, are the Congregational chapel at Melbourn (68) of 1717, and the Old Meeting-house at Gamlingay (42), parts of which date from the early 18th century.

Outstanding amongst the chapels of the later 18th century are three whose congregations derived from the itinerant preaching of the Rev. John Berridge, vicar of Everton, (Tetworth, detached) Hunts. The earliest of these is Fowlmere (40) of 1780, followed by Bassingbourn (2) of *c*.1791 and Duxford (33) of 1794. All these are of timber-framed construction and Bassingbourn is of particular note for the various enlargements made for a once-flourishing congregation, especially the large rounded end behind the pulpit. Of the last decade of the 18th century are also the former chapel in Downing Place, Cambridge (15), the former chapel of 1798 in Burwell (7) and the square brick Baptist chapel at Sutton (82) of 1791. The Quaker meeting-houses of this period are unspectacular, the earliest being at Swavesey (88) of 1719, others being Chatteris (24) of 1757 and the much-altered but still functioning meeting-house in Cambridge (17) of 1776–7.

Several chapels of the early 19th century are notable; Linton (60) of 1818 replaces a 17th-century meeting-house and has a spectacular line of monuments flanking the forecourt. Of particular interest was the Old Baptist Chapel in Willingham (102) of 1830, now demolished, for its apparently original semicircular seating plan. A general preference for plain or classically fronted chapels continued throughout the first half of the 19th century, as at Soham (77) of 1841 and later in Barrington (1) of 1856 and at Zion Chapel, Swaffham Prior (84) of 1862. The Gothic style was seen in the work of James Fenton at the Congregational chapel in Chatteris (23) of 1838, now re-fronted, and in the chapel of 1836 in March (66). The Wesleyan chapel of 1849 in Fordham (39) is cited by the Rev. F.J. Jobson as an appropriate design for an inexpensive village chapel.

Some of the more notable later chapels are in Cambridge, where the principal representative of the late 19th century and one of wider architectural importance is the Congregational 'Emmanuel Church' (16) of 1872–4 by James Cubitt, with a substantial tower dominating this part of Trumpington Street. The Baptists chose George Baines and Son to rebuild their chapel in St Andrew's Street (10) in 1903, unusually also with a tower, their more routine style appearing at Histon (51) with a matching chapel and Sunday-school of 1899 and 1901. The Wesleyans also supported the free Gothic style in their chapel on Christ's Piece, Cambridge (18) of 1913 by Gordon and Gunton. The Unitarian chapel in Emmanuel Road, of 1928 by R.P. Jones, although outside the scope of this survey, is also worthy of mention.

Building materials in the county principally comprise gault brick, or occasionally yellow facing brick, for walling and plain tiles or slate for roof coverings. Red brick of the early 18th century appears in the SW corner of the county at Gamlingay (42) and Melbourn (68). Clunch is restricted, in the buildings recorded, to the SE corner between Burwell (6, 7, 8), Fordham (39) and Isleham (56, 57), and pantiles are surprisingly rare and similarly located, in Soham (79), Swaffham Prior (83) and West Wratting (95). Timber-framing of a substantial kind appears in the three late 18th-century chapels at Bassingbourn (2), Duxford (33) and Fowlmere (40), all in the extreme S of the county, at Kingston (58), which is also the only remaining chapel with a thatched roof, and in a less robust form in several minor chapels of the early 19th century (69, 83, 95).

BARRINGTON

(1) CONGREGATIONAL (TL 395498). The church formerly meeting here originated in the late 17th century. It previously occupied a meeting-house on Boot Lane, 200 yards S of the present chapel. The chapel, built in 1856, is of gault brick with a three-bay pedimented front. The burial-ground surrounding the site of the earlier meeting-house contains some table-tombs and headstones of the early 19th century. (Chapel derelict 1972)

RCHM *County of Cambridge*. Vol. I *West Cambridgeshire* (1968) 8, monument (2) graveyard.

BASSINGBOURN

(2) Former CONGREGATIONAL (TL 334437). The meeting-house, built *c*.1791 for a congregation formed in that year probably as a result of the preaching of the Rev. John Berridge, was extended to the rear in the early 19th century and at the front later in the same century. The original structure has rendered timber-framed walls and a hipped tiled roof with raised centre valley; the first extension is similarly framed but its roof is slate covered; the front extension is in brickwork with a slated roof, gabled to the NE. The side walls of the original building have two tiers of windows in three bays, the upper windows having round-arched heads and wooden Y-tracery; this fenestration is repeated in the return bays of the front extension. The front has a central entrance and open timber porch, three upper windows of two lights below rectangular moulded labels, and a cusped circle in the gable.

The interior (originally $37\frac{1}{4}$ft square, enlarged to $48\frac{1}{2}$ft long) has a flat plaster ceiling divided by later ribs. A gallery around three sides was built in 1802 and the NE end re-sited in the late 19th century. It has a panelled front above an elaborately detailed entablature supported by Roman Doric columns; a roundel on the NE side is inscribed 'W.W. | FECIT | 1802'. The enlargement at the SW end is semicircular on plan and comprises a large vestry or school-room on the ground floor, and a room above now open to the chapel and occupied by the organ and choir seating. The roof of the original meeting-house has two trusses with a valley at collar level and four braced upright members below (cf. Fowlmere (40)). (Becoming derelict 1986)

Fittings – *Bootscraper*: next to vestry door. *Clock*: on gallery front, signed 'Willm. Andrews, Royston', 19th-century.

Congregational chapel, Barrington. (1)

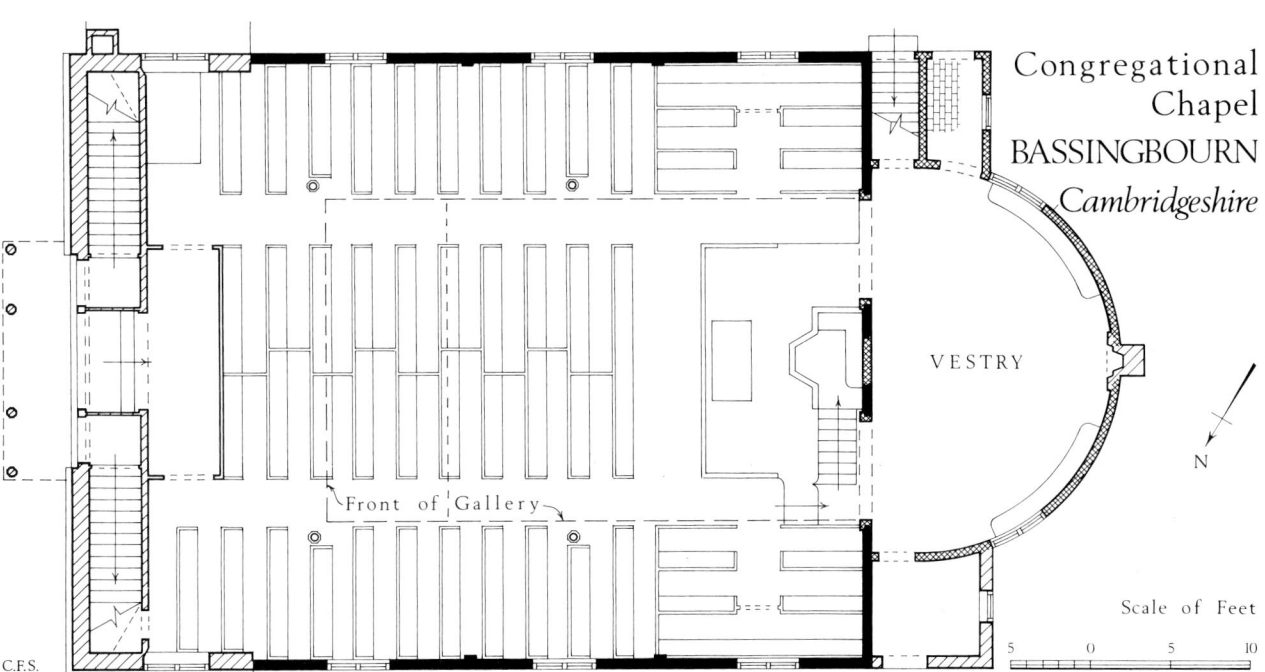

Former Congregational chapel, Bassingbourn. (2)

Monuments: in chapel on SE wall (1) Rev. Samuel Bull, 1826, first pastor. In burial-ground to NE (2) Thomas Prime, 1836, *et al.*, obelisk; also four table-tombs and other 19th-century monuments.

Cong. Mag. II (1819) 437–8. Rooke, R., *'Crown Him Lord of All': A History of Bassingbourn United Reformed Church* (1991).

BENWICK

(3) BAPTIST, High Street (TL 342903). The chapel, which stood nearly opposite the Wesleyan chapel, was demolished *c*.1970. *Monuments*: in burial-ground (1) Joseph Kittson, 18[23?], minister at Ramsey 33 years; (2) Fryer Richardson, 1829, *et al.*, stone pillar.

(4) WESLEYAN, High Street (TL 341903). Gault brick with hipped slate roof; three-bay front with tablet dated 1833.

BOTTISHAM

(5) Former INDEPENDENT (TL 550601). Timber-framed and weather-boarded chapel with gabled ends and tablet inscribed 'Erected 1819'. Two windows in each long side later boarded over. Superseded 1868 by new chapel 100 yards NNW.

RCHM *County of Cambridge.* Vol. II *North-east Cambridgeshire* (1972) 6, monument (2).

BURWELL

(6) BAPTIST (TL 588677). Gault brick front, side walls of clunch, hipped slate roof; built *c*.1845. Three-bay front with two tiers of segmental-arched windows. The interior has galleries around three sides, the side galleries added and all given open cast-iron fronts in 1874; original box-pews replaced since 1953.

Front.
Former Congregational chapel, Burwell.

Rear. (7)

(7) Former CONGREGATIONAL (TL 589665). The church, now meeting in other premises, originated in 1692, gathering jointly in Soham and Burwell; the latter became a distinct church in 1712. The meeting-house, now in commercial use, was built in 1798 much of the cost being met by John Taylor, a tanner, of Burwell. In 1866 it was much altered and re-fronted.

This is a long rectangular building of clunch with later brick dressings, a broad W front of gault brick, and a hipped slate roof. The W front of 1866 is of five bays with a pedimented centre bay between tall round-arched windows. The E wall has three similar windows, asymmetrically placed, probably replacing a pair of pulpit windows. The S wall has two plain windows with two circular gallery windows above; the N wall was similar before refenestration in 1866.

The interior has a gallery at the S end; before 1866 there were two end galleries and a cross gallery.

Monuments: in burial-ground, include (1) Robert Miller, 1773; (2) Thomas Cropley, 1795; (3) James Stephens, 1799.

Cong. Mag. II (1819) 438. RCHM *County of Cambridge*. Vol II *North-east Cambridgeshire* (1972) 25, monument (3).

(8) WESLEYAN, The Causeway (TL 588671). The chapel with walls of gault brick and clunch and a slated roof was built in 1835, originally having a three-bay front with round-arched doorway and windows; it was enlarged and one bay was added to the right in the later 19th century.

RCHM *County of Cambridge*. Vol II *North-east Cambridgeshire* (1972) 25, monument (4).

(9) Former PRIMITIVE METHODIST (TL 587674). The chapel has a three-bay pedimented front of gault brick, the bays separated by pilasters. Dated 1864.

CAMBRIDGE

(10) BAPTIST, St Andrew's Street (TL 453581). This congregation originated in 1721 as a major secession from the then Independent church at Hog Hill (*see* (15) below), meeting first in a converted stable and granary in the stone yard, where, in spite of initial difficulties, a Baptist church was formed. The first meeting-house was superseded in 1764 and its successor rebuilt in 1836. The existing chapel, built on the same site in 1903 to the designs of George and R. Palmer Baines, has walls faced with rough flints and ashlar dressings. It is in a free Gothic style with NE tower, and the interior, divided by timber arcades, has a polygonal apse and open timber roof.

Fittings – Chair: oak, with panelled back carved and inscribed 'D S 1670', given in 1938. *Monuments*: in chapel (1) Rev. Robert Roff, 1850, 12 years minister. In burial-ground N of chapel (2) Charles Foster, 1818, *et al.*, table-tomb; (3) Katharine (Smith) wife of William Eaden Lilley, 1842, table-tomb. *Plate*: includes a pair of two-handled cups of 1819; *see also* Teversham (89).

B.Hbk (1903) 377. Ivimey IV (1830) 450–8. Parsons, K.A.C. (ed.), *St Andrew's Street Baptist Church, Cambridge: 250th Anniversary* (1971). RCHM *City of Cambridge* Pt 2 (1959) 300–1, monument (66).

(11) EDEN CHAPEL, Fitzroy Street (TL 458586). The Strict Baptist church appears to have originated in a congregation which, in 1819, took the lease of an old meeting-house in Green Street (*see* (14)) and formed themselves into a church in 1823. The congregation removed to a new chapel on the present site in 1825, replaced by the present building in 1874. The chapel, of gault brick with a slate roof gabled at the front, stands above a basement.

Fittings – Inscriptions: inside front boundary wall, tablet from former chapel inscribed 'EDEN CHAPEL 1825'; a stone in front wall to the right of the entrance, now decayed, was inscribed 'JOHN FOREMAN minister 1825'. *Monuments*: in vestry (1) Lydia Tunwell Flack, 1839; (2) Susanna and Isabella Wybroe, 1836 and 1840; (3) John Cream, 1848. In forecourt (4) John Stittle, 1813, 'preacher of the Gospel for 30 years', wall monument from Green Street meeting-house; (5) Sarah Hindes, 1818; (6) Rob. Benton, 1837, and Rebecca his wife, 1817; (7) Mary Hempstead, 1849.

RCHM *City of Cambridge* Pt 2 (1959) 301, monument (69).

(12) ZION CHAPEL, East Road (TL 458583). The Baptist church originated in 1832 with the resignation of the Rev. William Allen, pastor at Eden Chapel, who commenced a new cause for which Providence Chapel, East Road, was opened in the following year (RCHM op. cit. below, monument (70), now demolished). Due to financial difficulties this was sold in 1837 but in the following year another chapel, now the school-room, was built in the same road. The chapel, built alongside its predecessor in 1877–8 to the designs of William Peachey of York, is of gault brick with dressings of red brick and stone; it has a tall gabled front to the street and galleries around three sides supported by cast-iron columns. The former chapel is of gault brick with a slate roof; the SW wall is divided into four bays with tall arched recesses embracing two tiers of altered windows. The NW front was added in 1879. The interior, now divided into two floors above a basement, has tall fluted columns of cast iron supporting the beams of a former gallery.

Anon., *Zion, One Hundred Years of Baptist Witness, 1837–1937* (1937). RCHM *City of Cambridge* Pt 2 (1959) 301, monument (67).

(13) Former BAPTIST, Chapel Lane, Chesterton (TL 463599). The chapel, now 'St Andrew's Church Hall', was built in 1844 for a congregation formed in that year which has since removed to Arbury Road. The walls are of gault brick and the roofs are slated. The original side walls of three bays have round-arched windows in similarly arched recesses; both ends are masked by later 19th-century extensions, that to the rear with wall arcades of three segmental-arched bays, the front taller, with a gable to the street of c.1863.

RCHM *City of Cambridge* Pt 2 (1959) 301, monument (68).

(14) Former CHAPEL, Green Street (TL 449585). A building on the S side of the street, of brickwork with two round-arched windows in the E wall, is now incorporated in the premises of Messrs Eaden Lilley and is entirely surrounded by other buildings. It comprises a former chapel with galleries around three sides supported by fluted columns of cast iron, and a fourth gallery added at the E end, above a basement storey. The chapel may possibly be that to which a Calvinistic Independent congregation migrated in 1818, when their lease of the old meeting-house in Green Street expired, and which in 1830 appears to have been occupied by Wesleyans.

The first meeting-house in Green Street stood on the N side, on the site of Nos 3, 4, and 5. It was built in the late 17th century for

Emmanuel Church (URC), Cambridge.

an Independent congregation which, following the accession of seceders from Hog Hill (*see* (15)) *c.*1696, became Presbyterian. It closed *c.*1778 and was reopened by Calvinistic Independents, when it became known as 'Stittle's Chapel' after the first minister whose monument (*see* (11)) was removed to Eden Chapel by the Strict Baptist congregation which had succeeded them in 1819. After its removal the meeting-house was demolished.

Atkinson, T.D., *Cambridge Described and Illustrated* (1897) 175–6. *CHST* IV (1909–10) 223–9.

(15) Former GREAT MEETING-HOUSE, Downing Place (TL 452582). A Presbyterian congregation bought the present site, then called Hog Hill, in 1687 and built the first meeting-house. In 1696 the church adopted a Congregational polity and the remaining Presbyterian supporters left to join the Green Street meeting. A secession in 1721 led to the formation of a Baptist congregation (*see* (10)). The present building, erected in 1790, remained in use until 1874, when the church removed to Trumpington Street; it is now the concert room of the University Music School.

The walls are of white brick and the roof is hipped and tiled. The SW front of three bays with a slightly projecting pedimented centre has been altered and a porch added in the late 19th century, but parts of three tall semicircular-headed windows remain. The interior (40¼ft by 50ft) with a gallery around three sides was entirely refitted in 1936. A lead rainwater-head at the S corner is dated 1790.

CHST IV (1909–10) 183–283. RCHM *City of Cambridge* Pt 2 (1959) 302, monument (71).

(16) CONGREGATIONAL, Trumpington Street (TL 448580). 'Emmanuel Church', built in 1872–4 for the congregation from the Former Great Meeting-house in Downing Place (now URC) was designed by James Cubitt. It is a large stone building in the Gothic style with a prominent E tower in which is a small gallery. The interior, purposely designed to avoid the obstruction of columns, has narrow aisles along the N and S sides and a polygonal choir apse at the W end.

Fittings – *Monuments*: in lobby (1) Rev. Joseph Sanders, 1788, 20 years pastor; (2) Joseph Thodey, 1835, brother of Rev. Samuel Thodey. *Plate*: includes four two-handled cups of 1698, 1705, 1711 and 1816.

Binfield, C., 'James Cubitt and Emmanuel Congregational Church', *Chapels Society Newsletter* I (1989–94) 80–4. *CYB* (1873) 424–6; (1874) 414. RCHM *City of Cambridge* Pt 2 (1959) 302, monument (71).

(17) FRIENDS, Park Street (TL 449588). The present site at the corner of Jesus Lane has been occupied by Friends at least since 1700, when Alice Docwra left an estate in Meeting House Yard in Jesus Lane in trust for the society. The meeting-house was rebuilt in 1776–7 but from 1795 to 1884 it was put to other uses and drastically altered before being reopened; it was further altered in 1926–7, 1948–50, and after 1963, when an annexe of 1894 was rebuilt. The meeting-house at the N end of the site is of brick in two storeys with the principal room at the upper level. Parts of the E wall date from the late 18th century, but this has been heightened and enlarged to the south.

Butler (1999) 32–6. RCHM *City of Cambridge* Pt 2 (1959) 302, monument (72).

(18) WESLEYAN, Christ's Piece (TL 454587). The chapel at the junction of Short Street and King Street was opened in 1913 to accommodate a society previously meeting in Hobson Street. The building, in a free Gothic style by Gordon and Gunton, was greatly altered internally in 1989 leaving only the chancel fittings intact. *Monuments*: reset from former chapel (1) Charles Vintner, 1881; (2) Susanna Scott, 1860; (3) William Baker, 1888, and Elizabeth his wife, 1882; (4) William Baker, 1856. *Organ*: in rear gallery, 1844, by William Hill, removed from Eastbrook Hall, Bradford, Yorks. West Riding (68), case altered.

Guite, J., *The Building of Cambridge Wesley 1904–1913* (1990). *Methodist Recorder* (21 March 1991). Tice, F., *The History of Methodism in Cambridge* (1966) 28–33.

(19) PRESBYTERIAN, Downing Street (TL 45155825). 'St Columba's', built 1890–1 for the Presbyterian Church of England (now URC), is a dour stone building by J. MacVicar Anderson, with nave, transepts and chancel. Prior to some internal rearrangement it had a gabled central pulpit between screens.

Knox, R. Buick, *St Columba's Church, Cambridge, 1879–1979* (1979).

[Pound Hill Chapel, RCHM *City of Cambridge* Pt 2 (1959) 302, monument (73), has been demolished.]

CAXTON

(20) BAPTIST, Ermine Street (TL 304582). The chapel, built in 1845 for a church formed in 1842, has walls of gault brick and a slated roof. The W front has a simple pediment, terminal pilasters, rendered platband, a central doorway and two upper windows lighting a W gallery. In a later 19th-century rear extension is an upper school-room opening to the chapel with an iron balustrade behind the pulpit. *Monument*: to Samuel Fordham, 1870, first pastor.

RCHM *County of Cambridge*. Vol. I *West Cambridgeshire* (1968) 37, monument (2).

BAPTIST CHAPEL, CAXTON CFS1972

CHATTERIS

(21) GENERAL BAPTIST, West Park Street (TL 393858). Built *c.*1835 for a church formed in 1785 by Joseph Scott, a former Countess of Huntingdon's minister, which previously met in a large barn. Gault brick W front with canted sides and pediment, three round-arched doorways and three windows above.

Wood (1847) 209.

(22) ZION CHAPEL, Park Street (TL 393859). The Strict Baptist chapel, built in 1839, was extended to the front in the late 19th century. The gabled N front of gault brick with dressings of red brick and stone is of three bays with two entrances. The original gallery with a panelled front remains unaltered and retains contemporary seating.

(23) CONGREGATIONAL, East Park Street (TL 394859). The chapel, dated 1838, was designed by James Fenton. It has an E front of yellow brick with canted sides separated by two-stage buttresses with gabled finials, and a low-pitched gable across the centre. There are two tiers of windows, the upper range having four-centred arched heads with labels and intersecting wooden tracery. The interior has a barrel-vaulted ceiling and exposed trusses. (URC) (Proposed 1994 drastically to extend the front, covering original elevation with a two-storey 'foyer')

Congregational chapel (URC), Chatteris. (23)

(24) Former FRIENDS (TL 391864). The former meeting-house, behind 76 High Street, was built in 1757; it was closed in 1922 and is now in commercial use. The building (originally 40½ft by 21½ft externally) was much altered in the late 19th century when the side walls were raised, the thatched roof replaced by slates at a lower pitch, sash windows inserted, and an extension built to the west. The original walling remains visible in the side walls with a segmental-arched doorway, now blocked, to the south.

Butler (1999) 36–7.

COMBERTON

(25) BAPTIST, Green End (TL 380565). Gault brick and slate with three-bay pedimented front, built 1868.

[A timber-framed barn (TL 382562) (RCHM *County of Cambridge*. Vol. I *West Cambridgeshire* (1968) 53, monument (17)) with evidence of late 19th-century dissenting use, has been demolished.]

COTTENHAM

(26) OLD BAPTIST CHAPEL, High Street (TL 451679). This formerly Independent congregation originated in the late 17th century largely through the work of Joseph Oddy (*see* (71)) and was initially associated with the church at Willingham (102), both becoming Baptist in the late 18th century. The present chapel, built in 1856 to replace one of 1781, is a large structure of gault brick with a slated roof, gabled front and two tiers of windows enclosed in tall round-arched wall arcades which continue at the sides; the interior has an original gallery around three sides and contemporary box-pews.

(27) EBENEZER CHAPEL, Rooks Street (TL 452679). The Strict Baptist chapel 'erected 1812, renovated 1899' is a plain building of gault brick with a slated roof. Three-bay gabled front with three doorways and lean-to wings with gallery staircases.

COVENEY

(28) PROVIDENCE CHAPEL (TL 490823). Gault brick and slate with round-arched doorway and two upper windows (now blocked) in gabled front wall. Square tablet dated 1845. Formerly Strict Baptist, now a farm store with all fittings removed. Gardner (1851) refers to the chapel as 'the property of Mr Waddelow Chambers ... appropriated to the use of the Christian Baptists'. *Monument*: in front of chapel, to Biddel Chambers, 1844, Jemima his wife, 1858, and Jemima infant daughter of Waddelow and Elizabeth Chambers (nd).

Gardner (1851) 497.

(29) WESLEYAN (TL 488821). Gault brick with red brick dressings, circular window in gable. Opened 1892.

DODDINGTON

(30) WESLEYAN, New Street (TL 399907). Gabled front of red brick, gault brick sides. Dated 1888.

DOWNHAM

(31) BAPTIST, Chapel Lane (TL 523838). Gault brick and slate with a broad three-bay front with two tiers of sash windows. The chapel is dated 1858; a tablet of 1788 from the former chapel is reset in the S gable wall. The interior has end galleries and an original pulpit with panelled back-board.

(32) WESLEYAN, Main Street (TL 520839). Gabled front of red brick with large Venetian window above entrance; dated 1907. Earlier building alongside, possibly the former chapel of 1877.

DUXFORD

(33) CONGREGATIONAL (TL 480462). An evangelical congregation gathered through the labours of the Rev. John Berridge, vicar of Everton, Hunts., fitted up a barn as a temporary meeting-house in 1793 and erected the present building in the following year. The chapel was enlarged to the front in 1859 by the addition of vestries with a school-room above, and in 1894 the interior was partly refitted. The original structure has rendered timber-framed walls and a hipped tiled roof. The front extension was demolished *c.*1977 and the original elevation reinstated; it had brick walls and a slated roof, gabled to the front, and a central entrance.

The interior (originally 37ft by 33ft) has a flat plaster ceiling with moulded cornice and galleries around three sides supported by cast-iron columns of 1894. The roof is carried by three trusses with a central valley at collar level discharging to the rear.

Bootscrapers: flanking later front entrance, pair, cast iron, of lyre pattern, *c.*1859. (URC)

Anon., *Duxford Congregational Church* (1924).

Congregational chapel (URC), Duxford. Restored front. (33)

ELSWORTH

(34) PROVIDENCE CHAPEL (TL 319637). The former chapel was built c.1831 for a Strict Baptist church founded in that year. The walls are of gault brick and the roof is hipped and slated. The N front is of three bays with a central round-arched doorway and two tiers of sash windows. In the S wall are traces of two tall windows altered in the mid 19th century when E and W galleries were added. The interior has an original N gallery and box-pews. A later school-room adjoins to the east. Burial-ground at rear with several large 19th-century monuments. (Derelict 1971, since converted to house)

RCHM *County of Cambridge.* Vol. I *West Cambridgeshire* (1968) 86, monument (2).

ELTISLEY

(35) WESLEYAN (TL 270596). Brick and slate, opened 1848, extended both ends; front dated 1879.

ELY HOLY TRINITY WITH ST MARY

(36) COUNTESS OF HUNTINGDON'S, Chapel Street, Ely (TL 540805). The chapel, built in 1802 to replace one of 1785, has brick walls and a slated roof with gabled sides. The broad S front of five bays with two tiers of sash windows has round-arched entrances in the slightly recessed end bays. The interior, refitted in the late 19th century, has a gallery along the S wall facing a wide segmental apse added to the N at the period of refitting.

Cong. Mag. II (1819) 502.

(37) WESLEYAN, Chapel Street, Ely (TL 539805). Brick and slate with tall round-arched windows in the side walls. Designed and built 1858 by Richard Freeman and Sons of Ely to replace a chapel of 1818; re-fronted by Josiah Gunton in 1891.

Jakes, E., *The Ely Methodists: 1774–1932* (1988).

FORDHAM

(38) CONGREGATIONAL, Mill Lane (TL 631707). The chapel of gault brick with two tiers of windows with renewed frames has a gabled front of three bays with round-arched upper windows. A large plaster panel above a later porch is painted with the date of erection, 1818. Galleried interior. Towards the rear is a detached school-room 'erected 1844'. *Monuments*: in burial-ground (1) James King, 1839; (2) Robert Harvey, 1847, and Elizabeth his wife, 1843; (3) Elizabeth (Connebee) wife of Rev. Martin Slater, 1841; (4) Robert Hunt, 1878, and Kerenhappuch, his widow, 1906; (5) William Smith, 1832, and Sarah his widow, 1841; (6) Rev. John Edward Cullen, 1878, and Matilda his wife, 1866; (7) Rev. Robert Gamble, 1868. *Sundial*: in blind window recess on S side.

Cong. Mag. II (1819) 502–3.

(39) WESLEYAN, Sharmans Road (TL 626708). The chapel built in 1849 is in a simple Gothic style recommended by the Rev. F.J. Jobson as a 'Village Chapel of the very plainest and least expensive style'. It was based on a design he had published in *The Watchman*, but possibly not erected under his supervision as there are a few design faults to which he refers. The chapel has walls of clunch with brick dressings, lancet windows and a porch at one side. The gabled front has a wood-framed window of three pointed lights and an inscribed band and circular light above.

Jobson (1850) 81–3.

FOWLMERE

(40) CONGREGATIONAL (TL 422456). The chapel, built in 1780 for a newly formed congregation, has rendered timber-framed walls with later brick pilaster buttresses, and a hipped roof formerly covered with plain tiles. The chapel was altered in the early 19th century, when a tall gabled projection was added between the front entrances slightly increasing the accommodation; a polygonal apse in brick was built at the opposite end in 1870 and a school-room and clock-tower with a 'public clock' were erected alongside the chapel c.1880.

The NW front has two doorways below later lean-to roofs and two round-arched windows above; there are two tiers of windows in the side walls. The interior (36¼ft square), largely refitted in the late 19th century, has a flat plaster ceiling with coved cornice and a gallery around three sides with a panelled front supported by later cast-iron columns. The roof is carried by two principal trusses and has a central valley at collar level. (URC)

Fittings – *Clock*: in clock-tower, by H. Sainsbury of London, bell 1880 by Mears and Stainbank. *Monument*: in front of chapel,

Congregational chapel (URC), Fowlmere. (40)

Rev. William Merchant, 1840, and Mary his widow, 1870, headstone. *Plate*: includes a pair of two-handled pewter cups, early 19th-century.

Rooke, R., *Mere Independendents: A History of Fowlmere and Thriplow United Reformed Church* (1996).

FULBOURN

(41) CONGREGATIONAL (TL 521558). This parish has long been the home of dissenting causes: two Baptist conventicles were reported in 1669 and Baptist and Presbyterian meetings existed in 1731. In 1851 some eight or ten private burial-grounds were said to exist, of which two or three then remained in use.

The Congregational chapel was built in 1810, heightened and enlarged to the S in 1841, and the S front rebuilt in 1862. It has walls of gault brick and a slate roof. The interior has galleries and pews of c.1841. (URC)

Fittings – *Clock*: on front of S gallery, signed Thomas Wilson, Cambridge, 1858. *Monuments*: in chapel (1) Thomas Hancock, gent., 'who at his own cost erected this chapel A.D.1810', also recording that John, Abraham and Joseph, sons of John and Ann Chaplin, placed it in trust in 1862; (2) John Chaplin, gent., 1833, signed 'Clayton, Camb.'. In detached burial-ground N of chapel (3) Susanna widow of Thomas Collier, 1799; (4) Thomas Hancock, 1732; (5) Elizabeth widow of Thomas Hancock, 1757; (6) Catherine wife of Thomas Hancock, 17[61?]; (7) Thomas Hancock 1783; (8) Thomas son of Thomas and Sarah Hancock, 1795, table-tomb; (9) John Chaplin, gent., 1833, table-tomb.

GAMLINGAY

(42) OLD MEETING-HOUSE (TL 238520). The congregation formed in the late 17th century under the auspices of John Bunyan and originally in membership with his Bedford church became autonomous in 1710. The church retained an open membership until 1793 being loosely regarded as Independent, becoming thereafter Baptist with a closed membership until 1909.

The meeting-house, which dates from the early 18th century but has been much altered, has walls of red brick and a hipped slate roof. The E front is largely original but a two-storeyed porch was added in the late 19th century; prior to this alteration it had three segmental-arched windows alternating with two similarly arched doorways to the lower stage and three windows above, the centre one round-arched and the others with flat-arched heads; in the

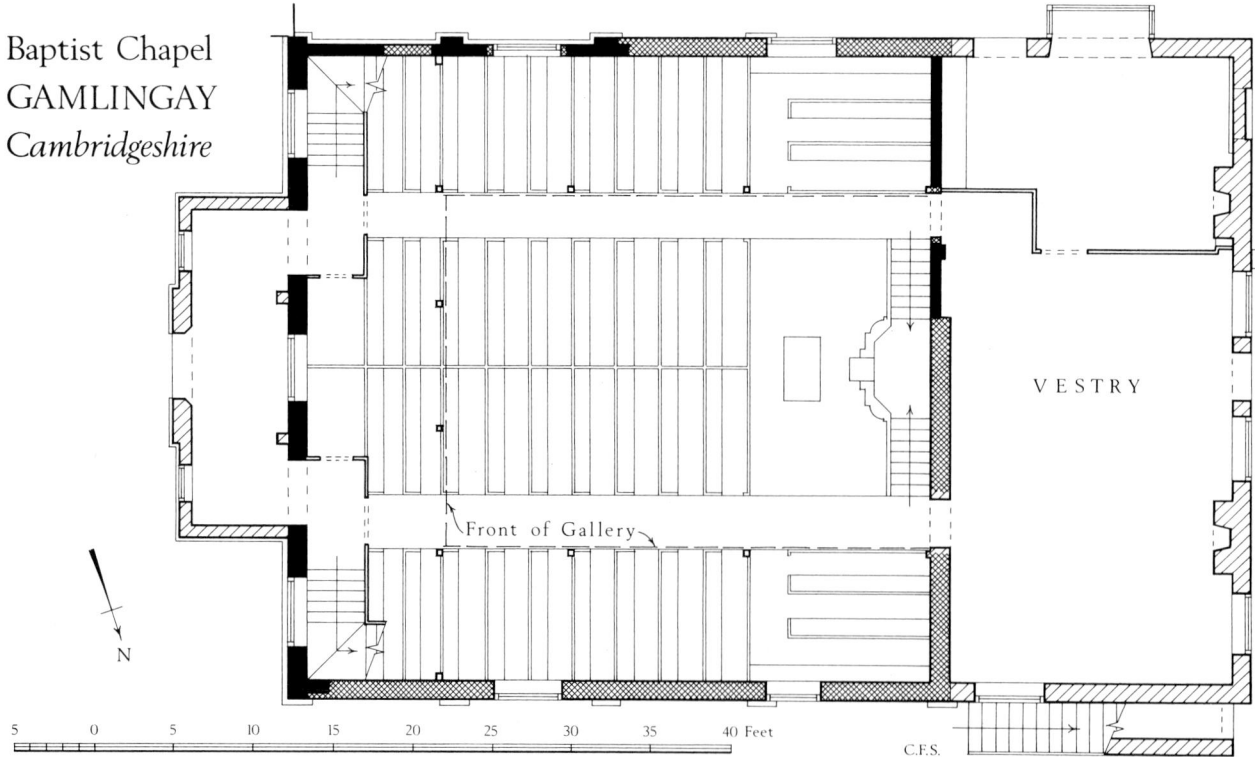

The Old Meeting-house, Gamlingay. Exterior before c.1881. (42)

wall are four wall-anchors inscribed with the numerals 1 7 9 6, at which date a front gallery was added and other alterations were contemplated, including perhaps a heightening of the walls. Two bays of walling contemporary with the front continue on the S side but the N and S walls have otherwise been largely rebuilt on the original foundations. A pair of vestries with former lecture-room above, approached by an external staircase, was added at the W end in 1858. The interior (39ft square) has a late 18th-century gallery around three sides supported by square columns; the seating was renewed in the late 19th century.

Monuments: in chapel (1) James Paine, 1831; (2) Mary Billing, 1760. In burial-ground (3) John Arnold, 1822, slate headstone signed 'Hull & Pollard, Leicester'.

Ivimey II (1814) 100–1. Tydeman, G.S., *A Brief History of Gamlingay Old Meeting Baptist Church* (1963). RCHM *County of Cambridge*. Vol. I *West Cambridgeshire* (1968) 103–4, monument (2).
[Zoar Chapel, RCHM *County of Cambridge*. Vol. I *West Cambridgeshire* (1968) 104, monument (3), has been demolished.]

GRANTCHESTER

(43) Former BAPTIST (TL 432559). The chapel, now an artist's studio, of brick with a pedimented front, is dated 1876.

GREAT EVERSDEN

(44) Former CONGREGATIONAL, Chapel Road (TL 366536). The chapel, now the village hall, was built in 1845 for a church which originated as a Presbyterian congregation in 1689 and was early associated with the cause at Barrington (1). The walls are of gault brick and the roof is slated. The NW front is pedimented and has three doorways and a cast-iron date tablet above the centre. The original gallery remains but the interior has otherwise been refitted.

RCHM *County of Cambridge*. Vol. I *West Cambridgeshire* (1968) 123, monument (2).

GREAT SHELFORD

(45) BAPTIST, High Street (TL 461521). The chapel of 1856 by J. Cowell has a gabled front of yellow brick with red brick dressings. Lancet windows predominate. *Monument*: in front yard to Benjamin James Evans, 1872, 6 years pastor.

Baptist Times (19 February 1987).

GREAT WILBRAHAM

(46) BAPTIST (TL 549579). The chapel, of gault brick with a slated roof, was built in 1833 incorporating a cottage or manse at the rear. The much altered W wall of three wide bays formerly had two doorways to the chapel and windows between and above, matching the surviving fenestration in the third S bay which formed the front of the manse. The gabled N end of three narrower bays was altered in the late 19th century by the insertion of a chapel doorway, at which period the W doorways were blocked and the windows altered.

GUILDEN MORDEN

(47) CONGREGATIONAL, Pound Green (TL 278441). Gault brick and slate with two tiers of round-arched iron-framed windows at the sides. Built 1840 but much altered at the front and a wide porch added in 1870.

HADDENHAM

(48) Former BAPTIST (TL 463755). This plain building of brick and slate, with a gabled E front, was built in 1817 and superseded by the present chapel in 1904. It has an irregular plan formerly with N and S galleries. *Monuments*: internally on W wall (1) James Biddall, 1854, signed 'Fuller, Ely'; (2) Thomas Rose, 1869, and Susanna Ashton his widow, 1870, signed 'Woolvine, Euston Rd., London NW'; (3) John Holland son of Thomas and Susanna Ashton Rose, 1852, and John Pitts Rose, infant, signed 'Hide, St Ives'.

HARSTON

(49) BAPTIST (TL 426513). The gault brick and polychrome chapel of 1870, by Morgan H. Davies of Abingdon, stands N of the site of the original meeting-house of c.1786. The latter had low walls, possibly timber-framed, with two entrances to the E and a steeply pitched hipped roof and was probably demolished after the erection of the present school-rooms by J.G. Robins in 1886. *Monuments*: in burial-ground (1) Joseph Sear, 1799; (2) Rev. George Compton, 1822, 30 years pastor, and Hannah his widow, 1826.

B.Hbk (1871) 258 (illus. wrongly captioned).

HASLINGFIELD

(50) PRIMITIVE METHODIST (TL 406521). Small gault brick chapel with three-bay gabled front of 1867.

HISTON

(51) BAPTIST, Station Road (TL 440631). The chapel and matching Sunday-school of 1899 and 1901 respectively stand on a site given by Stephen Chivers in 1899. The walls are of red brick with stone dressings and the roofs are tiled. Both are in the free Gothic style by George Baines and Son.

B.Hbk (1900) 376; (1902) 359.

(52) WESLEYAN, High Street (TL 438637). Gabled front with big quatrefoil-traceried window above timber porch; opened 1896.

CAMBRIDGESHIRE AND ISLE OF ELY

ICKLETON

(53) PRIMITIVE METHODIST (TL 490436). Three-bay gabled front of gault brick with date tablet of 1852 above round-arched entrance.

ISLEHAM

(54) BAPTIST, Pound Lane (TL 643746). The chapel was built in 1829 for a congregation formed in 1693 which, prior to 1806, was Independent; it was enlarged in 1838. The gabled front of gault brick is of three bays with a central doorway and two tiers of windows. An early 19th-century gallery remains inside but with later supports. Sunday-school at rear built 1888 with foundation stone in memory of the Rev. W.W. Cantlow, pastor, who in 1850 baptized the popular Baptist preacher C.H. Spurgeon at Isleham Ferry; this event is also commemorated by a modern memorial at the site of the ferry (TL 657755).

Fittings – *Monuments*: in chapel (1) Rev. John Reynolds, 1842, and Susannah his widow, 1847; (2) David Riste, 1828; (3) Elizabeth (Riste) Norman, 1844 (*see also* (55)); (4) Mary wife of the Rev. W.W. Cantlow, 1853. *Plate*: includes two two-handled cups, one of 1764 or 1766 and one of 1840.

Parsons, K.A.C. (ed.), 'The Church Book of the Independent Church (now Pound Lane Baptist) Isleham, 1693–1805', *Cambridge Antiquarian Records Society* Vol. 6 (1984).

(55) GENERAL BAPTIST, High Street (TL 644744). The chapel was built in 1811 by William Norman, one of a group of members from Pound Lane who had been briefly attracted by John Gisburne's preaching at Soham (*see* (79)) but who formed a separate church following Gisburne's support for Unitarianism. The chapel was enlarged in 1841 and two galleries were added later. The side walls are rendered and the front wall of yellow brick with brown brick dressings is not original. *Monuments*: in burial-ground (1) William Norman, 1824, 'who purchased this ground & erected this place of worship'; (2) Elizabeth widow of William Norman, 1844.

Audus, B., *et al.*, *High Street Baptist Church, Isleham: Ter-Jubilee Celebrations 1812–1962, Souvenir Programme* (1962). Wood (1847) 229.

Zoar Chapel, Isleham. In 1953. (56)

(56) ZOAR CHAPEL (TL 644745). The former chapel, now used for storage, was built in 1846 for a Strict Baptist congregation. It has walls of clunch with a gault brick front and hipped slate roof. The front wall has a central entrance, altered since 1953, which previously had a decorative fanlight. The name and date of the building are painted on a semicircular band above the doorway.

(57) PRIMITIVE METHODIST (TL 646744). Walls of squared clunch with yellow brick dressings and a hipped slated roof. Broad three-bay front with date '1840' in blind tympanum of round-arched entrance.

KINGSTON

(58) CONGREGATIONAL (TL 345554). The church (now URC) formed in 1840 occupies a small meeting-house with rendered timber-framed walls and half-hipped thatched roof, dating from the 18th century. The building appears to have been a cottage or outbuilding perhaps of two bays, extended to the rear and converted c.1840. Two tie-beams are exposed, that nearer to the E front having mortices for braces and a former partition.

RCHM *County of Cambridge*. Vol. I *West Cambridgeshire* (1968) 155, monument (2).

Congregational chapel, Kingston. (58)

LANDBEACH

(59) BAPTIST, High Street (TL 477645). The chapel built 1854 has walls of gault brick; the front has a pediment and terminal pilasters. There are two tiers of round-arched windows with cast-iron frames.

LINTON

(60) CONGREGATIONAL, Horn Lane (TL 560466). The church (now URC) which originated in the late 17th century formerly occupied a timber-framed meeting-house of 1698; this was replaced by the present chapel in 1818. The chapel, almost identical in design with that at Buntingford (Herts. (18)), of 1819, has walls of red brick rendered at the front and a slated roof. The gabled N front is of three bays with tall pilasters carrying semicircular arches above two tiers of openings; in the wider central bay are three grouped doorways with fanlights and a round-arched window above. The E wall has two recessed arches enclosing two tiers of windows.

Congregational chapel (URC), Linton.

Congregational chapel (URC), Linton. Former chapel. (60)

The interior has a small apse at the S end intended for the pulpit but now occupied by an organ. There is an original gallery around three sides but all the seating has been renewed. (Alterations to entrance lobby proposed 1995)

Fittings – *Chair*: in front of pulpit, carved back panels and armrests, late 17th-century, given 1955. *Clock*: on front of N gallery, signed 'Di[son?], Linton', early 19th-century. *Monuments*: in chapel (1) William Maling, 1720, Martha Jackson, 1740, Edmund Jackson, sen., 1742, Stephen Jackson, 1724, infant, Thomas Jackson, 1739, Edmund Jackson, jnr., 1774, William Jackson, 1784, slate tablet; also Martha Jackson, 1789, on separate piece below; (2) John Taylor, 1786, Mary his widow, 1810, and Edmund their son, 1804, signed 'W. Haselgrove'; (3) George Nichols, 1851, 40 years deacon, signed 'Swinton, Cambridge'; (4) Rev. Thomas Hopkins, 1839, 41 years pastor, signed 'Biggs, Sc. Bath'; (5) Ann Brightwell, 1781, and her sons John, 1787, and Thomas, 1803, signed 'J.P. Biggs fecit, Bath'. On front wall (6) Mary Taylor, 1824. In burial-ground E of chapel, now levelled and monuments re-sited, (7) Elizabeth wife of John Rolls, 1715, headstone with scrolled sides and winged cherub's head. The approach to the N front of the chapel is lined with a notable series of table-tombs of the early 19th century and later. *Paintings*: in vestry, water-colour sketch of former meeting-house, a smaller copy of this and one of the present chapel, all of the early 19th century. *Sculpture*: plaster bust inscribed 'Gulielmus Biggs Ætat 43. 1816'.

URCHSJ I (1973–7) 174–8.

LITTLEPORT

(61) INDEPENDENT, Globe Lane (TL 567869). Gault brick and hipped slate roof, narrow three-bay front with round-arched entrance, mid 19th-century.

(62) WESLEYAN (TL 566868). The earlier chapel, dated 1835, stands alongside its Gothic successor of 1889 by J. Gunton of London. The former has gault brick walls and a hipped slate roof; the front of three bays has two tiers of windows with flat-arched brick heads. The later chapel has a large window with perpendicular tracery over the entrance.

(63) Former PRIMITIVE METHODIST, Victoria Street (TL 570868). Gault brick with red brick dressings and slate roof hipped to rear; gabled front with ball finials to parapet, wide four-centred wall-arch to centre bay. Formerly dated 1845 but now converted to domestic use and inscriptions defaced.

LITTLE SHELFORD

(64) CONGREGATIONAL (TL 453514). The first chapel opened in 1823 appears to have remained the property of the heirs of the first minister who conveyed it to trustees in 1890. The present chapel seems to have been rebuilt on the same site at about that date.

CYB (1854) obituary of James Burgess.

LODE

(65) STRICT BAPTIST (TL 533627). Gault brick with slate roof, built 1832 but altered in the later 19th century by the addition of a tall two-storeyed and gabled front porch. The original gabled front, now partly covered, was of three bays with a wall arcade of three-centred arches, a triangular recess in the gable, and two tiers of windows. A school-room with lean-to roof and tall tapering chimney has been added at one side.

RCHM *County of Cambridge*. Vol.II *North-east Cambridgeshire* (1972) 74, monument (2).

MARCH

(66) CONGREGATIONAL, Station Road (TL 417969). The chapel, probably by James Fenton, was built in 1836 for a church formed

Congregational chapel (URC), March. (66)

in 1834. The building, of yellow brick has a wide gabled front, with canted angles and moulded labels to the windows. The original entrances are at the sides but a front porch was added in the late 19th century. The design closely resembles Fenton's chapel in Chatteris (*see* (23)). (Now jointly URC and Methodist)

MELBOURN

(67) ZION CHAPEL (TL 384446). A Baptist congregation existed in the late 17th century but its early history is obscure. The present chapel, dating from the mid 19th century, has walls of gault brick and a slate roof; it has been extended to the rear. The gabled front of three bays in two stages has three entrances with cast-iron brackets to moulded canopies. Inside is a continuous gallery, the return gallery behind the pulpit being an addition. Original box-pews remain to the lower floor. *Monuments*: (1) Rev. James Flood, 1857; (2) Stephen Hayes, 1865; (3) Rev. William Brinkley, 1834; (4) 'M.M.', 1850; (5) Maria Flood, 1850.

(68) THE OLD MEETING-HOUSE (TL 383444). The Independent church (now URC) originated in the late 17th century with a united congregation meeting in and about Chishill and Melbourn or Meldreth, with which Nathaniel Ball, ejected from Royston in 1662, was reputedly connected. The church at Melbourn separated from Chishill in about 1745. The meeting-house was built in 1717 and registered on 20 July in that year; it was enlarged to the front, heightened and reroofed in 1815 and extended to the rear *c.*1830. In 1865 a new chapel, designed by S.H. Moore, was built on the opposite side of the road and the old meeting-house was converted for Sunday-school use. About 1963 the later chapel was demolished and the former restored to use.

The building has brick walls and a hipped slated roof. The original fenestration remains visible only in the NE side wall, which had two upper and two lower windows, the former now replaced by three windows at a higher level. The SE front is entirely of 1815, of gault brick with a wide pilaster at each end, two double doorways with pediments, one sash window between and three above. The roof is surmounted by a domed polygonal lantern from which glazing bars have been removed.

The interior (37½ft square before enlargement) has original side galleries supported by turned oak columns; the SE end gallery of 1815 is carried by columns of pine. In the NW enlargement of

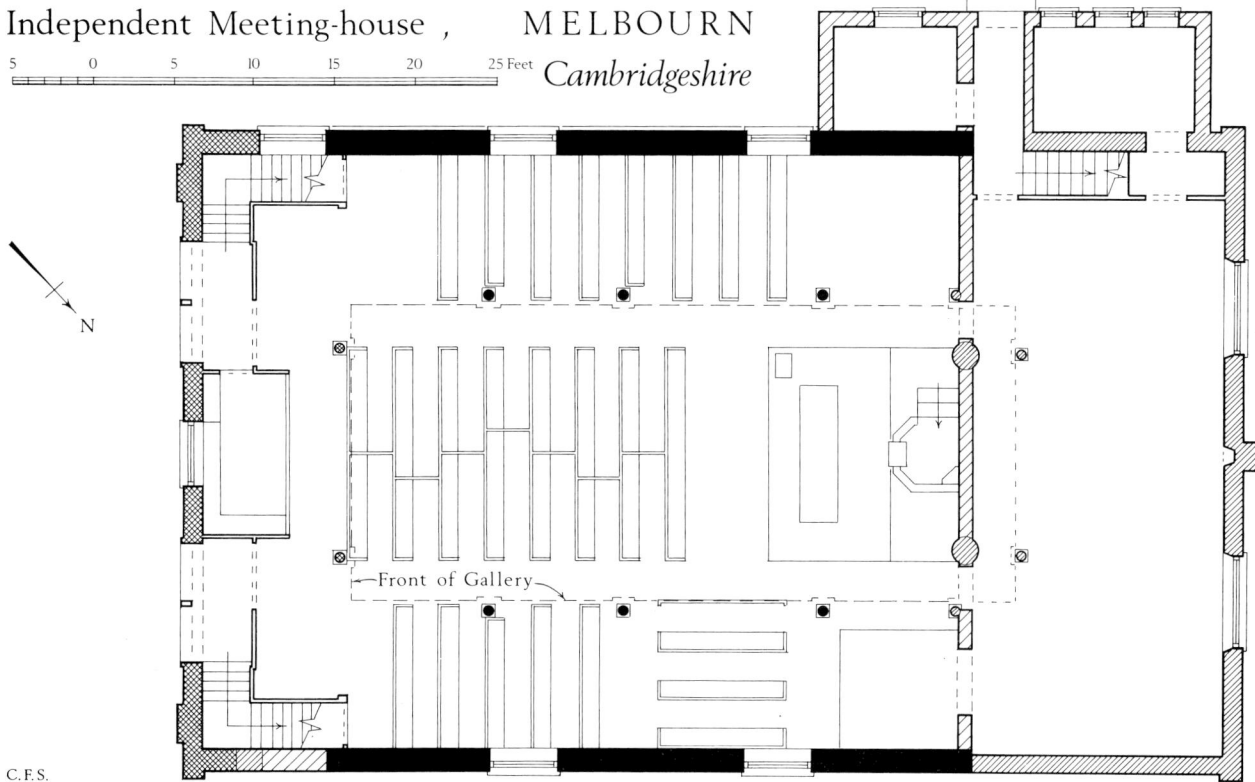

The Old Meeting-house, Melbourn. (68)

c.1830 the wall behind the pulpit was largely removed, the junction supported by two giant columns and the gallery returned behind them. In the restoration of 1963 a new partition was built on the line of the former back wall leaving the supports visible as half columns.

Fittings – *Clock*: on front of SE gallery, 'Parliament clock' with shaped dial and chinoiserie ornament on case, signed 'Thomas Kefford, Roystone', 18th-century. *Monuments*: on NW wall (1) Rev. William Carver, 1825, 32 years pastor. In SE pew (2) Mrs Sarah Nash, 1816; (3) Mrs Priscilla Woodham, 1779, William Woodham, 1785, and Mary his widow, 1804, Joseph Woodham, 1791, Sarah Woodham, 1824, and William Woodham, 1824, white marble tablet with cornice and shield-of-arms. In burial-ground to S three 18th-century headstones with scrolls and winged cherubs' heads. *Seating*: between front entrances, private pew with fielded-panelled partition on NW side. *Miscellanea*: silver medal with representation of SE front, 1815.

Chapple, G.P., and Palmer, W.M., *A Nonconformist Bicentenary Memorial* (1895). *CYB* (1866) 313–14. Rooke, R., *'Convinced That These Were God's People': A History of Melbourn United Reformed Church* (1994).

MELDRETH

(69) Former WESLEYAN (TL 382472). Small early 19th-century timber-framed chapel re-fronted in brick.

MILTON

(70) BAPTIST, High Street (TL 476627). The chapel built 1864 on 'land given by Isaac Coulson' has a pedimented front of gault brick with red brick dressings; there is a small porch between two round-arched windows with cast-iron frames. (Disused and most fittings removed 1993) *Monuments*: in chapel and small front burial-ground commemorating many members of the Coulson family.

OAKINGTON

(71) BURIAL-GROUND (TL 415649). A railed enclosure 50 yards NE of the parish church contains the following table-tombs with inscribed capstones, original panelled sides to the last, the others rebuilt in modern brickwork: (1) Henry Osland, 1711, 17 years minister at Willingham and Cottenham; (2) Joseph Oddy [Oddey], 1687, minister; (3) Francis Holcroft, 1691/2, minister.

(72) PARTICULAR BAPTIST (TL 413646). Gault brick and slate, three-bay gabled front, round-arched windows; dated 1865.

OVER

(73) STRICT BAPTIST, New Road (TL 374700). The church, believed to have originated about 1737 as an Independent congregation, was Baptist by 1778, in which year it joined the Eastern Association. The present chapel built in 1810 was rearranged internally in the mid 19th century and altered externally c.1920, when Tudor-style dressings were applied to the principal openings. The walls are of gault brick with later stone dressings and the roof is hipped and slated. The broad E front originally had two entrances with one window between and three above; the N doorway has been replaced by a window. The W wall, altered c.1850, formerly had two tall pointed-arched windows flanking a central pulpit, with two tiers of windows at each end.

The interior originally had the pulpit against the W wall and a gallery around the other three sides. In the mid 19th century the N gallery was removed, the S gallery brought forward and a W gallery erected; the pulpit was re-sited at the N end and given direct access from a N vestry. The gallery has a fielded-panelled front of the dates indicated. The pulpit has been renewed, but the door behind is of c.1850.

Fittings – *Inscriptions*: on brick N of E doorway 'R.A.1810'; on brick centrally on W wall 'TL'. *Monuments*: in chapel (1) Alice wife of Nathaniel Gifford, 1835, signed 'Cannam, St Ives'; (2) Nathaniel Gifford, 1845, signed 'Cannam, St Ives'; (3) Sarah (Lee) wife of Benjamin Catteel, 1818; (4) Rev. Thomas Lee, 1806, pastor, oval tablet signed 'Wm. Haselgrove, Cam'ge'; (5) Elizabeth widow of Thomas Lee, 1816, oval tablet matching last; (6) George Prudden, 1837, 28 years minister; (7) Susanna wife of George Prudden, 1828.

(74) PRIMITIVE METHODIST, The Lanes (TL 374706). 'Rehoboth Chapel', erected 1848, has walls of gault brick and a hipped slate roof; three-bay front with round-arched openings. Sunday-school 1883.

PARSON DROVE

(75) WESLEYAN (TL 374086). The chapel dated 1838, of brick with a slate roof, hipped to rear, was re-fronted in the late 19th century. The entrance was originally on the W side.

SOHAM

(76) BAPTIST, Red Lion Square (TL 594730). The church, formed in 1752 by members from Pound Lane, Isleham, (*see* (54)) is notable for the pastorate of Andrew Fuller (1775–82). The chapel was rebuilt in 1832. The walls are of gault brick and the roof is hipped and slated. The front wall of three bays has brick terminal pilasters with moulded capitals, two doorways with reeded architraves and circular paterae and two tiers of sash windows separated by a brick platband. The interior has a rear gallery to which side galleries were added in 1841; the original box-pews were replaced in 1898; the pulpit also dates from the late 19th century. An adjoining Sunday-school wing was built in 1887.

Monuments: on front wall, cast-iron tablets with scrolled tops (1) John Charles Ward, 1828, and Benjamin Hodgkins, 1833, pastors;

Baptist chapel, Soham. (76)

(2) Thomas Bartle, 1841, and Elizabeth wife of John Fordham, 1845, by G. Levet; (3) George Norman, 1836, pastor, and his wives, Elizabeth, 1815, and Ann, 1831.

BM XXIV (1832) 208, 450–1; XXIX (1837) 124; XXXIII (1841) 354. Ivimey IV (1830) 458–9, 581–2.

(77) CONGREGATIONAL (TL 592734). The chapel, rebuilt in 1841 for a congregation formed in 1692, has walls of gault brick with stone dressings and a slated roof. The pedimented S front of three bays with two tiers of sash windows is divided by tall brick pilasters with moulded capitals. The single doorway in the middle bay has a rectangular fanlight and surround with two fluted Ionic pilasters and dentil cornice.

The interior has a S gallery only with panelled front supported by two cast-iron columns; the seating was renewed in the late 19th century.

Congregational chapel, Soham. (77)

A hall and Sunday-school alongside the chapel were built in 1881. (Chapel closed 1994)

Fittings – *Bootscrapers*: at entrance, pair, of cast iron with anthemion-ornamented standards and claw feet. *Monuments*: headstones in front of chapel (1) William Slack, 1831, 34 years deacon, and Sarah his widow, 1834; (2) Edward Owers, 1844. *Organ*: by Bryson Bros & Ellis of London, presented 1901.

Cong. Mag. II (1819) 813–14. *EM* NS XX (1842) 295.

(78) PRIMITIVE METHODIST (TL 591736). Gault brick with red brick dressings, three-bay gabled front with tall central wall-arch enclosing entrance and three upper windows; 1869.

(79) Former UNITARIAN, 5–7 Hall Street (TL 592737). A serious division in the Baptist church following the adoption of Unitarian views by the minister, John Gisburne, led to his removal to form a new society, which joined the General Baptist Assembly in 1811. The chapel, opened April 1810, was closed in 1870 and subsequently converted into cottages. The walls are of brick and the roof is covered with pantiles. The front wall, which has been rebuilt, formerly had a tablet inscribed 'Unitarian Chapel built by Voluntary Subscription, 1809'. Traces of round-arched windows remain in the back wall.

Aspland (1850) 207–15, 221–7. *Monthly Repository* V (1810) 207–8. March (1835) 81–3. *Christian Life* XXVII (1902) 3, 10, 17, 31 May, 7 June.

STEEPLE MORDEN

(80) WESLEYAN (TL 287426). Gault brick and slate, built 1835 and enlarged to the front *c*.1863.

STRETHAM

(81) WESLEYAN (TL 513744). Red brick with gabled front and three grouped lancets above lean-to porch; 1885 by J. Gunton.

SUTTON

(82) BAPTIST (TL 442788). The chapel, dated 1791 on a stone in the E wall, is of gault brick with a hipped slated roof. The S front has been altered and now has a central doorway with three-centred arched head flanked by two segmental-arched windows and three windows above, all with renewed frames; the lower openings originally comprised two doorways with a window between. Two tall round-arched windows in the N wall flank the pulpit.

The interior ($33\frac{1}{2}$ft by $36\frac{1}{2}$ft) has a central circular post supporting the ceiling beams and a gallery around three sides. The lower seating and pulpit were renewed in the late 19th century but some original pews remain in the gallery. The roof structure consists mainly of common rafters, two pairs having collar-beams, but without true trusses.

SWAFFHAM PRIOR

(83) ZOAR CHAPEL, Rogers Road (TL 572647). Small Strict Baptist chapel erected 1821, in part rendered and timber-framed, but with a brick front and a pantiled roof. The E front is gabled and faces a small forecourt; along the S side is a mid 19th-century school-room with lean-to roof. The interior has a pulpit at the W end and shutters opening to the school-room on the S side.

Fittings – *Book*: manuscript music book inscribed 'Bottisham

Zoar Chapel, Swaffham Prior. (83)

Meeting-house February 1838'. *Clock*: on N wall signed 'H. Lickert, Cambridge'. *Communion Table*: in front of pulpit, with hinged flaps along the sides and removable desk top for music. *Monuments*: in chapel (1) Thomas Webb, 1868, nearly 48 years minister; (2) Charles Wilderspin, 1894, 20 years preacher; (3) Mary Waters, 1851, who 'was the first means of the Gospel being brought into this parish'. *Pitchpipe*: 19th-century. *Seating*: two ranks of open-backed benches in the chapel and similar seats in the annexe.

(84) ZION CHAPEL (TL 567639). The Strict Baptist chapel in the main street is dated 1862. It has walls of gault brick; the front is divided into three bays by brick pilasters, paired at the corners, carrying an entablature and pediment.

(85) Former WESLEYAN, Prior Fen (TL 532687). Gault brick with red brick banding, dated 1884.

SWAVESEY

(86) BAPTIST (TL 364679). 'Bethel Chapel', on the E side of the street, has walls of gault brick with red brick dressings. The front is of five bays divided by panelled pilasters. Dated 1868 'R. Hutchinson, architect'.

(87) STRICT BAPTIST (TL 363681). The chapel on the W side of the street was built in 1869 for a church formed in 1789. Gabled front of gault brick in three bays with two tiers of round-arched windows; 'Hannell & Robb, architects'.

(88) Former FRIENDS, Black Horse Lane (TL 361689). A meeting-house built in 1714 was rebuilt after a fire in 1719. This was altered in 1788 and minor repairs are recorded for several years in the early 19th century; it was sold in 1937 and is now in domestic use. The building, although much altered, appears to date from the early

Zion Chapel, Swaffham Prior. (84)

18th century; it has brick walls and a steeply pitched roof now slated but formerly thatched. The N front has a 19th-century gabled porch in front of the original entrance with two windows to the W with renewed frames and a doorway and window to the east. The S wall, partly covered by a wing at the E end, has a doorway between two windows with partly original wooden frames.

The interior (37¼ft by 18ft), probably once subdivided, is ceiled at collar level; traces of a mid 19th-century refitting are evident, including a match-boarded dado which rises at the W end behind the site of the former stand.

Butler (1999) 39.

TEVERSHAM

(89) BAPTIST (TL 500582). Gault brick with some red brick dressings and a slated roof; gabled front dated 1858. *Plate*: includes a two-handled cup of 1720, from St Andrew's Street, Cambridge (10), given 1921.

UPWELL

(90) Former PRIMITIVE METHODIST (TF 503028). Red brick with stone dressings, gabled front with round-arched windows. Defaced tablet, dated 1888.

WATERBEACH

(91) BAPTIST, High Street (TL 497653). A meeting-house which appears to have had rendered timber-framed walls and a tall thatched roof, built at the beginning of the 19th century 'on a site given by the lord of the manor', was the scene of C.H. Spurgeon's first ministry. The present chapel, which succeeded it, was built in 1863, with walls of gault brick and red brick dressings and a front of three bays with a pedimental gable and slightly recessed centre.

The interior has a gallery around three sides and a fourth gallery behind the pulpit now occupied by the organ.

Fittings – *Monuments*: in chapel (1) John Watts, 1860; (2) Henry Edwards, 1881, 25 years deacon, and Sarah his widow, 1892; (3) John Tebbit, 1866, and Mary his wife; also externally at sides of chapel, several early 19th-century headstones. *Plate*: pair of mid 19th-century Sheffield-plate cups, given by New Park Street church, Southwark, 1858. *Staircase*: externally at rear of chapel, leading to upper room, flight of eighteen steps with elaborately decorated cast-iron treads, risers and balustrade.

(92) BAPTIST, Chittering (TL 496699). Small isolated chapel on E side of road, dated 1858.

(93) Former WESLEYAN, Waterbeach (TL 497652). Brick with hipped slate roof. Much altered but retaining traces of earlier fenestration. Original tablet dated 1837 reset in ground near modern entrance. (Now Salvation Army Hall)

WESTON COLVILLE

(94) PRIMITIVE METHODIST, Weston Green (TL 624522). Brick and slate, altered front with original inscription bearing date 1847 and name 'Rehoboth'.

WEST WRATTING

(95) Former CONGREGATIONAL (TL 607520). Small chapel built c.1815 with rendered timber-framed walls and pantiled roof, enlarged to the front in brick and slate. The NE end, possibly altered in the mid 19th century, is apsidal and contains a later rostrum pulpit. Interior refitted in late 19th century. (Derelict 1974)

WHITTLESEY

(96) GENERAL BAPTIST, Windmill Street (TL 268974). Gault brick with hipped roof; three-bay front with tall round-arched windows. Built 1821, re-fronted late 19th century.

Wood (1847) 227.

(97) PARTICULAR BAPTIST, Gracious Street (TL 269974). 'Zion Chapel', built c.1836 for a church formed in that year, has walls of gault brick and a slated roof hipped to the rear. Three-bay front with pilasters and pediment, central entrance and tall round-arched windows.

Zion Chapel, Whittlesey. (97)

(98) WESLEYAN, Eastrea (TL 295972). Rendered brick and slate, opened 1848 but greatly altered.

WHITTLESFORD

(99) CONGREGATIONAL (TL 475481). Red brick with big lunette in front gable, of 1903 by H.S. Jardine. (URC)

WICKEN

(100) Former MEETING-HOUSE (TL 568707). 'A certain building adjoining Robert Aspland's house' registered for dissenters in August 1799 has been identified with a timber-framed and weather-boarded shed now converted to a garage in the grounds of 'Aspland House' (formerly 'The Chestnuts'). The building (19½ft by 15ft), which is associated with the early preaching of Robert Aspland jnr., the notable Unitarian Baptist minister, was

used also by Wesleyans for a short period in the early 19th century. The framing of the walls may be original but the roof and external cladding have been renewed.

Aspland (1850) *passim*. *Inquirer* (4 April 1981).

(101) Former PRIMITIVE METHODIST (TL 568708). Built 1866 superseding a chapel of 1835. Gault brick with gabled front and central entrance. (Closed 1944)

FMR PRIMITIVE METHODIST CHAPEL, WICKEN   CFS 1972

WILLINGHAM

(102) OLD BAPTIST CHAPEL, George Street (TL 404706). The church originated as an Independent cause in the late 17th century following the ejection of the rector, the Rev. Nathaniel Bradshaw, and was until *c*.1728 united with Cottenham. Sometime after the death of the Rev. Thomas Boodger in 1784 the church adopted a Strict Baptist polity and so remained until *c*.1975, when meetings ceased. The meeting-house, rebuilt in 1830 and standing on a restricted site, is a large building of gault brick with a hipped slated roof; the internal fittings are especially notable.

The W front is of four bays with two tiers of hung sash windows; the middle bays project slightly and have a pediment with moulded timber cornice and an oval tablet inscribed 'BAPTIST MEETING | Built by Subscription | 1830' within a wreath. In each of the end bays is a round-arched doorway of two orders. The E wall has three windows at two levels and the N and S end walls have each two upper windows only.

The interior has a semicircular gallery around three sides and a gallery across the W end. Two vestries are set between the front entrances with shutters opening to the chapel. With the exception of the conversion of the W gallery in 1930 to a small meeting-room the building is unaltered; it has original box-pews throughout, with numbered doors, arranged at both levels in a semicircular formation, and with a large table-pew in front of the pulpit. The gallery has a front of fielded panels divided by fluted pilasters above a moulded cornice and is supported by six cast-iron columns; it is approached by staircases next to the entrances with plain square balusters and doorways with three-centred arched heads at the lower landings. (Demolished *c*.1977–84)

Fittings – *Baptistery*: in floor below pulpit, rectangular with steps at N and S ends. *Monuments* and *Floorslabs*. *Monuments*: in chapel (1) Elizabeth wife of William Read, 1817, signed 'F & T Tomson, Camb.'; (2) Mary wife of John Fen, 1828, signed 'Tomson Camb.'; (3) John Rootham, 1827, '*Preacher* of the Cross of Christ in this place 38 Years', and John his infant son, stone tablet with moulded pediment, signed 'Gilbert, Cambridge'; (4) Ellis Munsey, 1845, minister 16 years, signed 'Wiles'. *Floorslabs*: at foot of pulpit steps (1) John Stevens, 1831; in aisle NE of the table-pew (2) Rev. Tho. Boodger, 1784, 30 years pastor, and Lettica his wife, 1783. *Pulpit*: mahogany, with concave sides and convex front.

CHST XII (1933–6) 120–30.

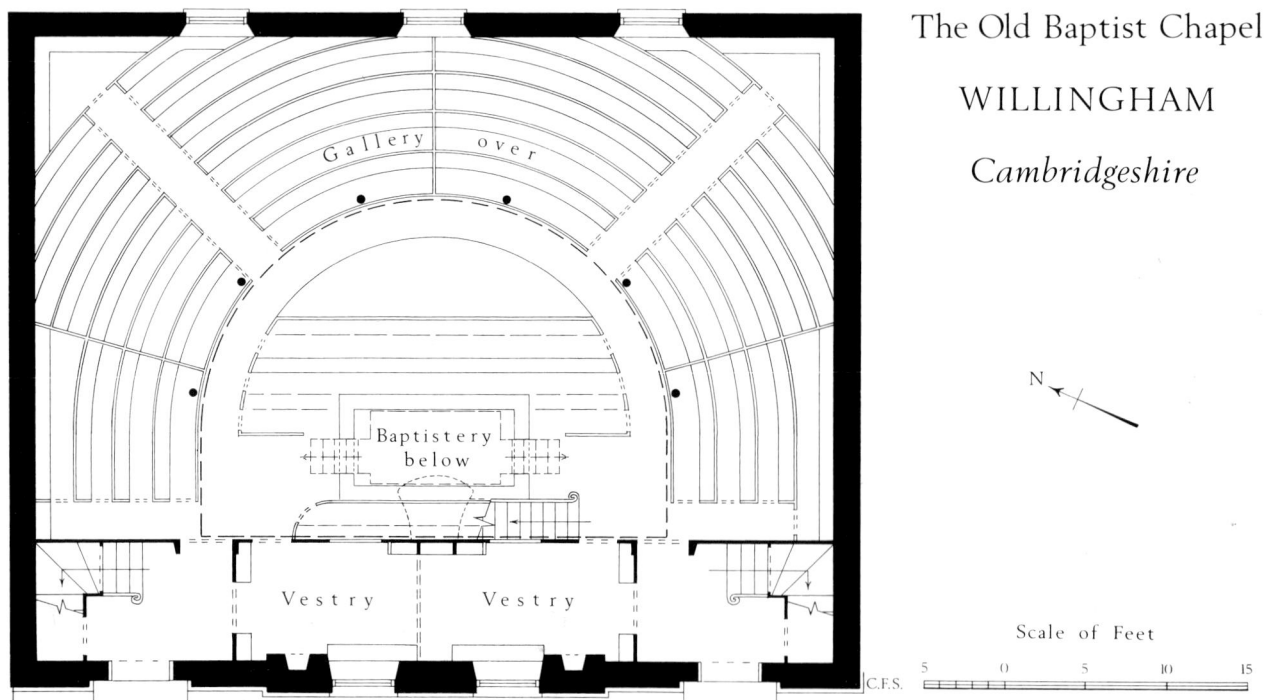

The Old Baptist Chapel
WILLINGHAM
Cambridgeshire

The Old Baptist Chapel, Willingham. (Demolished)

(103) THE TABERNACLE, George Street (TL 403705). A chapel 'formerly occupied by the Arian Baptist Church at Willingham' was taken by a new evangelical congregation in 1836 and enlarged. The Tabernacle, built in 1874 for a second Baptist congregation, perhaps that formed in 1836, stands opposite the foregoing; it is of gault brick with a gabled front flanked by entrance wings with open lattice parapets. (Rebuilt c.1989)

BM XXX (1838) 351. *Baptist Times* (19 April 1990).

(104) WESLEYAN, Church Street (TL 408705). The chapel facing the Green has a gabled front of gault brick with three arched bays enclosing a central doorway and two tiers of windows. Oval tablet dated 1851.

Wesleyan chapel, Willingham. (104)

WISBECH

(105) BAPTIST, Upper Hill Street (TF 462097). The present chapel of stone, in a 13th-century Gothic style with lancet windows and six-foil window in a transeptal gable facing the street, was built in 1859 for a Particular Baptist church which originated about 1690. United with this church since c.1961 is that of the General Baptists, formed 1655, who removed from their meeting-house of 1697 on the W side of Falcon Lane (TF 463096), now demolished, to a new chapel in Ely Place (TF 462096), built 1803, rebuilt 1873, also now demolished.

Ivimey II (1814) 99–100; IV (1830) 459–60. Taylor (1818) I: 138–41; II: 301–8, 407–8. Wood (1847) 185.

(106) Former BAPTIST, Victoria Road (TF 464091). Three-bay front of gault brick with gabled centre bay, dated 1856. (Now in commercial use)

(107) CONGREGATIONAL, Castle Square (TF 462096). The chapel built in 1818 for a newly formed congregation has a brick front of three bays with stone quoins, plinth and platband, brick parapet raised in the centre incorporating a date tablet, and two tiers of round-arched windows; the wide central doorway with rusticated surround is probably of later date. (URC)

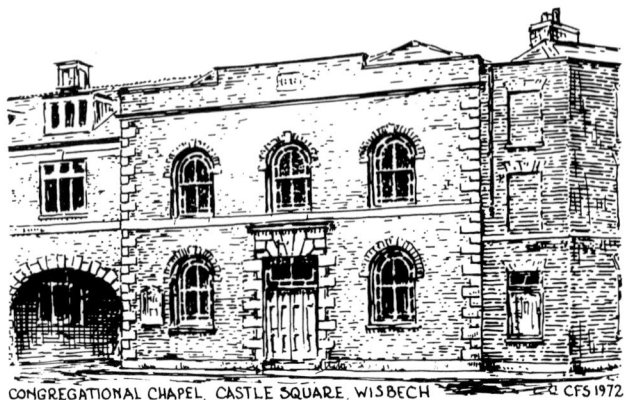

CONGREGATIONAL CHAPEL, CASTLE SQUARE, WISBECH   CFS 1972

(108) FRIENDS, North Brink (TF 458097). A meeting-house opened in 1711 was replaced by the present building in 1854 to the designs of Algernon Peckover. This has a front of gault brick with a doorway and three hung sash windows with moulded stone architraves and cornices supported by scrolled brackets.

Butler (1999) 40.

(109) WESLEYAN, The Crescent (TF 462095). Built c.1836, with a front wall of brown brick and stone quoins; gable and upper windows altered in the late 19th century.

WISBECH ST MARY

(110) PRIMITIVE METHODIST, Guyhirn (TF 401038). Small brick chapel of 1868.

(111) PRIMITIVE METHODIST, Murrow (TF 373069). Red brick with gabled front and large wall-arch enclosing the entrance and three upper windows. Dated 1875.

(112) Former PRIMITIVE METHODIST (TF 417079). Dated 1891, superseded by nearby chapel of 1926.

WITCHFORD

(113) BAPTIST (TL 498788). Small chapel of gault brick. Three-bay gabled front with round-arched windows; dated 1875.

ESSEX

The predominance of Congregational churches in this county, many of which trace their origins to Presbyterian causes linked with the names of ejected ministers, will be apparent from the monuments described, half of which were of this denomination. The large number of Friends' meeting-houses is also remarkable. Only a few Baptist chapels call for comment but the county is notable for the birthplace of C.H. Spurgeon, at Kelvedon, and for his conversion in the former Primitive Methodist chapel in Colchester (31).

No early meeting-house of any denomination remains in the county which has not suffered from at least an internal refitting in the 19th century, and several have been lost either by outright demolition, as at Abbess Roding (1) or by rebuilding, as at Saffron Walden (91), although in both these instances illustrations of the former buildings survive. The earliest remaining former Presbyterian meeting-house in the county, of 1707, is at Little Baddow (73) where the unusual arrangement of the original fittings may be deduced from the fenestration. A chapel of the same date at Bocking End, Braintree (9) has been enlarged, but a drawing of the original wide frontage with a series of parallel roofs and two tiers of windows contrasts interestingly with its much smaller contemporary some 20 miles to the south. Another notable building is at Terling (102) of 1752 which, although it has suffered greatly from internal rearrangement and the loss of most of its fittings, still retains its original chandelier. At Saffron Walden the General Baptist chapel (88) of 1744 remains, converted to a pair of houses, close to its much altered successor; the former congregation here was the only recently surviving representative of early 19th-century Unitarianism in the county, although the influence of Unitarian trustees at the Old Meeting in Colchester (28) is also of interest in the development of an orthodox secession in that town. The Particular Baptist chapel at Potter Street, Harlow (61), of 1756 has an unusually elaborate frontage and a remarkably flamboyant doorcase, but otherwise this chapel, too, has been greatly changed by extension and internal stripping.

Friends' meeting-houses in Essex form an important series, from the small but altered late 17th-century building at Stebbing (99) to the typical mid 19th-century planning of Epping (36) and Halstead (58). Particularly notable is Earls Colne (33), of 1733 or earlier, in which a narrow gallery was provided within the roof space, while the Chelmsford meeting-house (17) of 1823–4 is representative of the larger buildings required by more substantial urban meetings.

The early 19th century is dominated by the chapels designed by James Fenton of Chelmsford, principally for Congregationalists, of which Felsted (38) of c.1833–4 and Witham (119) of 1840 are amongst his best work; the more elaborate Wivenhoe chapel (121) of 1846 is strangely out of character. Other early 19th-century chapels include the former Congregational chapel at Manningtree (81) of 1823, distinguished by unusual rounded corners, a feature repeated in lesser degree at the front of the Wesleyan chapel at Brightlingsea (12) of 1843. This last is one of a group of chapels, others being Great Bentley (48) and Little Clacton (74), which have several features in common, but apart from these few Methodist chapels are of note; an exception is at Manningtree (82) with a pedimented front of 1807 subsequently embellished by a cupola. Methodists built a polygonal chapel with twelve sides in Maidenburgh Street, Colchester, in 1759 but it only survived until 1800. A few chapels built by a local denomination, 'The Peculiar People', are listed here of which the most complete is at Tillingham (111).

The later 19th century is represented by several Gothic Revival buildings; the work of Frederick Barnes of Ipswich at Lion Walk, Colchester (27), which in 1862–3 replaced an octagonal chapel of 1766, has itself now been largely rebuilt though his chapel at Halstead (57) remains; other examples include the work of Charles Pertwee at Great Dunmow (52), T. Lewis Banks at Hatfield Heath (65) and Charles Bell at Steeple Bumpstead (101), all of which take the place of older buildings.

Brickwork is common in Essex from the earliest times, the Friends' meeting-house at Stebbing (99) of 1674 includes some diaper patterning and carved brickwork for the date tablet. In the early 19th century gault brick is frequently used for the fronts of chapels with the sides built in cheaper red or yellow stock brick. Timber-framing clad with lath and plaster or weather-boarding is also used throughout the 18th century, the large Coggeshall chapel (24) of 1710, for which the contract survives, being specified to be finished in 'pebble-dash'. At Fordham (41) the Countess of Huntingdon's chapel of 1789 was originally weather-boarded, and at Maldon (77) the large Congregational chapel of 1801 is also timber-framed and finished with decorative pargeting. The older roofs are generally tiled, but slate is common from the early 19th century. No surviving use of thatch or pantiles was recorded.

ABBESS BEAUCHAMP AND BERNERS RODING

(1) Site of MEETING-HOUSE, Abbess Roding (TL 562119). A Presbyterian, latterly Congregational, church formed *c*.1698 at Rookwood Hall built a meeting-house half a mile N of the Hall in 1729–30 which survived until 1899, when services were transferred to a former preaching-station of 1887 in White Roding (*see* (117)). The site, W of Anchor Farm and adjacent to RCHM *Essex* II (1921) Abbess Roding, monument (3), is marked by a brick boundary wall. The meeting-house had a double roof hipped and supported internally by a pair of timber posts. The S front of four bays had two doorways in the end bays and two tiers of round-arched windows. *Plate*: in Colchester Museum, pair of two-handled cups 1747.

URCHSJ I (1973–7) 112–18.

Former meeting-house, Abbess Roding. (1)

ARDLEIGH

(2) WESLEYAN, Colchester Road (TM 053294). Brick with hipped slate roof; concealed behind late 19th-century Gothic front. Opened 1811.

BILLERICAY

(3) Former STRICT BAPTIST, 19 Chapel Street (TQ 675946). The small chapel, now 'Chapel House', built in 1798, has rendered walls and a tiled roof. It comprised a small chapel of two bays with an entrance in the gabled S end and cottage to the north.

(4) CONGREGATIONAL, Chapel Street (TQ 675943). The church (now URC) originated in the late 17th century as a Presbyterian congregation for which a house, 91 High Street, is claimed to have been licensed in 1672; it carries a modern commemorative tablet. The present chapel, built 1837–8, was designed by James Fenton. The walls are of gault brick and the roof is slated. Gabled front of three bays with prominent centrepiece rising above the sides and having thin corner buttresses and two stages of grouped lancets; gabled porches to right and left. Contemporary iron railings in front. *Monuments*: in burial-ground, include two square tombs with columned corners and urn finials (1) William Thorogood, 1860; (2) Charlotte daughter of Henry and Sarah Thorogood, 1861, *et al.*; also (3) memorial to Christopher Martin, Marie Martin, Solomon Power and John Langerman of Billericay, who sailed in the *Mayflower*, 1620, also to Peter Browne, erected 1920.

Taylor, W., *Calling the Generations: A History of the Independent Protestant Dissenters of Billericay (1672–1972)* (1972).

BRADFIELD

(5) WESLEYAN, Bradfield Heath (TM 140300). Red brick and slate, three-bay sides and gabled ends, bell-cote on SW gable above entrance, pointed-arched windows with keystones and Y-tracery. Opened 1850.

BRAINTREE AND BOCKING

(6) BAPTIST, Blyth's Meadow, Braintree (TL 758231). Gault brick and slate, pedimented three-bay front with platband, two tiers of three-light windows to centre bay, side bays with doorways and windows above; inscribed on cill of upper centre window 'REBUILT A.D.1833'. Galleried interior. Probably by James Fenton.

(7) CONGREGATIONAL, London Road, Braintree (TL 755228). Gault brick and slate; pedimented front of three principal bays separated by narrower recessed bays; paired entrances in end bays, two tiers of windows. Designed by James Fenton and formerly inscribed with date of erection, 1832, but altered 1860–70 with added embellishment to lower windows and door surrounds and intermediate windows inserted. Interior, altered *c*.1860–70, has a coved centre to the ceiling with exposed tie-beams. (URC) *Monument*: Rev. John Carter, 1864, 52 years pastor.

(8) CONGREGATIONAL, Church Street, Bocking (TL 762261). Low-built gabled front of gault brick, dated 1862. (URC)

(9) CONGREGATIONAL, Bocking End (TL 757234). The Independent church formed in 1699 erected a meeting-house in 1707 on part of Windmill Field; this remains incorporated in the present building. In 1818 the meeting-house was enlarged to the front and reroofed. The original E front was of red brick with two tiers of cross-framed windows below a parapet; the roof of five hipped sections was tiled. The present front of gault brick is of five bays with two tiers of round-arched windows, formerly with intersecting glazing-bars, and end entrances. The roof is now pyramidal, covered with slates and surmounted by an octagonal lantern. The rear W wall of early 18th-century brick has been altered and a vestry built against it, but traces remain of two round-arched windows formerly flanking the pulpit and of two smaller upper windows each side with flat-arched heads. The N and S walls are also of 1707 and have lobbies projecting at the sides on the line of the old frontage now providing access to gallery staircases.

The interior (46ft, enlarged to 51½ft, by 58ft) has a plaster ceiling of 1818 with a square central vault rising to the lantern. The seating and gallery front date from a late 19th-century refitting.

Fittings – *Communion Table*: in vestry, with turned baluster legs, early 18th-century. *Monuments*: in gallery (1) Rev. Thomas Craig, 1865, over 62 years pastor. Externally on W wall (2) Martha wife of Rev. Alexander Fletcher of Finsbury Chapel, London, 1843; W of chapel (3) private burial enclosure with high brick walls and segmental-arched entrance, tablet on front wall to Dorothy wife of Nathaniel Boosey, 1757, *et al.*; near NW corner of chapel (4) Thomas Shepherd MA, 1738/9, 39 years pastor, table-tomb. To the W of the chapel is a large burial-ground with many

Exterior before 1818.

Exterior after 1818.
Congregational chapel, Bocking End, Braintree.

monuments, including coffin-shaped box-tombs with head- and footstones of the early 19th century. *Paintings* and *Drawings*: in vestry, two oil portraits of ministers; also two water-colour drawings by E. Tabor (1) E front of chapel before alteration, dated 1818; (2) E front after enlargement, dated 1827, each with label recording their gift to the church in 1843 by Alexander Fletcher of Finsbury Chapel; also large drawing of interior after 1818 showing a former upper gallery.

(10) Former FRIENDS, Rayne Road (TL 755232). Stock brick and slate with gabled front of gault brick, central entrance with pilasters and entablature between two round-arched windows; secondary entrances each side. Built 1863 replacing a meeting-house of 1706. (Closed c.1950 and since used by the Salvation Army) *Inscription*: in boundary wall to S recording erection of wall in 1842.

Butler (1999) 175.

BRENTWOOD

(11) CONGREGATIONAL, New Road (TQ 595937). The chapel was built in 1847 for a congregation which first met in one of two former meeting-houses, both of which were closed by c.1800. The front is rendered and pedimented with a slightly projecting centre having four doorways and four round-arched upper windows with a lunette in the pediment; side entrances with windows over. (Demolition proposed 1978)

CYB (1847) 170, and obituary of Rev. David Smith.

BRIGHTLINGSEA

(12) WESLEYAN, Chapel Road (TM 092170). The chapel, of red brick with a hipped slate roof, was built in 1843 replacing a smaller timber-framed preaching-house of 1804. Front of three bays with central gablet, rounded corners and two tiers of pointed-arched windows with moulded labels; window frames, formerly with intersecting glazing bars, now drastically altered. Gabled porch with four-centred arched entrance. (For similar design *see* Great Bentley (48))

(13) NEW JERUSALEM CHURCH, Queen Street (TM 087169). This society commenced about 1809 and the first chapel was erected in New Street in 1814. The present chapel by E.C. Gosling was built in 1867–8. The walls are of gault brick with red brick dressings. The front of three bays has a stepped cornice, gabled centre bay and round-arched upper windows.

Hindmarsh (1861) 201, 217.

BURNHAM

(14) BAPTIST, Station Road, Burnham on Crouch (TQ 952956). The church claims a 17th-century date of origin. The present chapel, of 1904 by Searle and Hayes, is of brick, partly rendered, with precast 'patent stone' dressings.

B.Hbk (1905) 452.

CASTLE HEDINGHAM

(15) CONGREGATIONAL (TL 784354). The church (now URC) commenced in 1708 as a nominally Presbyterian society. The present chapel, rebuilt in 1842, possibly by James Fenton, has a front of gault brick and red brick sides. The pedimented front has two tiers of windows and two entrances with double doors; the three centre bays project slightly and have an inscribed blocking-course in the pediment. A detached school building behind the chapel is dated 1853. *Monuments*: in burial-ground (1) Mrs Mary Crown, 1736; (2) Rev. Baxter Cole, 1794. *Paving*: in front of chapel, radiating pattern of black and white pebbles, with date 1868. *Pulpit*: reputed to be that used by Isaac Watts, the Independent preacher, in former chapel, 18th-century.

CHELMSFORD

(16) STRICT BAPTIST, New London Road (TL 707065). 'Ebenezer Chapel', gault brick with lancet windows and slate roof; built c.1849.

(17) Former FRIENDS, Duke Street (TL 706070). The meeting-house, closed 1955 and since 1976 used as a library, was built in 1823–4 replacing earlier buildings near Baddow Road. The architect or surveyor is named in the building accounts as John Collis of Chelmsford. The walls are of gault brick and the roof is slated. The N front has a pediment with wide eaves, central portico with paired Doric columns and two tiers of blind window recesses. The side walls have each five round-arched upper windows; at the E side is a second entrance porch between minor rooms. The interior was originally divided into two rooms; the principal meeting-room to the S has rounded corners at each end of the stand.

Butler (1999) 175–8.

Former Friends' meeting-house, Chelmsford. (17)

CHIGNALL

(18) CONGREGATIONAL, Chignall Smealy (TL 660118). Small three-bay chapel of stock brick, built c.1843, greatly enlarged at one end in the late 19th century. (URC)

CHIGWELL

(19) CONGREGATIONAL, Chigwell Row (TQ 459931). Stock brick and slate, built 1804, altered or rebuilt 1845 and heavily embellished externally in the late 19th century. Three-bay front with pedimental gable and two tiers of windows. (URC) *Monuments*: in rear burial-ground (1) Rebecca widow of John Harris of Leominster, 1829, John Bellin, 1841, and [ ] his wife, 1833, broken panel from table-tomb; (2) Isaac Savill, 1862, and Frances his wife, 1835, broken headstone.

Mearns (1882) No. 44.

CHIPPING ONGAR

(20) CONGREGATIONAL, High Street (TL 552028). The formerly Presbyterian congregation (now URC) formed in the late 17th century following the ejection of the rector, John Lorkin or Larkin, built a meeting-house on the present site c.1720 which was rebuilt in 1833. The chapel, erected by John Sadd, contractor, of Maldon, stands behind a row of cottages on the E side of the street. The walls are of yellow stock brick with gault brick at the front, and the roof is slated. Three-bay pedimented front with central entrance and two tiers of windows. Four tall sash windows to side walls, front pair blind. Rear gallery, interior reseated in the late 19th century.

The cottages next to the street include a room above the arched approach to the chapel once used for a small academy attended by David Livingstone, the missionary.

Fittings – *Inscriptions*: on bricks of N and S returns of front wall, include date 'May 31 1833'. *Monuments*: in chapel (1) Rev. Isaac Taylor, 1829, Ann his widow, 1830, and Jane their daughter, 1824, late 19th-century tablet (related headstones now lie below the floor near the vestry; Jane Taylor was the author of the verses 'Twinkle, twinkle, little star…'); (2) Rev. Richard Cecil, 1863, minister 1838–47, Salome his wife, 1844, and their daughters Salome, 1843, and Lucy wife of Rev. John Hay, 1844.

CHRISHALL

(21) PRIMITIVE METHODIST, Crawley End (TL 446398). Built 1862, enlarged 1871. Large yellow-brick gabled front.

CLAVERING

(22) PRIMITIVE METHODIST, Hill Green (TL 481323). Three-bay gabled front of red brick with white brick dressings. Dated 1877.

COGGESHALL

(23) Former BAPTIST, Church Street (TL 851227). Low pedimented front of brick in three bays, built 1855.

Dale, B., *The Annals of Coggeshall* (1863) 227–8. Witard (1962) 66 and *passim*.

(24) CONGREGATIONAL, Stoneham Street (TL 850228). The Independent congregation was formed in the mid 17th century during the incumbency of Dr John Owen, later vice-chancellor of Oxford University. After the ejection of John Sames (or Sams) in 1662 dissenters met in a barn on the N side of East Street. The present site was acquired in 1710 and the meeting-house was erected in the same year; the building was enlarged in 1818 and 1834 and entirely refitted in 1882 and later under the direction of the Chelmsford architect, Charles Pertwee.

A building contract dated 16 May 1710, between Thomas Crosby of Bocking, carpenter, and Thomas Nicholls of Little Coggeshall, yeoman, and others, provides for a building 45ft long, 36ft broad, with walls 20ft high and having a front gallery 12ft wide and side galleries 9ft wide, the pews to be like those in Bocking meeting-house; the walls, timber-framed on a brick plinth, to be 'rough cast on laths … dash't with stones'.

The chapel is a large structure with rendered timber-framed walls and a slated roof. The W front is gabled, of four bays with two tiers of windows and a wide early 19th-century porch with two Greek Doric columns *in antis*; pediments were added to the upper windows and a lunette in the gable was replaced by a rectangular ventilator in the late 19th century. The side walls have four bays of windows in two tiers and at the E end is a two-storeyed vestry. The interior ($66\frac{1}{4}$ft by $44\frac{1}{4}$ft) has a gallery around three sides. Freestanding to the E is a mid 19th-century Sunday-school with a lecture hall of 1890 beyond. (The church is now jointly URC, Baptist and Methodist) (Interior of chapel subdivided c.1990)

Monuments: in W porch, three oval tablets (1) Thomas Heward, 1815, Elizabeth his wife, 1790, and Elizabeth their daughter, 1835; (2) William Leach, 1790; (3) John Wright, 1823; also (4) John Owen DD, vicar of Coggeshall 1646–51, late 19th-century brass tablet. In burial-ground to W (5–6) Thomas Unwin, 1810, Lydia his widow *et al.*, pair of table-tombs in railed enclosure.

CHST V (1911–12) 40–51. *CYB* (1891) 215. Dale (1863) op. cit. 187–225.

(25) Former WESLEYAN, Stoneham Street (TL 849226). Built 1882, superseding a small chapel in East Street. Gabled brick front with four-light plate-traceried window above porch.

COLCHESTER

(26) BAPTIST, Eld Lane (TL 99762505). The church formed in 1689 occupied hired premises in North Hill until 1711, when a building in front of the site of the present chapel was altered or rebuilt for use as a meeting-house. This was enlarged in 1810 but in 1834 it was reported 'dilapidated and unsafe' and a new building was erected on the site of an adjacent orchard. The chapel of 1834 has walls of red brick with a gault brick front and slate roof. The S front of three central bays with a central pediment and two end bays, has three wide doorways and three round-arched upper windows separated by brick pilasters. Two stone tablets are inscribed 'BUILT 1834' and 'RESTORED 1883'. The interior, with galleries supported by fluted cast-iron columns, was reseated in 1883. *Monument*: headstone reset externally against W wall, Thomas Steevens, 1802, pastor.

Blaxhill (1948) 15–16. Spurrier, E., *Memorials of the Baptist Church Worshipping in Eld Lane Chapel, Colchester…*(1889).

(27) CONGREGATIONAL, Lion Walk (TL 99722505). The Independent congregation (now URC) which originated about 1642 built a meeting-house in Moor Lane (Priory Street) which was placed in trust in 1692. This was superseded by a meeting-house on the present site (formerly Red Lion Walk) opened in 1766. The chapel was enlarged to the front in 1816 and rebuilt in 1862–3. The first chapel in Lion Walk, of brick and slate, was a regular octagon with two tall round-arched windows flanking the pulpit and two stages of windows in the other walls. The enlargement provided improved entrance facilities and a lengthened rear gallery. The chapel of 1862–3 in the Gothic style by Frederick Barnes of Ipswich is faced with polygonal masonry and has a corner tower and spire, the latter partly rebuilt after an earthquake in 1884. The interior has N and S arcades with galleries around three sides supported by cast-iron columns and a polygonal organ-apse at the E end behind the pulpit. (Chapel rebuilt c.1980 but retaining the steeple)

Fittings – *Model*: of octagon chapel, wood and paper, illustrating its condition prior to demolition, c.1862. *Monuments*: in

Congregational chapel (URC), Lion Walk, Colchester. (27)

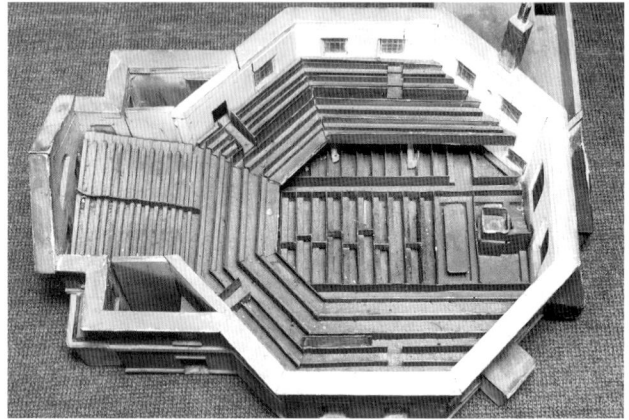

Model of former Octagon Chapel, Lion Walk, Colchester. (27)

burial-ground, several reset early 19th-century headstones. *Plate*: includes a set of four beakers, 1754–5.

Blaxhill, E.A., *History of Lion Walk Congregational Church, Colchester, 1642–1937* (1938). *CYB* (1863) 345–6.

(28) Former CONGREGATIONAL, East Stockwell Street (TL 997255). A Presbyterian congregation formed in the late 17th century built a meeting-house in Bucklebury Lane (St Helen's Lane) *c*.1692 'about midway on the south side of the lane'. In the early 19th century a sharp division occurred between the then Unitarian trustees and the minister, the Rev. Joseph Herrick, which was only resolved in 1816 by the former removing the roof of the meeting-house, causing the minister and his supporters to commence an orthodox cause in an adjoining street. The old meeting-house remained in Unitarian use until after 1823 and was later used by 'Swedenborgians' and by Wesleyan seceders; it was closed by 1880 and demolished in 1894.

The chapel in East Stockwell Street built for Mr Herrick's congregation in 1816–17 is a square building, enlarged to the front in 1835, with school-rooms added to the rear in 1867 and the interior reconstructed in the late 19th century; it was closed *c*.1970. The walls are of red brick with rendered dressings and the slate roof is surmounted by an octagonal lantern. The front of 1835 is of three bays with a pediment, central entrance with two Doric columns *in antis* and two tiers of windows.

Plate: two cups from the Old Meeting, given 1715 and 1717, now form part of the Colchester Civic Plate.

Blaxhill (1948) 10–14. Evans (1897) 51–2. *UHST* V (1931–4) 331–2.

Former Congregational chapel, East Stockwell Street, Colchester. (28)

(29) CONGREGATIONAL, Chapel Street (TL 994249). 'Headgate Chapel', attributed to W.F. Poulton, was built in 1844 for a congregation formed in 1843 by a few seceders from Lion Walk. Brick and slate with gault brick front of three principal bays with giant pilasters and pediment, round-arched doorways and two tiers of windows. Interior altered 1878, since refitted after fire damage.

(30) Former FRIENDS, St Helen's Lane (TL 997254). 'St Helen's Chapel', a late 13th-century building of rubble with ashlar dressings, brick lacing courses and a tiled roof, was used as an occasional meeting-house from 1701. In 1801 a new meeting-house was built in East Stockwell Street, successively replaced in 1872 by a building, now 'Rebow Chambers', in Sir Isaac's Walk, in 1938 by one in Shewell Road and again in 1971.

The former burial-ground, closed 1853, W of St Helen's Chapel, has brick boundary walls with tablets recording their erection in 1820. *Monuments*: reset around the boundary walls include (1) Ann and William Brockway, 1795, 1797; (2) Mary Ann Brockway, 1798.

Butler (1999) 179–83. Blaxhill (1948) 6–10. RCHM *Essex* III (1922) 50, monument (17).

(31) Former PRIMITIVE METHODIST, Artillery Street (TM 008247). Brick and slate, built 1839, front altered and gable added 1892; the original oval tablet reset over the entrance has been defaced. The chapel is notable for the conversion in 1850 of C.H. Spurgeon, which is commemorated on a monument within, erected 1897. The original pulpit is now in Spurgeon's College, London.

Kendall (1905) II: 239.

EARLS COLNE

(32) BAPTIST (TL 854289). Red brick with large wheel-window in gabled front. Built 1860 by a Mr Moore of London superseding a chapel of 1818, for a church founded in 1786. The first meeting-house, the conversion of two cottages, had an internal baptistery as early as 1795.

Spurrier, E., *Memorials of the Baptist Church Worshipping in Eld Lane Chapel, Colchester...* (1889) 33ff.

(33) FRIENDS, Burrows Lane (TL 856290). A meeting-house is said to have been built here in 1674 by John Garrod. The present structure could be of the early 18th century; a brick in the N wall is dated 1733. The walls are of brickwork with a pyramidal tiled roof. The W front was rendered and a porch added in the late 19th century, an original rear entrance with segmental-arched head remains blocked in the E wall between two windows, which have later served, for a time, as doorways.

The interior (30ft square) has a late 19th-century stand at the S side with traces of a window at its back. There are slight evidences of a former N gallery from which a narrow staircase in the NE corner rose to the roof space. A narrow gallery at ceiling level supported by two posts in the room below surrounded an octagonal opening 16ft across, now ceiled over, bounded by eight posts and a moulded handrail, parts of which remain, with plastered ashlaring and a ceiling at collar-beam level; a dormer window on the E side has been removed. (E wall and W porch now rebuilt)

Butler (1999) 185–6.

ELMSTEAD

(34) WESLEYAN, Elmstead Market (TM 065245). Red brick with yellow brick dressings; opened 1817, enlarged to front 1863 with decorative barge-boards; Sunday-school alongside dated 1872, in similar style.

EPPING

(35) CONGREGATIONAL, Lindsey Street (TL 462028). The formerly Presbyterian congregation (now URC) originated in the late 17th century and built the first meeting-house on the present site. In 1774 this had become much decayed and was rebuilt, the main part of the new structure being completed in one month and a day. This had brick walls with a domestic front of three bays with central pedimented doorway below a plain Venetian window and two tiers of segmental-arched windows; two cottages of two storeys and attics adjoined the sides of the chapel. In 1887 the front was entirely altered with a rendered Gothic façade designed by J. Winter of Epping, and the interior was refitted. About 1968 the wings and some of the later ornament were removed.

The surviving building (40¼ft by 27ft) incorporates the original structure of the 1774 chapel but retains little else of the period. Many monuments formerly in the chapel and burial-ground are listed in Wright op. cit. below, 91, 99, 106, 114–18. (Chapel reported rebuilt since 1970)

CYB (1888) 224. Wright, C., *Nonconformity in Epping* (1896).

(36) FRIENDS, Hemnall Street (TL 463023). Built 1850 to replace a meeting-house of 1705 on an adjoining site. The previous building, as described by Wright, 'had a rustic portico or verandah all round it, and was covered by a thatched roof extending beyond its walls down to the pillars which also supported it'. The present meeting-house has walls of stock brick with a gabled front and large tripartite semicircular-arched window and doorway combined. The plan comprises an entrance lobby flanked by minor rooms and with the meeting-room beyond.

Butler (1999) 187. Wright (1896) op. cit. 65–6.

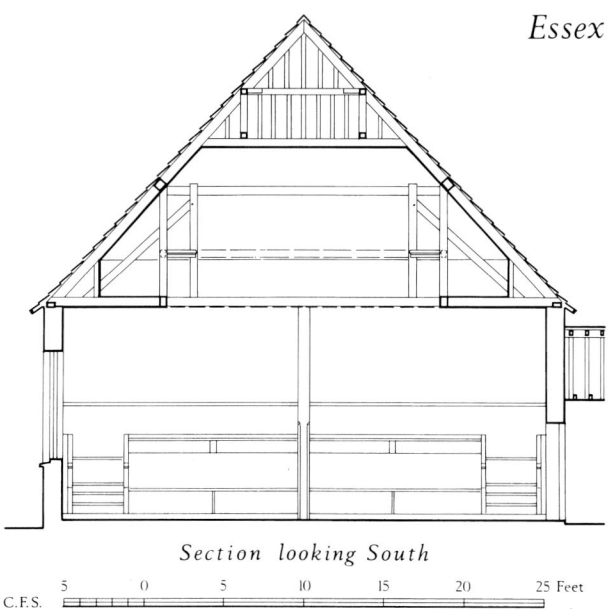

Friends' Meeting-house, EARLS COLNE *Essex*

Section looking South

EPPING UPLAND

(37) UNION CHAPEL, Epping Long Green (TL 435055). The first chapel, now 'Briar Cottage', built in 1834 for joint Baptist and Congregational use, stands 50 yards NE of the present chapel. It forms part of a row of two-storeyed brick cottages from which it is distinguished by having labels above the windows.

The present chapel, built 1862 from 'plans prepared by Mr Tarring' of London, has walls of stock brick with red brick dressings, the front is gabled and has a circular window above a small porch.

Wright (1896) op. cit.

FELSTED

(38) Former CONGREGATIONAL (TL 679204). The chapel built c.1833–4, probably by James Fenton, has brick walls and a slate roof. The front of gault brick in three bays with intermediate buttresses has two gabled porches and four-centred arched heads to the upper windows. The side walls of red brick in four bays, excluding the return bay of the front wall, have two tiers of windows. The interior has a gallery around three sides supported by iron columns. The ceiling is a segmental plaster barrel-vault with exposed trusses. (Converted to social use by 1993 and floor inserted) *Monuments*: in chapel (1) Rev. John Jonas Mark, 1869, first minister 1834–69. In burial-ground (2) William Ridley, 1852, and Martha his wife, 1837, table-tomb in railed enclosure.

(39) FRIENDS, Bannister Green (TL 694207). A small timber-framed and rendered meeting-house built in 1764 was demolished c.1940. The entrance and two square sash windows to the principal room were in the E wall; there was a smaller room in a wing at the rear. When recorded by the Royal Commission in 1914 it was in use as a Congregational chapel.

Butler (1999) 188. RCHM *Essex* II (1921) 75, monument (2).

FINCHINGFIELD

(40) CONGREGATIONAL (TL 684328). The chapel was built in 1779 for an Independent congregation, formerly Presbyterian, which originated in the late 17th century (now URC). The building was enlarged to the N in 1820, heightened and re-fronted. The walls are of brick and the roof is slated. Rendered S front of three bays with a pediment, central porch extended to each side and three tall round-arched upper windows. Side walls with two tiers of wide segmental-arched windows and a range of smaller

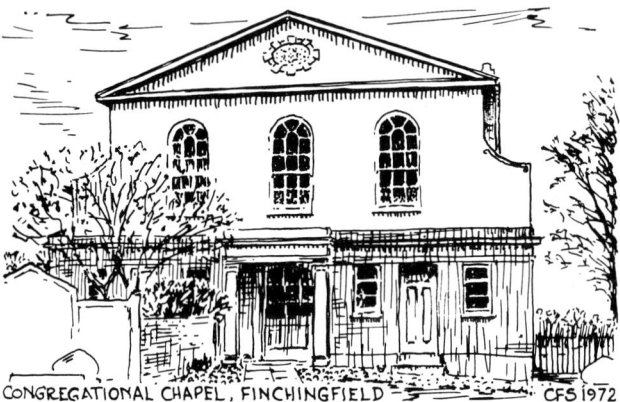

CONGREGATIONAL CHAPEL, FINCHINGFIELD — CFS 1972

Former Friends' meeting-house, Bannister Green, Felsted. (*Photograph 1914*) (39)

windows above. Galleried interior with an upper gallery along the E and W sides having an open cast-iron front supported by large iron brackets.

Fittings – *Inscription*: on brick in extension of E wall, 'IB 1820'. *Monuments*: in chapel (1) Joseph son of Rev. John Blackburn and Sarah his wife, 1819; (2) Humphrey Smith, 1824, recording a legacy of £500 for the support of the minister; (3) Mrs Sarah Bailey, 1781, recording a bequest for the support of the ministry.

FORDHAM

(41) Former COUNTESS OF HUNTINGDON'S (TL 931293). The chapel built *c*.1789 has timber-framed walls formerly weather-boarded but now mostly rendered, and a hipped tiled roof. The S front has two mid 19th-century windows to an inserted rear gallery and a later gabled porch. In the E wall are three tall sash windows; the W side is partly covered by a mid 19th-century school-room. A contemporary manse to the W, with a rendered timber frame with brick gables, of two storeys and attics, was demolished *c*.1971.

The interior (44ft by 29ft) has a rostrum pulpit at the N end with a balustraded top and Gothic panelling between buttresses below; the design is repeated on the ends of the rear pews and around a large table-pew in front of the pulpit. (Chapel converted to domestic use *c*.1983)

Fittings – *Baptismal Basin*: base metal, circular bowl with moulded base, late 18th-century. *Monuments*: in chapel Rev. John Harris, 1845, 'Minister of this place more than 50 years'. In burial-ground, several early 19th-century table-tombs.

Former Countess of Huntingdon's chapel, Fordham. (41)

FOXEARTH

(42) Former INDEPENDENT, The Street (TL 835446). The meeting-house, now a garage (31½ft by 21½ft externally), has rendered timber-framed walls and a hipped tiled roof with a coved plaster eaves cornice. It was built in the early 18th century and has four wooden cross-framed windows of that period in the exposed side wall; the opposite side is partly covered by a 19th-century cottage. The N front has a wide garage entrance and two windows with renewed frames. The interior has a dado of horizontal match-boarding and a plain plaster ceiling. *Monument*: in chapel on S wall, Rev. John Howard, 1836.

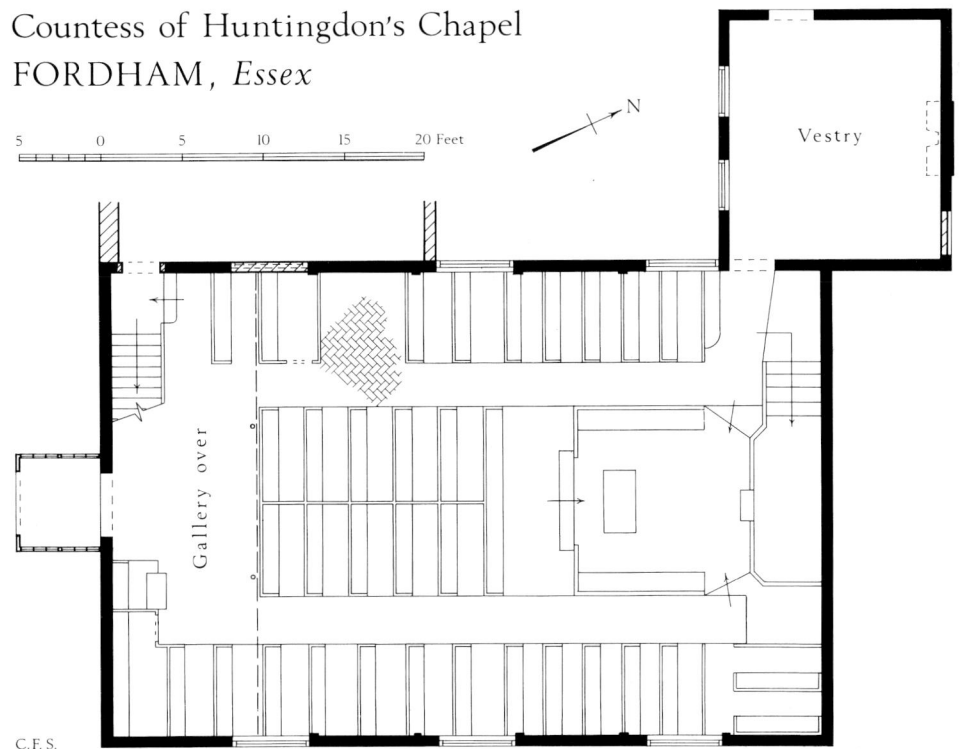

FRINTON AND WALTON

(43) CONGREGATIONAL, Walton on the Naze (TM 254217). The chapel in Station Street, designed by Charles Pertwee, was built in 1878 to supersede a chapel of 1836. It is faced in Kentish rag with Bath stone dressings and has a polygonal W end with pointed-arched entrance and gabled window above. (Now jointly URC/Methodist)

CYB (1878) 420.

(44) ZION CHAPEL, Walton on the Naze (TL 254217). The former Primitive Methodist chapel in Station Street, NE of (43), has a gabled brick front of three bays with cusped lancets; it is dated 1875.

GREAT BADDOW

(45) CONGREGATIONAL, High Street (TL 728051). The small gabled chapel of brick, built 1848, has been much altered and greatly enlarged. (URC)

GREAT BARDFIELD

(46) FRIENDS, Brook Street (TL 676305). The meeting-house, built 1804, has rendered timber-framed walls on a brick plinth and a hipped tiled roof. In the front wall are three sash windows and a wide doorway facing the burial-ground; there is a second entrance at one side. The interior comprises two rooms separated by shutters.

Behind to the NW, a low building of 16th-century origin, with rendered walls and tiled roof, with two shop fronts and dormer windows added, is believed to be the former meeting-house.

Butler (1999) 172–3. RCHM *Essex* I (1916) 14, monument (14).

FRIENDS MEETING-HOUSE, GREAT BARDFIELD — CFS 1972

(47) PRIMITIVE METHODIST (TL 676306). Gabled chapel of 1862 with adjoining school-room added 1903 in matching style. Red brick with dressings of yellow brick and decorative lozenges of black-painted brick in yellow brick surrounds.

GREAT BENTLEY

(48) WESLEYAN (TM 112220). Design similar to Brightlingsea (12) but with angle buttresses at the front corners; original tablet in front 'WESLEYAN | 1843'. (Rebuilt 1975)

GREAT BROMLEY

(49) WESLEYAN, Balls Green (TM 093243). Red brick with yellow brick dressings, gabled front of three bays with decorative bargeboards (cf. Elmstead (34)); c.1860–70.

GREAT CHESTERFORD

(50) CONGREGATIONAL, Carmel Street (TL 508429). Built 1841, enlarged to front in the late 19th century.

GREAT CLACTON

(51) WESLEYAN, Valley Road (TM 178164). Small chapel with rendered walls and pointed-arched windows; opened 1824 but much altered in the late 19th century.

GREAT DUNMOW

(52) CONGREGATIONAL, New Street (TL 628217). Red brick with white brick and stone dressings; triple-arched loggia below three graduated round-arched windows in front gable wall; built in 1869 by C. Pertwee replacing a meeting-house of c.1720. Some early 19th-century table-tombs remain in the burial-ground. Detached Sunday-school of 1864 by Thomas Gibbon of London. (URC)

CYB (1865) 311; (1871) 405–6.

(53) FRIENDS, New Street (TL 628216). Low brick walls with hipped slate roof; built 1833 to replace a meeting-house of 1706. Broad front and back walls of three bays with central entrances and intermediate recessed panels; segmental arch enclosing window above rear doorway. Central corridor between two equal-sized rooms.

Butler (1999) 184–5.

GREAT OAKLEY

(54) WESLEYAN, High Street (TM 194277). Rendered walls and hipped slate roof, opened 1817, Sunday-school built in front c.1860–70 and entrance re-sited. Original back gallery supported by two fluted columns; side galleries with iron-bracket supports added in the mid 19th century.

GREAT TOTHAM

(55) TOTHAM BARN CHAPEL (TL 853115). A small weatherboarded and thatched barn of the early 19th century has been fitted up as a meeting-house for an Evangelical Free Church.

GREAT WAKERING

(56) CONGREGATIONAL (TQ 947876). The chapel built 1889 has a gabled front of stock brick with dressings of red brick and terracotta. The previous chapel of 1822, which stood on the opposite side of the lane, has been demolished. (URC)

HALSTEAD

(57) CONGREGATIONAL, Parsonage Street (TL 815306). The Old Meeting (now URC) originated in the late 17th century as a Presbyterian society, a malthouse at Bois Hall, seat of Sir Samuel Taylor Bart., being licensed under the 1672 Indulgence. A meeting-house on the present site is said to have been built in 1718. In 1832, a second, or New, meeting was formed by secession for which a meeting-house (demolished c.1964) was built in High Street (TL 813306).

The present Gothic chapel of 1865–6 by Frederick Barnes stands on the site of the old meeting-house; the walls are faced with polygonal masonry and the roofs are slated. The N front is gabled and has a large traceried upper window of five lights, and entrances in flanking wings; a tower with broach spire stands back against the W side wall. (Spire demolished since 1972) A detached school-room, E of the chapel is dated 1894.

The interior has an open timber roof and galleries around four sides with cast-iron columns which rise above to support the roof structure. Shallow transepts to E and W have low benches in the gallery for use by children.

Fittings – *Clock*: on front of N gallery, Gothic case, signed 'Knight, Halstead'. *Glass*: rolled sheet glass impressed with diamond pattern. *Inscription*: on boundary wall to S, recording erection of S, E and W boundary walls in 1855. *Monuments*: in W transept (1) Rev. James Bass, 1829, 37 years preacher; (2) Rev. William Holman, 1730, 'who was near 30 years Pastor of the Church of Protestant Dissenters in this Town & was near 20 Years in writing ye Antiquitys of Essex', also Rebekah his wife, 1727, William their son, 1748, and Frances widow of the last, 1770; (3) Rev. Joseph Field, 1791, 35 years preacher, and Jane his widow, 1810. In burial-ground, many reset headstones and fragments including (4) Mrs Ann Bass sister of Rev. James Bass, [ ]; (5) Hannah wife of Owen Little, 1778, and Thomas their son, 1790; (6) George Asa, 1845, *et al.*, part of slate table-tomb; (7) Joseph Brown, 1797.

CYB (1866) 327–8.

(58) FRIENDS, Colchester Road (TL 816307). Brick with hipped slate roofs behind a parapet, built 1851 to replace an earlier building. Two identical rooms separated by folding shutters, low porch across front with a lobby between minor rooms. (Closed *c.*1971; in use for storage)

Butler (1999) 188–9.

(59) PRIMITIVE METHODIST, New Street (TL 810304). Big gabled front of red brick with gault brick and stone dressings; three-light window with intersecting stone tracery between pointed-arched entrances. Dated 1874.

HARLOW

(60) BAPTIST, Fore Street (TL 471115). The Baptist church in Harlow claims to date from the late 17th century. In the early 18th century it comprised three congregations, at Nazeing, Harlow and 'Sooson'. The chapel of *c.*1870 in Harlow village stands on a site, remote from the street, first occupied by a meeting-house built in 1764. The present building of gault brick with a gabled centre has Venetian traceried frames to the windows.

(61) BAPTIST, Potter Street (TL 473087). The chapel at Potter Street, built in 1756, was enlarged in the early 19th century by the addition of vestries and a school-room above; it was further enlarged and greatly altered internally in 1970.

The chapel has walls of red brick in English bond and the roof is covered with slates. The E front of three bays with an open pediment and wide eaves has two tiers of plain sash windows and a tripartite blind lunette in the pediment. The doorcase of carved wood is of exceptional elaboration with a swan-necked pediment and consoles. A long inscription panel, perhaps not original, is inscribed 'BAPTIST CHAPEL. ERECTED 1756'.

The interior (30ft square) has galleries around three sides with fielded-panelled fronts heightened in the early 19th century,

Baptist chapel, Potter Street, Harlow. (61)

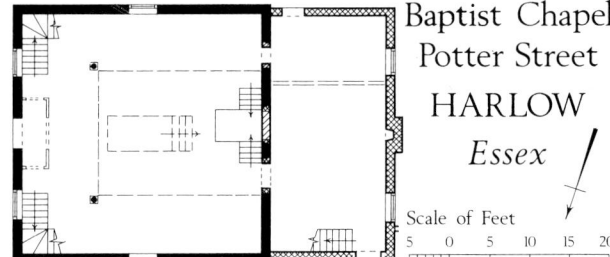

and supported at the corners by turned wood columns. The original W wall has a blocked doorway behind the pulpit formerly giving direct access from the later vestry, and shutters above opening to the Sunday-school. (Side galleries and W wall removed 1970) The roof is supported by three trusses with king- and queen-posts.

Fittings – *Baptistery*: centrally in floor with steps at W end. *Inscriptions*: on brick in W jamb of lower window S side, initials and date 1755; painted on brick inside E gable, 1760. *Monuments*: in chapel (1) Richard Perry, 1829, 'a Deacon of this church 48 years and a Member 70'; (2) Robert Blackman, 1855, Ann his widow, 1858, and Robert their son, 1857; (3) Rev. John Bain, 1831, 27 years pastor, and Mary his widow, 1839. Externally against S wall (4) Rev. John Nottage, 1776, 'First Minister of this Chapel and 20 years Pastor of the Church assembling here'; loose in burial-ground (5) John Wright, 1797, pastor, and Ann his widow, 1815. *Plate*: includes a pair of two-handled cups, 1760.

HARWICH

(62) Former CONGREGATIONAL, George Street (TM 260326). Built in the mid 19th century. Rendered walls and a hipped slate roof with bracketed eaves; the W front, partly concealed by later buildings, had two entrances with pointed-arched windows above. (Interior altered for commercial use)

Monuments: reset headstones at rear include one to Rev. Thomas Hill, 1854, 7 years pastor of Bathside Chapel, and his two children Harriet Emily and Edwin Alfred.

(63) Former WESLEYAN, Church Street (TM 260327). Rendered front of five bays with three-bay pediment and two tiers of plain sash windows with marginal glazing. Dated 1829 above central entrance.

(64) SALVATION ARMY, George Street (TM 260324). Brick citadel with castellated front, 1892.

HATFIELD BROAD OAK

(65) CONGREGATIONAL, Hatfield Heath (TL 527149). Knapped flint and stone, slate roof with octagonal flèche behind front gable; 1875–6 by T. Lewis Banks, replacing a timber-framed meeting-house of 1726. (URC)
 CYB (1877) 496–7.

HIGH EASTER

(66) Former CONGREGATIONAL (TL 622148). Stock brick and slate, N front of three bays with pilasters and rendered entablature, central entrance and two tiers of plain windows. Dated 1847 on parapet over centre bay and on brick at corner of E wall.

INGATESTONE AND FRYERNING

(67) CONGREGATIONAL, Ingatestone (TQ 648994). Red brick with gault brick front and slate roof; built in 1840 by James Fenton. Gabled SE front with two porches and a range of seven grouped lancets above. The interior has a rear gallery only but the fenestration allows for the addition of side galleries. The roof has exposed scissor trusses with short columnar struts. (URC) Inscriptions: on bricks in front wall, several names and initials, including, below centre window 'I.H.S.' above an anchor between initials and date '18A H40'. Reset in wall of rear outbuildings, tablet from previous chapel 'INGATESTONE|CHAPEL| ERECTED 1812|ENLARGED 1816'. Monuments: in chapel (1) Mary Norman, 1830; (2) Jane wife of Rev. Benjamin Hayter, 1833; (3) Rev. Benjamin Hayter, 1856, 32 years pastor (also monument in railed enclosure in front of chapel); (4) John Benson, 1825.

KELVEDON

(68) CONGREGATIONAL (TL 861188). The chapel 'erected 1853' has walls of red brick with gault brick dressings. The front is pedimented and the walls, divided into bays by brick pilasters, have tall round-arched windows with marginal glazing bars. A Sunday-school at the rear was built in 1879. (URC)

(69) Former FRIENDS (TL 864192). The meeting-house lies back on the NW side of High Street, between Nos 203 to 205, where the former entrance gates survive. The meeting-house built in 1802 is a large building of brick with a hipped roof from which the tiles have been stripped. The broad SE front is of four bays with the entrance in the second bay from the left and an oval window above. The burial-ground, now a lawn behind 198 High Street, has headstones reset around the boundaries. (Derelict 1994)
 Butler (1999) 191–2.

LANGHAM

(70) Former BAPTIST (TM 029335). A church formed here in 1754 was dissolved c.1939. The chapel, subsequently used as a social club, dates from the late 18th century. It has red brick walls and a hipped slate roof; two entrances in the longer front wall

FORMER BAPTIST CHAPEL, LANGHAM CFS 1972

with two sash windows between and three above; two arched windows in the back wall flanked the pulpit. The interior has a gallery around three sides, now floored over. Extensive burial-ground behind with 19th-century monuments.

(71) Former PRIMITIVE METHODIST (TM 016316). Red brick with hipped slate roof and round-arched windows; 'rebuilt 1860'. Bricks in front wall with dates 1816 and 1818 are reset from the former chapel.

LAYER BRETON

(72) FRIENDS (TL 946182). Low brick walls and slate roof, built 1827 and extended to W in 1852. The S front has a porch with a wide doorway and reeded architrave, between two sash windows, that to the W with original external shutters. Interior has lines of two former partitions W of the entrance, a stand at the E end and scrubbed pine benches with shaped arms and open backs; the walls are lined with match-boarding.
 Butler (1999) 192–3.

LITTLE BADDOW

(73) CONGREGATIONAL (TL 767078). The congregation, originally Presbyterian (now URC), numbers John Oakes, ejected minister of Boreham, Essex, amongst its first pastors. In 1707 a field called 'Bridge Croft' was conveyed to trustees as the site for a meeting-house and the present building was opened in that or the following year.

The chapel has brick walls and a tiled roof, gabled to N and S; the E front, in Flemish bond with glazed headers, is symmetrical and has a moulded brick cornice, a central rendered porch of later

Congregational chapel (URC), Little Baddow. (73)

Friends' meeting-house, Layer Breton. (72)

date, and two round-arched windows with original wooden frames and leaded glazing. The N wall has one similar window and two oval windows in the gable; a doorway with a segmental-arched head, perhaps intended for access to an end gallery, was blocked in the late 19th century.

The S wall, now largely covered by a school-room built in 1907, had two tall rectangular windows, one now blocked, flanking the present pulpit. The W wall has two tall round-arched windows balancing those on the opposite side; between them on the outer face are traces of a former timber-framed vestry with blocked doorway to the chapel and two oval windows inserted, after the removal of the vestry, flanking the site of a former pulpit which stood slightly S of the minor axis.

The interior ($44\frac{1}{2}$ ft by $24\frac{1}{4}$ ft) was much altered and refitted in 1888 when the pulpit was removed from the W side to the S end and three galleries were taken away. The original position of the pulpit appears from the fenestration to have been at the S end and a narrow N gallery opposite. In the mid 18th century the pulpit was removed to the W side mid-way between the N gallery front and the S wall, with the insertion of the two oval windows. The ceiling has a plaster barrel-vault of polygonal section with two exposed tie-beams.

Fittings – *Monuments*: in chapel (1) Rev. Stephen Morell, 1852; (2) Rev. Thomas Morell, 1892. Externally on E wall (3) Rachel King wife of Rev. William Parry, and their children Rachel and Edward, all 1791. In burial-ground (4) Catherine Jones, 1780; (5) Stephen Morell, 1824, Rev. Stephen Morell, 1852, *et al*. *Plate*: includes a two-handled cup of 1766 and a plain cup of 1774.

Marks, E.E., *A Brief History of the Congregational Church at Little Baddow* (1930). RCHM *Essex* II (1921) 152, monument (2). *Reform* (March 1986) 5.

Congregational Chapel, LITTLE BADDOW
Essex

LITTLE CLACTON

(74) WESLEYAN (TM 165191). The chapel dated 1861, of red brick with yellow brick dressings, has a hipped slate roof with front gablet, and pointed-arched windows with intersecting glazing bars. The design is comparable with earlier chapels at Brightlingsea (12) and Great Bentley (48), but smaller.

LITTLE WALTHAM

(75) CONGREGATIONAL (TL 708128). The chapel, built 1803, has rendered walls and hipped slate roof. The front wall has terminal

pilasters and a moulded entablature; there are two entrances with small windows above and a large round-arched window between. Two tiers of windows to side walls. Galleried interior, refitted. (URC)

MALDON

(76) BAPTIST, Butt Lane (TL 85280706). Yellow stock brick with red brick dressings; 1896 by P. Beaumont.

B.Hbk (1897) 317–18.

(77) CONGREGATIONAL, Market Hill (TL 851071). A house was licensed in 1672 for use as a Presbyterian meeting-place and the congregation (now URC) formally established in 1688 under the ministry of Joseph Billio, to whom is credited the provision of the first meeting-house on the present site in 1696.

The chapel, rebuilt in 1801 and enlarged to the front in the later 19th century, is a large building with timber-framed walls covered at the sides with decorative pargeting and a pantiled roof. The W front has a pedimented centre of three bays with an open loggia with Ionic columns and three round-arched upper windows; the side walls have two tiers of windows, the upper ones with round-arched heads.

The interior (82ft by $40\frac{3}{4}$ft) has a plaster ceiling coved at the sides above a moulded cornice and a continuous gallery with vestries below at the E end. The seating was renewed in the late 19th century but much of the original pulpit remains.

Fittings – *Monuments*: in vestibule (1) Rev. Simon Wilmshurst, 1800, 23 years pastor, Ann his first wife, 1779, and Mary his second wife, 1783. In loggia (2) Rev. Robert Burls, 1866, and Mary his wife, 1853; (3) Stephen Forster, 1811, 12 years pastor; also, in burial-ground, several table-tombs and other monuments of 19th-century date. *Portraits*: in vestry (1) Joseph Billio, born 1658, first minister, oil on canvas; (2) Robert Burls, pastor 1819–57.

(78) CONGREGATIONAL, Heybridge Basin (TL 871070). Timber-framed and weather-boarded chapel with double-gabled front. Built *c*.1850. (URC)

(79) FRIENDS, Butt Lane (TL 853070). Red brick with hipped slate roof, built 1820 on a new site to replace a meeting-house of 1707. Narrow W front with pedimented porch and three blind windows; five-bay sides with round-arched windows.

Butler (1999) 193–4.

(80) WESLEYAN, High Street (TL 854069). Big gabled front of brick with two-storeyed porch. Built 1861.

Methodist Recorder (6 February 1986).

MANNINGTREE

(81) Former CONGREGATIONAL, South Street (TM 107318). The chapel, built *c*.1823 for a church formed in that year, but now used by the Royal British Legion, has walls of red brick with a gault brick front and hipped slate roof. The design is unusual, with large rounded corners each with two tiers of sash windows; the entrance is in the E wall and there is a former gallery at this end.

(82) WESLEYAN, South Street (TM 107316). Gault brick and slate, opened 1807, much altered and refitted in the late 19th century. The original front of three bays with narrow blind wings has tall pilasters and an elaborate brick pediment, the entrance is central and there are two tiers of round-arched windows. A loggia between side porches with staircase wings behind and a prominent timber cupola were added *c*.1900. *Monument*: Ann wife of Samuel Hitchcock, 1841, buried in the Independent burial-ground, Tacket Street, Ipswich, signed 'Backhouse, Ipswich'.

RAYLEIGH

(83) BAPTIST, High Street (TQ 804904). The chapel appears to have been built in 1798–9 for a newly formed congregation, extended to the rear and partly refitted in the early 19th century and further altered in the second half of that century. The walls are of rendered brickwork and the roof is slated. The NW front is gabled, of three bays with round-arched windows above triple entrances. The sides, originally of three bays, have two tiers of segmental-arched windows.

Former Congregational chapel, Manningtree. (81)

Wesleyan chapel, Manningtree. (82)

The interior (34ft, extended to 56½ft, by 27ft) has a continuous gallery of the early 19th century with vestries below the SE end from which the pulpit was formerly directly accessible. The ceiling has a segmental plaster barrel-vault supported by a trussed rafter roof. (Chapel greatly extended to NE with additional rooms in 1981)

Monuments: in chapel (1) Rev. James Pilkington, 1853, over 50 years pastor; (2) Elizabeth wife of Rev. James Pilkington, 1840, signed 'T. Marsh, New Rd., London'; in burial-ground (3) George Good Uwins, 1835, and the above James and Elizabeth Pilkington.

(84) Former WESLEYAN, High Street (TQ 804905). Gabled brick front, 1885. (Now Salvation Army)

(85) PECULIAR PEOPLE, Eastwood Road (TQ 807904). Brick Gothic, c.1900. (Now 'Evangelical Church')

ROCHFORD

(86) CONGREGATIONAL, North Street (TQ 877906). The formerly Presbyterian congregation formed in 1690 built a meeting-house on the present site in 1740. The chapel, which has brick walls and a slate roof, incorporates the front and side walls of the original building (33ft square originally), but this was enlarged to the rear in 1838 and the front wall altered and rendered. The front is of three bays with two entrances and two tiers of windows. The galleried interior was refitted in the late 19th century.

Inscriptions: on bricks in side walls of rear extension, several names and the date 'August 18th 1838'. *Monument*: in chapel, Rev. Ebenezer Temple, 1841, 5 years minister, also externally, headstone to same laid flat.

ROYDON

(87) CONGREGATIONAL (TL 413101). The first chapel was built in 1798 and financed by the sale of £50 shares. The church, originally Baptist, was re-formed in 1811 and the chapel was rebuilt in 1851. Although much altered in 1936 the side walls, now rendered, have each two original round-arched windows with wooden Y-tracery. (URC)

Ackroyd, P., et al., *Congregational Church, Roydon* (1948).

SAFFRON WALDEN

(88) Former GENERAL BAPTIST, Hill Street (TL 540384). A General Baptist congregation, said to have been formed in 1711, built a meeting-house in 1744 on the S side of Hill Street which was superseded in 1792 by another set well back from the street SW of the former. In the 19th century the church supported a Unitarian ministry; it has since disbanded.

The earlier meeting-house, now converted to houses Nos 25 and 25a, has rendered pargeted walls and a hipped tiled roof. The wide front wall has two doorways and two tiers of sash windows, all with 19th-century details but probably representing the original openings.

The meeting-house of 1792 (35¼ft by 30ft externally) is a partly timber-framed building with rendered walls and double-hipped tiled roof with central valley at collar-beam level. The entrance was at the E end in a 19th-century porch, now removed, and there was a low lean-to vestry at the W end. Seven panels with applied moulding from the gallery front remain internally. The meeting-house was much altered in 1890 and later. (Now converted to commercial use with an entrance at the W end)

First chapel.

Second chapel.
Former General Baptist chapels, Saffron Walden. (88)

The former burial-ground, behind the first meeting-house, remains in part, much overgrown. Portions of three table-tombs survive, one to Joseph Eedis, 1816.

Evans (1897) 216.

(89) BAPTIST, Audley Road (TL 538382). The Particular Baptist church was formed in 1774 by seceders from the Independents in Abbey Lane, including the minister, Joseph Gwennap. The meeting-house built 1774–5, which stands behind the present chapel of 1879 by Searle, Son and Hayes, is described by Ivimey (op. cit. below) as 51ft square with a seating capacity of about 800. It has brick walls and wide eaves to the roof. The W front is covered by the later chapel; the E end has three round-arched windows reduced in height and a circular window in the gable; the side walls are of four bays with two tiers of windows, the upper windows having round-arched heads. Some early 19th-century headstones remain at the rear.

Ivimey IV (1830) 484.

(90) Former BAPTIST, London Road (TL 537380). The chapel dated 1822, apparently built for a Strict Baptist church, is of red brick with yellow brick dressings and has a slated roof with

wide eaves. The front has a simple pediment with defaced inscription tablets and an altered porch. The sides of four bays have sash windows set in wide round-arched recesses.

(91) Former CONGREGATIONAL, Abbey Lane (TL 536384). The Independent church (now URC) claims to have been formed in 1665 and the first meeting-house on this site was built in 1694. This was a square, probably timber-framed, building with rendered walls and a double-hipped tiled roof with central valley; the front wall had a central entrance and a round-arched window above under a narrow pediment.

The present chapel of 1811, builder William Biggs, has walls of red brick with a rendered front and slate roof. The front wall of three bays has a central arch rising into an open pediment, and three arched doorways behind a tetrastyle Ionic portico. The interior has an early 19th-century gallery around three sides but was otherwise refitted in 1890. The front of the original pulpit of Spanish mahogany is incorporated into the rostrum. Sunday-school, freestanding behind, built 1861.

Painting: in vestry, small water-colour sketch of former meeting-house.

Bocock, N.W., *The Abbey Lane Congregational Church, Saffron Walden, 1665–1933* (1933). CYB (1892) 217–18.

(92) FRIENDS, High Street (TL 537382). In the late 17th century Friends met in the back room of a cottage on or near the present site. The meeting-house, opened 1799 and drastically altered in 1969, has brick walls and a hipped tiled roof with a dentil brick eaves cornice. The rear W wall formerly had three bays of windows at two levels; a tablet dated 1798 remains on this wall. The interior (originally 37¾ft by 27¼ft) has been entirely refitted and the building has been extended to the front.

Butler (1999) 197–9.

SOUTHEND-ON-SEA

(93) CONGREGATIONAL, Nelson Street (TQ 881854). The chapel was built in 1866 to supersede one of 1806 which stood in High Street. It was designed in the Gothic style by W. Allen Dixon and has walls of Kentish rag with Bath stone dressings. The W end has a large wheel-window in the gable and a tower and spire above the principal entrance. The chapel was enlarged by E.J. Hamilton in 1889 by the addition of a second aisle and further rooms. (URC)

CYB (1866) 311; (1890) 218–19. Hodgkins, J.R., *The History of Cliff Town Congregational Church, Southend-On-Sea, 1799–1972* (1974).

(94) Former WESLEYAN, Park Road (TQ 876855). Gothic, faced with Kentish ragstone, with gabled front divided by two octagonal buttresses rising to coarse pinnacles; 1871 by E. Hoole. Hall at rear in similar style added 1902.

SOUTHMINSTER

(95) BAPTIST, Burnham Road (TQ 957996). Brick gabled front with grouped round-arched windows above porch. Dated 1861.

Former Congregational chapel, Saffron Walden. (91)

Congregational chapel (URC), Nelson Street, Southend. (93)

STANSTED MOUNTFITCHET

(96) CONGREGATIONAL, Chapel Hill (TL 514249). Gault brick partly rendered with two short towers above entrances; 1864–5 by Jasper Carvell (?Cowell) of London on site of 1698 Old Meeting-house. A drawing in the Essex Record Office of the former meeting-house shows a building set back on the N side of the road, originally 20½ft by 40ft externally, enlarged to the S by 14ft and with a smaller school building, formerly a barn, next to the road.

CYB (1867) 351. Essex Record Office, D/NC 2/13.

(97) FRIENDS, Chapel Hill (TL 510250). A modern building of 1957 stands on the site of a meeting-house of 1703. In the burial-ground are uniform headstones with dates including 1768, 1796 and 1800, and a larger tablet recording burials of the Day family 1712–84.

Butler (1999) 199, 200.

STEBBING

(98) CONGREGATIONAL (TL 661242). Robert Billio, ejected rector of Wickham Bishops, was licensed as a Presbyterian preacher here in 1672. The Independent church seems to have originated c.1715 with a 'lecture' supplied by a Mr Nottcutt of Thaxted, and a meeting-house was built about that time. The present chapel, perhaps an early 19th-century rebuilding, with rendered walls and slate roof, was enlarged to the front and refitted c.1864. Some tombstones of the late 18th century remain. (URC)

CYB (1864) 359.

(99) Former FRIENDS (TL 662241). The meeting-house dated 1674 was slightly altered and repaired in 1818; it was leased c.1920 and subsequently sold for use as a village hall. The walls are of brickwork in Flemish bond with glazed headers and some diaper patterning, and the roof is hipped and tiled with a small dormer at the W end; traces of a similar dormer at the E end remain in the roof structure. The original entrance front faces N and has a round-arched doorway, still with double doors in 1913 but now converted to a window; the arch has a keystone, imposts and a blind tympanum. Flanking the former doorway are two segmental-arched windows which still have their late 17th-century frames and ornamental catches. The E end has a central doorway with timber Doric porch and two windows of the early 19th century replacing windows lower and closer together. A brick platband incorporates, at the centre, a panel of bricks carved with the date 1674 in raised numerals; the platband continues around the other sides at a higher level.

One window in the W wall has been reduced in depth. The S wall had two windows matching those on the N side.

The interior (43¾ft by 24½ft) is divided into two rooms by an early 19th-century partition with sliding shutters. Other fittings, including the stand at the W end and open-backed benches, have been removed since 1913.

Butler (1999) 200–1. RCHM *Essex* I (1916) 282–3, monument (2).

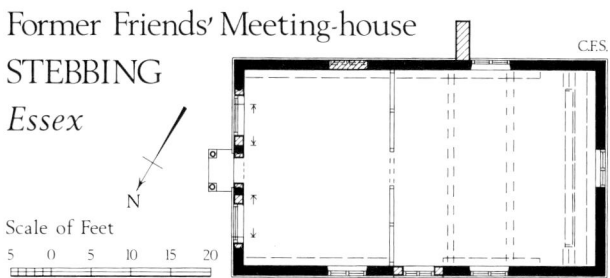

Former Friends' meeting-house, Stebbing. (99)

STEEPLE

(100) Former PECULIAR PEOPLE (TL 930027). Brick with three-bay gabled front dated 1877. (Converted to house)

STEEPLE BUMPSTEAD

(101) CONGREGATIONAL (TL 680411). Red and yellow brick, gabled front with octagonal turret and spirelet; 1883 by Charles Bell, replacing a square timber-framed and plastered meeting-house of 1800 which was re-fronted in brick in 1836.

CYB (1884) 414–15.

TERLING

(102) CONGREGATIONAL (TL 772149). Calamy (op. cit. below) says that the vicar, John Stalham, ejected in 1662, was a man 'of strict Congregational principles' who 'kept up a meeting in this place after he was turn'd out'. In 1714 the church (now URC) had the use of a tenement at 'the manor house of Okendon, in Terling … consisting of two lower or ground rooms and two chambers or upper rooms over, but is now laid open to the roof, and now used as a Dissenters Meeting House…' (Trust Deeds).

The present site was conveyed to trustees in 1752 and the meeting-house was erected in that year. A vestry was added at the rear in the later 18th century and the interior was entirely remodelled in 1895.

The chapel has brick walls with a platband and coved plaster eaves cornice, and a hipped tiled roof. The SE front is of three bays with a later porch and the end walls are each of two bays with two tiers of windows with original wood frames. The rear NW wall has two wide round-arched windows of three lights, now reduced in depth, which flanked the pulpit.

The interior ($25\frac{3}{4}$ft by $31\frac{1}{2}$ft) formerly had a gallery 'along the front', box-pews and the pulpit opposite the entrance. This was entirely altered in 1895, when the original hexagonal pulpit was cut down and reset at the SW end where two lower windows have been blocked, and the seating replaced by pitch-pine benches.

Fittings – *Chandelier*: brass, twelve-branch, surmounted by dove with olive branch and suspended by iron chain with lower hook in form of serpent, mid 18th-century. *Clock*: white circular dial, shaped case with chinoiserie ornament, signed 'Tho. Fordham', mid 18th-century (sold 1987). *Inscriptions*: many bricks with initials and dates, including – right of porch 'E.Clarke 1752'; on NE wall of vestry '17 J.S 84'. *Monuments*: in chapel on NW wall (1) Rev. William Kemp, 1844, 'pastor more than thirty years'; (2) late 19th-century panel recording burials below floor – John Dams, 1764, Elizabeth widow of Rev. William Kemp, 1852, their daughter Rachel, 1831, and sons James, 1835, and William, 1836. Externally on SE wall (3) Elizabeth widow of Thomas Willsdon of Fawler, Oxon., 1840; (4) Elizabeth Blyth daughter of Rev. William Kemp, [nd], *et al*. In burial-ground in front of chapel, (5) Mrs Jane Granger, 1807, *et al*., headstone with winged cherubs' heads; (6) Isaac Blyth, 1864, and Elizabeth his widow, 1868, obelisk; (7) Edward Blyth, 1831, *et al*.; (8) Charles Cousins, 1903, *et al*.; (9) John Cousins, 1870, and Sophia his wife, 1842, *et al*.; (10) Henry Willshier, 1844, and Elizabeth his wife, 1838; (11) 'Rev. Mr. Mosses Davies', 1766.

Congregational chapel (URC), Terling. (102)

TERLING CHAPEL *Essex*

Calamy (1713) II 304–5. Langstone, Miss M.R., *The United Reformed Church, Terling, Essex* (1988, typescript). Palmer (1802–3) II: 220. RCHM *Essex* II (1921) 228, monument (2).

THAXTED

(103) Former BAPTIST, Mill End (TL 613308). The chapel was built in 1813 for a newly formed congregation; it closed *c.*1865. The walls are of brick with a dentil eaves cornice and the roof is hipped and slated. The front of three bays has a wide arched recess enclosing the formerly pedimented entrance between two tiers of windows. The originally unfenestrated side wall facing the road has two shallow arched recesses. (Now in commercial use)

BM V (1813) 482; VI (1814) 352. Witard (1962) 58, 65–6.

(104) BAPTIST, Park Street (TL 612308). 'The New Baptist Meeting House' opened 1 January 1833 was enlarged to the front in the mid 19th century. The chapel, of brick with a slate roof, has a rendered pedimented front of three bays with central doorway and two tiers of windows; there are gallery entrances in the wings at each side. The interior, refitted in the late 19th century, has a gallery around three sides. *Monument*: in front of chapel, Rev. Edward Stephens, 1853, 6 years pastor, and Mary Anne his widow, 1889, headstone.

BM XXV (1833) 232.

(105) CONGREGATIONAL, Bolford Street (TL 609310). The chapel (now URC) is a large building of red brick with yellow brick dressings and a slate roof. The side walls incorporate work of *c.*1800 but this was extended to the rear, heightened and re-fronted in the late 19th century. The front wall has a triple-arched loggia

Baptist chapel, Park Street, Thaxted. (104)

entrance and three tall round-arched windows below a pediment. Some early 19th-century monuments remain in the burial-ground.

THORPE-LE-SOKEN

(106) BAPTIST (TM 179224). Timber-framed and weather-boarded chapel with hipped slate roof, built c.1802 for a church formed in that year. The front wall, refaced with pebble-dash, has a wide central doorway with pedimented canopy flanked by two tiers of sash windows. The interior is approximately square with a plaster ceiling slightly coved along each side. End gallery only, erected 1820, with some early 19th-century box-pews; late 19th-century rostrum pulpit with cast-iron balusters and lamp standards; in the vestry is a raised doorway formerly giving direct access to the pulpit. *Monuments*: in chapel (1) James Buckenham, 1837; in burial-ground (2) children of Matthew Harvey, 'many years Baptist minister of Horham, Suffolk,' also Sarah his wife, 1855.

(107) PRIMITIVE METHODIST (TM 181224). Low building with three-bay pedimented front, dated 1867.

THUNDERSLEY

(108) Former PECULIAR PEOPLE, 185 Daw's Heath Road (TQ 807889). The small weather-boarded chapel with gabled front and round-arched windows, built in 1852, was superseded c.1900 by a new building in Western Road and has been converted to a house. The front wall has been rendered and a modern porch built but it is otherwise unaltered externally.

Sorrell (1979) 27, 80, illus. facing 33.

THURROCK

(109) CONGREGATIONAL, Aveley (TQ 566802). The late 19th-century chapel on the N side of High Street supersedes a building of 1817. (URC)

CYB (1879) 306, obituary Rev. A. Brown.

(110) Former CONGREGATIONAL, High Street, South Ockendon (TQ 595831). The chapel built 1813 on the E side of the street has rendered brick walls and a hipped slate roof; three-bay front with two pointed-arched windows with wooden intersecting tracery; similar windows in the side walls. A row of early 19th-century headstones is reset against the N side. (Now in commercial use)

TILLINGHAM

(111) PECULIAR PEOPLE, South Street (TL 994034). Small chapel of c.1860–70 with timber-framed walls now rendered in pebble-dash but probably originally weather-boarded. Gabled front with round-arched doorway and windows; small upper window with inscribed tablet below obscured by overpainting. Four round-arched windows in side walls. Interior with wide wooden rostrum at E end and open-backed benches with cast-iron supports.

Sorrell (1979) 28, 32, 42, 49, 50.

Peculiar People's chapel, South Street, Tillingham. (111)

TIPTREE

(112) CONGREGATIONAL, Chapel Road (TL 903161). The 'Goodmans Green Meeting', founded in 1664 (now URC), built a meeting-house on this site in 1750 which was replaced by the present chapel in 1864. This building, of cruciform plan by Frederick Barnes of Ipswich, is of 'white' or grey brick with dressings of red brick. The front is gabled and has three tall graduated lancets above the entrance. *Glass*: the original glazing, which survives throughout, comprises sheets of 'Hartley's Patent imitation quarry glass' impressed with a diamond pattern to represent leaded lights.

CYB (1865) 308–9.

WALTHAM HOLY CROSS

(113) Former WESLEYAN, Waltham Abbey (TL 385006). The chapel in Monkswood Avenue was built in 1903; the walls are of red brick with stone dressings. The design is dominated by a large asymmetrically placed tower of slightly later date which serves as the principal entrance. (Now RC church)

WEST MERSEA

(114) Former CONGREGATIONAL, Mill Road (TM 015134). The chapel (now Baptist), rebuilt 1841 for a Union church formed 1805, has brick walls and a hipped slate roof; the front is partly obscured by a large modern porch.

(115) WESLEYAN, Mill Road (TM 015132). Gault brick with three-bay gabled front dated 1861.

WETHERSFIELD

(116) CONGREGATIONAL (TL 711313). The formerly Presbyterian congregation (now URC) originated in 1707. The present chapel dates from 1822, but has been greatly enlarged to the rear and a gable added to the front later in the 19th century. The walls are of red brick with a gault brick front and the roof is slated. The S front is of four bays with two doorways and four round-arched upper windows. The galleried interior has been refitted.

Monuments: in burial-ground, include many reset early 19th-century stones and a brick vault with monuments to the Legerton family dating from 1829.

WHITE ROOTHING

(117) CONGREGATIONAL, White Roding (TQ 564132). The chapel built in 1887 as a preaching-station of the church in Abbess Roding (*see* (1)) was enlarged in 1901, when all services were relocated here.

WITHAM

(118) STRICT BAPTIST (TL 822144). Gault brick and slate with three-bay gabled front of 1857.

(119) CONGREGATIONAL, High Street (TL 820144). The former meeting-house of 1715, enlarged twice in the late 18th century, had a singers' pew in the gallery opposite the pulpit said to have held 20 or 30 singers and musicians, and a table-pew in front of the clerk's seat below the pulpit.

The present chapel, erected 1840, with walls of red brick with a gault brick front and slate roof, is typical of the work of James Fenton of Chelmsford. The front is pedimented and has two doorways with tapered windows above flanking a two-tier centre bay with groups of three windows and parapet within the base of the pediment which is inscribed 'REBUILT A.D.1840'. 'Bicentenary Sunday Schools' at the rear are dated 1862. Interior of chapel refitted 1986. (URC)

Congregational chapel (URC), Witham. (119)

Inscription: on boundary wall to left 'This wall was built by Mr James Beadel and the trustees of the Independent chapel. 1854'.

(120) Former FRIENDS, Maldon Road (TL 823144). The meeting-house, built *c*.1809, now forms part of a Masonic hall. The walls are of brickwork and the roof is hipped and tiled. All external openings have been blocked or concealed by extensions but a few traces of segmental-arched windows remain visible in the NW wall.

Butler (1999) 205.

WIVENHOE

(121) Former CONGREGATIONAL, Quay Street (TM 038215). Rendered brick with some stone dressings, built 1846 by Thomas Sanford at his own expense to the designs of James Fenton of Chelmsford. The front, of three bays, has a pedimented centre between balustraded parapets. In the centre bay is an open porch with two columns, double doorways in splayed sides and a rear window incorporating a lantern; above is a three-light upper window with Roman Doric columns and entablature and tablet commemorating the donor.

The interior has a gallery around three sides, the front continues as an upper dado behind the pulpit with four pilasters rising from it to support a pedimented entablature and enclosing a memorial tablet. The plaster ceiling, lined in the later 19th century with 2ft-square pressed-steel plates, has at the centre an 8ft-square cast-iron Gothic-style ventilator. (Chapel derelict 1973)

Former Congregational chapel, Wivenhoe. (121)

Monuments: in chapel, behind pulpit (1) John Sanford, 1850, who paid for the erection of the British School on the site of the former chapel, and Thomas his brother, 1858, who built this chapel; above vestry door (2) Miss Mary Ann Sanford, 1873, recording a gift of £500 and her erection of 'six almshouses in this parish for the use of six aged females who will receive 6s. per week for their maintenance'.

CYB (1847) 166; (1857) 187, obituary of Rev. Samuel Hubbard.

WOODHAM FERRERS

(122) CONGREGATIONAL (TL 797001). Gabled front of brick with terracotta dressings; two pointed-arched doorways with window between and small terracotta panel dated 1882.

GREATER LONDON

The county of Greater London was created in 1965 by the amalgamation of the county of London, formed in 1888, with the previously unincorporated parts of the historic county of Middlesex and the metropolitan areas of the adjacent counties of Essex, Surrey and Kent. Central to this conurbation is the county of the City of London, jealous of its historic privileges, a hub of commerce and formerly home to a close-knit population among whom new ideas could readily find adherents. By the early 18th century over three dozen nonconformist meetings were active within the bounds of the City, principally of Presbyterians, Independents and Baptists. Some met in purpose-built meeting-houses usually constructed on leasehold sites but many used rented premises, including the halls of the Livery Companies. The fortunes of these societies cannot be discussed adequately here but the extent and the complexity of their operations can be traced in Walter Wilson's classic work *The History and Antiquities of Dissenting Churches and Meeting Houses in London, Westminster, and Southwark* (1808–14). Not a single one of these early meeting-places survives in recognizable form nor does any trace of nonconformist use remain in the now relocated Crosby Hall (176). Of those congregations which continued to meet within the square mile, one only, the City Temple (1), has stayed within the bounds of the City, while others moved away in the 19th century to Westminster (261), Islington (142, 147, 159), or further afield to Stoke Newington (92) or Leyton (242).

Beyond the confines of the City, the earliest meeting-houses of which some evidence remains recall the separate villages or enclaves with which the London hinterland abounded. In the borough of Southwark the fond but distant memory of Zoar Chapel was kept alive in the 'Church of the Pilgrim Fathers' (224), in which fact and fiction had become inextricably intertwined. More fortunate were the General Baptists of Deptford whose chapel (195) of *c.*1700 survived many changes, illustrative of the mixed fortunes of the congregation, until demolition *c.*1970. At Newington Green the Presbyterian meeting-house of 1708 (90) continues in religious use, although others of the early 18th century in Highgate (105) and further afield in Uxbridge (132) are no longer places of worship.

Some of the earliest of the surviving 18th-century chapels were erected by Huguenot congregations in the East End of London, of which that in Fournier Street, Spitalfields (233) is outstanding, though now sadly despoiled internally. All changed hands over the years, this and Parliament Court Chapel (234) became synagogues, and West Street Chapel, Seven Dials (45), after a period of Methodist use, became an Episcopal chapel. The East End of London also became the home of several Lutheran churches, of which St George's German Lutheran Church in Alie Street (241) of 1762–3 is the fortunate survivor. Foremost amongst the few late 18th-century chapels, and one of national importance, is Wesley's Chapel in City Road (157), which followed the traditional church layout of the day and served as a model for many other chapels of the Methodist Connexion.

The Society of Friends, whose presence within the City of London at the 'Bull and Mouth', Aldersgate Street, and subsequently at Devonshire House was not terminated until 1925 with the opening of Friends' House, Euston Road, has several late 18th-century meeting-houses of note in the outer districts, at Kingston (181) of 1773, Wandsworth (249) of 1778, and Isleworth (139) of 1785. The more rural type of meeting-house occurs at Winchmore Hill (69) of 1790, and at Uxbridge (134) of 1817. Later still, the further development of Quaker architecture is seen at Peckham (221), where the 1826 meeting-house, no longer in Quaker use, has a more formal urban character.

The rapid growth of the metropolis from the beginning of the 19th century gave rise to an unprecedented demand for chapel building, some of it speculative, for the ever-increasing number of congregations formed by subdivision, church planting, internal or doctrinal rivalry, or the cult of popular preachers. Greater competition demanded a more positive architectural expression than the restrained Georgian of the previous century and strong Classical elements were the accepted standard during the first few decades of the century. The pedimented colonnade of 1823 fronting Stamford Street Chapel, Southwark (225) was a bold statement for a Unitarian congregation at that date, but the stucco-fronted Portland Chapel of 1841 in St John's Wood (259) was well in keeping with the fashionable villas and terraces in the vicinity of Regent's Park. Baptists were particularly loyal to Classical architecture, the style chosen by their great preacher C.H. Spurgeon for the Metropolitan Tabernacle (223), but it was also preferred by Congregationalists when they were obliged to rebuild at Tollington Park in 1871 (149) and at the City Temple in 1873–4 (1).

The Romanesque or 'Lombardic' style was adopted by the Baptists in Bloomsbury for their chapel of 1845–8 by John Gibson (31) but with the majority of architects the Gothic style was preferred. All the most successful nonconformist architects contributed to the spate of chapel building and only a selection of their works can be cited here. John Tarring at Horbury Chapel (167) and later in Kentish Town (42) or Enfield (66); W.G. and E. Habershon at Hendon (12); Thomas Worthington at Rosslyn Hill (39); J. Wallis Chapman at Ealing (59); or W.D. Church with two notable chapels in Croydon (51) and Dulwich (219). To these must be added the very exceptional buildings for the Catholic Apostolic Church in Gordon Square (35) by J.R. Brandon and J.L. Pearson's at Paddington (255) and the elaborate if somewhat eccentric Church of the Ark of the Covenant at Stamford Hill (91) by Joseph Morris.

The large one or two thousand-seater chapels which dominate the religious scene in the late 19th century were not well suited to a scholarly Gothic treatment. A less rigid Lombardic or Italianate style was found preferable by W.F. Poulton for Westminster Chapel (260), while a more imaginative use of Gothic elements is seen in James Cubitt's Union Chapel Islington (151) or in Alfred Waterhouse's chapel at the King's Weigh House (261). A further change in the architectural climate is found at Upper Street, Islington (150), where Bonella and Paull used the Queen Anne style, and in the ubiquitous chapels by George Baines and Son in their ever-recognizable version of free Gothic. Several chapels of the early 20th century are of note, the foremost being the 'Free Church' in Hampstead Garden Suburb by (Sir) Edwin Lutyens (9), but C. Harrison Townsend's 'Free Church' at Woodford Green (210) and P. Morley Horder's Congregational chapel in Penge (27) are equally significant.

The planning of most chapels calls for little comment, but attention should be drawn to the former Surrey Chapel (226) a polygon of sixteen sides, and to the more common use of the octagon at Harecourt (147), Offord Road (152) and in the much later Wesleyan chapel at Raynes Park (199). The former Wesleyan chapel in Queensway, Bayswater (265), with a semicircular plan and two tiers of galleries, is notable for the skilful use made of a difficult narrow-fronted site. Some remarkable uses of materials are also worthy of mention, notably in the New Church at Anerley (29), entirely constructed of mass concrete; also the use of laminated timber trusses at West Ferry Road (239), the early fibrous plaster vault at Riggindale Road (194), patent stone dressings at Pentonville Road (146) and terracotta detailing in various places (187, 212, 266).

COUNTY OF THE CITY OF LONDON

(1) CITY TEMPLE, Holborn Viaduct (TQ 315815). The Congregational church (now URC) meeting in the City Temple is the last survivor within the boundaries of the City of London of the numerous nonconformist meetings which existed there from the mid 17th century. The church was gathered in 1640 by Dr Thomas Goodwin. In its early years it is believed to have met in Anchor Lane, off Thames Street, but from the late 17th century in a large meeting-house 'with three capacious galleries' in Paved Alley, a site on the W side of Lime Street at the N end. In 1755 the site, which was leased, had been sold by the freeholder to the East India Company for the enlargement of East India House; the church had made no adequate provision for an alternative meeting-place and the society was rent by internal disputes into two opposing factions. The smaller section, under the former pastor, John Richardson, moved to a chapel in Artillery Lane, Tower Hamlets (235), which they possibly rebuilt. The larger body were able to share Timothy Jollie's meeting-house in Miles Lane for morning worship and to use 'an old meeting-house in Hoxton Square' in the evening. This unsatisfactory state of affairs continued for ten years.

In 1766 a new but modest meeting-house was built in Camomile Street, off Bishopsgate Street, described as 'a good brick building, of a moderate size, with three galleries'. By 1805 the congregation was 'in a very low state', but their fortunes swiftly improved under a new minister, John Clayton, and larger premises were required. A central but confined site off the N side of Poultry was purchased from the City corporation for £2,000 and the Poultry Chapel was built in 1818–19, double the size of the former and seating 1,400. Here the church remained with growing consequence until the advent of another eminent preacher. In 1869 Dr Joseph Parker was persuaded to leave his pulpit at Cavendish Chapel, Manchester, on the expressed intention of the officers at Poultry Chapel 'to sell the property and erect a noble structure on the best available site that can be obtained'. Poultry Chapel was sold in 1872 to the Joint Stock Bank (Midland Bank, now the HSBC) and the present site on the S side of the new Holborn viaduct was bought from the City corporation.

The City Temple was designed by H.F. Lockwood (Lockwood and Mawson) to seat 2,500. The foundation stone was laid on 19 May 1873 and the building opened on the anniversary in 1874. It was severely damaged by bombing in April 1941, and the interior was entirely gutted although the front and rear walls have survived. The body of the chapel was reconstructed in 1955–8 to a new design by Frederick Lawrence, completed by Seely and Paget.

The walls of the original structure were of stone on a brick core. The chapel was, and in part remains, a building in the Classical manner of two superimposed orders, Roman Doric and Corinthian. The N front has a pedimented portico of three bays flanked by single bays containing gallery staircases, that to the right rising as a tower by two further stages, the uppermost surmounted by a small dome. The interior had a continuous gallery, very deep above the entrance, supported by cast-iron columns which were repeated above to carry a range of lunettes forming a clerestory. Notable amongst the fittings lost in 1941 was a large rostrum pulpit of stone and marble, the gift of the City corporation.

Clare, A., *The City Temple, 1640–1940* (1940). Hammond, B., et al., *The City Temple in the City of London* (1958). Marsh, J.B., *Memorials of the City Temple* (1877). Norwood, F.W., et al., *London's Great White Pulpit* (1924). Richards, (ed.) (1942) 50–1. Wilson I (1808) 212–50, 387–92.

BARKING

(2) BAPTIST, Linton Road (TQ 443843). The church founded in 1850 built its first chapel in Queens Road in 1851. That was superseded by the present chapel in 1893. This is of red brick with painted Bath stone dressings. The front is of three bays with giant pilasters supporting a segmental pediment intersected by a centre bay rising to a small triangular pediment. The roof, reconstructed in 1905 following an early structural failure, was originally segmental and constructed 'entirely of iron and concrete' by the Metallic Paving Company, evidently an early example of the use of reinforced concrete. Contemporary gates and railings remain in front.

B.Hbk (1895) 282–3. [Cowling, H.], *A Century of Christian Witness: Barking Baptist Tabernacle, 1850–1950* [1950]. Ivimey II (1814) 159. VCH *Essex* V (1966) 232, 245. Whitley (1928) No. 237.

Baptist Tabernacle, Barking. (2)

(3) Former FRIENDS, North Street (TQ 440845). Part of an existing building acquired for a meeting-house in 1673 was subsequently much altered and repaired. This closed in 1830 but was replaced in 1908, again for Quaker use, by the present meeting-house and mission hall designed by C.J. Dawson. This is of rendered brickwork with three ornamental Dutch gables at the front and a similar gable on the N side. (Converted to a Sikh temple in 1971)

A *burial-ground*, acquired 1672, now a public garden, remains to the W. It is partly bounded by brick walls and has a gateway at the E end. No monuments remain but Lidbetter (op. cit. below) illustrates a headstone to William Mead, 1713, and Sarah his wife, 1714.

Butler (1999) 173–4. Lidbetter (1961) 84. VCH *Essex* V (1966) 231–2, illus. facing 123.

BARNET

(4) CONGREGATIONAL, Wood Street, Barnet (TQ 244965). The congregation (now URC) which began as a Presbyterian society in the late 17th century built a meeting-house in Wood Street in 1709. This was closed in 1760 following the sudden defection of the minister and not reopened until 1797. The chapel was rebuilt in 1824 and superseded in 1890 by the present building.

The chapel, by George Baines, is of stone with a gabled front and corner tower and spire, of which the superstructure appears to have been rebuilt; the principal windows are of three lights with pointed-arched heads.

CYB (1891) 222; (1908) 154. Mearns (1882) No. 5. Urwick (1884) 258–72.

(5) BAPTIST, Creighton Avenue, East Finchley (TQ 271899). Of an ambitious scheme by George and Reginald Palmer Baines for a large chapel and separate Sunday-school in the free Gothic style only the latter was completed. This was commenced in 1902, of flint and brick with a wide segmental-arched window in the gabled front and contemporary iron finials to octagonal corner turrets. A much simpler chapel of 1930 by the same firm stands near by.

B.Hbk (1902) 353–5. Whitley (1928) No. 557.

(6) Former PRIMITIVE METHODIST, King Street, East Finchley (TQ 267899). Stock brick with red brick and stone banding, Gothic, by J. Willem; gabled front to E with memorial stone laid by Sir Francis Lycett. Extension to rear 1884.

(7) WESLEYAN, Ballards Lane, Finchley (TQ 258914). Red brick with corner tower and shingled spire, 1905. Former chapel to NE of 1879 by Charles Bell, stock brick, gabled front with two traceried windows between intermediate octagonal buttresses.

(8) PRESBYTERIAN, Finchley Road, Golders Green (TQ 251872). St Ninian. Brick with flèche, late Gothic, built 1910 for new congregation. *Plate*: includes a pair of two-handled cups in Sheffield plate, of the early 19th century. (URC, united 1979 with 'Trinity' Methodist)

PHSJ IV (1928–31) 259.

(9) 'FREE CHURCH', Hampstead Garden Suburb (TQ 254885). The 'Free Church', built for joint Baptist and Congregational use, was designed by (Sir) Edwin Lutyens to balance St Jude's church, on opposite sides of the central square. The foundation stones were

'Free Church', Hampstead Garden Suburb. (9)

laid 16 March 1911. It is a rectangular building of brick with stone dressings and a high tiled roof with a shallow dome above a short octagonal central tower. The outer walls are low with dormer windows, tall gabled ends to E and W and transeptal gables N and S of the tower. The interior is subdivided by tall Roman Doric columns into a short nave and aisles with piers supporting the tower above a central domed crossing. A short bay E of the crossing is occupied by the organ and pulpit, beyond which are minor rooms. There is a barrel-vaulted plaster ceiling above the nave and eastern bay.

Butler, A.G., *The Architecture of Sir Edwin Lutyens* (1950) Vol. II, 20, Pls XV–XVI, Photograph 80. Whitley (1928) No. 830.

(10) FRIENDS, North Square, Hampstead Garden Suburb (TQ 255886). Low L-shaped building of brick with hipped tiled roof; 1913 by Fred Rowntree in late 17th-century style.

Butler (1999) 395.

(11) BAPTIST, Finchley Lane, Hendon (TQ 235893). Brick with rubble and ashlar facing, cruciform Gothic, 1886 by J.E. Sears.

B.Hbk (1886) 342. Whitley (1928) No. 518.

(12) CONGREGATIONAL, Brent Street, Hendon (TQ 234891). The chapel, on the E side of the street, was built in 1854–5 in the 15th-century Gothic style by W.G. and E. Habershon. The walls are faced with Kentish ragstone and dressings of Bath stone. The W front is gabled and has a traceried window of five lights above a pair of entrances; the front is set between a pair of substantial octagonal turrets, designed to accommodate gallery stairs should they be required, and finished with lanterns having gablets over narrow lancets and heavily crocketed spires. (Demolished 1980)

Anon., *Hendon Congregational Church, 1854–1954: Centenary Booklet* (1954). *CYB* (1856) 266–8. Mearns (1882) No. 109.

Congregational chapel, Hendon. (Demolished) (12)

(13) Former FRIENDS, The Ridgeway, Mill Hill (TQ 228926). A meeting-house erected in 1678 and enlarged 1693 was closed in 1740. This was subsequently converted to cottages, 'Rosebank', now a single dwelling, 'Rosebank Farm'. The range of building is mostly timber-framed, of two storeys clad in weather-boarding and with a tiled roof; a barn at the NW end has also been converted to a house. No structural evidence of Quaker use remains visible.

Beck and Ball (1869) 308–10. Butler (1999) 408. RCHM *Middlesex* (1937) 73, Hendon monument (10).

(14) BAPTIST, Station Road, New Barnet (TQ 263962). Brick with Classical front in three bays with giant pilasters paired about centre bay to carry a raised central pediment. Built 1873. (Demolished 1983)

Whitley (1928) No. 505.

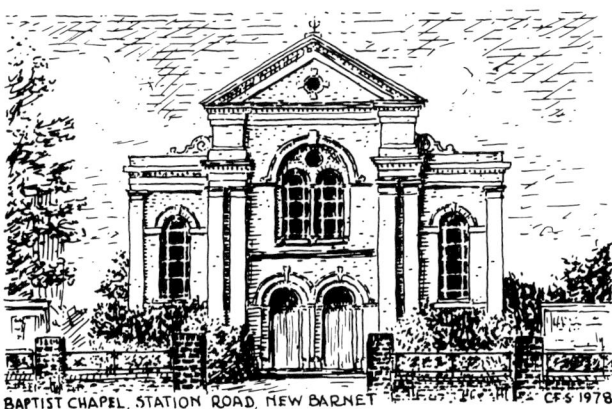

BAPTIST CHAPEL, STATION ROAD, NEW BARNET   CFS 1978

(15) BAPTIST, Ballards Lane, North Finchley (TQ 262919). Built *c.*1878; rubble and ashlar facing, gabled front, five-light window with circular tracery above entrance. Gallery stair to right with pyramidal roof.

Whitley (1928) No. 440.

(16) CONGREGATIONAL, Nether Street, North Finchley (TQ 262921). Built 1864–5 in the Gothic style by Searle, Son and Yelf, on ground given by J.H. Puget. Kentish rag with Bath stone dressings, four-light traceried window in gabled front and corner staircase tower tapered to square spire.

CYB (1865) 293. Mearns (1882) No. 92.

BEXLEY

(17) STRICT BAPTIST, Nuxley Road, Belvedere (TQ 490779). The chapel built in 1810 but bearing the date of the formation of the church in 1805 is a small building of rendered brickwork. The front, of three bays with round-arched upper windows, has a parapet with a large central panel between scrolls.

Chambers III (1956) illus. facing 97, 116–17. Whitley (1928) No. 91a.

(18) CONGREGATIONAL, Picardy Road, Belvedere (TQ 493786). Stock brick with dressings of coloured brick and stone, paired entrances under a trefoil arch in diaper surround; 1897 by Charles Pertwee replacing an iron chapel erected 1865.

CYB (1895) 180–1. Mearns (1882) No. 11.

(19) PRIMITIVE METHODIST, Picardy Road, Belvedere (TQ 494789). Small gabled chapel of brick with wheel-window with radiating colonettes; 1876 by W.G. Habershon & Pite.

(20) Former STRICT BAPTIST, 1 & 3 Bourne Road, Bexley (TQ 496737). The low building of rendered brickwork, greatly altered on conversion to two shops, was built in 1846, re-fronted c.1892 and superseded by a new chapel 50 yards NW in 1905. A tablet now reset outside the new chapel is inscribed 'Built 1846, Restored and Schools Erected 1893'.

Chambers III (1956) illus. facing 89, 111–12. Whitley (1928) No. 202.

(21) CONGREGATIONAL, Hurst Road, Bexley (TQ 492736). The Gothic chapel by George Baines was built in 1890 as a 'School Chapel' intended to form part of a larger scheme which was never completed. The walls are of Kentish rag with Doulton stone dressings. The gabled front has an octagonal corner turret and spirelet. (URC)

CYB (1891) 214.

(22) BAPTIST, The Broadway, Bexleyheath (TQ 487754). 'Trinity Chapel' was built to supersede a small chapel of 1827 on the S side of the street (demolished 1956). The new chapel, of 1868 by W.G. Habershon & Pite, has an impressive Classical S front of stock brick with rendered dressings. It is of three bays with giant Corinthian pilasters supporting a pediment with dentil cornices and surmounted by an acroterion.

Chambers III (1956) 110–11. Grace (February 1972) 16–17. Timpson (1859) 545. Whitley (1928) Nos 125, 475.

(23) Former WESLEYAN, North Street, Bexleyheath (TQ 493755). The chapel dated 1860, prominently facing one end of Chapel Road, is a small building of stock brick with red brick dressings and rusticated pilasters, a pediment with brick dentil cornices, and porch with serpentine barge-boards. Superseded in 1925 and now a Brethren meeting-room, 'Bethany Hall'.

(24) Former CONGREGATIONAL, Station Road, Sidcup (TQ 462720). Large Gothic chapel of ragstone with ashlar dressings and prominently cusped plate tracery; 1887–8 by George Baines. The previous chapel of 1879, in red brick, which became the school-room, lies behind. (Now in community use)

Mearns (1882) No. 192.

BRENT

(25) BAPTIST, Carlton Vale (formerly Canterbury Road), Kilburn (TQ 249831). Stock brick with pedimented front of three bays, giant pilasters and centre bay arched into pediment. Built 1865; annexe to rear dated 1872.

B.Hbk (1893) 146–7 obituary of the Rev. T. Hall. Whitley (1928) No. 399.

Baptist chapel, Carlton Vale. (25)

(26) PRESBYTERIAN, Craven Park Road, Harlesden (TQ 213837). The chapel of 1876 by Thomas Arnold, enlarged 1884, is of red brick with painted dressings; gabled front with four-light traceried window. (Now URC and Moravian)

BROMLEY

(27) CONGREGATIONAL, High Street, Penge (TQ 357700). The chapel built in 1912 for a church formed in 1908 is a notable example in the free Gothic style by P. Morley Horder. It is faced in stone and has a deeply recessed window in the gabled NE end facing the main road; at the opposite end is a short rectangular tower deeply buttressed on two sides. The plan comprises a nave with passage aisles, choir below the tower, and a polygonal communion apse. It has a small gallery at the NE end and a partly exposed crown-post roof with wall shafts supported on carved corbels between the segmentally pointed arches of the arcades. (URC)

CYB (1913) 145.

Trinity Chapel, Bexleyheath. (22)

Congregational chapel (URC), Penge, Bromley.

(28) CONGREGATIONAL, Crescent Road, Beckenham (TQ 380692). The church (now URC) first met in the Sunday-school of 1878 by J. Sulman. The present stone Gothic chapel of 1887–8 by J.W. & R.F. Beaumont has an elaborately detailed spire at one corner.

CYB (1877) 496; (1887) 254 and frontis. Mearns (1882) No. 9.

(29) Former NEW CHURCH, Waldegrave Road, Anerley (TQ 341703). This ambitious Gothic chapel of 1881–3 was 'designed and erected in concrete by W.J.E. Hanley', manager of the 'Concrete Building Company' of Blackfriars Road, London; the walls are entirely of red Portland cement concrete laid *in situ* with precast concrete details. It comprises a nave of four bays with polygonal chancel and vestries at the N end, a large gabled transeptal entrance to the E between octagonal towers with spires, formerly roofed in concrete, and school-rooms below. (Now converted to flats)

Anon., *The Jubilee of the Anerley Society of the New Church* (1933). *Concrete Quarterly* 89/90 (April/September 1971) 50–1.

Former New Church, Anerley. (29)

CAMDEN

(30) Former BAPTIST, Catton Street (TQ 305816). The church formerly meeting in 'Kingsgate Chapel' was derived from a Baptist meeting in Little Wild Street from which the majority of members seceded in 1736, refusing to accept allegations of misconduct made against the minister, Andrew Gifford, who was also assistant librarian at the British Museum. The first meeting-house was built on this site, which then formed part of the W end of Eagle Street, on the S side, in 1736; it was enlarged in 1760 and again in 1820 during the ministry of the Baptist historian, Joseph Ivimey. In 1856 Eagle Street Meeting-house was replaced by a new chapel with its front facing Kingsgate Street (now part of Southampton Row). This was a Gothic building with a front of three bays surmounted by a short octagonal turret. In 1900–2 the chapel was replaced by 'Baptist Church House', a large building by Arthur Keen to house the offices of the Baptist Union, and the church accommodated in a new Kingsgate Chapel, by the same architect, at the rear.

The former 'Kingsgate Chapel', on the site of the original Eagle Street Meeting-house, is a small octagonal building of brick with stone dressings; alongside the entrance is a tower giving access to the gallery. The interior was lit by a lantern on the roof and lunette windows at gallery level. In 1939 the gallery area was floored over and incorporated into the adjacent offices for use as a council chamber. (The church ceased to meet in 1961 and the chapel passed to secular use as 'Kingsgate House'. Baptist Church House was sold to London Underground in 1989 following relocation to Didcot)

Plate: set of twelve cups of unusual design, given by John Payne 1734; also flagon, 1765. Sold *c.*1965, one cup and flagon now at Bristol Baptist College.

Baptist Times (14 October 1982; 20 November 1986; 7 September 1989; 5 October 1989). *B.Hbk* (1903) 366–8. Champion, L.G., *Farthing Rushlight; The Story of Andrew Gifford, 1700–1784* (1961). Ivimey III (1830) 591–613; IV (1830) 337–42. Ward, A.T., *Kingsgate Chapel* (1912). Whitley (1928) No. 50.

(31) BAPTIST, Bloomsbury Street (TQ 300815). Bloomsbury Baptist Chapel was built in 1845–8 by (Sir) Morton Peto to a 'Lombardic' design by John Gibson. The walls are of gault or 'white' brick with stone dressings. The front has a central section of three bays between corner towers, three round-arched entrances and a large wheel-window centrally above. The centre was originally of two stages with a pediment, but an upper storey by H.F. Murrell was added in 1913 and the pediment replaced by an attic storey with a row of seven small windows. Until 1951 the towers were finished with octagonal spires and stone corner pinnacles. The galleried interior, originally seating about 1,400, was altered in 1963–4.

B.Hbk (1914) 511. Bowers, F., *A Bold Experiment: The Story of Bloomsbury Chapel and Bloomsbury Central Baptist Church, 1848–1999* (1999). *Civil Engineer and Architect's Journal* XI (May 1848) 129. Whitley (1928) No. 230.

(32) SOHO BAPTIST CHAPEL, Shaftesbury Avenue (TQ30028115). The chapel of 1887–8 by W. Gillbee Scott is of red brick with terracotta dressings, with exposed brickwork internally. The chapel built for a Strict Baptist church formed in 1791 was sold in 1916 to a church of the same denomination and renamed 'Gower Street Memorial' after their previous chapel.

B.Hbk (1888) 340–1. Paul I (1951) 27–60. Stonelake, R., *A City not Forsaken: A History of Christian Witness in Gower Street and Shaftesbury Avenue Chapel* (2000). Whitley (1928) Nos 67, 183.

Bloomsbury Baptist Chapel, Camden. Before 1913.

Catholic Apostolic church, Gordon Square, Camden.

(33) Former BAPTIST, Park Square East, Regent's Park (TQ 288823). The 'Diorama', which stood behind a seven-bay façade at the centre of a short terrace, was opened as a place of public entertainment in 1823. After closure in 1851 the lease was purchased by (Sir) Morton Peto, the building converted to a chapel and reopened in 1855 under the ministry of William Landels. Baptist use ceased in 1922. In 1987 it was under conversion for theatrical and related purposes.

B.Hbk (1900) 224–8. *The Times* 'Saturday Review' 5 February 1977. Whitley (1928) No. 279.

(34) Former CALVINISTIC METHODIST, Tottenham Court Road (TQ 295819). The chapel now used by the American Church in London stands on the site of Tottenham Court Road Chapel, first built for George Whitefield in 1756. The original square meeting-house, with a lantern on a pyramidal roof, was successively enlarged, sold in 1862, and reopened as a Congregational chapel in 1864. It was replaced in 1899 by a chapel by Rowland Plumbe, described as 'a Victorian rendering of Free Renaissance of the Netherlands'. That was destroyed by bombing in March 1945 and superseded by the present building in 1957. *Monument*: reset externally on N wall, Rev. Augustus Montague Toplady, vicar of Broadhembury, 1778. *Sculpture*: pottery, bust of the Rev. George Whitefield, by Enoch Wood, Burslem.

Belden (*c*.1930) 200–6. *CYB* (1865) 294–5; (1899) 155–6. Mearns (1882) No. 219.

(35) CATHOLIC APOSTOLIC, Gordon Square (TQ 297821). When in 1832 the minister Edward Irving was debarred from the Scotch Church, Regent Square, he opened a chapel in Newman Street which came to be regarded as the 'Central Church' of the Catholic Apostolic Church in London. By 1850, with the lease due to expire and the enlarged ritual of the church making greater demands on space, land was acquired at the SW corner of Gordon Square and an ambitious church of cathedral-like scale commenced, which was opened in December 1853.

This is a building of Bath stone with slate roofs, designed by J.R. Brandon in an early Gothic style, comprising a chancel, S chapel, N and S transepts, crossing, and nave with N and S aisles. To the E of the chancel is the 'English Chapel', intended to be ecclesiastically separate and under the direct charge of the Apostles. The church was never completed; a short tower at the crossing was intended to continue higher and to carry a spire to a height of 300ft. Two further bays at the W end of the nave were also envisaged and the W wall remains a 'temporary' brick structure. Many original fittings remain.

Beyer, W., *The Seven Churches in London* (1931) 6–10. Davenport, R.A., *Albury Apostles* (1970) 165–70. Drummond, A.L., *Edward Irving and his circle* (*c*.1935) 208–35 and *passim*. *The Ecclesiologist* XV (1854) 83–8. Survey of London XXI, *St Pancras: Part III* (Tottenham Court Road) (1949) 92, Pls 39–42.

(36) BAPTIST, Heath Street, Hampstead (TQ 264860). Brick with elaborate Gothic front in Bath stone, 1861 by C.G. Searle. Gabled front set between two heavily buttressed towers rising to octagonal turrets with spires.

Buffard, F., *Heath Street Baptist Church, Hampstead (1861–1961)* (1961). Whitley (1928) No. 333.

Baptist chapel, Heath Street, Hampstead. (36)

(37) Former CONGREGATIONAL, Lyndhurst Road, Hampstead (TQ 270854). Built 1883–4 for a congregation which first met in 1876 in a temporary building in Willoughby Road. Brick with Gothic windows, by Alfred Waterhouse; the front is semi-hexagonal with three gabled elevations, tapering towards the rear and with a Sunday-school behind. (Conversion to concert hall proposed 1983)

Briggs (1946) 45–7. *CYB* (1906) 188. Mearns (1882) No. 105.

(38) FRIENDS, Heath Street, Hampstead (TQ 264861). Rendered walls and tiled roof; semicircular porch on columns with copper-clad domed roof. 1907, by Fred Rowntree.

Butler (1999) 402–3.

(39) ROSSLYN HILL CHAPEL, Hampstead (TQ 268857). The Presbyterian congregation, which since the early 19th century has maintained a Unitarian theology, traces its probable origin to the support of Ralph Honeywood of Hampstead who *c*.1665 employed Daniel Evans, formerly of Jesus College, Cambridge, as his private chaplain. The Honeywood family continued to support the dissenting meeting and the first-known meeting-house was built in the early 18th century on a site adjoining their coach house, NW of the present chapel, on Red Lion Hill, now Rosslyn Hill. This was a building 45ft square, which in 1822 was held on a short lease; Wesleyan services were also being held there at that date.

Rosslyn Hill Chapel, Hampstead. (39)

The meeting-house was demolished as unsafe in 1828 and rebuilt. The present chapel, SE of the former, was commenced in 1862 and its predecessor converted for use as a school.

The chapel of 1828 is a small much-altered building of brick and slate standing on a concealed site close to its successor. The present chapel of stone in the Decorated Gothic style was designed by John Johnson and extended by Thomas Worthington in 1885 by the addition of an E chancel, minor rooms and a N aisle. The original work comprises a wide aisleless preaching nave of seven bays with S porch and organ chamber; the roof is slated and surmounted by a tall hexagonal flèche. The interior has an arch-braced timber roof; on the N side is an arcade of four bays to the aisle, at the W end is a narrow wooden gallery.

Fittings – *Clock*: in former chapel, 'Parliament clock', square dial with arched top, signed 'William Billinghurst, London', *c.*1792. *Font*: oak, by R.P. Jones, 1908, from Essex Church (175). *Glass*: in S windows of nave, 1867–71 possibly by Hardman, in N aisle by Holiday, Burne-Jones and others, in chancel by Wilson and Hammond. *Plate*: includes two two-handled cups of 1731 and 1764, a flagon of 1782 and a footed plate of 1709.

Evans (1897) 146–7. Ryde, F.M., Meadows, W. and Brandon-Jones, J., *Rosslyn Hill Chapel, A Short History, 1692–1972* (1972). Sharpe, H., *The Meeting House on Red Lion Hill and Rosslyn Hill Chapel Hampstead* (1914).

(40) CONGREGATIONAL, Pond Square, Highgate (TQ 284873). The church began with a late 18th-century secession from a Presbyterian meeting in Southwood Lane (105) meeting first in a 'small and obscure building' which was superseded by the present chapel on a new site in 1859. Pond Square Chapel (South Grove), by J. Roger Smith, is of stone in the Decorated Gothic style with a gabled front and octagonal tower and spire to one side. The interior has been partly refitted following amalgamation with a Presbyterian congregation from Cromwell Avenue, Haringey, in 1967. (URC)

CYB (1860) 236–7; (1897) 224–5, obituary of Josiah Viney. Mearns (1882) No. 111. Thompson, J., *Highgate Dissenters* (2001).

(41) Former WESLEYAN, Lady Margaret Road, Kentish Town (TQ 292853). The chapel of 1864–7 by John Tarring in the Gothic style has walls clad in Kentish rag with ashlar dressings. Gabled front with big traceried window above entrance; corner tower with spire; gabled side windows between stepped buttresses. Gallery around three sides with original seating, otherwise refitted. (Now RC)

Former Wesleyan chapel, Lady Margaret Road. (41)

(42) Former WESLEYAN, Prince of Wales Road, Kentish Town (TQ 281846). The large chapel on the N side of the road built in 1871 with a seating capacity of 900 is now occupied by the London Drama Centre. The S and W walls are faced in Bath stone but the E side is in brickwork. The S front is of five bays with an elaborately detailed pediment, Corinthian pilasters to the end bays and two columns of the same order *in antis* between to a recessed three-bay centre with round-arched doorways to the chapel and gallery staircases. The W wall is similarly divided by pilasters, with two tiers of windows to each of six bays. The interior has a gallery rounded to the S and supported by cast-iron columns. Behind the site of the pulpit is a wall-arch enclosing a small niche within an architectural setting. Minor rooms have been added below the side galleries.

(43) Former PRIMITIVE METHODIST, 55 Grafton Road, Kentish Town (TQ 286849). Stock brick with white brick pilasters and entablature. Three-bay front with altered centre bay replacing gable. (Now in commercial use)

Kendall (1905) II: 263.

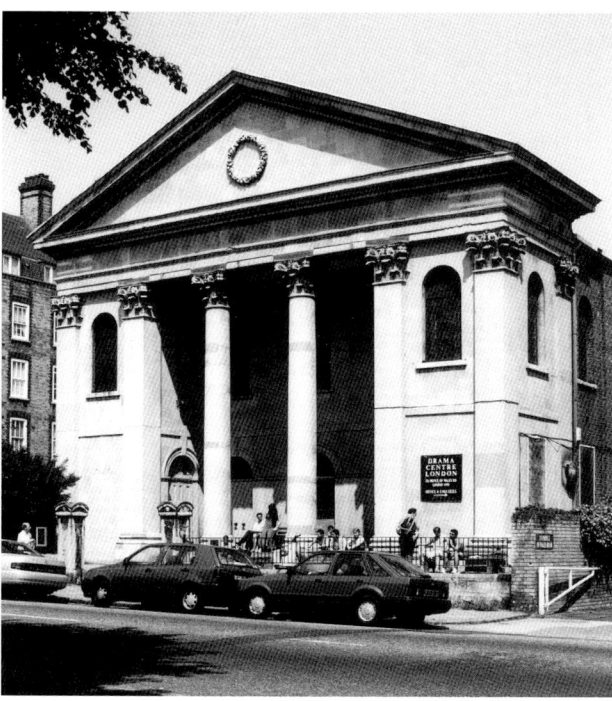

Former Wesleyan chapel, Prince of Wales Road. (42)

(44) WESLEYAN, Birkenhead Street, King's Cross (TQ 30358275). The chapel facing Birkenhead Street (formerly Liverpool Street) now known as Kings Cross Mission, Crestfield Street, from the street at the rear (formerly Chesterfield Street), was built c.1825–30 and subsequently enlarged to the rear to seat 900 persons. The much-altered and formerly pedimented NE front is of brick in five bays with a broad stucco platband between the principal storeys. Five tall round-arched upper windows have been altered and subdivided. The former central entrance has been enlarged but two original lower windows remain at each end of the façade. The formerly galleried interior has been entirely refitted and floors inserted.

Survey of London XXIV, *St Pancras: Part IV* (King's Cross Neighbourhood) (1952) 109–10.

(45) WEST STREET CHAPEL, Seven Dials (TQ 300810). The chapel said to stand on the site of an 'Episcopal Free Chapel' was built or occupied from 1700 by a Huguenot congregation who appear to have rented it from a private owner. In 1743 John Wesley secured the lease of the chapel from a charitable trust formed in 1728 and it remained in use as a Methodist chapel until 1798, when the society removed to a chapel in Great Queen Street. West Street Chapel was reopened in 1800 as an Episcopal chapel; it is now in commercial use.

The chapel of brick has a broad front to the street, possibly a rebuilding of 1799 when the chapel was refitted; the front is of four bays with tall round-arched windows, divided at gallery level and with doorways under the end windows. The interior, now subdivided and entirely refitted except for one gallery staircase, had in 1924 a gallery around three sides and a square lantern on the roof. (Roof structure entirely renewed)

Plate: now in Wesley's House, City Road, Islington, pair of cups with lengthy Latin inscription recording their gift by Peter

Fenowillet on 8 July 'MDCIIIC'[?1697] to the French congregation in West Street.

Dolbey (1964) 36–7. RCHM *London*. Vol. II *West London* (1925) 43–4, Holborn monument (3). Telford (1886) op. cit. 4–85. *WHSP* XVI (1927–8) 137–41.

(46) PRESBYTERIAN, Finchley Road, West Hampstead (TQ 257854). 'St Andrew's Church', now URC, was built in the Gothic style in 1903–4 by Pite and Balfour. It has walls of rock-faced stone and a prominent corner tower and spire.

CROYDON

(47) STRICT BAPTIST, Tamworth Road, Croydon (TQ 320657). The church which originated in the early 18th century previously met in a chapel of 1729 in Pump Pail. The present building of 1866 is of stock brick with rendered dressings. The front of three bays has terminal pilasters supporting a moulded pediment, central entrance with porch, and two tall round-arched windows. The interior has a low central pulpit with arched niche behind. *Clock*: plain circular dial and pendulum case, 18th-century, from previous chapel.

Chambers I (1952) 5–11. Whitley (1928) No. 46.

Strict Baptist chapel, Tamworth Road. (47)

(48) STRICT BAPTIST, West Street, Croydon (TQ 324650). 'Providence Chapel' was built 1847–8 for a church originating with the preaching of Francis Covell, a local tradesman. The walls are of stock brick, the front is pedimented and of three bays with an arch rising into the tympanum.

Chambers I (1952) 14–16. Paul V (1966) 1–33. Whitley (1928) No. 171.

(49) Former STRICT BAPTIST, Derby Road, Croydon (TQ 320660). Built 1876 and extended to front and side 1905.

Chambers I (1952) 11–12. Whitley (1928) No. 540.

(50) BAPTIST, Whitehorse Road, West Croydon (TQ 324666). The 'Tabernacle' of 1873 by J.T. Barker is of brick with stone dressings. The front is gabled and has quadrant porches in the re-entrant corners between the front bay and the body of the chapel. Earlier hall at rear in Lombardic style, dated 1870. *Organ*: by Father Willis.

Stockwell (c.1909) 76–82. Whitley (1928) No. 456.

(51) Former CONGREGATIONAL, Campbell Road/London Road, West Croydon (TQ 316670). The chapel, replacing a temporary building of 1865, was built in 1886 to designs by W.D. Church. It is an elaborately designed building of ragstone with Bath stone dressings in the 'Early Decorated' style, with nave transepts and an elegantly detailed corner tower and spire said to contain a 'peal of bells and chiming clock'. (Now used by an Asian congregation)

Cleal (1908) 136–9. *CYB* (1885) 255. Mearns (1882) No. 72.

(52) CONGREGATIONAL, Aberdeen Road, South Croydon (TQ 325647). Gothic with plate-traceried windows; 1870–1 by J.T. Barker.

CYB (1872) 409. Mearns (1882) No. 69.

(53) Former PRIMITIVE METHODIST, Wandle Road/Laud Street, Croydon (TQ 323651). Built 1857; rendered pedimented front, stock brick sides. (Altered for commercial use)

(54) Former PRESBYTERIAN, Oakfield Road, Croydon (TQ 323666). Built 1865, brick with elaborate wheel-window in E gable. (Closed 1939, now Masonic hall)

(55) PRESBYTERIAN, Croham Park Avenue (TQ 336641). 'St Paul's', 1905 by Charles Henman jnr. Gothic, red brick with stone dressings. Hall of 1909 is linked by a low wing at side. (URC)

(56) Former CHRISTIAN MISSION, Tamworth Road/Cairo New Road (TQ 319656). Brick front of three bays with terminal Corinthian pilasters supporting entablature and shrunken pediment. Presumably the Mission opened 12 January 1873. (Derelict 1997)

Sandall, R. *History of the Salvation Army* I (1947) 158.

(57) SALVATION ARMY, Booth Road (formerly Ellis-David Road), Croydon (TQ 319657). Red brick citadel with five-bay front c.1900; successor to the foregoing.

EALING

(58) BAPTIST, Church Road, Acton (TQ 201800). Brick with rendered front of five bays and pediment over three; 1864 by William Mumford. Front rendering possibly later; lower part strangely embellished with lighting bowls above entrances c.1930.

Whitley (1928) No. 385.

(59) BAPTIST, Castlebar Road, Haven Green, Ealing (TQ 177811). Large Gothic chapel of red brick with stone dressings; 1880–1 by

Baptist chapel, Castlebar Road, Haven Green. (59)

J. Wallis Chapman. The elaborate S front has a polygonal centre flanked on the left by a small circular wing and on the right by a vestigial tower with wide arched entrance formerly decorated with a surround of diaper and rising above to an octagon. The side walls have traceried windows below truncated gablets.

VCH *Middlesex* VII (1982) 159. Whitley (1928) No. 605.

(60) CONGREGATIONAL, Ealing Green (TQ 177804). Gothic, of coursed ragstone with gabled front between octagonal turrets, and separately gabled splayed bays. Brick sides. Built 1859–60 by Charles Jones, superseding an earlier chapel in The Grove. (Now jointly URC/Methodist)

VCH *Middlesex* VII (1982) 160. Mearns (1882) No. 80.

(61) Former WESLEYAN, Windsor Road, Ealing (TQ 180808). Gothic, with corner tower and spire, all faced with ragstone and ashlar dressings, gabled front with five-light traceried window; 1867–9 by Charles Jones & John Tarring. Wesleyan Memorial Hall alongside, 1925. (Transferred to Polish Catholic church, 1986)

VCH *Middlesex* VII (1982) 160–1.

(62) WELSH PRESBYTERIAN, Ealing Green (TQ 176803). Concealed behind cottage; brick with gabled front, dated 1908.

(63) SALVATION ARMY, Crown Street (TQ 199801). Red brick front with shaped gable, c.1900.

ENFIELD

(64) BAPTIST, Totteridge Road, Enfield Wash (TQ 359989). Stock brick with red and blue brick dressings, gabled front, dated 1871; Sunday-school 1893.

Whitley (1928) No. 439.

(65) BAKER STREET CHAPEL (TQ 330973). The chapel on the E side of Baker Street was built for a congregation formed in the late 17th century which was originally Presbyterian, became Congregational by the 19th century but appears to have transferred its allegiance to the Old Baptist Union c.1925. A chapel has stood on this site at least from 1702. The present building of 1862 in the Classical style by T.E. Knightley has walls of stock brick with stucco dressings. The W front has a pedimented portico with four giant Roman Doric columns and a central entrance beyond with windows over; in the pediment is a clock dial with foliage ornament in the surround. The S wall has five round-arched windows with moulded cornices and conjoined cills. The N wall is covered by other buildings. The interior has a W gallery supported by two cast-iron columns. The roof is open and supported by curved braces springing from corbels in the side walls. Behind the pulpit at the E end is a narrow arched recess and adjacent vestries.

CYB (1864) 279. Knight, G.W., 'Non-conformist Churches of Enfield', *Edmonton Hundred Historical Society*, NS 24 (1973) 4. UHST VI (1935–8) 251–2.

Baker Street Chapel, Enfield. (65)

(66) CONGREGATIONAL, Chase Side (TQ 323972). The congregation originated c.1780 when a former London hotelier opened his house for services and then built 'Zion Chapel' on this site. In 1791 the church divided, seceders building 'Chase Side Chapel' on an adjoining site to the S. The two factions reunited in 1871 and in 1874–5 erected the present 'Christ Church' on the site of Zion. This is a building in the Gothic style by John Tarring and Son, of brick faced with Kentish rag and Bath stone dressings. It has a prominent corner tower and spire with angle buttresses, corner pinnacles and lucarnes.

CYB (1876) 440–1. Knight (1973) op. cit. 4–6. Mearns (1882) No. 86.

Congregational chapel (URC), Chase Side, Enfield. (66)

(67) CONGREGATIONAL, Fox Lane, Palmers Green (TQ 309933). Red brick with stone dressings, free Gothic by George Baines and Son, built 1913 with slightly earlier Sunday-school adjacent. (URC)

CYB (1910) 151.

(68) CONGREGATIONAL, High Street, Ponders End (TQ 352958). A small chapel on the W side of the street said to have been built in 1768 and refitted c.1866 by Henry Fuller was demolished c.1957. It had a hipped roof and a broad front of four bays separated by pilasters, with round-arched windows and entrances in the end bays.

CYB (1866) 323. Mearns (1882) No. 177.

(69) FRIENDS, Church Hill, Winchmore Hill (TQ 313947). A meeting in existence by 1662 acquired the present site as a gift from John Oakley in 1682 for use as a burial-ground, and utilized a barn standing upon it as a meeting-house, which was more fully converted to that function in 1688. The present building, on the site of the former, was erected in 1790, enlarged in 1796 by the addition of a school-room, lobby and upper room, and in 1809 by the addition of a small 'Wash-house' behind the school-room.

The meeting-house has walls of stock brick and a slate roof. The S front is of three bays with a central entrance between a pair of sash windows with external shutters, and a simple pediment with

Friends' meeting-house, Winchmore Hill. (69)

blind circular recess carrying a modern painted inscription. The side walls have each a single sash window. The N wall is gabled and has a blind circle corresponding to that on the S front; attached at this end is a lower contemporary annexe, formerly caretaker's accommodation. The former school-room makes a wing to the E, lower than the meeting-house but with an attic room above; the S front has two sash windows, one on the site of a doorway, and a doorway to the right opening to the lobby and staircase.

The interior of the meeting-house (32ft by 28ft) has been refitted and the stand at the N end removed. Some wall benches remain.

Monuments: the extensive burial-ground to the W was enlarged to the N in 1821. Few monuments survive: two, to Dr John Fothergill, 1780, a founder of Ackworth School, Yorkshire, and Ann his sister, were removed to Ackworth in 1969; remaining monuments include (1) David Barclay (son of the Quaker, Robert Barclay, author of *Apology for the True Christian Divinity* (1678)), 1769; (2) David son of David Barclay, 1809; (3) John son of D. Barclay, 1787, and Susannah wife of John Barclay, 1805; (4) Sarah wife of Samuel Hoare, 1783; (5) Samuel Hoare, 1825.

Beck and Ball (1869) 299–301. Butler (1999) 433–4. King, A., *An Account of Winchmore Hill Meeting* (1957). White (1971) 17, 18, 104, 110.

(70) WESLEYAN, Green Lanes, Palmers Green (TQ 316937). 1912, by A.E. Lambert. Brick with stone dressings. Free Gothic, with gabled front between staircase wings.

(71) PRESBYTERIAN, Fox Lane, Palmers Green (TQ 307935). 'St George's', stock brick with stone dressings, gabled front and incomplete staircase tower to right with external pulpit. Interior of four bays with aisles. Built 1913. (URC)

(72) PRESBYTERIAN, Church Street (TQ 324967). 'St Paul's', stone Gothic with incomplete corner tower. Built 1907 but with hall at rear of 1901. (URC)

GREENWICH

(73) BAPTIST, Greenwich South Street (TQ 380769). The chapel of 1872 by C.G. Searle and Son is of brick with a gabled front divided into three bays by rusticated pilasters; Lombardic arcading below gable in centre bay. Gallery around three sides with cast-iron front.

Whitley (1928) No. 309.

(74) Former CONGREGATIONAL, Greenwich Road (TQ 378770). A Calvinistic society attached to the doctrines of George Whitefield was formed *c.*1750 and converted a timber barn for use as 'Greenwich Tabernacle'. The present site was acquired in 1799 and the 'New Tabernacle' was opened in 1801. This use ceased by 1924, when a Greenwich Road Memorial Chapel was built on a housing estate at Bellingham. The 'New Tabernacle' now serves as a coroner's office.

The walls are of stock brick with two tiers of round-arched windows. The NW front is of five bays with a three-bay centre and open loggia. A gallery around three sides is supported by piers. There is a small internal apse at the SE end.

Mearns (1882) No. 98. Timpson (1859) 363–6.

Former Congregational chapel, Greenwich Road. (74)

(75) CONGREGATIONAL, Rectory Place, Woolwich (TQ 431788). The prominently sited Gothic chapel of 1858–9 by Lander and Bedells has walls faced with ragstone and Bath stone dressings, except on the formerly concealed S side, which is of stock brick. The principal E entrance is flanked by separately roofed lobbies covering the gallery doorways; above the main entrance is a tall tower and spire with gablets above intended clock dials.

CYB (1859) 245–6; (1860) 253, 255. Mearns (1882) No. 248. Timpson (1859) 378–82.

(76) Former WESLEYAN, Calderwood Street (formerly William Street), Woolwich (TQ 433789). The chapel, built 1815–16, has a five-bay front of stock brick with two tiers of round-arched windows and a three-bay pediment raised above a parapet. A central porch is supported by a pair of Tuscan columns. An inscribed tablet carried by stone blocks dated 1816 has been concealed. At the rear is an original communion apse, since enlarged to accommodate an organ. (Converted after 1970 to a Sikh temple)

(77) PRESBYTERIAN, Woolwich New Road (TQ 436786). The congregation formerly meeting here originated in the late 17th century; it joined the Scots Presbytery in London in 1792 but in 1843 aligned itself with the Free Church of Scotland, later becoming a part of the Presbyterian church in England. The chapel of 1842 by T.L. Donaldson, in the Romanesque style with a central tower and broach spire, was demolished *c.*1968, and the church

Former Wesleyan chapel, Calderwood Street, Woolwich. (76)

(now URC) meets at St Mary's (Church of England), Greenlaw Street (TQ 431791).

Fittings – *Books*: Bible (Authorized Version) printed by Thomas Buck and Roger Daniel, Cambridge 1638. *Plate*: includes a pair of cups, 1800, inscribed '*Scotch Church Woolwich 1801*'. *Hatchment*: lozenge of arms believed to relate to Mrs Elizabeth Drake, d. *c*.1794, who left a bequest to support a dissenting minister in Woolwich. *Royal Arms*: oil on canvas, George III (1801–16).

Black (1906) 236–40, 273–4

HACKNEY

(78) BAPTIST, Queensdown Road, Clapton (TQ 348858). 'The Downs Chapel', of 1868 by Morton M. Glover, is in a Continental Romanesque style. The walls are of brown brick with dressings of coloured brick, stone and tile. The front has a gabled centre with a large wheel-window above a porch; at each side is a staircase wing rising as a rectangular tower of four stages with a steep hipped roof and pyramidal corner finials.

Whitley (1928) No. 457.

(79) CONGREGATIONAL, Lower Clapton Road (TQ 352855). 'Clapton Park Chapel' was built in 1869–71 for the church (now URC) formerly meeting at the Old Gravel Pit (85). The chapel is a large and ambitious building of stone with mixed Romanesque and Italianate detail by Henry Fuller. The front is rounded and set between a pair of octagonal stair towers with 'pepper-pot' roofs. In front is a semicircular vestibule over which is a row of round-arched windows. The interior has a gallery around three sides supported by cast-iron columns which rise above to carry an arcade of fifteen bays around the building.

The seating was removed in 1990 after the body of the chapel ceased to be used for worship. (Chapel now in community use; congregation continues to meet in Sunday-school buildings)

Congregational chapel (URC), Lower Clapton Road. (79)

Congregational chapel (URC), Lower Clapton Road. (79)

Building Design (January 1990, supplement); (25 May 1990). CHST X (1927–9) 160–6, 234–40, 267–76. CYB (1872) 403–4. Mearns (1882) No. 61.

(80) Former PRESBYTERIAN, Downs Park Road, Clapton (TQ 348856). Gothic, faced with ragstone; square tower with corner buttresses and pinnacles. Built *c*.1870–80. (Now New Testament Church of God)

(81) Former SALVATION ARMY, Linscot Road, Clapton (TQ 352857). The buildings of the London Orphan Asylum, of *c*.1823 by W.S. Inman, were purchased by William Booth and reopened in 1882 after conversion as the Congress Hall and International Training Centre. The four-bay Doric portico of the Asylum chapel, flanked by Doric colonnades linked to pedimented wings, remained from the earlier building. (Demolished except for portico and colonnades 1977–8)

(82) MABERLY CHAPEL, 47a Balls Pond Road, Dalston (TQ 334848). The chapel was built in 1825 for Independents by Henry Ashley on land owned by William Maberly. The front wall, of brickwork with later rendering removed, is in three bays with a simple pediment, and has two tiers of windows, an intermediate platband and two doorways with flat canopies. (Derelict 1996)

Mearns (1882) No. 138. Temple (1992) No. 17.

(83) Former GERMAN LUTHERAN, Ritson Road, Dalston (TQ 341849). The first Lutheran chapel in England was built in Trinity Lane, London, in 1672 following the granting of a Royal charter in 1669. Despite subsequent subdivisions and the formation of other Lutheran churches, the original German church continued to meet on that site until displaced for the erection of the Mansion House underground railway station. The church then removed to Dalston, where a German hospital was already established, building the present church by Habershon and Brock in 1875–6. This is of brick with stone dressings in a German Gothic style, comprising a nave and chancel with a tall tower and spire alongside. The front is gabled between square buttresses and pinnacles and has a large rose window above the entrance. *Reredos*: elaborately carved with segmental pediment supported by paired Corinthian columns, late 17th-century, now in the Victoria

and Albert Museum. (Closed c.1981; now used by West Indian congregation)

AMST 28 (1984) 92–113.

(84) Former PRESBYTERIAN, St Thomas's Square, Hackney (TQ 350843). The Presbyterian society in Hackney traced its origin to William Bates DD, ejected in 1662 as vicar of St Dunstans in the West. Bates preached to 'a society of Protestant Dissenters, who used to assemble in a large and ancient, but irregular edifice, situated in Mare Street, which was standing till the year 1773' which is believed to have been the conversion of several houses on the W side of the street. The society suffered a division in 1715 following the death of the minister, Matthew Henry, one section removing to the Gravel Pit (85). The remaining members, who eventually became Congregational, built a new chapel on the E side of Mare Street at the S side of St Thomas's Square, c.1772–3; it closed in 1896.

The new chapel, now barely recognizable following conversion to a cinema, has brick walls rendered to N and W. The chapel had a pedimented W front of c.1840, of three bays with giant pilasters and a Doric entablature between recessed bays. The original N wall has a platband at mid height and evidence of two tiers of former windows. The S wall may date from an early 19th-century enlargement. The former burial-ground to the S, now a public garden, is entered through a formal archway and retains several monuments.

Inscription: on stone tablet in N wall, 'St Thomas's Square, 1772'. *Plate*: pair of two-handled cups, 1700, and pair of plates, 1701, inscribed with the name of 'Mr Billio, minister'.

Evans (1897) 145. Palmer (1802–3) I: 115–20. Ruston, A.R., *Unitarianism and Early Presbyterianism in Hackney* (1980). Whitehead, J., *A Historical Sketch of … New Gravel Pit Church, Hackney* (1909).

(85) OLD GRAVEL PIT, Chatham Place, Hackney (TQ 352849). The meeting-house at the Gravel Pit was built in 1715 by seceders from the Presbyterian society in Mare Street following a disputed ministerial appointment. On the impending expiry of the lease in 1808–9 the then Unitarian congregation, under the ministry of Robert Aspland, built a new chapel (86) on a site further S, and the lease of their former chapel was taken in 1811 by an Independent church formed in 1804 and previously meeting in the hall of Homerton College; they may have been responsible for a partial rebuilding c.1853 before removing to a new chapel at Clapton Park (79). A second Congregational church leased the chapel in 1874.

The chapel has been greatly altered, refenestrated and partly rebuilt over a lengthy period of industrial use. The N and S walls are of yellow stock brick with dwarf buttresses and may incorporate some original material. The W front was of five bays with a pediment and three tall arched recesses enclosing two tiers of windows.

Aspland (1850) 220–30 and *passim*. Davies, J., *An Account of the Old Gravel Pit Meeting-house, Hackney* (1853). Mearns (1882) No. 99. Photographs, Hackney Borough Archives.

(86) NEW GRAVEL PIT, Chatham Place, Hackney (TQ 353847). When the church at the (Old) Gravel Pit was unable to secure an acceptable renewal of its lease, it bought a new site 270 yards S on which was built in 1809–10 an octagonal chapel designed by Edward Aiken. The chapel was rebuilt in 1858 in the Gothic style by H.A. Darbyshire. (Closed in 1969 and demolished. The site was under redevelopment for housing in 1974)

Anon., *Inscriptions from the New Gravel Pit (Unitarian) Churchyard, Paradise Place, Hackney, Middlesex* (1883). Aspland (1850) 220ff. Evans (1897) 145–6. Friends of Hackney Archives, *Hackney History* I (1995) 20–4. *Monthly Repository* IV (1809) 584; V (1810) 459[= 467].

(87) HAMPDEN CHAPEL, South Hackney (TQ 355842). The chapel on the W side of Lauriston Road (formerly Grove Street) was built in 1847 for an Independent congregation. It was in Baptist use from 1858 to 1927 but is now occupied by the Assemblies of God. The walls are of stock brick but the front is rendered in stucco. The front of three bays has a rusticated lower stage; the centre bay has a pediment with paired pilasters and a Venetian window above the entrance.

Whitley (1928) Nos 86a, 132, 302.

(88) Former CATHOLIC APOSTOLIC, Mare Street, Hackney (TQ 350842). Gothic; stock brick with decorative banding in W gable and stone dressings. Built 1873–4. (Greek Orthodox, 1974)

Beyer (1931) 12, 13.

(89) Former CONGREGATIONAL New Tabernacle, Old Street, Hoxton (TQ 332826). Set back on S side of street. Yellow stock brick with white brick quoins; three-bay pedimented front with three entrances and three round-arched windows above. 1844, by William Wallen & Son. (Closed by 1950, now in commercial use)

Mearns (1882) No. 53.

(90) NEWINGTON GREEN MEETING-HOUSE (TQ 329855). A Presbyterian meeting has been in existence at Newington Green since the late 17th century and several of the ejected ministers were at times associated with it: Samuel Lee took out a licence as a Presbyterian preacher at his house there in 1672; James Starkie (or Starkey) was minister there in 1690; and others were associated with a contemporary Independent meeting. The erection of a regular meeting-house did not take place until 1708. That building, which stands at the N side of the Green, was much altered in 1860 although the greater part of the original structure has survived.

The meeting-house has brick walls, mostly covered by 19th-century stucco, and a slated roof which replaces a hipped tiled roof with a high valley between parallel ridges. The S front of three bays has two round-arched windows replicating the originals but re-sited slightly to the W and embellished; the central entrance is set

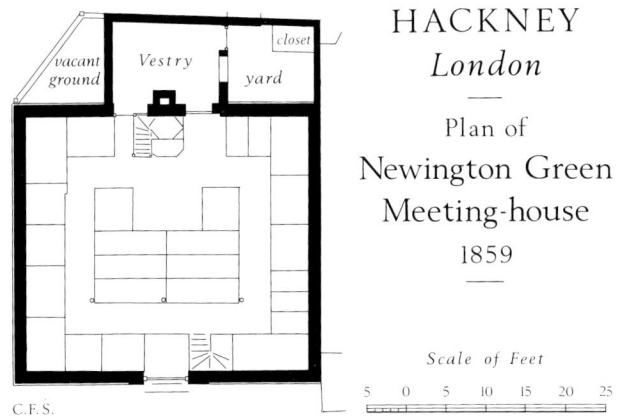

HACKNEY
London

Plan of
Newington Green
Meeting-house
1859

Newington Green Meeting-house
HACKNEY — Greater London

Exterior before 1860.

Exterior in 1945.
Newington Green Meeting-house. (90)

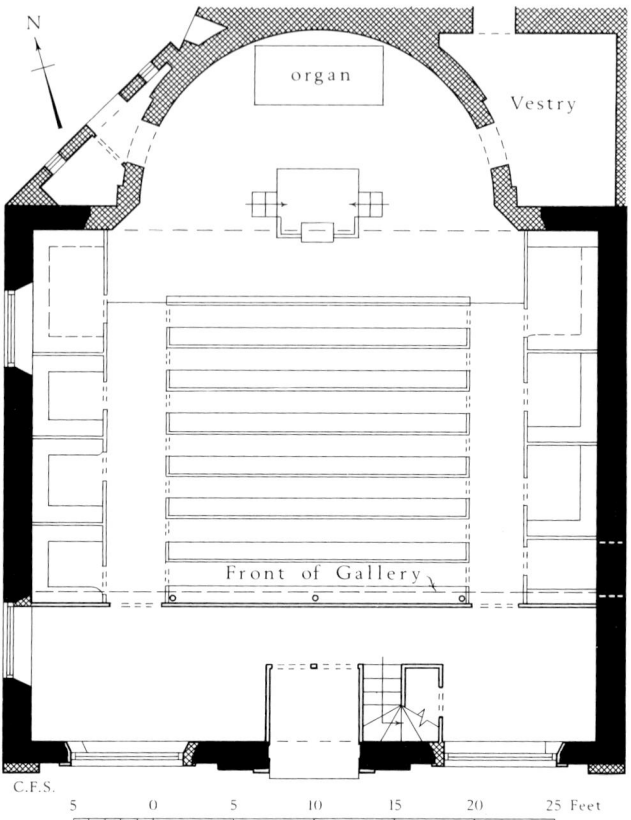

within a panel of thicker walling originally pierced by an oval window and surmounted by a small pediment. A large pediment of 1860, rebuilt in slightly erroneous facsimile in 1976, now extends across the full width of the front. The W wall has two upper and two lower windows unaltered in location but with round-arched heads added to the former; an oval window between them at the upper level has been blocked. The E wall is blank but traces of a blocked doorway to a formerly adjoining property was observed during repairs. The N wall was much altered in 1860 when a preaching apse was added on the site of a vestry and part of the wall removed; there was formerly a series of four upper windows with others below. Behind the meeting-house are school-rooms of 1887 by Chatfeild Clarke and Sons.

The interior (32¼ft by 35ft) has a plaster ceiling with a circular lay-light at the centre; there is a gallery across the S end only, supported by three cast-iron columns. The pulpit, originally set high against the centre of the N wall, was relocated in 1860 on the back of the apse but was later supplanted by an organ (now removed). The original 18th-century carved back-board remains in position. Some 18th-century box-pews survive at each side but the centre rank of pews was replaced in 1860.

Fittings – *Christening Basin*: green-veined marbled stoneware, shallow bowl on stem, early 19th-century. *Inscription*: externally on SW corner, tablet dated 1809. *Monuments*: internally (1) Richard Price DD FRS, 1791, 26 years minister, signed 'Clothier, New Road'; (2) Joseph Mundy Tapp, 1867; (3) Samuel Sharpe, 1881, 'author of the History of Egypt and translator of the Bible'; (4) Samuel Rogers 'the poet', 1855, 65 years a trustee; (5) Anna Laetitia Barbauld, 1825, signed 'R. Brown, 58 Great Russell Street'; (6) Rev. Thomas Cromwell PhD FSA, 1870, 25 years minister; (7) Andrew Pritchard FRS, 1882, 'author of *A History of Infusoria* and other scientific works'. *Plate*: includes a pair of two-handled cups of 1733.

Christian Freeman (1868) 152–4. Evans (1897) 154–5. RCHM London. Vol. II *West London* (1925) 92, Stoke Newington monument (2). Tarrant (1900) 5, 7. Tayler, J.L., *A Little Corner of London (Newington Green)* (1925).

(91) 'THE ARK OF THE COVENANT', Rookwood Road, Stamford Hill (TQ 341878). The church, now named 'The Church of the Good Shepherd', was built in 1895 for the Agapemonites whose principal settlement was at Spaxton, Somerset (*see Nonconformist Chapels and Meeting-houses in South-West England* (1991) 192, monument (148)). Under the leadership of the Rev. H.J. Prince, sufficient public interest and funds were attracted to

'The Ark of the Covenant', Rookwood Road, Hackney.

the cause to enable the erection of a large church near the metropolis in the evident expectation of creating wider support. After Prince's death in 1899 the leadership passed to the Rev. J.H. Smyth-Piggott, an ordained Anglican minister, who gained notoriety at his first service here in 1902 by claiming to be the Messiah. Occasional services continued until *c.*1926. The church was reopened in 1956 as 'The Primatial See of the Ancient Catholic Church'.

The church, of stone with Portland stone dressings, is in the Gothic style to a design by Joseph Morris, County Surveyor of Berkshire and a convert to Prince's beliefs. It comprises a large unaisled nave aligned NE–SW, with a polygonal sanctuary and a tall steeple above the SW entrance. It is particularly notable for the high quality of its glass and external sculptures, which reflect the millennarian beliefs of its builders. The tower, of four stages with corner buttresses and a battlemented parapet, is surmounted by a tall stone spire with gabled openings at the base and two annular bands of decoration. At the corners of the parapet are inscribed plinths carrying bronze emblems of the Evangelists; the same emblems are repeated in stone on the lower buttresses flanking the entrance; on the third stage of the tower are two roundels with representations of the flying scroll and the chariot of Elijah. The sanctuary has three windows each of two lights; it is ceiled with a wooden vault and is divided from the nave by a two-centred arch supported by marble columns. The nave is of five bays with an open roof supported by hammer-beam trusses resting on carved corbels and wall shafts; at the SW end is a narrow gallery. Beneath the sanctuary is a vestry and a larger room extending below one bay of the nave.

Fittings – *Glass*: the windows were designed by Walter Crane and executed by J.S. Sparrow, using glass manufactured by Britten and Gilson. The side windows of the nave have representations of flowers and fruit and are signed with small monogrammed figures of a crane and a sparrow. The principal window of four lights below the tower represents the sun rising above the waters with four angels carrying a scroll inscribed 'Then Shall the Sun of Righteousness arise with healing in his wings'. *Lectern*: carved wood with two supports in form of trees with roots and twisted branches and dove with outstretched wings. *Organ:* by Henry Willis & Sons.

Chapels Society *Newsletter* 1 (1989–94) 40–1, 52–5, 66. McCormick, D., *Temple of Love* (1962).

(92) BAPTIST, Stoke Newington Road (TQ 335858). 'Devonshire Square Chapel' perpetuates the memory of a meeting-house built on the site of 'Fishers Folly' behind Devonshire Square in the City of London by a Particular Baptist church claiming 1638 as its year of origin. That building, re-fronted *c.*1750 and rebuilt 1829, was purchased by the Metropolitan Railway Company in 1870 and the church, an amalgam of several congregations, removed to Hackney.

The chapel built 1870–1 at the corner of Walford Road, by T. Chatfeild Clarke, has tall round-arched windows. The building suffered bomb damage in 1940 but was partially reinstated in 1959. A lecture hall to the S is dated 1890.

Ivimey IV (1830) 317–21. Whitley (1928) Nos. 5, 6, 27, 29. Wilson I (1808) 400–54.

(93) GENERAL BAPTIST, Wordsworth Road, Stoke Newington (TQ 332856). Three-bay gabled polychrome brick front with bell-cote. Built 1894 for the mother church of 'The Old Baptist Union'.

Whitley (1928) 86–7, No. 598.

(94) ABNEY PARK CEMETERY, Stoke Newington (TQ 334868). The cemetery occupies the site and grounds of Abney House, the home of Sir Thomas Abney Bart., where Dr Isaac Watts found refuge for many years. The site was acquired in 1840 as of particular interest to nonconformists and was laid out for non-denominational use. Many dissenting ministers and other notable nonconformists are buried here. The mortuary chapel (derelict 1983) is a cruciform structure of brick with a central tower and spire. To the S of the chapel is a statue of Isaac Watts by E.H. Baily, erected 1845.

Barker, T.B., *Abney Park Cemetery* (1869). French, J., *Walks in Abney Park* (1883).

HAMMERSMITH

(95) BAPTIST TABERNACLE, Shepherd's Bush Road (TQ 235797). The chapel, of red brick with terracotta dressings in a free Gothic style, was begun in 1892 but only completed in 1907. The original design appears to have been by J. Wallis Chapman, although the architect for the completion is named as Percival W. Hawkins. The broad W front to the street is gabled and has a SW corner tower with dragon gargoyles and short shingled spire, balanced by a minor wing on the NW; the flanking wings have foundation stones laid on 3 November 1892. The wide entrance is approached by a steep flight of steps.

B.Hbk (1908) 528–9. Whitley (1928) No. 704.

(96) Former CONGREGATIONAL, Castletown Road, Fulham (TQ 246783). The S front and two bays only remain of the Gothic chapel of 1882–5 by James Cubitt and J.M. Brydon. Coursed stone gabled front, three graduated paired lancets above entrance and flying buttresses above side aisles. (Now an Indian cultural centre)

The Building News (28 April 1882).

(97) Former ALBION CHAPEL, Dalling Road, Hammersmith (TQ 226786). The chapel was built for a Congregational church formed 1774 which met from 1784 in Ebenezer Chapel, King Street, but removed to the present site in 1855. The chapel may be of this date, although it is reported to have been built, or more probably refurbished, in 1891–2 by F.W. Stocking. The E front, of brick, has a pediment across three bays supported by giant Tuscan pilasters. (Now occupied by the Salvation Army)

Mearns (1882) No. 104; (1883) No. 103.

(98) Site of FRIENDS, Furnival Gardens, Hammersmith (TQ 228783). The Friends meeting-house of 1765 in Lower Mall was entirely destroyed in 1944 and a new building erected on another site. The location of the former is marked by a sunken garden and inscribed modern sundial.

Beck and Ball (1869) 261–4. Butler (1999) 401–2. Cundy, H.W., *Hammersmith Quakers' Tercentenary 1677–1977* (1977). Lidbetter (1961) Fig. 32, Pl. XVII.

(99) WESLEYAN, King Street, Hammersmith (TQ 226786). 'Rivercourt', stone Gothic with ragstone facing, corner tower and spire, traceried windows below gables. 1875, by Charles Bell.

(100) Former METHODIST NEW CONNEXION, North End Road, Fulham (TQ 249779). Red brick with stone dressings,

gabled front between staircase wings; 1887–8 by A.H. Goodall. (Now furniture store)

(101) Former PRIMITIVE METHODIST, Furber Street (TQ 226791). Brick with gabled S front dated 1892, granite columns flank arched entrance. Annexe to N 'erected 1870 rebuilt 1905'. (Now an Evangelical church)

(102) Former FREE METHODIST, Walham Grove, Fulham (TQ 252774). Yellow brick with stone dressings, crudely Gothic. Built 1865–6. (Now Kensington College of Business)

(103) Former WELSH PRESBYTERIAN, Effie Road, Fulham (TQ 253771). Stone-faced with gabled front partly covered by polygonal porch containing entrances to chapel and gallery stairs. Of 1900–1 by Edward Avern. (Now London Academy of Performing Arts)

(104) Former PRESBYTERIAN, Leysfield Road (TQ 224795). 'St Andrew's', built 1870 by Edmund Woodthorpe for the United Presbyterian Church, is a substantial Gothic building of stone with a tower at the E end of four stages with parapet and tall pinnacles at the corners. (Now St Andrew Bobola's Polish Roman Catholic church)

Mackelvie (1873) 503.

HARINGEY

(105) Former MEETING-HOUSE, Southwood Lane, Highgate (TQ 284876). The Presbyterian society for which this was built appears to have been formed in the late 17th century by William Rathband, ejected vicar of South Weald, Essex. Heterodoxy came early to the congregation, which in c.1769 appointed the deist, David Williams, as minister; about 1778 many members left to support a newly built Calvinistic chapel in the same road (40) but the weakened society continued to meet until 1798. In 1806 Unitarians made an unsuccessful attempt to reopen the building and in 1809 the lease was sold to Baptists supported by the Eagle Street church (30); it was renamed Highgate Tabernacle and continued until c.1960–70. Now a library for Highgate school.

The meeting-house, of the early 18th century, has brick walls with later rendering; the main roof is hipped and slated. It was extended 8ft to the front c.1809. The front wall of five bays divided by pilasters has a pediment over three previously open bays, closed and altered 1836. Above the doorways in the end bays are cast-iron lamp brackets of the early 19th century. In the rear wall are three round-arched windows, two of which flanked the pulpit. The interior (originally 23¼ft by 49¾ft) probably had separate end galleries, the present gallery, rounded into the front extension, is of 1836.

Aspland (1850) 217. *CHST* V (1911–12) 4–13. *Monthly Repository* I (1806) 550. Whitley (1928) No. 100.

(106) BAPTIST, Tottenham High Road (TQ 339909). The chapel of 1826 by J. Clark has walls of stock brick with rendered dressings and a hipped slate roof. The front of three bays projects slightly at the centre and has a porch supported by paired Doric columns. Round-arched upper windows have conjoined imposts and moulded arched heads.

VCH *Middlesex* V (1976) 360. Whitley (1928) No. 130.

Baptist chapel, Tottenham High Road. (106)

(107) BAPTIST, Muswell Hill Broadway (TQ 289897). Red brick and stone, Gothic with staircase tower at corner rising to an octagon with a short spirelet. 1901, by George and Reginald Palmer Baines.

B.Hbk (1901) 357; (1902) 363. Whitley (1928) No. 795.

(108) BAPTIST, Bounds Green Road, Wood Green (TQ 305908). Free Gothic, faced with white flints and red brick dressings; square corner tower with small turret at one corner. Timber arcades. 1907, by George Baines and Son.

B.Hbk (1908) 532. Whitley (1928) No. 432.

(109) BROOK STREET CHAPEL, Tottenham (TQ 339901). Brethren meeting-room, opened 1839. Brick with gabled W end and circular upper window.

VCH *Middlesex* V (1976) 361.

(110) CONGREGATIONAL, Queen's Avenue, Muswell Hill (TQ 284897). Gothic, with walls rendered in pebble-dash and stone dressings. Intended corner tower completed to lower stage only. 1900, by P. Morley Horder. (URC)

CYB (1899) 153–4; (1900) 148–9.

(111) Former CONGREGATIONAL, Lordship Lane, Wood Green (TQ 312904). Large Classical chapel of stock brick with elaborately detailed pedimented front of three bays with Corinthian pilasters and circular window over entrance rising into pediment; upper mouldings of pediment removed. 1864, by Lander and Bedells. (Closed c.1964)

FORMER MEETING-HOUSE, SOUTHWOOD LANE, HIGHGATE CFS 1974

CYB (1864) 268. Mearns (1882) No. 247. VCH *Middlesex* V (1976) 357, 361.

(112) CONGREGATIONAL, Whitefield Tabernacle, Wood Green (TQ 293906). The chapel in Alexandra Park Road, of 1907 by Mummery and Fleming-Williams, is a cruciform building of brick and stone in a free Gothic style with a central flèche. It was intended to form part of a larger scheme and named in honour of Whitefield Tabernacle (145), whence some of its members came. (URC)

CYB (1908) 160. VCH *Middlesex* V (1976) 362.

(113) CONGREGATIONAL, High Road, Wood Green (TQ 309914). Red brick and terracotta, built 1909–10 with Sunday-school of 1901 alongside.

CYB (1903) 156.

(114) FRIENDS, Tottenham High Road (TQ 339904). A meeting-house of 1714 on this site was rebuilt in 1831 and superseded in 1960 by shops with a penthouse at the rear to serve as a meeting-house. Some wall panelling and benches remain from the earlier building. The burial-ground at the rear retains some reset headstones.

Butler (1999) 422–4. Collie, M.A., *Quakers of Tottenham, 1775–1825* (1978).

(115) Former WESLEYAN, Archway Road, Highgate (TQ 286880). The chapel of 1905 by W.H. Boney is of red brick with stone dressings and has a gabled front with lancet windows and nook shafts in Early English style, flanked by octagonal corner buttresses. (In use as a community centre in 1977)

(116) WESLEYAN, Colney Hatch Lane, Muswell Hill (TQ 286901). Brick with stone dressings, corner tower with octagonal upper stage. Built in 1900; adjacent hall built in 1904.

(117) WESLEYAN, 'St Marks', Tottenham High Road (TQ 338891). Concealed behind a range of shops but dominated by an entrance tower, all of the 1930s, are the much rebuilt remains of the Gothic chapel of 1867 and Sunday-school of 1915.

(118) Former WESLEYAN, Trinity Road, Wood Green (TQ 307909). The foundation stone of 'Trinity Chapel', laid on 20 April 1871 by Sir Francis Lycett, records that this was 'the first chapel commenced by the aid of a Fund to promote the erection of fifty Wesleyan Methodist chapels in London and its suburbs to each of which Sir Francis engaged to give one thousand pounds'. Gothic, with walls of stock brick with stone dressings. Clock-tower and spire at W corner. (Now in use by Greek Orthodox church, but much rebuilt after a fire in 1986)

(119) Former PRESBYTERIAN, Muswell Hill Broadway (TQ 287896). The chapel of 1902–3, in a free Gothic style by George and Reginald Palmer Baines, has walls faced in white flint with red brick dressings; corner tower with spirelet. (Proposed conversion to public house 1995)

HARROW

(120) Former BAPTIST, Byron Hill Road, Harrow-on-the-Hill (TQ 150871). The first chapel on this site, built in 1812, was rebuilt in 1864. It was enlarged in 1872 by the addition of a wing and rooms for the Sunday-school. In 1908 the church removed to a new Gothic chapel by McKilliam and Proctor in College Road and the Byron Hill chapel has since passed into commercial use.

Former Wesleyan 'Trinity Chapel', Wood Green. (118)

The chapel of 1864 has a gabled front of brick with a large circular window above the porch; the Sunday-school has a matching gabled front and is joined to the chapel by a wing with a ventilating flèche on the roof.

B.Hbk (1908) 516. John, S.T.H., *The Harrow Baptist Church, 1806–1956* (1956). Whitley (1928) No. 99.

(121) BAPTIST, Paines Lane, Pinner (TQ 123898). Brick with stone dressings in free Gothic style, 1909–10 by Spalding, Spalding and Myers. Corner tower with shingled spirelet. (United Free Church)

B.Hbk (1909) 511, 513. VCH *Middlesex* IV (1971) 263. Whitley (1928) No. 312.

(122) BAPTIST, High Street, Wealdstone (TQ 153899). Brick and terracotta, with prominent corner tower in Perpendicular Gothic style, 1905, by John Wills and Sons.

B.Hbk (1905) 481. Whitley (1928) No. 534.

(123) CONGREGATIONAL, Hindes Road, Harrow (TQ 151886). The chapel, built in 1929 for a church tracing its ancestry to the historic Silver Street Church in the City of London, incorporates

a stone reset internally inscribed 'Falcon Square Chapel 17th May 1842'. (URC)

Mearns (1882) No. 48. VCH *Middlesex* IV (1971) 263. Wilson III (1810) 3–125.

(124) Former WESLEYAN, Lower Road, Roxeth (TQ 148870). The chapel was built *c.*1856 replacing one of 1810; it was superseded in 1905 by a new chapel in Bessborough Road and is now occupied by a Welsh Congregational church. The walls are of gault brick with round-arched Romanesque windows and detailing, including a band of intersecting arcading to the lower stage at the front. The front is gabled and has a slightly projecting central feature.

Former Wesleyan chapel, Roxeth. (124)

(125) WESLEYAN, Locket Road, Wealdstone (TQ 155901). Red brick with stone dressings; a large Gothic window of ten lights with intermediate buttresses spectacularly overarches the W doorway. Opened 1904.

HAVERING

(126) BAPTIST, London Road, Romford (TQ 509885). 'Salem Chapel', adjoining St Andrew's Road, is dated 1847. Stock brick with painted dressings, three-bay front with open pediment on paired pilasters to centre bay and tapered jambs to upper windows.

Whitley (1928) No. 156.

(127) UPMINSTER OLD CHAPEL, St Mary's Lane (TQ 556866). The chapel was built in 1800 and a Congregational church formed in 1801. In 1911 the church removed to a new building (*see* (128)) and the chapel passed into use by the Brethren. In 1996 it was under repair for the Havering Christian Fellowship.

This is a small timber-framed structure with rendered walls possibly originally weather-boarded, and a later brick front of 1847 which is also rendered. The N front is gabled and has a central entrance with an open porch having a pair of Tuscan columns below a moulded entablature. Above the entrance is a lunette window with panel over carrying Classical ornament. The entrance is flanked by a pair of false windows with Tudor labels and by panelled corner pilasters, all of the late 19th century.

The interior (about 50ft by 26ft) has a N gallery, possibly of

1827, supported by a pair of Ionic columns and with pilasters against the side walls; the gallery was enlarged forwards *c.*1847 and refitted, the earlier part having two steeply raked banks of seating for children, separated by a tall screen, and standard seats in front. Most of this seating has been removed. The ceiling, otherwise flat, rises above the gallery with a barrel-vault springing from the side purlins, exposing one roof truss with later embellishment. The lower seating, renewed in the late 19th century, has been removed; the pulpit, of like date, has a bowed front and rounded back-board.

(128) CONGREGATIONAL, Station Road, Upminster (TQ 560867). Built 1910–11 to replace the foregoing, Gothic by T. Stevens, faced with Kentish rag and Bath stone dressings. Double-gabled transepts and gabled end to road with four-light traceried window. An intended tower at the SE corner remained unbuilt. (URC)

CYB (1911) 151. [Smith, C.W.], *A Short History of Upminster Congregational Church, 1911–61* [1961].

HILLINGDON

(129) BAPTIST, Harefield (TQ 054909). 'Union Chapel', built in 1834, has walls of stock brick and a slated roof. The gabled W front is rendered and has a central doorway with round-arched surround between two hung-sash windows with pedimented heads, the embellishment possibly dating from a renovation of 1885. At the back of the chapel is a later lean-to vestry. There is a small W gallery.

Jarvis (1953) 88–92. Stuart (1907) 108–9. Whitley (1928) No. 149.

(130) WESLEYAN, Harefield (TQ 054910). The chapel was built privately in 1864 by Robert Barnes, a former mayor of Manchester, who had commenced to hold services in 1863 in his coach house at Guttersdean Farm (The Grove). It passed to Wesleyans in 1869 on Mr Barnes's removal from the district. The walls are faced with flint and stone dressings. Gabled front with large wheel-window above porch. School hall added to S in 1906.

Jarvis (1953) 82–7.

(131) BAPTIST, Harlington (TQ 087776). A 'Congregational Baptist Church' was formed in 1798 by a congregation which had been in existence for about 40 years. The meeting-house, apparently private property, was given to the church by John Atlee in 1799, immediately enlarged and an internal baptistery constructed. A new chapel was built on the opposite side of the road in 1879 and the former building was converted for use as a Sunday-school.

The former meeting-house of c.1775 is of brick with a slated roof hipped to the rear. It was extended to the front by one bay and heightened in 1799 and further altered in 1879. The E front is gabled and partly covered by a later porch with two blocked doorways. The S side of three bays has two tiers of round-arched windows; the N wall is covered by later building. The interior (originally about 26ft by 29ft), now converted to a church hall, has a children's gallery at the W end behind the site of the pulpit.

The present chapel, by W. Ranger, is of brick with a rendered front of five bays and pedimented centre bays with urns.

Fittings – *Inscriptions*: in former chapel, on brick reset over internal doorway in N wall 'IA·1775·SH'; on bricks in W front 'JA 1799' and other initials. *Model*: of present chapel, possibly architect's model, cork. *Monuments*: in front of former chapel, ten headstones, reset, early 19th-century and later. *Plate*: pewter, late 18th-century, including two plates inscribed 'Harlington Chapel'.

Whitley (1928) No. 85a.

(132) THE OLD MEETING-HOUSE, High Street, Uxbridge (TQ 055844). Presbyterian meetings assisted by several ejected ministers were held from the late 17th century on private premises. In 1716 part of the present site at the W end of High Street was taken on a 99-year lease and William Thurbin, a local builder, contracted to erect 'a good substantial Meeting House'. In 1753 the site was enlarged and the freehold acquired. In 1833 the church adopted a Congregational polity. The meeting-house was extended in 1867, when additional rooms were added at the SW end, and the whole building was subjected to a major programme of alteration and enlargement in 1882 by John Sulman. In this the building was heightened, re-roofed and given a new entrance at the SW end. Following amalgamation with a Methodist congregation in 1972 the church (now URC) moved to a new chapel, 'Christ Church' in Belmont Road, and the former meeting-house was converted to secular use as 'Watts Hall'.

The building has walls of brickwork, now partly rendered, and roofs covered with slates and tiles. The original front faced NW and had a central doorway between two round-arched windows; these windows remain with their original frames, a third matching window replaces the doorway and a fourth is within the SW extension. The SE wall has no openings. The NE wall, partly obscured by later vestries, has been rebuilt above the original eaves line replacing a double gable. The SW front, entirely of 1883, is dominated by a plain corner staircase tower with pyramidal roof.

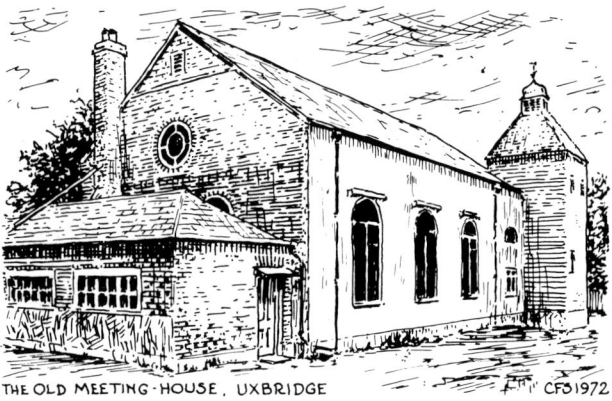

THE OLD MEETING-HOUSE, UXBRIDGE   CFS 1972

The interior (originally 30¼ft by 41ft) was entirely refitted in 1883; the pulpit may have been against the SE wall at first but it has long been sited at the NE end between two round-arched windows into which vestry doorways have been inserted.

Plate: includes a pair of two-handled cups of 1738 and a plate of 1740.

Jarvis (1953) 15–22. Pearce, K.R., *Old Meeting Congregational Church, Uxbridge, 1662–1962* (1962). VCH *Middlesex* IV (1971) 91–2.

(133) PROVIDENCE CHAPEL, The Lynch, Uxbridge (TQ 054841). An Independent congregation formed c.1777 built a chapel in 1795–6 of which one of the trustees appears to have been William Huntington SS (*see* Sussex (64)). This had a gabled front of three bays with two tiers of round-arched windows; it was enlarged and given a stucco front with pilasters and a raised central pediment in 1850. The church united with the Old Meeting (132) in 1962. (Chapel was demolished in 1969)

Fittings, at Old Meeting-house – *Model*: cardboard, showing 1850 front, manse and surrounding burial-ground. *Plate*: tall beaker of 1772 from the Congregational Church, Uxbridge, Mass., U.S.A., given 1930.

Jarvis (1953) 23–9. Mearns (1882) No. 226. Summers (1905) 69. VCH *Middlesex* IV (1971) 92–3.

(134) FRIENDS, Belmont Road, Uxbridge (TQ 057843). A meeting in existence by 1676 acquired land for a burial-ground in 1678 and erected a meeting-house on the site in 1691. This was rebuilt in 1755 and replaced by the existing building in 1817.

The meeting-house of stock brick with a hipped slate roof is four bays in length with a SW front of three bays and a central porch; the windows have round-arched heads and hung sashes. The interior comprises two rooms separated by a passage between movable screens and with outer doorways in the side walls. The principal meeting-room at the NE end has a flat plaster ceiling with coved borders. The original early 19th-century stand and wall benches remain.

Sculpture: attached to side of porch, fragment of late 18th-century churchyard monument with cherubs' heads below celestial crown, reused as small ledger stone.

Beck and Ball (1869) 285–6. Butler (1999) 425–7. Jarvis (1953) 49–54. Trott, C., *The Story of Uxbridge Quakers from 1658* (1970). VCH *Middlesex* IV (1971) 93.

(135) Former WESLEYAN, New Windsor Street, Uxbridge (TQ 053840). Brick with gabled front and octagonal corner buttresses. Front of three bays formerly with pointed-arched windows and central doorway, dated 1847 on quatrefoil above central window. (Closed 1930. Heightened and refenestrated. Converted to Masonic hall 1952)

Jarvis (1953) 30–6. VCH *Middlesex* IV (1971) 93–4.

(136) Former BAPTIST, Money Lane, West Drayton (TQ 057794). The chapel built in 1827 and enlarged c.1839 was superseded by a new building in Swan Lane (TQ 060798) in 1924–5. It subsequently passed to industrial use but has now been converted into dwellings.

The front, which may be of the date of enlargement, is of stock brick and has two tall round-arched windows flanking a central

Providence Chapel, Uxbridge. (Demolished)

entrance covered by a later porch. A parapet with terminal blocks and a central brick panel in front carrying a small raised pediment with moulded dressings has been rebuilt in altered form.

BM XIX (1827) 576; XXXV (1843) 371–2. VCH *Middlesex* III (1962) 205. Whitley (1928) No. 136.

HOUNSLOW

(137) CONGREGATIONAL, Boston Manor Road, Brentford (TQ 176777). The church worshipping here claims to have been formed in 1694. In the early 19th century Unitarian beliefs prevailed but *c*.1850 the chapel 'passed into the possession of the Independents'. The chapel suffered severe damage by bombing in 1944 and was reinstated in 1955 to a reduced height.

The chapel, built in 1782, has walls of stock brick; the roof is covered with corrugated asbestos. The front is of three bays with a central round-arched doorway with fanlight between two matching former entrances, now blocked but with fanlights remaining. In the upper walling, now lowered, were three low rectangular windows to the gallery and a large pediment with dentil cornices, enclosing a circular window, and a brick bell-cote or ventilator at the apex added in the late 19th century. The side walls, of three bays with round-arched windows, had upper windows similar to those in front. The interior (41½ft by 31½ft), formerly galleried, retains some late 19th-century fittings. A Sunday-school alongside the chapel, of 1871 by John W. Smithies, was enlarged in 1906. (URC)

Gates and *Gate Piers*: in front of chapel, tall brick piers with moulded capping and stone pineapple finials; late 18th-century; contemporary wrought-iron gates. *Inscription*: on tablet in rebuilt front gable 'DEO|HOC|TEMPLUM|ERAT|ÆDIFICATUM |ET DEDICATUM|A.D.1782' *Monuments*: externally, reset at side of chapel (1) Robert Gray, 180[1 or 9]; (2) William Watkins, 1802, *et al.*; (3) Henry King, 1809, *et al.*;(4) William Wilson, 1809, 'many years coachman[?] to H.R.H. The Prince of Wales'; (5) Rev. Matthew Bradshaw, 1792, Mary his widow, [nd], and Jane[?] their daughter, 1790; in front of chapel inside boundary wall (6) William Prince, 1802; (7) Mrs Sarah Walmsley, 1802; (8) Jane wife of James Montgomery, 1826, table-tomb.

Hadfield (1825) 162. Mearns (1882) No. 22. VCH *Middlesex* VII (1982) 159–160.

Congregational chapel (URC), Hanworth Road, Hounslow. (138)

(138) CONGREGATIONAL, Hanworth Road, Hounslow (TQ 139756). The chapel 'rebuilt 1835' was probably designed by James Fenton of Chelmsford. The walls are of stock brick, the front has a wide pediment over three bays, the centre bay projects slightly and has an entrance between paired pilasters and a group of three arched windows above. The side walls have triplets of windows at two levels. There are slight indications of enlargement to the rear, said to be of 1864–6. (URC)

Monuments: in small burial-plot alongside include (1) [ ] Worsley, late of High Wycombe, *et al.*, early 19th-century brick table-tomb with coped stone slab; (2) Joseph Faulkner, 1839, *et al.*, low table-tomb.

Mearns (1882) No. 115.

(139) FRIENDS, Quakers' Lane, Isleworth (TQ 163768). The meeting-house built in 1785 suffered bomb damage in 1940 and the front wall has been rebuilt to the original design. The walls are of stock brick and the roof is covered with slates. The NE front is of five bays; the doorway in the penultimate bay to the left has a flat moulded canopy supported by shaped brackets; to the right is a round-arched window between two blind arched recesses.

The interior comprises a single meeting-room (25ft by 21¾ft) with entrance lobby and inner room to the SE having a gallery over with shutters opening to the main room and an attic above. The staircase has at its upper level a late 18th-century balustrade with turned newels. Early 19th-century cloakrooms, now altered, flanked a small courtyard to the SE; an additional room was built on the SW side in 1957. The roof is supported by three king-post trusses.

Congregational chapel, Boston Manor Road. In 1945. (137)

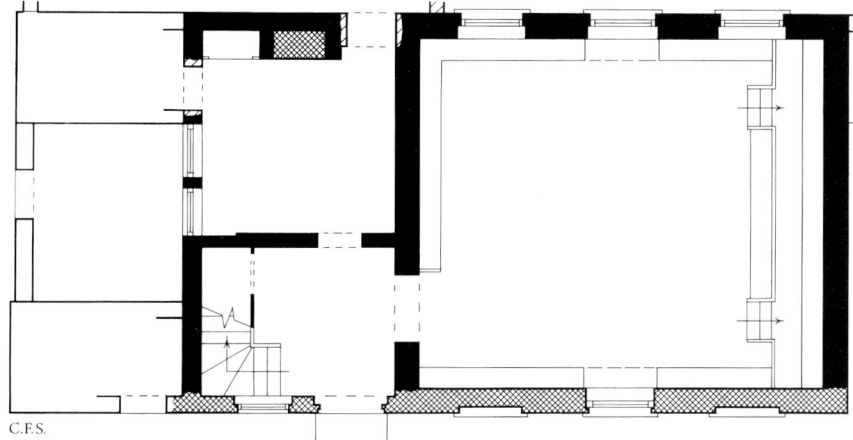
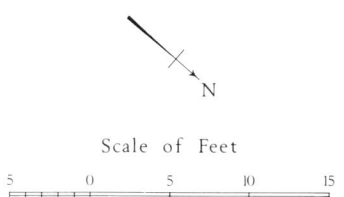

Friends' Meeting-house, Quakers' Lane, Isleworth
HOUNSLOW
Greater London

Friends' meeting-house, Isleworth. (139)

Inscription: on lintel of SE doorway '21 4 M⁰ 1785'. *Monument*: in burial-ground, to Benjamin and Sarah Angell 'the donors of this ground' and other early Friends interred between 1787 and 1872. *Seating*: open-backed benches with cast-iron supports, late 19th-century.

Beck and Ball (1869) 286–7. Butler (1999) 376–7. Wilding, J. (ed.), *Brentford & Isleworth Friends Meeting House, 1785–1985* (1985).

(140) WESLEYAN, Bell Road, Hounslow (TQ 137755). The chapel dated 1879 is of brick with a stuccoed front of three bays with rusticated corner pilasters. The central bay is pedimented and has a porch with paired Roman Doric columns and a large round-arched window above.

ISLINGTON

(141) Former BAPTIST, Camden Road (TQ 300853). The chapel was built in 1853–4 for the Baptist Metropolitan Chapel Building Society. It was designed in a late Gothic style by C.G. Searle and is faced in Kentish rag with ashlar dressings. The front is gabled and flanked by octagonal staircase towers originally carrying spires. Above the ogee-canopied central entrance is a traceried window of six lights. The chapel was converted for use as a hostel in 1989–90 but the church continues to meet in the former 'Lecture and School Rooms' of 1858 at the rear.

Temple (1992) No. 58. Whitley (1928) No. 274.

(142) BAPTIST, King's Cross Road (TQ 308829). 'Vernon Chapel' was built in 1843–4 for a church of complex ancestry (Whitley (1928) No. 36) then meeting in Fetter Lane in the City of London. It was reopened by the present church in 1861. The chapel is of brick with a front of three bays separated by buttresses surmounted by obelisk finials; in the gabled centre bay is an uncusped traceried window. Above the entrances in the side bays are blind windows.

Temple (1992) No. 14. Whitley (1928) Nos 36, 105a, 332.

(143) Former BAPTIST, Moreland Street, formerly Charles Street (TQ 319828). Built 1868–9 by Finch Hill & Paraire as 'Spencer Place Chapel' for Baptists formerly meeting in Goswell Road. Brick with round-arched windows and tower above entrance; much altered and reduced in height 1958. (Now an office)

Temple (1992) No. 11. Whitley (1928) No. 105a.

(144) Former CONGREGATIONAL, Junction Road (TQ 292864). The chapel built in 1867 for a newly formed congregation was designed by W.F. Poulton. It is faced with Kentish rag with Bath stone dressings. The plan comprised a wide preaching nave with polygonal transepts and chancel and was intended to have a corner tower and tall spire, of which only the base was built. The front is gabled and has two porches with traceried windows above. (Now Hindu cultural centre)

Mearns (1882) No. 113. Temple (1992) No. 74.

(145) WHITEFIELD TABERNACLE, Tabernacle Street (TQ 329824). George Whitefield erected a temporary wooden preaching-house on this site, 220 yards N of John Wesley's recently opened 'Foundery', in 1741. In 1752–3 this gave way to a large, square, galleried Calvinistic Methodist Tabernacle with pyramid roof and square central lantern. The church became Congregational and the Tabernacle was superseded in 1868–9 by the existing building

standing on one corner of the former site. Gothic, by C.G. Searle and Son, with triple-arched entrance to Leonard Street and large traceried window over. (Closed 1958; since in commercial and scholastic use)

CYB (1870) 380. Mearns (1882) No. 54. Seymour (1839) I: 198ff. Temple (1992) No. 13.

(146) Former CONGREGATIONAL, Pentonville Road (TQ 307830). The chapel of 1853–4 in the Gothic style by Henry Hodge stands on a confined site behind other buildings S of King's Cross Road. The walls are of ragstone with dressings of 'Ransome's patent siliceous stone'. (Now Welsh Congregational)

CYB (1856) 270–1. Mearns (1882) No. 171. Temple (1992) No. 29.

(147) HARECOURT CHAPEL, St Paul's Road (TQ 323849). The Congregational church (now URC), in existence by the late 17th century, first met in the City of London where a meeting-house and manse were built in Hare Court off Aldersgate Street *c.*1688. This was superseded in 1772 on the same site by 'a good substantial square building, of rather a small size' with a front of four bays with two tiers of round-arched windows and two pedimented doorways in the end bays. The interior was galleried around three sides and there was a cellar below which was let for storage.

When the church resolved to leave the City a chapel in St Paul's Road 'then in course of erection' by the London Congregational Chapel Building Society was purchased. The chapel, opened 1857, is in the Gothic style by W.G. and E. Habershon. The plan is octagonal with gabled wings on three sides and a pyramidal roof originally surmounted by an octagonal ventilator and spirelet. (Chapel destroyed by fire 20 December 1982)

Plate: an early set of beakers and plates engraved with the arms of donors is unlocated.

CYB (1856) 262–3. Marsh, J.B., *The Story of Harecourt* (1871). Mearns (1882) No. 123. Temple (1992) No. 34 and pp. 129–30. Wilson III (1810) 277–303.

(148) Former INDEPENDENT, Rawstorne Street (TQ 317829). Built 1828, closed by 1837 and subsequently much altered. Brick with three-bay front and central entrance.

Temple (1992) No. 12.

(149) Former CONGREGATIONAL, Tollington Park (TQ 309871). The church which met here until *c.*1959 originated in the late 17th century under Daniel Burgess, building a chapel in New Court, Carey Street (Westminster), in 1705. In 1865 the chapel was purchased compulsorily for the erection of the Law Courts. The new chapel, not completed until 1871, was designed by C.G. Searle, a deacon of the church. It is a large Classical building of brick with stone dressings with a tetrastyle portico of giant Corinthian columns and ornate pediment, fronting a façade of five bays with three doorways each with a segmental pediment.

Former Congregational chapel, Upper Street. (150)

Union Chapel, Islington. (151)

The interior, which remains largely intact, has a gallery around three sides, rounded to the rear. There are basement rooms below.

The chapel was sold in 1959 and the church removed to other premises but disbanded in 1976. (Now RC Church of St Mellitus)

B.Hbk (1871) 257–8. *CYB* (1871) 413; (1872) 405. Mearns (1882) No. 215. Temple (1992) No. 47. Wilson III (1810) 492–545.

(150) Former CONGREGATIONAL, Upper Street (TQ 317838). The first chapel in this location was built in 1814–15 for a church previously meeting in Church Street (Gaskin Street). As a result of proposed street improvements the site was compulsorily purchased and the present building erected in 1888. This is a large structure of brick in the Queen Anne style by Bonella and Paull, in which the chapel is raised above a basement school-room. The street frontage is gabled and has a tall bay window at the apex. (Closed 1979 and converted to offices)

The Building News (20 December 1889). Dixon, L.D., *Seven Score Years and Ten: The Story of Islington Chapel during One Hundred and Fifty Years, 1788–1938* (1938). Mearns (1882) No. 127. Temple (1992) No. 35.

(151) UNION CHAPEL, Compton Terrace (TQ 317846). The 'Evangelical Union Church', Congregational since 1847, originated in 1799 in non-denominational evangelical meetings held in a former chapel in Highbury Grove (163). The present site was acquired in 1806; the first chapel, which had a Classical front of five bays with a three-bay pediment and cupola, was re-fronted in 1861 with a portico of six giant Ionic columns.

The existing chapel, which replaced the earlier buildings in 1876–7, was made necessary by the continued increase in congregations during the pastorate of the Rev. Dr Henry Allon (1843–92). The chapel is a large structure of red brick with stone dressings and a tiled roof. It was designed in the Gothic style by James Cubitt and is an exemplar of his published views on the planning of buildings for congregational worship. The W front is dominated by a tall and substantial tower above the entrance, completed in 1889. The body of the chapel is square with stone piers supporting an octagonal wooden ceiling and galleries set back behind the arched bays. The pulpit is on the E side with the organ in a bay behind, concealed behind a screen. Behind the chapel is a large Sunday-school and lecture hall.

Union Chapel, Islington. (151)

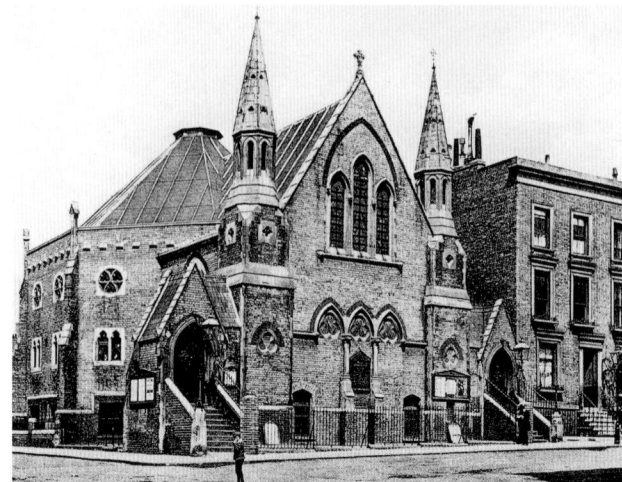

Former Congregational chapel, Offord Road. (152)

Fittings – *Lighting*: remains of extensive ring of gas jets around walls. *Organ*: by Henry Willis. *Pulpit*: octagonal, of stone with panels and enrichment of alabaster, green marble and onyx.

Anon., *Union Chapel, The Story of A Hundred Years* (1899). *CYB* (1876) 447–8. Cubitt, J., *Church Design for Congregations* (1870). Mearns (1882) No. 126. Temple (1992) No. 19.

(152) Former CONGREGATIONAL, Offord Road (TQ 308843). The chapel, built 1856–7 for seceders from Caledonian Road chapel, was designed in the Gothic style by Lander and Bedells. The walls are of brick with stone dressings; the gabled front is flanked by turrets, formerly capped by octagonal spirelets, and gabled entrances of which only one remains. The body of the chapel behind is octagonal with a pyramidal roof having a concealed lantern at the apex. The interior, which was galleried and has a school-room below, has been subdivided. Since 1919, when the church amalgamated with Union Chapel, the chapel has been in commercial use.

CYB (1857) 239–40. Mearns (1882) No. 124. Temple (1992) No. 28.

(153) CLAREMONT CHAPEL, Pentonville Road (TQ 313832). The former Congregational chapel was built in 1819 with the support of Thomas Wilson; in 1902 it became the Central London Mission, but in the 1960s it passed into secular use. It is now occupied by the Crafts Council. The walls are of brick and the front was rendered in stucco and embellished *c*.1860. The front is of three bays, the centre bay is brought forward and carries a pediment; the principal entrance has an original open porch supported by pairs of Ionic columns. Interior subdivided.

Inscription: stone in external W wall of chapel '[ ] IN WESTWARD OF THIS WALL BELONGS TO T. W. 1819'. *Railings* and *Gate Piers*: adjacent to road, cast-iron with Classical decoration to piers, 1819.

Mearns (1882) No. 172. *RIBA Journal* (November 1991) 52–4. Temple (1992) No. 31.

(154) WOODBRIDGE CHAPEL, Hayward's Place, Clerkenwell (TQ 31638227). The chapel standing on part of an estate earlier left for the support of almshouses in Woodbridge, Suffolk, was built in 1832–3 for a Calvinistic Independent congregation, possibly one under the ministry of John Latchford, which formerly met in Bartholomew Close (Non-parochial registers). The building was transferred in 1894 to John Groom for use as a mission hall. It is now used by a medical mission, which continues to hold services.

The walls are of brick with two tiers of windows above a basement. The front is of four bays with a wide central entrance between paired pilasters. The interior, refitted in the late 19th century and now ceiled at gallery level, has a flat plaster ceiling above and a gallery on three sides rounded at one end. The gallery has an open iron balustrade. Below the chapel is a former storage cellar with access gates remaining in the railings on the E side.

Monument: in chapel, to John Alfred Groom, 1919, pastor 52 years, founder of the Crippelage, London, and Orphanage, Clacton-on-Sea. *Notice Boards*: on front wall, two plaster panels with moulded surrounds. *Railings*: externally on S and E sides, *c*.1833.

Temple (1992) No. 9. Wilson III (1810) 388.

(155) Former CALVINISTIC METHODIST, Chadwell Street (TQ 314829). 'Providence Chapel' built in 1823–4 swiftly passed in 1827 to a succession of other occupants (see (156)) until in 1853 it was taken by the present Strict Baptist church and renamed 'Mount Zion'. The front, set between two houses, is rendered in stucco. It is of four bays with a two-bay pedimented centre and two doorways behind a tetrastyle Ionic portico; the upper windows have round-arched heads.

Black (1906) 246–8. Temple (1992) No. 3. Whitley (1928) No. 247.

Former Northampton Tabernacle, Amwell Street.   (156)

(156) Former NORTHAMPTON TABERNACLE, Amwell Street (TQ 312827). The chapel was built in 1835 by John Blyth for seceders from the Countess of Huntingdon's Spa Fields Chapel, who first met in Providence Chapel, Chadwell Street (see (155)). It closed in 1847 and was converted for a Roman Catholic mission (now Church of SS Peter and Paul). Elaborate brick front of three bays with rendered dressings; central entrance between Ionic pilasters with full Venetian window over. The interior retains much of its original gallery on three sides, slightly reduced in length, and supported by cast-iron columns.

Temple (1992) No. 1.

(157) WESLEY'S CHAPEL, City Road (TQ 328823). The first Methodist preaching-house in Moorfields was opened in 1739 and fashioned out of the ruins of a derelict foundry. 'The Foundery' stood on the E side of Windmill Street, now Tabernacle Street, about 100 yards S of Wesley's Chapel. By 1775 growing needs, dilapidation and street improvements made the provision of a new chapel imperative, the site immediately opposite Bunhill Fields burial-ground (164) was acquired, and the chapel built in 1777–8 to a design which can be ascribed to no single architect although the names of George Dance, James Peacock, and others who may have had some involvement have been suggested.

The chapel, originally intended to lie behind a continuous terrace of housing (including Wesley's house) fronting City Road but which was never completed, is a large building of brick with minimal stone dressings and a hipped slate roof. The W front is five bays in width with a three-bay pedimented centre and two tiers of round-arched windows. The central doorway was originally flanked by pilasters supporting a segmental pediment, replaced in the early 19th century by the present portico with paired Greek Doric columns and entablature. Other alterations to the front, many dating from 1891, include a rebuilding of the brick parapet, a continuation in stone of the frieze of the central pediment, replacement of the window frames, and the imposition on the façade of brick quoins and other rustication. At the E end is an apse of stone with three round-arched upper windows below a fluted frieze.

The interior (83ft by 58ft) is designed in accordance with the plan of contemporary Georgian parish churches, with a communion apse at the E end and pulpit centrally in front. The space is not subdivided but a gallery around three sides is supported by columns, originally of wood (reset against the W wall) but replaced by jasper in the major alterations of 1891. The plaster ceiling is elaborately decorated, replicating the original which was destroyed in a fire in 1879. Below the chapel is an extensive crypt now converted to a 'Museum of Methodism'.

Fittings – *Communion Table*: concealed within modern boxing. *Glass*: stained glass of c.1888 in apse, and elsewhere later, by various artists including in S wall a memorial window of 1901 by A.O. Hemming to the architect W.W. Pocock, d.1899. *Monuments*: in chapel, numerous wall monuments of the late 19th century. In crypt, some monuments affixed to walls and many headstones worn and relaid flat as paving; in SW corner seven private burial vaults with panelled cast-iron doors, one with oval plaque to Mrs Sarah Mortimer, 1838. Externally, in burial-ground E of chapel, monument surmounted by obelisk and urn marking grave of John Wesley, 1791, and other ministers. *Pulpit*: originally of three tiers but reduced to two in 1864; gift of Mr Andrews of Hertford.

Wesley's Chapel, City Road, Islington.

Wesley's Chapel, City Road, Islington. (157)

Reredos: in apse, tripartite with pedimented centre, panels (altered) inscribed with Lord's Prayer, Creed and Decalogue.

AMST 38 (1994) 15–29. Dolbey (1964) 45–52. McMurray, N., *The Stained Glass of Wesley's Chapel* (1988). Stevenson, G.J., *City Road Chapel, London, and its Associations* (1872). Temple (1992) No. 4. Woodward, M., *One at London: Some Account of Mr Wesley's Chapel and London House* (1966).

(158) PRIMITIVE METHODIST, Caledonian Road (TQ 306847). Yellow brick with red brick dressings; 1870 by T. and W. Stone.
Temple (1992) No. 57.

(159) UNITARIAN, Upper Street (TQ 317841). The formerly Presbyterian congregation originated in the late 17th century in the City of London, meeting successively at Rutland House, Meeting-house Court, and finally on the S side of Little Carter Lane, just S of St Paul's Cathedral, where a meeting-house was built in 1733–4 to designs by George Sampson. The society erected a new Gothic chapel, 'Unity Church', by T. Chatfeild-Clarke in Upper Street, Islington, in 1860–2 which was destroyed in 1940. A small chapel was built on the rear part of the site in 1958. *Plate*: includes four two-handled cups of 1766, inscribed as the property of the congregation in Carter Lane, also four plates of 1720, given by Samuel Palmer to the Dissenting congregation in the Old Jewry in 1733.

Evans (1897) 148–9. Temple (1992) No. 36 and p. 131. Titford, C., *History of Unity Church, Islington, London* (1912). Wilson II (1808) 105–64, 172.

(160) Former SANDEMANIAN, 18a Furlong Road (TQ 313849). Rusticated stucco front with two round-arched windows at front and central porch. Built *c.*1886. Interior subdivided. (Closed 1947; now Conservative club 'Lesson Hall')
Temple (1992) No. 24.

(161) Former SANDEMANIAN, No. 3 Highbury Crescent (TQ 316848). Brick, of two storeys with basement, possibly a conversion but with tall windows to first-floor meeting-room, for a church meeting until 1901 in a chapel of 1862 in Barnsbury Grove. (In minimal use 1983, closed before 1988)
Temple (1992) p. 116.

(162) Former NEW CHURCH, Camden Road (TQ 303856). The chapel was built in 1873 for a 'Swedenborgian' Society previously meeting in Cross Street, Hatton Garden. It is a large building in the Gothic style by Edward C. Gosling comprising an aisled nave with transepts, apsidal chancel and a tall corner tower and spire. The walls are faced with Kentish rag with ashlar dressings. The apex of the spire has been removed. The society moved to High Barnet in 1954. (Now an arts centre)
Hindmarsh (1861) 169–74. Temple (1992) No. 59.

Former New Church, Camden Road. (162)

(163) Former UNITARIAN, 18 Highbury Grove (TQ 320851). A small chapel built *c.*1793 by the Rev. Hugh Worthington was closed in 1796 but reopened in 1799 by the founders of Union Chapel (151). In 1806 it was much altered or partly rebuilt on conversion to a house. Classical stucco front of three storeys set back between adjoining houses, one now demolished.

Anon., *Union Chapel, The Story of a Hundred Years* (1899), 8. Temple (1992) No. 49.

(164) BUNHILL FIELDS BURIAL-GROUND, City Road (TQ 327823). Land at Bunhill Fields was enclosed in 1665 by the lessees, the Corporation of London, for use as a burial-ground under the management of Henry Tyndall. The ground, not being episcopally consecrated, became much used by the then large number of nonconformist churches in the City, many of whose ministers and

others were commemorated on the monuments with which it was once filled. *Monuments*: many headstones, table-tombs and other monuments remain in the S half of the ground but the N sector has been largely despoiled of memorials. Many inscriptions are barely legible but some earlier transcriptions have been published. Monuments include John Bunyan, 1688, renewed 1862, Dr Daniel Williams, 1716, Susanna Wesley, 1742, Dr John Gill, 1771, Dr John Rippon, 1836, and many more. The burial-ground was closed in 1853.

CYB (1870) 427–8. Jones, J.A., *Bunhill Memorials* (1849). Light, A.W., *Bunhill Fields* (2 vols, 1915, 1933). RCHM *London*. Vol. II *West London* (1925) 19, Finsbury monument (3).

(165) FRIENDS BURIAL-GROUND, Bunhill Fields (TQ 325823). The ground lying W of the foregoing was first acquired in 1661 and subsequently enlarged. The present extent only comprises the E portion of the former site. The only monument is a small late 19th-century headstone to George Fox, the founder of the Society of Friends, 1690, the location of whose grave is unknown. A small memorial hall built in 1881 at the N end of the ground was destroyed by bombing *c.*1940 but the caretaker's house remains.

Beck and Ball (1869) 329–34. Butler (1999) 380. Edwards, G.W., *The Quaker Burial Ground, Bunhill Fields, London* (pamphlet, *c.*1950). Temple (1992) No. 2.

KENSINGTON AND CHELSEA

(166) BETHESDA CHAPEL, Kensington Place (TQ 253804). Modest chapel of 1824, occupied as 'Silver Street Chapel' by various Baptist congregations and since *c.*1886 by a Strict Baptist church formed in 1866. Stock brick with rendered front; central round-arched doorway with fanlight, covered by later porch. Interior, refitted late 19th century, now horizontally divided.

Survey of London XXXVII, *Northern Kensington* (1973) 86. Whitley (1928) Nos. 127, 410.

(167) Former CONGREGATIONAL, Kensington Park Road (TQ 251806). 'Horbury Chapel', of 1848–9 by John Tarring, was built to relieve overcrowding in a chapel in Hornton Street. Ragstone-faced Gothic having two towers with short spires flanking the gabled front; broad nave with transepts and altered galleries. (Closed 1935 and renamed 'Kensington Temple' by Elim Pentecostal church)

CYB (1849) 215. Horne, C. Silvester, *A Century of Christian Service: Kensington Congregational Church 1793–1893* (1893) 89–93. Mearns (1882) 162. Survey of London XXXVII, *Northern Kensington* (1973) 247–9.

(168) CONGREGATIONAL, Allen Street, Kensington (TQ 253794). Large chapel built 1854–5 for a church (now URC) which originated in 1793 and previously met in a chapel in Hornton Street. Grand Classical design in stone by Andrew Trimen with pedimented portico supported by giant Corinthian columns above a rusticated base. Very wide interior with galleries supported by thin cast-iron columns with leaf capitals. Centre bay of ceiling slightly raised for ventilation.

Fittings – The upper part of the elaborate mahogany pulpit and the choir seats remain but re-sited; the pulpit was originally central. *Organ*: by Father Willis.

CYB (1856) 261. Horne (1893) op. cit. Mearns (1882) No. 130.

(169) TALBOT TABERNACLE, Talbot Road (TQ 249813). Built 1887 on an enclosed site for a Baptist, later Independent Evangelical, congregation. Romanesque style in red brick and terracotta, by W.G. Habershon and Fawkner, with rounded front to S. (Under conversion 1997 to community arts centre)

Survey of London XXXVII, *Northern Kensington* (1973) 330. Whitley (1928) No. 544.

(170) WELSH CONGREGATIONAL, Radnor Walk (TQ 274782). Stuccoed front with pilasters to centre bay and lunette windows adjacent. Built *c.*1880 for church formed 1859.

Mearns (1882) No. 41. Huws, I.O., *Hanes Eglwys Radnor Walk, Chelsea, Llundain, 1859–1959* (1959).

(171) CHRISTIAN SCIENCE, Sloane Terrace (TQ 280788). 'The First Church of Christ Scientist' stands on the site of a Wesleyan chapel of 1811–12 by W.F. Pocock. It was built in 1904–9 in a free Byzantine style by R. Crisholm. The broad front is of ashlar with an entrance centrally in an arcade of five bays and a row of seven

First Church of Christ Scientist, Sloane Terrace. (171)

arched windows of two lights above. At the E end is a tall clock-tower with a domed and balustraded upper stage. (Advertised for sale, February 2000)

(172) WESLEYAN, King's Road (TQ 273781). The society meeting here originated in the late 18th century; in 1790 they hired one of the dancing rooms of the former Ranelagh Gardens followed by a slaughterhouse in Lower George Street which was fitted up as a preaching-house. In 1811–12 a large chapel ('55ft by 50ft') was built in Sloane Terrace which was succeeded by a chapel in Chelsea Manor Street in 1903. This suffered bomb damage but was rebuilt in 1983; the school premises, of red brick in three storeys, remain at the corner of King's Road. *Monuments*: formerly at Sloane Terrace (1) Peter Kruse, 1857, signed 'Cusworth, Stamford Hill'; (2) Rev. John Gaulter, 1839; (3) Mrs Elizabeth Parker, 1834, recording a legacy of £100; (4) Samuel Elsdale, 1809, recording a benefaction of £500. The last three tablets are signed 'E. Hatchard, Ebury Street'.

Anon., *Methodism in Chelsea to 1963* (1963).

(173) WESLEYAN, Lancaster Road (TQ 240811). The Gothic chapel of 1879 by Alexander Lauder has walls of 'white' brick with stone dressings. The SW gabled front has a window of six lights with a buttress at the centre surmounted by the figure of an angel bearing a crown and palm branch; to the right is a tall thin buttressed spirelet and rounded staircase projections to each side.

Survey of London XXXVII, *Northern Kensington* (1973) 355.

(174) MORAVIAN, King's Road (TQ 267777). In 1750 Count Zinzendorf purchased Lindsey House, Cheyne Walk, as a residence and to serve as a focus for missionary work abroad. The house was remodelled in 1753 by Sigismund Gersdorf, the ground behind, being the former stable yard, was laid out as a burial-ground to serve the London congregation then meeting in Fetter Lane, and the stables on the N side were rebuilt as a chapel. An ambitious proposal was mooted to create a large settlement extending further to the NW, beyond the present King's Road, as well as to the NE of Lindsey House and to build a larger chapel, but the death of the Count at Herrnhut in 1760 halted any further progress and in 1774 the major part of the estate was sold. During the 19th century the chapel was leased to the parochial Park Chapel as a national school; it is now used as artists' studios and a small chapel has been formed in a NE annexe.

The former chapel, on the NW side of the burial-ground, was built or reconstructed *c.*1753 but the rear wall is buttressed and rendered and may be earlier. The walls are of brickwork and the roof is hipped and tiled, with wide eaves supported by shaped wooden brackets. The broad SE front of five bays has three segmentally arched windows between two doorways in the end bays, one greatly enlarged. The end walls each formerly had a window matching those in front. The interior (24½ft by 56ft) has been divided by partitions into three separate rooms. The roof is supported by four original queen-post trusses with wind-braces.

Moravian chapel, King's Road, Chelsea. (174)

The burial-ground is divided by paths into four sections with male burials on the SW and female on the NE side. *Monuments*: on front wall of chapel, modern tablets replacing but not replicating former monuments (1) Christian Renatus Count of Zinzendorf and Pottendorf, 1752; (2) Count Henry LV Reuss Koestritz, 1846, his wife Maria Justina, 1828, and their elder son Count Henry LXXIII Reuss Koestritz, 1855; (3) Maria Theresa wife of Rev. George Stonehouse, 1751. In burial-ground, rectangular marker stones, including (4) John Cennick, 1755, modern replacement.

[England, J.], *A Short Sketch…of the…Moravian Church…in London and District* (1889). Podmore, C. (ed.), *The Fetter Lane Moravian Congregation, London, 1742–1992* (1992). RCHM *London*. Vol. II *West London* (1925) 15, Chelsea monument (17). Survey of London IV, *Chelsea: Part II* (1913) 46; XI *Chelsea: Part IV* (The Royal Hospital) (1927) 90–8.

(175) UNITARIAN, Palace Gardens Terrace, Kensington (TQ 255805). 'Essex Church', 1886–7 by T. Chatfeild Clarke and Son, is the successor to Essex Street Chapel in the Strand, a former auction room rented in 1774, and subsequently purchased, by the Rev. Theophilus Lindsey, who in 1773 had resigned the living of Catterick, Yorkshire, on professing a conversion to Unitarian beliefs. The chapel was reconstructed in 1777–8 but entirely altered on the removal of the congregation; the site is now occupied by Essex Hall.

The new building in Kensington, built to accommodate the Essex Street congregation and one of more recent formation from Notting Hill, is of red brick with stone dressings in the Gothic style. It comprises a large preaching nave with shallow transepts, a polygonal chancel and an incomplete corner tower at the front enclosing a staircase to a rear gallery. The quality of some of the fittings is exceptional.

Fittings – *Font*: wood and brass, hexagonal, surrounded by angels with outstretched wings; cover with finial formed by a trinity of winged cherubs' heads; by Ronald Potter Jones, in memory of his mother, 1904. *Lamp*: pendent, brass with circle decorated with cherubs' heads. *Monument*: externally, polished granite and stone pillar with figure of seated boy, inscribed to commemorate the 'Originators of Sunday Schools, 1580–1780', dated 1880. *Pulpit*: octagonal, carved wood cornice, canopy enriched with winged cherubs; elaborate desk of beaten copper with vine decoration. *Reredos*: inlaid in carved wood surround with centre figure of Christ; a tablet in the floor of the chancel records that the reredos, pulpit and choir stalls were dedicated by Ronald Potter Jones in memory of his father, Charles William Jones, 1908.

(Essex Church was demolished 1978 and replaced by a smaller chapel. Most of the fittings were dispersed: lamp to Dr Williams's Library; font, choir stalls and pulpit to Rosslyn Hill Chapel, Hampstead; organ to Brighton; and communion table and chairs to Manchester College, Oxford)

Evans (1897) 150. *Nonconformist Music Magazine* IV (1891) 54. Rowe, M., *The Story of Essex Hall* (1959). Williams, R., *Essex Church in Kensington 1887–1987: History of a Unitarian Cause* (1987). Wilson III (1810) 479–91.

(176) CROSBY HALL, Chelsea (TQ 270776). Crosby Hall, rebuilt on this site in 1909–10, was part of the house of Sir John Crosby, built *c*.1466, which stood on the E side of Bishopsgate Street, close to the church of St Helens in the City of London. In the late 17th century the interior was subdivided and an upper floor, approached by an external staircase, was occupied as a meeting-house by a Presbyterian congregation which continued to meet there until 1769, when their lease expired and the society disbanded; the meeting-house was subsequently used by James Relley, the Universalist, until his death in 1778.

AMST XXVI (1982) 227–43. Clapham, A.W., and Godfrey, W.H., *Some Famous Buildings and their Story* (*c*.1912) 121–38. RCHM *London*. Vol. II *West London* (1925) 14, Chelsea monument (10). Wilson I (1808) 329–61.

KINGSTON UPON THAMES

(177) BAPTIST, Union Street (TQ 180693). Seceders from the Independent meeting opened a small meeting-house '40ft by 22ft' in 1790 which was superseded by the present chapel in 1864. Rubble with ashlar dressings, gabled W front with five-light traceried window. At the NW corner is a short octagonal turret and spire.

Chambers I (1952) 67. Cleal (1908) 186. Ivimey IV (1830) 537. Whitley (1928) No. 78.

(178) STRICT BAPTIST, Cowleaze Road (TQ 183697). 'Providence Chapel' was built 1845 for seceders from the foregoing. Stock brick with three-bay gabled front; extended by one bay to the rear.

Chambers I (1952) 68. Whitley (1928) No. 197.

(179) CONGREGATIONAL, Eden Street (TQ 180691). A Presbyterian society emerged in the years following the ejection in 1662 of the vicar, Richard Mayo. Out of this an orthodox Independent church arose in 1775, probably as a result of theological differences, and the original society ceased to meet after 1806. The Independents first met in a house in Brick Lane and built the first chapel on the present site in 1803.

The chapel, rebuilt in 1856, is a Classical building by Barnett and Birch. The walls are of stock brick with Portland cement dressings. The front is of three principal bays with giant pilasters supporting a Doric entablature and pediment; in each bay is a round-arched doorway with a window over; flanking bays with rusticated quoins, blind at the front, accommodate the gallery staircases which have separate entrances in the return walls. The interior has a coffered ceiling and an original horseshoe-shaped gallery extending only half the length on each side. The ground floor slopes down gently towards the pulpit. In the vestibule is a *brass* of 1912 commemorating the Rev. Richard Mayo. (URC) (Interior reported altered and gallery removed since 1975)

Cleal (1908) 181–91. *CYB* (1857) 254–5. Mearns (1882) No. 140. Sturney, A.C., *270 Years, The Story of Kingston Congregational Church* (1932). Sturney, A.C., *The Story of Kingston Congregational Church* (1955).

(180) Former CONGREGATIONAL, Maple Road, Surbiton (TQ 179677). The chapel of 1854, by James Wilson of Bath, has walls of stock brick with some stone dressings in the Romanesque style. The front is gabled between two short square towers with a strongly battered second stage. The chapel was superseded in 1865 by a larger one to the NE by A.J. Phelps. (Later chapel now demolished. The earlier building survives in commercial use)

Cleal (1908) 300–5. *CYB* (1865) 308. Mearns (1882) No. 212.

(181) FRIENDS, Eden Street (TQ 182692). The first meeting-house built 1673 is believed to have stood at the corner of Heathen Street and Back Lane (now Eden Street and Union Street). The present meeting-house of 1773 is concealed behind a hall and caretaker's house of 1901 and 1930 on the SE side of Eden Street. The walls are of brickwork and the roof is hipped and covered with slates. The SE wall has three tall sash windows, that at the centre now altered and incorporating a doorway below.

The interior (36ft by 27ft) originally incorporated a small meeting-room with gallery over at the SW end but is now undivided. A burial-ground at the rear, acquired in 1806, has uniform headstones reset against the boundary walls.

Beck and Ball (1869) 311–15. Butler (1999) 591–3. Pulford, J.S.L., *The First Kingston Quakers* (1973).

LAMBETH

(182) BAPTIST, Coldharbour Lane (TQ 325764). 'Denmark Place Chapel' is named after a site at the junction of Coldharbour Lane and Denmark Hill. A chapel built there in 1802 was leased in 1823 to a new congregation which removed in 1825 to the present newly built chapel 150 yards S. Side galleries were added in 1832 and other 'improvements' made in 1869. The walls are of stock brick with some later rendering at the front. The NW front is of five bays with a pediment (original cornices destroyed since 1961), four pedimented doorways and three round-arched upper windows within tall arched bays.

Fullerton, W.Y., *The Church under the Hill…* (nd. c.1923). Whitley (1928) Nos. 89a, 126.

(183) BAPTIST, Courland Grove (TQ 298765). 'Zions Hill Baptist Chapel' dated 1840 is a small chapel of stock brick. The gabled front has three arched bays enclosing two tiers of windows. Recessed central porch with Ionic columns *in antis*.

Stockwell (c.1909) 60. Whitley (1928) No. 165.

(184) Former BAPTIST, 27 Belmont Close (TQ 295756). 'Garner Chapel' was built 1852–3 but precipitately sold in 1860 to the Bible Christians, the church being obliged to erect a new chapel further N in Fitzwilliam Road. It was no longer in use by 1888 and now serves in part as the Oddfellows Hall. Stock brick with three-bay pedimented front, two tiers of round-arched windows and porch dated 1852.

'Ebenezer Chapel', Fitzwilliam Road (TQ 294759) built for this congregation in 1861, is a plain building of brick with a gabled front and stepped buttresses dividing the side bays.

Paul I (1951) 61–83. Whitley (1928) No. 262.

(185) Former BAPTIST, Grafton Square (TQ 293756). The chapel was built in 1882 for a church founded in 1787 which earlier met in a chapel on the SE side of Clapham Common. The walls are of stock brick with dressings of red brick and stone and the roofs are tiled. The gabled N front is set back between two square staircase towers with pyramidal roofs and has an open balustraded porch. The chapel built to seat 900 is now used by a Pentecostal church.

Baptist Messenger (1882) 135; (1883) 25–6. Stockwell (c.1909) 52–9. Whitley (1928) No. 76.

(186) BAPTIST, South Lambeth Road (TQ 304768). The chapel built 1866 for a newly established church has walls of stock brick with rendered dressings. The E front has a pedimented portico supported by four Corinthian columns, lacking in entasis, between flanking bays. The back of the portico forms a high recessed porch with three doorways and upper windows. In 1972 the interior had a continuous round-ended gallery with an open cast-iron balustrade.

Whitley (1928) No. 412.

(187) BAPTIST, Solon Road (TQ 303753). 'Kenyon Baptist Chapel' was designed by William Higgs, Treasurer of the London Baptist Association, who died in 1883 prior to its erection. The chapel was built in his memory in 1884–5 at the expense of his family. The walls are of brickwork with a front of Yorkshire stone and terracotta dressings throughout by J. Stiff & Sons of Lambeth. The front is gabled, of three bays divided by buttresses; in the centre bay are three pointed-arched entrances with marbled columns below gablets and a large traceried upper window of five lights with Decorated tracery. The galleried interior, five bays in length, has walls of exposed polychrome brickwork and an open timber roof. *Monument*: in vestibule, to William Higgs, 1883, 22 years deacon at the Metropolitan Tabernacle.

B.Hbk (1885) 360–1. Whitley (1928) No. 654.

(188) CONGREGATIONAL, St Matthew's Road, Brixton (TQ 310749). 'Trinity Chapel', built 1828, was first served by a minister in the Countess of Huntingdon's Connexion. Various internal alterations were carried out in 1850, school-rooms extended in 1866 and the chapel refitted in 1874 and later. The walls are of stock brick. The W front of three bays with a moulded

Trinity Chapel, Brixton. (188)

cornice has a slightly recessed centre with a stuccoed porch having two Greek Doric columns *in antis*, segmental-arched lower windows and three round-arched upper windows set in arched recesses. The sides are of four bays. The interior has a gallery around three sides, rounded to the W, with an open cast-iron balustrade of the late 19th century. *Monument*: in chapel, Rev. Samuel Elridge, 1882, 42 years pastor.

Adjacent to the chapel on the S are a hall and minor rooms dated 1875.

At the end of the 19th century an abortive proposal was made to build a larger chapel on land to the E facing Effra Road. A design by George and R.P. Baines is illustrated in *CYB* (1900) 144–5, and another figures in Cleal (1908) facing 318.

Cleal (1908) 260–2. Mearns (1882) No. 25.

(189) CHRIST CHURCH, Westminster Bridge Road (TQ 312794). The Independent church meeting in Surrey Chapel, Blackfriars Road (226), on which the expiry of the lease was imminent, acquired this site at the junction of Westminster Bridge Road and Kennington Road and employed Paull and Bickerdike to design a large Gothic chapel, built 1873–6. The seating capacity was 2,500. The plan comprised an octagonal auditorium with gabled transepts, a corner tower and spire (which alone survives post-war rebuilding) and a large hall. The 'Lincoln' tower, so named in gratitude to its American benefactors, is of stone in four stages and has corner pinnacles, the spire is banded in stars and stripes. (Now jointly Baptist/URC as 'Christ Church and Upton Chapel')

Briggs (1946) 41. Cleal (1908) 217–24. *CYB* (1874) 425–7. Mearns (1882) No. 239.

(190) CONGREGATIONAL, Stockwell Green (TQ 307760). 'Stockwell New Chapel', so called to distinguish it from the earlier chapel-of-ease, was built in 1798 on the S side of Stockwell Green. The chapel was greatly enlarged and much rebuilt in the mid 19th century. The original chapel was of brick with an elongated octagonal plan; the NW side wall alone survives, of three bays with two tiers of round-arched windows, of which the lower are set in arched recesses. The reconstructed chapel of 1849–50 by James Wilson has a rendered NE front of three bays with a pediment and Ionic pilasters and a forward-projecting staircase tower to the left which since 1954 has been reduced to the general height.

The interior, widened to the SE in 1850, has a gallery around three sides with an open balustraded front of cast iron of *c*.1881 and iron columns which rise to support the roof structure. Queen-post trusses remain in the roof from the original chapel; the SE extension is separately roofed. (Chapel reported sold 1987)

Fittings – *Brasses*: (1) Rev. David Thomas, 1875, 31 years minister; (2) commemorating the marriage here on 16 June 1855 of William Booth, founder of the Salvation Army, and

Christ Church, Westminster Bridge Road, Lambeth. Interior before rebuilding.   (189)

Christ Church, Westminster Bridge Road, Lambeth.

Stockwell New Chapel, LAMBETH, Greater London

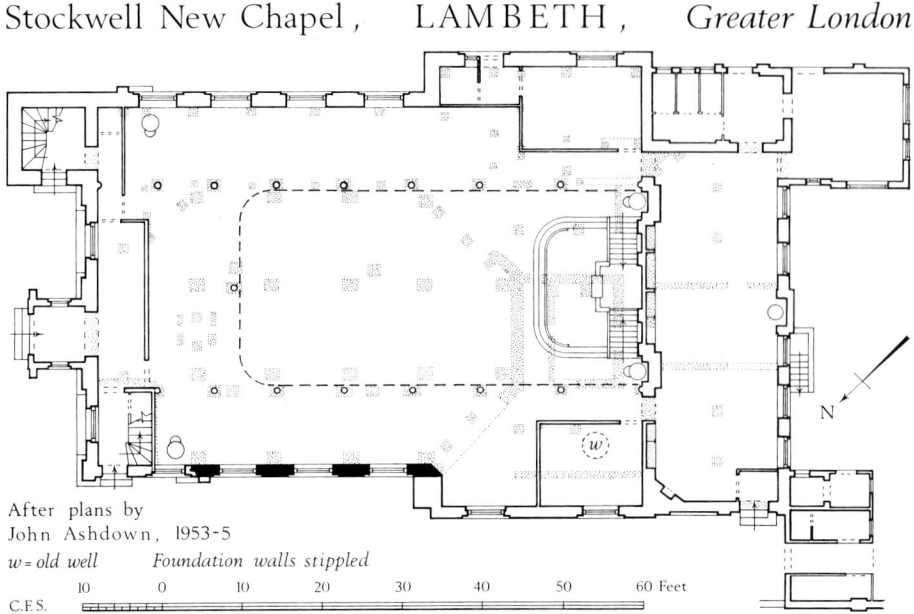

After plans by John Ashdown, 1953-5
w = old well   Foundation walls stippled
C.F.S.

Catherine Mumford, erected 1955. *Monuments*: in chapel, behind pulpit (1) Rev. Thomas Jackson, 1843, first pastor [removed before 1979]; in burial-ground reset headstones and fragments, also (2) Rev. Thomas Jackson, 1843, 43 years pastor, Jane his wife, 1825, Jane their daughter, 1855, buried in Norwood Cemetery, and William their second son, 1856, brick tomb with stone capping.

Cleal (1908) 225–33. *EM* NS XXI (1843) 273. Mearns (1882) No. 204.

(191) Former CONGREGATIONAL, Chapel Road, West Norwood (TQ 321716). Built 1820 to replace a small chapel of 1806. Brick with possibly later rendered pedimented front of three bays with paired Ionic columns to central porch. Round-arched bays in side walls enclosing two tiers of windows, later Sunday-school wing behind. (Derelict 1976, now residential)

Cleal (1908) 79–82. Mearns (1882) No. 157.

(192) CONGREGATIONAL, Streatham High Road (TQ 301711). Red brick with stone dressings. Gothic with battlemented tower; 1900–1 by James Cubitt. Sunday-school hall of 1911 adjacent. (URC)

Cleal (1908) 344–6. *CYB* (1901) 161–2.

(193) WESLEYAN, Knights Hill, West Norwood (TQ 319715). Squared rubble with gabled front, Romanesque details in round-arched front windows and side doorway. Opened 1841.

(194) UNITED METHODIST, Riggindale Road (TQ 295713). Built in 1900 by F. Wheeler & E. Speed. Red brick with stone dressings. Low gabled front with splayed double porch. Interior said to have widest fibrous plaster barrel-vaulted ceiling for its date. Former chapel to left, now hall, of *c*.1880 in Jacobean style, red brick with decorative pargeting in gable.

LEWISHAM

(195) GENERAL BAPTIST, Deptford Church Street (TQ 373775). The original General Baptist meeting in Deptford was formed before 1679. It appears to have had a chequered existence during the 18th century and may have ceased to meet regularly after 1779, causing the General Baptist Assembly in 1797 to enquire into the state of the trust. As a result of renewed interest the meeting was amalgamated with another General Baptist church of early origin which had met in Fair Street, Horsleydown and elsewhere, but which from 1781 shared a meeting-house in Worship Street, Shoreditch. The Deptford premises were repaired and reopened in 1801 by the two churches which formally united in 1804. From this period the church supported a Unitarian ministry.

The meeting-house (described as inspected in 1969) standing 60 yards E of St Paul's Church dates from *c*.1700 but has been much altered. The walls are of brickwork and the hipped roof, which has a central valley, is covered in tiles to the rear section but with slates at the front. The original building was probably a timber-framed and weather-boarded structure of traditional type; in the mid 18th century the outer walls were cased or partly rebuilt in brickwork leaving the principal posts in place and leaving undisturbed a headstone of 1711 against the S wall. In a later major repair, possibly 1801, the wall posts were replaced by brick piers cut into the earlier brickwork and the lower window openings carefully blocked.

The E front is of three bays with round-arched upper windows and a blocked window centrally below and two porches of 20th-century date incorporating original doorcases with carved wooden consoles supporting a moulded cornice. The windows and buttresses to this wall have red brick surrounds and it is possible that it may have been entirely rebuilt. The rear W wall is partly covered by a late 19th-century vestry with a lean-to roof. The exposed part of this wall at the S end has a brick platband of three courses; there is a dentil brick eaves cornice, which also continues half-way along the S side. Two upper windows remain and possible traces of a pulpit window. The N and S end walls have each two upper windows, those on the S with segmental-arched heads, and traces of lower windows distinguishable only by the blocking in English

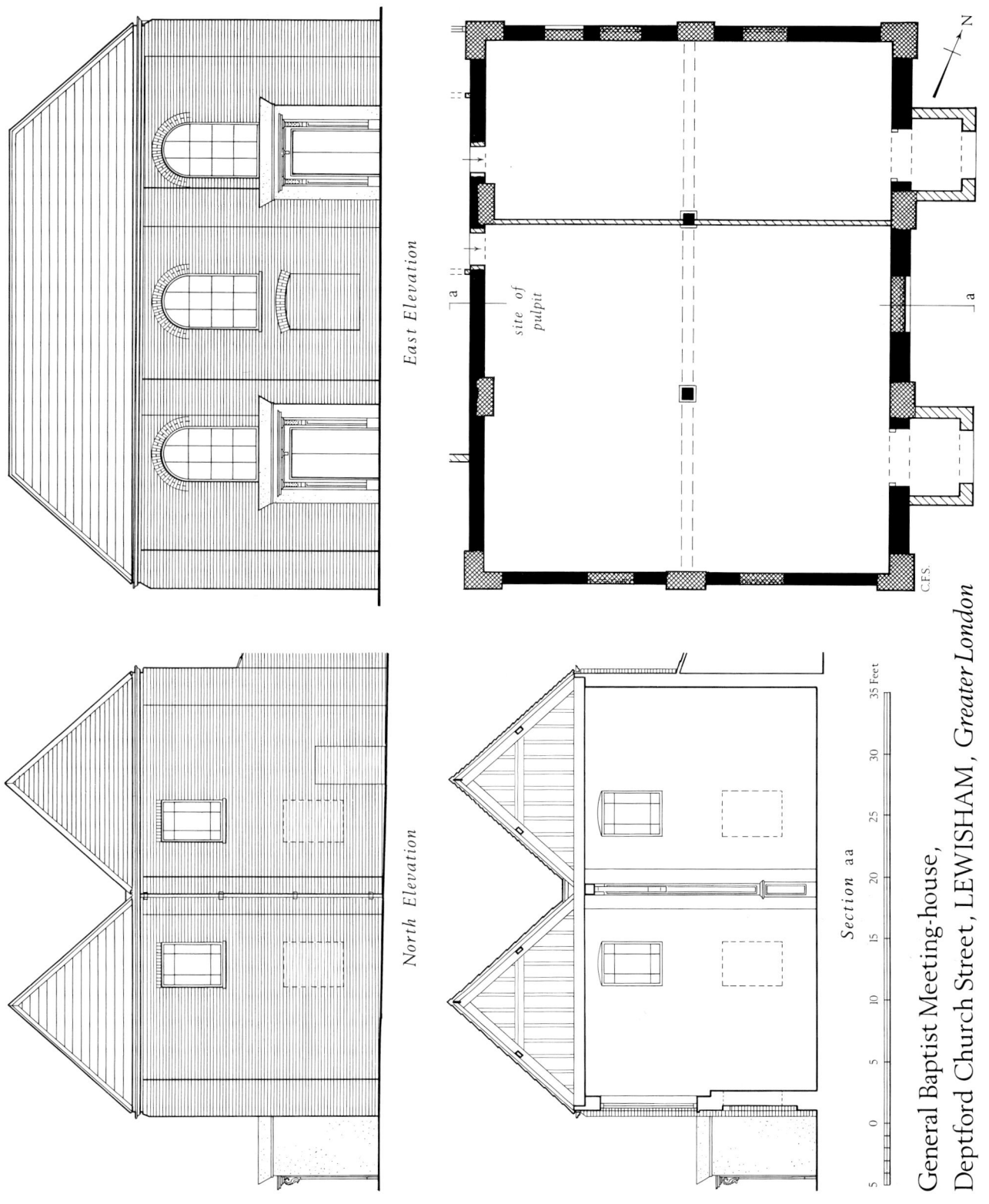

General Baptist Meeting-house, Deptford Church Street, LEWISHAM, *Greater London*

bond which contrasts with the generally Flemish bond of the main walling.

The interior (32¾ft by 43¼ft) has been subdivided leaving only the N bay available for worship; the remainder has an inserted floor and retains no fittings. No evidence remains of former galleries but it is probable that end galleries and possibly a cross gallery were once provided. The roof is supported by two tall softwood posts carrying the valley beam; each has a high panelled dado of early 18th-century character and straight upper braces with added ornamentation. (The meeting-house was derelict in 1969 following damage by fire; the site has since been entirely cleared and the area grassed over)

Monuments: in chapel at N end, on E wall (1) Sarah daughter of Samuel Brent of Blackheath, 1870; on N wall (2) Sarah Ambrosia (Croke) widow of Rev. William Moon, 1846, and their children Sarah Jane first wife of Rev. John Omer Squier (21 years pastor), 1834, Elizabeth widow of Rev. J.E. Fletcher of Crewkerne, 1871, and Charlotte first wife of Rev. T.B.W. Briggs of Dover, 1847, signed 'Yeatman & Sons, W. Norwood'; (3) Rev. Michael Castle Gascoigne, 1888, Mary Mercy Ockendon [his widow] 1895, and Fanny Alicia, their daughter, wife of Thomas Chambers, 1892; (4) Rev. Egbert A. Carlier, 1953, minister 1912–39, and his son Egbert C. Carlier, 1956, Treasurer 1939–56, Secretary of General Baptist Assembly 1947–56; on W wall (5) Robert Lloyd Jones, 1837, commander of the *Margaret West*, died at Batavia; (6) Arthur Kingsford, 1850, died Sydney, NSW, Australia, on board the ship *Francis Ridley*; (7) Rev. William Moon, 1823, pastor 'upwards of twenty years', signed 'B. Smith'; (8) William Leigh son of John Carslake of Sidmouth, died at Greenwich 1834, aged 15, signed 'J. Clark, Exeter'; externally built into S wall (9) Mary wife of Tristram Bradshaw, 1711, headstone; built into W wall at S end (10) Jane wife of John Yeomans of this town, 1730; also in burial-ground to W a few decayed table-tombs and other monuments of the 18th century and later.

Evans (1897) 144. Timpson (1859) 345–7. Whitley (1928) Nos. 2 and 28. Wilson IV (1814) 256–63.

(196) ZION CHAPEL, New Cross Road (TQ 370770). Built 1846–7 for Strict Baptist seceders from a Huntingtonian Chapel 'Ebenezer' in King Street. The chapel stands on the S side of the road, set back between a pair of houses. The front is of three bays with giant pilasters and a pediment. The interior has a gallery around four sides with an open balustraded front of cast iron. Vestries were added to the rear in 1864 by S.K. Bland; chapel re-fronted and internally refitted 1876.

Grace (November 1992) 19–21. Timpson (1859) 354–5. Whitley (1928) Nos. 177, 194.

(197) CONGREGATIONAL, Deptford High Street (TQ 373773). A meeting-house of 1702, rebuilt 1756, was superseded in 1862 by a large chapel by Francis Pouget. The church closed *c*.1969. *Plate*: includes a pair of two-handled cups of 1708, a pair of standing cups of 1715, and plates of 1703 and 1707.

CYB (1863) 341. Mearns (1882) No. 76. Timpson (1859) 347–53.

(198) PRESBYTERIAN, Brockley Road, Lewisham (TQ 367754). 'St Andrew's', Gothic of 1882 by J. McKissack & W.G. Rowan. Squared ragstone and ashlar dressings. Prominent tower and spire. (URC)

Presbyterian chapel (URC), Brockley Road. (198)

MERTON

(199) WESLEYAN, Worple Road, Raynes Park (TQ 233694). Erected 1914, in free Byzantine style by Withers and Meredith. Brick with stone dressings; octagonal plan with large lunette windows in front and side gables; domed staircase wings at front corners. Galleried interior with contemporary fittings.

NEWHAM

(200) BAPTIST, Romford Road, Forest Gate (TQ 407850). Brick with gabled front and octagonal lantern; large wheel-window above wide former entrance. Of 1881 by J.W. Chapman. Sunday-school behind, 1899.

Whitley (1928) No. 619.

(201) BAPTIST, The Crescent, Stratford (TQ 391848). Gothic chapel of grey brick and stone with tall stone pinnacles at the front corners, built *c*.1855–60. Adjacent hall dated 1861.

Whitley (1928) Nos 269, 564.

(202) BRICKFIELDS CHAPEL, Welfare Road, Stratford (TQ 393842). The church, now URC, which originated in the late 17th century as a Presbyterian society, previously occupied a meeting-house in Salway Place. In 1773–5, shortly before the lease was due to

expire, the society was reconstituted as an Independent church and in 1776, with financial assistance from John Fleming, a local benefactor, a new chapel was built on the present site.

The chapel, of rendered brickwork, has been much altered. It originally had a pedimented W front with a central pedimented doorway between two tall rectangular windows; the side walls of four bays had two tiers of windows, the upper range with round-arched heads. A small Sunday-school building was added to the rear in 1868. In a major reconstruction in 1896 the chapel was reroofed and two short staircase towers with pyramidal roofs added to flank the front entrance. In a further reconstruction in 1950–2, following wartime damage, side galleries that had been added in 1896 were removed, the side walls were lowered in height by 6ft, the windows reduced to a single tier and the roofs of the staircase towers rebuilt.

The interior has a rear gallery with late 19th-century cast-iron balustrade. No other internal fittings of interest remain. In 1986 the surrounding burial-ground was denuded of its monuments.

Bedford, D.R., *A Hope That Never Fades: The Story of … Brickfields, 1662 to 1992* (1992). Mearns (1882) 209. VCH *Essex* VI (1973) 128–9.

(203) Former CONGREGATIONAL, Sebert Road, Forest Gate (TQ 407854). The chapel of 1884 by Francis Sturdy superseded one of 1856 which stood in Chapel Street, Forest Lane (TQ 403853). Yellow stock brick with red brick and painted stone dressings. Five-bay front with gable across three bays and flanking wings, one rising to a domed octagonal turret.

[Busby, C.E.], *Hitherto Henceforth 1856–1956* (1956). CYB (1857) 231. Mearns (1882) No. 94.

(204) Former CONGREGATIONAL, Romford Road, Forest Gate (TQ 402850). Built 1883, by T. Lewis Banks. Knapped flint with red brick dressings. Gothic with corner tower and short spire. Hall at rear dated 1890.

CYB (1883) 385–6. Mearns (1882) No. 225.

(205) Former PRIMITIVE METHODIST, Upton Lane, Forest Gate (TQ 404845). Simple late 19th-century brick Gothic chapel. (Now in commercial use)

(206) UNITARIAN, West Ham Lane, Stratford (TQ 391842). Small chapel of grey brick with rusticated brick quoins and rectangular tower of three stages. Built 1869, by T. Chatfeild Clarke.

Christian Freeman (1869) 74, 75. Evans (1897) 155–6.

REDBRIDGE

(207) CONGREGATIONAL, Nightingale Lane, Wanstead (TQ 405886). The chapel, of stone in the Gothic style by John Johnson, was first erected in the Euston Road in 1856–61 as the Anglican district church of St Luke but in 1865 it was compulsorily purchased by the Midland Railway Company in connection with the building of St Pancras Station. The fabric of the building was then sold to the newly formed Congregational church in Wanstead (now URC), who re-erected it with some modifications on the present site. These reduced the length of the nave by one bay, shortened the chancel, omitted the clerestory and a spire, and reduced the size of the S porch. The front has a vestigial tower with corner buttresses and flanking gabled ends to the aisles formerly with octagonal turrets and spires at the corners. Detached hall at rear, 1896 by E.M. Whitaker.

Unitarian chapel, West Ham Lane. (206)

CYB (1867) 367–8. Mearns (1882) No. 236. Speedyman, D., *et al.*, *Wanstead United Reformed Church: 125 Years, 1865–1990* (1990).

(208) WESLEYAN, Derby Road, Woodford (TQ 400909). The chapel of 1876–7 by Charles Bell was built for seceders from the Free Methodist society (*see* (209)). Brick with stone dressings and gabled front in the Gothic style.

(209) Former FREE METHODIST, High Road, Woodford Green (TQ 401922). The first chapel on this site was built *c*.1852 for a society which had recently seceded from the Wesleyans. The chapel was rebuilt in 1869. In 1874 some members reverted to their original allegiance (*see* (208)), the remainder were joined by Congregational seceders and formed a 'Union Church' (*see* (210)). The building was converted to a Working Men's Club in 1904 following the erection of the new chapel in High Elms. The former chapel, which faces S, is of brick and has an altered tower at the SE corner originally surmounted by a square spire. A side doorway with shell hood incorporating the monogram 'WMC' was inserted at the base of the tower in 1904.

Galey, R.L., *The History of the Woodford Green United Free Church* (1968).

(210) 'FREE CHURCH', High Elms, Woodford Green (TQ 400922). A 'Union Church' with a Congregational polity was formed in 1876 of disaffected Free Methodists, seceders from a Congregational church and some Baptists. The popular novelist Joseph Hocking was minister from 1900 to 1910. In 1947 the church was reconstituted as Woodford Green United Free Church, incorporating members from Woodford Congregational church.

The chapel of 1903–4 by C. Harrison Townsend is of red brick with yellow terracotta dressings. The gabled E front has a deeply splayed arch enclosing a lunette window above a pair of entrances and at the NE corner the lower storey of an uncompleted tower. The sides have short aisles crossed by flying buttresses and shallow gabled transepts. The interior, partly faced with marble, has N and S arcades with semicircular arches and a barrel-vaulted ceiling.

Galey (1968) op. cit.; also *Transactions Woodford & District Historical Society*, Pt XIII. VCH *Essex* V (1966) 356–7.

RICHMOND UPON THAMES

(211) Former CONGREGATIONAL, Sheen Lane, Mortlake (TQ 205757). The meeting-house built in 1716 but in commercial use since 1901 was demolished *c*.1995. It stood on the E side of the road immediately S of the railway. It formerly had a brick front with corner pilasters, parapet with segmental pediment over, and a central entrance below a round-arched window.

Anon., *1662–1962: East Sheen Congregational Church* (1962). Cleal (1908) 191–201. *EM* NS XIV (1836) 406. Mearns (1882) No. 190.

(212) CONGREGATIONAL, Vernon Road, Mortlake (TQ 206756). Built 1901–2 by Howgate and Keith replacing the foregoing; brick with terracotta dressings in free Gothic style with octagonal corner turret. (URC)

CYB (1901) 160.

(213) BETHLEHEM CHAPEL, Church Terrace, Richmond (TQ 17957470). The chapel was built in 1797 by John Chapman, a market gardener formerly of Hounslow Heath and later of Petersham, for a Calvinistic Independent congregation; it was opened by William Huntington SS. Some modifications appear to have been made during the 19th century including the addition of porches, the provision of an apse at the N end and the erection of a vestry.

The walls are of yellow stock brick with some stone dressings and the broad E front is rendered in stucco; the roof is hipped and slated. The front is of three bays with semicircular arches enclosing sash windows. The principal entrance is in a porch projecting to the left of the frontage; a secondary entrance balances this to the right. The W wall, which is covered by later buildings, has no original windows but one has been added at the centre and there is a blocked doorway to the vestry. The S wall is partly covered by a roof above a paved passage from which there is a central doorway to the chapel.

The interior (29¼ft by 21¼ft) has a coved plaster ceiling which together with a shallow apse at the N end may date from the late 19th century. At the S end is a gallery of early 19th-century date with contemporary seating; it was originally supported by three turned wood columns, one of which survives; a central column has been replaced by a pair of cast-iron posts. A stair to the gallery is contrived partly within the S passage. The apse to the N probably replaces a second external passage to the vestry; it is flanked by two small vestibules one serving the vestry at the NW corner.

Inscription: above doorway in S porch 'BETHLEHEM CHAPEL BUILT IN THE YEAR 1797'. *Pulpit*: of the early 19th century, contemporary with the gallery.

(214) CONGREGATIONAL, The Vineyard, Richmond (TQ 180745). The chapel of 1830–1 by John Davies was extended to the front and otherwise enlarged in 1853 by Joseph James. The original design was in the Romanesque style with an entrance at one side. The extension in grey brick retains many of the original features with three round-arched upper windows and a small circular window in the gable but adds a small central porch. Paired arches at the end of a side annexe remain from the original design.

Bethlehem Chapel, Richmond. (213)

Congregational chapel, The Vineyard, Richmond. (214)

Cong. Mag. (February 1833) frontis. *CYB* (1854) 281–2. Mearns (1882) No. 181.

(215) PRESBYTERIAN, Little Green, Richmond (TQ 179751). Tall Gothic chapel by W. Wallace, 1884–5; of brick with stone dressings and octagonal flèche on roof; paired windows between massive buttresses in the W wall overlook the Green. (URC)

(216) UNITARIAN, Ormond Road, Richmond (TQ 179746). Gothic, 1896. Brick with yellow terracotta dressings. Five graduated lancets are enclosed by an arch in the gabled end; apse at rear.

SOUTHWARK

(217) GROVE CHAPEL, Camberwell Grove (TQ 330762). The chapel by D.R. Roper was built in 1819 for a newly formed Calvinistic Independent church under the ministry of Joseph Irons. The walls are of stock brick with some repairs following war damage, and the roof is hipped. The E front is of five bays with slightly projecting end bays and lower wings for gallery stairs added in 1839; central entrance with secondary entrances in end bays and tall round-arched upper windows.

The interior has a gallery around three sides. The pulpit was lowered in the mid 19th century but the original upper desk remains; in the wall behind is a lunette window. The roof is supported by queen-post trusses with dwarf king-post trusses across the corners to support the hips.

Grove Chapel, Camberwell Grove. (217)

Monuments: in chapel (1) Richard Pope, 1853, 25 years deacon, Sarah Bloomfield his first wife, 1834, and Caroline his second wife, 1852; (2) Thomas Bradbury, 1905, 31 years pastor; (3) Rev. James Jay, 1875, 21 years pastor; (4) Rev. Joseph Irons, 1852, 33 years pastor, Mary Ann his first wife, 1828, Mary Ann their eldest daughter, 1833, and Lucy his second wife, 1862; (5) Samuel Carter, 1827, 'one of the twelve who first united here' and who 'laid the foundation stone of this chapel March the 15th 1819'.

Cleal (1908) 111–13. Lock, J., *The History of Grove Chapel, Camberwell* (1919).

(218) Former CONGREGATIONAL, Wren Road, Camberwell Green (TQ 327767). The chapel built 1852–3 to supersede the 'Mansion House Chapel' is in the Gothic style, with a gabled front dominated by two octagonal staircase towers and stone turrets with truncated spires. Galleried interior. (Latterly in commercial use. Demolished before 1997)

Monuments: in chapel (1) Rev. John Burnet, 1862, 32 years minister; (2) Stephen Westbrook, 1897.

Cleal (1908) 63–7. Mearns (1882) No. 32.

(219) Former CONGREGATIONAL, Barry Road, Dulwich (TG 340740). Large Gothic ragstone chapel with prominently sited corner tower and spire, by W.D. Church. Built 1890–1. (Converted to hospice *c.*1986) Adjacent Sunday-school, now chapel, used by joint URC/Methodist church.

Cleal (1908) 166–70. *CYB* (1890) 215–16. Mearns (1882) No. 77.

(220) Former BURIAL-GROUNDS, Long Lane, Bermondsey (TQ 332794). Quakers meeting in Horsleydown, whose meeting-house stood at the NE end of Horsleydown Fair Street, acquired a site in Bermondsey, ⅜ mile S, in 1697 for use as a burial-ground. This was closed in 1854 except for the reburial in 1860 of remains from a former Friends burial-ground in Worcester Street, Southwark. In 1895 it was converted into a public garden; it is now a playground. Adjacent to it on the E was a smaller nonconformist burial-ground of another denomination, possibly of mid 18th-century origin, but now conjoined to the former.

Inscriptions: In S wall of Friends burial-ground (1) recording dates of purchase and closure, erected by Six Weeks Meeting, 1895; (2) recording erection of boundary wall, 1789; in S wall of former burial-ground to E (3) 'This Wall being 29 feet and 3 inches in length is the Property of and was built by Iohn Savidge 1749 & 1750'.

Monuments: in E burial-ground only, of the late 18th and early 19th century, including (1) Elizabeth wife of William Peacock, fellmonger, 1834, headstone; (2) vault of William James and Edward Pierse, 1837, reset capstone.

Beck and Ball (1869) 216–23, 236–8. Butler (1999) 406, 436. White (1971) 57.

Baptist chapel, Rye Lane, Peckham. (222)

(221) Former FRIENDS, Highshore Road, Peckham (TQ 341765). The meeting-house opened in 1826 was extended to the rear in 1843–4. The walls are of stock brick and the roof slated. The front, set back between contemporary wings, is of three bays with a pediment, three upper windows and an open loggia covering a central entrance; the wings are of two storeys with retiring rooms below caretaker's accommodation and an upper classroom. The meeting-house is undivided. (Sold 1962, subsequently in Post Office use)

Beck and Ball (1869) 224–5. Butler (1999) 410–11. Lidbetter (1961) Fig. 7. White (1971) 96–7.

(222) BAPTIST, Rye Lane, Peckham (TQ 342765). The chapel of 1863 by S.K. Bland was built to replace a chapel demolished for railway construction. The walls are of stock brick, the front is of three bays with corner pilasters and a central pediment, dated 'MDCCCLXIII', supported by giant freestanding Tuscan columns. Memorial stones below the columns commemorate 'the Old Baptist Chapel erected 1819' and the 'New Baptist Chapel erected 1858' [*sic*].

Stockwell (*c*.1909) 161–9. Whitley (1928) No. 113.

(223) METROPOLITAN TABERNACLE, Newington Butts (TQ 319789). The Tabernacle was first built in 1859–61 for the rapidly growing Baptist church formerly meeting in New Park Street under the pastorate of C.H. Spurgeon. The original building seating 4,908 was by W.W. Pocock in a grand Classical style with cast-iron arcades supporting double galleries; it was intended to have domed towers at each corner, but these were omitted in the finished work. The Tabernacle was destroyed by fire in April 1898 except for the portico and outer walls, which were incorporated into a new building designed by Searle and Hayes. This closely followed the former although reducing it slightly in length. The new building was destroyed by bombing in *c*.1942 and entirely rebuilt in 1959, incorporating only the grand pedimented portico of six giant Corinthian columns. The former side bays, which housed the gallery staircases, have been replaced by wings of three bays which conceal the utilitarian post-war structure lying behind.

B.Hbk (1901) 356–7. Hayden, E.W., *A Centennial History of Spurgeon's Tabernacle* (1962). Pike, G.H., *The Metropolitan Tabernacle...* (1870). Spurgeon, Mrs C.H., *et al.*, (eds), *C.H. Spurgeon's Autobiography* II (1899) 311–33. Whitley (1928) No. 44.

(224) CONGREGATIONAL, Great Dover Street (TQ 327793). 'The Church of the Pilgrim Fathers', claiming a tenuous descent from societies formed in the 17th century or before and having links with a church meeting in Zoar Chapel, Zoar Street, and elsewhere, built a chapel in New Kent Road in 1864. This was destroyed by

Metropolitan Tabernacle, Newington Butts. In 1911. (223)

bombing in 1939–45 and replaced in 1957 by a modest multi-purpose building at the corner of Great Dover Street and Spurgeon Street.

Fittings – *Plate*: includes four beakers, one of 1691 and three replicas of 1766, 1769 and 1772, and two plates of 1788. *Pulpit*: from Zoar Chapel, now in the Bunyan Museum, Bedford.

CHST III (1907–8) 153–4. Cleal (1908) 1–16. Mearns (1882) No. 195. Wilson IV (1814) 188–90.

(225) Former UNITARIAN, Stamford Street (TQ 314803). Two Presbyterian societies, both of which originated in the late 17th century but had accepted a Unitarian theology by the early 19th century, united in 1823 erecting a new chapel on the S side of Stamford Street. One of the constituents met first in Tothill Street, Westminster, moving during the pastorate of Dr Calamy to a new meeting-house in Long Ditch or Princes Street near Westminster Abbey, replaced by a smaller building in the late 18th century which closed in 1818. The second society first met near the Maze in Southwark, moving in 1703 to a meeting-house in St Thomas's Street. The new chapel, opened 12 October 1823 and possibly to be ascribed to John Rennie, was demolished in 1964 with the exception of the surviving wide pedimented hexastyle portico in the Greek Doric style fronting the street. There were originally two doorways within the portico with windows between.

Evans (1897) 141–3. *Monthly Repository* XVIII (1823) 419, 556, 607, 631. Wilson IV (1814) 57–118, 294–319.

Former Unitarian chapel, Stamford Street. (225)

(226) SURREY CHAPEL, Blackfriars Road (TQ 317800). The chapel built in 1782–3 in Surrey Street, later Blackfriars Road, was destroyed by bombing *c*.1940–2. It was built for the Rev. Rowland Hill, whose evangelical preaching and liturgical services attracted a considerable following. After his death in 1833 he was followed by the Rev. James Sherman of St Mary's Chapel, Reading, Berks. (*see Nonconformist Chapels and Meeting-houses in South-West England* (1991) 14–15, monument (49)), under whom the society became more specifically Congregational. With the approach of the termination of the lease of the site the church erected Christ Church, Westminster Bridge Road (*see* (189)) opened in 1876. For the remainder of the lease until 1883 the chapel was occupied by Primitive Methodists, who then built another chapel near by retaining for it the name 'Surrey Chapel'. The former building then passed into commercial use and subsequently became a boxing stadium.

The original Surrey Chapel was a polygonal sixteen-sided building of brick. The outer walls had two tiers of windows with a platband between and a moulded cornice and parapet. The principal entrance was on the W with a porch, Venetian window over and a pediment above; gallery staircases abutted the N and S sides. The interior had a continuous octagonal arcade around the gallery front supporting a polygonal lantern over the centre space and a flat ceiling above the gallery.

Cleal (1908) 217–24. Davies, C.M., *Unorthodox London* (2nd ed. 1876) 130–5. Edwards, F.G., 'A Celebrated Nonconformist Organist: Benjamin Jacob, of Surrey Chapel', *Nonconformist Musical Journal* III (1890) 57–8, 71–4. Richards, (ed.) (1942) 76. Senior, B., *A Hundred Years at Surrey Chapel* (1892). Seymour (1839) II: 319–22.

(227) Former CONGREGATIONAL, Browning Street (TQ 324786). 'Locks Field Meeting House', Clayton's Chapel or York Street Chapel, was built in 1789–90 and variously altered during the mid 19th century and in 1875. After 1894 responsibility for its use was transferred to the London Congregational Union, who developed it as a mission hall, naming it 'Browning Hall' after Robert Browning who was baptized here in 1812 and attended services in the chapel during his youth. The street name was similarly changed in 1921.

The chapel, which stood on the S side of the street W of Morecambe Street, was demolished and replaced by housing *c*.1990–5. The walls were of brickwork with some later rendering. The N front was of five bays with a three-bay pediment and round-arched upper windows; a wide mid 19th-century porch covered the lower part. The original plan was rectangular (53ft by 22ft) with a semicircular S end possibly added and a later annexe on the W. There was a small burial-ground S of the chapel.

Monument: relocated on cleared land to the E is a tomb chest on dwarf legs to Richard Holbert, 1804, Captain James Wilson, 1806 [his son-in-law], and Anna Francis Wilson, [1815?], daughter of the last.

Cleal (1908) 67–73. Mearns (1882) No. 233. Robinson, (ed.) (1997) xci, 23. Survey of London XXV, *St George the Martyr and St Mary Newington, Southwark* (St George's Fields) (1955) 101–2 (plan), Pl. 82b.

(228) Former BERESFORD CHAPEL, Walworth (TQ 323778). The former Congregational chapel on the S side of John Ruskin Street (formerly Beresford Street) is of brick with a rendered front of five bays with a pedimental gable and two tiers of round-arched windows. It was built in 1818 for the popular preacher Dr Edward Andrews on his failing to be appointed to the charge of Camden Chapel (230). It was attended as a child by John Ruskin, who described it with its plain interior as 'the Londinian chapel in its perfect type'. After the removal of the congregation to Sutherland Chapel (229) in 1841 this became an Episcopal chapel. (Latterly in commercial use. Demolished 1997)

Cleal (1908) 105. Robinson, (ed.) (1997) xxxiii, 22. Ruskin, J., *Praeterita* (1889) I: paras 79, 81, 152.

(229) Former SUTHERLAND CHAPEL, Liverpool Grove (TQ 324781). The former Congregational chapel was built in 1842 to replace 'Beresford Chapel', which had become financially embarrassed. It stands on the E side of Walworth Road, from which it was originally approached, but is now only visible from Liverpool Grove. Continuing financial problems, the nature of the site and the changed character of the district led to its closure in 1904. It has since served as a cinema and for other commercial and industrial purposes. The walls are of stock brick with sides of five bays having round-arched windows and a polygonal E end. The W front of three bays, rendered in cement with giant Doric columns *in antis* to the centre bay, has an overall entablature but all pediment details have been removed.

Cleal (1908) 104–11. *EM* NS XX (1842) 547. Mearns (1882) No. 232. Survey of London XXV, *St George the Martyr and St Mary Newington, Southwark* (St George's Fields) (1955) 103.

(230) CAMDEN CHAPEL, Peckham Road, Camberwell (TQ 335768). The chapel built for the Countess of Huntingdon's Connexion in 1795 was enlarged in 1814 and a chancel in the Byzantine style was added in 1854. It was demolished *c.*1951. The walls were of brick; the front of five bays with entrances in lower wings had a stone-faced tripartite central feature with rusticated lower stage and upper part with Doric pilasters and entablature.

Lock (1919) 6–11. Ruskin (1899) op. cit. II: para. 157.

(231) WESLEYAN, Bermondsey Street (TQ 332793). Bermondsey Central Hall, 1899–1900 by Charles Bell, rebuilt internally 1968. Front of red brick and terracotta with wide arched entrance and square superstructure with pyramid roof.

SUTTON

(232) WESLEYAN, Cheam Road (TQ 259640). Large stone Gothic chapel of 1906–7 by Gordon and Gunton. Prominently sited at W entrance to town centre with dominant corner tower and open corona spire. Nave with passage aisles, transepts and polygonal apse, and ancillary buildings to north. Original branched electric-light fittings. Glass in chancel commemorating Cuthbert Bainbridge of Lower Cheam, 1915.

TOWER HAMLETS

(233) Former HUGUENOT, Fournier Street (TQ 33878181). The former chapel at the corner of Fournier Street (previously Church Street) and Brick Lane, built in 1743, was designed by Thomas Stibbs as a chapel-of-ease to the French church in Threadneedle Street. In 1809 it was leased to the 'London Society for Promoting Christianity among the Jews' but in 1819 the lease passed to the Wesleyans, in whose occupation it remained until 1897. The chapel was then converted to a synagogue but by 1976 it had been further transformed by conversion to a mosque.

Former Huguenot chapel, Fournier Street. (© *London Metropolitan Archives*)

The walls of brick with stone dressings have two tiers of windows separated by a platband. The broad S front facing Fournier Street is of six bays with a four-bay pedimented centre, round-arched upper windows, segmental-arched below, and doorways with round-arched heads, pilasters and entablatures, in the penultimate bays. The E end is of three bays with a pediment and a Venetian window centrally in the upper stage. The fenestration of the N wall largely follows that to the S; the W wall is partly covered by adjacent properties.

The interior (54ft by 80ft) has been entirely altered. Although the orginal layout is uncertain, when in Methodist use it had galleries along the E, S and W sides supported by Doric columns and a Doric entablature below panelled fronts. The pulpit and a five-bay reredos stood centrally against the N wall. On conversion to a synagogue the E gallery was partly removed to allow the Ark to be positioned against the E wall. On further conversion to a mosque the interior fittings were removed and an upper floor inserted at gallery level. *Sundial*: in S pediment, dated 1743 with motto 'umbra sumus'.

Survey of London XXVII, *Christ Church and All Saints* (Spitalfields and Mile End New Town) (1957) 221–5, Pls 40–1.

(234) Former HUGUENOT, Sandys Row (TQ 33478168). 'Parliament Court Chapel', originally entered from the narrow alley of that name, was built in 1763–6 replacing an earlier meeting-house; it was built for a French Protestant congregation which, after regrouping, left the building *c.*1786. In 1792 it was let to Universalists under Elhanan Winchester followed by William Vidler, who retained possession in spite of a considerable secession in 1801 on his profession of Unitarian opinions; that society removed in 1824, later becoming the South Place Ethical Society, and was succeeded by Scotch Baptists and others. In 1870 the chapel was converted to a synagogue with a new W entrance facing Sandys Row.

The original building has brick walls and round-arched upper windows. The E end has a small central projection of later date with a small upper window, altered internally to accommodate the Ark; either side are segmental-arched lower windows incorporating minor doorways, and gallery windows above. An extension on a polygonal site at the W end, has a central doorway and three storeys of small round-arched windows to minor rooms.

The interior (48ft by 36ft) has a gallery around three sides with four Roman Doric columns and a Doric entablature. The side galleries are original but the W gallery is inserted, replacing one at the opposite end. The ceiling is coved around all sides, pierced for the window heads and carried on short lengths of moulded cornice. The E end is occupied by the Ark, an elaborate feature with Corinthian pilasters supporting a full entablature below a semi-dome.

Aspland (1850) 325. Chapels Society *Newsletter* I (1989–94) 24. Conway, M.D., *Centenary History of the South Place Society* (1894). Radcliffe, S.K., *The Story of South Place* (1955) 1–13. Survey of London XXVII, *Christ Church and All Saints* (Spitalfields and Mile End New Town) (1957) 36–7. Whitley (1928) Nos 74, 77.

(235) Former INDEPENDENT, Artillery Lane (TQ 33508168). The chapel which served Independents and Baptists, but was used as a synagogue from 1896 to 1948, has latterly been used as a warehouse. It was built in the mid 18th century on an irregular site immediately E of Parliament Court Chapel. The walls are of brickwork and the front, altered in 1950, was of seven bays with three entrances with pedimented surrounds, segmental-arched windows between and round-arched windows above. The interior, totally gutted in 1989 during renovation, retains the timber structure of a domed ceiling with central lantern.

Survey of London XXVII, *Christ Church and All Saints* (Spitalfields and Mile End New Town) (1957) 37–8.

(236) Former INDEPENDENT, Hope Street Chapel (TQ 33808213). The chapel, probably dating from the late 18th century, was built behind houses 93–5 on the W side of Hope Street (now Wilkes Street). It was converted to a synagogue in 1903 but was in use as a bakery in 1978. The walls are of brickwork, rendered at the front, but without any architectural pretensions. The interior has a gallery around three sides.

Survey of London XXVII, *Christ Church and All Saints* (Spitalfields and Mile End New Town) (1957) 113.

(237) CONGREGATIONAL, Pott Street, Bethnal Green Road (TQ 349826). The large chapel of 1849 in the Gothic style by John Tarring, originally with a corner tower and spire, survives in a severely mutilated state. (URC)

CYB (1850) 197–8. Mearns (1882) No. 16.

(238) Former CONGREGATIONAL, Mansford Street (TQ 345827). The chapel built in 1880 was sold in 1889 to the London Domestic Mission Society (Unitarian). The W front, in the Lombardic style by W.D. Church, is of stock brick with dressings of stone and stucco; three bays with gable, paired entrances and wheel-window above. The interior has a W gallery with open cast-iron balustrade. *Monuments*: in chapel (1) Elizabeth Jacqueline Garrett, [undated *c.*1910], large tiled picture in pre-Raphaelite manner, possibly by Doulton; (2) Charles Loftus Corkran, missioner, 1901.

CYB (1880) 417–18, engraving incorrectly captioned 'Pendlebury'. *Inquirer* (5 January 1889; 12 April 1986; 3 January 1987). Mearns (1882) No. 14.

(239) Former PRESBYTERIAN, West Ferry Road, Isle of Dogs (TQ 372789). St Paul's, built 1859 for the Presbyterian Church

Former Presbyterian chapel, West Ferry Road. (239)

in England, is a small chapel of polychrome brickwork in the Byzantine style by Thomas E. Knightley. It is four bays in length and has a clerestory carried internally by laminated timber trusses. The front is of three stages with a central round-arched entrance, and two arcaded upper stages.

Wilkinson, E., *London: Docklands* (1998) 96–7.

(240) Former FRENCH CHAPEL, 2a Hanbury Street (TQ 338819). The chapel built *c*.1719 for a French congregation was also used by a German church; it housed a Baptist church *c*.1845–52, United Free Methodists from 1858 and since 1887 has been a parish hall for the parish of Christ Church, Spitalfields. The N front is obscured by an extension of 1864 by C.McJ. North, but some early brickwork remains at the rear.

Survey of London XXVII, *Christ Church and All Saints* (Spitalfields and Mile End New Town) (1957) 190–1.

(241) ST GEORGE'S GERMAN LUTHERAN CHURCH, Alie Street (TQ 340812). The church built in 1762–3 for a German Lutheran congregation has walls of stock brick and a slated roof. The S front is of three bays with a pedimental gable. The centre bay breaks forward and formerly rose to a Classical steeple (demolished since 1957) with clock dial below and a weather vane of St George at the apex. In the centre bay is a Venetian window with a blind lunette above; the flanking bays have each a doorway with a round-arched window over. The side walls have two tiers of windows, round arched above and segmentally arched below. The church was extended to the N by one bay, possibly in 1766, in which year a two-storeyed vestry wing was added against the E side.

The interior has a gallery around three sides supported by Tuscan columns; the gallery fronts have moulded entablatures below panelling. (Church transferred to Historic Chapels Trust, 1999)

Fittings – *Benefaction Boards*: two groups of three, with dates from 1829. *Inscriptions*: on brick panel below upper window of vestry, names and initials with date 'Aug 21 1766'. *Monuments*: several wall monuments of the late 18th century and later include (1) Dederick Beckman, 1766, William his son, 1764, Henry Beckman, 1765, and Mrs Margaret Magdalene Beckman, 1787; (2) Edward Heinrich Sieveking, 1868, and Emerentia Louise Franziska (Meyer), 1861, buried Abney Park Cemetery, tablet with shield-of-arms; (3) Dr Louis Cappel, 1882, pastor; (4) Dr Gustavus Anthony Waschel, 1799, first pastor, his wife and three children (unnamed) and his son John Christian, 1819, resident surgeon at the smallpox hospital at St Pancras, tablet with shield-of-arms. *Pulpit*: centrally at N end, shaped desk with back-board and canopy surmounted by dove; twin staircases with reading desk W of pulpit and matching false desk to E, fronted by gilded reredos to communion table decorated with vine leaves and black-letter inscription within laurel wreath. *Royal Arms*: above pulpit carved and gilded wood, George III, *c*.1763. *Tables of Decalogue*: on wall flanking pulpit, in enriched frames surmounted by winged cherubs' heads.

WALTHAM FOREST

(242) CONGREGATIONAL, Langthorne Road, Leyton (TQ 385862). The church (now URC) which originated in the late 17th century first met in premises on the E side of Fetter Lane in the City of London, on a site later occupied by a Moravian chapel. In the early 18th century the church removed to a chapel on the W side, remaining there until 1894, when greatly depleted congregations persuaded the members to move to Leyton where they united with an existing congregation already occupying an iron chapel.

The present chapel, in a domestic style by P. Morley Horder, was built in 1899–1900; it is of brick rendered in pebble-dash with stone dressings. The chapel, which is barrel vaulted and has galleries on three sides, stands above basement classrooms.

Mearns (1882) No. 49. Pye-Smith, A., *Memorials of Fetter Lane Congregational Church* (1900). Wilson III (1810) 420–71.

(243) NEW MEETING-HOUSE, Walthamstow (TQ 367889). A meeting-house for dissenters opened in 1695 and replaced in 1740 stood on the N side of Marsh Street (now High Street). In 1786 the minister, Joseph Fawcett, was suspected of heterodox beliefs resulting in a major secession. The seceders erected a new meeting-house on the S side of the street and formed themselves into a Congregational church. The New Meeting continued to occupy these premises until 1871, when they erected a large Gothic chapel on the site of the Old Meeting-house, closed 1835. The new chapel, by John Tarring, remained until 1965 when it was demolished and the church (now URC) united with another meeting in Orford Road.

The New Meeting-house of 1786–7 was leased to Primitive Methodists in 1875 and subsequently sold to them; it remained in Methodist use until 1973, when it was sold for commercial use. The walls are of stock brick and the front was altered and embellished in stucco *c*.1875. The N front is gabled, of three bays with a central doorway and two tiers of windows; above the

St George's German Lutheran Church, Alie Street. (241)

entrance is a Venetian window, which is the principal surviving feature of the original design. The side walls of four bays with round-arched windows set in arched recesses below blind panels remain unaltered except for the replacement of the window frames. The building was extended to the S in the early 19th century and later, partly oversailing the burial-ground. The interior (51½ft by 33ft), refitted in the late 19th century, has a deep N gallery with cast-iron vine scroll decoration to the upper part of the front.

Monuments: in the burial-ground at rear, 38 monuments were recorded and the inscriptions, mostly of the early 19th century, were published by the Walthamstow Antiquarian Society in 1969; some have since been destroyed or defaced. (1) James Hall, 1844, Rachael his wife, 1812, Elizabeth, [ ], and Sarah, 1864, their daughter[?s], also 'Razafy, a Christian refugee from Madagascar…, 1840', table-tomb in railed enclosure; (2) Sarah Love (Hunt) wife of Antonio da Costa, of Token House Yard, London, merchant, a native of Portugal, 1821, and their son Francisco Love da Costa, 1821, headstone. *Plate*: two cups of 1787.

Batsford, M.E., *Nonconformity in Walthamstow* I (1977) 'Congregationalists & Baptists'. Budden, H.D., *The Story of Marsh Street Congregational Church, Walthamstow* (1923). Hanson, S., Law, A.D., and Tonkin, W.G.S., *Marsh Street Congregations*, Walthamstow Antiquarian Society, Publication No. 11 (1969). Mearns (1882) No. 229.

(244) FREE METHODIST, Markhouse Road, Walthamstow (TQ 366882). 'Lighthouse Chapel' of brick, built 1893, has a circular tower at one corner rising to a truncated spire surmounted by a beacon. Galleried 'music hall'-style interior, altered.

Chapels Society *Newsletter* I (1989–94) 57–8.

WANDSWORTH

(245) BAPTIST, Werter Road, Putney (TQ 241752). Large Italianate chapel of 1884 by [ ] Johnson. Gault brick with stone dressings; gabled centre, large window with Venetian tracery between end bays terminating in dwarf turrets.

Whitley (1928) No. 563.

(246) Former CONGREGATIONAL, Upper Richmond Road, Putney (TQ 238751). The chapel, built 1861 for a congregation seceding from one at the Platt Chapel in 1857, was designed by Charles R. Gribble. It is of ragstone with Bath stone dressings in the Decorated Gothic style and was intended to have a tower and spire. The gabled front has two entrances and a traceried window of five lights. Now the 'Goodrich Theatre'.

Cleal (1908) 233–9. *CYB* (1862) 322–3.

(247) Former CONGREGATIONAL, Mitcham Road, Lower Tooting. The former 'Defoe Chapel', built 1776, used by Primitive Methodists from 1902 but latterly a shop, appears to have been demolished, as has its successor of 1904–5 in the same street (TQ 277712; rebuilt by URC). The former is said to have had a 'pedimented Classical front'.

Cleal (1908) 208–17. Mearns (1882) No. 218.

(248) CONGREGATIONAL, East Hill, Wandsworth (TQ 262747). The church formed in 1811 first met in a former Huguenot chapel of possibly 17th-century date in High Street (demolished 1882–3) which had been purchased and repaired by the Evangelical Association in 1808. The chapel on East Hill, of 1859–60 in the Gothic style by J.G. Stapleton, was much enlarged in 1875–6 by the addition of a nave leaving part of the earlier structure as a transept. A Sunday-school in a matching style was added alongside in 1882–3.

Cleal (1908) 245–52. *CYB* (1856) 253–5; (1860) 252. Mearns (1882) No. 234.

(249) FRIENDS, Wandsworth High Street (TQ 258746). The meeting-house, which stands concealed behind later buildings on the S side of the street, was built in 1778. The site was acquired in 1673 and the first meeting-house erected or converted from existing buildings. The present meeting-house has brick walls and a hipped tiled roof with high central valley. The S wall facing the burial-ground has three sash windows with segmental-arched heads. The entrance in the E wall is protected by a later covered passage. The interior (34ft by 30ft) has a two-stage stand at the W end, extended N and S; some wall benches have been removed.

Adjacent to the N is a smaller, possibly later, women's meeting-house, now largely refitted, with a former fireplace at the W end. The buildings fronting the street, refaced in 1927, comprise classrooms and caretaker's accommodation.

Fittings – *Graffiti*: on back of benches in meeting-house, scratched initials and dates, including 'EHB 2 of May 1781' and 'T. Rickman'. *Inscription*: externally on S wall of meeting-house, tablet inscribed 'REBUILT | 1778.'. *Monuments*: in burial-ground, plain round-topped headstones of early 19th century and later. Also, reset tablet in E boundary wall, a tablet inscribed 'Here lyeth y̆ͤ | Body of | JOAN STRINGER | the giver of | the Ground | who dyed in | the year | 1697.'.

Beck and Ball (1869) 318–27. Butler (1999) 427–8. Lidbetter (1961) Fig. 6, Pl. XLIII.

Friends' meeting-house, Wandsworth High Street. (249)

(250) WESLEYAN, Upper Richmond Road, Putney (TQ 236752). The chapel of 1881–2 by James Weir is of stock brick with stone dressings. Tall corner tower with pinnacles and battlements; five separately gabled windows face the road. Ancillary rooms by Albert Dawkins added 1907. Interior damaged by flying bomb 1944 and reinstated.

Farmer, L., *The Putney Story: A History of Putney Methodism* (1970).

(251) HUGUENOT BURIAL-GROUND, East Hill (TQ 263748). The burial-ground associated with the considerable Huguenot

Welsh Baptist chapel, Eastcastle Street.

community living in Wandsworth from the late 17th century was acquired *c*.1680 as an additional parochial burial-ground. The monuments, now mostly illegible, are fully recorded in Squire (1886) op. cit. below.

Shaw, R.A., Gwynn, R.D, and Thomas, P., *Huguenots in Wandsworth* (1985). Squire, J.T., 'The Huguenots in Wandsworth in the County of Surrey and their Burial Ground at Mount Nod', *Proceedings of the Huguenot Society of London* I (1886) 229–42, 261–312.

CITY OF WESTMINSTER

(252) BAPTIST, Abbey Road, St John's Wood (TQ 265831). The chapel set between a pair of related three-storeyed houses is of red brick with stone dressings. The bowed front with a three-bay gabled porch is flanked by a pair of square towers with octagonal pyramidally roofed upper stages. At the rear is a shallow apse. Built 1863–4 by W.G. Habershon and Pite. (Towers partly demolished since 1984)

Stott, W., *A Ministry of Twenty-five Years in London* (*c.*1887). Whitley (1928) No. 359.

(253) WELSH BAPTIST, Eastcastle Street (TQ 292814). 'Capel Bedyddwyr Cymreig', dated 1889, is closely set between former houses on the N side of the street. The front of brick and stone is of four principal stages with a three-bay colonnade of tall Corinthian columns fronting a recessed lower part with a pair of balustraded stairs to the chapel and gallery. The interior of the chapel has a coved ceiling with clerestory lighting, galleries and original fittings. There are two tiers of rooms above the chapel and a basement below.

John, W.P., and Hughes, G.T., *Hanes Castle Street A'r Bedyddwyr Cymraeg yn Llundain* (1959). Whitley (1928) No. 311.

(254) Former BAPTIST, Westbourne Grove (TQ 251811). The chapel of 1853 but much enlarged to each side in 1866 is by C.G. Searle, in the Gothic style with walls faced with ragstone and ashlar dressings. The S front is gabled between octagonal turrets and later side bays. (Now used by the International Christian Fellowship)

Survey of London XXXVII, *Northern Kensington* (1973) 271–2.

(255) CATHOLIC APOSTOLIC, Maida Avenue (TQ 264820). The second largest of the Catholic Apostolic churches in London stands on the SE side of Maida Avenue. It was built in 1891–4 in the Gothic style by J.L. Pearson. The walls are of red brick with stone dressings and the roofs are tiled and surmounted at the crossing by a tall lead-covered flèche. The end wall facing the street is pierced

Catholic Apostolic church, Maida Avenue.

by a tall arched recess between square turrets with octagonal tops and spires, enclosing a small apsidal baptistery; to the left is an arcaded entrance linked to a clergy house and to the right the base of an uncompleted tower.

The plan comprises an aisled nave and transepts, chancel and ambulatory with polygonal apse, and flanking chapels. The roofs are stone-vaulted throughout. Many original fittings survive.

Beyer (1931) 18–23. *Country Life* (3 September 1987) 192–3. Quiney, A., *John Loughborough Pearson* (1979) 206–9.

(256) CHRISTIAN SCIENCE, Curzon Street (TQ 288803). The Third Church of Christ Scientist has a grandly self-confident entrance façade in Portland stone facing the end of Half Moon Street. Tall columns flank the entrance with an arch rising into an attic storey over which presides a Classical steeple. Built 1910, by Lanchester and Rickards.

Nicholson and Spooner (*c*.1910) 190.

(257) PADDINGTON CHAPEL, Old Marylebone Road (TQ 274817). The Congregational chapel was built in 1813 largely at the instigation and the personal expense of Thomas Wilson. The walls are of brickwork with a stone front. The original front of three bays with two tiers of round-arched windows and a triple entrance feature was replaced in 1869 by a front of five bays with a three-bay portico with giant Corinthian columns. The chapel was extended forwards in 1899 in an Italianate style by Alfred Conder, with a five-bay pedimented centre between staircase towers with domed tops. The interior with a gallery around three sides was also refitted. (Demolished 1981; one lone gate pier survives in front of site)

Monuments: in chapel (1) George Douglas Macgregor, 1899, 30 years pastor, and Maria Johnston his widow, 1899; (2) James Stratten, 1872, 42 years pastor; (3) Rev. J. Ossian Davies, 1916, 5 years pastor; (4) Rev. Isaac Morley Wright, 1896; (5) Samuel Pooley, 1887, 23 years City Missionary.

CYB (1900) 203–4; (1901) 164. [Green, P.], *Paddington Chapel 1813–1963* (1963). Mearns (1882) No. 167.

(258) CRAVEN CHAPEL, Foubert's Place (TQ 293811). The Congregational chapel, built in 1822 at the expense of Thomas Wilson, survives in a greatly altered state. The building, believed to be by Robert Abraham, has walls of stock brick with rendered dressings. The front of three bays with a slightly projecting centre has been refenestrated; it formerly had a central pediment, a pedimented doorcase, and round-arched upper windows rising from a platband about 4ft higher than at present. The side wall of six bays with end bays breaking forward has been similarly altered. It passed briefly into Methodist use in 1894 but has since served commercial interests.

Christian Instructor (Supplement, 1822) 716–17. *CYB* (1875) 431–2. Mearns (1882) No. 64. *Survey of London* XXXI, *St James, Westminster: Part II* (North of Piccadilly) (1963) 200–1.

(259) PORTLAND CHAPEL, St John's Wood Terrace (TQ 271834). The former Congregational chapel, now in commercial use, was opened in 1841. The walls are of brick with a stuccoed front having a pedimented portico with four giant Corinthian columns between narrow flanking bays. The central doorway has a round arch with keystone and fanlight. Above the pediment is a square base as for a short tower.

EM NS XX (1842) 85. Mearns (1882) No. 188.

Portland Chapel, St John's Wood Terrace. (259)

Westminster Chapel, Buckingham Gate.
Before rebuilding of tower. (260)

Westminster Chapel, Buckingham Gate. (260)

(260) WESTMINSTER CHAPEL, Buckingham Gate (TQ 293794). The first Congregational chapel on this site, built in 1841 for the Metropolis Chapel Building Fund Association, was a simple Classical building seating 1,500, with a pedimented front and open centre bay with two Ionic columns *in antis*. The rapid growth of the congregation under its first pastor, Samuel Martin, brought with it the need for the present much larger chapel designed by W.F. Poulton of Reading. The new building in the Lombardic style, opened in 1865 and seating 2,400, has walls of stock brick with some red brick and Bath stone dressings. The NE front facing Buckingham Gate (formerly James Street) is gabled and has an arcaded entrance below a range of round-arched windows; flanking bays contain gallery staircases, that to the right rising to a tall thin tower originally finished with a steep pyramidal spire which became unsafe and was refashioned *c.*1935.

The interior comprises a large round-ended auditorium with a ribbed ceiling and paired iron-framed upper windows between attached columns; two tiers of galleries with cast-iron fronts are carried along the sides, the lower gallery being continuous. Circular windows light the lower gallery with shorter windows below. A recess at the NE end above the entrance was intended to accommodate the organ, re-sited at the opposite end behind the pulpit in 1879. The pulpit comprises a circular platform with a lower communion platform in front. Behind the chapel are numerous minor rooms, vestries and a lecture hall.

Fittings – *Monument*: William Brooke, 1856. *Organ*: 1879 by 'Father' Willis, reconstructed and enlarged 1920. *Sculpture*: bust of Samuel Martin, first pastor, d.1878.

CYB (1847) facing 158; (1866) 325–6; (1879) 330–2. Lloyd-Jones, D.M., *Westminster Chapel (1865–1965), Centenary Address* (1965). Mearns (1882) No. 240.

(261) KING'S WEIGH HOUSE CHAPEL, Duke Street (TQ 284810). The Congregational church formerly meeting here originated in the 17th century in the City of London as a Presbyterian society, becoming Independent about 1780. Meetings were held in a building in Cannon Street or St Martin's Lane until 1697 when a

Former King's Weigh House Chapel, Duke Street, Westminster. (© *A.F. Kersting*)

new and larger meeting-house was erected above the King's Weigh House in Little Eastcheap; the congregation, which became the second largest in London, rebuilt their premises at the Weigh House in 1794 remaining there until 1832 when the site was required for road development. A new chapel was then built on Fish Street Hill from which the church was obliged to move in 1882 for the construction of Monument Station. After some delay, agreement was reached to amalgamate with a small congregation meeting in a chapel in Robert Street (now Weigh House Street) and to rebuild on an enlarged site. The church continued to worship here until 1965, when the remnant of the congregation united with Whitefield Memorial Church, Tottenham Court Road (34). The chapel now serves as the Ukrainian Catholic Cathedral.

The new King's Weigh House Chapel was designed by Alfred Waterhouse and opened in 1891. The walls are of red brick with light buff terracotta dressings and a tiled roof. The W front facing Duke Street is gabled, with three round-arched entrances, between a taller three-storeyed NW wing and a tall tower and spire at the SW corner. The body of the chapel is oval and has two tiers of windows. The interior has a shallow domed ceiling; there was originally a continuous gallery with an organ at the E end behind the pulpit but in 1903 the organ was divided and ritualistic fittings began to be introduced to a reordered E end, presaging the liturgical changes during the idiosyncratic ministry of W.E. Orchard (1914–32).

Fittings – *Baptismal Basin*: circular bowl with gadrooned base and rim, London assay, 1697. *Plate*: includes a set of six cups, 1696–1705 (two now at Bala-Bangor College, Bangor), and a plate with scalloped edge of 1749.

Briggs (1946) 42–5. Kaye, E., *The History of The King's Weigh House Church* (1968). Mearns (1882) Nos 52, 182. Survey of London XI, *The Grosvenor Estate in Mayfair: Part II* (The Buildings) (1980) 87–9. Wilson I (1808) 148–204.

(262) WESLEYAN, Hinde Street (TQ 284814). The first chapel on this site, of 1810 by the Rev. William Jenkins, had a front of five bays with a three-bay pediment and two tiers of round-arched windows. This was superseded in 1886 by the present chapel by James Weir. It is a large building of grey brick with Portland stone dressings in the Renaissance style with a two-stage open portico to the S of three bays with paired columns and a pediment between staircase bays, that on the SW corner rising to an octagonal tower and spire. The interior has a panelled ceiling coved to E and W and divided by ribs. There is a gallery around three sides. At the N end is an arched pulpit recess with semi-dome and paired Corinthian columns; the pulpit, formerly with rear access only, has an arcaded front supported by a corbel. Below the chapel is a large schoolroom with substantial circular piers and columns supporting the superstructure.

Fittings – *Glass*: the windows are glazed with large original sheets of etched patterned glass. *Monuments*: in chapel (1) William Corderoy, 1860, and Mary his wife, 1857; (2) Adam Clarke LL.D, 1832; (3) Rev. Thomas Stanley, 1832, Superintendent; (4) Francis Calder, 1857, nearly 48 years Trustee Steward, and Sarah his wife, 1854; (5) John Scott, 1870, and Sarah his wife, 1865, parents of Rev. John Scott of Ceylon; (6) Rev. Abraham Eccles Farrar, 1849, late Superintendent; (7) William Johnson, 1889, signed 'Dottridge'; in basement (8) William Corderoy, 1860, 'who

Wesleyan chapel, Hinde Street.   (262)

laboured in this School 31 years'. *Seating*: in gallery, original pews; lower seating removed 1978.

The Building News (4 November 1887). Curnock, N., *Hinde Street Chapel, 1810–1910* (1910). Dolbey (1964) 160–1. Telford, J., *Two West-End Chapels* (1886) 86–278.

(263) WESTMINSTER CENTRAL HALL, Broad Sanctuary (TQ 300796). The Wesleyan 'Central Hall', a multi-purpose building incorporating chapel and offices, on the site of the Westminster Aquarium, was designed by Lanchester and Rickards and opened in 1912. It is a steel-framed building faced in stone, heavily rusticated, in a free Classical manner, dominated by a massive angular dome.

(264) Former WELSH PRESBYTERIAN, Charing Cross Road (TQ 299810). The chapel which was built in 1887 to replace one in Nassau Street (now Gerrard Place) lost by the construction of Shaftesbury Avenue was designed by James Cubitt in the Romanesque style. The E front has two separately gabled bays between the entrances. Above the chapel is a short octagonal tower with paired arched openings. (Interior altered in 1984 on conversion to secular use)

Survey of London XXXIII, XXXIV, *St Anne, Soho* (1966), XXXIII: 308–9; XXXIV: Pl. 25b.

(265) Former WESLEYAN, Queensway (TQ 259808). The chapel, built in 1868, was occupied from 1909 to 1946 by the West London Ethical Society, briefly leased to a Unitarian Fellowship,

and purchased by the present owners in 1954; it is now the Roman Catholic Church of Our Lady Queen of Heaven. The W front of white brick with stone dressings and Gothic detailing has a recessed centre between staircase bays; the main entrance, reached by a rebuilt flight of steps from the street, is set in an arcade of five pointed-arched bays above which are two tiers of windows with a gable over a central traceried window of four lights.

The interior, semicircular on plan above a basement, has two tiers of galleries supported by cast-iron columns; the S wall, against which the pulpit formerly stood, is blank. The original seating remains throughout.

(266) FRENCH PROTESTANT CHURCH, Soho Square (TQ 296813). The church which had met from the mid 16th century in Threadneedle Street removed in 1843 to a new building in St Martin's le Grand. After being obliged to make way for an extension to the General Post Office, the church acquired the present site on the N side of Soho Square and commissioned (Sir) Aston Webb to design a new building. This was opened in 1893. The front is of brick and terracotta with an arched central entrance and flanking windows below a gabled centre between separately roofed turrets; on the roof is a tall flèche.

The interior, faced with buff terracotta, comprises an aisled nave with four bay arcades and clerestory windows, and an apse at the N end.

Painting: portrait of the Rev. John de Lepine, d.1714. *Royal Arms*: Stuart, carved in wood. *Sculpture*: on tympanum of entrance, carving in mediaeval style commemorating the granting by Edward VI in 1550 of a charter of asylum to Huguenot refugees from France, erected 1950.

Batisse, F.A., *Londres Huguenot: sur les pas des huguenots français à trayers Londres…* (1978). RCHM *London*. Vol. II *West London* (1925) 121, Westminster monument (23). Survey of London XXXIII, XXXIV, *St Anne, Soho* (1966), XXXIII: 62–3.

(267) Former FRENCH PROTESTANT, Monmouth Road (TQ 255811). Small chapel built *c*.1861–6 of brick with stuccoed front of three bays with a pediment and corner pilasters. Round-arched doorway raised up above semi-basement. (Now Jehovah's Witnesses)

(268) CHURCH OF SCOTLAND, Crown Court (TQ 304811). The first Presbyterian meeting-house on this site was built in 1719. It was enlarged in 1847 and re-fronted in an elaborate Romanesque manner. This was replaced in 1909 by the present building by Eustace Balfour (Balfour and Turner), which has a broad front of red brick and Portland stone in an Elizabethan style, of six bays with three tiers of windows, the end bays projecting slightly.

Fittings – *Communion Plate*: reported given by Duchess of Manchester, 1842–8. Wilson (op. cit. below) refers to *Portraits* in vestry of two ministers, John Freeland, 1747–51 and Thomas Oswald, 1752–73; Black (op. cit. below) notes a *Royal Arms* (? George I) on panel below gallery (now over communion table).

Anon., *Crown Court, Church of Scotland, WC2* (1971). Black (1906) 75–111. Wilson IV (1814) 3–10.

(269) SWEDISH LUTHERAN CHURCH, Harcourt Street (TQ 274817). Built in 1910 in restrained Gothic style based on a sketch by Axel Haig. Portland stone front with tall gabled centre and flèche between three-storey wings. Swedish Royal Arms below W window of first-floor chapel.

Fittings – from former Swedish Church of 1728 in Prince's Square (Swedenborg Square) Wapping (demolished), include *Chandelier* dated 1770, *Font* and *Pulpit*.

HERTFORDSHIRE

Although only a relatively small number of early chapels and meeting-houses survives it is a measure of the continued strength rather than the weakness of dissent in the county. Many congregations which originated in the earliest years of nonconformity remained sufficiently strong to rebuild or enlarge their premises leaving little visible trace of their antiquity. Several ejected ministers gathered congregations in the years following the Restoration from which churches, principally of the Independents, eventually emerged. The county is fortunate in possessing the earliest Friends' meeting-house in the country, at Hertford (38), built in 1670 and clearly designed to be capable of conversion to a house, which it closely resembles in outward appearance, should the need arise. Two other meeting-houses also remain from the end of the 17th century, though no longer in religious use. In St Albans the Old Meeting-house in Lower Dagnall Street (61) was built in 1697–8, in brick, for an affluent Presbyterian congregation which adopted Unitarianism in its later days. At about the same date a congregation mainly of Independents built a timber-framed meeting-house at Box Lane near Hemel Hempstead (31) which in its structure contrasts strongly with the former although both are similar in size and layout.

The 18th century is represented by a small re-sited and interestingly secluded chapel at Braughing (16), but more notably by the 'Old Independent Chapel' in Ware (80). A former General Baptist chapel in Tring (74) of 1751, long converted to secular use, was demolished during the course of this survey. A small Quaker meeting-house dating from 1718 remains in Hemel Hempstead (35), but also of Quaker interest is Baldock (9) of *c.*1750 or earlier, and the denomination is represented in the early 19th century at Berkhamsted (14) of 1818 and Hoddesdon (45) of 1828 at which elements of Classical formality make their appearance.

The Baptist chapel at New Mill (78) of 1818, replacing a much enlarged earlier meeting-house, is characteristic of the early 19th-century chapels of the western part of the county while the number of Baptist meetings in and around Tring is also notable. Other Baptist chapels include Akeman Street, Tring (76) of 1832 and Zion Chapel, Kings Langley (48) of 1835. The Congregational chapel at Buntingford (18) of 1819 is of interest for its simple triple-arched front, a feature also found at Linton (Cambs. (60)) of 1818 and St Ives (Hunts. (38)), but of greater pretension is the Independent chapel in Spicer Street, St Albans (64) of 1811–12 by the architect William Jenkins.

Works by named architects using the fashionable styles of the day become more prominent from the mid 19th century, one of the most spectacular being the classically fronted Baptist chapel in Hitchin (39) of 1844 by John Davies, repeating his 1841 design for the Baptist chapel in Abingdon, Berks. (*see Nonconformist Chapels and Meeting-houses in South-West England* (1991) 1–2, monument (1)). The short-lived Romanesque style appears at Ware (81) in the Congregational chapel by John Brown, but the Italianate Romanesque was adopted in 1876–8 by J. Wallis Chapman for the largest Baptist Chapel in the county in 'Beechen Grove', Watford (85). Poulton and Woodman's Congregational chapel in Bishop's Stortford (15) of 1859–60 is of particular note as being a precursor in style and date of Westminster Chapel, London (Greater London (260)), by the same firm.

Several chapels in the Gothic style must be mentioned, one of the earliest being the Wesleyan chapel in Baldock (10) of 1853. Equally of note are the Congregational chapels in Hertford (37), by T. Smith and Son, and at Sawbridgeworth (67), of 1862–3 by Poulton and Woodman, also the Baptist chapels at Hemel Hempstead (33) of 1861 by Joseph James, and, towards the end of the century, in St Albans (62) of 1884 by Glover and Salter. The freer use of the Gothic style in the early 20th century appears here as elsewhere in the buildings by George Baines and Son, for Baptists at Breachwood Green, King's Walden (49) of 1904 and in Hertford (36) of 1906, while the influence of the Arts and Crafts Movement is seen in H.G. Ibberson's Baptist chapel, part of a proposed larger scheme, at Chorleywood (21) of 1906, and in the Friends meeting-house in Letchworth (50) of 1907, a free interpretation of the late 17th-century meeting-house at Brigflatts, Yorks., West Riding (*see Nonconformist Chapels and Meeting-houses in the North of England* (1994) 305, monument (358)).

The principal building material in the county is brick, which was in use from an early date particularly in urban contexts but timber-framing remained an option at least until the end of the 18th century for less prominent locations. Stone only appears with the mid 19th century and remains comparatively rare. Roofs generally are covered with clay tiles.

HERTFORDSHIRE

ABBOTS LANGLEY

(1) Former BAPTIST, Hunton Bridge (TL 083006). The chapel built 1851 originally had a low gabled front; it was re-fronted in brick in 1893 and given an elaborately shaped gable and matching porch. (Now used as a stained glass studio)
Stuart (1907) 106–7.

(2) Former BAPTIST, Bedmond (TL 099039). 'Bethesda Chapel', dated 1859, has a gabled front with brick pilasters flanking the porch and a round-arched iron-framed upper window. (Derelict 1994)
Whitley (1928) No. 273.

ALDBURY

(3) BAPTIST (SP 965126). The chapel, hidden behind cottages 39–43 Stocks Road, was built c.1827. Three-bay brick front with central round-arched doorway between two tiers of windows.

ARDELEY

(4) Former CONGREGATIONAL, Wood End (TL 325255). The chapel adjoining Chapel Farm was built in 1820 and rebuilt in 1862. It has walls of red brick with yellow brick dressings and a gabled E front. The date tablet from the first chapel is reset low down in the rear wall near the NW corner.
CYB (1876) 333–4, obituary of D.E. Ford. Urwick (1884) 769–70.

ASHWELL

(5) STRICT BAPTIST, Gardiners Lane (TL 266397). Gault brick, gabled front with shaped barge-boards and porch with four-centred arched entrance. Registered 1847.

(6) CONGREGATIONAL (TL 269397). The church, formed 1767 in the wake of local preaching by John Berridge, vicar of Everton, (Tetworth, detached), Hunts., built a new meeting-house c.1793. The chapel was burnt down and rebuilt in 1850–1. The N front of red brick with gault brick dressings is of three bays with giant pilasters supporting an open pediment into which the centre bay is arched. *Inscriptions*: on bricks incorporated in E and W walls, many names including two, low down on W side, with date 1829. *Monuments*: in front burial-ground (1) Sarah Ripshire, 1841; (2) Thomas Christy, 1829; (3) Eliza daughter of William and Eliza Kirbyshire, 1828, *et al.*; (4) Catherine wife of George Pitty, 1838.
Urwick (1884) 781.

(7) FRIENDS BURIAL-GROUND (TL 269396). A meeting-house built in 1679 and closed in 1836 was demolished in 1860 following storm damage. The meeting-house stood at the N end of the burial-ground which is bounded on the other three sides by walls of gault brick erected in 1860. Some plain round-topped headstones remain, to Thorne, Warboys and others, with dates from the early 19th century.
Butler (1999) 252.

(8) Former WESLEYAN, Church Lane (TL 268397). Built 1833; converted to two cottages, No. 1 and adjacent, following the erection of a new chapel further S in 1880 (demolished 1979). Rendered walls with gabled E front, much altered.

BALDOCK

(9) Former FRIENDS (TL 244341). The meeting-house standing in a lane off the E side of Church Street was largely built c.1750 possibly incorporating at the N end part of its predecessor acquired in 1696. The walls are timber-framed, rendered externally and the roof is tiled. The principal section (32ft by 20½ft) is of three bays with one window of three lights in each bay on the W side and one centrally in the opposite wall. The S end is gabled. An annexe at the N end, which may have been partly domestic, has three shuttered openings to the meeting-room and a staircase to an upper room. The main meeting-house is undivided and ceiled. The stand was at the S end and the walls have a high dado of vertical boarding. The roof of common rafters has clasped purlins but no regular trusses. In the burial-ground to the E are a few fragments of 19th-century headstones.
Butler (1999) 252–3. Urwick (1884) 568–70.

Former Friends' meeting-house, Baldock. (9)

(10) WESLEYAN, Whitehorse Street (TL 245340). The chapel opened 1853 replacing one of 1795 has walls of red brick with rendered dressings. The S front is gabled and subdivided by two octagonal buttresses which rise to open stone lanterns with ogee caps; above the central entrance is a window of four lights with cusped tracery. In the flanking bays and the side walls are windows of two lights with cusped Y-tracery. The interior is ceiled at collar level and has arcades supported on slender columns and trusses with Gothic ornamentation. There is a gallery to the S and a low rostrum at the opposite end; all fittings date from 1853.

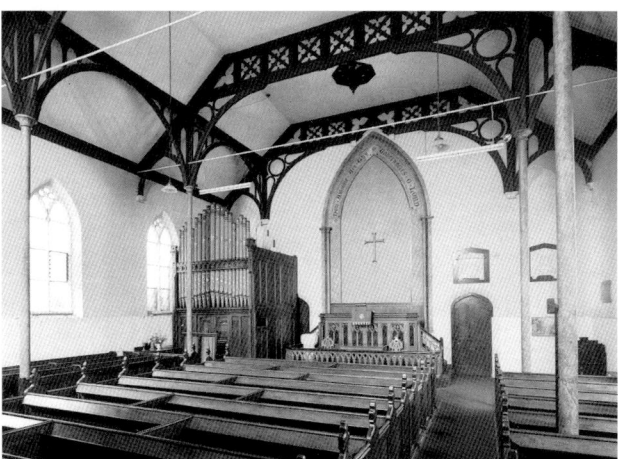

Wesleyan chapel, Baldock. (10)

The walls are of grey brick at the front with red brick sides. The E front is gabled with panelled terminal pilasters and three round-arched bays enclosing two tiers of windows and a central entrance. The side walls have each four tall round-arched windows with wooden Y-tracery frames. At the back is a triple-gabled vestry.

The interior has a single E gallery supported by two octagonal wood columns and approached by twin staircases each with a dog-gate at the bottom. The roof is supported by four queen-post trusses. (Chapel closed c.1990, interior gutted and vestry demolished on conversion to house)

Fittings – *Glass:* in centre lights of Y-traceried windows, clear glass triangle on coloured background alternately red and yellow. *Inscription*: in front gable 'Erected 1841'. *Monuments*: on front wall (1) James second son of J.G. Wilson of London, 1844; in burial-ground (2) William Savell, 1848, table-tomb; also several wooden cruciform grave markers of late 19th century and after. *Pulpit*: polygonal, reduced in height and pedimented back-board removed. *Seating*: in gallery, centre rank of box-pews, open-backed benches with shaped ends at sides; lower seating renewed in late 19th century.

Sunday Times 'Style' (5 November 1995) 28. Urwick (1884) 739. Watts (1978) 30.

BERKHAMSTED URBAN

(13) GENERAL BAPTIST, High Street, Berkhamsted (SP 996077). The church formed in the mid 17th century later constituted one section of a joint church including congregations at Chesham,

General Baptist chapel, Berkhamsted. (13)

(Interior altered since 1982) *Monuments*: in chapel (1) Thomas Hine, 1857, and Elizabeth his widow, 1868; (2) Joseph Swannell Hine, 1856, and Emily his widow, 1893. *Railings*: in front of chapel, original gateway with cast-iron standards.

BARKWAY

(11) CONGREGATIONAL (TL 385359). Gothic chapel of 1884 by W.D. Church, replacing a building of 1785.

Urwick (1884) 733.

BARLEY

(12) Former INDEPENDENT (TL 399386). The chapel was built in 1841 for a highly Calvinistic congregation which separated from an existing Independent church in 1829. The church disbanded in 1873 and the chapel was sold to Congregationalists in 1889.

Bucks., and Tring, Herts. A meeting-house erected in 1691, possibly rebuilt in 1722, and enlarged in 1840, stood in Water Lane with a burial-ground in The Wilderness. It was superseded by the present chapel in 1864. This is a building in the Gothic style, of grey brick with red brick and stone dressings, and a tower and octagonal stone spire at one corner.

Hayden, R., (ed.), *English Baptist Church Records: I. The General Baptist Church of Berkhamsted, Chesham and Tring 1712–1781* (Baptist Hist. Soc., 1985). Taylor (1818) I: 233, 327–9; II: 440–6. Wood (1847) 207.

(14) FRIENDS, High Street, Berkhamsted (SP 987080). The meeting-house built in 1818 for Friends formerly meeting near Tring has walls of stock brick and a hipped slate roof. The front is symmetrical with two round-arched windows and a large porch room, rebuilt 1964. The interior was formerly divided into two rooms by a partition with shutters.

Butler (1999) 253–4.

BISHOP'S STORTFORD

(15) CONGREGATIONAL, Water Lane (TL 488215). The church (now URC) originated in the late 17th century. In 1712 a barn in Water Lane was converted to a meeting-house and that was replaced in 1767 by a larger chapel, 44ft by 40ft, which stood on the NE corner of the present site.

The chapel built in 1859–60 to seat 800 adults and 300 children was designed by Poulton and Woodman of Reading in an Italianate

Congregational chapel (URC), Bishop's Stortford. (15)

Congregational chapel (URC), Bishop's Stortford. (15)

style with walls of white brick and Bath stone dressings. The oval plan resembles that of the slightly later Westminster Chapel, (Greater London (260)) by the same architects. There are two tiers of windows with cast-iron frames, arranged in groups of three, and square staircase towers flanking the entrance at the S end.

The interior has a coved ceiling divided by plaster ribs. Two tiers of galleries are carried around three sides, the upper gallery supported by cast-iron brackets, the lower additionally by spirally twisted columns; the ironwork is by 'Watts'. The pulpit at the N end has been partly reconstructed and the original seats to the lower floor and first gallery have lost their doors. The roof is supported by four queen-post trusses.

Fittings – *Benefaction Boards*: over inner doorways, modern, recording benefactions of 1744 by Ann Phillips 'for the support of the minister of the meeting of Protestant Dissenters assembling in Water Lane'; and others of 1759, 1763, 1866 and 1917. *Inscription*: below window NE of pulpit, brass recording a restoration in 1930 by Sir George Oakley, architect. *Monuments*: in chapel (1) Rev. John Angus, 1801; (2) Rev. William Chaplin, 1844.

CYB (1861) 276–7. Lewis, M.G., *The Congregational Church, Water Lane, Bishop's Stortford, 1662–1962* (1962). Urwick (1884) 705–6.

BRAUGHING

(16) CONGREGATIONAL, Fleece Lane (TL 394253). The Rev. Robert Billio, ejected rector of Wickham Bishops, Essex, is credited with encouraging the formation of the church. In the early 18th century meetings were held in a former barn or granary but in 1762 the present site, 'the bottom end of the garden of Fleece house', was acquired and the meeting-house erected. This is a rendered timber-framed building claimed to have originated as a barn located 'between Datchworth and Hitchin', associated with the preaching of John Bunyan; in 1719 the barn was acquired by a dissenting congregation at Datchworth and re-erected at Petits; and when that congregation declined it was removed to Braughing.

The chapel is a small rectangular timber-framed building of four bays (18ft by 36½ft) with a tiled roof gabled E and W and rendered walls. The front faces S and has an entrance in the E end bay. The E wall has two gallery windows below the tie-beam and one centrally above; the W wall, which is partly weather-boarded, was similarly fenestrated but the windows have been blocked. The interior originally had galleries at each end but the W gallery was removed, the pulpit re-sited at the W end and the interior refitted in 1885. The principal structural posts have shaped heads and curved braces to tie-beams.

Fittings – *Fontlet*: square bowl decorated with biblical scenes, on wooden stem, late 19th-century. *Monuments*: in chapel (1) Catherine daughter of Thomas and Sarah Webster, 'lost in the wreck of the Tayleur off the island of Lambay in the Irish Channel on the 21st of January, 1854, in the 25th year of her age'; in burial-ground (2) Rev. William Henry Woodward, 1841, 8 years pastor, and Mary his widow, 1858; (3) Rev. Daniel Bocking, 1811, and Susanna Daking, 1830; (4) Mary wife of Rev. Daniel Bocking, [ ]; (5) Joseph Judd, 1832, and Sarah his daughter, 1824. *Painting*: in vestry, oil portrait of Rev. William Barnes, 1895, by M. Baddeley.

Hertfordshire Countryside (February and March 1971). Urwick (1884) 576, 673–4.

(17) WESLEYAN, The Street (TL 396251). Gabled front with angularly arched windows. Opened 1883.

BUNTINGFORD

(18) CONGREGATIONAL, Baldock Lane (TL 361294). A meeting-house built in 1785 was destroyed by fire in 1819 and replaced by the present chapel (now URC). This has a gabled S front of yellow stock brick, of three round-arched bays with giant pilasters, three grouped doorways in the centre and a round-arched upper window between two plain sashes to light the gallery.

The interior has a gallery around three sides built or altered in the mid 19th century, with panelled front curved at each end but partly cut away to allow the introduction of a large organ on the W side. The pulpit is set in front of a shallow arched recess in the N wall.

Fittings – *Clock*: on front of S gallery, signed 'Linsell, Hadham'. *Monuments*: in chapel, on N wall (1) Charles Cole, 1818, currier, signed 'J. P. Biggs, fecit, Bath'; (2) James Sutton, 1824, Susannah his widow, 1834, and Maria their eldest daughter, 1838, signed 'Gilbert, Camb'; on E wall (3) Suddy Mumford, 1838, Ann his widow, 1858, and Mrs Susanna Foster their daughter, 1834, signed 'D. Peck, Hertford'; (4) Suddy Mumford son of above Suddy and Ann, 1860, signed 'David Peck'; on W wall (5) Thomas Peggram, 1854, and Maria his wife, 1851; (6) Rebecca widow of Charles Cole, 1823. In burial-ground E of chapel (7) Hannah daughter of [ ], 1797; (8) Elizabeth wife of [ ], 1791; (9) Sarah daughter of Thomas and Ann Morris, 1790; (10) table-tomb, inscription worn, *c.*1800; (11) James Sutton, 1824, nearly 30 years deacon. *Pulpit*: polygonal, supported on four columns, 1819, enlarged.

Cong. Mag. II (1819) 125, 252.

Congregational chapel (URC), Buntingford. (18)

HERTFORDSHIRE

BUSHEY

(19) CONGREGATIONAL, Church Walk (TQ 135952). The congregation (now URC) formed in 1809 built a chapel in 1814 which was superseded by another in 1850. The present building of 1904–5 on the site of its predecessor was designed by P. Morley Horder in a simple brick Gothic style with a corner tower formerly surmounted by a spire. (Internal alterations proposed 1989) *Monuments*: in burial-ground, some headstones of the early 19th century and later have been reset, including (1) Frances only daughter of Rev. John Fernie of Brewood, Staffs., 1841; (2) Mary wife of Rev. D. Hillier, [1847?]; (3) Eliza wife of William Pettingell of Mount Street, London, 1824.

CYB (1905) 128. Urwick (1884) 399.

CHIPPERFIELD

(20) BAPTIST (TL 042018). The church was formed in 1820 following an interest commenced by preachers from Chenies, Bucks. The chapel built in 1837 was enlarged in 1859 and largely refashioned in 1866 including a gabled front and corner staircase tower with pyramidal roof. The original side walls remain but extended by one bay to the front; the rear NE wall retains traces of two former windows flanking the pulpit. The interior has a single SW gallery.

Fittings – *Inscriptions*: on bricks externally in SE wall 'H. Biggs 31 March 1837', 'T.D. Biggs, 31 March 1837', and many undated names. *Monuments*: in chapel (1) Rev. Edward Steane DD, 1882, former Secretary of Baptist Union; (2) Richard Taylor, 1875; (3) Rev. S. Couling, pastor 1872–85; (4) George Freeman, 1850, deacon; in burial-ground (5) William son of Jesse and Sarah Wallinger, 1876, wooden grave-board; (6) James Jordan, 1856, butcher, headstone. *Plate*: pewter, set of flagon, two cups and two plates, the flagon and cups inscribed '*The Gift of Richard Davis to the Communicants of the Dissenting Meeting at Chipperfield, Herts 1st August 1821*'.

Urwick (1884) 451. Watts (1978) 26. Whitley (1928) No. 116.

CHORLEYWOOD

(21) BAPTIST, Hillside Road (TQ 023958). A new chapel and Sunday-school were designed by H.G. Ibberson to occupy a site on a housing estate developed by James Beckley, who was also a major benefactor to the chapel. The chapel was never built and the school erected in 1906 has remained in use as a meeting-house with the addition of a hall in 1934. The school/chapel of brick with some rendering and a slate roof is lit by a series of tripartite lunettes in the side walls. It is designed in the Arts and Crafts tradition and contains some fittings and small tapestries of the period.

B.Hbk (1906) 481–2. *The Builders' Journal* (3 May 1905). *Chorleywood Free Church, Hillside Road; 1905–1965, Diamond Jubilee Year Book* (1965).

(22) Former PRIMITIVE METHODIST, Colleyland (TQ 026962). Built 1893 superseding a building in Solesbridge Lane. Red brick with yellow brick dressings; gabled E front with doorway between lancets and paired lancets in side walls. Interior with large two-centred arch behind rostrum pulpit and small vestry behind. Many inscribed tablets on outer walls. (Sold 1970–1, all inscriptions violently defaced; converted to Arts Centre)

Former Primitive Methodist chapel, Chorleywood. (22)

COLNEY HEATH

(23) WESLEYAN, Sleapshyde (TL 202069). Small three-bay chapel of rendered brickwork, gabled E front with later porch. Opened 1840.

COTTERED

(24) Former CHAPEL (TL 318293). Brick with low gabled front; tablet inscribed 'Built by Voluntary Contributions'. Possibly the Congregational Mission Chapel of 1843.

DATCHWORTH

(25) Former WESLEYAN, Burnham Green (TL 263164). Originally an infant school, built 1843, inscription on gable end. (Now village hall)

FLAUNDEN

(26) Former BAPTIST (TL 017010). 'Union Chapel' was built in 1830 and a Baptist church formally constituted in 1836; this briefly united with a church at Chipperfield in 1850 but was re-formed eight years later. In 1985 the church united with one in Bovingdon and the chapel was closed. The chapel is a low building of brick with a broad front to the S, extended one bay to the W, and a Sunday-school built at the E end in 1891. (Converted to house 1987)

Baptist chapel, Hillside Road, Chorleywood. (21)

GREAT GADDESDEN

(27) Former BAPTIST, Jockey End, Gaddesden Row (TL 039135). 'Ebenezer Chapel' built 1845, of brick with gabled NW front; three tall round-arched front windows with outer arches of stone. Gallery above entrance, box-pews with doors removed. (Closed c.1976 and converted to workshop) *Monuments*: externally on SW wall (1) Ellen Knowles, 1870, 'who willed the first lamps to this place of worship'; in burial-ground NE of chapel, three late 19th-century wooden grave-boards (2) illegible; (3) Elizabeth wife of Charles Walters, 1874; (4) Emily wife of John Newton, 1865, exceptionally elaborate monument with buttressed and spired end posts (loose and damaged 1994).

(28) WESLEYAN, Jockey End, Gaddesden Row (TL 040137). Small chapel of rendered brickwork, opened 1845. Arched canopy over entrance.

HARPENDEN URBAN

(29) Former CONGREGATIONAL, Amenbury Lane, Harpenden (TL 134141). The chapel on the S side of the lane was built in 1840 for a church formed in 1822 which originated in meetings held in a recently established Dissenting grammar school. The chapel (now in commercial use) has a pedimented brick front of three bays with two tiers of windows, altered 1887. Following the erection of a new chapel in 1896–7 (*see* (30)) the former chapel was used for a brief period as a Sunday-school.

Skinner, Mary, *Gathered Together: A History of Harpenden United Reformed Church* (1990).

(30) CONGREGATIONAL, Vaughan Road, Harpenden (TL 136143). The chapel built in 1896–7 for the congregation from the foregoing (now URC) was designed by Arthur Anscombe in a free Gothic style. The walls are of red brick with stone dressings. The principal entrance at the N end is covered by a porch above which an octagonal ventilating turret in the gable provides an architectural feature. The interior has a wide nave with passage aisles and an arched organ-recess at the S end. A Sunday-school hall was added at the S end in 1903–4.

Skinner (1990) op. cit.

HEMEL HEMPSTEAD

(31) BOX LANE CHAPEL, Boxmoor (TL 037057). Although much speculation has been indulged in regarding the origins of the Presbyterian, latterly Congregational, society formerly meeting here it can only be said that it probably originated in the late 17th century and was in existence for some years prior to the erection of the meeting-house. This building is described as 'lately erected' in the first trust deed of 1697 although a reported ledger stone of 1694, now missing, may indicate a slightly earlier date. The building remained substantially unaltered until c.1836–7 when it was 'repaired and altered', an old vestry demolished, and a porch and school-room built. Further substantial changes in 1876 greatly altered both the internal and external appearance of the building. The site is additionally of interest for Roman funerary remains uncovered in the burial-ground in 1837.

(The chapel was drastically altered with the loss of all fittings and much remaining character in 1972 on conversion to a house. It is here described as existing prior to that date; the drawings show the wall framing as exposed during conversion.)

The walls are timber-framed with later brick infilling concealed externally by a harsh concrete rendering; the roof, covered with decorative tiling, is of double construction with half-hipped ends and a central valley. Gables were added to front and rear in the 19th century. The front faces SE and has two early 19th-century round-arched windows with wooden frames of three lights and leaded glazing; a central porch of 1836–7 is gabled and has stepped angle buttresses and an ogee-arched doorway. In the later gable is a circular window and a small tablet at the apex inscribed 'Rebuilt 1690 Restored 1876'. There is a similar circular window in the rear gable. A small vestry occupies a restricted site at the rear. The end walls to NE and SW have each two lunette windows above tie-beam level and two lower windows; the SW end is partly covered by a 19th-century school-room with lean-to roof.

The interior (33ft by 40½ft) has two oak posts of octagonal section supporting the valley beam, concealed within rectangular boxing in the late 19th century or before. The ceiling has a wide segmental plaster barrel-vault with a cross vault to the added front and rear gables; it is shaped around the original braces from the central posts but braces from the wall posts in the front and rear walls had previously been removed. A narrow gallery along the SE side was constructed in the late 19th century, approached by a staircase in the school-room; it is supported by four columns of pine with traditional moulded caps and bases. Galleries may earlier have existed against the end walls. Behind the pulpit on the NW side is a shallow recess in the later brickwork contemporary with the present vestry; the former vestry of rubble has a lozenge of brickwork ornament on its formerly external NE face.

Fittings – *Clock*: on SW wall above inner doorway to school-room, 'Parliament clock' with octagonal dial and pendulum case decorated with oriental hunting scene, signed '*Edward Pinchbeck LonDon* [sic]', 18th-century. *Communion Table*: oak (2ft by 6ft) with turned baluster legs, front stretcher with moulded edge and supported by shaped brackets, 18th-century. *Glass*: in circular window behind pulpit, simple floral emblem of red, yellow and white glass, early 19th-century. *Inscription*: on small softwood panel from former pew, fixed to screen below gallery, brass upholstery nails making a heart above '17 ℞ 08'. *Lighting Fittings*: fixed to NW face of boxing of each of the two main posts, wrought-iron support to 18in-long wooden candlestick and iron hood above, early 19th-century. *Monuments*: no monuments remain within the chapel but a floorslab said to have been recorded in 1892 is claimed to have commemorated the Rev. Thomas Whitehead, who 'died 18 August 1694' and was 'upward of 15 years pastor'. In burial-ground NE of chapel (1) Mary Ann wife of Robert Oliver of Felden, 1876; (2) 'JFG 1845, CG 1856'; (3) William Henry Austin, 1851, and Jane his daughter, 1875, with footstone 'WHA 1851, JA 1875'; (4) 'TC 1877'; (5) George Austin, 1865, and William his brother, 1868; (6) Mary daughter of Thomas and Mary Knowlton, widow of Edward Hill, 1832, with footstone 'MH 1832'; (7) Mrs H. Montague, 1870, and Sarah her daughter, wife of J.W. Harberd, 1874, with footstone 'HM 1870, SH 1874'; (8) 'FM 1854, HM 1855'; (9) 'AH 1864'; also three late 19th-century headstones against SE wall. *Notice Board*: on porch, overpainted but retaining traces of 19th-century service times,

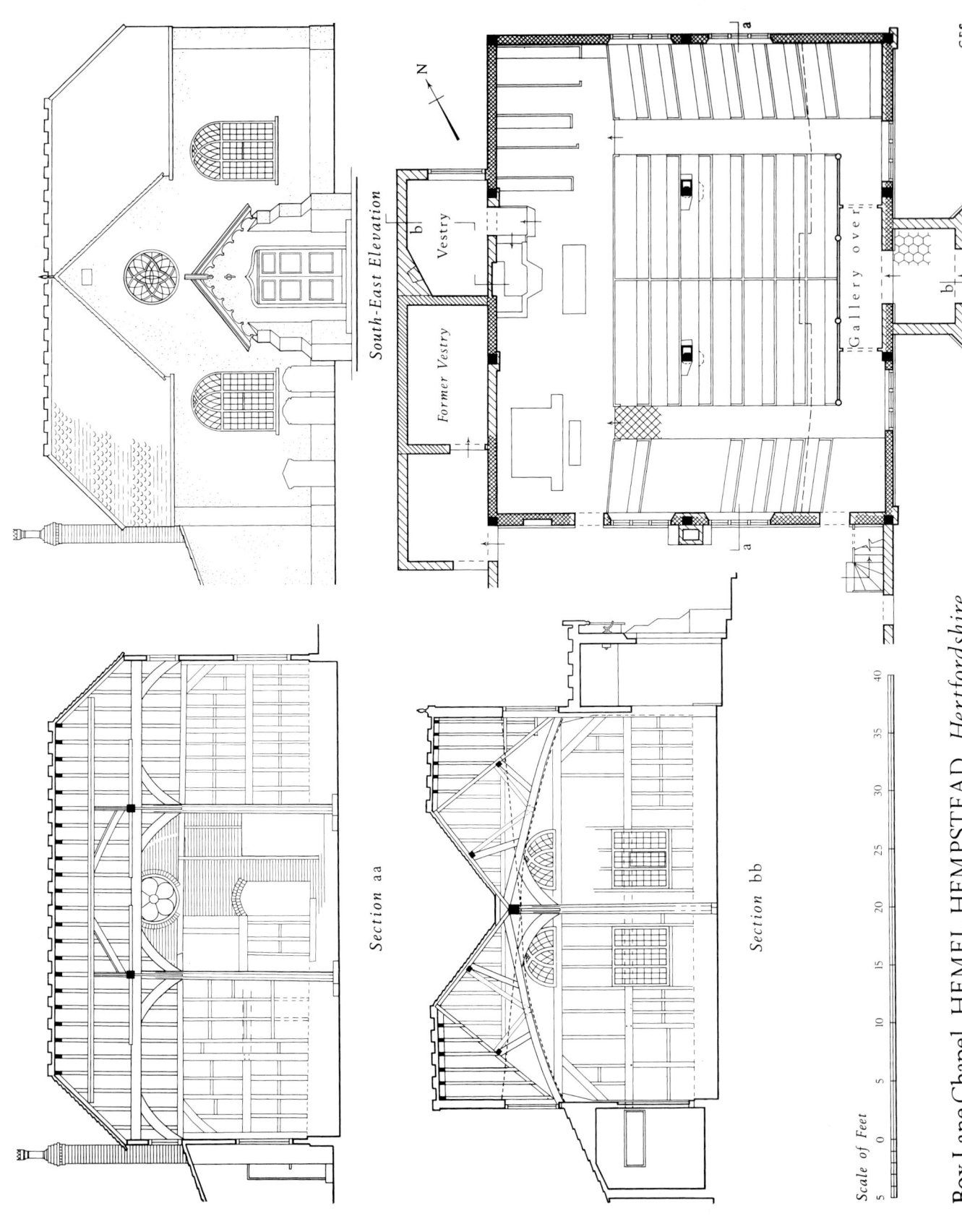

Box Lane Chapel, Boxmoor, Hemel Hempstead. (31)

'Lords Day Mor'g at ¼ to 11 o'Cl, after'n at ½ past 2 o'Cl, Ev'g at ½ past 6 o'Cl, Thursday [½] past 5 o'Cl'. *Plate*: includes two pewter plates by Benjamin Blackwell, of the mid 18th century. *Pulpit*: two tiers of bolection-moulded panels, 19th-century possibly incorporating earlier work.

Archæologia XXVII (1839) 434; XXXIV (1852) 394–8. Briggs (1946) 18. Pope, F.G., and Sabey, B.W., *Box Lane Congregational Church, 1600–1950* (1950). Urwick (1884) 382–90.

(32) BAPTIST, Boxmoor (TL 048059). The first chapel on this site was built in 1825 and a Particular Baptist church formed in the following year; the chapel was of brick with a hipped roof, the front of three bays had a segmental-arched doorway between two tiers of sash windows separated by a platband. The present chapel of brick and stone in the Gothic style said to be by J. Neale of Bristol was built in 1864. It has a square corner tower with octagonal slated spire and corner spirelets. The interior has an open roof supported by four hammer-beam trusses resting on sculptured corbels. A gallery around three sides is supported by cast-iron columns by 'A. Munro, Iron founder, Bristol'. *Monuments*: in burial-ground, (1) Mary Carey, 1842, and Mrs Ann Hobson, 1843, 'sisters of William Carey DD, missionary…', also Hannah Potto daughter of the above Mrs Hobson, 1864; (2) James Church, 1840, and Jane his widow, 1844.

[Johns, S.T.B.], *Boxmoor Baptist Church, 1826–1976* [1976]. Urwick (1884) 391–2.

(33) BAPTIST, Marlowes (TL 056075). The Baptist church in Hemel Hempstead originated in the mid 17th century. In 1711 one rood of land was acquired in Bury Road for a burial-ground and in 1731 a new meeting-house was erected 'to the rear of the Rose and Crown ph, in High Street'. The site of the latter is now converted to a public garden (TL 057079) and some re-sited monuments remain visible. That chapel was a square building with hipped roof and central valley, four-bay front and two tiers of windows.

The present chapel in Marlowes, opened 1861, was designed by Joseph James in the Gothic style. The walls are of stock brick with stone dressings. The gabled front has two traceried windows above the entrance.

Notice Board: loose in chapel, inscribed 'Marlowes Chapel', with service times, late 19th-century.

Cook, W.G.S., *Marlowes Baptist Church, Hemel Hempstead* (1961). Urwick (1884) 441–2.

(34) SALEM CHAPEL, Two Waters (TL 055056). The Strict Baptist church was formed in 1817 and the chapel, in Featherbed Lane, was built in the following year. This has rendered brick walls and a hipped slate roof. The front faces SE and has two sash windows to the chapel with a cottage to the right and extension to the left incorporating a gallery. The pulpit at the NE end has a polygonal front with reeded panels and original back-board. (Closed 1990)

(35) FRIENDS, St Mary's Road (TL 058079). The present site, described as 'a plot of land 44 yards by 18½ yards belonging to the Bell Inn in High Street' with access through the inn yard, was acquired in 1718 largely superseding a meeting-house 2 miles NE at Wood End (approximately TL 083099). The meeting-house erected in 1718 has brick walls and a hipped tiled roof. The W front has a central entrance (blocked since 1948) and two tiers of sash windows, those S of the entrance have been conflated into taller round-arched windows; the fenestration of the E wall has been similarly altered. The interior (41½ft by 21½ft) was altered and refitted in 1958 following a period of minimal use between 1905 and 1949. Two newel posts from the former stand have been reused in a modern staircase.

Anon., *250th Anniversary of the building of the Friends' Meeting House, Hemel Hempstead* (1968). Butler (1999) 256.

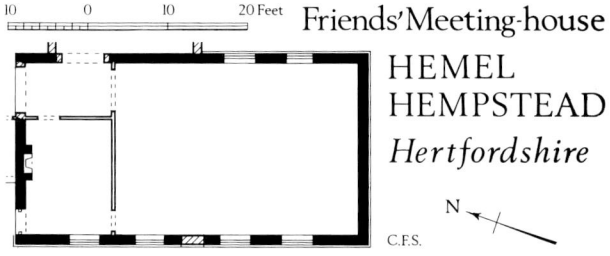

HERTFORD

(36) BAPTIST, Cowbridge (TL 323129). Brick with big seven-light segmentally arched front window with perpendicular tracery and octagonal corner turrets. 1906, by George Baines and Son.

B.Hbk (1906) 488. Lake, E., *Hertford Baptist Church 1897–1987* (1987).

(37) CONGREGATIONAL, Cowbridge (TL 324128). The church (now URC) formed in 1673 had a meeting-house near Christ's Hospital until 1796 when it was demolished to enlarge the school. The present site was then acquired and a new meeting-house erected which was replaced by the present building in 1863. The chapel, designed by Thomas Smith and Son, is in the Gothic style with walls faced with flint and dressings of yellow brick and Bath stone. It comprises a nave and aisles with wooden arcades on cast-iron columns and a continuous clerestory.

CYB (1863) 317, 320. Skinner, R.O., *The History of the Hertford Congregational Church* (1923). Urwick (1884) 542–7.

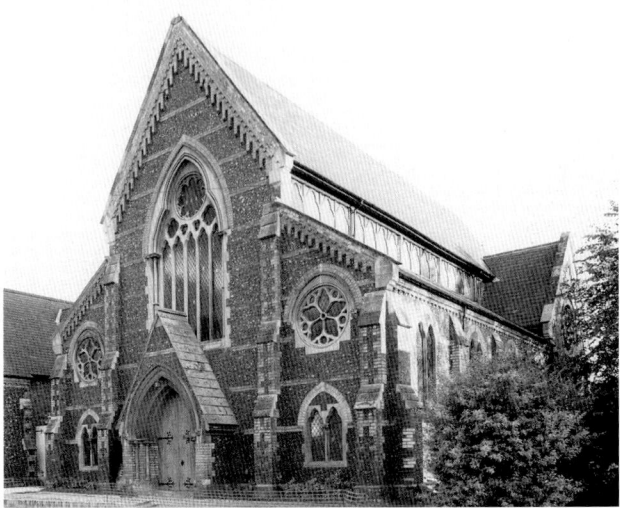

Congregational chapel (URC), Cowbridge, Hertford. (37)

(38) FRIENDS, Railway Street (TL 328127). The first meeting of the Society of Friends in Hertford was held in 1655 and land for a burial-ground was acquired on the W side of Port Hill (TL 323131) in 1661. The present site, which comprised cottages and land in 'Back Street', was bought in 1669 and placed in trust specifically for Quakers. The meeting-house (42ft by 34¾ft externally), for which detailed building accounts survive, was erected in 1670. The walls are of brickwork and the roof is tiled. The design closely follows that of a two-storeyed house of the period to which it could if necessary have been converted, with twin gables to the NW front and a substantial chimney-breast against the SW side. The rear half of the roof is aligned at right angles to the front and has NE and SW gables. This exterior conceals a single large room rising the full height of the building with a freestanding post supporting the roof structure and a gallery at the SW end.

The front wall has a single window of three lights in each of the gables and a range of small windows below which is repeated at the rear. The windows at the extreme NE ends of the front and back walls were formerly doorways but blocked in 1717 when it was decided to make a double door and porch on the NW side and to close the two doors next to the [minister's] gallery and make windows instead. These lower windows appear to have been cross-framed but blocked in the lower halves in 1737 when it was agreed 'to get all the wooden windows round the meeting-house plastered quite up to the glazed lights', perhaps signifying that the lights below the transoms were unglazed and closed by shutters; two windows in the rear wall have been reopened below the transom but with the lower parts of the frames renewed.

N front.

Interior from SW.
Friends' meeting-house, Hertford.

The interior has a gallery ('loft' or 'upper gallery') at the SW end with lobby below. The staircase in the S corner has a straight string and flat shaped balusters. The gallery, divided by a partition into two rooms, one with a fireplace, has shutters opening to the meeting-room; the opening was enlarged, possibly in 1815, by lowering the cill, and reusing the shutters sideways as earlier graffiti on them indicate. The lobby has a wide fireplace in the SW wall and shutters opening to the meeting-room. The stand at the NE end has been enlarged but the wall seat and that first in front appear to be unaltered.

The 'Small Meeting-house', a detached building to the N, now 'The Priory Rooms', was built for women Friends in 1737. This was specified to be '21ft long by 18ft wide' externally, but it has been much rebuilt. It is of brick and tile with a hipped double roof and centre valley; the S and W walls remain and have one window of three lights to the W and a two-light window and wide doorway on the S side.

Fittings – *Books*: over 50 volumes of early Quaker and other works including (1) *A large and complete concordance of the Bible in English...*, by Samuel Newman, 'now teacher of the Church of Rehoboth in New England', printed for Thomas Downes and Andrew Crook (1650); (2) three volumes of late 17th-century tracts, including William Bayley, *To the Camp of Israel...called Quakers in England...* (1675); (3) Samuel Fisher, *The Testimony of Truth Exalted* (1679); (4) John Milton, *Paradise Regained* (1720); (5) *The Works of William Penn* (1726); (6) *Journal of the Life of Thomas Story* (1747); (7) Joseph Besse, *A Collection of the Sufferings of the People called Quakers* (1753).

Clock: on gallery front, signed 'E. L. Simmons, Coleman St., London', early 19th-century. *Chair*: oak, with turned legs, scrolled arm-rests and back panel carved in low relief, 17th-century. *Ironwork*: on doors in gallery and catches of lower windows, late 17th-century. *Seating*: benches in meeting-room, unpainted deal, with shaped ends, 18th-century and later.

Butler (1999) 256–8. Rowe, Violet A., *The First Hertford Quakers* (1970).

HITCHIN

(39) BAPTIST, Tilehouse Street (TL 181290). The congregation originated in the mid 17th century largely under the influence of the preaching of John Bunyan. The church formed in 1669 included both Baptists and Independents but the latter withdrew in 1677. The first regular meeting-house was built in the vicinity of the present chapel in 1692 and variously altered and enlarged during the 18th century. When its materials were offered for sale in 1844 its dimensions were given as '46ft by 36ft and 18ft high'.

The present chapel, designed by John Davies and closely resembling his Baptist chapel in Abingdon, Berks. (*see Nonconformist Chapels and Meeting-houses in South-West England* (1991) monument (1)), was built in 1844 and is of brick with a stucco front. The N front is of three principal bays with four attached Roman Doric columns *in antis* carrying a full Doric entablature and pediment; in each bay is a round-arched doorway and sash window above. The side walls of six bays have two tiers of windows.

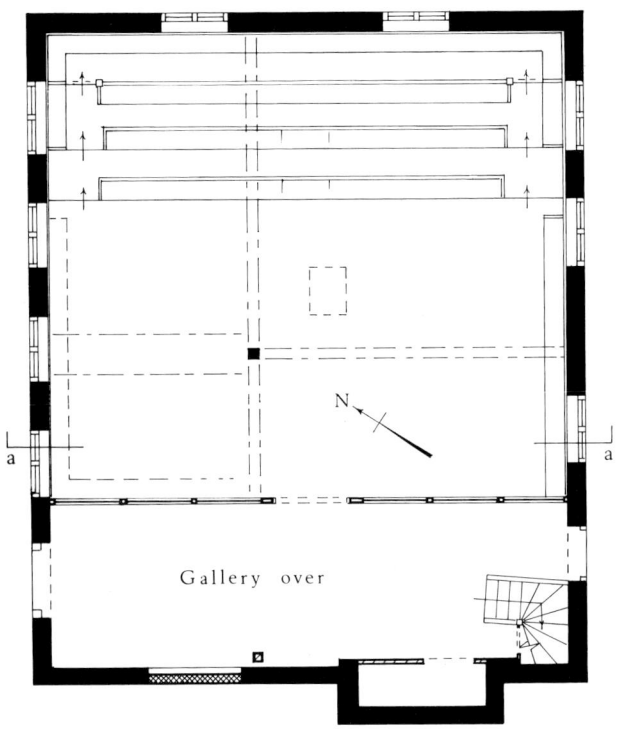

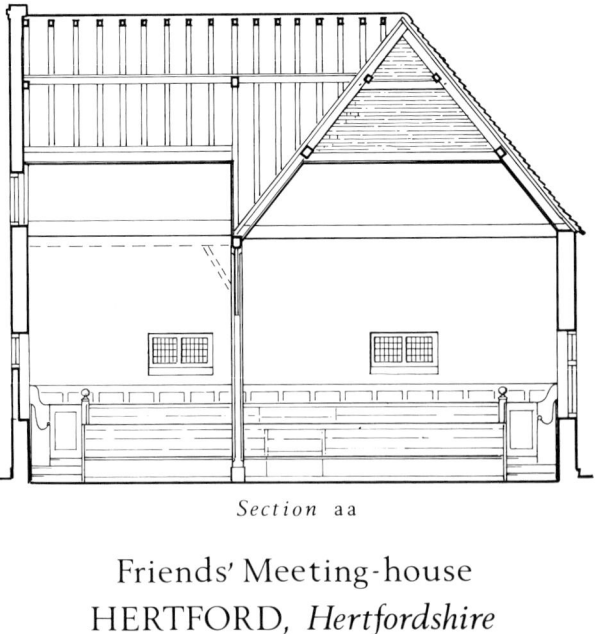

Section aa

Friends' Meeting-house
HERTFORD, *Hertfordshire*

The interior has a gallery around three sides supported by reeded cast-iron columns. The seating and pulpit were renewed in the late 19th century.

Fittings – *Gates* and *Gate Piers*: at main entrance, of cast iron with Greek anthemion ornament to openwork piers and scrolled overthrow. *Monuments*: externally on W wall (1) Agnes Beaumont (Mrs Story), 1720, member of John Bunyan's Bedford Church from 1672, erected 1812; in extensive burial-ground to rear (2) John son of John Foskett, 1713, headstone with winged cherub's head, loose.

BM XXXVI (1844) 470–1. *Hertfordshire Mercury* (29 June 1844). Hine (1929) II: 44–96. Ivimey II (1814) 197. Urwick (1884) 645–9. Watts (1978) 9–10, 19.

(40) BETHEL CHAPEL, Queen Street (TL 186290). Strict Baptist; with rendered gabled front dated 1869.

(41) BAPTIST, Walsworth Road (TL 190294). The site was first occupied by a mission hall erected in 1867. A General Baptist church in connection with Tilehouse Street was formed in 1869; the present Gothic chapel of red brick with stone dressings by J. Wallis Chapman was built in 1875–6. Sunday-school on site of mission hall built 1914.

Anon., *Souvenir Brochure 1869–1969* (1969). Hine (1929) II: 95. Watts (1978) 19.

(42) CONGREGATIONAL, Queen Street (TL 186289). The congregation which separated from Tilehouse Street in 1677 built their first meeting-house on this site (formerly Dead Street or Back Street) in 1690. This was a large rectangular building of brickwork with a hipped tiled roof supported internally by tall pillars; it had galleries around three sides and a pulpit between two tall round-arched windows in the back wall. The meeting-house was rebuilt in 1855; the new chapel of yellow brick has a front of three bays with giant rusticated pilasters supporting a pediment. (Demolished 1970) *Monuments*: headstones of the 18th and 19th centuries remained stacked in the burial-ground in 1970.

Hine (1929) II: 97–134. Urwick (1884) 649–50.

(43) Former FRIENDS, Brand Street (TL 183293). A meeting-house in Cod-piece Alley (later Meeting-house Alley) was built in 1694; this was superseded in 1840 by the present building designed by Samuel Whitfield Dawkes. The meeting-house, now occupied as local government offices, has rendered walls and a hipped roof. The SW front of five bays with plain sash windows has a long low

Baptist chapel, Tilehouse Street, Hitchin. (39)

HERTFORDSHIRE

porch of three bays in front originally flanked by open loggias. The interior comprises two meeting-rooms divided by a screen with four pilasters and three bays of shutters. The larger room to the NW, converted to a council chamber, retains its original stand. Further buildings have been added at one end.

Burial-ground: across the road to SW, has uniform round-topped headstones including dates 1762, 1763. A new meeting-house was built on this site 1958–9.

Butler (1999) 258–60. Hine (1929) II: 135–237, reissued (1929) as *A Mirror for the Society of Friends*. Urwick (1884) 638.

(44) Former WESLEYAN, Brand Street (TL 184293). The chapel built 1834, altered and re-fronted 1870, has a SW front of grey brick with stone dressings. Three-bay centre with three arched entrances between wings. (Demolished *c*.1971) *Monuments*: reset on front wall (1) Thomas Ward, 1839; (2) Sophia Ward, 1836.

Hine, R.L., *The Story of Methodism at Hitchin in 1834–1934* (1934). Poole, H., *et al.*, *Old Hitchin, Portrait of an English Market Town* (1976).

HODDESDON

(45) FRIENDS, Lord Street (TL 372088). A meeting-house was built in 1828 to supersede a building of 1697 in Marsh Lane (now Essex Road) which survived until 1956 converted to a pair of cottages. The new meeting-house has walls of stock brick and a slate roof. The simple Classical front has a pedimented centre between low wings and a central doorway with cornice supported by decorative consoles. The interior has a small entrance passage between two retiring rooms; the single meeting-room beyond has a stand at the S end. *Monuments*: in burial-ground to S, uniform round-topped stones, the earliest is to Catherine Manser, 1829.

Butler (1999) 260–1. Urwick (1884) 496–8.

Friends' meeting-house, Hoddesdon. (45)

ICKLEFORD

(46) WESLEYAN (TL 185321). Brick with gabled front dated 1850.

KIMPTON

(47) BAPTIST, Perry Green (TL 145190). 'Union Chapel', gabled front of yellow brick with red brick dressings; erected 1886.

KINGS LANGLEY

(48) STRICT BAPTIST, Waterside Road (TL 075029). 'Zion Chapel' dated 1835 has walls of rendered brickwork and a hipped slate roof. Front of three bays with round-arched windows. Interior refitted in late 19th century, semicircular reeded front of original pulpit incorporated in later rostrum.

KING'S WALDEN

(49) BAPTIST, Breachwood Green (TL 151220). In the early 18th century a large meeting of dissenters existed at Bendish, 1 mile E, relocating, according to Ivimey (1814), in 1787 at Coleman Green, which he calls 'about a mile off'. In that year a barn in King's Walden parish was registered as a meeting-house. The present church claims to be the successor to the Bendish meeting. It was described in 1827 as 'Coleman Green' and is said by Watts (1978) to have originated with the resumption of regular services at an old chapel in Breachwood Green. The chapel was replaced in 1831 by another on the present site and superseded in 1904 by the existing building. The previous chapel had brick walls and a hipped slate roof; the front was of three bays with entrances in the end bays below round-arched upper windows, and a plain sash window in the centre bay with date tablet above.

Baptist chapel, Breachwood Green. (49)

The present chapel of 1904 by George Baines and Son is of red brick with white brick dressings in a late Gothic style with ornamentation typical of this firm of architects. The front has a gabled centre with a segmental-arched window of seven lights above paired entrances.

Fittings – *Bible*: ('Breeches Bible', 1562, not examined). *Monuments*: in burial-ground, Rev. Richard Elliot, 1833, 'late missionary in Demerara'; also three wooden grave-boards dated 1896, 1897, 1900. *Pulpit*: loose below gallery, simple square wooden box, the front and one side of 17th-century oak planks, the door, with iron hinges and remains of 17th-century bolt, is fixed to a wooden corner post with shaped top; back and other side later; inscription on back 'Bunyan's Pulpit 1658'. This pulpit is claimed to have been originally in the meeting-house at Bendish and to have been retained because of its supposed historic interest.

B.Hbk (1905) 452. *BM* XIX (1827) 576. Ivimey II (1814) 188. Watts (1978) 27.

LETCHWORTH

(50) FRIENDS, South View (TL 219319). The meeting-house, 'Howgills', of 1907 by Robert Bennett and Wilson Bidwell, was built as a private house for Julia Reckitt incorporating a large meeting-room which, together with the house, she transferred to the Society of Friends. The building follows in its basic design that of the 17th-century meeting-house at Brigflatts, Yorks., West Riding (*see Nonconformist Chapels and Meeting-houses in the North of England* (1994) 305, monument (358)), but with generally taller proportions and larger windows to the meeting-room. The walls are rendered with stone dressings and the roof is tiled. The interior has a gallery on two adjacent sides and a gated staircase but is without a stand.

Butler (1999) 262.

(51) WESLEYAN, Norton Way South (TL 221323). Brick, in free Gothic style with minimal ornament. Opened 1914.

MUCH HADHAM

(52) CONGREGATIONAL (TL 427186). Small chapel of stock brick with red brick dressings; gabled front with rose window and stone pinnacle at apex. Built 1872–4 to design by Habershon and Brock.

CYB (1847) 164; (1875) 440.

NETTLEDEN WITH POTTEN END

(53) STRICT BAPTIST, Potten End (TL 018091). Small chapel built 1835 on concealed site. Brick, gabled front with oval window above porch. Interior with gallery at entrance, otherwise refitted. *Monuments*: in chapel, painted wood (1) William Moores, 1872, 16 years pastor; (2) Thomas Wood, 1854, 24 years pastor; in burial-ground (3) Thomas Wood, 1854, 24 years pastor, and Jane his wife, 1848.

Grace (August/September 1995) 17–19.

PRESTON

(54) BAPTIST (TL 180248). 'Bunyan Chapel' built 1877 apparently by Foster family. Red brick gabled front with narrow round-arched windows.

REDBOURN

(55) MOUNT ZION, Fish Street (TL 107121). The chapel first built in 1802 by Congregationalists was enlarged or rebuilt to double its size in 1807 and further enlarged by re-fronting in 1865. A secession in 1869 led to the formation of a separate Baptist church which, in recent years, has acquired the chapel for its own use. Gabled brick front with rendered dressings.

Urwick (1884) 301. Watts (1978) 30, 44.

(56) WESLEYAN, North Common (TL 105122). Brown brick with red brick banding. Pointed-arched windows in gabled front; school-rooms below chapel. Built 1876.

RICKMANSWORTH URBAN

(57) BAPTIST, High Street, Rickmansworth (TQ 061945). The church began as a secession in 1822 from a congregation at Mill End. The present chapel, opened 1843, is of brick with a gabled front and pointed-arched windows with intersecting tracery. The interior has a rear gallery only, supported by cast-iron columns.

BM XXXV (1843) 584. Watts (1978) 20. Whitley (1928) Nos 51a, 123a.

(58) WESLEYAN, High Street, Rickmansworth (TQ 063945). The first chapel on this site, built in 1843, was replaced in 1866 by a chapel by Mr Pearson of Rickmansworth, of brick with stone dressings. It comprises a chapel with hall adjacent and an octagonal staircase tower with slated spire. The E end is polygonal with gabled sides carried internally on squinch arches. The interior, of four bays, has arched-braced trusses ceiled at collar level and supported by a series of head corbels with Gothic foliage. There is a W gallery. (Demolished *c*.1980)

Weeden, S.E., *Living Flame: A Short History of Methodism in Rickmansworth between 1816 and 1966* (1966).

ROYSTON

(59) NEW MEETING-HOUSE, Kneesworth Street (TL 355409). The Congregational church formerly meeting here originated as a secession in 1791 from the Old Meeting in John Street whose chapel, rebuilt 1843, has been demolished. The two congregations reunited in 1922. The seceders built their meeting-house in 1791–2, enlarging it to the front in the early 19th century.

The original building ($36\frac{1}{2}$ft, enlarged to 54ft, by $32\frac{3}{4}$ft) is of rendered timber-framed construction, partly cased in brickwork; the hipped M-roof with upper valley discharging to the rear is covered in tiles; two round-arched windows in the rear W wall flank the pulpit. The gabled E front of grey brick is of three bays with pilasters, carrying a tall wall-arch to the centre bay enclosing the entrance and a round-arched upper window.

The interior has a plaster ceiling with acanthus-leaf decoration to the cornice; two columns support the wall plate on the line of the original E wall.

Monument: in vestry, Rev. Thomas Towne, 1830, 36 years pastor, also Livesay Mary, 1809, three infants, Thomas, Jacob and Anne [nd], and Mary, 1822, children of Rev. Thomas and Mary Towne. *Pulpit*: possibly incorporates some original material.

Urwick (1884) 813–14.

(60) Former UNITARIAN, Upper King Street (TL 355406). The congregation was formed in 1832 with the support of John George Fordham, who fitted up a chapel in outbuildings at the rear of his house in Back Street (now 47 Upper King Street). The chapel, opened 23 September 1832 by the Rev. W. Clack of Soham,

Former Unitarian chapel, Upper King Street, Royston. (60)

Cambs., occupies the W part of a range of timber-framed and weather-boarded buildings, mostly of a single storey but heightened at the W end, possibly in 1832. The interior (36½ft by 14½ft) retains no original fittings; it was extended by 11ft to the E into the adjoining lower buildings. The chapel was closed in 1895 and has subsequently been used as a workshop. (Derelict 1975)

Christian Life XXVII (1902) 10 May; XXVIII (1903) 23 May. *Christian Reformer* XVIII (1832) 475. Evans (1897) 215. *Inquirer* (24 April 1875) 269–70 obituary of J.G. Fordham. Ruston (1979) 17–24.

ST ALBANS

(61) OLD MEETING-HOUSE, Lower Dagnall Street (TL 145072). The Presbyterian society originally meeting here was formed in the late 17th century following preaching in the city by several of the ejected ministers. In 1794, the acceptance of Arian preaching by the majority of the congregation led the orthodox members to leave and to form a separate society. The Old Meeting then developed on Unitarian lines, becoming much reduced by the mid 19th century, disbanding in 1861; after some use by other denominations and a brief attempt to resume Unitarian services the meeting-house was sold in 1895.

The Old Meeting-house, built in 1697–8 and now in use as offices and greatly altered, has brick walls with later rendering and a hipped tiled roof with a central valley and moulded-wood eaves cornice. The N front, set back behind a small formerly walled forecourt, is of three bays. Before alteration it had a platband at mid-height, an entrance in the left-hand bay with a small window above; the right-hand bay was probably similar but covered by a

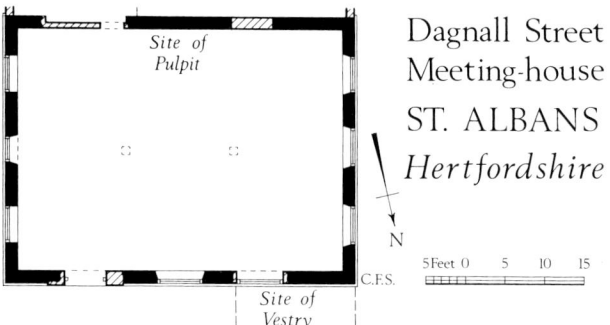

Exterior in late 19th century.

The Old Meeting-house, Lower Dagnall Street, St Albans. (61)

later vestry; and in the centre was a tall window, possibly altered. The E wall, also of three bays with a platband, had a small doorway in the centre with a narrow window above between wider windows. All openings had segmental-arched brick heads. The S wall, exposed internally in an adjacent structure, still retained its original appearance in 1968 with exposed brickwork, a platband of two courses at mid-height, and two wide segmentally arched windows flanking the site of the pulpit.

The interior (30ft by 40¼ft) has been subdivided and a floor inserted at gallery level. Urwick (1884) describes the interior before closure: 'Within, a deep gallery runs along three sides, and the pulpit with communion pew below occupies the fourth, commanding a clear view of every seat below and above. The massive roof of solid oak beams, ceilinged off, is supported by two strong, tall, tree-like pillars of timber'. No trace of the pillars was observed but the roof structure remains unaltered; this comprises two parallel roofs with collar-beam trusses separated by a central valley; the framing of the ceiling is also original.

Evans (1897) 215–16. Ruston, A.R., *Old Presbyterian Meeting House St Albans: The Story of a Building* (1979). Ruston (1979) 5–16. Urwick (1884) 188–207. Urwick, W. *Centenary Memorial [of the Congregational Church Sunday-School, St Albans]* (1894) 1–22.

(62) BAPTIST, Upper Dagnall Street (TL 146073). The Baptist church meeting in St Albans was originally a section of a church centred on Kensworth, Herts., 12 miles NNW, formed in the

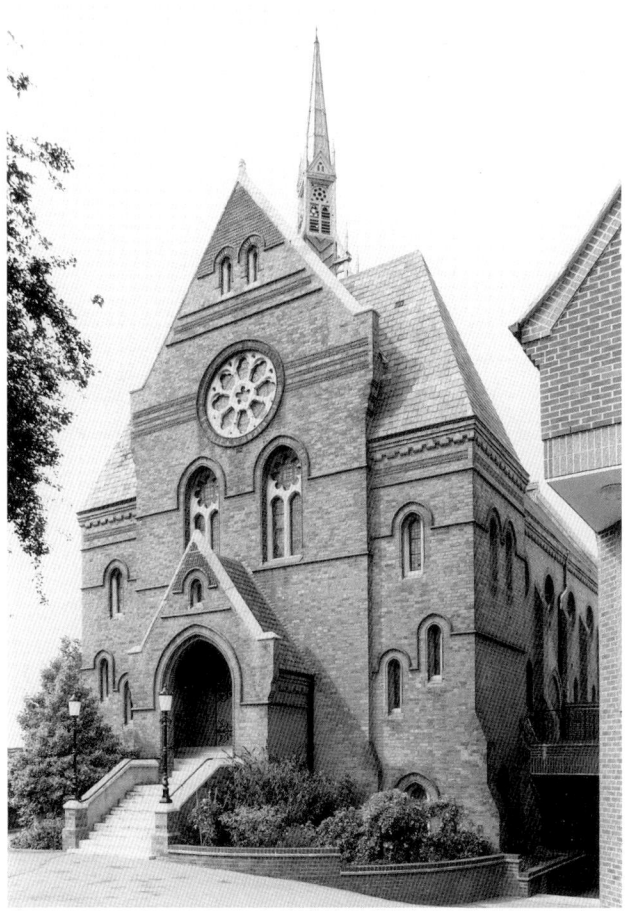

Baptist chapel, Upper Dagnall Street, St Albans. (62)

mid 17th century. By 1713 St Albans had become a principal centre for this congregation and a meeting-house was built in 1720. This was enlarged in 1759 and altered and repaired in 1819, its size being given by Ivimey (1830) as '36ft by 34ft'. The present chapel, on the site of the former, was built in 1884 to a design by Glover and Salter (Morton M. Glover). This is a tall building of brick with steeply pitched roofs and a prominent flèche on the ridge. The S front has a gabled centre between staircase wings. The interior has a S gallery and polygonal N end, beyond which is an open baptistery.

Fittings – *Communion Table*: oak, with turned columnar legs, early 18th-century. *Light Fittings*: original circular fretted gas pendants, 1884. *Monuments*: externally W of chapel, early 19th-century headstones and other monuments, mostly reset or fragmentary, including (1) John Lewis, 1808, Mary Ann his wife, 1849, *et al.*, square column; (2) Sarah wife of William Upton 'minister of this chapel', 1838, and Elizabeth their daughter, 1845.

B.*Hbk* (1886) 337–8. Ivimey II (1814) 168–78; IV (1830) 506–7. Watts (1978) *passim*.

(63) Former BRETHREN, Lattimore Road (TL 151070). The meeting-room built at the cost of Mrs Worley of New Barns in 1865 is a framed structure with weather-boarded cladding. The wide front is gabled and has two round-arched windows and a central doorway with small circular window above. At the rear is a slightly later annexe of similar construction but with walls rebuilt in brickwork. The roof of the meeting-room is supported by five iron skeleton trusses comprising tension rods and T-section diagonal compression members with bolted joints. (Burnt down *c*.1993)

(64) INDEPENDENT, Spicer Street (TL 145072). The orthodox seceders from the Old Meeting-house, Lower Dagnall Street (61), who commenced a separate meeting in 1794, fitted up a small barn in 1795. The chapel in Spicer Street, built in 1811–12 to designs by William Jenkins, has brick walls and a slate roof. The pedimented W front of three bays has a central entrance with canopy supported by iron brackets perhaps replacing columns, two round-arched lower windows and two small gallery windows. The E wall is partly covered by an organ chamber of 1892. To the N of the chapel is a Sunday-school built 1863, enlarged 1888.

The interior (46ft by 36ft) has a gallery around three sides supported at the rear by timber columns but by cast-iron columns at the sides. The pulpit and seating were all renewed in the late 19th century.

Fittings – *Clock*: on front of W gallery, signed 'John Galer, St Albans', early 19th-century. *Monuments*: in chapel (1) Rev. William Urwick MA, 1905, 15 years pastor, author of *Nonconformity in Hertfordshire*, etc.; (2) Rev. John Harris, 1871, 37 years pastor; in rear burial-ground, head- and footstones reset flat in concrete.

Harding, F.A.J., *Three Hundred Years of Christian Witness in St Albans, 1650–1950* (1950). Urwick (1894) op. cit. under (61).

SANDON

(65) Former CONGREGATIONAL, Roe Green (TL 318338). The chapel was built in 1868 for a church originating at Red Hill in the mid 17th century but now united with Walkern URC. A small chapel formerly standing at Red Hill (TL 301331) has been demolished. The chapel at Roe Green, built on land given by H. Fordham, was paid for partly out of a charity established by John Brett in 1747 for supporting local dissenting worship. The walls are of yellow brick with red brick dressings; the front is gabled and has a central porch with a double-arched window above.

Kelly, *Directory of Hertfordshire* (1933) 243. Urwick (1884) 815–19. VCH *Hertfordshire* III (1912) 270.

SARRATT

(66) BAPTIST (TQ 043994). Stock brick with gabled front facing the Green. Built 1895.

Urwick (1884) 336. Watts (1978) 29. Whitley (1928) No. 191.

SAWBRIDGEWORTH

(67) CONGREGATIONAL (TL 480147). A society of Baptists and Independents registered a place of worship in or about 1797 and a mixed church was formed in 1817. The first chapel erected in 1814 was enlarged in 1826 and replaced by the present building in 1862–3. This was designed in the Gothic style by Poulton and Woodman of Reading, whose chapel at Milton Regis, Kent (Kent (125)) had been visited by the building committee and approved as a model for the new building. The walls are of stock brick with dressings of coloured brick and stone. The E front is gabled and has to the N a square tower with pyramidal spire.

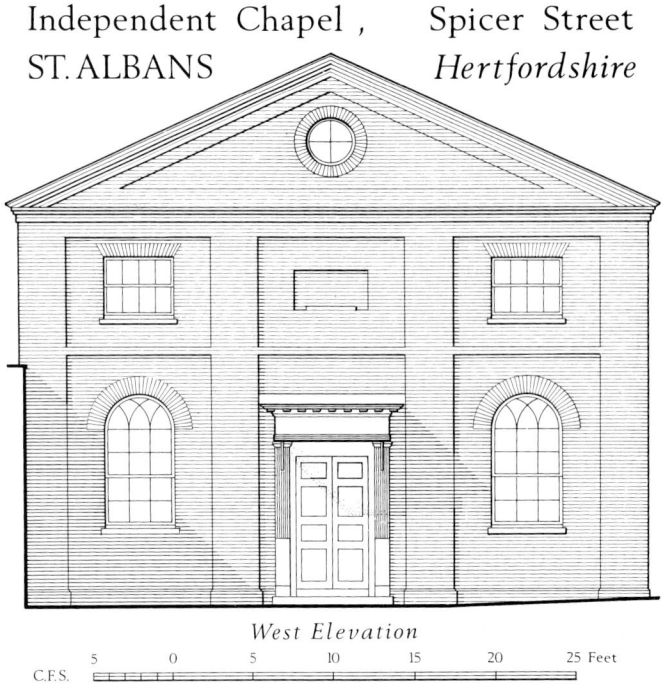

Independent Chapel, Spicer Street
ST. ALBANS *Hertfordshire*

West Elevation

The interior comprises a rectangular preaching nave with organ-apse at the W end; alongside to the N is a Sunday-school aisle separated from the chapel by an arcade of four bays with double columns having shafts and bases of cast iron and closed by movable wooden screens. A detached block of classrooms dated 1911 stands N of the chapel.

Floorslab: inside SE entrance, Herbert Tyler, 1845, 28 years minister. *Inscription*: below E window, date '1862' in quatrefoil.

CYB (1863) 323, 326. Guest, E., *The Congregational Church, Sawbridgeworth, Hertfordshire* (1963). Urwick (1884) 687.

SHENLEY

(68) WESLEYAN, London Road (TL 190006). The chapel opened 1839 has been heightened and enlarged to the front. *Inscriptions*: on two stones in boundary wall of forecourt 'This wall is built on T. Carters Ground …' with dimensions and date 1840.

STANDON

(69) CONGREGATIONAL, Puckeridge (TL 384231). Built 1834, replacing a temporary building brought from Datchworth two years before. Cheap brick Gothic chapel with stone pinnacle at apex of front gable. (Pinnacle and other dressings stripped since 1970)

Urwick (1884) 674.

THERFIELD

(70) CONGREGATIONAL (TL 336373). Flint with yellow brick dressings; front of three bays with low gable, doorway and large upper window altered c.1867. Interior refitted. *Monument*: in burial-ground to N, Edward Rant Bird, 1857, Mary his widow, 1885, *et al*., table-tomb.

Urwick (1884) 822–3.

TRING RURAL

(71) BAPTIST, Long Marston (SP 899157). Three-bay front of red brick with white brick pilasters and two tiers of round-arched windows. Hipped roof. Dated 1869.

(72) Former WESLEYAN, Long Marston (SP 898155). Red brick with yellow brick dressings and hipped slate roof. Three-bay front with segmental-arched doorway, inscribed panel above dated 1864. (Closed by 1996)

Durley (1910) facing 26.

(73) Former PARTICULAR BAPTIST, Wilstone (SP 905140). Small broad-fronted chapel of brick with hipped roof, dated 1837. Three-bay front with round-arched openings. Later cottage attached. (Now converted to two cottages)

TRING URBAN

(74) Former GENERAL BAPTIST, Frogmore Street, Tring (SP 923115). The church which since 1889 has met in a chapel in High Street (77) was a section of the Berkhamsted church formed in the mid 17th century. The meeting-house built in 1751 and enlarged to the front in 1839 stands on the W side of the street. The walls are of brickwork and the roof of the earlier part is hipped and covered with tiles; the later roof is slated. This is a small broad-fronted building (16ft, extended to 24ft, by 28ft externally). The front of 1839 is of yellow brick with a half hip to the truncated gable; it is of three bays with two tiers of windows, the lower openings replaced by a shop front. The rear wall of the original meeting-house behind has two tall windows with altered round-arched heads flanking the site of the pulpit and two upper windows to light N and S end galleries; a fragment of a pre-existing timber-framed building is incorporated into the N end of this wall. The interior has been subdivided. (Largely rebuilt as two cottages since

Former Baptist Chapel, Frogmore Street, TRING. C.F.S. 1975

1975 retaining only parts of the 1839 extension) *Inscription*: on S wall of extension 'Built 1751, Enlarged 1839'.

Chapman, L.G. (ed.), *English Baptist Records, I: The General Baptist Church of Berkhamsted, Chesham and Tring, 1712–1781* (1985) *passim*. Taylor (1818) I: 328; II: 440–3. Watts (1978) 11, 22. Wood (1847) 207.

(75) Former STRICT BAPTIST, Akeman Street, Tring (SP 923112). 'The Tabernacle' or Upper Baptist Chapel, set back in The Terrace (now Tabernacle Yard) off the W side of the street, was associated with the church at New Mill (78). The site, then Levatts Yard, appears to have been bought in 1799 and registered in April 1800 when a building was fitted up, described as 'a small place ... on the premises of John Levatt, in Akeman Street'. The building has a tall forebuilding of brick, of domestic appearance, with an E front of three bays, three tiers of windows and a central round-arched entrance. The chapel behind is a plain structure of a single storey, gabled to the rear, with two sash windows flanking the site of the pulpit. The forebuilding was built or adapted *c*.1807 to provide additional accommodation including two tiers of galleries with panelled and reeded fronts. Since closure in 1897 the premises have been used for social purposes. (Derelict 1975, demolished *c*.1979) *Inscription*: on brick in N wall 'TB 1799'.

Watts, D.R., in *Hertfordshire Countryside* (February 1979) 46–51.

(76) STRICT BAPTIST, Akeman Street, Tring (SP 923113). The chapel was built in 1808 for seceders from the church at New Mill (78), and others, who commenced meetings at Frogmore End in 1801; it was rebuilt in 1832. The chapel is a square building of red brick with a pyramidal slated roof. The E front of three bays divided by plain pilasters has a wide round-arched entrance, similarly arched upper windows, and two lower windows with segmentally arched heads set in semicircular-arched recesses.

The interior, largely refitted in the late 19th century, has a gallery around three sides; adjacent to the rear is a galleried Sunday-school of *c*.1900.

Inscription: on tablet above entrance 'ERECTED 41 by 35ft. 1808 REBUILT 51ft. SQ^{RE} 1832' *Monuments*: in front yard, pair of obelisks (1) James Page, 1851, 5 years pastor; (2) Richard Glover, 1861, 26 years pastor.

Watts (1978) 15, 19. Watts (1979) op.cit. Urwick (1884) 466.

(77) BAPTIST, High Street (SP 922113). The chapel in the Gothic style by W. Huckvale was built in 1889 for the congregation from

Strict Baptist chapel, Akeman Street, Tring. (76)

Frogmore Street (74). It has a three-bay gabled front of purple brick with stone dressings.

(78) BAPTIST, New Mill (SP 925126). The Particular Baptist church purchased premises in 1699 which were converted to a meeting-house. After a brief period of closure in the mid 18th century the meeting was revived and a new meeting-house erected soon after 1775, described by Ivimey (1830) as '31ft by 25ft' and 'repeatedly enlarged'. The present chapel, built 1818 ('62ft by 40ft including the vestries'), stands on the site of the former. The walls are of brickwork and the roof is hipped and slated. The front and sides are of three bays with two tiers of segmentally arched windows; the entrance, centrally at the front, has a round-arched head. The interior has an original gallery around three sides but was otherwise refitted in 1912.

Attached W of the chapel is the Sunday-school dated 1897, built from the proceeds of the sale of 'The Tabernacle'; beyond this are two early 19th-century cottages and an extensive burial-ground.

Fittings – *Monuments*: in chapel (1) John Sutton, 1800; (2) John Rees, 1815, pastor, and John his infant son, 1815; (3) Daniel Clarabut, 1833, 17 years pastor; (4) John Clement, 1812, nearly 24 years pastor; (5) Henry Blaine, 1788, 13 years pastor; (6) Louis R. Foskett, 1894, 7 years pastor; externally, headstones reset into rear wall of Sunday-school (7) John Fulks, 1840, *et al.*; (8) Abigail wife of James Lawrence, 1813; (9) Robert Garneth, sen., 1778; (10) Robert Cox, 1813, and George son of Robert and Elizabeth Cox, 1812; (11) Martha wife of William Butcher, 1810, and William their son, 1812; in burial-ground (threatened with partial clearance 1988) numerous monuments of the early 19th century

Baptist chapel, New Mill, Tring Urban. (*Water-colour, 1853*) (78)

and later. *Painting*: small water-colour of 'New Mill Chapel' signed 'J.A. Grange, 1853'.

Anon., *A Brief History of the Baptist Church, New Mill, Tring, Hertfordshire* (1883). Anon., *A Concise History of the New Mill Baptist Church, Tring* (1955). Ivimey IV (1830) 507–8. Urwick (1884) 465–6. Watts (1978) 10, 15, 19.

WALKERN

(79) CONGREGATIONAL (TL 291266). Rendered walls with masonry lining, gabled front with round-arched iron-framed window above entrance, built 1810. (URC/Methodist) *Monument*: in burial-ground, Mary Ann wife of James Hilton, 1841.

Urwick (1884) 615–16.

WARE

(80) Former CONGREGATIONAL, Church Street (TL 357145). The Old Meeting, described in the early 18th century as Presbyterian, was formed in the years following the ejection in 1661 of the vicar, John Young. In 1778, after the death of the minister, the church divided over the question of a successor, and the supporters of the former assistant pastor appear to have separated, building a new chapel in that year; the fate of the other section is unrecorded.

The 'Old Independent Chapel' in Church Street or Dead Lane, built in 1778, was closed in 1918 on amalgamation with the church in High Street (81); it has subsequently served a variety of secular purposes. The walls are of brickwork and the roof, hipped around a high central valley, is covered in late 19th-century decorative tiling. The S front of three bays has a central doorway and two tiers of windows, all are round-arched and have stone surrounds of the mid 19th century. Windows in the side walls have original segmental-arched heads. The N wall, covered by a later vestry, has two large round-arched windows, now blocked, which flanked the pulpit.

The interior (39¼ft by 38¼ft) probably had a gallery around three sides, now with an inserted floor; one original wall seat with shaped supports remains in the gallery. The roof is supported by

Old Independent Chapel, Church Street, Ware. (80)

two M-trusses of softwood with queen-posts and a valley at collar level discharging to the north.

Monuments: in small burial-ground to W (1) Thomas Adams, 1787, and Martha his widow, 1798, headstone; (2) Samuel Stevens, 1806, *et al.*, large flat slab; (3) James Harradence, 1842; (4) Ann Harradence, 1822, and her sons William, 1815, and Thomas, 1826; (5) Martha Harradence, 1828, and James William her son, 1835.

Urwick (1884) 719–20.

(81) CONGREGATIONAL, High Street (TL 359144). This congregation (now URC/Methodist) originated in 1788 with evening services introduced by Richard Gridley; a church was formed in 1811 under his nephew R.G. North and a meeting-house erected in 1816. The present chapel, in the Romanesque style by John Brown of Ware, was built in 1859. The walls are of brick and stone; the front wall, faced in rusticated masonry, has a round-arched doorway and windows and a wheel-window in the gable. In front of the chapel is a contemporary Sunday-school, enlarged 1884. The chapel has a S gallery and chancel to N flanked by a vestry and organ recess.

Fittings – *Glass*: throughout, a complete series of contemporary windows by Chance, patterned quarries with coloured borders in the side windows and more elaborate painted glass at the N end. *Inscriptions*: on two stones in front gable '1816', 'Rebuilt 1859'; internally below N window, foundation stone laid 25 November 1858 by D.W. Wire, Lord Mayor of London, and name of 'John Brown, Surveyor and Builder'. *Monuments*: on E wall of chancel (1) Rev. Richard Gridley North, 1825; (2) James Clements, 1839, *et al.*; (3) Sarah wife of James Beadle, 1814, *et al.*; (4) Rev. George Pearce, 1858, and Elizabeth Sarah his wife, 1843.

Auld, F., *Centenary of the Rebuilding of the High Street Congregational Chapel, 1859–1959* (1959). *CYB* (1860) 257–8; (1935) 259. Urwick (1884) 720–1.

(82) WESLEYAN, New Road (TL 35951440). Stock brick, 1839, enlarged to front in red brick *c*.1900.

(83) SALVATION ARMY, Baldock Street (TL 356145). Brick with precast concrete dressings. Citadel style with battlemented parapet rising to gable at centre. Dated 1907.

WARE RURAL

(84) Former WESLEYAN, Wareside (TL 394157). Late 19th-century chapel of brick with gabled front and wide pointed arched entrance. (Converted to house)

WATFORD

(85) BAPTIST, Clarendon Road (TQ 110967). Baptist meetings in Watford are believed to have existed from the mid 17th century and to have had links with Particular Baptist churches in London and subsequently at Hemel Hempstead. In 1707 the constituent sections of the Hemel Hempstead church agreed to separate and the members in and about Watford were reorganized as an autonomous society. The first known meeting-house built in 1721, illustrated in a sketch of 1771, stood in Beechen Grove a short distance SE of the present chapel; it was a small brick building of three bays with a central entrance and two tiers of windows. This was enlarged by about 13ft to the front in 1810 but replaced in 1835 by a larger chapel '58½ft by 45½ft' on the same site.

The present chapel, retaining the name 'Beechen Grove', was built on an adjacent site in 1876–8 to a design in the Italianate Romanesque manner by J. Wallis Chapman. This is a large building of brick with a tall tower with pyramidal roof above the NW entrance. The NW end is apsidal; at the SE end is a smaller communion apse and a circular two-storeyed vestry. The body of the chapel has arcades with passage aisles, a deep NW gallery, and high boarded ceiling.

The former chapel, converted to a Sunday-school in 1878, extended to the front and altered internally in 1899, was demolished *c*.1963 for town redevelopment. (The present chapel was subdivided internally in 1987 with an inserted floor providing an upper hall with chapel below)

Baptist Times (24 September 1987). Stuart (1907). Whitley (1928) No. 9.

(86) STRICT BAPTIST, Derby Road (TQ 113965). 'The Tabernacle', built 1887, is of brick with a gabled front flanked by two recessed entrances surmounted by circular turrets with conical roofs.

Whitley (1928) No. 446.

(87) BAPTIST, Chalk Hill/London Road (TQ 121954). 'Bushey Baptist Chapel' in 'New Bushey', now Oxhey, was built in 1882 for a church formed in 1870. The building is of brick with a stone front in the Gothic style by W.H. Syme. Gabled entrance with

Congregational chapel (URC), High Street, Ware. (81)

HERTFORDSHIRE

paired doors; in paving in front of each a pair of cast-iron grilles inscribed 'Patent metal scraper-mat G. Tidcombe & Son, Watford'.
  Whitley (1928) No. 472.

(88) WESLEYAN, London Road, Oxhey (TQ 123954). Red brick with indecisive corner tower; 1904 by Bell and Meredith.

WELWYN

(89) STRICT BAPTIST, Mimram Walk (TL 232162). 'Ebenezer Chapel' dated 1834, hidden in a narrow alleyway, is no longer the 'plain discreet Late Georgian' building described by Pevsner in Buildings of England. Rendered walls, altered entrance, plastic-framed windows.

Pevsner, N. rev. Cherry, B., *Hertfordshire* (Buildings of England) (2nd ed. 1977) 395.

WHEATHAMPSTEAD

(90) CONGREGATIONAL (TL 175139). Red brick with coloured brick and stone dressings; wooden arcades with clerestory. Built 1876–7. (URC)

WIDFORD

(91) Former CONGREGATIONAL (TL 421153). Brick, gabled front with pointed-arched entrance. Dated 1898. (Sold 1969 and heavily converted to house)

'Beechen Grove' Baptist chapel, Clarendon Road, Watford.   (85)

HUNTINGDON & PETERBOROUGH

(Cambridgeshire)

The county of Huntingdon, with its general pastoral character, has not had any marked impact on the history of nonconformist architecture. As the native county of Oliver Cromwell, who was born at Huntingdon in 1599, it may, however, claim a not inconsiderable share in the national fortunes of the 17th century and in the development of organized dissent. Very few ministers in this county were ejected from their livings in 1662, and none founded any separate meeting. The formerly Presbyterian congregation in St Ives (40) and the Baptist church meeting in Warboys (53) both claim to have roots going back to the Commonwealth; the origins of the Great Gransden meeting (15, 16) can be traced to one of those widely spread churches which were a feature of country areas in the late 17th century, and the now defunct Quaker meetings at Earith (6) and St Ives (41) were of similar antiquity; but most of the other churches were formed no earlier than the late 18th century. The preaching of John Berridge, the peripatetic 'methodist' vicar of Everton (1755–93), whose parish church (RCHM *Huntingdonshire* (1926) 269–71, Tetworth monument (1)) stood in a detached corner of the county, and of Henry Venn, who became vicar of Yelling (1771–97) following a successful evangelical ministry in Huddersfield, Yorks. West Riding (*see Nonconformist Chapels and Meeting-houses in the North of England* (1994) 279, monument (219)), had a great influence on the awakening of a religious interest from which 19th-century nonconformists continued to profit. The early fruits of this activity can be seen at Great Gidding (13) while the origins of the cause at Houghton (20) are of considerable interest at a later period.

With few exceptions the buildings listed are of brick, usually gault brick, and the roofs are covered with slates. In only six examples were tiles recorded, and apart from two minor instances the absence of pantiles is notable. The timber-framed meeting-house at Hail Weston (18) of 1759, although fragmentary, shows East Anglian affinities, but the paucity of buildings dating from before 1800, only four of which remain (13, 16, 18, 41), precludes any general comment. In the early 19th century the three-bay front with a hipped roof, as at Earith (7), was popular, but the variant of a gable and the addition of brick pilasters, as at Somersham (48) lasted longer into the century, the pilasters becoming, as at Yelling (60) in 1850, mere divisions between recessed panels, a design which is repeated in 1880 at Stanground South (50) with no more than the inevitable late-Victorian embellishment. Of the more sophisticated chapels of the Gothic revival, the 'Free Church' in St Ives (40) of 1863 by John Tarring is of particular merit; his other work in the county, at Huntingdon (*see* (22)), has been demolished. The brick Wesleyan chapel at Eaton Socon (8) in the Romanesque style is also worthy of attention.

The SOKE OF PETERBOROUGH, which was appended to the historic county in 1965, contains very little of note. Besides the city of Peterborough only the parishes of Ailsworth and Castor are represented here, and the former chapel in Priestgate, Peterborough (28), is the principal object of interest for its unusual entrance feature utilizing an existing building behind which the body of the chapel lies concealed.

AILSWORTH

(1) FREE METHODIST (TL 117988). Gault brick walls with red brick dressings to cornice of front pediment. Three-bay front with round-arched openings. Dated 1860.

BLUNTISHAM

(2) BLUNTISHAM MEETING-HOUSE (TL 368746). The meeting originated in 1784 when Mr Coxe Feary commenced to hold services in private houses and later in a barn, where on 28 December 1786, 26 persons united together as a church. Mr Feary adopted Baptist views in 1791 and the cause is now regarded as belonging to that denomination.

The first meeting-house was commenced 10 April 1787 and opened 26 October the same year with Mr Feary as first pastor. It was built of red brick with a tiled roof and originally measured 40ft by 31ft but it was enlarged by 14ft to the rear in 1797, increasing the depth to 45ft. A vestry was added in 1805, and an additional gallery for the Sunday-school children in 1817. Drawings show a double-gabled front of three bays with two doorways and two tiers of windows. The interior had galleries on three sides and box-pews, with a table-pew in the centre aligned along the longer axis of the enlarged building. The singers' pew was at the rear at ground level.

The old meeting-house was demolished in 1874 and the present building erected on its site was opened on 9 June 1875. This was designed in an attempt to retain some of the character of its

Former meeting-house, Bluntisham. (2)

predecessor, including the double-gabled front, and incorporates some of the materials of the former. The walls are of brickwork and the roof tiled; the front gables have narrow barge-boards and finials; a wide porch across the front has three gabled entrances. Reset in the front wall is the original date tablet, inscribed 'This HOUSE built by Subscription AN° 1787'. The interior has galleries on three sides supported by turned wood columns which rise to ceiling level, some of which may be reused from the former building.

Fittings – *Collecting Shovel*: wood, with two handles, side-opening box with spring catch, 19th-century. *Monuments*: in chapel (1) Rev. Coxe Feary, 1822, 35 years pastor; (2) William Asplan, 1847, 60 years deacon; (3) Rev. John Edmund Simmons, 1868, 38 years pastor, and Rev. Samuel Green, 1840, co-pastor and pastor, 1819–30. *Paintings*: (1) exterior of former meeting-house, water-colour by H. Jackson; (2) water-colour of interior of former meeting-house, unsigned. *Photograph*: of small thatched Baptist chapel at Woodhurst, Hunts. (TL 3176), built 1798, demolished 1902. (Other fittings including a 'tuning fork' or pitch-pipe are reported to be in St Ives Museum)

Dixon, R.W., *A Century of Village Nonconformity at Bluntisham, Hunts, 1787 to 1887* (1887).

BROUGHTON

(3) BAPTIST, Causeway Road (TL 282780). Gault brick and slate, three-bay gabled front with round-arched doorway and oval tablet, erected by B. How, sen., 1861.

CASTOR

(4) CONGREGATIONAL (TL 123986). Stone with slate roof, three-bay gabled front. Built 1848.

Coleman (1853) 377–8. RCHM *Peterborough* (1969) 66.

CATWORTH

(5) WESLEYAN (TL 086732). Common brick and slate, two windows in longer walls. Opened 1838, much altered and upper part rebuilt.

EARITH

(6) Former FRIENDS (TL 382749). The first meeting-house of *c*.1729 was rebuilt in 1774 to accommodate the members from a former meeting at Bluntisham. It was again rebuilt in 1818 but demolished *c*.1960–70. A modern house stands on the site.

Butler (1999) 272. Dixon (1887) 72–94. Whitten (1897) 60–3.

(7) Former WESLEYAN, Chapel Road (TL 385749). Gault brick with hipped slate roof. Three-bay two-stage N front with central doorway; tablet below altered upper window inscribed 'WESLEYAN CHAPEL ERECTED 1828'. *Bootscraper*: wall bracket. *Inscriptions*: on bricks in E and W walls, names, initials and date '1828'.

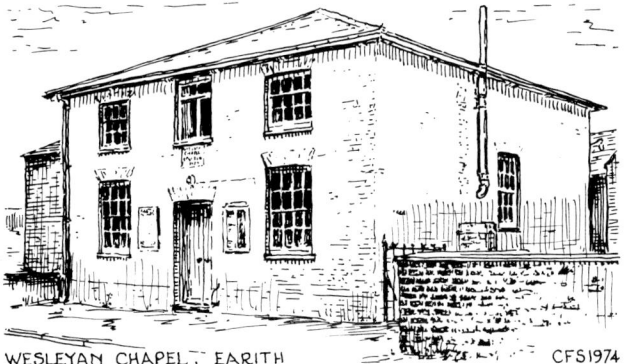

EATON SOCON (*formerly Bedfordshire*)

(8) Former WESLEYAN (TL 169586). The chapel, built in 1850, has walls of yellow brick and a slate roof. The gabled W front has a central round-arched doorway with Romanesque detail, flanked by two windows of similar character and five above. A circular tablet in the gable with altered inscription dated 1850 was partly defaced when the chapel was closed and sold *c*.1974.

ELLINGTON

(9) JIREH CHAPEL (TL 159718). The chapel (derelict 1972) stands on the W side of the Green. It was first built in 1833 and rebuilt in 1847 for a Particular Baptist church. The walls are of gault brick and the roof is covered with slates. The S front has a pedimented gable, two tiers of round-arched windows, the lower ones blind, and a central doorway with two tablets above carrying the chapel name and date of re-erection. The original pews and table-pew remain but the pulpit was remade in the late 19th century. *Monument*: on E wall, to Thomas Sutton Rowlatt, 1917, now fallen off, has earlier incomplete palimpsest inscription on reverse to William Brice, 1758, and Elizabeth his wife, 1747.

Chambers IV (1963) 126–7.

ELTON

(10) WESLEYAN, Middle Street (TL 085939). The chapel 're-erected 1864' has a three-bay front of rubble with ashlar dressings; this has two tiers of round-arched windows, rusticated corners and a cornice and parapet with ball finials and a shaped gablet at the centre. *Railings*: in front of chapel, of cast iron on a panelled iron plinth, *c*.1864.

Former Wesleyan chapel, Eaton Socon. (8)

FENSTANTON

(11) STRICT BAPTIST, Church Street (TL 319687). The small chapel built *c.*1836 for a new congregation has been superseded by a new building on the opposite side of the road. The old chapel is a low structure with rendered walls and a pantiled roof; two sash windows face the road.

Chambers IV (1963) 106–7, Pl. 19a.

(12) CONGREGATIONAL, Chequer Street (TL 318687). The chapel, which replaces an earlier building, was erected in 1874 to a Gothic design by James Tait. Rock-faced stone with tiled roof; gabled porch with thin turret alongside formerly completed with a square spire, but now much reduced in size and interest. Interior of three principal bays and triple-arched end with polygonal apse beyond. (URC)

CYB (1875) 440.

GREAT GIDDING

(13) PARTICULAR BAPTIST (TL 118830). The chapel was built in 1790 for a church which originated about 1779 and previously met at Winwick; the site was placed in trust for Particular Baptists on 20 January 1790 and the building registered on 13 October in that year. It has walls of coursed rubble and a hipped slate-covered roof. The broad S front of three bays has two doorways and two tiers of windows, all with flat-arched heads and keystones. The window frames have been altered. Two tablets below the eaves carry a continuous inscription 'THIS BUILDING WAS ERECTED BY SUBSCRIPTION of FRIENDS | FOR A PLACE of WORSHIP 1790'. The E and W walls have wood cross-framed windows at ground and gallery level. Two round-arched windows in the N wall flank the pulpit and have moulded architraves and key-blocks internally. A vestry of brick and pantile was added at the NW corner in the 19th century.

The interior (24ft by 32ft) has a gallery around three sides

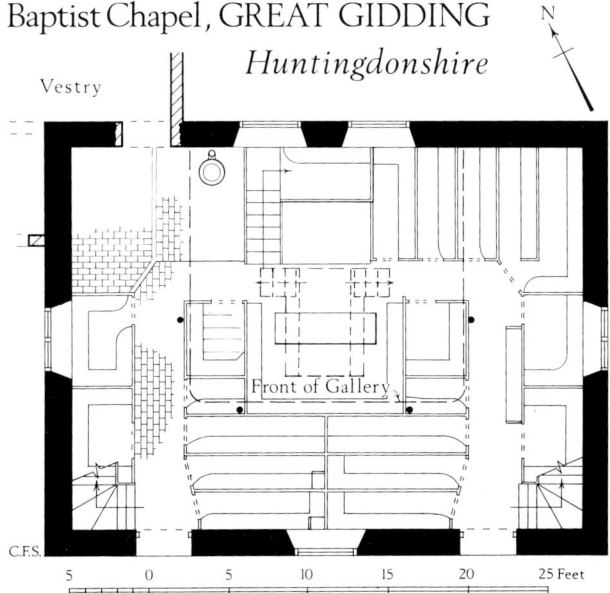

S front.

Interior before removal of fittings.
Particular Baptist chapel, Great Gidding.

supported by turned wood columns: the front has plain panels with a moulded capping. The table-pew in the centre of the chapel is now open to the N and has a baptistery below.

Fittings – *Graffiti*: on outer walls, names, initials and dates including 'I. Rippon, 1790' and 'Thomas Shamley, 1796'. *Monuments*: on front wall, Joseph Norris, 1871, 9 years minister; also 19th-century monuments in burial-ground to N and S. *Pulpit*: the ogee-headed back-board of the former hexagonal pulpit remains on the N wall, other woodwork reused in late 19th-century rostrum. *Seating*: original box-pews with plain panelled sides on ground floor; singers' pew in S gallery.

(The entire fittings of the lower floor, pews and pulpit, were totally removed and destroyed in 1992 under the protection of the Ecclesiastical exemption from listed building legislation.)

Chambers IV (1963) 126.

(14) Former WESLEYAN (TL 118832). Brick and slate, 'opened 1847' but rebuilt in late 19th century. Sunday-school, built in 1906. (Closed *c*.1980)

GREAT GRANSDEN

(15) Former MEETING-HOUSE and BURIAL-GROUND, West Street (TL 269559). The church now meeting in Providence Chapel (*see* (16)) originated as one of the extensive group of nonconformist societies gathered in the late 17th century by Francis Holcroft. In 1694, when the church book begins, meetings were being held here and at Croydon, Cambs.; in the early 18th-century 'Evans List', the cause appears under the latter place as a society of Independents. In 1734 the church was reorganized as Particular Baptist and, shortly afterwards, *c*.1735, the present chapel was built on a new site.

The former meeting-house is believed to be represented by a cottage, 'The Old Meeting-house' No. 20 West Street (Eltisley Road). This is a rendered timber-framed and thatched building of the early 17th century which, although without structural evidence of its supposed use, could well have served that purpose.

The 'Old Burial-ground', adjacent to the cottage on the E side, is a small parcel of ground containing two headstones of the mid 18th century and several others of more recent date. The latter include one to Anne Dutton, 1765, widow of pastor Benjamin Dutton, who 'generously left an endowment for the preaching of the gospel in this village', erected 1887.

RCHM *Huntingdonshire* (1926) 122, monument (22).

(16) PROVIDENCE CHAPEL, Sand Road (TL 273558). The Particular Baptist chapel built *c*.1735 for the church formerly meeting in West Street (15) has brick walls and a hipped tiled roof. The front wall, with brick plinth and dentil cornice, has a central doorway with bracketed hood and two tiers of segmental-arched windows separated by a platband. Two windows in the rear wall flanking the pulpit have been blocked.

The interior (30½ft square), largely refitted *c*.1900, has two round wood columns with square heads and bases supporting the roof structure. A gallery along two adjacent walls was added later in the 18th century and has a plain panelled front above a fluted Doric frieze; the fenestration allows for the return of the gallery along the NE wall but this does not appear to have been erected.

Fittings – *Clock*: on front of NW gallery, black and gold with octagonal dial and Chinese decoration on case, by Thomas Kefford

Providence Chapel, Great Gransden. (16)

of Royston, mid 18th-century. *Library*: A 'valuable library of puritanic books, left by the celebrated Mrs Ann Dutton' does not survive. *Monuments* and *Floorslabs*. *Monuments*: in chapel on SE wall (1) Robert Skilleter, 1831, *et al.*; in front of chapel (2) Timothy Keymer, pastor 1755–72, headstone; *Floorslabs*: (1) 'R.S.1831'; (2) 'Ed.S.1832'.

B.Hbk (1891) 146–7, obituary of Frederick King. Chambers IV (1963) 124, Pl. 24a. Ivimey IV (1830) 509–10. Typescript notes from *The History of Great Gransden*.

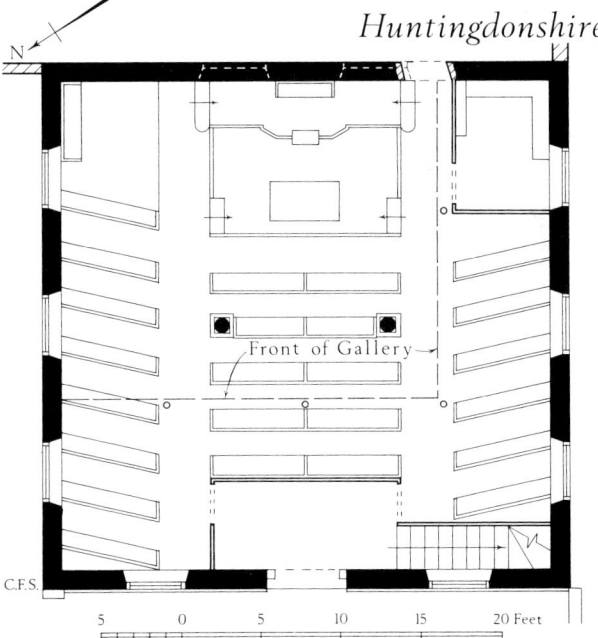

GREAT STAUGHTON

(17) Former BAPTIST (TL 133645). 'Union Chapel', built 1871, of yellow brick with tile banding, has a gabled front with porch and to one side a squat tower of two stages with a spire. (Now in secular use)

Former Baptist chapel, Hail Weston. (18)

HAIL WESTON

(18) Former BAPTIST (TL 164622). The Baptist chapel, closed c.1969, was built in 1759 by a few persons who had removed from Great Staughton; it was enlarged c.1780 and refitted in 1844. The original building was a small timber-framed structure, 20ft by 37ft, gabled to E and W and entered as at present on the S side. The two gable walls of this survive up to the original collar-beam and have each one low window to the ground floor divided in the centre by an intermediate post, and a window above the tie-beam, all with renewed frames. About 1780 the chapel was extended to the N in brick and tile to its present size (30½ft by 37ft). The original ceiling line at collar-beam level was continued over the extension and the N purlin of the old roof supported by two substantial timber posts which rise behind the gallery fronts. The N rear wall has two round-arched windows flanking the site of the pulpit and two tiers of smaller sashes at each side. The gallery of c.1780 has a front of fielded panelling and retains its original seating of plain benches with open backs and shaped ends. In 1844 the front wall had become dangerous and was rebuilt in gault brick to some 4ft higher than the original and the ceiling level continued up to it; the front roof was then rebuilt and covered in slates. The ground-floor seating has been entirely destroyed but part of the fielded-panelled pulpit of c.1780 remains. (Chapel derelict 1972)

Fittings – *Baptistery*: centrally in front of pulpit. *Communion Table*: two legs on horizontal bearers with braces to top,

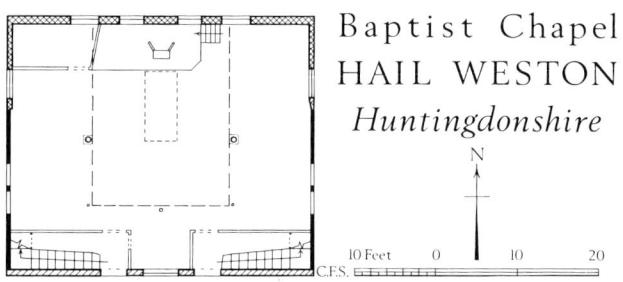

Baptist Chapel
HAIL WESTON
Huntingdonshire

18th-century. *Inscriptions* and *Scratchings*: on gallery woodwork, seat in S gallery 'WB 1782'; handrail of SW staircase 'S.WARD 1786', 'W.WARD 1784'. *Monuments*: in burial-ground N of chapel, early 19th-century and later.

Page (1953) 8–10. MSS with Mr Walter Page, Hail Weston.

HOLYWELL-CUM-NEEDINGWORTH

(19) WESLEYAN, Needingworth (TL 340720). Yellow brick and slate, gabled front of three bays with central arch rising into gable and inscribed 'Wesleyan Chapel 1888'.

HOUGHTON AND WYTON

(20) HOUGHTON CHAPEL (TL 281721). The chapel was built in 1840 at the expense of Potto Brown, a flour miller, who with Joseph Goodman had been instrumental in establishing

Houghton Chapel. (20)

nonconformist preaching in the village. These gentlemen were much influenced by some aspects of Quaker doctrine but the church, nominally a Union church during the 19th century, long maintained an Independent polity. The chapel remained in private ownership until 1875.

The walls are of gault brick with a wooden eaves cornice, and the roof is slated. The E front has a bracketed pediment, central porch and tall round-arched windows which are repeated in the side walls. A vestry was added in 1860 and an organ chamber was built on the N side in 1877. The interior was altered in the late 19th century but retains at the E end a gallery built c.1842–3 for the use of the Sunday-school. When first built the chapel had box-pews and a raised platform across the full width of the W end with two reading desks but no pulpit. In front of the platform were seats facing the congregation in the manner customary in a Friends' meeting-house. In accordance with the views of the original proprietor the usual ordinances were not at first observed. (Converted 1986 to a URC conference centre)

Bootscrapers: pair, portable, with lyre-shaped upstand and rectangular tray with re-entrant corners.

Bell, H., *A Jubilee Memorial of the Union Chapel, Houghton, Huntingdon*, (1890). Goodman, N., Tebbutt, C.P., and Dixon, R.W., *Potto Brown, the Village Philanthropist* (1878). *Reform* (April 1986).

HUNTINGDON AND GODMANCHESTER

(21) Site of BAPTIST CHAPEL, Godmanchester (TL 247706). The Particular Baptist chapel in Cambridge Road has been demolished since 1963 and the forecourt made into a public garden. The chapel is said to have been built c.1796 but appears to have been much altered and re-fronted in the later 19th century. Some fragments of brickwork remain together with a former Sunday-school wing dated 1868. In the forecourt are several *Monuments*: including (1) William Scandrett, 1841, 17 years pastor, and Hannah his widow, 1858; loose, near school (2) Thomas Godwin, 1877, 16 years pastor, former wall monument.

Chambers IV (1963) 104–5, Pl. 18. Pack, T., *A Faithful Standard Bearer...* (1931).

(22) Former UNION CHAPEL, Grammar School Walk, Huntingdon (TL 239719). The chapel, now in commercial use, was built in 1826 for a joint Baptist and Independent church founded in 1823. About 1868 the church removed to a new building, 'Trinity', a large Gothic edifice with tower and spire by John Tarring (demolished c.1970) and the former chapel was converted for use as a British School. It has walls of light brown brick and a hipped slate roof. The front and side walls are of three bays with two tiers of hung-sash windows; two round-arched windows in the rear wall flank the site of the pulpit.

CYB (1869) 321. Millard, J.H., *A Jubilee Memoir of Trinity Church, Huntingdon...* (c.1873).

KIMBOLTON

(23) Former UNION CHAPEL, Thrapston Road (TL 098680). The chapel was built in 1852 for a united Baptist and Congregational church of which the former denomination claimed an existence from 1692, being the only 'anabaptist' meeting in the county referred to in the 'Evans List'. The building, now a public hall, has walls of gault brick and a slate roof. The front wall with three round-arched bays rising into an open bracketed pediment has a central doorway with rusticated stone surround.

(24) Former MORAVIAN (TL 100678). The chapel, obscurely sited in a minor street, has brick walls rendered at the front, and a slate-covered roof. The front half of the building was erected in 1823 and originally had two entrances in the NW wall and two upper round-arched windows. A foundation stone at one corner of this wall is dated 'APRIL 15 1823'. The chapel was enlarged to the rear in 1836. The interior has a gallery around three sides with original seating and staircases adjacent to the former entrances. (Closed c.1974 and conversion to house proposed)

Fittings – *Clock*: on front of NW gallery, signed 'Peacock, Kimbolton'. *Pulpit*: in crude Gothic style with ogee arches below, c.1823.

England (1888) 38–9, Pl. XVII.

Former Moravian chapel, Kimbolton. (24)

OLD WESTON

(25) WESLEYAN (TL 100774). The chapel, opened 1839, of brick with a hipped tiled roof, stands in a retired position on the E side of the main road.

ORTON WATERVILLE

(26) PRIMITIVE METHODIST (TL 157963). Three-bay gabled front of yellow brick with red brick bands and dressings. Dated 1880.

PETERBOROUGH

(27) CONGREGATIONAL, Westgate (TL 190990). Gothic chapel by R. Moffat Smith with twin spirelets flanking entrance, six-light traceried window at front and gabled side bays. Built 1859 for a congregation gathered c.1776 which previously met in a chapel on the opposite side of the road. (URC/Methodist)
Coleman (1853) 352–6. *CYB* (1860) 233.

(28) Former CONGREGATIONAL, Priestgate (TL 191986). The chapel was built in 1864 for a congregation formed about 1861 by some members from the chapel in Westgate. In 1948 it became a joint Congregational/Presbyterian church. The chapel, designed by W.G. Habershon and Pite, stands behind a pre-existing two-storeyed domestic range in the centre of which has been intruded an arched entrance surmounted by a pedimented tower and short spire.
CYB (1865) 307.

(29) Former WESLEYAN, Dogsthorpe (TF 190012). Small chapel of brick and pantile built 1833, enlarged or rebuilt 1898.

(30) Former PRIMITIVE METHODIST, Newark (TF 209005). Three-bay front of red brick with yellow brick pilasters, dated 1870.

(31) WESLEYAN, Werrington (TF 173034). The chapel, dated 1835, has brick walls and a hipped slate roof. The S front of yellow brick has a two-storeyed porch incorporating a staircase to the S gallery. A vestry was added to the W in 1878.
RCHM *Peterborough* (1969) 60.

Wesleyan Methodist Chapel, Werrington
PETERBOROUGH *Huntingdonshire*

(32) Former PRIMITIVE METHODIST, Werrington (TF 173031). Red brick walls with yellow brick pilasters and hipped slate roof. Front originally of three bays with tablet over doorway inscribed 'PRIMITIVE METHODIST JUBILEE CHAPEL 1870'; fourth bay to W later. (Now a workshop)

PIDLEY CUM FENTON

(33) BAPTIST, Church End, Pidley (TL 328782). The chapel, which has figured as a preaching-station of Bluntisham and later of Somersham, dates from the mid 19th century. It has low walls of gault brick and a slate roof. Five round-arched windows face the road.

RAMSEY

(34) SALEM CHAPEL, High Street (TL 288850). The Strict Baptist chapel was built in 1857 at the insistence of David Irish, formerly minister at Warboys, when he accepted the pastorate of the Ramsey church. The walls are of gault brick and the roof is slated. The pedimented front of four bays is divided by three plain rendered pilasters with bracket capitals. Two wide semicircular arches open to an exposed vestibule from which similarly arched doorways lead into the chapel and to gallery staircases in the

Former Congregational chapel, Priestgate. (28)

front corners. A tablet in the pediment is inscribed 'SALEM 1857'. The interior has a gallery around three sides with open ironwork front; the original seating remains with box-pews to the ground floor and open pews above.

Chambers IV (1963) 111.

(35) WESLEYAN, High Street (TL 286850). Gault brick with minimal stone dressings, Gothic with SE turret and pyramidal spire; opened 1899.

(36) Former CHAPEL, High Street (TL 287849). Located SSE of (35) is a former chapel converted in 1911 for use as a Drill Hall by the Huntingdonshire Territorials and now in commercial use. It dates from c.1830 and has gault brick walls and a hipped slate roof. The front of three bays has a round-arched entrance and two tiers of hung-sash windows. Two widely spaced round-arched windows flank the site of the pulpit. A gallery around three sides has been removed.

ST IVES

(37) PARTICULAR BAPTIST, East Street (TL 314714). The chapel on the SW side of the street, adjoining Crown Place, is of brick with a gabled front. The central entrance set between two small windows has a debased Classical surround; above it is a round-arched upper window and an oval tablet inscribed 'erected 1839, enlarged 1862, 1887'.

Behind the chapel, facing Crown Place, is the 'Particular Baptist Sabbath School erected 1887', and on the opposite side of East Street a range of former *almshouses*, 'The Pilgrims' Rest', erected 1885 'in connection with the Particular Baptist Meeting House'.

Chambers IV (1963) 107, Pl. 19b.

(38) Former CHAPEL, Chapel Lane (TL 314711). The chapel, now in commercial use, has brick walls and a slate roof. The gabled front with three round-arched bays enclosing two tiers of windows closely resembles the Congregational chapels at Linton, Cambs. (60), of 1818, and Buntingford, Herts. (18), of 1819, and is of similar date. The interior has been much altered but traces of a stepped gallery remain at one end. This may have been the General Baptist chapel, purchased in 1806 but possibly re-fronted.

Taylor (1818) II: 308–15, 408–9. Wood (1847) 192.

(39) Former INDEPENDENT, Free Church Passage (TL 314712). The building, dated 1811 on the keystone of the doorway, has walls of gault brick. The front is of five bays with two tiers of windows; the entrance in the end bay to the right has a round-arched head, the four lower windows have segmental-arched heads, the five upper windows are round-arched.

(40) 'FREE CHURCH', Market Hill (TL 314712). The Congregational church in St Ives claims to have been founded in 1642 and was at first regarded as Presbyterian; in the mid 19th century it became a 'Union Church' incorporating a Baptist element. The chapel erected 1863–4 in a 14th-century Gothic style to designs by John Tarring is prominently situated; it has brick walls faced in stone, and a slate roof. The entrance is surmounted by a tower with a tall broach spire incorporating a 'town clock'. Three windows in each side wall have gablets above. An apse at the SW end was designed to provide a large vestry with organ and singers' gallery over. The interior was subdivided and entirely refitted in 1979–81.

CYB (1866) 319. *Reform* (February 1981).

Congregational 'Free Church' (URC), St Ives, with statue to Oliver Cromwell. (40)

(41) Former FRIENDS, Chapel Lane (TL 314711). The meeting-house stands on the S side of the lane. Part of the land was transferred by a deed dated July 1690 and is described as '32 yards long and 11ft [?yards] broad, being part of a piece of freehold land in St Ives, whereupon a cottage formerly stood, burnt in the fire at St Ives in April 1689, abutting North on a common lane'. This was recorded in the minutes of the Huntingdonshire Monthly Meeting in June 1691 as a gift from John Peacock. The meeting-house built in 1691 was heightened in 1725 (described as 'rebuilt') and a list of subscribers is preserved. Some repairs were carried out in 1756 at a cost of £10 8s. 9d. and in the same year a subscription was proposed 'for closing up one of the galleries'. In 1787 the meeting was united with that at Swavesey, Cambs. In 1861 the meeting-house was reported closed, but some Quaker use continued until c.1930. It has since passed to the Boy Scouts Association.

The walls of the meeting-house are of dark red brick and the double roof is hipped and covered with tiles; a flat roof now spans the former central valley. The NE wall facing Chapel Lane has a slight offset 4ft below the eaves and above it is a blocked square window. There are indications externally and in the internal wall plaster that this wall was formerly gabled from the level of the offset. The front wall, approached through a rebuilt gateway, has a brick plinth, two tiers of windows separated by a platband, and original entrances, now blocked, at each end. Two of the three ground-floor windows have renewed frames; the third has been altered to form a wide entrance. Four upper windows retain their original wood frames and two have rectangular leaded glazing in iron casements with ornamental latches. The upper part of the wall dates from 1725, but the lower stage appears from the difference in style and spacing of the windows to be the original work of 1691. A modern brick annexe at the SW end replaces a staircase which gave direct access to the SW gallery.

The interior (48½ft by 24½ft) is rhomboidal on plan, with a ceiling height of 15ft. The double roof has a central valley supported by three turned wood columns with moulded stops to square heads and bases, and ogee-moulded cornices. The two end columns date from the heightening of 1725; that to the SW is inscribed 'IA 1725'. The middle column, inserted in 1756, is inscribed 'EH/IW 1756/SA/IS'. There are slight indications of a former gallery at the NE end, removed c.1756. At the SW end is a deep gallery enlarged when the outer staircase was built, perhaps c.1800. The gallery front has two ranges of vertically sliding shutters with reeded panels. No other fittings now remain but photographs taken since Quaker use ceased show a stand with three tiers of plain panelling at the NE end, probably of the late 18th century, and some loose benches with open backs and shaped ends; externally, some uniform round-topped headstones with early 19th-century dates have also disappeared.

Butler (1999) 274–5. MS records in Cambs. Record Office.

(42) Former PRIMITIVE METHODIST, East Street (TL 313715). Gault brick with pointed arch in gabled front; dated 1895. (Now offices)

Former Friends' Meeting-house, ST. IVES, *Huntingdonshire*

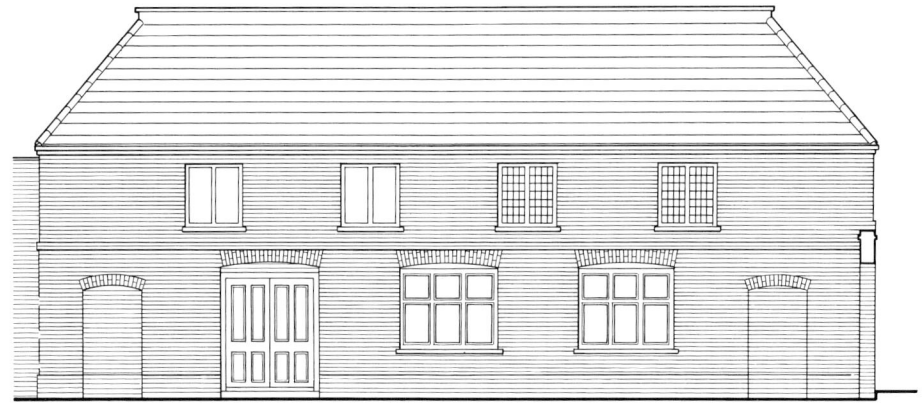

South-East Elevation

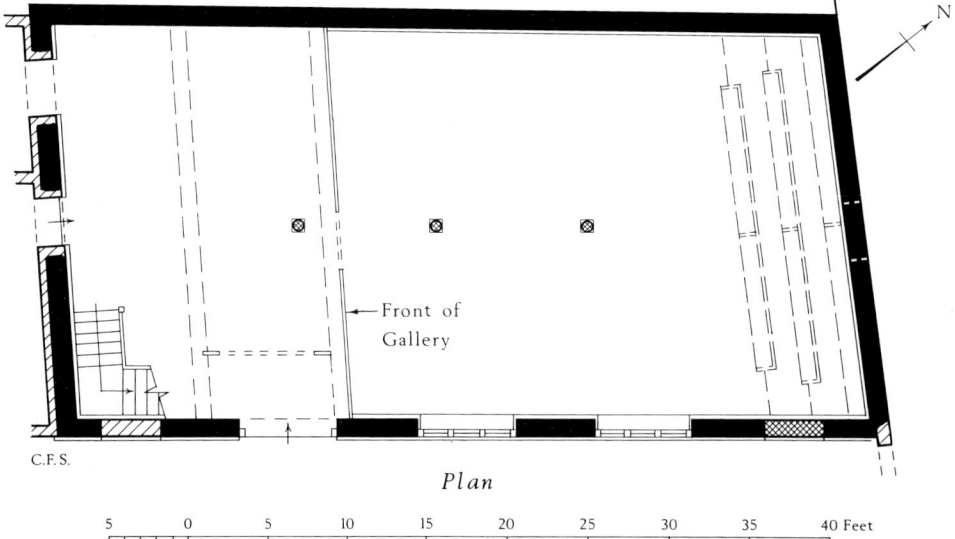

Plan

ST NEOTS

(43) STRICT BAPTIST, New Street (TL 183604). The church originated in the late 18th century and the first chapel was built on this site in 1800. This was rebuilt in 1816, enlarged to the rear and a gallery added in 1821, and further altered and a wide front porch built in 1897. The walls are of gault brick, rendered at the front, and the hipped roof is covered with slates. The front and sides were originally of three bays with two tiers of windows. The gallery, around three sides, has an open ironwork front of c.1897. Many early 19th-century wall monuments have been re-sited outside on the N wall.

Chambers IV (1963) 98–9, Pl. 17b. Page (1953) 12–13.

(44) CONGREGATIONAL, High Street (TL 184604). The Independent church (now URC) was founded in 1691. A meeting-house built in 1718, described as 'a square red-brick, unattractive building', stood behind the present chapel which superseded it in 1888, but survived until c.1968 when it was destroyed by fire. A few fragments of the earlier foundations remain. It had been re-fronted in 1844 in three bays with a pediment and entrances in wings at the sides.

The chapel of 1888, designed by Edward J. Paine, is of red brick with stone dressings. Facing the street is a prominent tower of four stages with pinnacled corner buttresses and a short spire.

Cooper, R.D., *The History of the Old Meeting House, St Neots, 1691–1890* (1890). *CYB* (1889) 225–6; (1890) 212–13; (1893) frontis. Page (1953) 8–9.

(45) WESLEYAN, Huntingdon Street (TL 185604). A chapel, 47ft square, built in 1793 with front added 1861, was demolished c.1970.

Dolbey (1964) 95.

SAWTRY

(46) WESLEYAN (TL 168836). Brick and slate, opened 1833, re-fronted and refenestrated 1927.

SOMERSHAM

(47) BAPTIST (TL 361779). On S side of main road near centre of village. Brick walls and tiled roof; the N front is gabled and has a central segmental-arched doorway with round-arched blind window over, flanked by two tiers of segmental-headed windows with renewed frames. Small oval tablet in gable inscribed 'BUILT A.D. 1812'. Three-bay sides, extended to rear. Original gallery; pulpit and seating renewed in the late 19th century.

(48) WESLEYAN, Parkhall Road (TL 361781). Chapel of gault brick with slate roof. Front wall of three bays with central entrance and two tiers of segmental-arched windows, divided by brick pilasters with stepped capitals supporting simple entablature and pediment with tablet inscribed 'WESLEYAN CHAPEL A.D.1845'. Interior with rear gallery only, late 19th-century fittings, and inserted suspended ceiling.

SPALDWICK

(49) UNION CHAPEL (TL 131728). An Independent church existed in the early 18th century which in 1773 was described as having a Baptist minister but 'the congregation Independent'. This became predominantly Baptist in the 19th century.

The chapel, erected in 1844, has walls of gault brick with stone dressings and a slate-covered roof. The S front has a bracketed pediment, three closely set round-arched upper windows with cills continuing across the façade as a platband, and two similarly arched doorways below with a window between. The interior has a deep S gallery, original open pews and table-pew, and a late 19th-century rostrum pulpit.

Monument: on E wall, Rev. John Manning, pastor 1793–1842, 1855.

Union Chapel, Spaldwick. (49)

STANGROUND SOUTH

(50) BAPTIST, Chapel Street (TL 201973). Yellow brick with red brick dressings, three-bay panelled front wall with dentil cornice and pediment. Dated 1880.

STILTON

(51) Former WESLEYAN, Church Street (TL 162893). The chapel, opened in 1848, is now in industrial use. The walls are of gault brick and the roof slated. The N front has a moulded brick parapet, three round-arched bays enclosing two tiers of windows and a central porch.

Wesleyan chapel, Somersham. (48)

FORMER WESLEYAN CHAPEL, STILTON CFS 1974

TOSELAND

(52) WESLEYAN (TL 239626). Small chapel with gault brick walls and slate roof; gabled front with lancet windows and single-stage buttresses. Opened 1849.

WARBOYS

(53) STRICT BAPTIST (TL 309802). A Baptist church has met in and around Warboys since 1647. In its earliest years this was closely linked with a Baptist meeting at Fenstanton and from 1714 to 1828 the two societies constituted a single church. By the early 19th century meetings in Warboys had ceased but were recommenced in private rooms. In 1828 the Warboys members of the Fenstanton meeting formed themselves into a separate church and occupied a barn formerly used by Wesleyans. In 1831 the barn was demolished and replaced by the present chapel. The front wall of gault brick was then of three bays with two tiers of flat-arched sash windows and a central doorway with round-arched head in two orders. The roof was hipped and slated. Galleries were added c.1832–6 and in 1842 the central doorway was converted to a window and the flanking windows to a pair of narrower entrances.

The chapel was renovated and extended to the front in 1898–9 following the visit of a delegation to the chapel in New Street, St Neots (43) to inspect the work there. Apart from the brickwork of the side and rear walls little now remains visible of the 1831 structure; the windows in the side walls were entirely remade and the gabled front of red brick with pointed-arched entrance and three graduated lancets above is entirely of 1898–9. The interior has a suspended ceiling at gallery level.

Monuments: in burial-ground, of the early 19th century and later, include one to David Irish, 26 years pastor here and 8 years at Salem Chapel, Ramsey, 1863.

Chambers IV (1963) 109–11, Pl. 20a. *Grace* (June 1992) 17–18. Hyde, H.A., *The Warboys Baptists* (1963).

WINWICK

(54) Former CONGREGATIONAL (TL 104808). Small chapel of 1865 now used as a hall. Three-bay pedimented front of gault brick with wide rusticated corner pilasters, round-arched windows and gabled porch.

WISTOW

(55) Former CONGREGATIONAL, Manor Street (TL 280811). The chapel, now 'Wistow Village Hall', was built c.1864. The walls are of gault brick with a tall front gable and entrance in gabled surround; pointed-arched windows with iron frames at the sides.

YAXLEY

(56) STRICT BAPTIST, Chapel Road (TL 182920). Gault brick with three-bay gabled front and wavy barge-boards. Tablet inscribed 'Jireh 1860'.

Chambers IV (1963) 122, Pl. 23b.

(57) CONGREGATIONAL (TL 187921). The chapel built 1812 for a newly formed church (now URC) has walls of gault brick and a hipped slate roof. The front is of three bays with two tiers of round-arched windows and a blind window above the central entrance. The doorway has brick pilasters and a semi-circular arch and fanlight. Between the upper windows are two tablets inscribed 'ERECTED AD 1812 / BY VOLUNTARY CONTRIBUTION'.

(58) WESLEYAN, Chapel Road (TL 182921). Gault brick and slate; rectangular brick labels to windows; dated 1844.

(59) FREE METHODIST, Main Street (TL 183921). Gault brick and slate; five-bay gabled front dated 1859.

YELLING

(60) BAPTIST (TL 256626). Chapel of gault brick and slate, built 1850 but refitted 1883, replaced an earlier chapel on another site. The front wall of three panelled bays with segmental-arched doorway and windows has a frieze of paired bricks and a plain steeply pitched pediment. *Monuments*: above pulpit, (1) Rev. Henry Bottle, first pastor, 1859; in burial-ground (2) Rev. Henry Bottle, 1859, and Mary his widow, 1868.

BM XLII (1850) 770.

Baptist chapel, Yelling. (60)

KENT

This county, exhibiting a wide variety of nonconformist denominations, is particularly notable for the early spread of General Baptists. The church meeting in Eythorne (54) claims an origin in the early 17th century although a change of site and denominational orientation has left it devoid of any major architectural interest. A more substantial physical presence remains of the congregation in Deal (38) where the late 17th-century meeting-house has survived, although in an altered state. In Canterbury the General Baptists had the use of part of the Blackfriars monastery (23) while in Smarden, where the burial-ground remains (127), they appear to have made use of an existing house. The chapel of 1716 at Bessels Green (28) continues in use by its now Unitarian congregation and stands in a large burial-ground. The remotely situated former chapel at Headcorn of 1741 (74) is also of interest in conjunction with its successor of 1819 (75) standing in the village. The most notable chapel of the denomination is in Dover (42) where the fashionably Classical building of 1819 has an elongated octagonal plan.

Presbyterian and Independent meeting-houses of the early 18th century remain in Tenterden (140) and Maidstone (88), and a small former chapel in Tunbridge Wells (107). The chapel of 1706 in Sandwich (117) most closely resembles many in other parts of the country with its double-roofed construction supported by a pair of timber posts; Tenterden, although still vernacular has been enlarged with a brick front; Maidstone, which has a square plan, is more advanced in design as is to be expected in an urban environment.

The later 18th century is marked by the proliferation of denominations. Particular Baptists at Bessels Green (29) broke away from the older General Baptist meeting and erected their own chapel in 1770. In Cranbrook Strict and Particular Baptists converted a pair of cottages in 1787 (33). Congregationalists working amongst the naval fraternity of Bluetown in Sheerness built a large chapel in 1784 (122), and in Broadstairs the old St Mary's Chapel (18) continued to be worked by Independents. The earliest Quaker meeting-house still standing in the county is in Rochester, built 1780–1 (105), and of comparable date, 1788, are the fragmentary remains of a Methodist chapel at St Peters, Broadstairs (21), which has associations with John Wesley. The Countess of Huntingdon's Connexion also figures here with late 18th-century former chapels at Faversham (56) and Dartford (36).

The most unusual chapel of the early 19th century is Providence Chapel, Cranbrook (34), built for the Calvinistic Independent followers of William Huntington SS, and variously enlarged at first-floor level. The Strict Baptist chapels of the period, though generally small, vary a great deal in character, from the simple weather-boarded chapel of *c*.1802 at Stone (134) and the equally plain brick-built Providence Chapel at Frittenden (65), to the strangely sited Zoar Chapel in Canterbury (24) perched on a former water tower on the town walls.

The more architecturally pretentious chapels of the early 19th century exhibit the earlier preference for simple Classical detail, the former Congregational chapel at Wingham (150) of 1835 being a typical design by James Fenton. Two Wesleyan chapels by William Jenkins, in his usual style, remain in Canterbury (26) and at Rochester (106), the former the victim of internal 'improvement' and the latter no longer in use. Congregationalists in Tunbridge Wells (110) expressed themselves in an exceptionally robust manner, in marked contrast to some smaller contemporary chapels. The former chapel in Swanscombe (137) should be noted for its picturesque grouping between a pair of contemporary cottages, all faced with knapped flints. Also remarkable of this period is the Bible Christian chapel 'Cardiphonia' at Hartlip (71), built by private patronage and containing an unusual series of panels with scriptural texts.

In the mid 19th century the Baptists of Ramsgate chose the Romanesque style for their chapel (101) but the Gothic style in all its forms came to dominate the remainder of the century. It appears in its simplest unsophisticated and still 'Gothick' state in Margate (95) in the former Wesleyan chapel of 1811, and in that of 1823 in Maidstone (91). F.J. Jobson, the Methodists' principal apologist for the style, designed a small chapel in Aylesford (6) of 1851, which accords with his strictures for simple village chapels, and W.W. Pocock was responsible for a double-towered chapel of 1844–5 in Dartford (37). The principal chapels of the later 19th century were built for Congregationalists, by John Tarring at Rochester (104) and Sevenoaks (120) and by W.F. Poulton, later Poulton and Woodman, in Ashford (5), Herne Bay (77), Margate (93) and Milton Regis (125), all of which bear the recognizable style of their architects. Lesser known is the Church of the New Jerusalem, for which a Gothic Church of some pretensions with a substantial tower was built by private means in 1881 at Snodland (131). And more strange but still worth recalling is the now demolished 'Jezreel's Tower' in Gillingham (66) built in 1885, but never completed, for the Christian Israelites, and a reminder of one of the extremes to which enthusiasm can extend.

The building materials in use in the county include timber-framing, of which both early and late examples appear. The traditional form is at Tenterden (140), but later less substantial framing clad in weather-boarding occurs at Dartford (36), Cranbrook (33, 34), Bredgar (15) and Coxheath (87). Brickwork is common throughout the county, but stone, except in rubble form, is rare before the 19th century. Slate and tiles for roofing are equally abundant.

APPLEDORE

(1) WESLEYAN, The Street (TQ 955295). Small brick chapel dated 1836 but with later features.

ASH

(2) CONGREGATIONAL (TR 287584). Yellow brick with polychrome dressings; gabled front with big pointed wall-arch enclosing two tiers of windows. Late 19th-century, replacing chapels of 1806 and 1849. Sunday-school adjacent, 1882 by W.R. King.

CYB (1901) 174, obituary of J.B. Dadd. Timpson (1859) 403.

ASH-CUM-RIDLEY

(3) BAPTIST, Ash Green (TQ 600653). 'Ebenezer Chapel', rebuilt 1889, is of brick with a gabled front. The church was formed in 1843.

ASHFORD

(4) BAPTIST, Station Street (TR 01154275). A General Baptist church which originated in the mid 17th century became Calvinist by *c.*1700. In July 1746 'a newly erected building in Marsh Lane' (St John's Lane) was registered for Baptists; it was rebuilt in 1830.

The present chapel of 1881 is of yellow brick with red brick dressings. The front is of three bays with a wide round-arched entrance and giant Corinthian pilasters supporting an entablature and parapet raised over the centre bay. At the rear facing St John's Lane is the former chapel of 1830 with a refenestrated front of three bays, plain pilasters and small pediment over the centre.

Chambers III (1956) 52–3. *BQ* VII (1934–5) 34–8. Ivimey IV (1830) 514–16.

(5) CONGREGATIONAL, Church Road (TR 010427). An Independent church formed in the early 19th century and loosely linked to the Countess of Huntingdon's Connexion claimed descent from an earlier Presbyterian society in existence from the late 17th century. A chapel, built in 1821, was transferred to the Countess's Trustees in 1823 but reverted to a Congregational trust in 1865, when it was rebuilt.

The chapel, in the Gothic style by W.F. Poulton of Reading, was opened in 1866. It has stone walls and a slated roof. The E front is gabled and has a four-light window with plate tracery; there are two entrances at the front, above that to the right is a short tower with octagonal upper stage and spire. Alongside to the N is a contemporary school hall designed for incorporation into the chapel should the need arise. (Demolished *c.*1974)

Congregational chapel, Ashford. (Demolished) (5)

Box, E.S., *Ashford (Kent) Congregational Church* [1962]. *CYB* (1865) 290. Timpson (1859) 508–10.

AYLESFORD

(6) Former WESLEYAN, Rochester Road (TQ 732590). The chapel built in 1851 follows, with slight variations, F.J. Jobson's design for a simple village chapel. The walls are faced with polygonal masonry and the roof is slated; the front to the road is gabled and has in it three graduated lancets. The sides have each a gabled porch and lancet windows, and at the further SE end is a polygonal apse. The interior, converted to office use *c.*1991, remains undivided at the SE end but the other half towards the road has been floored at the level of the original back gallery.

Jobson (1850) 81–3.

BARHAM

(7) WESLEYAN, Derringstone (TR 206493). Rendered walls with exposed flint and brick at one side and slate roof hipped to rear; simple pedimented front of three bays with round-arched doorway and tablet dated 1836.

BETHERSDEN

(8) STRICT BAPTIST (TQ 930404). 'Union Chapel', built 1806, is of brick with a three-bay gabled front and small porch; the doorway and front windows all have three-centred arched heads. The chapel has been extended to the rear.

Chambers III (1956) 12–13.

BIDDENDEN

(9) STRICT BAPTIST, Bounds Cross, Lashenden (TQ 849410). 'Ebenezer Chapel', built 1879–80, is of brick with a three-bay gabled front and two-bay sides. The interior is lined with matchboarding and has a boarded ceiling at collar level. At the entrance is a gallery supported by two iron columns. The original fittings remain throughout.

Fittings – *Communion Table*: with removable singers' desk standing on top, late 19th-century. *Monument*: in burial-ground, John Kemp, 1932, 52 years pastor, and Malvina his second wife, 1941, headstone. *Pulpit*: supported on two posts. *Stabling*: for six horses and other beasts.

Chambers III (1956) 15–16. Kemp, J., *Memoir of John Kemp* (1933).

BOROUGH GREEN

(10) STRICT BAPTIST (TQ 609573). The chapel built in 1817 on recently enclosed common land has been entirely altered by enlargement in all directions. The original building was square with a hipped roof and concealed central valley. A deep gallery was added on the W side in 1832 and a matching gallery to the E at a later date; in 1850 the chapel was extended to the S front by 12ft and further enlargement was made to the rear early in the 20th century. The walls are rendered and have round-arched windows with uniform glazing of *c.*1910. The S front is gabled.

Chambers III (1956) 82–4. Ivimey IV (1830) 514.

BOUGHTON MALHERBE

(11) STRICT BAPTIST, Grafty Green (TQ 872488). The chapel built privately *c.*1833 is a low brick building with a broad front of three bays; the roof, half-hipped at one end, is covered with patent tiles replacing slates. The front windows formerly had external shutters. Above the doorway is the painted inscription 'JEHOVAH JIREH | A PARTICULAR BAPTIST CHAPEL'.

Chambers III (1956) 15.

BOUGHTON UNDER BLEAN

(12) WESLEYAN, Boughton Street (TR 056594). The chapel built in 1844 has plain brick sides with lancet windows. The front is a wild Gothic extravaganza, of three bays with octagonal buttresses topped by pinnacles; the centre bay, brought forward, rises to a square turret supported by flying buttresses and formerly completed with a spire. Above the pointed-arched doorway is an elaborately cusped and traceried window of four lights with an ogee hood-mould. (Closed 1981 and converted to art gallery)

Methodist Recorder (Winter Number, 1903) 60.

Wesleyan chapel, Boughton Street. (12)

BRABOURNE

(13) STRICT BAPTIST, Brabourne Lees (TR 081403). 'Bethel Chapel', built 1818, has timber-framed walls with tile hanging to the sides but later rendering in front. The front is gabled and has a plain porch and two small round-arched upper windows. *Monuments*: in burial-ground (1) Joseph Skinner, 1841, first pastor, and Sarah his widow, 1850; (2) railed enclosure next to porch with seven headstones to families of Horton and Marchant.

Chambers III (1956) 54–5.

KENT

BRASTED

(14) Former BAPTIST (TQ 469550). Red brick and stone with gabled front, large circular window with plate tracery over entrance and triangle of timber-framing with cusped decoration above. Built 1886, by John Wills of Derby. (Converted to house)
B.Hbk (1886) 339.

BREDGAR

(15) Former WESLEYAN, Silver Street (TQ 876604). Built 1811. Weather-boarded chapel with half-hipped tiled roof. The S end has a wide entrance and two small gallery windows; two large sash windows in each side wall. Superseded by new chapel (now demolished) in 1868 and used for Sunday-school. (Now store)

Former Wesleyan chapel, Silver Street, Bredgar. (15)

BRENCHLEY

(16) Site of STRICT BAPTIST, Matfield Green (TQ 659416). A chapel built 1811 and enlarged 1826 was superseded by a new building on another site in c.1934. The former 'Ebenezer Chapel' was demolished in 1937 but the burial-ground remains. *Monuments*: former wall monuments fixed to fragment of walling (1) Mrs Ann Wells, 1844; (2) John Carr, 1851, and Elizabeth his widow, 1852; (3) William Ansell, 1851; (4) Thomas Hanbury, 1854, Mary his widow, 1855, also Elizabeth and Mary Hanbury, both 1841; in front burial-ground (5) William Finch Waller, 1866, 50 years a Baptist minister; (6) Charlotte wife of H[enry] Bartholomew, pastor, 1878, in railed enclosure.
Chambers III (1956) 72–5, Pls facing 54, 55. Paul V (1966) 308–21, Fig. 320.

(17) Former BAPTIST, Brenchley Road (TQ 667418). Timber-framed and weather-boarded with barge-boards; triangular-headed windows. Built late 19th century or after.

BROADSTAIRS

(18) ST MARY'S CHAPEL, Albion Street (TR 398679). This site is claimed to be that of the mediaeval chapel of Our Lady of Bradstow (alias Broadstairs). Following the Reformation, part of the by then ruined building became the private property of the Culmer family who exhibited strong support for the Puritan cause. How far worship compatible with these sentiments may have been carried on here from the early 17th century as has been assumed has yet to be proved but it seems that the old chapel was fitted up as a place of worship by Joseph Culmer in 1691 and that preaching services were held in association with the Presbyterian or Congregational Meeting in Ramsgate. In 1825–8 the chapel was repaired and enlarged, or more probably rebuilt, by its then owner, Mrs John Goodwin, and evangelical liturgical services were held assisted by ministers from the Countess of Huntingdon's Connexion and others. In 1871 a new Congregational chapel was built at The Vale for the use of a newly formed church. St Mary's Chapel continued in minor use until being sold in 1926 for use as a parish room. It now serves as a store for an adjacent shop.

The chapel stands on the SE side of the street partly concealed behind a later building leaving the SW end wall and part of the NW wall visible. The walls are of coursed flint, knapped on the principal sides, with dressings of yellow stock brick; the roof is hipped and covered with tiles. The entrance from the street was through a doorway with two-centred arch of brick set in a gabled flint boundary wall with a stone tablet above inscribed in early 19th-century characters 'ST MARYS CHAPEL. 1601.'. This entrance has been partly reconstructed and the tablet reset above a window over the entrance in the main wall. This window and two at an upper level at the SW end have pointed-arched heads of brick and wooden Y-tracery frames. Also in the SW end are the reset early 17th-century arched head of a doorway and a domestic window of five lights with mullions and transom.

The interior is an irregular parallelogram (about 34ft by 17½ft). A record of painted texts, and verses by Richard Baxter, obscured by whitewash in 1797, must relate to the previous chapel which was evidently supplanted in the 'enlargement' of 1825–8 when a gallery, now removed, is said to have been built.

St Mary's Chapel, Broadstairs. (18)

Monuments: in chapel on NE wall (1) Medmer Goodwin, 1832, and Martha his widow, 1832; (2) John Culmer Hurst, 1830, and George Lushington Hurst, 1833; (3) Mary Goodwin, 1836.

Anon., *Congregationalism in Broadstairs: A Brief Survey of 1601 to 1951* [1951]. Briggs (1946) 20–1. *CHST* VII (1916–18) 44–8.

(19) Former STRICT BAPTIST, 58 High Street (TR 395679). 'Providence Chapel', now a sale room, was first built in 1790 for a church formed in 1760. The walls are of stock brick, rendered at the front, and the roof, hipped to the rear, is slated. The windows throughout have simple pointed-arched heads. The front is gabled and has a high rusticated plinth, a doorway between two windows and one above, with a quatrefoil in the pedimented gable; two rendered panels are inscribed 'Erected 1790', 'Restored 1909'.

The interior (35½ft by 27½ft) has a single gallery at the entrance supported by a pair of wooden columns of the early 19th century. Two windows in the back wall flank the site of the pulpit.

Buffard (1963) 90, 109, 122. Chambers III (1956) 30–1.

(20) Site of BAPTIST, Shallows (TR 374688). A chapel, built in or before 1750 for a branch of a church meeting in Canterbury, closed in 1800 and was largely demolished in 1856. It stood on the NW side of Shallows Lane and is said to have measured 34ft by 16ft. The site is occupied by a shed which may incorporate part of the structure. A commemorative stone, renewed 1932, stands adjacent to the lane.

Chambers III (1956) 25–8, facing 23. Ivimey IV (1830) 512–13.

(21) Former METHODIST, St Peters (TR 380684). On 28 November 1788 John Wesley reluctantly preached at 'a little preaching-house being just built at St Peters (two miles from Margate)', an appointment which he found 'utterly inconvenient, on many accounts'. Evidently the cause did not prosper because in 1797 the chapel was let to a section of the Baptist church formerly meeting at Shallows (*see* (20)). The freehold was sold to the Baptists in 1816 (who still worship here), and the chapel was enlarged in 1834.

The chapel stands immediately SW of the parish church and was originally approached from an alley alongside the Wheatsheaf Inn. Of the original building (about 20ft by 40ft externally, greatly enlarged to the rear and at one end in 1834, and extended to the front in 1938), two walls of brickwork remain. The broad front facing SE has been heightened; it had a central entrance with round-arched head between two similarly arched windows, that to the right replaced by a taller window in the 19th century.

Monuments: in burial-ground (1) Martin Cramp, 1822, Mary his wife, 1819, Rev. Thomas Cramp, 1851, pastor, Rebecca his first wife, 1803, Frances his second wife, 1864, *et al.*; (2) John Brook, 1864, 18 years Baptist minister at Broadstairs, *et al.*

BM XXVI (1834) 439–40. Chambers III (1956) 28, 30. Curnock, (ed.) (1938) VII: 450. Ivimey IV (1830) 512–13.

BURHAM

(22) WESLEYAN, Church Street (TQ 726621). Stock brick with red brick dressings; gabled front with two-light pointed-arched window with brick Y-tracery above porch. Opened 1847.

CANTERBURY

(23) Former GENERAL BAPTIST, Blackfriars (TR 149581). The remains of the Blackfriars monastery were purchased in 1658 by a Huguenot surgeon, Peter de la Pierre, who permitted their use by a Baptist church. In the early 18th century a new meeting-house and cottage were built at the SW end of the surviving mediaeval monastic hall with ground to the S for a burial-ground. The chapel was closed in 1913 and the contents dispersed.

The walls are of brickwork; in each side wall are tall round-arched windows for the meeting-house and two tiers of cottage windows adjacent. The interior was described in 1900 and 1905 as having high box-pews with a centre aisle, a baptistery below a large centre pew, a choir gallery at the back and a pulpit approached directly from the vestry with hexagonal canopy above.

Monuments: in burial-ground, a few fragments of early 19th-century headstones survive in a neglected state. To the S of the former meeting-house is one table-tomb raised above a vault, to Rev. Samuel Kingsford, 1821, 40 years pastor, Sarah his wife, 1782, *et al.*

Evans (1897) 40–1. Maguire, L.J. (ed.), General Baptist Assembly, occasional papers: *Church Book 1711–1721* No. 11 (1990); *Registers 1780 to 1836* No. 17 (1992); *Church Book 1660 to 1695* No. 18 (1992). Taylor (1818) I: 351. Taylor, A.F., *The Free Churches of Canterbury* [1926] 5–19. *UHST* V (1931–4) 70–7.

(24) STRICT BAPTIST, Burgate Lane (TR 152577). 'Zoar Chapel' stands on the 'Water Tower', a bastion of the city walls. It was built in 1802 in connection with the city water supply and converted in 1845 for a church formed in 1838 by secession from one which was meeting in a former Methodist chapel, the 'Pepper Pot' or 'Round House', in King Street. The building has brick walls, rounded at the rear to follow the outline of the bastion. The front is gabled and has above the entrance a large shield-shaped tablet with the chapel name surmounted by a civic crown.

Chambers III (1956) 38–9. Taylor [1926] op. cit. 23.

Strict Baptist chapel, Burgate Lane, Canterbury. (24)

(25) FRIENDS, Canterbury Lane (TR 151577). In 1687–8 Friends bought three small tenements in Canterbury Lane and built a meeting-house on the land at the back. This was altered or reconstructed in 1773. In the mid 19th century the cottages in front were replaced by a new building with two entrances and two

Exterior (© *Kenneth Gravett*).

Interior (1942).
Wesleyan chapel, St Peter's Street, Canterbury.

tiers of windows. The meeting-house was destroyed by bombing in 1942. The present meeting-house was erected on a new site in The Friars (TR 148580) in 1956.

Burial-ground: Showler (1970) 33, 49, refers to a disused burial-ground with a small grave-keeper's cottage at 5 Forty Acres Road, St Dunstans, acquired 1661.

Butler (1999) 179–80. Lidbetter (1961) 10. Showler (1970) *passim*. Taylor [1926] op. cit. 50–1.

(26) WESLEYAN, St Peter's Street (TR 147580). Methodist preaching commenced *c*.1750 and the first preaching-house, built in King Street, was opened by John Wesley in 1764. This was a small dodecagonal building '40ft in diameter' known as the 'Round House' or the 'Pepper Box', and constructed from materials from the demolished St Andrew's Church. It was superseded in 1811 but continued in various occupations until demolition *c*.1864.

The present chapel by William Jenkins is dated 1811. The walls are of yellow stock brick, with a NE front of five bays, two tiers of round-arched windows and a pediment over the three middle bays which project slightly. The central doorway with an open timber porch was supplemented in the late 19th century by additional entrances in the adjacent bays. The interior retained the essential elements of its original layout until 1956 with a continuous gallery, tall central pulpit, and communion apse with circular window behind. Alterations in 1956 saw the culmination of several generations of 'improvements' which seriously compromised the integrity of the interior, including the removal of the SW half of the gallery, alteration and re-siting of the pulpit and the total redesigning of the SW end.

Dolbey (1964) 128, 161–3, Pl. 21. Vickers, J.A., *The Story of Canterbury Methodism* (1961).

CHATHAM

(27) BAPTIST, Clover Street (TQ 758677). 'Zion Chapel' was built in 1821 for a church claiming a foundation date of 1644. The front wall is rendered, of three bays with two tiers of round-arched windows and a small pediment over the centre bay. Porch supported by two Greek Doric columns. Basement rooms below chapel. 'Zion Sabbath School' at rear dated 1858. (School demolished 1979)

Chambers III (1956) 92–3.

CHEVENING

(28) GENERAL BAPTIST, Bessels Green (TQ 509556). This congregation, which originated about 1640, owes its origin to the work of William Jeffery, pastor of a church meeting in or about

General Baptist chapel, Bessels Green. (28)

Bradbourne, a hamlet about 1 mile N of Sevenoaks. The present site has been occupied since 1716, in which year the meeting-house was opened. In 1766–9 the meeting suffered from doctrinal disputes resulting from the appointment of John Stanger as assistant pastor who was dismissed in 1769 and founded a separate congregation (*see* (29)). The original society subsequently followed other General Baptist churches in the South-East in becoming Unitarian in the 19th century.

The meeting-house, standing within a large burial-ground, has brick walls and a hipped tiled roof. The building is rectangular and aligned N–S (43¼ft by 22¾ft externally); the N end, now a vestry, was formerly a cottage and a later caretaker's cottage adjoins to the north. The E front has three cross-framed windows to the left of the present entrance, the N of which is on the site of the original entrance. Adjacent to the present entrance is a small window below the eaves; to the right is a single bay with heightened upper window and a later bay now part of the larger cottage and with a similarly heightened upper window. The S end wall, now covered by tile hanging, formerly had two windows flanking the pulpit. There are two principal windows in the W wall.

The interior of the meeting-house (30¾ft by 19¾ft) has been entirely altered and retains little of its original character. An early photograph shows it seated with box-pews and with an hexagonal canopied pulpit between windows at the S end, none of which survives. A gallery at the N end has also long disappeared. The ceiling, formerly of plaster, coved on all sides, was replaced by match-boarding in the late 19th century.

Baptistery: An external baptistery adjacent to the road 50 yards W was constructed in 1733; it was described in 1936 as 'a brick lined pool in a hollow approached from either side by curved steps which meet in one broader set leading to the pool'. The site, now in the front garden of a house, 'The Bastry', has been filled in but some remains may still lie below the ground.

Fittings – Chandelier: brass, single tier of twelve branches, 18th-century. *Chair*: with two arms, rectangular back panel carved with lozenge decoration, late 17th-century. *Clock*: on W wall, octagonal dial with single hand, long pendulum case, referred to in Church Book 'The clock was put up in the Meeting-house 26 March 1718'. *Communion Table*: with turned baluster legs and renewed top, early 18th-century. *Monuments*: in burial-ground, several monuments of the 18th century and later including (1) William King, 1748; (2) Stephen Colgate, 1764, minister, and Mary his wife [nd]; (3) Jane wife of John Fuller, and daughter of Rev. John Briggs, 1841. *Plate*: pair of pewter cups with hemispherical bowls, 18th-century.

BQ XXVII (1978) 300–20. Chambers III (1956) 78–81. Crosby III (1740) 97–9. Evans (1897) 14. Ivimey II (1814) 223. Taylor (1818) I: 108, 280, 351. *UHST* III (1923–6) 153–4; IV (1927–30) 157–8; VI (1936–7) 103–15, 213–21. Whitley (1928) No. 25.

(29) PARTICULAR BAPTIST, Bessels Green (TQ 507554). This church originated with the dismissal of John Stanger as assistant minister of the General Baptist church who was found guilty of entertaining Calvinistic beliefs. The meeting-house built in 1770 has brick walls and a tiled roof half-hipped at each end; it incorporates a small cottage for the minister. The broad NE front has a symmetrical elevation of three bays with round-arched windows and a cottage to the right of two storeys and attics. The SE end wall

PARTICULAR BAPTIST CHAPEL, BESSELS GREEN CFS 1972

has a round-arched window and above it a small window, formerly a lunette, to light attic rooms above the chapel. There are two round-arched windows in the rear SW wall, now covered by later building.

The interior (36ft by 24ft), refitted in the late 19th century, has a gallery of that period at the SE end. (Reordered and extended to SW 1998)

Monuments and *Floorslab*. *Monuments*: in chapel, Rev. John Stanger, 1823, 'the Founder of this Church'; in burial-ground, many monuments of late 18th century and after. *Floorslab*: Rev. John Stanger, 1823, and Mary his second wife, 1835, pentagonal tablet.

BQ XXVII (1978) 300–20. *New Baptist Magazine* I (1825) 121–4, 211–12.

(30) CHIPSTEAD CHAPEL, High Street, Chipstead (TQ 502561). An early 17th-century timber-framed building of two bays, probably of domestic origin, was converted to a nonconformist chapel in the mid 19th century. The walls are rendered externally and entirely refenestrated but much of the original timber structure remains inside. (Under reconstruction for domestic use 1995)

CHISLET

(31) WESLEYAN, Boyden Gate (TR 222656). Brick with three-bay gabled front dated 1841.

CRANBROOK

(32) Former GENERAL BAPTIST, High Street (TQ 774360). A church in existence by 1648, which was dissolved in 1873, formerly met in or behind a timber-framed Wealden house, 'The Old Studio', on the opposite side of the road from the later chapel.

The chapel on the N side of the road, dated 1807 and opened 1808, latterly 'The Cramp Club', is of brick and has a gabled front with narrow recessed end wings and ball finial on the gable; there are three round-arched upper windows. The lower half is covered by a modern extension which replicates the lost part of the elevation.

Buffard (1963) 65–6. Chambers III (1956) 18. Maguire, L.J. (ed.), General Baptist Assembly, occasional papers: *The General Baptist Church Meeting at Cranbrook, Kent: Register of Births and Deaths 1682–1837* No. 24 (1995). Taylor (1818) I: 283.

(33) STRICT BAPTIST, St David's Bridge (TQ 778359). The church originated in 1780 by secession from the Independent church and first met in a private house. The present chapel was

Former General Baptist chapel, High Street, Cranbrook. From lithograph. (© *Nicholas Cooper*) (32)

converted in 1787 from a pair of timber-framed cottages; the walls are covered with weather-boarding and the roof, half-hipped at the ends, is covered with plain tiles. The NE front wall has three round-arched upper windows and a porch with a pair of doorways, one serving the gallery. There are two similar windows in the back wall.

The interior (28¼ft by 19¼ft) retains some traces of blocked openings in the plaster lining of the front wall. There is a gallery at the SE end. The pulpit at the opposite end dates from the early 19th century and has fluted supports and a round-arched back panel. A small vestry projects beyond the back wall and has shuttered openings towards the chapel.

Fittings – *Baptistery*: centrally in floor. *Clock*: signed 'Ballard, Cranbrook'. *Communion Table*: plain table with two supports and lower bearers, surmounted by four-sided desk for singers. *Monument*: externally, George Stonehouse, 1814, pastor 'upwards of 30 years', headstone. *Seating*: box-pews removed 1967.

Chambers III (1956) 18–19.

(34) PROVIDENCE CHAPEL, Stone Street (TQ 776360). The congregation formerly meeting here appears to have originated around Isaac Beeman, a deacon of the Baptist church who left in 1795 to meet with others 'in a small building off Stone Street'. The new cause was supported by William Huntington SS, a native of Cranbrook who in 1803 met the expense of erecting a timber-framed chapel standing on top of the original meeting-room, now the school-room. In 1808 the chapel was extended to the W and an E gallery erected; shortly afterwards, in 1818, it was enlarged by 12ft to the N, and finally in 1828 further extended on that side with a polygonal front designed by Thomas Dearn. The church remained Calvinistic Independent or Huntingtonian until 1909 when it was reorganized as Strict Baptist.

The chapel stands on a concealed site behind other buildings.

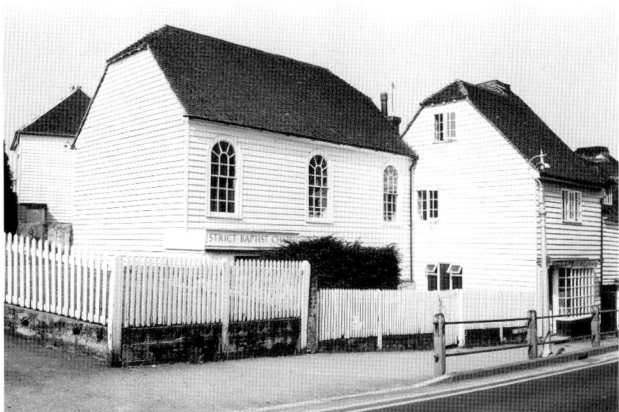

Strict Baptist chapel, St David's Bridge, Cranbrook. (33)

Providence Chapel, Stone Street, Cranbrook. (34)

The walls are timber-framed and clad with plain weather-boarding except at the front on which the boarding is grooved to resemble masonry jointing. The roofs are slated. Most of the structure is at first-floor level supported by the brick walls of the original meeting-room, freestanding columns and later infilling. The front has seven facets with five round-arched sash windows, the centre window now blocked internally. The chapel is approached by two external covered staircases.

The interior has a flat plaster ceiling with exposed beams demarcating the various stages of enlargement and a circular ventilator. There is a gallery around three sides with a panelled front supported by marbled timber columns. (Chapel closed 1987, some fittings removed to Cranbrook Museum)

Fittings – *Baptistery*: below floor in front of pulpit, with brick substructure exposed below, built 1914. *Clock*: on front of S gallery, signed 'Smith, Cranbrook'. *Collecting Shovels*: pair with enclosed boxes and short handles, inscribed 'Providence Chapel'. *Pictures*: in vestry (1) small portrait of William Huntington SS, oil on wood, one of three by Francis Burrell, 1803; (2) portrait of William Huntington SS standing in pulpit, vernacular style, oil on wood; (3, 4) two portraits of Isaac Beeman; (5) print of (1) engraved by J. Godby, 1813; (6) print of portrait of Huntington, published 1786; (7) view of interior of chapel, lithograph by 'Thos. D.W. Dearn Archt.', 1829. *Plate*: electroplate set from Galeed Chapel, Brighton, Sussex. *Pulpit*: polygonal front with applied reeded mouldings, supported by two marbled columns. *Seating*: original open-backed benches with later infilling to backs, early 19th-century. *Miscellaneous*: (1) pair of steel-rimmed spectacles in green case, once the property of William Huntington SS. (2) Communion ticket, Providence Chapel, London.

Chambers III (1956) 20–4. [Honeysett, R.J.], *Providence Chapel, Cranbrook, 1803–1953* [1953]. Paul V (1966) 243–67. Wright (1909) *passim*.

(35) CONGREGATIONAL, High Street (TQ 776361). The formerly Presbyterian society had a meeting-house converted in 1710 from a pair of houses; this was subsequently altered by the erection of a gallery and vestry and superseded by the present chapel on a new site in 1857. This has a gabled front of gault brick with Gothic windows; the side walls of red brick have continuous wooden clerestories.

Timpson (1859) 443–6.

DARTFORD

(36) ZION CHAPEL, Priory Hill (TQ 538742). The chapel was built privately in 1794 by John Wellard of Eynsford and leased to the Countess of Huntingdon's Connexion. This use ceased in

Providence Chapel
CRANBROOK
Kent

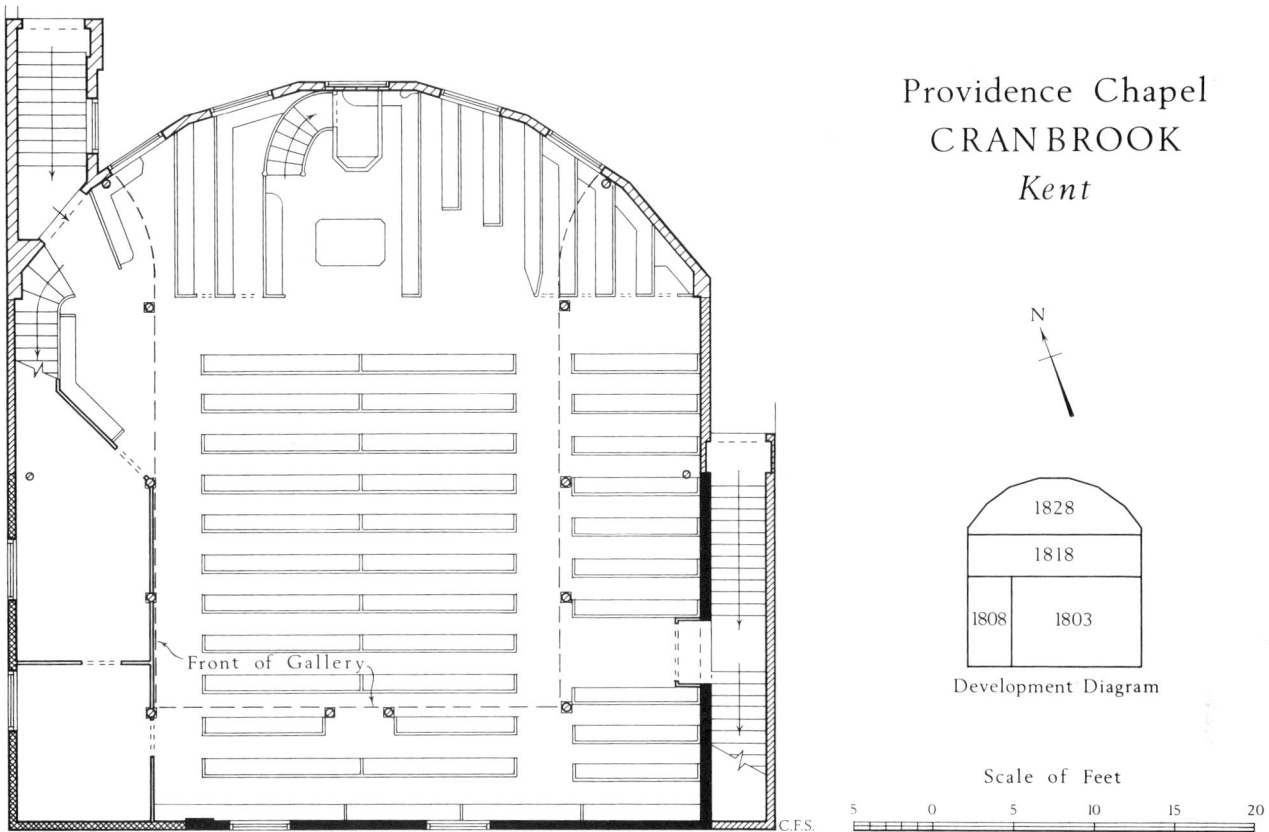

1821 after a period of decline and it was used for a time as a National School. In 1847 the present Strict Baptist church commenced meeting in the chapel, which they ultimately purchased in 1918.

The chapel (31¾ft enlarged *c*.1800 to 42¾ft, by 24¼ft externally) is a timber-framed building clad in weather-boarding and with a hipped roof covered with pantiles. The broad W front, which originally had two large sash windows between a pair of doorways, has been extended by one bay to the S and variously altered. Two large windows in the N end wall have been blocked. The interior has a N gallery with panelled front.

Chambers III (1956) 107–8. Timpson (1859) 451–3.

Wesleyan chapel, Spital Street, Dartford.   (37)

(37) WESLEYAN, Spital Street (TQ 540741). The chapel built in 1844–5 to designs by W.W. Pocock has a front of gault brick and yellow stock brick sides. The front is gabled with a three-light lancet window above triple entrances, flanked by a pair of towers with tall lancet windows; the towers have battlemented parapets and prominent crocketed stone pinnacles at the corners. (Pinnacles destroyed since 1972; proposal to subdivide interior reported 1989)

DEAL

(38) Former GENERAL BAPTIST, 120a High Street, formerly Lower Street (TR 377529). The chapel, now converted to a private house, was built c.1688 by Samuel Taverner, Governor of Deal Castle during the Commonwealth, who later joined the Baptist church in Dover. The original congregation, which became Unitarian in its latter days, survived until 1910 after which the chapel was put to a variety of secular or religious uses.

The chapel stands on low ground well below the present street level; it is a small rectangular building with walls of coarse brick and a tiled roof. The broad W front of four bays has been variously altered: in the late 19th century by the application of a rendered façade with terminal pilasters, moulded cornice and pedimental blocking-course, and in the late 20th century when the windows, formerly with segmental-arched heads, were given pointed-arched heads and Regency glazing. The interior retains no original features, but a *floorslab* to Samuel Taverner, 1696, is believed to be concealed below the present floor.

Evans (1897) 65. Hague and Hague (1986) 44.

Former General Baptist chapel, High Street, Deal. (38)

(39) Former BAPTIST, Nelson Street (TR 375531). The chapel, now 'Nelson Hall', was built in 1814. It is set back from the street behind a railed forecourt. The front, altered or 'improved', is stuccoed and of mid 19th-century appearance, of three bays with two tall round-arched sash windows and a central porch.

BM VII (1815) 263; VIII (1816) 220.

(40) Former CONGREGATIONAL, High Street (TR 376530). The first meeting-house, built in 1689, was of brick and tile with a double roof and end galleries; it measured 34ft by 41ft. A new chapel erected in 1804 and enlarged in 1808 was replaced by the present building on the same site in 1882. The present chapel, now converted to social use, is a large building of brick with stone dressings in the Gothic style by Joseph Gardner of Folkestone. The gabled front is flanked by a pair of slightly recessed staircase towers with octagonal upper stages and tall slate-covered spires. *Monuments*: in burial-ground S of chapel, several decayed headstones of the 18th century and later; also a monument to William Royson, 1771, Lieutenant Governor of Greenwich Hospital, and Elizabeth his widow, [1780?], urn on pedestal.

CYB (1882) 404–5. Timpson (1859) 404–13. Walford, E. (ed.), *Walford's Antiquarian [Antiquarian Magazine]* VIII (1885) 225.

DODDINGTON

(41) Former WESLEYAN (TQ 934572). Brick with segmental-arched windows, dated 1903. (Now village hall)

DOVER

(42) ADRIAN STREET CHAPEL (TR 319414). The General Baptist congregation, which had become Unitarian by 1800, was formed in the mid 17th century. One of its earliest supporters was Samuel Taverner, a former Governor of Deal Castle, who had moved to Dover in 1665 and in 1672 licensed a room in his house near the Market Place. In 1681 he was ordained pastor. In 1745 a meeting-house near Market Lane was purchased to replace the earlier room and that remained in use until the erection of the present chapel.

Adrian Street Chapel was built to accommodate the increased numbers attracted to the preaching of Benjamin Marten, appointed pastor in 1800. The building, erected in 1819–20, was designed by Thomas Reed, described in the *Monthly Repository* XIV (1819) 338 as 'building surveyor to Government for the coast of Kent and Sussex' who 'on account of his firm attachment to Unitarian principles, has very kindly and gratuitously drawn our plans and superintended the work'. The plan is an elongated octagon; the walls are of gault brick and stock brick, the hipped and slated roof has a central flat and wide bracketed eaves. The principal front faces E and has plain paired pilasters below a pediment; in both the longer walls to the E and W is a large tripartite window within a semicircular enclosing arch; other windows, in two tiers, have round-arched heads. The outer doorways are in the SE and SW angles with a doorway between leading to vaults below the chapel. A vestry of two storeys is attached at the N end with which a later school-room block (now demolished) was connected. A detached manse formerly lay to the south.

The interior has a plaster ceiling. At the S end is a gallery with a concave panelled front. The N end has a shallow apse now occupied by an organ but originally by the pulpit which was accessible at a high level directly from the vestry. Within the apse at either side were two doorways, now superseded by one cut through the E end of the wall, for access to the vestries. The lower vestry was subdivided and has in each part a corner fireplace and an outer doorway; the W doorway is now blocked. The roof over the chapel is supported by queen-post trusses. Below the chapel an irregular space remains, reduced by the construction of burial vaults, together with a central mass of brickwork probably the base of the baptistery.

Fittings – *Books*: bible, printed by John Archdeacon, Cambridge, 1789. *Glass*: plain window glass was replaced by inappropriate hammered glass following a fire in 1987. *Inscriptions*: on keystone

Adrian Street Chapel, Dover. (42)

of principal window at front, date '1819'; on keystone of corresponding window at rear, initials and date 'R.S / 1819'.

Monuments: in chapel, on W wall (1) Margaretta daughter of Robert Smith MD of Maidstone, 1854; (2) Rev. John Marten, 1880, 'A Messenger of the General Baptist Churches 1861–1880', buried in Saffron Walden cemetery, brass; (3) Charles Woodland Chitty, born 1874 died 1979, and Ernest Chitty, 1966; on NW wall (4) Robert Tiffin, 1874, and Clara his daughter, 1900; (5) Thomas Barker Wawne Briggs, 1883, 35 years minister; (6) Benjamin Igglesden, 1873, and Mary his widow, 1888; on NE wall (7) Elizabeth Ann (Marten) widow of George Igglesden, 1872, also Priscilla (Marten), 1873, wife of John Marsh, and Rachel Jane Marten, 1903; on E wall (8) Rev. Benjamin Marten, 1823, 'pastor of this General Baptist Church …'; (9) Elizabeth widow of Rev. Benjamin Marten of Barfrestone, 1856; (10) George Igglesden, 1835, and his children Clara, 1835, and Selina, 1836.

Externally on S wall (11) Roger Squire, 1834, Elizabeth his first wife, 1824, and Elizabeth Minter his second wife, 1845; (12) Elizabeth Ann (Marten) widow of George Igglesden, 1872, and Priscilla (Marten) wife of John Marsh, 1873; in plinth (13) Benjamin Marten of Barfrestone, 1823, pastor for nearly 30 years, 'leaving a widow and 12 children to lament their loss', also Elizabeth his widow, 1856, and their sons, Benjamin, 1840, Samuel Flint, 1848, Joseph Seaton, 1852, Edward, 1854, and Stephen Love, 1863; (14) family vault of William Kitchin inscribed on wall above to William Kitchin, 1825, Frances his widow, 1838, and Ann their daughter, 1859[?]; in plinth of vestry (15) vault of John [ ]; (16) Edward Philpotts; on W wall of chapel (17) Henry Knight, 1832, his two sons Richard Leadbetter, 1826, and Henry, 1826, and Elizabeth Harmer Knight, 1826. In small burial-ground at rear of chapel, about half-a-dozen headstones, including (18) George Pear, 1822, and Tryphena his wife [date gone]; (19) John Slaughter, 1844, and Ann Goodwin Slaughter his wife, 1829, 'leaving Mary Ann his 2nd wife and eleven children to lament their loss'; at one side of the path leading to the front of the chapel are six further headstones.

Painting: loose, oil painting of exterior showing roof surmounted by a domed clock-tower, for which no structural evidence exists, mid 19th-century. *Plate*: plated base metal, set of two cups, three plates, and one flagon; flagon inscribed 'in commemoration of the passing of the Dissenters' Chapels Bill 1844'. *Pulpit*: with elaborately curved sides and base, formerly cantilevered from back wall of apse, 1819, re-sited. *Seating*: box-pews to lower floor, slightly altered; some benches in gallery.

Christian Freeman (December 1870) 182–3. Evans (1897) 75–6. Ivimey IV (1830) 511. Maguire, L.J. (ed.), General Baptist Assembly, occasional papers: *A History of the General Baptist Church meeting in Dover, in the County of Kent…, by B. Marten (1802)* No. 16 (1992). *Monthly Repository* XIV (1819) 337–8; XV (1820) 318. Taylor (1818) I: 273–80, 350. *UHST* VI (1935–8) 157–8.

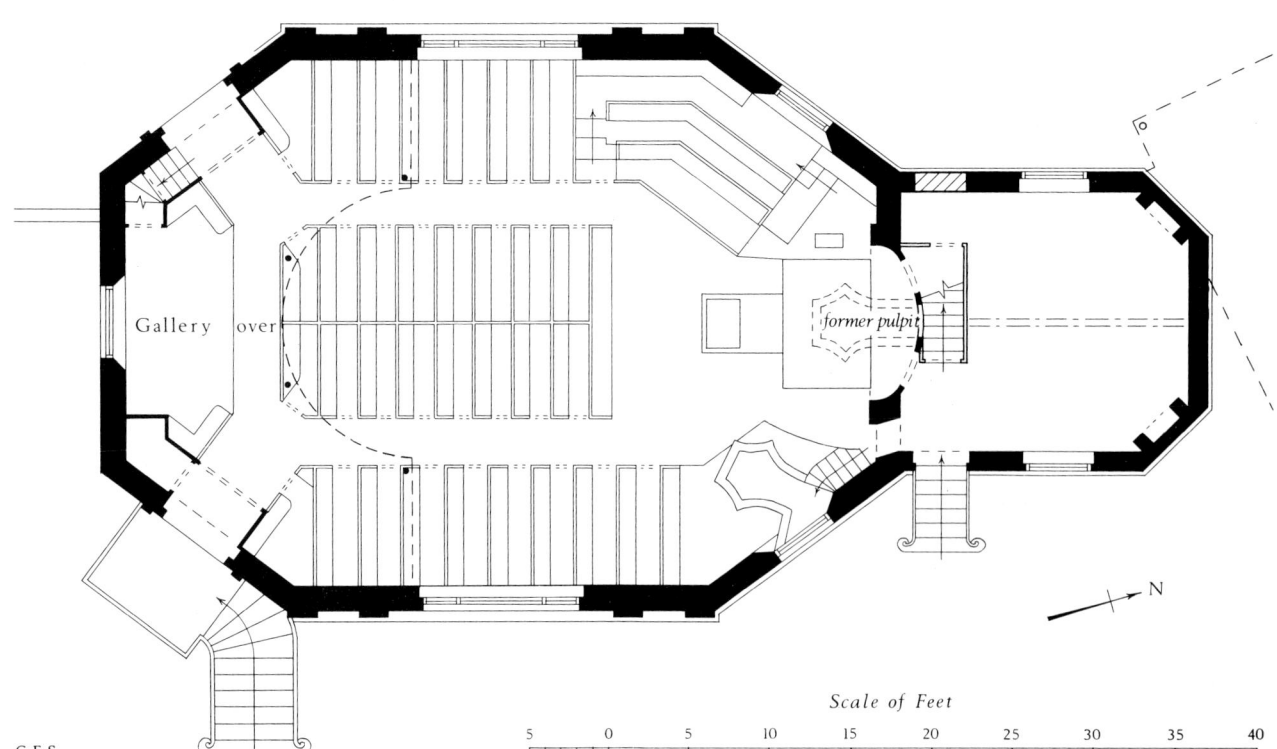

Adrian Street Chapel, DOVER — Kent

(43) BAPTIST, Biggin Street (TR 318417). Salem Chapel has a rendered front of three principal bays with a pediment; lower stage rusticated, upper stage divided by Corinthian pilasters. Built 1840, re-fronted 1879. (Demolished c.1975)

BM XXXII (1840) 533.

(44) Former WESLEYAN, London Road (TR 312422). Brick with hipped slate roof, concealed behind stuccoed front of three bays with pedimented centre having two Ionic columns *in antis*. (Now a social club) *Inscriptions*: over front entrance 'Wesleyan Centenary Chapel 1839' (defaced); on two bricks in side wall 'E Dyer | 1839'.

(45) WESLEYAN, Tower Road (TR 311418). Tower Hamlets Mission, opened 1850, occupies a small hall with rendered gabled front but sides built of brick rubble.

EAST PECKHAM

(46) STRICT BAPTIST (TQ 668487). 'Providence Chapel' dated 1855 has a gabled front with later rendering and two pointed-arched windows with intersecting glazing bars.

Chambers III (1956) 75.

(47) WESLEYAN (TQ 667487). Red brick with yellow brick dressings; 1886 by S.W. Haughton of East Grinstead.

EASTRY

(48) BAPTIST (TR 310546). 'Zion Chapel', built 1824 as a preaching-station for Eythorne, is a small brick building with a hipped slate roof; three-bay front with tall sash windows and recent porch.

Miller (1924) 65–7.

(49) Former WESLEYAN, Mill Lane (TR 308547). Brick with hipped roof; round-arched doorway in front and two blocked upper windows with new window pierced between. Re-sited tablet inscribed 'Providence Chapel 1822'.

EDENBRIDGE

(50) EBENEZER CHAPEL, High Street (TQ 443463). The timber-framed and weather-boarded chapel, with later brick gable end, was built in 1808 by John Tyler for Calvinistic Independents. The church later became Strict Baptist. (Conversion to social use proposed 1994)

Chambers III (1956) 88–9, Pl. facing 112.

EGERTON

(51) Former STRICT BAPTIST, Potter's Forstal (TQ 891466). The chapel of brick with a slate roof was built in 1825 and enlarged to the front in the mid 19th century. The front is gabled, of three bays with sash windows and a later porch. (Derelict 1974)

Chambers III (1956) 11–12.

ELHAM

(52) WESLEYAN, High Street (TR 177441). The Wesleyan Centenary Chapel of 1839 stands adjacent to its predecessor of 1814. Both have fronts of three bays; the earlier chapel is of brick with a hipped roof, the later building, with side walls of banded flint and brick, has a rendered pedimented front divided by pilasters. *Inscription*: on two bricks below eaves of earlier chapel 'WMxR | 1814'. *Monuments*: headstones (1) William Johnson, 1859; (2) Ann wife of Ephraim Coleman, 1832; (3) John Page, 1855; (4) Richard Foreman, 1861.

EYNSFORD

(53) BAPTIST (TQ 542658). A preaching-house was opened in 1796 by John Stanger of Bessels Green (*see* (29)). The present chapel, on the earlier site, is entirely of 1906 in a free Gothic style by Tait and Hobbs of Dartford. *Monuments*: in burial-ground (1) John Nevile, 1873, many years pastor at Sutton-at-Hone, and Elizabeth his widow, 1885; (2) William Hodsoll, 1835, and Ann his widow, 1875.

B.Hbk (1907) 494–5. *New Baptist Magazine* I (1825) 212. Whitley (1928) No. 83.

EYTHORNE

(54) BAPTIST (TR 283494). A General Baptist church is claimed to have been in existence here by the early 17th century. Prior to 1755 the church, in membership with the General Baptist Association, met in a cottage in Coldred Road, demolished 1901. The first regular meeting-house was built adjacent to this cottage in 1755. Within the next 30 years the church had transferred its allegiance to the Particular Baptists.

In 1804 a new site was acquired on Langdown and the present chapel erected; it was enlarged to the front in 1842. The walls are of brick with two tiers of round-arched windows, the front is rendered and the roof is hipped and tiled. The front wall is of three bays with a low gable and a blind window above a modern porch. The interior, which has a continuous gallery, was reseated in 1900.

Chambers III (1956) 42–54. Miller (1924). Taylor (1818) I: 281–2; II: 96, 138. Wood (1847) 176.

FAVERSHAM

(55) BAPTIST, St Mary's Road (TR 018613). Big gabled front of yellow stock brick with red and blue dressings; foundation stone laid by C.H. Spurgeon, 1872.

Weeks, W.R., *A Hundred Years and More: The History of Faversham Baptist Church*, Faversham Papers No. 14 (1977).

(56) Former COUNTESS OF HUNTINGDON'S, Partridge Lane (TR 015615). A preaching-house was opened in 1787 and the present chapel opened two years later. This was supplied by preachers in the Countess's Connexion until 1828, when a Congregation church was formed. In 1879 the church removed to a new chapel in Newton Road and the former chapel passed into secular use. The walls are of brick with two tiers of windows in the side walls, the upper ones formerly with round-arched heads. The front is gabled but largely obscured by later staircase wings and other additions; the chapel was also extended to the rear in the 19th century.

Timpson (1859) 435–7.

(57) CONGREGATIONAL, Newton Road (TR 017612). The chapel built in 1878–9 by Joseph Gardner of Folkestone to replace the foregoing is an elaborate composition with giant Corinthian columns supporting a pediment with full entablature, and quadrant staircases filling the spaces between the portico and recessed wings. (Demolished c.1975)

(58) WESLEYAN, Preston Street (TR 015610). Gothic chapel built 1861 with walls of rubble with ashlar dressings. The front has three

gabled bays separated by buttresses with plain pinnacles. The central entrance and triple window above are set within a tall arched recess. The flanking bays have cross finials to the gables, gabled secondary entrances and circular windows above with plate tracery. The side walls have separately gabled bays. The interior was subdivided horizontally in 1980 when the former Congregational Church (57), now URC, united with this congregation.

Wesleyan chapel, Preston Street, Faversham.　　　　(58)

(59) Former SALVATION ARMY, Stone Street (TR 015612). Restrained gabled front of brick with large lunette above entrance. Dated 1906.

FOLKESTONE

(60) BAPTIST, St Michael's Street (TR 232361). A Particular Baptist church which had been meeting since *c.*1720 was joined in 1728 by seceders from the General Baptist Church of Hythe and Folkestone. In 1729 the enlarged society acquired land at Mill Bay, or 'The Bayle', and built a meeting-house '45ft by 20ft'. That was superseded in 1790 by the present chapel but by 1797 the church had returned to its former building and leased the new chapel, then known as 'Zion', to the Countess of Huntingdon's Connexion. The latter society was re-formed as Congregational *c.*1824 and removed to a new chapel (62) in 1857. Zion was eventually sold in 1878 to another Baptist church.

The chapel is a square building of brick with a pyramidal tiled roof. The front wall covered with later rendering is of three bays with a central doorway and two tiers of round-arched windows. There are similar windows at the centre of each side wall and two rectangular pulpit windows at the rear.

The interior (32¾ft square) is lofty and has a pair of probably later posts, slightly off centre, to support the roof structure. Original galleries around three sides are supported at the rear by a pair of marbled timber Tuscan columns but at the sides by iron columns. The chapel was much refitted in the late 19th century and the walls and ceiling lined with match-boarding; it was further refurbished in 1983 for Evangelical Baptists following closure *c.*1973.

Chambers III (1956) 48–51. *Grace* (December 1983) 5. Ivimey IV (1830) 511–12. Paul V (1966) 280–7. Timpson (1859) 510–13.

Salem Chapel, Rendezvous Street, Folkestone.　　　　(61)

(61) SALEM CHAPEL, Rendezvous Street (TR 22903605). The Baptist church which formerly met at Mill Bay (*see* (60)) built their first chapel on this site in 1845. The present chapel of brick with a grand stuccoed Classical façade was built in 1873 to the designs of Joseph Gardner. The front of three principal bays has a central pedimented portico supported by pairs of Corinthian columns, with a wide round-arched entrance and three balustraded windows above. There is a lecture hall below the chapel. (Sold 1987 following removal of church to Hill Road; now a public house)

Baptist Times (22 October 1987; 10 September 1998).

(62) CONGREGATIONAL, Tontine Street (TR 230362). The church which originally met in Zion Chapel (60) built the present chapel in 1856–7. This is in the Gothic style by Joseph Gardner.

The walls are faced in ragstone and the roof is slated and has a small wooden bell-cote behind the front gable. The chapel was enlarged in 1885, possibly by one bay to the front, and has a galleried aisle on one side with separately gabled upper windows.

Timpson (1859) 510–13.

(63) CONGREGATIONAL, Radnor Park (TR 222362). Large Gothic chapel (now URC) of stone with ashlar dressings, wide unaisled nave with separately gabled side windows and corner tower. Built 1897–8 to designs by Joseph Gardner. The interior was partly reconstructed in 1984 with additional rooms below a deep gallery at the N end. *Inscription*: brass on communion table to 'Joseph Gardner Architect of this church who died before its completion', presented by his widow and family.

CYB (1897) 178; (1898) 162–3.

(64) WESLEYAN, Grace Hill (TR 229362). Stone Gothic with gabled front, and thin corner tower with octagonal upper stage and spire; 1865–6 by Joseph Gardner. (Demolished *c*.1978)

FRITTENDEN

(65) PROVIDENCE CHAPEL, Pound Hill (TQ 817411). The small chapel was built in 1805 by a Mr Mitchell who preached there from 1814 to 1821. The building remained in private hands until 1876 when it was placed in trust for Strict Baptists. It has brick walls and a slate roof. The front has two tall sash windows to the chapel with doorway between; to the right is a later cottage or annexe with a vestry and kitchen for the chapel on the ground floor. The interior of the chapel, largely refitted in the late 19th century, formerly had a segmental plaster ceiling. The table-pew in front of the pulpit may be original; there is no baptistery. *Monuments*: in chapel (1) David Southon, 1847; externally (2) Thomas Clifford, 1872, and Louisa his widow, 1892.

Chambers III (1956) 14–15.

GILLINGHAM

(66) CHRISTIAN ISRAELITE, Chatham Hill (TQ 777670). 'Jezreel's Tower', a square building of brick and concrete, of loosely Elizabethan character, was begun in 1885 by the followers of the preacher 'J.J. Jezreel' who failed to complete it. (Demolished *c*.1961)

Homan (1984) 77. Rogers, P.G., *The Sixth Trumpeter* (1963) 36ff.

GOUDHURST

(67) WESLEYAN (TQ 723380). Red brick with yellow brick dressings. Gabled front with tall round-arched windows; central entrance re-sited. Dated 1878.

GRAVESEND

(68) BAPTIST, Windmill Street (TQ 648738). 'Emmanuel Chapel' built in 1843 has a rendered front of three bays with a pediment and two tiers of windows. The side walls are of yellow stock brick. Rendering of front renewed and some details removed since 1951.

BM XXXIII (1841) 575–6.

(69) Former STRICT BAPTIST, Peacock Street (TQ 650739). 'Zoar Chapel', of brick with low pedimented front, was built in 1846 to the designs and partly at the cost of I.C. Johnson, 'founder of the cement works at Greenhithe'.

Chambers III (1956) 98.

Providence Chapel, Pound Hill, Frittenden. (65)

HADLOW

(70) STRICT BAPTIST, Court Lane (TQ 635499). Red brick with gabled S front, pointed-arched window above small porch. Built 1830.

Chambers III (1956) 87.

HARTLIP

(71) BIBLE CHRISTIAN (TQ 837638). 'Cardiphonia Chapel' was built in 1820–1 on ground provided by William Drawbridge, a local magistrate, who retained ownership of the building treating it much like a private chapel. The walls are rendered and the roof is covered with slates; the plan is a double square to which a hall was added at the rear in 1907. The E front wall has a central doorway, originally with a pediment over but replaced by a porch in the early 20th century. The side walls have each two windows of two lights with wooden pointed-arched tracery below a square head with a moulded label. There is a small private entrance on the N side now internal and covered by an outbuilding.

The interior was refitted c.1907 when the W wall was replaced by a screen and a window of three lights reset from it in the N wall of the hall. The pulpit was originally placed centrally along the N wall with seats facing towards it at each end and a private pew for the family of William Drawbridge at the W end.

(Since 1972 the chapel has been unsympathetically 'repaired', the roof re-covered in patent tiles, the porch rebuilt, the windows on the S side replaced and stripped of their external labels, and other windows reglazed with large panels of obscured glass)

Fittings – *Glass*: in reset window at N end of hall, formerly in W wall of chapel, at head of centre light, oval panel, much decayed, bearing a crest of feathers bound with a double band and issuing from a coronet, with motto scroll below, also oval panels and quarries with formal decoration; in head of one window on N side contemporary glass with floral quarries. *Inscriptions*: internally, a series of nine devotional panels entitled, on N wall – 'Jesus Christ | GOD [above former site of pulpit] | Holy Ghost'; on S wall – 'Faith | Hope | Charity'; on W wall – 'Brethren | Our departed Friends'; and above E doorway – 'May God bless our [King]' [altered to Queen].

Bible Christian chapel, Hartlip. (71)

Baldwin, R.A., *A History of Hartlip Methodist Chapel* (c.1970). Bourne (1905) 88–9.

HAWKHURST

(72) BAPTIST (TQ 759308). The chapel of 1892 by G.F. Hawkes of Birmingham is of red brick with painted stone dressings. The front, which is gabled with intermediate stepped buttresses rising to pinnacles, has a triple-arched entrance loggia with an elaborate pointed-arched window above with a circular pattern of cusped tracery; on a band below the window is the inscription 'The Meeting House of the Baptist Church 1892'.

B.Hbk (1894) 299–300.

Baptist meeting-house, Hawkhurst. (72)

HAWKINGE

(73) UNION CHAPEL, The Street, Up Hill (TR 216402). A Baptist chapel was opened in Hawkinge in 1824. The earliest part of the present building is an annexe alongside the chapel with a tablet above the entrance inscribed 'Union Chapel 1832'. The chapel, of brick with stone dressings, was largely or entirely rebuilt in the Gothic style in 1873. It has a gabled front with a short clock turret at one corner and a polygonal apse at the rear. The side wall is rendered. *Bootscrapers*: incorporated in front boundary wall, three large recesses with curved scraper bars, c.1873.

BM XVI (1824) 487.

HEADCORN

(74) Former GENERAL BAPTIST, Love Lane (TQ 84954405). The church now meeting in Station Road (*see* (75)) appears to have been a section of one formed in the mid 17th century based on Biddenden which later formed separate churches. The present site, ¾ mile E of the village, was purchased in 1736 and a meeting-house built which was registered in 1741.

The former meeting-house (32½ft by 24¾ft externally), now a

pair of cottages, is a timber-framed structure of which the upper half is now covered with tile hanging and the lower walls rebuilt in brickwork. The roof is hipped and tiled and retains its original form with a central valley discharging to the S but concealed by a continuous roof across the N front. The building was converted to a single cottage after the erection of a new chapel in 1819; it was subdivided in the 1920s and has since been extended and greatly altered. Conversion to a cottage included the insertion of a central brick chimney-stack with a lobby entrance on the N side and horizontal subdivision.

The *burial-ground*, adjacent to the E, is a long narrow strip of land alongside the lane bounded by hedges and a ditch. It contains numerous monuments of the mid 18th and 19th centuries. These include three headstones with identical scrolled tops and oval panels (1) Edward Love, 1808, 43 years pastor, and Jane (Budgin) his wife, 1807; (2) Robert Pyall, 1820, 29 years pastor, and Henrietta his wife, 1810; (3) Elizabeth Igglesden, 1817; also (4) John Coupland, 1815, 8 years assistant minister; (5) James Cowper, 1761; (6) Johnathan Clark, 1809, [minister], Grace his widow 1826, and their children, Johnathan, 1825, Hannah wife of William Wood, 1803, and Sarah, 1849. (For full record *see* Boorman (1978), op. cit. below.)

BQ XXIV (1971–2) 30, 79, 84, 86; XXVII (1977–8) 311. Boorman, K.C., *The General Baptist Graveyard, Love Lane, Headcorn, Kent* (Headcorn Local Hist. Soc, *c.*1978, reprinted in Maguire, L.J. (ed.), General Baptist Assembly, occasional papers: *The General Baptist Church Meeting at Headcorn, Kent: Composite Register of Births, Deaths & 1731 to 1837* No. 23 (1995). Buffard (1963) 65, 67, 125. *Monthly Repository* XIV (1819) 515–16. Taylor (1818) I: 350. *USHT* VII (1939–42) 65.

(75) GENERAL BAPTIST, Station Road (TQ 836442). The chapel which superseded the foregoing on a new site in 1819 is a plain building of brick extended to the N in 1978. The S front is of three bays with pedimental gable and two tiers of windows; the lower windows and central doorway have round-arched heads. The interior, refitted in 1978, has a back gallery only, supported by two cast-iron columns. (Front rebuilt in facsimile, 1998) *Inscription*: tablet in front gable inscribed 'UNITARIAN | BAPTIST | CHAPEL | 1819', the first word painted out *c.*1870 following a reversion by the church to its earlier Trinitarian position. *Monuments*: in burial-ground, late 19th-century headstones have been re-sited.

HERNE BAY

(76) BAPTIST, High Street (TR 178683). Low pedimented front of brick with rendered dressings; three conjoined round-arched windows between Corinthian pilasters, entrances in wings. Built 1879, hall added alongside 1885.

(77) CONGREGATIONAL, Mortimer Street (TR 179683). The congregation (now URC) originated in 1822 when a chapel was built for Calvinistic dissenters. In 1837 a former Episcopal chapel was acquired but in the following year some members left to resume worship in the former building, 'Union Chapel'. In 1854 a Wesleyan chapel on part of the present site was bought by the seceders who erected the existing chapel, by Poulton and Woodman, in 1864. This has brick side walls but the N front is of

General Baptist chapel, Headcorn. (75)

Kentish rag; the front is gabled with intermediate buttresses, a pair of gabled porches and a central pointed-arched window of five lights with cusped tracery. *Inscription*: tablet in outer wall of church hall, facing High Street, reset 1933 from earlier chapel, 'The ground on which this chapel stands was the gift of Geo. Burge Esqr. 1852'.

CYB (1863) 320. Timpson (1859) 524–7.

(78) WESLEYAN, High Street (TR 177683). Tall chapel with gabled front, staircase wings, corner tower with broaches to octagonal upper stage and spire. The whole, including the spire, faced with polygonal masonry. Of 1885 by Charles Bell.

HERNHILL

(79) WESLEYAN, Dargate (TR 081616). Red brick with low gabled front of three bays, dated 1840.

HORSMONDEN

(80) PRIMITIVE METHODIST (TQ 704404). Flemish bond brickwork with glazed headers, hipped slate roof. Broad front with two segmental-arched windows, former central entrance blocked and re-sited in lean-to wings. Date stone '1846' on site of original entrance.

HOUGHAM WITHOUT

(81) WESLEYAN, West Hougham (TR 265402). Rendered walls and hipped slate roof. Three-bay front dated 1840 with tall windows and arched doorway with blind tympanum, all with rusticated surrounds. Interior reseated; original pulpit with bowed front, panelled back-board with reeded pilasters and broken pediment.

HYTHE

(82) WESLEYAN, Rampart Road (TR 160347). Stone with quatrefoil-traceried window in gable end and octagonal corner turret. Built 1897–8 replacing a chapel of 1845. A memorial in the vestibule lists burials 1847–58.

IGHTHAM

(83) WESLEYAN, Chapel Lane (TQ 592567). The chapel dated 1848 has stone walls with stone galleting and brick dressings. The front of three bays with a pedimental gable has a later porch. The windows have stone tracery added in the late 19th century.

LAMBERHURST

(84) STRICT BAPTIST (TQ 674360). Small brick chapel built 1816, with three-bay front, pedimental gable, doorway with hood supported by paired brackets and round-arched windows with blind tympana. The interior, partly reseated, has a gallery at the entrance supported by two octagonal posts. Behind the pulpit is a vestry with a second timber-framed vestry added above it c.1900 and only accessible by a stair behind the pulpit.

Chambers III (1954) 86–7.

LEIGH

(85) Former INDEPENDENT (TQ 547463). The chapel built 1871, now used by the Royal British Legion, was designed by George Devey for Samuel Morley for use by an Evangelical Free Church. After Morley's death in 1886 it passed to the Established Church, but closed before 1914. The chapel, in a late Gothic style, of red brick with blue brick diaper and stone dressings, is four bays in length with gabled ends. A large hall in a matching style stands detached to the rear.

Homan (1984) 69.

LENHAM

(86) CONGREGATIONAL, Maidstone Road (TQ 897522). The chapel (now URC) of 1951 by George Baines and Son stands on the site of one of 1824. *Monuments*: in burial-ground (1) Rev. James Oakshett, and two children, James Owen and Ellen Taylor Oakshett, all 1837; (2) John Wilson, 1848, deacon, and Ruth his widow, 1869, capstone of table-tomb.

Timpson (1859) 504–8.

LOOSE

(87) CONGREGATIONAL, Coxheath (TQ 757511). Small timber-framed chapel of 1825 with weather-boarded sides and flush-jointed boarding to front. Gabled front of three bays with round-arched windows and circular window above porch.

Timpson (1859) 343, 503.

MAIDSTONE

(88) EARL STREET CHAPEL, Market Buildings (TQ 759558). The Presbyterian society may owe its origin to the influence of, *inter alia*, Thomas Wilson, perpetual curate of Maidstone, who died 1651 and his successor John Crump, ejected 1662. In 1672 Lady Tayler's house in St Faith's Green was licensed for Presbyterians while the chancel of St Faith's Church has been claimed to have housed the congregation prior to the erection of a permanent meeting-house. An orthodox secession occurred in 1745 following which the majority increasingly accepted a Socinian and ultimately a Unitarian doctrine.

'Earl Street Chapel' in Market Buildings, formerly 'Mitre Yard', was built in 1736. It is a square building of brick with a pyramidal roof covered with tiles. The walls have wide clasping pilaster buttresses at each corner, a narrow plinth and a stepped brick eaves cornice. The E front of three bays originally had doorways in the outer bays (of which the bootscrapers remain in place), replaced by windows and a central doorway substituted in 1921, the date on the lintel of the doorway. Three segmental-arched upper windows are original; below the middle window is a stone with the date 1736. The side walls each of three bays have two tiers of windows. The W wall has been pierced by a shallow pulpit recess also of 1921.

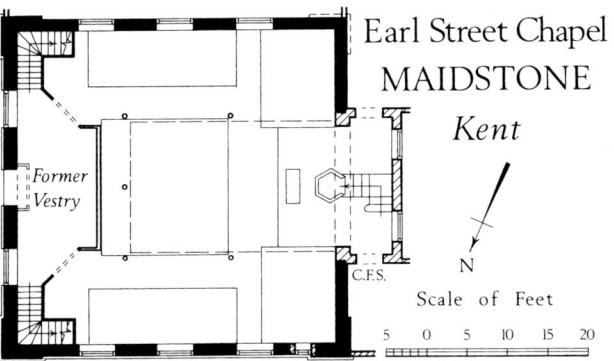

The interior (39ft square), reseated in the late 19th century, has a gallery around three sides with a fielded-panelled front supported by five columns with moulded caps and bases. The roof is supported about a central king-post with naturally forked base.

Fittings – *Clock*: on gallery front, signed 'Bartlett, Maidstone', 19th-century. *Inscriptions*: on bricks at sides of original entrances, initials and one possible date 1725. *Pulpit*: hexagonal with fielded-panelled sides and inlaid ornament, on flared stem; original stair reconstructed; the former back-board with arched and keyed panel flanked by fluted pilasters has been reset in the vestibule. *Sculpture*: plaster statue (41in.) of Rev. A.M. Harris (1780–1820).

Evans (1897) 162–4. Knighton, Miss G.L., *Three Hundred Years of Religious Freedom, 1662–1962* (1962). Timpson (1859) 333–5.

Earl Street Chapel, Maidstone. (88)

(89) Former BAPTIST, Union Street (TQ 762560). 'Bethel Chapel', now the Salvation Army Citadel, was built c.1833 for a Baptist church formed by a secession from a church meeting in King Street. The congregation removed to new premises in Knightrider Street (TQ 761554) in 1906–7. The rendered front of three bays with two tiers of windows and a pedimental gable was embellished in the late 19th century.

BM XXX (1838) 214.

(90) FRIENDS, Wheeler Street (TQ 762561). The meeting-house was built in 1811–12 for a recently re-established meeting; it was variously altered and enlarged during the 19th century and later leaving much of the original front obscured. The walls are of red brick and the roof is hipped and slated. The interior originally comprised one principal room with a smaller room at one end below the loft or gallery. (Demolished c.1975 for a public car park)

Butler (1999) 284–5. Showler, K., *The Society of Friends in Kent* (1970) 17–18.

(91) WESLEYAN, Union Street (TQ 761561). The chapel was built in 1823 replacing one registered in 1802. The rendered front of five bays with a three-bay pediment has been systematically altered leaving little beyond a row of pointed-arched upper windows, from which the original intersecting glazing has been removed, to recall its earlier character. The lower part of the front is covered by a crudely Classical part-open porch. Interior refitted. A large burial-ground in front of the chapel, formerly replete with monuments, has been laid bare; a few headstones are reset against a boundary wall.

MARGATE

(92) BAPTIST, New Street (TR 354709). The chapel built c.1825, replacing one of 1770, has walls of stock brick and a rendered front of five bays with two tiers of pointed-arched windows. A porch was added to the front and separate gallery entrances constructed in 1843. A new entrance at the rear facing Cecil Square was constructed in 1899 comprising an elaborate Gothic annexe of three bays with traceried windows and a flèche, by H.T.A. Chidgey.

B.Hbk (1901) 355–6. BM XXXV (1843) 372; XXXVI (1844) 92. Chambers (1956) 28–9. Ivimey IV (1830) 513.

(93) CONGREGATIONAL, Union Crescent (TR 355709). Gothic with corner tower and stone spire above entrance, walls faced with Kentish rag. 1860, by Poulton and Woodman. (URC)

CYB (1859) 252–3.

(94) Former FRIENDS (TR 362697). 'Draper's Almshouses', erected in 1709 as a benefaction from Michael Yoakley, was the location of a Quaker meeting from 1710 which for 200 years from 1750 met in an almshouse adjacent to the 'Clock House'. A few late 19th-century ledger stones in the courtyard mark a former burial-ground.

Butler (1999) 285–6. FHSJ XIV (1917) 146–56.

(95) Former WESLEYAN, Hawley Square (TR 355708). The former chapel of 1811, now in commercial use, has a broad stuccoed front of five bays with 'Gothick' porches in the end bays, three windows with square labels between and five pointed-arched windows above. The windows have inserted tracery of the late 19th century. Adjacent to the left is the former Sunday-school of 1896 by R. Dalby Reeve.

Homan (1984) 74.

(96) WESLEYAN, Northdown Road (TR 361711). Stone with prominent corner tower, 1875–8 by Drewe and Bower.

(97) WESLEYAN, Birchington (TR 304690). Simple Gothic chapel of 1830 of yellow stock brick with battlemented parapet to gabled front; slender three-stage clock-tower above central entrance. Basement below chapel.

Wesleyan chapel, Birchington. (97)

MEOPHAM

(98) STRICT BAPTIST, Meopham Green (TQ 638650). Mount Zion chapel, built 1828, is of brick with a three-bay gabled front. The refitted interior has a single rear gallery added in 1836.

Chambers III (1956) 103–5. *Grace* (November 1978) 11.

MERSHAM

(99) Former WESLEYAN, Frithgate (TR 037370). Rendered gabled front dated 1846, with round arch enclosing central entrance and upper window. *Monument*: in small burial-ground, William son of Samuel and Mary Bayley, 1808.

MINSTER

(100) WESLEYAN (TR 311644). Brick with rendered dressings; gabled front of three bays with pointed-arched windows below labels. Altered inscription tablet dated '1850'.

RAMSGATE

(101) BAPTIST, Cavendish Street (TR 382650). The Particular Baptist church first met in a chapel in Hardres Street acquired in 1832, possibly from the Strict Baptists. The present chapel of 1840 by J. Wilson in a robust Romanesque style has walls of gault brick with rendered dressings. It has a broad NE front to the street of seven bays with entrances in the end bays; the gabled centre bay is surmounted by a finial of grotesque proportions and flanked by stout buttresses with turreted tops. Adjacent to the right is a Sunday-school of 1900.

The original layout had the pulpit against the centre of the longer rear wall and small galleries at each end; this was altered c.1900 when the pulpit was re-sited at the SE end and the chapel reseated. The two galleries, which remain intact, have arcaded fronts supported by cast-iron columns. The pulpit is similarly ornamented in a lavish Romanesque manner comprising a wide rostrum with central desk and lower communion platform with matching balustrade.

Glass: in all windows, borders of red glass, multicoloured glass in tops of windows and roundels with six-pointed stars.

BM XXV (1833) 380, 567; XXXII (1840) 584, 673–5. Chambers III (1956) 31–3.

(102) CONGREGATIONAL, Meeting Street (TR 380651). The congregation formerly meeting here which originated as a Presbyterian society in the late 17th century had a meeting-house in Queen Street. The first chapel on the present site, built in

Baptist chapel, Cavendish Street, Ramsgate. Pulpit.   (101)

Baptist chapel, Cavendish Street, Ramsgate.   (101)

1743, was replaced by 'Ebenezer Chapel' in 1838–9. The chapel of gault brick with rendered dressings was designed by 'two members of the church, G.M. Hinds and W. Woodland'. The front wall of seven bays with two tiers of pointed-arched windows has a wide pediment over five bays; the three middle bays, bounded by octagonal buttresses, have a pair of shield-shaped tablets inscribed 'Founded AD 1662', 'Erected AD 1838'.

The interior has tall galleried arcades of seven bays with cast-iron columns and four-centred arches. The ceiling has a pointed barrel-vault over the central space. (Now URC/Methodist, meeting in Hardres Street)

Fittings – *Fontlet*: Gothic pattern on octagonal pedestal, c.1840. *Monuments*: in chapel (1) Rev. George Townsend, 1837, one of the founders of the London Missionary Society; also externally several reset headstones of the late 18th century and after. *Pulpit*: c.1838. *Seating*: complete set of box-pews, the lower pews have mahogany capping.

Hurd, A.G., *These Three Hundred Years* (1962). Timpson (1859) 421–31.

ROCHESTER

(103) Former INDEPENDENT, Strood (TQ 738691). 'Zoar Chapel' has a gabled brick front of three bays with two tiers of sash windows all set within arched surrounds. In the low gable is a quatrefoil inscribed 'In Honour to GOD | 1796'. The interior has a rear gallery. *Monument*: below front window, externally, Rev. Thomas Drew, 1853, 40 years pastor. (Derelict 1972)

Timpson (1859) 321–2.

(104) CONGREGATIONAL, The Vines, Maidstone Road (TQ 744682). The chapel was erected in 1853–4 for a church (now URC) gathered by the Rev. Dr Jenkyn but who soon afterwards felt obliged to leave and commence another meeting in a chapel on Star Hill. The chapel at The Vines is a rectangular building six bays in length in the Gothic style by John Tarring. The walls are faced with ragstone and ashlar dressings. The gabled front of three bays is divided by buttresses and has gabled entrances in the end bays.

CYB (1856) 258; (1859) 204, obituary of T.W. Jenkyn. Timpson (1859) 317–20.

(105) FRIENDS, Northgate (TQ 743686). The burial-ground described as 'a piece of ground … in Pompe lane' was conveyed to Friends in 1675 and a meeting-house built in the following year. The meeting-house was superseded by the present building on another part of the ground in 1780–1. This has brick walls and a hipped tiled roof; the NW front in Flemish bond brickwork with glazed headers has three sash windows and a later porch below the middle window. An extension to the left of two storeys was built c.1812.

Butler (1999) 287–8.

(106) Former WESLEYAN, St Margaret's Bank (TQ 750679). 'Bethel Chapel', now in commercial use, was built in 1810 to designs by William Jenkins. It has brick walls. The front of five bays has a three-bay pediment and two tiers of round-arched windows; the central doorway and lower windows have been covered by a lean-to extension since 1963.

ROYAL TUNBRIDGE WELLS

(107) Former PRESBYTERIAN, Little Mount Sion (TQ 58353885). The chapel registered in 1721 was built for a society originating in the late 17th century which had previously met in a ballroom at Mount Ephraim House. With the advent of other denominations the society declined and the chapel closed in 1814. Prior to that date Wesleyans had met in the building, and a Congregational church occupied the chapel from 1830 to 1848. It is now in commercial use and has been much refurbished in recent years.

The chapel, which is approximately square on plan, has brick walls now rendered externally; the roof, probably formerly hipped and tiled, has been rebuilt to a lower pitch. The N, S and W walls have each four tall round-arched windows; the E wall is blank. The original entrances were below the end windows on the W side; one original doorway with a pair of fielded-panelled doors remains at the N end covered by a later porch.

Chambers III (1956) 68. Strange (1949) 15–17. Timpson (1859) 462–71. *WHSP* X (1915–16) Pl. facing 197.

Former Presbyterian chapel, Little Mount Sion.   (107)

(108) HANOVER CHAPEL, Hanover Road (TQ 58353980). The Strict Baptist church was formed in 1834 following cottage meetings. The chapel built in that year was designed by Henry Kewell, pastor and architect. The gabled front with wide eaves is

of red brick of three bays with two tiers of round-arched windows and a central porch. The name and date of the chapel appear on a circular tablet in the gable.

Chambers III (1956) 65–7.

(109) REHOBOTH CHAPEL, Chapel Place (TQ 583389). The chapel was built in 1851 for a Strict Baptist congregation formed in 1848. The congregation had dispersed by 1873 and the chapel passed to another similar group. The walls are rendered and the roof is slated. The gabled front has terminal pilasters, a slightly projecting centre bay with a pair of arched doorways, and two tiers of round-arched windows. (Closed 1994 and converted for commercial use)

Chambers III (1956) 69–71.

Former Congregational chapel, Mount Pleasant Road, Royal Tunbridge Wells. (110)

Rehoboth Chapel, Chapel Place, Royal Tunbridge Wells. (109)

(110) Former CONGREGATIONAL, Mount Pleasant Road (TQ 584396). The congregation formed in 1830 first met in Mount Sion Chapel (107), building the present chapel in 1846–8. This is a large Classical building of stone with a hexastyle Tuscan portico, added in 1866, and three round-arched entrances at the front. The side walls are of six bays divided by pilasters, each bay with one tall round-arched window. At the rear is a Sunday-school of 1866. (Converted to a multiple store since 1972, rear wall removed to incorporate the former school and two floors inserted)

Strange (1949) 26–7. Timpson (1859) 463–71.

(111) COUNTESS OF HUNTINGDON'S, Mount Ephraim (TQ 58253995). The Countess acquired a house at Mount Ephraim and built her first chapel in 1769. This timber-framed building, enlarged in the early 19th century, had a gabled front with battlemented parapet and Gothic windows. The chapel was replaced in 1867 by 'Emmanuel', stone Gothic with corner tower and spire by Wimble and Taylor of London. *Monuments*: in burial-ground (1) George Lidbetter, 1843, and Delia his widow, 1859, sarcophagus with claw feet; (2) short stone pillar with ball finial, inscribed 'Near this spot stood and preached that eminent servant of God, George Whitefield, at the opening of the original chapel built by Selina, Countess of Huntingdon. July 23, 1769'. (Chapel demolished 1974)

Seymour (1839) II: 124–47 *passim*. Strange (1949) 23–5. Timpson (1859) 472–7.

(112) WESLEYAN, Vale Road (TQ 583390). Meetings which commenced in the Presbyterian chapel, where John Wesley preached on several occasions, were continued in a new chapel on this site built in 1812. The present chapel by Charles Bell, opened 1873, has a gabled front faced with polygonal masonry, corner buttresses rising to tall finials, and a triple-arched porch raised high above street level.

Strange (1949) 19–20. Timpson (1859) 465.

(113) Former 'FREE CHURCH', Mount Ephraim (TQ 583399). 'St John's Free Church' was built 1899–1901 for seceders from the nearby Countess of Huntingdon's chapel under their minister the Rev. James Mountain. The building eventually passed to the Presbyterian Church of England (now 'URC St Andrews with Mount Pleasant'). The building, by H.M. Caley, which includes chapel, Sunday-school and manse, is an amorphous structure of brick with Gothic details.

B.Hbk (1899) 385; (1902) 372–5. Strange (1949) 13, 18.

RUCKINGE

(114) WESLEYAN (TR 026336). Rendered walls and low gabled front dated 1839.

ST NICHOLAS AT WADE

(115) WESLEYAN, Down Barton Road (TR 263666). A preaching-house was registered for Methodists in 1777. The present chapel,

built in 1822, has brick walls and a gabled front of three bays with small blind upper windows as if for a potential gallery. (Derelict 1974)

SANDHURST

(116) BAPTIST (TQ 809280). A meeting-house built in 1731 was enlarged in 1844 but replaced by the present chapel in 1853. This is of red brick with white brick dressings; the front has a pedimental gable and is divided into three bays by wall arcading embracing two tiers of windows. The N side wall is similarly subdivided into four bays. The interior has a W gallery adjacent to the entrance and an E gallery with shuttered front behind the pulpit; the fittings are of pitch-pine.

Chambers III (1956) 61–2.

SANDWICH

(117) THE OLD MEETING-HOUSE, Cornmarket (TR 329582). Several nonconformist meetings existed in Sandwich in the later 17th century of which the Independents seem to have been the most active. Among their preachers was the ejected minister, Comfort Starr, who in 1672 attempted unsuccessfully to license a chapel belonging to St Bartholomew's Hospital as a meeting-house. By the early 18th century Independents and Presbyterians appear to have had their respective pastors but it seems likely that they combined in the erection and use of this meeting-house which was built in 1706. During the 18th century the society, which was regarded as Presbyterian, rapidly declined until c.1796 the minister, [? James Milnes] 'an Arian', was persuaded to sell his interest to two orthodox Independents who placed the building in a new trust and appointed a Congregational minister. The meeting-house was refitted in 1845 and a Sunday-school room built, in 1873–8 cottages in front were removed and further internal changes made, in 1885 the building was reported to be in a very dilapidated state and the need for further repairs in 1897 led to consideration of the possible advantage of its substitution by a 'new iron chapel' and further repairs. (URC)

The meeting-house of 1706 has walls of rubble with later rendering and the roof, which is hipped about a central valley, is covered with tiles. The E front has a central entrance between two tall windows reduced by partial blocking to narrow slits. The side walls each of two bays have two tiers of windows. Two altered windows in the rear wall flank the pulpit.

The interior (37¼ft by 42ft), much refitted, has two cylindrical posts with moulded capitals supporting the N–S valley. There is a gallery around three sides, the cross gallery possibly added. A vestry formerly below the gallery in the NE corner was removed 1875 but traces of a corner fireplace remain.

Inscription: brass plate fixed to one of the two principal posts claiming them as being gifts from French refugees, 1685, unproven.
Plate: includes a two-handled cup of 1757 and a pair of plates of 1708.

Timpson (1859) 399–403. Wilson III (1810) 229.

(118) Former WESLEYAN, 60 King Street (TR 332580). A small preaching-room in Lucksboat Street (now upper part of King

The Old Meeting-house, Cornmarket, Sandwich. (117)

Street) was in use from 1776; in 1788, because of its inadequacy, John Wesley was offered the use of one of the dissenting chapels. A chapel on or about this spot of possibly early 19th-century date is incorporated in the present building. It previously had a gabled front of three bays with a central arched entrance and two tiers of windows. Methodist use ceased in 1870 and the building has been re-fronted with two bay windows above a shop front.

Curnock, (ed.) (1938) VII: 449.

(119) Former PRIMITIVE METHODIST, Moat Sole (TR 328580). Yellow brick with shaped gable above three-bay front. Two tall round-arched window recesses are filled with smaller round-arched cast-iron window frames below flat-arched heads. Foundation stone laid 9 September 1862.

SEVENOAKS

(120) CONGREGATIONAL, St John's Hill (TQ 531560). The Chapel built 1865–6 was designed by John Tarring. The walls are faced with Kentish ragstone with Bath stone dressings; the front is gabled and has a central tower of three stages above the entrance with parapet and corner pinnacles; spire removed 1880. The side walls have separately gabled windows. (URC)

CYB (1866) 307; (1899) 161–2, obituary of A.B. Attenborough. Homan (1984) 86.

SEVENOAKS WEALD

(121) WESLEYAN (TQ 527509). Small brick chapel opened 1843, extended to front.

SHEERNESS

(122) BETHEL CHAPEL, Chapel Street, Bluetown (TQ 912750). The Congregational church formerly meeting here may have originated about 1725. The work was greatly strengthened in the mid 18th century by the preaching of George Whitefield and others and a meeting-house was built for the society in 1763 above houses in High Street. Among those who interested themselves in the cause was William Shrubsole, a master mastmaker, who took upon himself the duties of pastor and for whom the present building was commenced in 1784.

The chapel, now in industrial use, is said to have been originally 42ft by 36ft but extended in length by 15ft to its present size in 1787. Among the many alterations recorded during the 19th century is a major internal refitting and the provision of a new roof in 1838, further reseating in 1873, and the replacement of window frames in 1893. The chapel was sold c.1921 when the church removed to a school-room in Hope Street (see (123)).

The chapel, standing on the N side of the street, has brick walls and a half-hipped mansard roof latterly covered in roofing felt. The side walls, extended to the front and possibly to the rear, have two tiers of narrow windows. The S front has a truncated gable, a pair of round-arched doorways with keystones and imposts, with a segmental-arched window between and a tripartite window above with arched and keystoned centre. The front wall is partly obscured by the former manse built 1812, a house of three storeys overlooking the small forecourt. At the rear is a Sunday-school wing of stock brick built c.1848.

Inscriptions: on cill and apron of upper window 'HE SHALL

Bethel Chapel, Bluetown, Sheerness. (122)

ESTABLISH IN HIS STRENGTH | 1787 | BETHEL CHAPEL'; on keystone of upper window 'W+S | 1787' for William Shrubsole.

Gordon, J., *History of the Congregational Churches of Sheerness, Queenborough, Minster, and the Isle of Grain, from the Year 1725 to 1898* (1898) 17–70. Sears, A.T., *James Prankard, Minister of the Bethel Independent Chapel, Sheerness, from 19th February 1811 to 11th January 1838 with Extracts from his Church Book* (1962). Timpson (1859) 482–8.

(123) CONGREGATIONAL, Hope Street, Mile Town (TQ 920748). The Sunday-school to which the church from the foregoing moved c.1921 comprises two adjacent buildings of brick with gabled fronts. The earliest has a central entrance between a pair of round-arched windows and a tablet in the pedimental gable inscribed 'BETHEL CHAPEL | SUNDAY SCHOOL | 1832'. The other, dated 1882, now serves as the chapel. (URC)

SHORNE

(124) PRIMITIVE METHODIST, Shorne Ridgeway (TQ 692703). 'Zion Chapel' dated 1838 has a low gabled front of brick with arched doorway between sash windows.

SITTINGBOURNE AND MILTON

(125) CONGREGATIONAL, Milton Regis (TQ 902645). A congregation gathered by a Countess of Huntingdon's Connexion minister in 1789 built the first 'Paradise Chapel' in 1790; this was variously enlarged and then replaced by the present building in 1860. The walls are of yellow brick with stone dressings in the Gothic style by Poulton and Woodman. Above the entrance is a short tower and slated spire. Alongside the chapel is a separately roofed two-storeyed Sunday-school, heightened 1865, extended 1880. (URC)

KENT

Congregational chapel (URC), Milton Regis. (125)

CYB (1861) 273–6. Jones, J.B., *The History of Paradise Chapel, Milton, Kent* (1910). Timpson (1859) 493–6.

(126) CONGREGATIONAL, Sittingbourne (TQ 906637). Gothic chapel of 1865, probably by Poulton and Woodman, stone with tower and spire above entrance; gabled front with sharply pointed lancets. Wooden clerestory. (URC)

SMARDEN

(127) Former GENERAL BAPTIST (TQ 874429). The General Baptist church at Smarden was part of a scattered church meeting at a variety of locations in and around Biddenden. One of these appears to be the timber-framed house of 16th-century origin known as 'The Meeting-house'. This is of two storeys with a hipped tiled roof and central chimney; the front is tile-hung to the upper floor but underbuilt in brickwork. *Monuments*: in adjacent burial-ground include (1) George Kenhelmn, 1751, 30 years 'Elder of the Church of General Baptist Meeting in Smarden and Stapleherst', Elizabeth his widow, 1767, and daughters Mary and Dinah; (2) Matthew Vane, 1763, minister and elder, Sarah his widow, 1803, and Sarah his daughter 1833.

Buffard (1963) 29–30, 67. Taylor (1818) I: 283, 349–50. Wood (1847) 210.

(128) GENERAL BAPTIST, High Street (TQ 882424). 'Zion Chapel', built in 1841 for the foregoing, has rendered walls and a slate roof. The front of three bays has a pediment supported by four pilasters, a central pedimented doorway and two tall windows. There is a gallery at the entrance.

(129) TILDEN CHAPEL (TQ 873411). A Particular Baptist chapel built on this site in 1726 had a broad front of three bays and a hipped roof. The present chapel, which replaced it in 1892, is a plain brick building with gabled front. *Inscription*: triangular tablet reset on front of porch 'This | Is : the : Gift : of | Iames Tilden of high | Halden in Kent Yeaman | and Was Built In the year 1726'. *Monuments*: in burial-ground, many monuments of mid 18th-century date and later including (1) Jenkin Hague of Folkstone, Gent., 1777, and Susan his wife, 1774, table-tomb.

Chambers III (1956) 3–9.

SMEETH

(130) STRICT BAPTIST, Brabourne Lees (TR 085406). 'Zion Chapel' built 1838 has walls of stone with brick dressings; the front is gabled.

BM XXX (1838) 261, 305. Chambers III (1956) 54–5.

SNODLAND

(131) NEW JERUSALEM CHURCH, High Street (TQ 704617). The church was built in 1881 largely by the Hook family for a society formed c.1865. The building is faced with Kentish ragstone and comprises a nave, two-bay chancel, and four-stage tower above the principal entrance. (Disused by 1995)

New Jerusalem Church, Snodland. (131)

STAPLEHURST

(132) STRICT BAPTIST, Chapel Lane (TQ 787432). 'Providence Chapel' built in the early 19th century has weather-boarded timber-framed walls and a tiled roof. A lower wing, perhaps a former cottage, adjoins to the S, and another cottage is attached on the N side.

Chambers III (1956) 13–14.

(133) CONGREGATIONAL (TQ 786431). A chapel built in 1825 to replace a timber-framed meeting-house was superseded by the present chapel in 1889. The front, of brick and stone, is a crude conglomeration of Gothic details. (URC)

CHST V (1911–12) 278–81. Timpson (1859) 439–43.

STONE-CUM-EBONY

(134) EBENEZER CHAPEL, Stone (TQ 940282). The Strict Baptist chapel built c.1802 is attached to one end of an earlier house. The chapel is timber-framed with weather-boarded walls and a tiled roof. There is a small porch at the NE end. The interior is entirely lined in match-boarding.

Chambers III (1956) 63–4.

SUTTON-AT-HONE

(135) STRICT BAPTIST (TQ 557696). 'Bethesda Chapel', of brick, built c.1842, has a gabled front of three bays with two tiers of windows.

Chambers III (1956) 114. Whitley (1928) No. 179.

SUTTON VALENCE

(136) CONGREGATIONAL, Broad Street (TQ 815492). A chapel of 1794, enlarged 1821, was replaced in 1873 by the present Gothic building by Sulman and Rhodes. The walls are faced with ragstone; there is a short tower and spire above entrance. (Closed 1975; since used by school)

CYB (1873) 426. Timpson (1859) 498–503.

SWANSCOMBE

(137) Former CONGREGATIONAL, High Street, Greenhithe (TQ 587751). A small chapel first built in 1801 but enlarged or rebuilt c.1819 and later enlarged to the front is now in commercial use. The chapel is set between a pair of contemporary cottages, Nos 17 and 21 High Street, with its front formerly recessed behind a small forecourt. The front walls of the cottages are faced with finely jointed knapped flint and the façades and openings surrounded by rusticated bands of natural flints. The front of the chapel as extended forward probably repeats the design of the original gabled front with two pointed-arched upper windows, but the flint facing is coarser and brick dressings have been substituted for the rusticated flintwork; a lean-to porch with a pair of doorways covers the lower stage. The side and rear walls, including the formerly exposed walls of the cottages facing the forecourt, are of stock brick.

The interior of the chapel, originally two bays in length, has a pair of round-arched wall recesses at each side and a similar recess to the rear where the pulpit was set below a large lunette. The extension to the front incorporated a gallery and had a small vestry below with a corner fireplace; the ceiling was extended and pierced by two plaster domes for ventilation.

Homan (1984) 61. Timpson (1859) 541–2.

(138) CONGREGATIONAL, Ingress Vale (TQ 596748). The chapel in Knockhall Road, built in 1860, was enlarged 1862. (URC)

Ebenezer Chapel, Stone. (134)

KENT

SWINGFIELD

(139) BIBLE CHRISTIAN, Swingfield Minnis (TR 214430). Flint with galleted joints and brick dressings; gabled front dated 1845, later porch. Windows in side walls only.

TENTERDEN

(140) OLD MEETING-HOUSE, Ashford Road (TQ 886337). The society, apparently in existence by the late 17th century, of mixed but predominantly Presbyterian sympathies, had accepted Unitarian preaching by the early 19th century. Although early records are lacking the present site seems to have been occupied since the early 18th century.

The meeting-house built c.1700, of timber-framed construction with tile hanging above a brick plinth, was extended to the front in 1746 in mathematical tiles but later re-fronted in brickwork; the roof is tiled with half hips to each side concealing parallel valleys. The E front of three widely spaced bays approximately replicating the 1746 elevation has a central entrance with double doors in a pedimented surround; the three upper and two lower windows have segmental-arched heads and renewed frames. The side walls have each two lower windows with hung sashes and upper windows with 18th-century casements. The W wall, covered by later building, has two windows, now internal, flanking the pulpit.

The interior (originally 29ft by 39¼ft) was increased in depth to 38¼ft in 1746 in which year the meeting-house was (re)registered (perhaps repairing a previous omission), the size being then given as '40ft by 39ft'. There are galleries around three sides with fielded-panelled fronts. The roof, ceiled at collar level, is supported by two trusses on the line of the side galleries, the tie-beams being extended E into the new work and additional upper posts with wavy braces added to support the superstructure.

Fittings – *Clock*: on front of E gallery, 'Parliament clock' with shaped dial, signed 'George Thatcher, Cranbrook', mid 18th-century. *Communion Plate*: includes two two-handled cups with S-shaped sides and embossed decoration, 1661, 1668 (sold 1974). *Font*: Gothic, octagonal with columnar base, c.1855, brought from Unitarian chapel, Kentish Town, London, 1937. *Inscriptions*: in SW corner on wood nailed to S wall, initials 'IP SP HR TH WH AC'; on brick in outbuilding, reset, '1781 HT'. *Library*: in SE vestry, many leather-bound volumes of the late 18th century and later, numbered and stamped 'Tenterden P.U.C. Library'. *Monuments*: in small rear burial-ground, headstones and brick vaults of the early 19th century. *Pulpit*: centrally against W wall, hexagonal with fielded-panelled sides on shaped base, with tall narrow back-board and high canopy with dentil cornice, inlaid soffit, ogee top and ball finial; stair to S with turned balusters. *Seating*: entirely renewed in late 19th century.

Chambers III (1956) 58–61. Evans (1897) 241–2. *UHST* XX (1991–4) 81–97.

TEYNHAM

(141) Former WESLEYAN (TQ 950626). The former chapel, now shop, on the N side of the main road was built in 1841; brick with rendered front, altered pedimental gable and three upper windows. A new chapel was built in 1928 alongside the Sunday-school of 1868 in Green Street (TQ 951624).

TONBRIDGE

(142) WESLEYAN, East Street (TQ 592466). Brick with dressings of yellow brick and stone. Long frontage to street combining Gothic chapel of 1872 by Cattermole and Eade and Sunday-school of 1897.

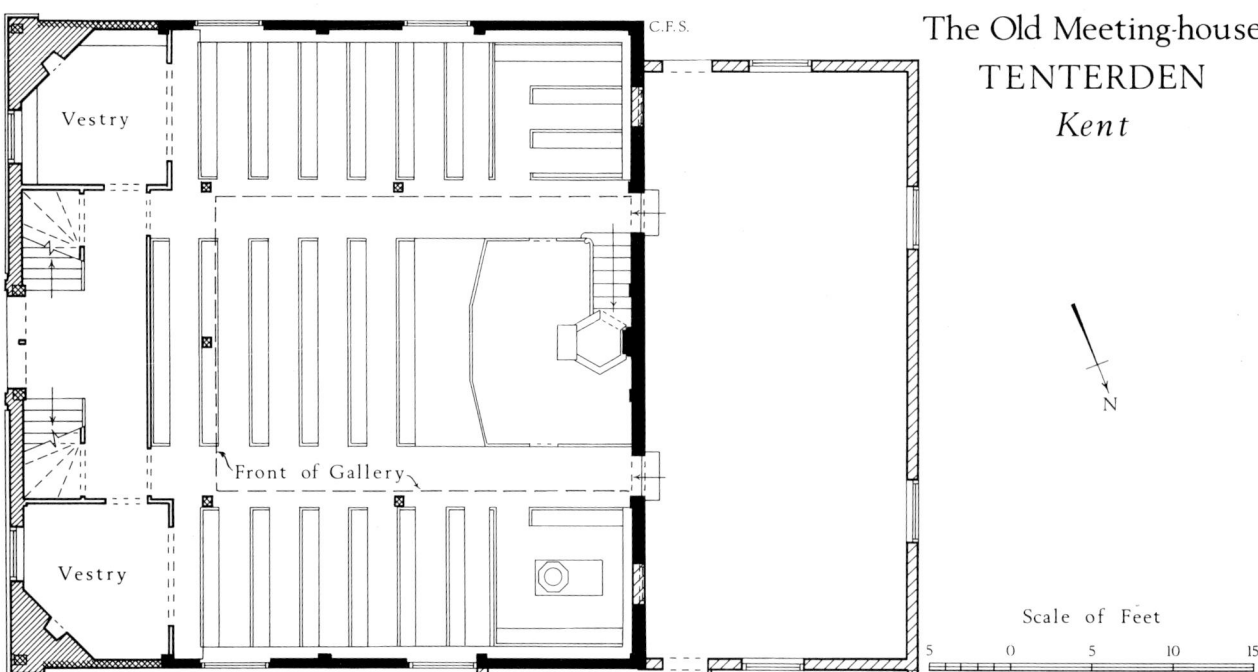

The Old Meeting-house TENTERDEN Kent

The Old Meeting-house, Tenterden.

WESTERHAM

(143) CONGREGATIONAL, Fullers Hill (TQ 445541). The congregation previously met from 1836 in a small wooden chapel built by Wesleyans in 1824; the present chapel dated 1839 has a rendered front of three bays with pilasters and a full pediment. There are no galleries; the sides have each three round-arched windows set high in the wall. Refitted in the late 19th century.

Pickford, C., *1839 1939 Westerham Congregational Church Centenary 'One Hundred Years' Souvenir Booklet* (1939). Timpson (1859) 527–9.

WEST MALLING

(144) BAPTIST, Swan Street (TQ 683578). Two tiers of pointed-arched windows with renewed frames in three-bay rendered and gabled front of 1836.

Chambers III (1956) 84–5.

WHITSTABLE

(145) BAPTIST, Middle Wall (TR 105666). Plain chapel of 1875, extended to front in 1911 in heavy neo-Classical style.

(146) Former CONGREGATIONAL, High Street (TR 107664). A small wooden chapel of *c*.1795 was replaced by a brick chapel in 1833; this was destroyed by fire in 1854 and the present building erected on the site. 'Zion Chapel', opened 1855, has a rendered front, three-bay centre with Corinthian pilasters supporting an entablature arched over the centre bay, and lower wings of two bays with Ionic pilasters. (Converted to theatre, 1982)

The church (now URC) now meets in the detached Sunday-school of 1891 in Middle Wall.

CYB (1856) 269. Timpson (1859) 522–4.

(147) WESLEYAN, Argyle Road (TR 107663). Brick front of three bays with two tiers of round-arched windows and short pediment. 1868, by T.G. Cozens.

(148) Former PRIMITIVE METHODIST, Albert Street (TR 108668). Rendered gabled front with two tall sash windows and stepped entrance. Dated 1864.

(149) SALVATION ARMY, High Street (TR 106665). Heavily detailed gabled front of 1887.

WINGHAM

(150) Former CONGREGATIONAL (TR 243578). The church 'gathered by Samuel Elgar Toomer' originated in 1807 and met from 1812 in a former General Baptist chapel. The present building, converted to a house *c*.1994, was designed by James Fenton of Chelmsford and built in 1835; a Sunday-school was added in 1855. The pedimented front is of yellow stock brick, the

Former Congregational chapel, Whitstable. (146)

Former Congregational chapel, Wingham. (150)

sides are of red brick and the roof is slated. The front of two stages has broad terminal pilasters and a central feature with triple windows which rises into the pediment and carries the date of erection. The entrances in the outer bays have paired doors and windows above. The interior (prior to conversion) was without galleries although capable of receiving them; the rostrum pulpit and pews were of the late 19th century.

Fittings – *Glass*: in central windows of front wall, coloured borders, alternately red and blue, or purple and gold. *Monuments*: in chapel (1) Samuel Toomer Esq. of Wingham, 1844, 'who at his own expense provided this chapel, grounds and manse and put the same in trust for the use of the Independent denomination'; (2) Rev. Samuel Elgar Toomer of Preston Court, 1870, founder, 53 years pastor, builder of chapels at Preston and Stourmouth; in burial-ground in front of chapel (3) Samuel Toomer, 1844, Sarah his wife, 1839, Joseph his brother, 1853; also his son, Rev. Samuel Elgar Toomer, 1870, Ann Elgar his first wife, 1828, Sophia daughter of Joseph Toomer, his second wife, 1863, *et al.*, square stone plinth inscribed on four faces, surmounted by urn.

CYB (1871) 357–8, obituary of Rev. S.E. Toomer. [Rook, H.J.], *A Brief Memoir of Samuel Toomer Esq., late of Wingham, Kent* (1844). Timpson (1859) 514–19.

WYE

(151) WESLEYAN, Bridge Street (TR 053467). The chapel built in 1869 has walls of red brick with yellow and black dressings; the gabled front of three bays has a central doorway with small circular window above and two pointed-arched windows with cast-iron latticed frames. Interior refitted. Small hall in similar style adjacent.

LINCOLNSHIRE

Although in area the second largest English county, Lincolnshire was for long relatively thinly populated with few large towns and an indifferent rural economy which did little to encourage the growth of religious observance. In Epworth in the early 18th century not more than one per cent of the population attended the church communion, a condition evident in a report on his parish by the rector, Samuel Wesley (VCH *Lincolnshire* II (1906) 72). The rector noted the absence of Papists and Presbyterians from his parish while acknowledging the presence of some 'Anabaptists and Quakers', and it is these denominations, whose strength lay mainly in rural areas, that appear to have been the most active of the early dissenters. In Lincolnshire the General Baptists were particularly successful, gathering themselves into churches which embraced areas of considerable extent of which that in the Isle of Axholme, which included a congregation at Epworth, was but one; another was in the 'South Marsh', centred around Alford, one of whose congregations had the use during the Commonwealth of Northolme Chapel, the parish church of Wainfleet St Thomas. Many General Baptist meeting-houses remain in the county of which the earliest and architecturally the most interesting is at Monksthorpe (121), built on a remote site in 1701. The former chapel at Maltby le Marsh (180) of 1776 is of an entirely domestic appearance, and the former chapel at Gosberton (106), which may be contemporary with it, represents the minimal requirements of a small society. At South Killingholme (229), the only other 18th-century building recorded here of this denomination, the rebuilt chapel of 1792, not only displays its purpose a trifle more readily but serves as a reminder of the paucity of Particular Baptist influence in the county at an early date, only Horncastle (148) of 1767 being similarly attributable; at South Killingholme the joint use of the building by both wings of this church is remarkable.

Friends' meeting-houses, although less numerous in their survival, include several of importance. The earliest Quaker building in the county, in Lincoln (170), is dated 1689 although now much changed in appearance including an unusual arcaded aisle added in the 18th century. The best-preserved meeting-house, at Brant Broughton (49), dated 1701, is on the eastern edge of the county as is that of the early 18th century in Gainsborough (98).

A few Presbyterian congregations arose in the late 17th century of which that in Stamford (239), after a period of some uncertainty, became Congregational, while Lincoln (168) and Gainsborough (96) followed the more usual paths towards a Unitarian ministry: only the Lincoln chapel now remains from the 18th century, greatly altered in the course of its chequered history. Of greater interest is the case of Kirkstead Abbey Chapel (159), served for a century by Presbyterian preachers and the subject of an important and lengthy legal action for the recovery of a private endowment.

The predominance of Methodist chapels in Lincolnshire in the 19th century, whose proliferation, second only to Cornwall, may similarly be attributed, though in lesser degree, to the failure of the older denominations to attract a scattered rural population, serves also as a proper monument to John Wesley, the prime mover of the Connexion, who was born at the rectory in Epworth in 1703. The earliest remaining Methodist preaching-house here, built at Raithby (211) in 1779 by Robert Carr Brackenbury, is notable not only for its unprepossessing external appearance but also for the quality of its internal appointments. More representative of the society in its early years is the former chapel in Gainsborough (99), hidden behind other buildings and outlasting its much grander successor, while North Scarle (200), dating from the years immediately following Wesley's death, points forward to the many village chapels of utilitarian simplicity which met the needs of a subsequent generation.

Small three-bay chapels, with a central doorway between windows in the longer front wall and a hipped roof, abound throughout the county; nearly all belonged to Wesleyan societies and have dates mainly between 1820 and 1870, although the former Congregational chapel at Barrow upon Humber (19) of 1780 is a forerunner of the type on a larger scale. Larger and more elegant Methodist chapels of the period include especially Louth (177) of 1835, while the contemporary Congregational chapels at Caistor (57) of 1842 and Pinchbeck (207) of 1840 also deserve notice. The two Strict Baptist chapels at Deeping St James (74) and Stamford (238) both have historical associations with notable pastors, while at Long Sutton (175) is a rare instance of the introduction of heterodox elements into the General Baptist New Connexion; the new doctrines of Universalism on which the earlier church at Long Sutton foundered were taken up more successfully by a society in Boston, where the small former chapel (43) survives, though superseded in 1819–20 by the best of the early 19th-century Lincolnshire chapels, in Spain Lane (44) for the, by then, Unitarian society.

Chapels of the later 19th century and after are not greatly remarkable although several are recorded here. The most notable of the smaller chapels is at Haconby (124) built for dual denominational use and with an unexpected galleried interior. Architecturally impressive are the Wesleyan chapel at Market Rasen (184) of 1863 with its giant portico, and the Congregational chapel in Newland, Lincoln (169) of 1876 by Bellamy and Hardy in the Gothic style with a particularly successful galleried interior, while the Primitive Methodist chapel in High Street, Lincoln (172) of 1905 has little difficulty in outshining its smaller and older Unitarian neighbour across the street.

Most of the buildings recorded have brick walls, only relatively few examples of stone construction being found. Pantiles are commonly used on roofs throughout the county as well as plain tiles with slate on later work; no thatched roofs remain, although Monksthorpe (121) is reported to have been thatched until 1847.

ABY WITH GREENFIELD

(1) WESLEYAN, Aby (TF 410786). Red brick with yellow brick dressings; gabled front with graduated lancets and intermediate buttresses rising to octagonal pinnacles. Erected 1895.

ALFORD

(2) CONGREGATIONAL, Chauntry Road (TF 452758). The first meeting-house, built 1795, was extended to the S in 1845 and a new chapel attached at the opposite end in 1876, leaving the former to serve as school-rooms. The original building (30ft by 24¾ft) has brick walls with two round-arched windows facing the road and a third window in the extension with a pair of blocked round-arched doorways between and an end entrance covered by a later porch. The chapel of 1876 by J. Tait of Leicester is a small building of brick and tile with Gothic windows and a flèche.

Barker (1860) 28–9. *CYB* (1877) 499.

(3) Former WESLEYAN, Chapel Street (TF 455762). The chapel, now a Masonic hall, of brick with a rendered front and hipped slate roof, was built in 1819. Three-bay front with arched centre bay enclosing lower window and altered date tablet. Two doorways, one removed, and two round-arched windows above. 'Wesleyan Centenary Sunday School 1839' to north.

(4) WESLEYAN, West Street (TF 453760). The chapel opened 1865 is a large Gothic building of gault brick by W. Botterill of Hull. The gabled front has three doorways with gabled surrounds, traceried upper windows and a prominent finial at the apex. The sides of five bays have two-stage buttresses. *Inscription*: loose tablet from former chapel, inscribed 'BETHELL CHAPEL 1841'.

ALKBOROUGH   *Humberside*

(5) WESLEYAN (SE 882217). Brick and slate, gault brick front of two bays divided by three tall pilasters with Ionic capitals; pedimented gable with a tablet dated 1840.

Wesleyan chapel, Alkborough. (5)

(6) Former PRIMITIVE METHODIST (SE 882216). Red brick with yellow brick dressings, gabled front with three round-arched windows above entrances; defaced tablet. Built 1864.

ALVINGHAM

(7) WESLEYAN, Highbridge Road (TF 363913). Low building of brick, erected 1836; originally two bays long, enlarged to front in late 19th century.

(8) Former PRIMITIVE METHODIST, Church Lane (TF 363912). Brick with hipped slate roof, broad three-bay front with round-arched openings and tablet dated 1848.

Wesleyan chapel, West Street, Alford. (4)

LINCOLNSHIRE

ASLACKBY AND LAUGHTON

(9) Former BAPTIST, Aslackby (TF 084303). Red brick with yellow brick dressings and round-arched windows; built in the late 19th century, transferred to Methodists in place of the (now demolished) Wesleyan chapel of 1863. (Converted to house by 1993)

Leary and Vickers (1984) 23.

ASWARDBY

(10) WESLEYAN (TL 379703). Brick with hipped slate roof, round-arched doorway in E end with two small gallery windows above; pairs of segmental-arched windows in other walls with marginal glazing. Opened 1842.

AUTHORPE

(11) WESLEYAN (TF 401811). Broad three-bay brick front and hipped roof; round-arched windows with intersecting glazing bars. Dated 1862.

BARDNEY

(12) Former WESLEYAN, Bardney (TF 118693). Brick with two tiers of pointed-arched windows; built 1837, front altered c.1900. In 1994 the church occupied a small brick chapel of 1903 in Church Lane. (?Former chapel demolished)

(13) WESLEYAN, Bardney Dairies (TF 135740). Broad front of gault brick with hipped slate roof, dated 1857; three bays with two more added.

Wesleyan chapel, Bardney Dairies. (13)

(14) Former WESLEYAN, Southrey (TF 137668). Brick with hipped pantiled roof, originally a broad three-bay front, one bay rebuilt larger; savagely defaced inscription tablet above original entrance. Opened 1838.

(15) Former PRIMITIVE METHODIST, Wragby Road (TF 123700). Broad front of gault brick, three bays with defaced tablet above entrance. Built 1838. (Now used by Salvation Army)

BARKSTON

(16) WESLEYAN, West Street (SK 928416). Brick and pantile, broad three-bay front with segmental-arched openings; the pews, formerly stepped up to the left of the central entrance, have been replaced. Opened 1832.

BARLINGS

(17) WESLEYAN, Scothern Road, Langworth (TF 062765). Brick with hipped pantiled roof, broad three-bay front of gault brick with entrance in slightly projecting centre bay covered by later side-entry porch; red brick sides. Opened 1854.

BARNETBY LE WOLD   Humberside

(18) WESLEYAN, West Street (TA 058093). Brick with paired lancets and gabled entrance, built 1879.

BARROW UPON HUMBER   Humberside

(19) Former CONGREGATIONAL, Lords Lane (TA 071210). The chapel (in use 1971 as a Salvation Army hall) has brick walls and a hipped pantiled roof. The 'New erected Independent chapel at Barrow' was registered in July 1780. The broad E front is of three bays with two pointed-arched windows with intersecting glazing bars and a round-arched doorway with later timber surround. There are two similar windows in the W wall and a circular window high in the S wall above the site of the pulpit. A Sunday-school (derelict 1971) was added at the S end in the late 19th century.

The interior (34ft by 30¼ft) has a flat plaster ceiling. Box-pews incorporating late 18th-century panelling are stepped up to the right of the entrance.

Monuments: two headstones relaid as floorslabs (1) Rev. Abraham Greenwood, 1827, died at Immingham, and Susanna his widow who died at Barrow [1828] (*see also* monument at South Killingholme (229)); (2) Mary wife of Rev. Abraham Greenwood (son of the foregoing), 1850.

Barker (1860) 30. *BQ* II (1924–5) 84–9.

Former Congregational chapel, Lords Lane,
Barrow upon Humber. (19)

(20) WESLEYAN, High Street (TA 07162123). Four arched bays of red brick with yellow brick dressings, two tiers of round-arched windows, doorways in end bays. Built 1868 on the site of the former chapel built in 1780. Small brick and pantile Sunday-school adjacent with broad three-bay front of 1838.

Former Congregational chapel, Chapel Street, Barton-upon-Humber. (21)

BARTON-UPON-HUMBER *Humberside*

(21) Former CONGREGATIONAL, Chapel Street (TA 03002205). A barn was registered by Independents in June 1766; the present chapel of 1806 is a tall building of dark brick with a slate roof, three-bay front with pedimental gable and two tiers of round-arched windows. The interior has a round-ended gallery; most of the original fittings remain intact.
  Barker (1860) 29–30.

(22) WESLEYAN, Chapel Street (TA 03052199). The first preaching-house, built in Cottage Lane in 1788, was superseded in 1816 by the first chapel on the present site. The second chapel, built in 1860–1, is a large building of grey brick. The front is of five bays with giant pilasters and a large pediment, three doorways and two tiers of round-arched windows.
  WHSP VIII (1911–12) 129ff.

BASSINGHAM

(23) WESLEYAN (SK 911600). The chapel dated 1839 is a square building with walls of red brick and a pyramidal slate roof; the principal windows are at the upper level.

BAUMBER

(24) WESLEYAN (TF 223742). Red brick with hipped roof and broad three-bay front dated 1844; door and window arches have parallel voussoirs in V formation. Pulpit to right of entrance, raised seating to left.

BELCHFORD

(25) WESLEYAN, Chapel Lane (TF 294755). Red brick, yellow brick dressings; gabled front with porch, dated 1871.

(26) Former PRIMITIVE METHODIST, Chapel Lane (TF 293756). Small brick chapel built 1834 at junction with Ings Lane; converted to garage.

BELTON *Humberside*

(27) WESLEYAN, High Street (SE 785072). Big gabled front with three-light traceried window above entrance; dated 1879. By T. Brownlow Thompson.

BICKER

(28) Former WESLEYAN (TF 225378). Three-bay N front of red brick with broad pilasters, gabled parapet with shield-shaped tablet dated 1846.

BILLINGHAY

(29) Former PRIMITIVE METHODIST (TF 154551). Three-bay gabled front, all windows blocked; dated 1850.

(30) WESLEYAN, Tattershall Bridge (TF 194560). Red brick with yellow brick dressings; gabled three-bay front with round-arched windows and gabled porch. Opened 1852.

BILSBY

(31) Former WESLEYAN (TF 473764). Low walls of red brick with hipped slate roof, two pointed-arched windows in each side wall. Dated 1835 on partly defaced tablet over blocked entrance.

BINBROOK

(32) Former WESLEYAN, High Street (TF 211937). Red brick with dressings of yellow brick and stone; built 1877.

(33) Former PRIMITIVE METHODIST, High Street (TF 210938). Yellow brick front with altered gable and two tiers of round-arched windows. Built 1836, inscription defaced.

BLYTON

(34) Former WESLEYAN (SK 851947). Gabled end with simplified Venetian window between flanking porches; dated 1822. Later Sunday-school of matching design adjacent.

LINCOLNSHIRE

BOLINGBROKE

(35) WESLEYAN, Old Bolingbroke (TF 352650). Red brick and slate with broad three-bay S front; gabled W end facing road with wavy barge-boards and two windows with splayed lintels and keystones. Dated 1845. *Monuments*: W of chapel (1) Thomas Chatterton, 1877; (2) Martha wife of last, 1864; (3) Thomas Chatterton, 1851.

(36) Former PRIMITIVE METHODIST (TF 351561). Dated 1859, now used for storage.

BONBY   *Humberside*

(37) WESLEYAN (TA 004153). Dark brick with hipped slate roof; three-bay front with round-arched windows and tablet above doorway dated 1813. Refitted in late 19th century.

BOSTON

(38) GENERAL BAPTIST, High Street (TF 328436). The date 1651 claimed for the formation of this church is that at which four members of a separatist society which began about 1644 'in the South Marsh parts of Lincolnshire' formed themselves into a Baptist church. The church met in various places around Boston and for a time had the use of Northolme Chapel, the former parish church of Wainfleet St Thomas. A revival in the Boston congregation in 1763 resulted in the erection of a new meeting-house in Goat Street which was opened by Dan Taylor in 1764 and enlarged in 1777. The church joined the New Connexion on its formation in 1770.

The present chapel, built in 1837 on a new site on the E side of High Street and enlarged in 1841, may be the work of James Fenton. It has a gabled front in grey brick of three bays separated by stepped buttresses, two gabled porches and upper windows with four-centred arched heads and moulded labels.

Crosby III (1740) 78. Taylor (1818) II: 124–32, 194–6, 281–4, 397–8. Wood (1847) 182.

(39) Former CONGREGATIONAL, Grove Street (TF 331443). The chapel (closed *c*.1950–60) was built in 1819 for a newly formed congregation; it has brick walls and a hipped slate roof. Three-bay front with two tiers of windows, a formerly pedimented central entrance and a moulded cornice (now removed) and parapet inscribed 'GROVE STREET CHAPEL 1819'.

Barker (1860) 30–1. *Cong. Mag*. II (1819) 443.

(40) Former CONGREGATIONAL, Red Lion Street (TF 328443). The chapel was built in 1868 to replace a Romanesque chapel of 1850 erected for a faction which left Grove Street Chapel in 1847. Yellow brick with red brick and stone dressings and large plate-traceried rose window in gabled front; by C.J. Innocent and Brown of Sheffield. Closed by 1972.

Barker (1860) 31–2. *CYB* (1868) 338.

(41) WESLEYAN, Red Lion Street (TF 328444). The Methodist society, in existence by 1759, built a preaching-house in Wormgate in 1764; a new chapel was built in Red Lion Street *c*.1808 and replaced 1839–40 by Stephen Lewin's Wesleyan Centenary Chapel. This last, severely damaged by fire in 1909, had a five-bay Ionic colonnade between terminal pavilions. The present chapel by Gordon and Gunton, opened 1911 but incorporating part of the former structure, has a bowed front between towers. *Monuments*: in burial-ground include (1) William Binfield, 1849, with two staves of musical notation, signed 'Slight & Smith'; (2) Robert Hubbert, 1873, 'one of the founders and trustee of the Centenary Chapel', Maria his wife, 1854, and Ann Hubbert, 1890.

Leary, W., *Methodism in the Town of Boston* (1972).

(42) Former FREE METHODIST, Pump Square (TF 32954405). Rendered three-bay front with altered gable, built 1856, with a smaller Sunday-school adjacent of 1872. Closed 1962.

(43) Former UNIVERSALIST, Chapel Row (TF 332442). This small meeting-house was built in 1804 for a society formed in 1802 'upon the principles of the Universalists'. The first pastor was ordained 9 April 1802 by William Vidler and Richard Wright, both of whom, together with this society, were shortly to declare themselves Unitarians. The meeting-house 'on the Main Ridge' was registered for 'Independents' in August 1804 and it remained

Former Congregational chapel, Grove Street, Boston. (39)

Former Universalist meeting-house, Chapel Row, Boston. (43)

in use until 1820 when Spain Lane Chapel was opened. The building was then sold for use as a Quaker meeting-house, closed 1836, again sold 1851 and subsequently housed Baptists, Free Methodists, a school, and was latterly in use as a garage or store. The walls are of common brick and the roof is hipped and covered with slates and pantiles. The broad W front is of three bays with two round-arched windows and a central doorway formerly with a pedimented surround. The roof at the S end is half-hipped and may have abutted other property. *Inscription*: oval stone tablet over entrance, inscribed 'THIS | Meeting-House | BUILT | 1804'; overpainted 'MR A[BBO]TT'S ACADEMY'.

Butler (1999) 363.

(44) SPAIN LANE CHAPEL (TF 32954382). Built in 1819–20, and opened 21 June 1820, for the then Unitarian congregation from Chapel Row (*see* (43)). It is a neatly designed chapel of brick with a hipped slate roof with wide eaves. The S front, of red facing bricks with stone dressings, is of three bays with rusticated quoins, two tiers of windows and a central doorway; the lower openings have round-arched heads of two orders and intersecting glazing bars. Above the entrance is a large plain stone panel. The side walls have each three sash windows with cambered heads and three short blind window recesses above, possibly intended to be opened had side galleries been required. At the back are two round-arched windows set high in the N wall and an inscription between, on two stones, 'BUILT | MDCCCXIX'.

The interior has a high plaster ceiling with moulded cornice. At the S end is an original gallery with paired brackets below a panelled front supported by four fluted wooden Doric columns; the staircase in the SE corner has a central wooden newel.

Spain Lane Chapel, Boston. Gallery staircase. (44)

The seating was largely replaced in the early 20th century but some earlier fragments remain in the gallery. The pulpit, which is original, is a low rectangular box with panelled and veneered sides supported by four dwarf columns. A low crypt below the chapel, approached externally from the N, does not appear to have been used for burials.

Several *monuments*, including table-tombs of the early 19th century, remain in the burial-ground.

Bolam (1962) 13–16. Evans (1897) 27. *UHST* IV (1927–30) 277–8.

BOURNE

(45) GENERAL BAPTIST, West Street (TF 094202). The church was formed in the late 17th century by separation from the Spalding society. An earlier meeting-house, built in 1717, was enlarged in 1807 and replaced by the present chapel in 1835. This has an ashlar front, red brick sides and a hipped slate roof. The S front is of three bays with two tiers of round-arched windows between wide terminal pilasters and has a moulded cornice with blocking-course

General Baptist chapel, West Street, Bourne. (45)

inscribed with the date of erection. Galleried interior refitted in late 19th century.

    Taylor (1818) II: 416–19. Wood (1847) 192.

(46) WESLEYAN, Abbey Road, formerly Star Lane (TF 097202). The chapel of brick with a rendered front, built 1839 by Thomas Pilkington, replaced a chapel of 1812 which stood to the rear. The date tablet of the former is reset in the outer wall of a detached church hall built 1965. The front of three bays with a pediment supported by giant pilasters has two tiers of rectangular windows with arched glazing bars. A rear gallery was added in 1867; there are no side galleries.

Wesleyan chapel, Abbey Road, Bourne. (46)

(47) BAPTIST, Dyke (TF 105225). Red brick sides, yellow brick gabled front with wooden canopy above entrance. Built 1878, enlarged to rear.

Baptist chapel, Dyke, Bourne. (47)

BRADLEY *Humberside*

(48) Former WESLEYAN (TA 240063). Brick with hipped slate roof and broad three-bay front; built 1849. (Fittings removed)

    Lester (1890) 112.

BRANT BROUGHTON AND STRAGGLETHORPE

(49) FRIENDS, Brant Broughton (SK 916542). The meeting-house on the S side of Meeting-house Lane adjacent to a burial-ground acquired in 1673 has walls of stone with some timber-framing and later brickwork, and a pantiled roof. The building incorporates fragments of the walling of a timber-framed barn of three bays which, with a narrow strip of ground to the E and stables to the N, was transferred to Friends by Thomas Robinson by deed of gift dated 28 March 1702; the deed also refers to one bay S of the barn of which Friends were to have occasional use. Two posts of the barn structure remain each side of the internal partition with braces to a beam at gallery level. About 1701–2 the barn was encased in stone and the present S and E walls and part of the W wall are of this date. The meeting-house was much refitted in the early 19th century and the stables, the N wall and the S gable were rebuilt in brickwork.

The E front has two doorways with timber lintels and two windows to the right with similar lintels and external shutters; the windows have original wooden cross-frames of the early 18th century but the doors are a century later in date, the original main doors of two leaves having been altered and rehung in a doorway on the N side of the stable passage. Above the principal doorway is a stone tablet inscribed ' T^{R}S | 1701' for Thomas and Sarah Robinson.

The interior (37¾ft by 16ft) is divided by a wooden screen with

Friends' meeting-house, Brant Broughton. (49)

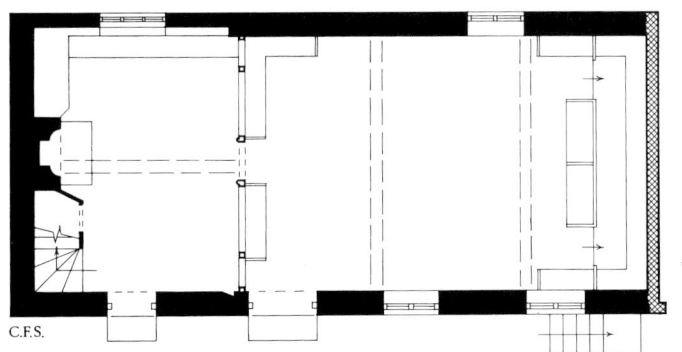

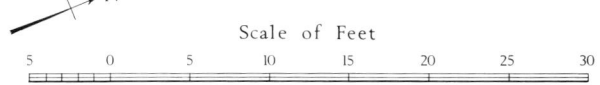

Friends' Meeting-house
BRANT BROUGHTON
AND STRAGGLETHORPE

Lincolnshire

shutters having a small room to the S with an 18th-century fireplace and a loft or gallery above, also heated. The principal room has a stand at the N end and open-backed benches of the early 19th century.

Mounting Steps: against N end of E wall, brick, early 19th-century.
Sundial: on S gable wall, stone, early 19th-century.
Butler (1999) 363–4.

(50) WESLEYAN REFORM, Brant Broughton (SK 917545). The chapel dated 1862 on N side of Maltkiln Lane is of brick with a hipped slate roof. Tall round-arched windows in three-bay S front and on E side.

BRIGG *see* GLANFORD BRIGG

BRIGSLEY *Humberside*

(51) PRIMITIVE METHODIST (TA 254017). Broad three-bay brick front, dated 1873.

BROUGHTON *Humberside*

(52) WESLEYAN, High Street (SE 963087). The chapel, dated 1849, has walls of coursed limestone rubble and a hipped slate roof. The front formerly had two doorways now altered to round-arched windows and a new entrance built at one side. Extended to rear.

BURGH LE MARSH

(53) BAPTIST, The Causeway (TF 503649). Brick with hipped tiled roof, built 1836.

BURTON UPON STATHER   *Humberside*

(54) FRIENDS' BURIAL-GROUND, Thealby (SE 895182). Small rectangular enclosure bounded by stone walls; no monuments.

Butler (1999) 369.

BURWELL

(55) Former PRIMITIVE METHODIST, Buttercross (TF 354796). The 18th-century Buttercross, an octagonal brick building surrounded by arched openings with pediments, was enclosed and heightened in the 19th century. It served for a time for Methodist services but is now 'Burwell Church Hall'.

Kendall (1905) I: 454. Leary and Vickers (1984) 12.

CADNEY   *Humberside*

(56) PRIMITIVE METHODIST, Howsham (TA 045044). Brick with hipped slate roof, built 1838; three-bay front refaced 1883.

CAISTOR

(57) Former CONGREGATIONAL, Church Street (TA 117013). The chapel, dated 1842, has walls of yellow brick, except the W side which is red, with rendered dressings and a slate roof. Three-bay pedimented S front with brick terminal pilasters, rendered and tapered intermediate pilasters and two tiers of windows with tapered architraves and matching doorway. Interior, altered in the late 19th century, has a S gallery. (Converted since 1971 for a school library)

Barker (1860) 47. Mumby, E.H., 'Methodism in Caistor' (Typescript in Dr Williams's Library, 1961) 20–4.

Former Congregational chapel, Caistor.   (57)

(58) WESLEYAN, Chapel Street (TA 11780138). Red brick and slate; tall pedimented front of three bays with giant pilasters and grouped round-arched windows. Built 1842, by 'Mr Mason of Brigg', interior altered 1871.

Lester (1890) 105–6. Mumby (1961) op. cit.

(59) Former PRIMITIVE METHODIST, Plough Hill (TA 118012). Brick with gabled front and grouped lancets. Defaced tablet. Built 1867–8.

CARRINGTON

(60) WESLEYAN, New Bolingbroke (TF 308580). Brown brick with hipped pantiled roof. Broad three-bay N front with round-arched windows with marginal glazing bars; dated 1825.

Wesleyan chapel, New Bolingbroke.   (60)

CAYTHORPE

(61) WESLEYAN, Chapel Lane (SK 937484). Rubble with slate roof; opened 1844.

CHAPEL ST LEONARDS

(62) PRIMITIVE METHODIST (TF 555725). Brick with three wide round-arched windows facing road. Opened 1836, much altered.

CLAXBY

(63) Former WESLEYAN (TF 111949). Long building with brick labels to windows. Built 1836. (Converted to public hall)

CLAYPOLE

(64) Former WESLEYAN, Chapel Lane (SK 847491). Brick with hipped pantiled roof; three-bay front with small tablet dated 1835 above doorway.

(65) Former PRIMITIVE METHODIST (SK 847490). Brick with three-bay front behind railed forecourt; opened 1897.

CLEETHORPES   *Humberside*

(66) PRIMITIVE METHODIST, Grimsby Road (TA 300093). 'Beaconsthorpe' Methodist chapel, red brick with stone dressings. Built 1913–14 in a free Gothic style with a tapering corner tower and thin spire.

CONINGSBY

(67) GENERAL BAPTIST (TF 226584). The chapel was built in 1862 for a church which, in conjunction with Tattershall, was in existence by 1657. Previous chapels were built in 1720 and 1813. Three-bay front in polychrome brickwork with tall yellow brick pilasters, arched entablature to centre bay, and altered pediment.

Taylor (1818) I: 137, 218, 319. Wood (1847) 228.

LINCOLNSHIRE

Primitive Methodist chapel, Grimsby Road, Cleethorpes. (66)

(68) WESLEYAN, Dogdyke Road (TF 224577). The first known preaching-house was hired in 1755; in 1779 John Wesley preached in a newly erected chapel, the predecessor of the present building. The chapel, built in 1825, is a plain structure with walls of brown brick and a hipped slate roof; it has two tiers of round-arched windows in three bays to the front and sides. A large porch was added and the interior greatly altered in 1906.

Marshall, J.C., *Coningsby Methodist Church 1755–1960* (1960).

(69) Former PRIMITIVE METHODIST, Coningsby Moor (TF 245568). Small chapel of brown brick with hipped pantiled roof. Single sash window to right of doorway. Dated 1850.

(70) WESLEYAN, Moor Side (TF 246580). Brick and pantile with two-bay sides, opened 1840, enlarged to rear and re-fronted 1888.

CONISHOLME

(71) FREE METHODIST (TF 403956). Brown brick with hipped slate roof; broad three-bay front with round-arched windows irregularly divided by pilasters. Dated 1856.

CROWLAND

(72) WESLEYAN, Nene Terrace (TF 259080). Three-bay pedimented front with gault brick pilasters. Dated 1868.

CROWLE   *Humberside*

(73) GENERAL BAPTIST, Mill Road (SE 774132). A section of the Isle of Axholme church met at Crowle in the 17th century. A school-chapel was built in 1820 as a preaching-station of the Epworth church and replaced in 1879 by the present buildings. These are of rendered brickwork and comprise a chapel and adjacent Sunday-school with similar gabled fronts and round-arched windows.

Wood (1847) 209.

General Baptist chapel, Crowle. (73)

DEEPING ST JAMES

(74) STRICT BAPTIST (TF 149096). The chapel was built for Frederick Tryon, vicar 1838–9, on his seceding from the Established Church. The walls are of brick and the roof slated; the front is gabled and has three recessed bays enclosing two entrances and one upper window. A tablet in the gable is inscribed 'CAVE ADULLAM 1839'. The interior, partly refitted, has a rear gallery with fielded-panelled front. *Monument*: in chapel, to Frederick Tryon, 1903, 'pastor for more than 63 years'.

Chambers IV (1963) 117–18. *Grace* (April 1984).

DOGDYKE

(75) Former WESLEYAN, Chapel Hill (TF 207542). Brick with hipped pantiled roof and broad three-bay front, now rendered. Built 1846. (Converted to cottage)

DUNHOLME

(76) Former WESLEYAN, The Green (TF 025793). The former chapel on the S side of The Green was built in 1841, closed *c.*1852 and converted to a pair of cottages. Brick with hipped pantiled roof.

(77) FREE METHODIST (TF 023793). The chapel of gault brick with a broad three-bay front and hipped pantiled roof was built *c.*1852, a school was added alongside in 1868 and the entrance re-sited.

LINCOLNSHIRE

DUNSTON

(78) Former WESLEYAN, Middle Street (TF 065630). Three-bay brick front, built 1832. (Altered and converted to cottage)

(79) PRIMITIVE METHODIST, Chapel Lane (TF 064628). 'Jubilee Chapel', of brick with a broad three-bay front, was built in the mid 19th century and enlarged to the front in 1870.

EAST BARKWITH

(80) WESLEYAN (TF 168815). Brick with hipped slate roof; the broad three-bay front, divided by pilasters, has round-arched openings and a tablet above the entrance dated 1860. Lunette behind pulpit left of entrance, stepped seating to right. (Derelict 1974)

EAST KIRKBY

(81) WESLEYAN (TF 335622). Brick, three-bay front with labels over windows; dated 1862. Sunday-school of 1908 attached.

EASTOFT   *Humberside*

(82) PRIMITIVE METHODIST (SE 806164). Three-bay front of red and yellow brick with contemporary Sunday-school alongside. Dated 1869.

(83) Former CHAPEL, High Street (SE 806165). Fifty yards N of the above. Brick, inscribed 'Rebuilt 1854'. Possibly for the Methodist New Connexion, the only other congregation registered in the 1851 census.

EASTVILLE

(84) Former PRIMITIVE METHODIST (TF 402568). Three-bay gabled front dated 1876.

EPWORTH   *Humberside*

(85) GENERAL BAPTIST, Station Road (SE 774045). A church meeting in the Isle of Axholme was in existence by the late 17th century, chiefly centred on Epworth and Butterwick. A meeting-house is said to have been built in Epworth in 1760. The present chapel of 1857, of brick and slate, has a gabled three-bay front with round-arched openings, terminal pilasters and entablature. A detached school building of basically similar design but segmental-pointed windows is dated 1881.

Taylor (1818) I: 319; II: 425–8. Wood (1847) 209.

(86) WESLEYAN (SE 78150385). John Wesley, who in 1742 stood on his father's tombstone in the parish churchyard and addressed an enthusiastic assembly, returned in 1758 to preach 'in the shell of the new house'. In 1772 'a lately erected building called the Preaching House' was registered for 'Independents' but apparently refers to the earlier chapel or its successor. A new chapel of red brick built in 1821 was superseded by the present building in 1888–9; this is a large Gothic chapel by Charles Bell, of stone and slate with a tower rising to an octagonal turret and spire above the main entrance.

Curnock, (ed.) (1938) IV: 305.

(87) METHODIST NEW CONNEXION (SE 78150395). Red brick with stone dressings and slate roof, gabled front with two-light

Wesleyan chapel, Epworth.   (86)

Gothic traceried windows; porch partly demolished. Built 1860 to commemorate Alexander Kilham, founder of the Methodist New Connexion, born in Epworth in 1762. (Disused since 1944)

FIRSBY

(88) WESLEYAN (TF 456631). Isolated chapel of red brick with stone dressings; large circular window with cusped tracery in gabled front. Built 1902 by Gordon and Gunton.

FISKERTON

(89) Former WESLEYAN (TF 047722). Three-bay brick front with pilasters; built 1837. (Converted to house since 1967 and refenestrated)

FLEET

(90) GENERAL BAPTIST, Fleet Hargate (TF 397249). The first chapel on this site was built in 1764 for a society which originated at Holbeach c.1681 as a branch of the Spalding church; the society met at Fleet from 1690 but also held meetings at Lutton and Gedney. The chapel at Fleet was enlarged in 1782, 1803, 1830 and 1842 and was replaced by the present building in 1876; this has a tall three-bay gabled front of brick with stone dressings and tall round-arched bays enclosing two tiers of windows. *Monuments*: in burial-ground, include (1) Susan wife of Benjamin Anderson, 1799; (2) Mary (Anderson) wife of Thomas Lee, 1799; (3) John Ewen, 1782, and Ann his widow, 1802; (4) Matthew Hursthouse, 1780, with circular inscription panel surmounted by a basket of roses between two cherubs' heads; (5) Mrs Sarah Hursthouse, late 18th-century, rectangular panel between Ionic columns with segmental pediment above.

Taylor (1818) I: 217, 317; II: 121–3, 197, 286–91, 398–401. Wood (1847) 208.

FOLKINGHAM

(91) WESLEYAN, Chapel Lane (TF 071336). Brick with later rendering and hipped pantiled roof. Entrance at E end incorporates a tablet dated 1841; side walls of two bays with two tiers of sash windows; one round-arched window in W wall behind rostrum pulpit. The E gallery, supported by two wooden columns, retains original box-pews but without their doors.

FRISKNEY

(92) WESLEYAN, Friskney (TF 472558). The chapel, of brown brick with a hipped slate roof, is a large building with a three-bay front with two tiers of windows between terminal pilasters. There were originally two round-arched doorways, now converted to windows, and a large circular window between which has been altered to a doorway. Three upper windows have round-arched heads and a tablet below the centre window is inscribed 'Wesleyan Centenary Chapel 1839'. The interior has a horseshoe-shaped gallery with a complete set of box-pews and a slightly lower singers' gallery behind the pulpit; the lower seating and rostrum pulpit date from the late 19th century.

Wesleyan chapel, Friskney. (92)

(93) WESLEYAN, Friskney Fen (TF 432571). Small chapel of brick with broad three-bay front, now rendered, and hipped pantiled roof. Opened 1836.

FULBECK

(94) PRIMITIVE METHODIST, Washdyke Lane (SK 946502). Plain building of brick and slate, gabled front with pointed-arched doorway and window. Built 1825, 'restored 1899'.

FULSTOW

(95) PRIMITIVE METHODIST, Main Street (TF 328971). Brick and slate with three round-arched windows in side wall facing road; entrance at N end with partly defaced tablet dated 1836.

GAINSBOROUGH

(96) BEAUMONT STREET CHAPEL (SK 817897). A chapel was built about 1701 for a Presbyterian congregation formed in the late 17th century which later became Unitarian. This was superseded in 1928 by a new chapel in Trinity Street, 700 yards S (SK 817890), which was closed in 1974. The former chapel, now demolished, stood on the W side of Beaumont Street. It is described in the earliest deed as 'that house or building lately erected in a place called Ratten Row in Gainsborough' and placed in trust for Congregationalists, Independents or Presbyterians. This was a plain building of brick with three round-arched sash windows facing the street, a doorway to the left, and a segmental-arched gallery window in the S wall. The interior had been greatly altered in 1907–9. *Plate*: includes three two-handled cups of 1691, 1695 and 1718.

Clark-Lewis, W.R., *The Foundation and History of Beaumont Street Church, Gainsborough* (1912). Evans (1897) 91–2. *UHST* VI (1935–8) 379–80.

(97) CONGREGATIONAL, Church Street (SK 815901). The chapel of hard red brick with stone dressings in a free Gothic style by R.C. and E.R. Sutton was built in 1896 to commemorate the 17th-century preacher John Robinson. The expressed intention 'to reproduce as far as possible, a structure with the distinctive marks and characteristic features of the Meeting-houses of the date in which he [Robinson] lived' has been very freely interpreted. (URC)

CYB (1895) 186.

(98) FRIENDS, Market Street (SK 816899). The meeting-house standing on the S side of the street near the junction with Beaumont Street has brick walls and a pantiled roof with

Friends' meeting-house, Gainsborough. Rear. (98)

gabled ends. It was built in 1704 and has a stone with this date in the S wall. Alterations in 1809, 1876 and 1951 have not greatly affected the original structure (35ft by 24½ft externally) but the N wall is now largely concealed by extensions of 1876.

The principal elevation facing S has two windows with flat-arched brick heads, that to the E reduced in width, and further to the right an upper window with a blocked window below. The E wall has a central doorway with 19th-century wood frame and a window above. Two windows in the N wall are covered by later buildings. The interior has a gallery and screens at the E end and a stand opposite. The fittings appear to have been entirely renewed in the 19th century. There is a small burial-ground to the south.

Butler (1999) 365–6.

(99) Former METHODIST, Little Church Lane (SK 814900). The former preaching-house standing on the E side of an alley off the N side of Lord Street has brick walls with dentil brick eaves cornices and a gabled roof re-covered in corrugated asbestos. It was erected c.1785 and continued in use until 1804, when it was superseded by a chapel in Beaumont Street or North Street, itself rebuilt in 1968.

When originally constructed the only openings to the ground floor were two symmetrically placed doorways in the S wall; above these was a range of five windows with two more at the same level in the E and W gabled end walls. It is probable that the pulpit stood against the N wall and that there were small galleries against the other three sides. Before religious use ceased much rearrangement took place; one of the S doorways was replaced by a window and other windows were pierced at that level, a new entrance was made in the W wall and the pulpit removed to the E end. The galleries were also altered to provide two narrow N and S galleries and a deeper gallery at the W end. The building has long been in commercial occupation and many other minor changes have been made to the fenestration.

The S wall has two doorways with semicircular arched heads in 9in. brickwork, that to the E now occupied by a window; to the W of each doorway a round-arched window has been inserted, the arches cut through the brickwork without voussoirs. At gallery

Former Methodist chapel, Little Church Lane, Gainsborough. (99)

level are the remains of five segmental-arched windows, that at the W end lengthened to form a warehouse doorway and subsequently blocked; the next window remains glazed; the third and fourth are blocked and a small window pierced between; the fifth is glazed. Of these the central window, now lacking its brick arch, may have been altered while the chapel was still in use.

The N wall is blank but a centrally placed upper window was blocked when a fireplace and chimney were built against it internally; it may have been pierced to give additional light to the pulpit, the opposite S window being blocked to prevent glare.

The W wall is gabled, the upper part of the gable being rebuilt; there is a wide semicircular-arched doorway to the ground floor, added when the interior was rearranged, and at gallery level two segmental-arched windows, later altered or blocked, were inserted asymmetrically towards the N end of the wall.

The E wall, with brick tumbling below the rebuilt apex of the gable, has two blocked windows similar to those in the W wall and likewise asymmetrically towards the N, the probable reason being to allow more light on the N side which was otherwise devoid of original windows. Two round-arched windows to the ground floor, now concealed by a lean-to shed, may be secondary.

The interior (16½ft by 30ft) retains few original features. The structure of the later gallery remains with two N–S beams supporting the W gallery and beams of lesser scantling supporting the two side galleries which taper towards the side walls as they approach the E end. The roof structure is original and has pegged collar-beam trusses with clasped purlins; it was formerly ceiled below the collars.

Leary, W., *Methodist Chapels in Lincolnshire: The Eighteenth Century* (typescript, 1976). *WHSP* VI (1907–8) 67–70 (chapel wrongly identified).

GEDNEY

(100) GENERAL BAPTIST, Gedney Broadgate (TF 405226). The chapel was built in 1839 for a branch of the Fleet society, extended to the rear and three-bay gabled front added in 1868. Small boundary stone in side wall inscribed 'Not the Extent within 9 Inches'.

Wood (1847) 208.

(101) Former FRIENDS, Church Gate (TF 401242). A meeting-house given by Stephen Willoughby in 1698 appears to have occupied this site and to be referred to in a contemporary deed of 'admission to one cottage and one acre of land in Gedney in Churchgate abutting North on Church Gate'. The existing structure may be a rebuilding of the early 18th century, but the meeting-house was greatly altered to its present form in 1846–7 when it was heightened, refitted and a cottage added at the E end.

The walls are of brick and the roof is slated. The S wall has openings in the older lower walling only, comprising two doorways with a window between near the W end and three windows to the right all with segmental-arched heads. The N wall facing the road has the remains of a central window only to the lower part with a range of four sash windows in the heightening. The W end is gabled and surmounted by a substantial brick chimney-stack; a wide round-arched doorway with wooden pedimented surround, and two arched upper windows, date from the mid 19th century.

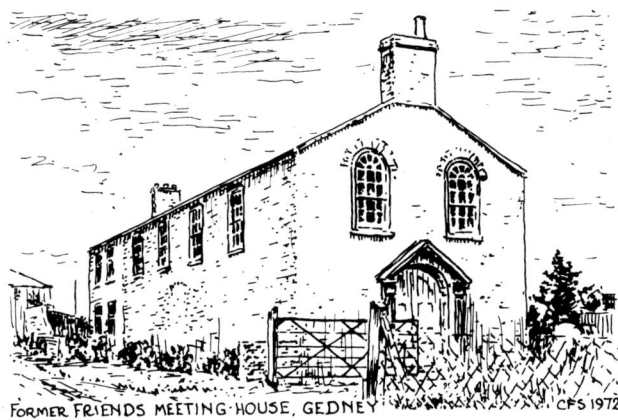

FORMER FRIENDS MEETING-HOUSE, GEDNEY CFS 1972

The interior (46¾ft by 17¼ft) has a gallery at the W end with shutters above, and formerly below; the outline of the stand is visible at the E end. (Reported demolished c.1981 and bungalows built on site)

Monuments: in burial-ground to S, three large ledger stones, one ?1847, others later.

Butler (1999) 366.

GEDNEY HILL

(102) GENERAL BAPTIST, Hillgate (TF 339114). A chapel built here in 1811 by a section of the Fleet church was rebuilt in 1883. Brick and slate, gabled front with lancets.

Wood (1847) 211.

GLANFORD BRIGG *Humberside*

(103) Former CONGREGATIONAL, Wragby Street, Brigg (TA 001073). Built 1813; brick with rendered gabled front partly concealed by a lower entrance bay added over the forecourt in the late 19th century. Horseshoe-shaped gallery with later organ gallery and minor rooms at rear. *Monument*: in chapel to

Former Wesleyan chapel, Brigg. (104)

LINCOLNSHIRE

Jonathan Spring, 1831, 'one of the founders of this chapel', *et al*. (Under conversion to auction rooms 1980)

Barker (1860) 32–3.

(104) Former WESLEYAN, Bridge Street, Brigg (SE 997071). Three-bay pedimented front of yellow brick with giant pilasters and two tiers of windows with tapered jambs. The interior has been converted for commercial use with a floor inserted at gallery level; decorative plaster ceiling roses remain. Built 1840.

GLENTHAM

(105) Former WESLEYAN (TF 000902). Brick, rendered front with stone lining and hipped roof. Built 1821. (Refenestrated and converted to house)

GOSBERTON

(106) GENERAL BAPTIST (TF 244313). The society, in existence by the late 17th century as a section of the Spalding church, became autonomous about 1762. In 1784, when the church joined the New Connexion, a debt of £60 was reported which may have been occasioned by the erection of a meeting-house. The present chapel of red brick with yellow brick dressings and a slate roof is dated 1866. Alongside is the smaller former chapel of *c*.1784. This has brown brick walls and a pantiled roof. The N front (32½ft wide) is of three bays with a segmental-arched doorway between similarly arched windows; it was extended to the E in 1837 and a gallery built at that end.

Taylor (1818) II: 294–300 and *passim*. Wood (1847) 184.

GOXHILL   *Humberside*

(107) Former WESLEYAN, Howe Lane (TA 102213). Built 1828 but re-fronted *c*.1852. Three-bay front with pedimental gable, in red brick with yellow brick dressings, defaced tablet above inserted garage doors.

(108) PRIMITIVE METHODIST, Chapel Street (TA 103216). Big gabled front of yellow brick with red brick dressings, two gabled porches and three tall traceried windows; dated 1891.

(109) SABBATH SCHOOL, Chapel Street (TA 103215). Low front of three bays with inscribed tablet above entrance with name and date 1859.

GRAINTHORPE

(110) WESLEYAN (TF 383973). 'Ebenezer' chapel, built 1818, has walls of brown brick with patent tiled roof; the gabled front of three bays has two tiers of round-arched windows. Two doorways in gabled porches replaced a central entrance in the late 19th century.

(111) FREE METHODIST, High Street (TF 384972). Three-bay front of brick with hipped slate roof; asymmetrically spaced doorway and windows have splayed lintels with moulded keystones. Tablet dated 1854.

GRANTHAM

(112) ZION CHAPEL, 23a Castlegate (SK 91523595). The former Calvinistic Independent chapel is entirely concealed behind other buildings; it is approached through an archway with double doors and a reeded architrave of the early 19th century. The chapel was built in 1792 possibly for a congregation connected with Thomas Barston of Grantham, a friend of William Huntington SS.

The walls are of brickwork and the roof, which is hipped at the E end, is covered in pantiles; the building has been slightly extended to the E where a flight of stone steps, now covered, rises to the entrance. There is one round-arched window in both N and S walls and two windows at the W end flanking the site of the pulpit. The interior, gutted since the chapel closed *c*.1971, had a gallery at the E end. (Converted to gymnasium)

Monument: in chapel on S wall, to Thomas Toms 'an eminent Believer', 1818, oval tablet.

(113) CONGREGATIONAL, Avenue Road (SK 915358). The chapel (now St Peters Hill URC) was built in 1869–70 in the Gothic style by James Tait. At one corner above the principal entrance is a thin tower and spire.

CYB (1870) 380.

(114) WESLEYAN, Finkin Street (SK 915359). Methodists met from 1787 in a building in Back Lane, removing in 1803 to a new chapel in Finkin Street which was enlarged in 1827. The present chapel built in 1840 is a large building of stone with ashlar facing to the principal sides and a slate roof. The S front, altered in the early 20th century by the addition of staircase wings and a colonnaded entrance, has round-arched upper windows, a moulded cornice and a pediment with the denominational name in giant lettering. The side walls are of five bays, those to the W having arched recesses enclosing the windows. The interior has a continuous round-ended gallery.

(115) Former PRIMITIVE METHODIST, Commercial Road (SK 915354). Rendered pedimented front with three arched bays enclosing central entrance and two tiers of windows. Erected 1837, enlarged 1876.

(116) SALVATION ARMY CITADEL, London Road (SK 916354). Boldly battlemented brick front with octagonal turret and arched centrepiece; *c*.1900.

GREAT GONERBY

(117) WESLEYAN, Spring End (SK 894383). Brick and pantile, rendered gabled front with tablet dated 1835, otherwise much altered or rebuilt.

(118) Former PRIMITIVE METHODIST, Green Street (SK 896384). Red brick with dressings of gault brick and stone; pedimented front with double-arched entrance between tall arched windows and circular light above. Shaped tablet dated 1873. Sunday-school opposite dated 1886.

GREAT LIMBER

(119) Former WESLEYAN, Grasby Road (TA 129085). Brick with hipped slate roof; broad front of three bays separated by broad pilasters. Tablet over entrance dated 1841.

Lester (1890) 110.

(120) Former WESLEYAN, Grasby Road (TA 131086). The successor to the foregoing built 1892–3 is in the Gothic style with a three-light traceried window in the end gable. (Converted to house)

General Baptist meeting-house, Monksthorpe, Great Steeping. (121)

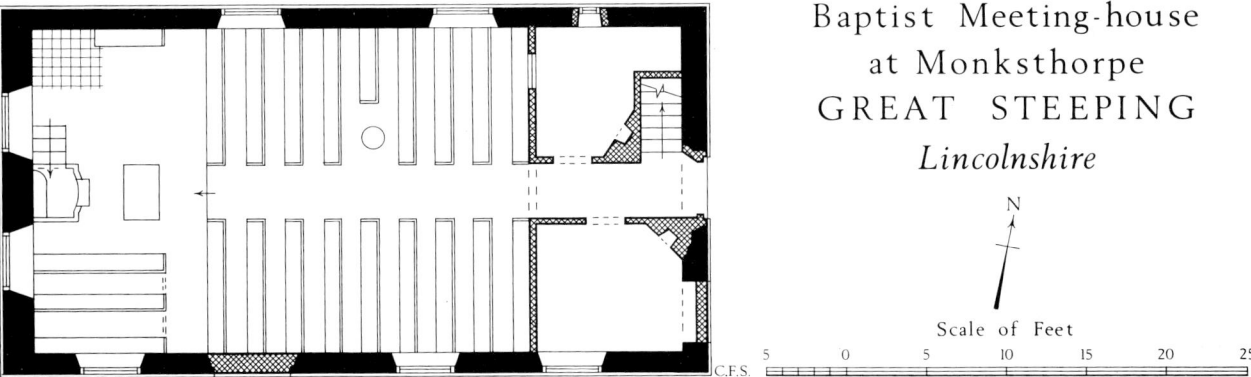

Baptist Meeting-house at Monksthorpe
GREAT STEEPING
Lincolnshire

GREAT STEEPING

(121) GENERAL BAPTIST, Monksthorpe (TF 450654). The congregation at Monksthorpe, which has long been associated with the church at Burgh le Marsh (53), appears to have been formed in the late 17th century. The first trust deed of the present remote site is said to be dated 1701 being the gift from Hugh Hyscoghe or 'Ayscough', attorney-at-law, to the people called Baptists, for ever, of the land for a burial-ground and 'for the purposes of building a meeting-house to worship God in'.

The meeting-house has brick walls in English bond with a tall plinth and a steeply pitched roof covered with pantiles which are said to have replaced thatch in 1847. The S wall has three segmental-arched windows with the original frames replaced by

General Baptist meeting-house, Monksthorpe, Great Steeping. Monument to Joseph Harpam. (121)

hung sashes in the 19th century; a wide similarly arched doorway was blocked at the time of this alteration (since reopened). The N wall has two regularly spaced windows of a similar pattern and two like windows in the W wall now flank the pulpit; the brickwork of the W gable is slightly recessed and has in it an access door to the roof space. The E wall has a small chimney-stack above the recessed brickwork of the gable. A central doorway and window above were inserted in the mid 19th century; the carefully blocked site of an earlier doorway is visible near the S end of this wall. A low range of buildings to the NE in brick and pantile includes a former cottage and a stable with three stalls.

The interior (40¼ft by 20¼ft) was almost entirely refitted in 1847 when two vestries with an entrance passage and gallery above were built at the E end and a new pulpit, with bowed front and two turned columnar supports, erected between the W windows. The location of the earlier pulpit is uncertain but may have been between the N windows. The seating of open-backed benches with two box-pews near the pulpit also dates from 1847.

Baptistery: externally, E of meeting-house, with slightly bowed brick sides and tiled base, possibly of 19th-century date in present form, with later repairs.

Fittings – *Collecting Shovels*: two, with flat octagonal box and single handle, 19th-century. *Monuments* and *Floorslabs*. *Monuments*: in burial-ground, several of 18th-century date with traditional decoration, including (1) Joseph Harpam, 1783, headstone with winged cherub's head and flowers; *Floorslabs*: in chapel, at E end below pulpit (2) 'Hugh Ayscough Gent.' Attorney at Law, 1704, 'he was the first promoter of this building and gave the ground on which it stands…'; near N wall (3) Thomas Ashley, 1800.

Dowse, J., *The History of Monksthorpe and Burgh Baptist Churches, Lincolnshire* (1910) [duplicated typescript reprint] 4–5. Taylor (1818) II: 106, 126.

GREAT STURTON

(122) Former WESLEYAN (TF 214767). Brick with gabled end and porch. Built 1883. (Derelict)

GRIMSBY   *Humberside*

(123) Former CONGREGATIONAL, Hainton Avenue (TA 275086). 'Welholme Mission Church and Sunday School' of red brick with yellow terracotta dressings was built in 1894 in a simple Gothic style by Herbert G. Scaping of Grimsby. A larger chapel was added in 1907 in a free Gothic style by G. Bell, Withers and Meredith. The latter (now 'The Welholme Galleries') has a prominent corner tower and thin spire.

CYB (1895) 185–6; (1908) 156–7.

HACONBY

(124) BAPTIST and former PRIMITIVE METHODIST (TF 106254). This small brick chapel is remarkable for its size, the completeness of its fittings and the joint denominational use for which it was built. The narrow gabled front has a round-arched doorway with fanlight between two windows formerly with hung sashes and a tablet in the gable inscribed 'Baptist and Primitive Methodist Chapel erected by W. Brown A.D. 1867' (the words 'and Primitive Methodist' have been painted out). In the rear wall is a single pointed-arched window behind the pulpit.

'Baptist and Primitive Methodist' chapel, Haconby.   (124)

The interior (24ft by 13½ft), ceiled at collar level, has galleries along each side wall with open balustraded fronts supported by turned wood columns; the galleries are approached by separate staircases adjacent to the entrance but are also linked by a later cross gallery. The pulpit is an original rostrum with balustraded front matching the galleries. The seating comprises open-backed benches to the ground floor with plain backless benches in the galleries. Iron hat-pegs line the wall at both levels on the right-hand side only. (Now only in Baptist use)

HAGWORTHINGHAM

(125) Former WESLEYAN (TF 344695). The chapel built 1839 has brick walls; the front of three bays has a round-arched doorway, small upper windows and a full pediment. (Closed 1968 and partially converted for domestic use)

(126) Former PRIMITIVE METHODIST (TF 346696). Broad front with doorways in end bays and five round-arched windows between. The interior comprises chapel to left and smaller room to right. Dated 1875.

HALTON HOLEGATE

(127) WESLEYAN (TF 415646). Brown brick and slate, gabled front formerly with two doorways and window between; built 1837, altered and extended at side 1937. The interior has no galleries; the floor slopes down towards a rostrum pulpit.

HAMMERINGHAM

(128) WESLEYAN (TF 309669). Brown brick with hipped slate roof, originally with broad three-bay front, extended and entrance re-sited at end in late 19th century. Opened 1840.

HATCLIFFE *Humberside*

(129) Former WESLEYAN (TA 214008). The former chapel, opened 1837, has brick walls; the front of three bays has stepped buttresses, but all other features have been obscured by drastic conversion to domestic use.

HAXEY *Humberside*

(130) Former WESLEYAN, Haxey (SK 771999). The former chapel with rendered walls and hipped roof, now converted to a house and post office, was built in 1814. Greatly altered.

(131) Former WESLEYAN, Low Burnham (SE 780022). Brick and slate, gabled front with two doorways, one blocked, and tablet dated 1848.
   Lindley (1969) Pl. 64.

(132) PRIMITIVE METHODIST, Low Burnham (SE 780022). South of (131); three-bay front with gabled centre to parapet and round-arched openings. Built 1872, superseding a chapel of 1836.

(133) Former METHODIST NEW CONNEXION, Westwoodside (SK 756997). A small three-bay chapel of brick with gabled parapet carries a tablet inscribed 'Ebenezer Chapel 1846'. A larger chapel stands alongside. The first chapel on this site was built in 1802.

(134) PRIMITIVE METHODIST, Westwoodside (SK 754995). Broad three-bay front of red brick with yellow brick dressings. Dated 1861.

HEAPHAM

(135) WESLEYAN, Common Lane (SK 876883). Small but elaborate chapel of 1896 of red and yellow brick with a hipped slate roof and decorative ridge tiles. Contemporary window glass.

HECKINGTON

(136) Former WESLEYAN (TF 143441). Red brick with hipped roof and two tiers of windows. Defaced tablet dated 1835. Now 'St Andrew's Church House'.

Wesleyan chapel, Common Lane, Heapham. (135)

(137) WESLEYAN REFORM, Eastgate (TF 144441). Gault brick with hipped pantiled roof. End entrance with pair of curved doors in reeded surround; external shutters to side windows. Dated 1852.

(138) Former PRIMITIVE METHODIST, Heckington Fen (TF 184459). Red and yellow brick; three-bay gabled front with arch enclosing doorway and small circular window above. 'Rebuilt 1873'.

HEIGHINGTON

(139) WESLEYAN (TF 029694). The chapel of coursed stone with a three-bay front and later rendered porch was built in 1848. The pulpit and two tablets of Decalogue of earlier date are recent insertions.

HELPRINGHAM

(140) PRIMITIVE METHODIST, The Green (TF 139407). Brick with circular window of plate tracery above later lean-to porch. Dated 1883.

HEMINGBY

(141) Former WESLEYAN, Chapel Lane (TF 238746). Broad four-bay front of red brick with pointed-arched windows and gabled porch. Dated 1859.

HOGSTHORPE

(142) WESLEYAN (TF 536721). Red brick with yellow brick dressings and hipped roof. Front of three bays with giant pilasters carrying segmental arches enclosing paired upper windows. Dated 1863.

HOLBEACH

(143) GENERAL BAPTIST, Albert Street (TF 360247). The chapel, built in 1845 for a section of the Fleet church, has brick walls covered with a harsh cement rendering. Pedimented front of three bays with round-arched windows and doorway with scrolled handrails.
   Taylor (1818) II: 399. Wood (1847) 208.

LINCOLNSHIRE

(144) WESLEYAN, Holbeach Drove (TF 325123). Brick with hipped pantiled roof; end entrance with round-arched head and fanlight. Dated 1833.

(145) Former PRIMITIVE METHODIST, Holbeach Bank (TF 355274). Three-bay front with pedimental gable and round-arched windows. Dated 1864.

(146) WESLEYAN REFORM, Albert Street (TF 360246). Brick gabled front with three round-arched upper windows in arched recesses, altered below. Dated 1853.

HORKSTOW

(147) Former PRIMITIVE METHODIST (SE 987185). Brick Gothic, of the late 19th century. (Now motor repair workshop)

HORNCASTLE

(148) Former BAPTIST, Cagthorpe (TF 258694). The chapel built in 1767 for a newly formed Particular Baptist church, although claimed (1851 census) to have been 'rebuilt in 1839', was heightened and extended to the W at about this date; it is now used as a Salvation Army Hall. The chapel (originally 32½ft by 24¼ft externally) has brick walls with ashlar quoins to the E front and at the NW corner. The gabled E end has a central entrance with segmental-arched head and a later wood surround. The N and S walls have each two original windows to the lower stage with segmental-arched heads and keystones and two windows in the later walling above, all with hung sashes. An extension of 6ft at the W end links the chapel to an earlier house. Inside is a deep gallery with a fielded-panelled front divided by fluted pilasters. *Monuments*: externally on N wall (1) John Hill, 1779, 13 years pastor; (2) Thomas Lamb, 1811, and Frances his wife, 1810.

Former Baptist chapel, Horncastle. (148)

(149) Former CONGREGATIONAL, Queen Street (TF 262696). The chapel erected in 1822 to replace a smaller building opened the previous year has brick walls and a hipped roof. Three-bay front and sides with two tiers of segmental-arched sash windows and central entrance in later porch. 'Independent Sunday School' behind of 1825, rebuilt 1874. *Monument*: in front burial-ground, Rev. John Pain, 1844, 23 years pastor, and Esther his widow, 1868.
  Barker (1860) 39–40.

HORSINGTON

(150) WESLEYAN (TF 190684). Brick with hipped pantiled roof, broad three-bay front with large tablet dated 1837 over later porch; one bay added to left.

HOUGH-ON-THE-HILL

(151) Former WESLEYAN, Gelston (SK 914452). A small three-bay chapel of 1839 with adjacent cottage, converted to house since 1957, heightened, refenestrated, and entrance re-sited; only the partly defaced date tablet remains unchanged.

HUMBERSTON   *Humberside*

(152) Former WESLEYAN, Church Lane (TA 312053). Three-bay chapel built 1835, of brick with hipped slate roof; E front with round-arched windows, blocked doorway and renewed oval tablet inscribed 'Wendover Hall 1909'. Superseded by new chapel in Humberston Avenue (TA 309053) in 1907 and converted to public hall. 'Wesleyan Sunday school 1896' adjacent to north.

HUNDLEBY

(153) WESLEYAN (TF 390664). Gabled front of gault brick with clasping corner buttresses and pinnacles, pointed-arched windows and porch. Dated 1871.

HUTTOFT

(154) WESLEYAN, Sutton Road (TF 513767). Broad front of five bays with central gabled porch and pointed-arched windows; built 1856. Later vestry to left.

INGHAM

(155) WESLEYAN, High Street (SK 949835). Brick with hipped roof, round-arched windows and end entrance incorporating upper window. The Sunday-school behind, of coursed rubble with broad three-bay front and arched openings, may be the original chapel opened 1836 with the present chapel added in the mid 19th century.

IRBY IN THE MARSH

(156) Former PRIMITIVE METHODIST (TF 474632). Brick with hipped pantiled roof, defaced tablet dated 1837 above altered end entrance; two windows to each side wall.

KEADBY WITH ALTHORPE   *Humberside*

(157) WESLEYAN, Althorpe (SE 834096). Gabled front with round-arched windows and tablet dated 1864.

KEELBY

(158) WESLEYAN, Yarborough Road (TA 164104). Red brick with yellow brick dressings; gabled front with four-light traceried window and two porches now crudely conjoined. Opened 1867.
  Lester (1890) 108.

KIRKSTEAD

(159) THE ABBEY CHAPEL (TF 190614). The chapel is a notable building of stone dating from the early 13th century which formed a subsidiary place of worship to the Cistercian abbey church.

The abbey was suppressed in 1537, the site being granted to the Duke of Suffolk, and by the early 18th century all the abbey buildings with the exception of the chapel had been demolished or had fallen into ruin. The chapel, said to have been a 'donative', seems to have been used for Protestant worship at least by 1626, the date of the former pulpit. Josiah Rock, ejected rector of Saundby, Notts., is said by Calamy to have 'got into a Priveledg'd Place in the Gift of Esquire [John] Disney, where he preach'd publickly without Conforming', the place being tentatively identified by A.G. Matthews as Kirkstead. The association with the Disney family, who were Presbyterians, seems, however, to have commenced in 1685 on the marriage of Daniel Disney with Catherine Fiennes-Clinton in which year a Presbyterian minister was appointed to the chapel. Dr John Taylor was minister here 1715–33. On the death in 1790 of the Rev. John Dunkley a new owner, Richard Ellison, sought to prevent further Presbyterian use which ceased in 1793–4, their uncertain tenure being exacerbated by a failure to maintain a trust. The protracted legal argument that followed succeeded only in recovering an endowment settled on the ministry by Daniel Disney in 1720 and confirmed by his will of 1732; this judgement enabled the erection of a new chapel at Woodhall Spa (*see* (285)). The Abbey Chapel then passed to Anglican use, some minor repairs being carried out in 1843, but structural neglect led to its closure about 1876. The building was restored to use as 'St Leonard's Church' following major repairs in 1913–14 when the low hipped roof was replaced by the present gabled roof and the vaulted interior was entirely re-mediaevalized. Prior to 1914 the interior retained a full set of box-pews and had, reset centrally at the E end, an octagonal *pulpit,* now at the old parish church of All Saints, Walesby, Lincs. (TF 138924), with carved back-board and canopy, dated 1626.

Fittings – *Communion Table*: loose in roof space (1980), damaged, small oak table with turned legs and shaped brackets below upper rails, early 17th-century. *Monuments* and *Floorslabs. Monuments*: in burial-ground, include (1) Sarah Moore, 1783; (2) John Warter, 1699; (3) Charles Warter, 1769; (4) Mary wife of John Warter, 1786; (5) John Warter, 1781; *Floorslabs*: in chapel (1) Henry Fines Esq., 1676, and Jane his widow, 1689; (2) Edward Fines grandson of Henry Fines, 1753; (3) John [?son of] Benjamin Harrison 'Curate of this Parish' and Elizabeth his wife, [1750?]; (4) 'M.S.1790'. *Plate*: (in Lincoln cathedral treasury) (1) beaker, with short tapered sides inscribed H^{F}I for ?Henry and Jane Fines, London assay 1658; (2) sweetmeat dish, perhaps used as christening bowl, London assay 1653.

Anon., *The Kirkstead Story* (1968). *Archaeological Journal* XL (1883) 296–302. *The Builder* (1 March 1912). Calamy, E., *An Abridgement of Mr Baxter's History of his Life and Times...* (1713) II: 526. Evans (1897) 123–4. Matthews, A. G., *Calamy Revised* (1934) 414. *Monthly Repository* VIII (1813) 81–6. *PHSJ* VI (1936–9) 25–9. *Thoroton Society Trans.* XIV (1910) 45–9.

KIRTON (in Holland)

(160) Former GENERAL BAPTIST (TF 304387). The chapel, now used as a fire-engine house, was built in 1840 but leased and later sold to an Independent congregation in 1846. Rendered brick walls and slate roof hipped to rear. Gabled front with altered entrance; pointed-arched windows with intersecting glazing bars. Small burial-ground at rear with *monuments* to (1) Samuel Smeeton of Kirton House, 1860, and Eleanor his widow, 1877; (2) Samuel Smeeton, 1888, *et al.*

Barker (1860) 40. Wood (1847) 232.

(161) Former WESLEYAN, Kirton Holme (TF 262419). Built in 1820 with a new chapel erected alongside in 1903, now in Anglican use. Walls of dark brick and a hipped pantiled roof. All windows altered in 1903 and end entrance covered by a porch linking the two buildings. Gallery next to entrance.

KIRTON IN LINDSEY   *Humberside*

(162) GENERAL BAPTIST, St Andrew's Street (SK 935986). Built 1897 for a church claiming 1663 as its year of origin. The previous chapel of *c.*1815 stood in Church Street.

Taylor (1818) II: 315–18, 409–10. Wood (1847) 183.

(163) WESLEYAN, Wesley Street (SK 936986). The chapel opened 1842 has walls of coursed limestone with a gault brick front and

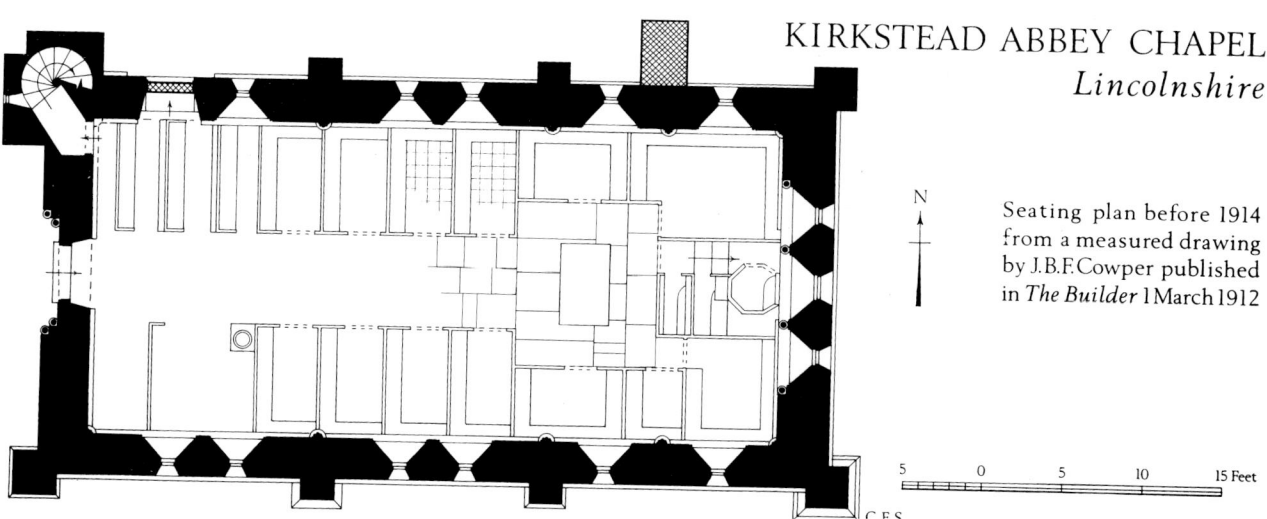

KIRKSTEAD ABBEY CHAPEL
Lincolnshire

Seating plan before 1914 from a measured drawing by J.B.F. Cowper published in *The Builder* 1 March 1912

hipped slate roof. The front wall is of three bays with two tiers of windows and giant pilasters with entablature and parapet. Above the central entrance is a defaced tablet formerly inscribed in large characters 'WESLEYAN'.

Sunday-school, 200 yards SE (SK 937985), now a cottage, is a small single-storey building of brick and pantile with three-bay front and tablet inscribed 'WESLEYAN | SUNDAY SCHOOL | FOR CHILDREN | OF ALL | DENOMINATIONS | 1827'.

LEADENHAM

(164) Former WESLEYAN (SK 950522). Brick with hipped slate roof, broad front with three sash windows in arched recesses and entrance right of centre with defaced tablet dated 1841. (Closed 1964)

LEGBOURNE

(165) PRIMITIVE METHODIST (TF 369844). Brown brick with yellow brick dressings, gabled front with five graduated lancets. Dated 1892.

Betjeman (1952) 116 (details incorrect).

LEGSBY

(166) Former WESLEYAN (TF 134852). Broad front of brown brick with yellow brick dressings and hipped roof. Three widely spaced round-arched windows and gabled porch. Built 1839.

LEVERTON

(167) WESLEYAN (TF 397472). Small wayside chapel, plain gabled front dated 1858.

LINCOLN

(168) HIGH STREET CHAPEL (SK 97357055). The chapel was built c.1726 for a Presbyterian congregation formed in the late 17th century, one of the principal supporters being Daniel Disney of Kirkstead (see (159)). The society was very weak by the late 18th century and after 1792 the chapel was used by Calvinistic Methodists. When in 1803 the latter attempted to gain absolute possession the trustees ejected them, reopening the place for worship of a Unitarian character which has continued apart from three periods of disuse between 1902 and 1923. The chapel has suffered from alternating periods of neglect and revival but the basic 18th-century structure remains.

The walls are of brick with later rendering above a stone plinth and the roof is hipped and slated. Prior to c.1900, when a pediment was added to the front wall, a porch built, and the front windows altered, the walls rendered and the roof covering changed, the W front had a central doorway with small flat hood between a pair of segmental-arched windows. The side walls each have two tall round-arched windows, the foremost pair, re-sited after the above alterations, may replace two tiers of windows. The rear fenestration has also been altered and probably had two tiers of windows at the ends of return galleries with a pair of pulpit windows between.

The interior (30ft by 36¼ft) has a flat plaster ceiling and two wooden columns of circular section with moulded capitals supporting the main N–S beam of the roof. The pulpit, formerly against the E wall, has been re-sited in the NE corner and a gallery on the W side, which probably continued along the N and S walls, has been removed. The original roof structure remains although modified in the 19th century; it formerly had two small valleys

Friends' meeting-house, Park Street, Lincoln. Interior in 1855. (170)

above the columns, and trusses with collars and clasped purlins. (Chapel repaired and realigned 1987)

Monuments: in chapel (1) William Bedford jnr., 1841; externally, on S wall (2) Maria wife of Rev. [George St?] Clair, 1852, oval tablet; in front path (3) Joseph Reynolds, 1813; (4) [ ], Mrs Ann Staden widow, 1745, and Ann wife of Andrew Kippis sen., 1757, broken headstone.

Evans (1897) 131–2. *Inquirer* (6 June 1987). *UHST* II (1919–22) 1–31.

(169) Former CONGREGATIONAL, Newland (SK 97357130). A chapel built in High Street in 1820 for a newly formed congregation (now URC) was superseded in 1840 by the first chapel in Newland. In 1876 a larger chapel was built alongside to the designs of Bellamy and Hardy of Lincoln and the former building converted for use as a 'commodious lecture-hall and classrooms, answering alike for school purposes, tea-meetings, &c.'. (*CYB* op. cit. below)

The chapel of 1840 is of brick and slate with a gabled front of yellow brick added *c.*1876. The earlier front, with three graduated lancets in the centre, and side bays with gabled porches and paired lancets above, was the work of James Fenton. The present chapel of brick with stone facing to the principal elevations is a large building in the Gothic style with a gabled S front from which the finer details of ornament have been removed. It has at the centre a large traceried window of five lights, and to the right a tower with broach spire above the entrance. The interior, of unusually elaborate composition, is divided by arcades of six bays with substantial iron columns which support the fronts of the side galleries and rise to pointed arches with a pointed barrel-vault over the centre space.

Barker (1860) 41–3. *CYB* (1877) 493–4 and frontis. Hill, Sir Francis, *Newland Congregational Church 1820–1974* (1979).

(170) FRIENDS, Park Street (SK 974714). This site appears to have been in Quaker occupation since the mid 17th century; a deed of gift dated January 1652/3 (Lincoln Record Office, Soc.Fr.A/14) refers to a stable with yard or garden adjoining in the Pott Market in Newland, St Martin's parish, and a later deed of 1669, possibly

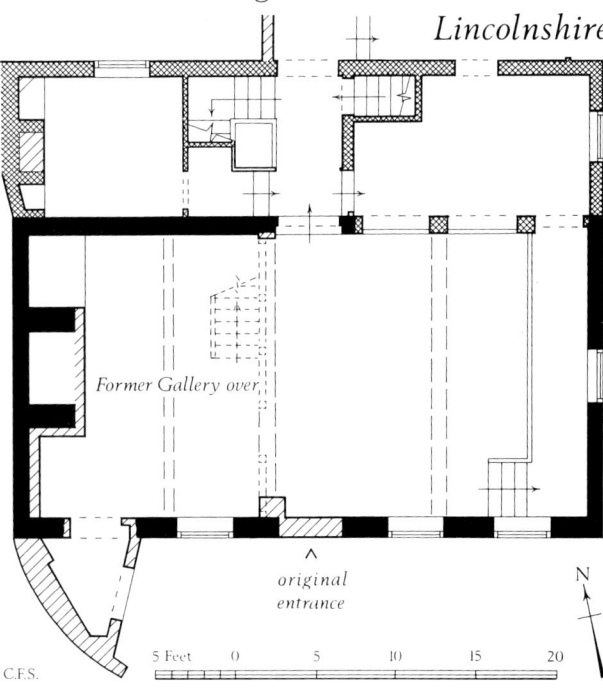

Friends' meeting-house, Park Street, Lincoln. Interior in 1855. (170)

relating to the enclosure of a burial-ground, refers to this land as enclosed by stone walls, 34 yards N–S, 26 yards at N end and 12 yards at S end. A meeting-house built on this plot in 1689–90 at a cost of £60 was belatedly registered at Quarter Sessions on 1 December 1706, located as in the first deed.

The meeting-house, which is substantially of 1689–90, has brick walls now rendered in pebble-dash and a gabled roof covered with pantiles but which, prior to the 19th century, appears to have had a covering of plain tiles. The principal alterations have been the addition in 1717 of lean-to accommodation on the N side incorporating a small cottage to the W, a considerable internal refitting c.1855, and the erection in 1910–11 of a second meeting-house or hall at the E end. Prior to the mid 19th-century alterations the S front had a central doorway between pairs of cross-framed windows and a pair of smaller windows above the W pair; the entrance was moved to the W end of this wall in 1855 and the window frames replaced by sashes. The gabled E and W walls have, in the former, one window now internal behind the stand and one above, and in the latter a small attic window in the gable.

The interior (34½ft by 17½ft) was, prior to 1855, divided by a screen with shutters having a gallery at the W end approached by a staircase in the smaller room; the lower rooms have now been conflated and the gallery, which has an attic room above, is incorporated into the caretaker's accommodation. The meeting-room has a dado of plain panelling and the stand has an open balustraded front. The N extension provides at the E end additional seating space raised above a cellar and having a plain arcade of two arches opening to the main room with a smaller arch at one end of the stand. Adjacent to the cottage is a staircase with open well, straight string and turned balusters which rises to a semi-attic above the meeting-room.

Pictures: two small pencil sketches of interior facing E and W, the former inscribed 'drawn in 1855 and repaired and altered immediately after'.

Butler (1999) 367–8. *Lincolnshire Life, County Annual* (1966) 59.

(171) WESLEYAN, Bailgate (SK 977721). Gabled front of stone in three bays divided by buttresses. 1879, by Bellamy and Hardy.

(172) PRIMITIVE METHODIST, High Street (SK 973706). Built in 1905 as 'Portland Place Memorial Chapel'; brick with rusticated stone dressings, flamboyant Classical detail and asymmetrical domed tower.

Leary, W., *Methodism in the City of Lincoln* (1969) 37–8.

LISSINGTON

(173) FREE METHODIST (TF 108833). Small chapel of painted brickwork with porch against gabled end; dated 1863.

LITTLE HALE

(174) PRIMITIVE METHODIST, Chapel Lane (TF 146416). Three-bay chapel of brick and pantile; built 1837, extended by one bay in c.1887.

LONG SUTTON

(175) GENERAL BAPTIST, West Street (TF 431228). A society formed about 1773 by Henry Poole, previously minister at Fleet, built a meeting-house in Lutton in 1776 (*see* (179)); Poole later adopted Universalist views and the church became Unitarian. A new society, which was initially a branch of the Fleet society, was formed about 1818 and the present chapel was built in 1841. The walls are of brick and the roof is pantiled. The wide gabled front of gault brick terminated by stepped buttresses has a central pointed-arched doorway between tall paired lancets and three graduated lancets above.

Taylor (1818) II: 197–8, 285–6. Whitley, W.T., *Minutes of the General Assembly of the General Baptist Churches in England* (1910) II: 5, 265. Wood (1847) 182, 196, 231.

LOUTH

(176) Former GENERAL BAPTIST, Cannon Street (TF 328875). The chapel (closed c.1928), now offices, 'Cannon Street House', on the S side of Northgate, was built in 1827 superseding a former Countess of Huntingdon's chapel bought by the New Connexion in 1800. A two-storeyed Sunday-school block in red brick was added against the E front in the late 19th century.

Barker (1860) 43. Taylor (1818) II: 410–13. Wood (1847) 205.

(177) WESLEYAN, Eastgate (TF 328875). The chapel built in 1835 has walls of brown brick with stone dressings. The front wall of six bays with entrances in slightly projecting penultimate bays and narrow end bays has two tiers of round-arched windows separated by a platband, with conjoined cills to the upper windows and panels with a swag ornament below. A parapet above the middle bays carries the denominational name and date in raised characters.

Wesleyan chapel, Eastgate, Louth. (177)

The tall interior has a continuous gallery with panelled front supported by cast-iron columns. Early 19th-century box-pews remain throughout, some of the rear seats being raised above the general floor level. In the late 19th century the pulpit was replaced by a rostrum which is supported by Corinthian columns and has a communion table immediately beneath. (Interior totally gutted and refitted 1977) *Monument*: in chapel, Rev. Thomas Galland MA, 1843.

Country Life (30 January 1975). Leary, W., and Robinson, D.N., *A History of Methodism in Louth* (1981).

LUSBY

(178) WESLEYAN (TF 339679). Small double-cube chapel of brick with a hipped slate roof, plain pilasters and narrow flat-arched windows. Tablet above entrance inscribed 'Rebuilt & Enlarged 1842' and recording the extent of the ground belonging to the trustees.

LUTTON

(179) Former GENERAL BAPTIST, Chapel Bridge (TF 427235). The chapel close to the boundary of Long Sutton was built in 1776 for a church formed in 1773 which became Unitarian (*see also* (175)). The chapel, closed *c*.1930, demolished *c*.1970, had brick walls and a hipped roof; the broad front was of three bays with two Venetian windows flanking a pedimented round-arched doorway with a lunette above.

Country Life LXXXVIII (December 1940) 164 Pl. 7 (wrongly captioned). Hague and Hague (1986) 44. Wood (1847) 182, 196.

MALTBY LE MARSH

(180) Former GENERAL BAPTIST (TF 463810). A Baptist congregation is believed to have met here from the late 17th century as part of the 'South Marsh' church. In 1773 fifteen members of the older society seceded to join the New Connexion and the present chapel was built for them in 1776. The church, never large, was so reduced by 1816 that the building was temporarily shared with a group of Johnsonian Baptists.

The chapel is a small brick building of domestic appearance with a hipped pantiled roof. The broad S front of three bays has two tiers of segmental-arched sash windows and a central entrance. The N wall has two upper and two lower windows and the end walls are blank; a vestry wing is attached to the east. The interior ($20\frac{1}{4}$ft by $33\frac{1}{4}$ft) was partly refitted in the late 19th century when the pulpit was removed from the N wall to the W end and a W gallery was probably removed leaving only the original E gallery intact. The pulpit is hexagonal with fielded-panelled sides; some contemporary panelling has been reused in the pews and as a dado around the walls. (Chapel closed *c*.1978 and converted to house)

Chandeliers: four, brass, with moulded stems surmounted by eagles, and fluted sconces. One with four upper and eight lower branches and gadrooned ornament on the stem; three smaller with five branches only. Also two sconces attached to pulpit. Late 18th-century. (In private possession)

Monuments: in chapel on N wall (1) William Robinson, 1882, recording a bequest of £200; (2) David Dent, 1787, 'He was many Years a respectable Member of this Christian-Society: and in the Year 1776 erected this Meeting-House at his own expence: and bequeathed it with the adjoining Burying-Ground for the use of the General-Baptists for ever'; (3) Rev. James Kiddall, 1862, 37 years pastor 'and preached the Gospel Free of Charge', signed 'Stark, Louth'. In burial-ground (4) John Walmsley, 1796, headstone.

Taylor (1818) I: 319; II: 196–7, 284–5, 398. Wood (1847) 182.

Former General Baptist chapel, Maltby le Marsh. (180)

(181) WESLEYAN (TF 467816). Yellow brick with blue brick dressings, built 1873. Former chapel of 1837 opposite, converted to house 'Hillcrest'.

MANBY

(182) WESLEYAN, Chapel Lane (TF 397872). Broad three-bay front, brick with hipped roof, round-arched openings and tablet dated 1847.

MAREHAM ON THE HILL

(183) Former WESLEYAN (TF 285680). The chapel dated 1853 replacing one of 1836 on another site has a gabled front with two windows and former entrance at one side. (Closed 1967 and converted to domestic use)

GENERAL BAPTIST CHAPEL, MALTBY LE MARSH   CFS·1972

LINCOLNSHIRE

Wesleyan chapel, Market Rasen. (184)

Wesleyan chapel, Messingham. (189)

MARKET RASEN

(184) WESLEYAN, Chapel Street (TF 107889). 'Centenary Chapel', built 1863, of red brick with dressings of stone at the front and of yellow brick at the sides. The front facing Union Street has three round-arched doorways in rusticated surrounds each with a window above and a pedimented tetrastyle portico with Ionic columns.

MARTIN

(185) Former WESLEYAN (TF 12305995). The chapel, dated 1860, on the N side of the main street has a three-bay gabled front of yellow brick with round-arched bays enclosing two tiers of windows.

(186) Former PRIMITIVE METHODIST, Mill Lane (TF 122600). The chapel, originally of a single storey, had a broad front of three bays facing the lane; above the blocked central doorway is a tablet dated 1837. The building was heightened in the mid 19th century and converted to a house after 1879.

(187) Former PRIMITIVE METHODIST (TF 123599). The chapel on the S side of the street opposite (185) was built in 1878–9 to supersede (186). It has a gabled brick front with a short central tower above the entrance.

MARTON

(188) WESLEYAN (SK 840821). Brick and pantile with three-bay gabled front. Dated 1814 on reset tablet in front wall; extended to front and altered *c*.1860.

MESSINGHAM   *Humberside*

(189) WESLEYAN, Church Lane (SE 892047). Brown brick with hipped pantiled roof; broad three-bay front with two tiers of windows, plain central doorway and oval tablet above dated 1821. Sunday-school of 1869 adjacent.

METHERINGHAM

(190) WESLEYAN, High Street (TF 069616). Rock-faced stone with ashlar dressings; paired entrances under segmental arch and window of five lancets above. Built 1907, by A.E. Lambert.

MINTING

(191) WESLEYAN (TF 183738). Broad three-bay front, much altered 1895; original tablet dated 1838 reset in S gable.

MORTON

(192) BAPTIST (TF 095240). Red brick with polychrome dressings; gabled front with round-arched windows. Foundation stone 1875.

MOULTON

(193) WESLEYAN (TF 307243). Brick with low-pitched hipped roof. Three-bay S end with segmental-arched openings and small circular window above entrance; one larger window in each side wall; two upper windows and circular light at N end. Opened 1830.

(194) PRIMITIVE METHODIST, Moulton Seas End (TF 322275). Brick with hipped roof, end entrance with tablet above doorway dated 1835.

Primitive Methodist chapel, Moulton Seas End. (194)

NETTLETON

(195) WESLEYAN (TA 111002). The society commenced in 1795 with meetings in private houses. The chapel, first erected in 1800 but rebuilt in 1848, is a low building of brick with later rendering, the roof is pantiled. The chapel (30¼ft by 18¼ft externally) may have had a three-bay front but it has been much altered, refenestrated, and a Sunday-school added in 1912. The roof is supported by king-post trusses.

Lester (1890) 113–14.

NEW LEAKE

(196) WESLEYAN, Spilsby Road (TF 402573). The chapel of brown brick and slate with a segmentally arched end entrance and two gallery windows over with tablet between, is dated 1838. A Sunday-school at the rear is dated 1848. *Fontlet*: pottery, Winchester Cathedral type.

NORMANBY BY SPITAL

(197) Former WESLEYAN, Normanby (TF 001882). Rendered walls and hipped pantiled roof; front and sides divided into three bays by plain pilaster buttresses; traces of shield-shaped tablet above central entrance. Built 1813, closed 1862, much altered.

(198) Former FREE METHODIST, Normanby (TF 002882). Gabled front between porches; dentil brick enrichment above all windows. Built 1864.

NORTH KYME

(199) WESLEYAN (TF 153523). Gabled W front with polychrome decoration and tall arched windows. Dated 1874. A cottage with a broad rendered front of three bays with a hipped roof on the opposite side of the road may be the previous chapel of 1848.

NORTH SCARLE

(200) Former WESLEYAN (SK 849669). The chapel, built 1799–1800, was registered 13 August 1800 as a 'new erected building the property of William Storr'; it was superseded by a new chapel near by in *c.*1900 and has since served minor secular purposes. The walls are of brick and the roof is pantiled. The broad front wall has two round-arched doorways with fanlights, a wide sash window between with segmental-arched head and small gallery windows above the entrances. The gabled end walls with block-bonded joints to the better quality brickwork of the front wall have each one small window to the lower stage. Two larger upper windows in the back wall flank the site of the pulpit.

The interior (22¾ft by 30¼ft) has a plaster ceiling with three tie-beams. The original gallery remains around three sides with a panelled front supported by chamfered posts and approached by staircases in the front corners, one of which has been removed. Traces of former seating remain in the stepped gallery floor.

Dolbey (1964) 98.

(201) Former UNITED METHODIST (SK 849671). Red brick with hipped roof, pointed-arched windows and later porch. Dated 1874.

NORTH THORESBY

(202) WESLEYAN, Station Road (TF 292984). Red brick and slate, with tall narrow segmental-arched windows; gabled front with group of three windows above later porch. Built 1846 replacing a chapel of 1821.

Lester (1890) 88–90.

OSGODBY

(203) Former PRIMITIVE METHODIST (TF 077926). Brick and pantile. Low gabled front, heads of two windows survive above inserted garage door; defaced tablet. Built 1842.

OWSTON FERRY   *Humberside*

(204) WESLEYAN, High Street (SE 811002). 'Centenary Chapel' dated 1837, of brick and pantile, has a gabled front of three bays with terminal pilasters formerly rising to panelled tops: these, with the gable coping, have been removed. Two tiers of round-arched windows with a simple Venetian window above the central entrance.

Lindley (1969) Pl. 61.

(205) Former PRIMITIVE METHODIST, High Street (SE 811001). Brick with hipped slate roof; built 1850 replacing a chapel of 1838, enlarged to front 1870. Three-bay front with two tiers of windows, much altered on conversion to house.

PARTNEY

(206) WESLEYAN, Maddison Lane (TF 411684). Brick and pantile, former entrance in gabled W wall; later porch and vestry wing project to south. Opened 1835. (Derelict 1974)

PINCHBECK

(207) INDEPENDENT, Money Bridge (TF 215256). A congregation was gathered in 1785 by a student from Trevecca College and a church formed in the following year. The first chapel on this site was built in 1787, enlarged in 1817, and a school-room added in 1834. The present chapel built in 1840 is a large building of brick with a hipped slate roof and two tiers of sash windows with flat-arched heads and keystones. The W front of three bays has a round-arched doorway with fanlight and tablet above with the dates of erection and alteration. The side walls, also of three bays,

Former Wesleyan chapel, North Scarle.   (200)

are divided by broad pilasters; in the rear wall is a large lunette window. The school-room wing of 1834, a low building of brick and pantile, projects at one side. The interior has a rear gallery only, the lower seating was replaced in the late 19th century. *Monuments*: externally against S wall (1) Thomas Lawrence, 1846, and Olive his wife, 1836; (2) John Bell, 1841.

Barker (1860) 45–6.

POINTON AND SEMPRINGHAM

(208) WESLEYAN, Pointon (TF 116319). Brick with hipped pantiled roof; broad three-bay front with segmental-arched openings. Dated 1842.

POTTERHANWORTH

(209) Former WESLEYAN (TF 058662). Gault brick with hipped pantile roof; broad three-bay front with round-arched openings; slightly enlarged to the left. Built 1831.

(210) Former PRIMITIVE METHODIST (TF 058662). Chapel immediately E of (209) built 1830, of brick and pantile with altered front and tablet 'Enlarged 1872'.

RAITHBY

(211) METHODIST (TF 374670). The chapel occupies the upper floor of an outbuilding in one corner of the stable yard of Raithby Hall. The Hall and chapel were built in 1779 by Robert Carr Brackenbury, an itinerant Methodist preacher and wealthy supporter and friend of John Wesley. Wesley visited Raithby on 5 July 1779.

The chapel has brick walls and a hipped slate roof. The SE side facing the gardens of the Hall is of domestic appearance, of three bays with two tiers of windows separated by a brick platband, a round-arched doorway in the centre opens to a stable with six stalls below the chapel and there is a similarly arched window above between two windows with flat-arched heads, all with hung sashes. The upper windows on the opposite side are similar to the last and in the NE wall are two upper windows flanking the pulpit.

The SW front to the stable yard was altered in the early 19th century when a plain forebuilding was erected to enclose the formerly open outside staircase. The front now has a wide round-arched entrance closed by common coach-house doors, and a triple sash window above under a high relieving arch; the extended side walls are decorated with ball finials. The formerly exposed frontage, now internal, has a double staircase with moulded timber handrails against the later walls from which turned wood balusters have all been removed. The principal entrance at the head of the staircase has a moulded surround with a pediment and small fluted brackets at the sides, fielded-panelled reveals, and a pair of fielded-panelled doors.

The interior (41ft by 18ft) has a coved plaster ceiling with a moulded cornice and a panelled dado around the walls. The pulpit opposite the entrance has been replaced by a rostrum and communion enclosure with balustraded fronts, possibly reusing material from the staircase; the original octagonal canopy and fielded-panelled back-board remain; the base of the octagonal stem of the former pulpit is visible in the floor below the rostrum.

The seating was largely renewed or reconstructed in the 19th century and two pews flanking the pulpit were removed and their materials reused in box-pews at the rear of the chapel. *Collecting Shovels*: pair, overall length 38in.

Dolbey (1964) 76–7. *WHSP* XX (1935–6) 170–3.

SALTFLEETBY ST PETER

(212) WESLEYAN (TF 425890). Chapel on N side of Mar Dyke, red brick and slate with three-bay front having round-arched windows with rusticated stone voussoirs; opened 1848. (Demolished 1974)

SCAMBLESBY

(213) WESLEYAN (TF 280784). Brick and slate with pointed-arched windows in yellow brick surrounds. Tablet in front wall dated 1835. Small three-bay rear wing. Later gabled wing added to NE 1868.

SCOTHERN

(214) WESLEYAN (TF 035775). Gault brick with hipped roof. Broad three-bay front with round-arched windows and former central doorway. Dated 1858.

SCOTTER

(215) Former WESLEYAN (SE 886010). The chapel of brick and pantile, built 1815, has a broad front of three bays with inserted shop front, two tiers of windows and an oval date tablet in the SE end. The gabled end walls have stone copings and kneelers. Two windows in the rear wall flank the site of the pulpit.

The interior has an inserted floor but retains the original gallery structure around three sides with splayed corners and panelled front.

(216) Former PRIMITIVE METHODIST, Hobb Lane (SE 885009). Gault brick with hipped slate roof; built 1849, closed 1966 and much altered on conversion to shop. An earlier chapel of 1819 in Long Street, sold to the Methodist New Connexion in 1849, has been demolished.

SIBSEY

(217) PRIMITIVE METHODIST, Northlands (TF 347533). Brick with hipped slate roof; three-bay front with later porch, two gallery windows and altered tablet dated 1837.

PRIMITIVE METHODIST CHAPEL, NORTHLANDS   CFS 1974

Exterior from stable yard.

Upper doorway to chapel.

Methodist chapel, Raithby.

LINCOLNSHIRE

SKEGNESS

(218) BAPTIST, Beresford Avenue (TF 567631). The congregation first occupied a prefabricated iron chapel, 'St Paul's', formerly owned by the Free Church of England, now the church hall. An ambitious but unexecuted design for a new chapel by George Baines was eventually supplanted in 1911 by the present building by John Wills and Sons. This is of red brick and stone with a corner tower and gabled end with a window of five lights with perpendicular tracery.

B.Hbk (1895) 304; (1899) 382; (1902) 366; (1911) 515. *Baptist Times* (2 October 1986).

(219) WESLEYAN, Algitha Road (TF 567633). Red pressed brick with stone dressings; gabled front with four-light traceried window over entrance and long flanking wings. 1881–2, by Charles Bell.

SKIDBROOKE WITH SALTFLEET HAVEN

(220) WESLEYAN, Saltfleet (TF 454938). Rendered brick with hipped pantiled roof; broad front with three round-arched windows with intersecting glazing bars and later porch. Opened 1815, enlarged 1867.

SKILLINGTON

(221) WESLEYAN (SK 898257). Stone with hipped slate roof; broad three-bay front with round-arched windows and boldly carved inscription with date 1847 above central entrance. (For a chapel of similar design and date *see Nonconformist Chapels and Meeting-houses in Central England* (1986) 132, monument (78), Stonesby, Leics.)

SLEAFORD

(222) CONGREGATIONAL, Southgate (TF 068458). The chapel was built in 1867–8 to replace a meeting-house of 1776 which stood in Hen Lane 'at the terminus of a dirty lane … only approachable by a plank of wood over a stream of water' (Barker (1860) 49). Plain Gothic chapel of stone and slate by W.G. Habershon and Pite; gabled front with twin porches, nave and aisles divided by arcades with cast-iron columns supporting a wooden clerestory and open crown-post roof. (URC)

Barker (1860) 47–9. *CYB* (1867) 363.

SNITTERBY

(223) WESLEYAN, Chapel Lane (SK 985947). Brick with hipped roof, minimal three-bay front with segmental-arched openings. Built 1840.

SOUTH COCKERINGTON

(224) FREE METHODIST, Chapel Lane (TF 380891). Low red brick walls and hipped roof; two sash windows with tablet between dated 1855; end entrance.

SOUTH FERRIBY   *Humberside*

(225) WESLEYAN, Farishes Lane (SE 987211). Broad three-bay front of brick with round-arched windows and tablet dated 1839 above later porch.

SOUTH KELSEY

(226) Former WESLEYAN, Caistor Road (TF 043982). The chapel on the S side of the road, now converted to a house 'The Old Chapel', dates from the early 19th century. The walls are of brick covered with later rendering and the roof is pantiled and hipped at the W end. The N front is of three principal bays with two tiers of windows and later porch. There is one round-arched window in the W wall. The interior has been subdivided except the W bay, which remains open to its original height.

(227) WESLEYAN, Brigg Road (TF 043985). Red brick with gabled ends; pointed-arched windows with intersecting glazing bars. Built 1879.

(228) Former FREE METHODIST (TF 043982). Former chapel opposite (226), red brick with gabled front, *c*.1870–80.

SOUTH KILLINGHOLME   *Humberside*

(229) GENERAL BAPTIST (TA 158156). A church in existence by 1686 included members from a wide area who held meetings in several villages including Killingholme. The present site was given to the church in 1747 under the will of Thomas Wakeham, pastor *c*.1720–47, and the first meeting-house was then erected; an increase in support led to its rebuilding in 1792. Calvinistic doctrines which began to penetrate the society from that date culminated in the formation in 1796 of a separate Particular Baptist

Congregational chapel (URC), Sleaford.   (222)

General Baptist chapel, South Killingholme.   (229)

church, of which Abraham Greenwood became the pastor and which had the use of the chapel on Sunday mornings. This separation probably ceased after Greenwood's death.

The chapel opened 10 November 1792 is a simple rectangular building of brickwork in irregular bond with a pantiled roof having tumbled gables at the E and W ends. The E end has a central segmental-arched doorway with the date of erection on a small tablet above. The N and S walls have each two windows with semicircular-arched heads of red brick and renewed frames. At the W end is a lower wing probably intended as the minister's house but now serving as a vestry; this is of similar materials to the chapel and has two former attic windows, now blocked, in the W gable and a chimney-stack above.

The interior ($33\tfrac{3}{4}$ft by $21\tfrac{1}{2}$ft), which has a boarded ceiling, was refitted in the late 19th century. Pews and the rostrum pulpit with baptistery in front are of this period; there is no gallery. Two doors, each with four fielded panels, open to the vestry.

Fittings – *Collecting Shovels*: two, one with rectangular box and long handle, 20in. overall. *Monuments*: in chapel (1) Rev. George Crooks, 1878, 35 years minister; in burial-ground (2) John Hannath, 1799, pastor; (3) Martha wife of Thomas Smith, 1792; (4) Susannah wife of Joseph Fowler, 1793; (5) Rev. Abraham Greenwood, 1827, 'one of the founders of the Baptist Missionary Society at Kettering, 2nd October 1792', 55 years a minister, 33 in this place (*see also* monument at Barrow upon Humber (19)).

BQ II (1924–5) 84–9. Taylor (1818) II: 198–201, 291–4, 401. Wood (1847) 183.

SOUTH WILLINGHAM

(230) Former WESLEYAN (TF 194834). Brick with hipped slate roof; originally three-bay front with round-arched windows, dated 1834; extended one bay with gabled end in the late 19th century.

SPALDING

(231) GENERAL BAPTIST, Chapel Lane (TF 246227). A church that appears to have originated in the mid 17th century, by 1688 included members from Spalding, Bourne and Haconby. The first meeting-house on the present site, built 1689–91, was destroyed in the town fire of 1715. The new chapel of that date is said by Taylor to have been inelegant, 'the interior had an unfinished appearance: the pulpit was clumsy; the pews, few; and the floor, brick'; this was replaced in 1811 by a larger building and superseded in 1828 by the present chapel, which was further enlarged in 1843 and 1855.

The walls are of dark brickwork and the roof is hipped and slated. The end wall facing Chapel Lane, now rendered, has a wide round-arched doorway altered to a window, and a Venetian window above between two plain sash windows. The side walls of four bays with two tiers of windows have been extended by two bays to the rear, the chapel being now entered at the back from Swan Street. The adjacent 'Baptist School' is dated 1865.

Monuments: reset against side wall of school, five headstones, (1) Thomas Mason[?], 1799, with winged cherub's head between urns; (2) Elizabeth widow of Rev. William Burgess, late of Fleet, 1820; (3) Isabella Cannon, 1829; (4) William C[   ], early 19th-century; (5) Rebecca wife of John Armstrong, 1816.

Taylor (1818) I: 106, 216–18, 317–19; II: 99, 114–21, 413–16.

Watkinson, A.J., *A Short History of the Spalding Baptist Church, 1646–1946* (1946). Wood (1847) 192.

(232) CONGREGATIONAL, Pinchbeck Road (TF 248229). The chapel was built in 1821 for a new congregation gathered by a student from Hoxton Academy following an unsuccessful attempt to begin a Particular Baptist interest; it was re-fronted in 1910. The front wall is of brick of three bays with two tiers of round-arched windows, an original tablet 'INDEPENDENT CHAPEL 1821' is reset above the central entrance, and there is a long, uninterrupted balustrade on the wall top. Sunday-school alongside of 1856, three bays with pilasters and pediment. (URC)

Barker (1860) 49–53.

(233) FRIENDS, Double Street (TF 250228). The meeting-house stands on part of the site of a burial-ground acquired in 1698 when existing buildings were converted for use as a meeting-house. The present building of 1805 is of brick with a hipped roof, it was re-fronted and a slate roof replaced by tiles in 1965. The SE front wall, which follows the original design, has a central pedimented doorway between two tiers of segmental-arched windows and the original tablet above with the date 1805 in a beaded oval frame and another 'Restored 1965'. The rear end wall facing the street has a single wide lunette and in each side wall is a segmental-arched sash window. The interior is divided into two principal rooms separated by shutters.

Fittings – include early 19th-century open-backed benches and a table with turned legs of the early 18th century.

Butler (1999) 368–9.

Friends' meeting-house, Spalding. (233)

(234) PRIMITIVE METHODIST, Little London (TF 237211). Rendered brick, three-bay gabled front with two tiers of windows and large oval tablet dated 1842. School to S built 1866.

SPILSBY

(235) Former CONGREGATIONAL, Hundleby Road (TF 395662). The chapel of white brick with a gabled front having rusticated brick quoins and a tall central arch was built in 1865–6 to a design by Kennedy and Daglish of Glasgow. By 1889 it had been sold for use as a Masonic hall; it is now in commercial use.

CYB (1866) 307.

Wesleyan chapel and manses, Spilsby. (236)

(236) WESLEYAN (TF 403661). The chapel of 1878 by Charles Bell forms the centre of a composition including a pair of identical detached manses to right and left. The gabled front of gault brick is divided into three bays by stepped buttresses and has a wide six-light window with cusped circular tracery above the entrance.

STAMFORD

(237) Former GENERAL BAPTIST, No. 13 Bath Row (TF 02700695). Meetings commenced in 1828; a church of six members was formed in the following year and on 20 September 1829 a public baptism in the River Welland attracted considerable interest. The chapel built in 1835 was closed in 1846 on the failure of the cause and was converted to domestic use. The walls are of rubble and the roof is hipped and covered with stone slates. The end wall facing the street retains evidence of a central doorway between the present wide segmental-arched windows; two gallery windows above have been lengthened. Some original segmental-arched windows remain in the E wall but the fenestration has been greatly altered.

RCHM *The Town of Stamford* (1977) 30, monument (38). Wood (1847) 228, 235–6.

(238) STRICT BAPTIST, North Street (TF 030073). The chapel built 1834 by John George de Merveilleux remained private property until 1862; J.C. Philpot, editor of the *Gospel Standard* was pastor 1841–64. The chapel was largely rebuilt in 1901 although some portions of the earlier rubble walling remain.

Chambers IV (1963) 116–17. Paul III (1958) 132–80. RCHM *The Town of Stamford* (1977) 30, monument (39).

(239) CONGREGATIONAL, Starr Lane (TF 032073). Presbyterian meetings commenced in the late 17th century, Joseph Cawthorn, ejected rector of St George's Church, being licensed here in 1672 when two private houses were registered as meeting-places, and Edward Brown and John Richardson, also ejected from livings in Stamford, both continued to preach in the vicinity. A meeting-house in St Paul's Street, destroyed by rioters in 1714, was superseded in 1720 by the first building on the present site, which had been acquired in 1719. In March 1774 Independents registered a chapel which they had built in All Saints' parish, possibly for a separate congregation. In 1817 the Presbyterian society, which had suffered from a long period of decline, was re-formed as a Congregational church (now URC) and the meeting-house was rebuilt two years later.

The chapel has walls of red brick with a stone plinth and a hipped slate roof. The S end has a wide segmental-arched entrance to a formerly open lobby, with the date 'MDCCCXIX' and three round-arched windows above. The W wall facing the street is of four bays with round-arched windows at gallery level; similarly arched windows below, but in two orders of brickwork, were originally blind, corresponding to four blind lunettes in the opposite wall. A tall gallery around three sides with a panelled front rounded to the S is supported by eight cast-iron columns with Doric capitals. Much of the original seating remains, principally box-pews, with some low benches for children in the SE and SW corners of the gallery.

A stone gateway S of the chapel with four-centred arched opening, formerly part of the Corn Market arcade, was rebuilt here in 1862 and is inscribed on the E side as a memorial to the 1662 ejection.

Barker (1860) 17–18, 54–5. RCHM *The Town of Stamford* (1977) 30, monument (36).

(240) WESLEYAN, Barn Hill (TF 028072). Two preaching-houses were registered by Methodists in 1800. The first chapel on Barn Hill, which remains behind its late 19th-century successor, was registered in December 1803 and built at the cost of Miss Frances Treen, Robert Carr Brackenbury being an original trustee. A gallery was added in 1838 and the building extended to the front. It has rubble walls with an ashlar front and slate roof. The SW front of 1863 incorporates architectural elements from the earlier frontage including two round-arched windows with keystones and a Venetian window above the later entrance; three stone panels also reset are carved with emblems representing Faith, Hope and Charity. The present chapel, partly concealing the former, was built in 1886 by J.T. Ward.

Love-feast Cups: three from a set of four tall two-handled glass cups engraved 'Trinity Methodist Chapel, Stamford. Love Feast', 19th-century.

RCHM *The Town of Stamford* (1977) 30, monument (37).

Former Wesleyan chapel, Barn Hill, Stamford. (240)

STOW

(241) WESLEYAN (SK 882819). Brick with pantiled roof; side walls originally of two bays, enlarged to front and tablet dated 1824 reset above round-arched entrance.

STURTON BY STOW

(242) Former FRIENDS, High Street (SK 889808). The meeting-house on the S side of the street was built in 1861 but after 1895 it passed to Methodist use; it has subsequently been greatly altered on conversion to a bungalow but may be distinguished by the superior quality of its brickwork. The original entrance in the gabled end wall has been blocked; above it is a tablet formerly inscribed 'Friends Meeting House 1861' over which is a small lozenge with this date and the initials I B for Joseph Burtt who gave the site.

Burial-ground: 200 yards E, rectangular plot containing several large trees and seventeen uniform headstones with dates from the 1860s.

Butler (1999) 369.

(243) Former WESLEYAN, Till Bridge Lane (SK 890804). Brick with gabled end to road; built 1805.

(244) Former PRIMITIVE METHODIST, Fleets Lane (SK 892806). Small brick chapel with gabled front and traces of two round-arched windows above pair of inserted garage doors. Dated 1854.

SUTTERTON

(245) Former GENERAL BAPTIST (TF 286361). A house which had recently been registered by Methodists was in 1802 used for General Baptist preaching. A meeting-house was built and opened 29 September 1803 and in 1808 the society, formerly united with Gosberton, became autonomous. The present chapel was built in 1825 and enlarged, possibly by the addition of a gallery, in 1839. The walls are of brick and the roof is hipped and slated. The E front of three bays has a central round-arched doorway with open pediment between two round-arched windows and three plain sash windows above; the side walls each have two windows at each level; in the back wall are two windows flanking the pulpit with a lean-to vestry below. A gallery around three sides has a fielded-panelled front and staircases in the front corners. The tall pulpit of *c*.1825 has a bowed front supported by a pair of columns. The lower seating was renewed in the late 19th century.

The 'General Baptist Sunday School', 100 yards S, is dated 1882. (Chapel closed *c*.1972 and since converted to house with loss of fittings and some monuments in burial-ground)

Monuments: in burial-ground to N include (1) Rev. John Bissill, 1844, 'founder of the General Baptist Cause in this Village and Minister Thirty-Five years', and Nancy his widow, 1849, daughter of the Rev. Dan Taylor, slate table-tomb with panelled sides; (2) Elizabeth widow of the Rev. W. Bampton, 'the first General Baptist Missionary to India', 1871, Edward Bissill, 1857, and Ann his widow, 1862, slate panels from table-tomb; (3) George Everson, 1810, headstone with cherub's head.

New Baptist Magazine I (1825) 435. Taylor (1818) II: 403–6. Wood (1847) 207.

Former General Baptist chapel, Sutterton. (245)

(246) Former WESLEYAN, Spalding Road (TF 281356). The chapel built 1845 has a low brick front of three bays with pilasters and a pediment with dentil cornices.

LINCOLNSHIRE

SUTTON ON SEA

(247) WESLEYAN, Alford Road (TF 520818). Red brick with stone dressings; octagonal corner turret with dwarf spire. Contemporary iron railings. Built 1910 by John Wills and Son.

SUTTON ST JAMES

(248) GENERAL BAPTIST (TF 395183). The chapel opened 1834 replaces one built 1814 for a society formed in 1813 as a branch of Fleet and later of Tydd St Giles, Cambs. Brick and slate with grossly altered rendered front; small dated tablet above arched doorway with fanlight.

Taylor (1818) II: 399, 407. Wood (1847) 192.

(249) WESLEYAN (TF 397184). The chapel of red brick with a gault brick front is dated 1841. The front is of three bays with pilasters and a pediment.

SWABY

(250) Former WESLEYAN, Pinfold Land (TF 379773). Built 1839. Brick with hipped roof; end entrance replaced by wide opening; one round-arched window in each side wall. *Inscriptions*: on loose tablets (1) 'Wesleyan Chapel 1839'; (2) 'Wesleyan Chapel A.D. 1866'; (3) 'Free Methodist chapel 1869'.

(251) Former WESLEYAN SUNDAY-SCHOOL (TF 378773). The Wesleyan chapel of 1866, successor to (250), has been demolished. The Sunday-school at the rear remains, converted to a village hall.

SWINESHEAD

(252) WESLEYAN, High Street (TF 236405). The chapel, built 1845, has brick walls and a pantiled roof hipped to the rear. The front is gabled, of three bays with round arches enclosing two sash windows with intersecting glazing bars and a central porch of the late 19th century. Converted to Sunday-school when a larger chapel was built alongside in 1908 but restored to use after the latter was demolished c.1986.

TATTERSHALL

(253) WESLEYAN, Lodge Road (TF 211579). Red brick with gabled front; narrower end bay with four-centred arched doorway under square label and two-light traceried window above. Opened 1849.

TEALBY

(254) WESLEYAN (TF 156906). Rubble with brick quoins and hipped pantiled roof with dentil brick eaves cornice; two pointed-arched doorways in front with segmental-arched windows above and tablet dated 1819. One pointed-arched window in each side wall and two at rear. (Conversion to house proposed 1994)

(255) Former PRIMITIVE METHODIST (TF 15659070). Now a cottage, 'Durdans'; in the front wall is the outline of a large pointed-arched window and a similarly arched doorway to the left. Tablet inscribed 'PRIMITIVE METHODIST CHAPEL 1846' now reset in garden path.

(256) Former CHAPEL (TF 15629077). Opposite (255), brick with lunette-shaped recess in gable; converted to cottages. Mid 19th-century.

Wesleyan chapel, Tealby. (254)

(257) Former FREE METHODIST (TF 15559067). Red brick with yellow brick dressings; gable end to road with tablet dated 1867. Converted to house c.1900.

THEDDLETHORPE ST HELEN

(258) PRIMITIVE METHODIST (TF 478887). Red brick with hipped slate roof; three-bay front irregularly divided by pilasters. Dated 1852. Sunday-school adjacent 1888.

THIMBLEBY

(259) Former PRIMITIVE METHODIST (TF 235700). Broad three-bay brick front formerly dated 1857. Central entrance blocked.

THORNTON CURTIS   *Humberside*

(260) Former WESLEYAN (TA 088178). Red brick with minimal stone dressings; three lancets in gabled front with defaced quatrefoil tablet above dated 1850.

THORPE ON THE HILL

(261) Former WESLEYAN, Lincoln Lane (SK 908656). Brick with hipped pantiled roof and broad three-bay front with altered entrance. Built 1842, superseded by present chapel 1909.

TIMBERLAND

(262) WESLEYAN (TF 119585). Small but elaborately finished chapel of 1878; red brick with blue and yellow brick dressings. Gabled front of three bays with Venetian-tracery windows.

TOYNTON ALL SAINTS

(263) WESLEYAN (TF 392639). Brown brick with yellow brick dressings, three-bay front with later porch. Built 1860, extended 1939 reusing two original windows from end wall. Match-boarded interior.

TOYNTON ST PETER

(264) WESLEYAN (TF 402632). Brown brick with hipped pantiled roof; broad front originally with two doorways and larger window between now converted to central doorway. Gallery around three sides with original box-pews; cast-iron columns, lower seating and rostrum all later. Opened 1811.

UPTON

(265) WESLEYAN, High Street (SK 869869). Rendered brick walls and pantiled roof; two sash windows in each side wall. Opened 1822. Original entrance in gabled end covered by lower extension of c.1840.

WADDINGHAM

(266) PRIMITIVE METHODIST, Silver Street (SK 982961). The chapel built in 1815 was extended to the front by one bay in 1859. Brick with three-bay front, gabled parapet and round-arched windows.

WAINFLEET ALL SAINTS

(267) Former FRIENDS, High Street (TF 498590). The meeting-house built in 1775 at a cost of £70 to replace one in Wainfleet St Mary (*see* (269)) stands behind Nos 45–6 High Street. It was sold in 1949 having long fallen out of use and was converted to a garage. The building has brick walls and a pantiled roof. The E front, entirely altered since 1955, had a central doorway in a small wooden porch between two hung-sash windows. The W wall is blank. The N and S walls are gabled with brick tumbling and two-course brick platbands at the base of the gables. At the N end is an external chimney-breast and in the S gable a single segmental-arched window. The interior (30¼ft by 18½ft) is ceiled at collar level and has a blocked fireplace at the N end. No evidence remains of the former disposition of the fittings.

Butler (1999) 370–1.

(268) PRIMITIVE METHODIST, Wainfleet Bank (TF 470593). Red brick with hipped pantiled roof; round-arched doorway with fanlight and large tablet above with date 1838 and text 'Come in thou blessed of the Lord wherefore standest thou without'. Two segmental-arched windows in longer side walls.

Primitive Methodist chapel, Wainfleet Bank. (268)

WAINFLEET ST MARY

(269) FRIENDS' BURIAL-GROUND, Haven Bank (TF 479591). North of early 19th-century 'Quaker Cottage', bounded N by road, E by track and drain, hedges W and S removed; in use by 1718, when it is mentioned in the will of John Baldock who left two rooms in his house and adjoining premises to be converted to a meeting-house for Quakers. No monuments.

Lincoln Record Office: Soc.Fr.A/25.

WALCOT NEAR BILLINGHAY

(270) Former WESLEYAN, The Smoot, Walcot (TF 130565). The former chapel, 100 yards W of its successor, has brick walls and a hipped roof. It has been much altered on conversion to a pair of cottages but the original tablet dated 1820 remains in the front wall.

(271) Former WESLEYAN, Walcot (TF 131565). Gault brick with three-bay gabled front, round-arched openings and lunette with border inscription dated 1869.

WELBOURN

(272) WESLEYAN, High Street (SK 967543). Brown brick with hipped roof, broad front of three bays divided by recessed panels with serrated brick eaves cornices, central doorway with tablet above dated 1839 flanked by two tiers of segmental-arched windows.

WELBY

(273) Former WESLEYAN (SK 974384). Coursed rubble and slate; broad three-bay front with round-arched windows, gabled porch, and tablet dated 1866.

WELLINGORE

(274) Former WESLEYAN, High Street (SK 984566). Red and yellow brick, gabled front with tall centre bay dated 1887 'Jubilee'.

WELTON

(275) WESLEYAN (TF 010798). Coursed rubble with hipped roof, broad three-bay front with gabled porch. Opened 1815 but refenestrated in late 19th century.

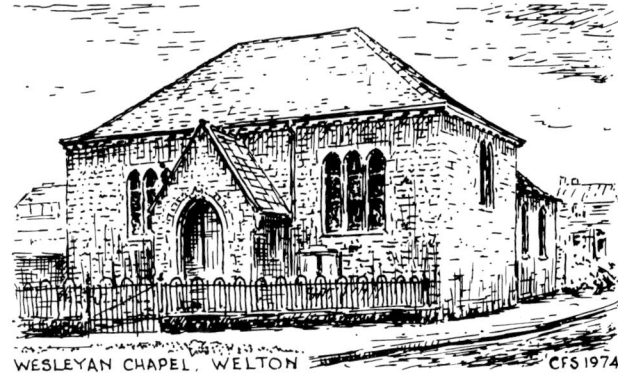

WESLEYAN CHAPEL, WELTON   CFS 1974

WEST BUTTERWICK *Humberside*

(276) WESLEYAN, North Street (SE 835059). Rendered brick with hipped pantiled roof, round-arched end entrance and three windows in each side wall. Built 1871 on site of 1836 chapel.

LINCOLNSHIRE

(277) Former PRIMITIVE METHODIST (SE 833058). Brick with hipped pantile roof, two round-arched windows in N wall. Built 1846.

WHAPLODE

(278) WESLEYAN, Dowsdale Bar (TF 285100). Small chapel with gabled porch, built 1897 replacing a chapel of 1841.

(279) Former WESLEYAN, Saracen's Head (TF 340271). The chapel of brown brick with a hipped slate roof, was built in 1825 and later doubled in width. The front wall had a single doorway with round-arched window above, a second doorway and window were added to the left in the enlargement and later a single central entrance was substituted; there is one round-arched window in each end wall and two windows in the rebuilt back wall. *Inscriptions*: on defaced tablet below original front window, 'Methodist CHAPEL 1825'; on brick below later front window 'J. SLATOR'.

Dolbey (1964) 174–5.

(280) Former WESLEYAN REFORM, Saracen's Head (TF 339272). Brick with hipped slate roof, windows altered, formerly with round-arched heads. *Inscription*: on semicircular tablet above entrance '1866 WESLEYAN [altered to UNITED] REFORM CHAPEL'.

(281) WESLEYAN, Whaplode (TF 328243). Brown brick with hipped slate roof, built 1838; formerly with two tiers of windows but entirely refenestrated with pointed-arched windows and gabled porch added.

(282) WESLEYAN, Whaplode Drove (TF 315139). Square chapel of brown brick with a pyramidal slate roof, extended and wide pointed-arched windows inserted centrally in S front and W side (cf. (161)). Mid 19th-century (dates of 1844 and 1862 are claimed), extended to E 1902.

WILDMORE

(283) WESLEYAN, New York (TF 246551). Red brick with yellow brick dressings; gabled front with tall centre bay and round-arched windows. Opened 1872.

WILLOUGHTON

(284) PRIMITIVE METHODIST (SK 931931). Gault brick front with red brick dressings, two tiers of round-arched windows. Built 1866 replacing a chapel of 1837.

WOODHALL SPA

(285) PRESBYTERIAN, Mill Lane (TF 178624). The chapel was built in 1821 as the successor to Kirkstead Abbey Chapel (*see* (159))

Presbyterian chapel (Unitarian), Woodhall Spa. (285)

following the recovery in 1812 of the former endowment, for a Unitarian Presbyterian congregation. The chapel is a low building of brown brick with a slate roof and plain doorway in the E end with date tablet in the pedimented gable; there are two segmental-arched windows in each side wall and a former cottage of two storeys at the W end. The interior has plain open-backed benches. *Monuments*: in chapel (1) Richard Wright, 1836, Unitarian Missionary, minister 1827–36; (2) Rev. Griffith Roberts, 1857, minister 1837–57; (3) Robert Holden, 1909, minister 51 years.

Evans (1897) 123–4. *Inquirer* (15 November 1980, 10 July 1982). *UHST* VII (1939–42) 74–5.

WORLABY *Humberside*

(286) WESLEYAN (TA 014139). Plain brick gabled front, originally with two doorways and windows over, central circular window with border inscription dated 1858.

(287) Former PRIMITIVE METHODIST (TA 01471375). Red brick with hipped slate roof and broad three-bay front with round-arched openings, dated 1853.

WRANGLE

(288) WESLEYAN (TF 433512). Brown brick with hipped slate roof. Two tiers of round-arched windows to sides, altered below and blocked above. Opened 1842.

YARBURGH

(289) Former WESLEYAN (TF 351932). Brick and pantile, with segmental-arched window in gabled end wall. Built 1818.

NORFOLK

Few counties can match Norfolk for the richness and diversity of its nonconformist history or the quality of its greater chapels and meeting-houses. The return of separatists from Holland to form an Independent church in Norwich in 1643 (152) with a branch in Great Yarmouth (88), and the commencement of another church in Guestwick (96) in 1652, are examples of nonconformist societies whose continued existence and growth enabled them to erect substantial meeting-houses in the later years of the 17th century. Although nothing of that period remains at Great Yarmouth, the Old Meeting-house in Norwich of 1693 is a building of national importance with a sophisticated brick frontage as befits its location, while at Guestwick the timber frame of the 17th-century meeting-house remains interestingly encased in later brickwork. The only other major building of the later 17th century, the Friends' meeting-house at Gildencroft in Norwich (158), survives merely as a fragment following wartime destruction, but it was comparable in size and quality with the Old Meeting-house. The Presbyterian society in Norwich, formed shortly after the Restoration, soon required equally substantial premises which were erected close to the Old Meeting-house but replaced in 1754–6 by the Octagon Chapel (159), another building of great architectural importance. Large meeting-houses were not confined to the towns: the chapel at Oulton (167), built in 1731 for an existing Independent congregation, stands in as remote a situation as is possible to imagine. Other smaller chapels of this period include the Congregational chapel in Wymondham (239) of 1715, now much enlarged, and the former General Baptist chapel at Smallburgh (186) of 1712, now in Methodist use.

Many Quaker meeting-houses of the 18th century and later remain in the county, although some, no longer in use, have suffered from alteration. Notable amongst these are the mid 18th-century meeting-houses at Mattishall (135) and Diss (49) and the 'Swafield' meeting-house at North Walsham (149) of 1772. Principal amongst the early 19th-century meeting-houses is Upper Goat Lane, Norwich (157) of 1826 by J.T. Patience.

A small timber-framed chapel of the mid 18th century which remained remarkably complete at the time of this survey, but which has since lost much of its character on conversion to a house, is the former Presbyterian Chapel at Hapton (209). The late 18th-century Wesleyan chapel at Little Walsingham (125) is of considerable architectural interest while the Independent chapels in South Creake (189) of 1779 and Briston (19) of 1775 are additionally notable as originating with the benefactions of private individuals. Although the Calvinistic Methodist Tabernacle in Norwich (156) of 1752 has been demolished the survival of another small chapel of that denomination at Forncett (72) is worthy of mention, as is the speculative nature of the origin of a chapel in Aylsham (4), built in 1789 for possible Methodist use, though soon after taken by the Baptists. The Baptist chapel at Claxton (34) of 1765 exemplifies the degree of expansion needed for a growing congregation.

Several Baptist chapels of the early 19th century include country chapels, such as Necton (141) of 1802, Kenninghall (115) of 1807, Carlton Rode (29) and Neatishead (140) both of 1811, and others. 'Stepney Chapel' in King's Lynn (117) of 1840–1 is representative of the work of the architect James Fenton. The Baptist chapel at Worstead (235) is also notable both externally and for the large box-pews in the side galleries. The Congregational chapel at Denton (42) of 1820–1 is of much interest. The former Unitarian chapel in Diss (46) is the successor to an earlier chapel in Suffolk.

The most significant late 19th-century chapels include the Baptist chapels in Diss (47) and Swaffham (201), similarly designed with twin towers in an Italianate style, a feature repeated in the former King Street Independent chapel in Great Yarmouth (90), all being built between 1855 and 1859. The unusual Primitive Methodist Temple in Great Yarmouth (94) of 1875–6 was demolished during the course of this survey. Most notable of the Classical chapels of this period is the Congregational chapel in Princes Street, Norwich (153) of 1868–9 by Edward Boardman, who also re-fronted a chapel in Harleston (172). Gothic Revival chapels include the Congregational chapels of Great Yarmouth (89) and East Dereham (61), of 1870 and 1874 respectively. More unusual and pointing the way to the freer architectural practices of the following century is the small Wesleyan chapel at Overstrand (168) designed by (Sir) Edwin Lutyens.

Available building materials were limited by the comparative absence of good building stone; timber-framing appears in some of the earlier chapels (96, 104, 209) but brickwork is ubiquitous. Near the coast pebbles are sometimes used as a facing material, as at Bacton (7) and Holt (106–8) and flint was also generally available, usually with brick dressings. Clay lump was found at Gissing (81) and Kenninghall (116) in the 19th century. Roof coverings were often of plain tile or more frequently of pantile, either red or dark glazed, throughout most of the period.

NORFOLK

ACLE

(1) PRIMITIVE METHODIST (TG 402102). Three-bay gabled front with serrated brick cornices. Two round-arched entrances flank central window. Dated 1883.

ATTLEBOROUGH

(2) Former CHAPEL, Chapel Road (TM 043952). Rendered walls with three-bay gabled front outlined in brickwork. Possibly the former Primitive Methodist chapel of 1839. (In use by Salvation Army, 1971)

(3) PRIMITIVE METHODIST (TM 044950). Brick, in the Gothic style with short corner tower. Built 1913 by A.F. Scott & Son.

AYLSHAM

(4) Former METHODIST, White Hart Street (TG 194270). The chapel, now Baptist, was built by a 'speculative Baptist in the expectation of its being used by John Wesley's connexion'. It was registered for Methodists on 10 October 1789 but given up a year later and Baptists supported by the Rev. Joseph Kinghorn of Norwich commenced meetings there, forming the present church in 1791.

The chapel has brick walls and a hipped pantiled roof. The broad N front, which has a high brick plinth, was originally of three bays with two tiers of windows and a central doorway. In the mid 19th century a matching bay was added to the E, the window heads replaced by splayed lintels, and the entrance re-sited in a porch at the W end of the front wall. The original door-frame, reset on the E face of the porch, has an eared architrave, triple keystone and bracketed cornice. School-rooms were added at the E end under a separate roof in 1876. The original fenestration of the S wall, with four lower windows and two gallery windows above, indicates a layout with E and W galleries and pulpit opposite the entrance.

The interior (originally 28¾ft by 35ft) was partly refitted in the mid 19th century and the pulpit re-sited. Only the W gallery remains, with plain panelled front supported by two posts; the gallery pews incorporate some late 18th-century panelling.

Fittings – *Brasses*: in porch, three shield-shaped tablets (1) Priscilla Roberts, 1839; (2) Louisa Connold, 1843; (3) Sarah Ebbetts, 1833. *Inscription*: on brick in N wall close to line of extension, 'EP.1826'. *Monuments*: in chapel, include (1) Frederic Thomas Connold, 1844, *et al.*; (2) John Pedder, gent., 1827, Frances his widow, 1831, and Ann Harvey her sister, 1822, recording that 'Ann Harvey and Frances Pedder were Baptised in this parish on a personal profession of faith April 22nd 1791 and became the founders of the Baptist Church in this place'; (3) Robert Harvey, 1842; (4) Isabella wife of Rev. C.T. Keen, 1853.

Browne (1877) 567.

(5) WESLEYAN, White Hart Street (TG 195270). One end of a range of brick buildings including two adjacent houses. Chapel opened 1844, front rebuilt 1910.

(6) WESLEYAN REFORM (TG 196274). 'The Tabernacle', red brick with yellow brick dressings; three-bay front with large pediment. Foundation stone 'S+J 1868'; chapel extended to rear 1910.

Wesleyan Reform chapel, Aylsham. (6)

BACTON

(7) BAPTIST (TG 350334). The meeting-house was registered 13 July 1822. The walls are faced with pebbles and have brick dressings; the roof is pantiled. The pebbles are coursed in the E wall but set at random in the W front. The front wall has two segmental-arched windows and a later porch between; to the left a former entrance with a small window above has been carefully blocked to match the adjacent walling. An extension at the S end includes a vestry and gallery over; further buildings adjoin N and S. Interior refitted late 19th century. *Monuments*: in burial-ground, of the early 19th century and later, include one to Sarah Ann Pestell, 1838.

BANHAM

(8) Former WESLEYAN (TM 063877). Flint with brick dressings and pantiled roof, wide three-bay front formerly dated 1822. (Converted to cottage and drastically refenestrated)

(9) PRIMITIVE METHODIST (TM 067885). Brick and pantile, gabled three-bay front altered in the late 19th century with white brick dressings and large shaped tablet dated 1837.

BAWDESWELL

(10) WESLEYAN (TG 047208). Brick and pantile with hipped roof, narrow three-bay front with round-arched openings; tablet dated 1829.

(11) Former PRIMITIVE METHODIST (TG 048209). Brick, flint and pantile, gabled front with round-arched doorway and small tablet dated 1856.

BEESTON WITH BITTERING

(12) FREE METHODIST, Beeston (TF 908159). Small chapel of brick, with modern flat roof and round-arched doorway. Opened 1817; dated brick in front wall.

BEETLEY

(13) PRIMITIVE METHODIST (TF 969179). Red brick with white brick and stone dressings, three-bay gabled front, 1871.

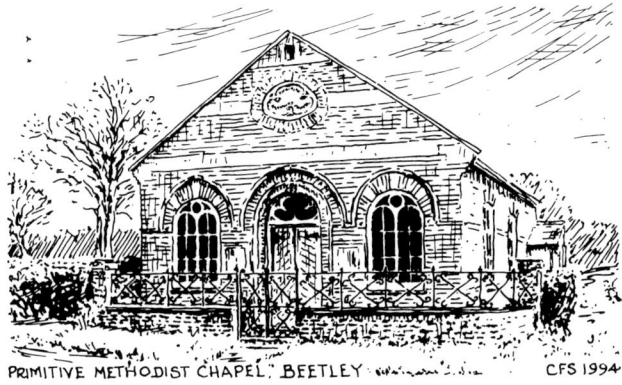
PRIMITIVE METHODIST CHAPEL, BEETLEY   CFS 1994

BESTHORPE

(14) PRIMITIVE METHODIST (TM 070974). Red brick with yellow brick dressings; three-bay gabled front with segmental pediment above central entrance. Built 1866.

BINHAM

(15) PRIMITIVE METHODIST (TF 983395). Brick and slate, three-bay gabled front with small lunette in gable. Dated 1868.

BLAKENEY

(16) Former WESLEYAN (TF 030439). Brick with hipped pantiled roof, built 1812, heightened 1846. Chapel sold to Methodist Reformers 1846. Sunday-school wing added by United Methodists 1903.

BRADENHAM

(17) PRIMITIVE METHODIST, East Bradenham (TF 924087). Three-bay gabled front with decorative barge-boards; porch between narrow round-arched windows. Dated 1877.

BRIDGHAM

(18) Former WESLEYAN, Chapel Lane (TL 960860). Flint and brick, built 1834, enlarged in the late 19th century and after. (Now village hall)

BRISTON

(19) INDEPENDENT, The Lane (TG 061327). The chapel and adjacent manse were built in 1775 by Miss Elizabeth Frankling, later wife of William Grieves, and placed in trust for (?Calvinistic) Methodists in 1778 on condition that she personally received all the income from the property in exchange for keeping it in repair. In 1783 the Independent minister at Guestwick, John Sykes, was additionally appointed minister at Briston and the two trusts and both churches were subsequently combined as a single unit while retaining both places of worship.

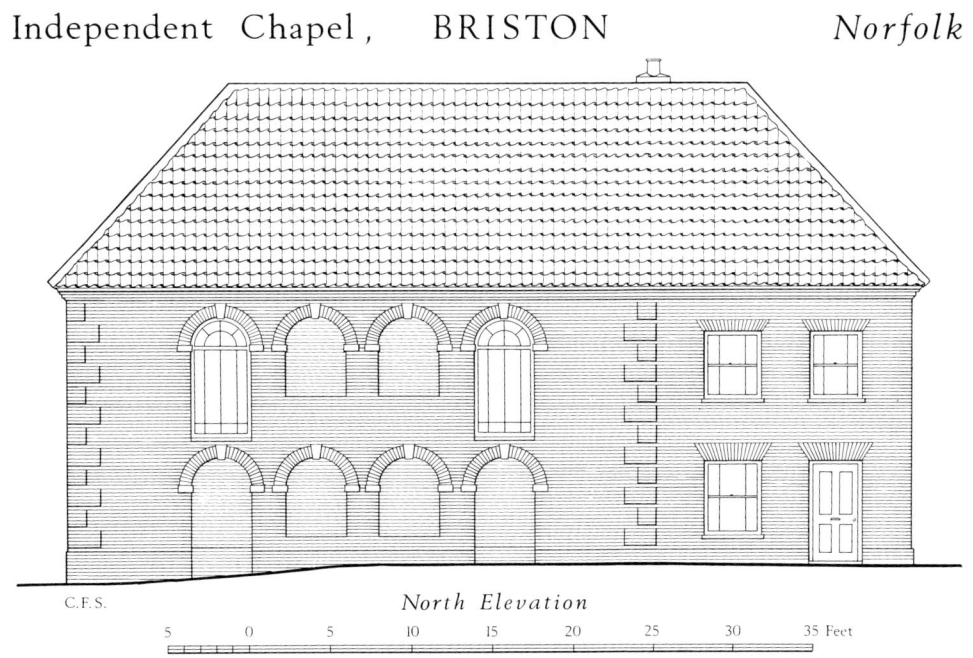
Independent Chapel, BRISTON   Norfolk
North Elevation

The chapel and house form a single structure of brick under a hipped and pantiled roof. The N front of the chapel facing The Lane is bounded by brick quoins and has two round-arched doorways with a pair of windows between and four windows above, all blocked except two upper windows which have been lengthened. The adjoining house has a front of two bays with flat-arched heads to the doorway and windows. The E wall is blank except for an inserted doorway with round-arched head, keystone and impost blocks as those in the front wall. The S wall of the chapel has four windows at the upper level only, the centre pair with cills set slightly lower than the others. The house projects to the S beyond the extent of the chapel.

The interior (18½ft by 32¾ft) was entirely altered and reoriented in the late 19th century with the pulpit at the W end opposite the later entrance. There are no surviving galleries but E and W galleries with a pulpit against the S wall may have comprised the original layout. The flat plaster ceiling is coved on all sides above a moulded plaster cornice. At the rear, adjacent to the house, is a small vestry of the late 18th century with fielded-panelled inner door.

Fittings – *Inscription*: between upper windows of front wall, brick inscribed '17 WG 75'. *Insurance Plaque*: above dated brick, 'Sun No. 409286'. *Monuments*: in chapel (1) Aquila Robins, 1833; in burial-ground at rear, many headstones now loose, including (2) John Goldsmith, 1823, Mary his wife, 1786, *et al. Plate: see* Guestwick (96).

Anon., *Guestwick-Briston 1652–1952* (*c*.1952). CHST XXI (1971–2) 74–6.

(20) WESLEYAN, The Lane (TG 060328). A school-room built about 1782 was used for Methodist services; it was replaced by the present chapel in 1811–12. This is a square building of brick with a pyramidal roof covered in pantiles. The front wall is of three bays with two tiers of windows with flat-arched heads and a central doorway with early 19th-century surround. The interior (about 34ft square) has an original gallery above the entrance; the seating was renewed in the late 19th century. *Monuments*: in chapel (1) Ann wife of Joseph Hill, 1812; in burial-ground (2) Mary Allen, 1800, and Mary Weston her daughter, 1800; (3) brick table-tomb, early 19th-century.

(21) Former PRIMITIVE METHODIST (TG 063320). Flint with brick dressings and hipped pantiled roof. Built 1832, enlarged and possibly heightened in 1891. (Converted to house since 1972)

BROOKE

(22) BAPTIST, High Green (TM 281987). The chapel of brick but covered with modern rendering has at the front a crow-stepped gable, windows with Tudor labels and a porch with a stepped gable and octagonal buttresses surmounted by plain pinnacles. On two shields in the spandrels of the wooden frame of the porch doorway is the date 1831 although the chapel appears to have been built in 1841, in which year a church was formed. The interior has a plain plaster ceiling with one ceiling rose. The pulpit, opposite the entrance, has a gallery behind with open-backed seating; in front is a table-pew with baptistery beneath.

BM XXXIII (1841) 349. Norfolk Record Society *Religious Worship in Norfolk* LXII (1998) 184.

Baptist chapel, High Green. (22)

BUNWELL

(23) PRIMITIVE METHODIST, Bunwell Street (TM 119041). Red brick with yellow brick dressings and dark pantiled roof; three-bay gabled front with rusticated corner pilasters and round-arched openings. Inscribed band below gable with date 1876.

BURGH ST PETER

(24) Former WESLEYAN, Mill Road (TM 468934). Small chapel possibly built 1815, rebuilt 1835 and re-fronted in the late 19th century. (Converted to house *c*.1979)

BURNHAM MARKET

(25) Former CONGREGATIONAL, North Street (TF 833423). Red brick with gault brick front and three-centred arched windows. Built 1807, remodelled *c*.1860.

Browne (1877) 355–6.

BUXTON WITH LAMMAS

(26) BAPTIST, Buxton Heath (TG 237211). 'Heath Chapel', built about 1796 for a church formed in that year, has been demolished apart from a small outbuilding of the early 19th century. *Monuments*: on front wall (1) lozenge-shaped tablet inscribed 'SH/1832'; in burial-ground (2) William Barton, 1837, and Frances his wife, 1837; (3) Samuel Parker, 1864.

(27) Former FRIENDS, Lamas (TG 242229). The meeting-house was built *c*.1720. The meeting closed in 1858 and the building was subsequently used by Methodists and the Wesleyan Reformers but latterly for storage.

This is a relatively long and low building (43¾ft by 22½ft externally) with walls of red brick on a tall plinth and a pantiled roof. The N wall facing the road has two later or enlarged windows with altered frames. The S wall facing the burial-ground has a segmental-arched doorway and four windows with original moulded wood frames and square mullions. The E and W walls are gabled, the former having a single window with original wood frame in the gable, the latter having two upper windows, both blocked, and a blocked, possibly inserted, doorway asymmetrically below.

The interior has a boarded ceiling inserted in the late

Former Friends' Meeting-house
BUXTON WITH LAMMAS
Norfolk

South Elevation

19th century. No original fittings appear to survive. (Converted to house since 1981)

Monuments: in overgrown burial-ground to S of meeting-house, include (1) Mary second wife of John Wright, 1691, Richard their son, 1775, and Grace (Smythies) his wife, [ ], John Wright of Esher, son of the last, 1798, and Mary (Leach) his wife, 1770, Ann (Seamur) wife of John Wright, 1685, John their son, 1728, and Elizabeth his wife, 1739, Richard Wright son of the last, 1777, and his three wives Elizabeth (Kirby), 1739, Mary (Fulcher), [ ], and Phebe (Fuller), 1781, also John Wright of Buxton, 1717, monument with large coped top, late 19th-century; (2) John Wright, 1853, and Ann his widow, 1856; (3) John Wright, 1871, and Anne his wife, 1861; (4) Mary daughter of John and Ann[e?] Wright, 1889; (5) Isaac Sewell, 1878, and Mary his wife, 1884; (6) Anna daughter of Isaac and Mary Sewell, 1878, authoress (grave reported destroyed 1984); loose against S wall of meeting-house (7) Ransome Bransby, 1881; (8) Mary Harford, 1839, and Esther Harford, 1857; (9) Elizabeth Harford, 1872, and James Harford her brother, 1876.

Butler (1999) 444–5.

CAISTER-ON-SEA

(28) PRIMITIVE METHODIST (TG 524118). Three-bay pedimented front of gault brick dated 1865.

CARLETON RODE

(29) BAPTIST (TM 118930). The meeting-house was built in 1811 at the expense of John Barnard of Carleton Rode for a Baptist congregation originating in 1774 which was formed as a distinct church in 1812. The walls are of brickwork with later rendering and the roof is hipped and covered with dark glazed pantiles. The front is of three bays with two tiers of windows and the remains of a brick platband which continues along the side walls. A change in wall thickness visible internally may indicate that the building has been extended to the rear.

The interior has a gallery around three sides. Pulpit and seating were renewed in the late 19th century.

BM III (1811) 517.

Primitive Methodist chapel, Caister-on-Sea. (28)

Baptist chapel, Carleton Rode. (29)

CASTLE ACRE

(30) Former GENERAL BAPTIST (TF 819152). The chapel built in 1841 was enlarged in the late 19th century when a new chapel was erected at the W end and the former converted for use as a Sunday-school. The front of three bays is of brickwork and the side walls of flint with brick dressings. (Now occupied as a youth club)
Wood (1847) 231.

(31) PRIMITIVE METHODIST, Bailey Street (TF 818151). Red brick with yellow brick dressings, three-bay gabled front with paired lancets below semi-circular arched heads. Dated 1878.

CATFIELD

(32) PRIMITIVE METHODIST (TG 386217). Rendered brick with hipped slate roof. Opened 1838; tablet in gabled parapet with dates '1826–1929'.

CAWSTON

(33) Former WESLEYAN (TG 137240). The chapel dated 1829, now occupied by the Wesleyan Reform Church, has been extended by one bay to the rear. The 1851 census claims a date of 1816 for the chapel and includes apposite comments from the Wesleyans and the Reformers about their recent divisions.
Norfolk Record Society *Religious Worship in Norfolk* LXII (1998) 92–3.

CLAXTON

(34) Former BAPTIST (TG 336027). The chapel was built for a Particular Baptist church which originated in the mid 18th century. It was erected mainly at the expense of the first pastor, Henry Utting, and registered on 13 April 1765 as a 'new built house in Claxton, against the road to Ashby'. Of this building only the W wall survives following a major rebuilding in the mid 19th century and a subsequent heightening and reroofing.

The walls are of red brick and the pyramidal roof is covered with dark glazed pantiles and surmounted by an iron finial. The upper twelve courses of brickwork are in a lighter brick and have been painted to match the rest. The S front has two doorways, a blocked window between and others at each side; above is a range of five windows, the end ones lengthened. The original W wall, covered by a lean-to vestry of c.1778–1808 and pierced by later openings, may have been the front wall of the first chapel; it appears to have had two doorways close set at the centre with single windows to right and left.

The interior (now 43ft square) has a gallery around three sides with a fielded-panelled and marbled front supported by square chamfered posts. The ceiling is boarded above a moulded wood cornice. (In 1972 the chapel was in use for storage)

Fittings – *Baptistery*: in floor on E–W axis of first chapel and perhaps central to that building. *Clock*: on front of N gallery facing final site of pulpit, marbled case only, early 19th-century. *Monuments* and *Floorslabs*. *Monuments*: in chapel on S wall (1) Job Hupton, 1849, itinerant preacher in the Countess of Huntingdon's Connexion from 1785, pastor 1794–1849; in vestry (2) Thomas Giles, 1778, headstone reset; in burial-ground W of chapel (3) Mary wife of James Hupton, 1826, headstone; (4) Job Hupton, pastor, 1849, Elizabeth his [?first] wife, 1819, and Frances his third wife, 1874; also many headstones of the early 19th century and later; *Floorslabs*: in chapel (1) Rev. Henry Utting, 27 years pastor, 1792, *et al.*; (2) William Nichols, 1799; (3) Sarah Nichols, 1790; in vestry (4) Thomas Giles, 1808.
Browne (1877) 564–5.

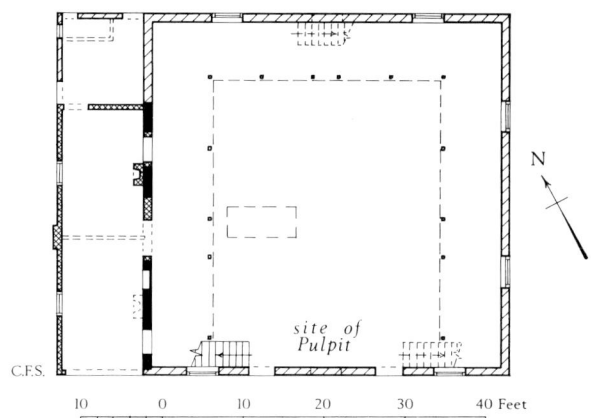

Former Baptist Chapel, CLAXTON   *Norfolk*

CLEY NEXT THE SEA

(35) Former WESLEYAN (TG 045439). Gault brick with gabled front and two tiers of windows between broad corner pilasters. Porch with two Roman Doric columns *in antis*. Built 1839 as 'Wesleyan Centenary Chapel'; later United Methodist. (Sold 1973 and since converted to house)

COLBY

(36) WESLEYAN (TG 229296). Three-bay brick front with simple pedimented gable, 1846, extended to rear 1891.

COLTISHALL

(37) Former WESLEYAN, Rectory Road (TG 271199). Walls of knapped flint with gault brick front and hipped slate roof.

Former Baptist chapel, Claxton.   (34)

Three-bay front with two tiers of sash windows, central doorway with fluted Doric pilasters and pediment, and defaced inscription panel above formerly dated 1842. Single gallery at entrance. Now used by Brethren as 'Bethesda Hall'.

(38) FREE METHODIST, Chapel Lane (TG 273199). Gabled front with round-arched windows; dated 1878.

CORPUSTY

(39) PRIMITIVE METHODIST (TG 114300). The chapel built in 1859 is of brick with the E front of large knapped flints with flint galleting and brick dressings. The roof is hipped and pantiled. The chapel, originally three bays in length, was extended to the N by one bay in 1911 and the E windows, formerly in two tiers, replaced by tall round-arched windows.

COSTESSEY

(40) BAPTIST (TG 173118). The chapel was built in 1822 for a society in existence from 1797. The walls are of brick and the roof is hipped and slated. The W front was of three bays but the central entrance was blocked in the late 19th century and a new doorway made in the N end wall. There is a vestry centrally on the E side. The interior may originally have had end galleries and pulpit to the E, but only the N gallery remains.

CROMER

(41) BAPTIST, Church Street (TG 221422). The chapel of 1902 by A.F. Scott has an elaborate Gothic front of three bays of brick with terracotta dressings. Open lobby at front with inscription above arched entrance 'The Meeting House of the Baptist Church'.

B.Hbk (1904) 376–7.

DENTON

(42) CONGREGATIONAL (TM 279885). The church meeting here (now URC) which may have originated in the mid 17th century acquired the present site and built the first meeting-house in 1701. The existing building, erected in 1820–1, has walls of red brick and a hipped slated roof. The S front of three bays has entrances in the end bays with crudely designed wooden porches each with two columns supporting a flat canopy with reeded architrave and circular paterae. The three upper windows and one between the entrances have flat-arched heads and hung sashes. The side walls are each of three bays. The N wall has two upper windows and is partly covered by a lean-to vestry.

The interior has a gallery around three sides with a plain panelled front supported by slender iron columns. Many of the original unpainted box-pews remain throughout but a large railed table-pew in front of the pulpit was constructed in the late 19th century. The pulpit, against the N wall, is approached directly from the vestry by a doorway at ground level and a short flight of stairs within the chapel.

Fittings – *Chair*: formerly at Guestwick chapel (96), with carved panelled back and head rail, shaped arms and turned supports, 17th-century. *Communion Table*: formerly at Guestwick chapel (96), small table, with square chamfered legs and renewed top, 2ft 3in. by 2ft 8in. over frame, late 17th-century.

Monuments: in chapel (1) Rev. Edward Hickman, 36 years minister, 1841; (2) Anna Maria Devereux, accidentally drowned at Tarussovo, Russia, 1884, and interred in the Protestants' cemetery, Moscow; externally, on N wall (3) Rev. Mr Nathaniel Holmes, late of Guestwick, 1732, and Elizabeth his first wife, 1723; on E wall (4) Joseph Parker, 1834, and Mary his wife, 1825; in burial-ground W of chapel many monuments of 18th century and later, including (5) Samuel Rix, 1745, and Mary his widow, 1778, brick table-tomb; (6) Nathanael Rix, 1714, small headstone with death's head; (7) Elizabeth Rix, 1717, similar to last; (8) Samuel Rix, 1723, headstone with death's head; (9) Daniel Thompson, 1772, and Prisc[illa?] his widow, 1776, brick table-tomb; (10) Jane wife of Rev. John Hurrion, late of Denton, 1737, headstone with concentrically curved inscription; (11) Rev. Mr Samuel Hurrion, late of Beccles, 1763, Deborah his widow, 1789, and Rev. John Hurrion, late minister of Southwold, 1793; (12) Rev. Mr Thomas Wickes, 1733; against W wall of vestry (13) Deborah Robinson, 1732, headstone with winged cherub's head.

Plate: three pewter plates with touch of George Holmes, mid 18th-century. *Pulpit*: hexagonal with panelled sides and reeded corners, early 19th-century.

Browne (1877) 333–42. *EM* NS XX(1842) 3,5.

DEOPHAM

(43) PRIMITIVE METHODIST, Deopham Green (TM 043995). Rendered side walls possibly on timber-frame, with gabled brick front, dated 1837.

Baptist meeting-house, Cromer. (41)

DERSINGHAM

(44) METHODIST NEW CONNEXION (TF 693301). Small chapel of 1851 incorporating part of an earlier structure. Rubble with brick dressings and three-bay gabled front. The site slopes away to the rear allowing external access to a room below the back of the chapel.

(45) Former PRIMITIVE METHODIST (TF 687308). 'Bethel Chapel' dated 1878 is of mixed materials; the gabled front is faced with pebbles and brick dressings, the side walls are built of large squared stone blocks. (Now in secular use)

DISS

(46) PARK FIELDS CHAPEL, Park Road (TM 115797). The former Unitarian chapel, now a Masonic hall, was built in 1822 for an originally Independent congregation which previously met at Palgrave, Suffolk (122), where a meeting-house had been erected in 1697. The chapel in Diss has brick walls, now painted externally, and a hipped roof covered with slates. The S front is of three bays with an open pedimented porch supported by four Roman Doric columns. The side walls are each of two bays with windows set in arched recesses. *Burial-ground*: see Palgrave, Suffolk (122).

Evans (1897) 71–2. *Monthly Repository* XVI (1821) 629; XVII (1822) 446; XVIII (1823) 171. *UHST* VI (1935–8) 149–51.

(47) BAPTIST, Denmark Street (TM 115799). The first Baptist meeting-house in Diss, opened in 1789, was a small building 18ft by 36ft with a gallery at each end; it was enlarged to 36ft square in 1798 by the addition of a further gallery. The church suffered a secession in 1822 when the pastor, William Ward, left and erected a separate Baptist Tabernacle on his own land.

The present chapel of 1859 in an Italianate style by W. Woods has walls of gault brick. The gabled front with two tiers of round-arched windows is set between a pair of corner towers (cf. Swaffham (201)). Sunday-school to left dated 1926. (Tower parapets rebuilt since 1971 omitting upper cornices)

Browne (1877) 566–7. Ivimey IV (1830) 524–6.

(48) CONGREGATIONAL, Mere Street (TM 117797). A chapel built in 1835 in Castle Street was soon superseded by the present larger building (now URC) opened in 1839. Red brick with a gabled front having a battlemented porch and pointed-arched windows with wooden tracery. Three-bay sides with stepped buttresses and two tiers of windows with square labels.

Interior without galleries, much altered *c.*1962 with lowered ceiling. Three-bay wooden arcade behind pulpit formerly with shutters opening to rear school-room. *Monument*: Rev. Joseph Field, 42 years pastor, 1880.

[Baker, K.J.], *Diss United Reformed Church, 1835–1985* [1985]. Browne (1877) 363.

(49) FRIENDS, Frenze Road (TM 120800). The meeting-house was built in 1745 superseding one of 1697. The walls, of red brick with some glazed headers in the sides and rear, have a low plinth and an eaves cornice with two lines of dentils and serrated brickwork. The roof is hipped and covered with dark glazed pantiles. The broad S front is of three bays with a central doorway below a pedimented hood and a pair of segmental-arched windows with hung sashes with renewed frames possibly replacing earlier cross-framed casements; the arch of the right-hand window has been rebuilt. The W wall has a small central doorway blocked in the late 18th century with glazed headers but reopened 1981. The rear wall has, close to each end, a smaller segmental-arched cross-framed window with a gallery window over. Attached to the E end is a large room of 1897 and later.

The interior (19ft by 32¾ft) formerly had end galleries and a stand centrally on the N wall. It now has a single W gallery with fielded-panelled front, with a central supporting column on a

Baptist chapel, Denmark Street, Diss. (47)

Friends' meeting-house, Frenze Road, Diss. (49)

Congregational chapel (URC), Denton. (42)

Former Park Fields Chapel, Park Road, Diss. (46)

NORFOLK

square panelled base. The gallery staircase in the SW corner has twisted balusters and a newel of the mid 18th century.

Fittings – *Inscriptions* and *Scratchings*: on bricks at E end of front wall below eaves, 'SB 1745', 'RH 1745', '17 EH 45'; internally, on wall panelling W of front entrance 'W.H Novr 10th 1775', '*Elizabeth Howell July 18 1779*'. *Monuments*: in burial-ground, uniform round-topped headstones, 19th-century and later. *Stand*: at E end, 19th-century (removed 1981).

Butler (1999) 438–9.

(50) Former FREE METHODIST, Park Road (TM 116797). Three-bay front with wide rusticated corner pilasters and pediment with semicircular arch above central upper window. Late 19th-century. (Demolished since 1971)

DOCKING

(51) WESLEYAN (TF 770369). Brick with hipped pantiled roof, three-bay front with two tiers of round-arched windows. Opened 1821, altered and possibly heightened in later 19th century.

(52) Former PRIMITIVE METHODIST (TM 770369). Immediately E of (51), brick with tall round-arched windows, three-bay front with wide central entrance, defaced tablet dated 1836, and parapet with gabled centre. (Demolished *c.*1973)

DOWNHAM MARKET

(53) Former PARTICULAR BAPTIST, London Road (TF 612029). The chapel, now a Masonic hall, was first built *c.*1800 and much enlarged in 1844. The walls are of rubble, mostly rendered, but with some exposed brickwork at the N end of the E side; the roof is hipped and slated. The entrance is at the N end between a pair of blocked windows; the E wall is largely covered by a later annexe but in the W wall are five segmental-arched windows.

BM XXXVII (1845) 30.

(54) Former STRICT BAPTIST, Priory Road (TF 611031). 'Zion Chapel', built 1849 but probably rebuilt 1882, is now a Salvation Army hall. Brick walls with traces of earlier work; round-arched windows.

(55) Former FRIENDS, Bridge Street (TF 608032). The meeting-house was built in 1700 for a meeting settled in 1699. It suffered several periods of disuse, 1796–1814, 1872–4 and 1881–1905, and passed out of use in 1937. The walls are of brickwork in English bond with a rubble plinth at the front and one end; the roof, formerly thatched, was rebuilt to a lower pitch, and is now covered with slates. The N front has been refenestrated and originally had a central entrance with one window to the right only; one segmental-arched window in the rear wall is original. The gabled E wall has a pair of later windows and traces of two in the gable, their segmental-arched brick heads partly cut across by the lowering of the roof. At the S end of the W wall is a blocked doorway; the remainder of this wall is covered by an adjoining cottage. The interior (45¾ft by 24ft) has no original fittings; it was formerly subdivided by a screen into two separate rooms. (Now a county library)

Monuments: in burial-ground to S (1) Ann wife of [Simon?] Collins, 1750; (2) Daniel Goddard, 1727; (3) Thomas Goddard, 17[..]; (4) Thomas Goddard, 1710; (5) Grace Circhen, 1750;

FORMER FRIENDS MEETING-HOUSE, DOWNHAM MARKET CFS1972

(6) William Circhen, 1770; also four substantial headstones to the Doyle family, of 19th-century date.

Butler (1999) 440.

(56) Former WESLEYAN, Cannon Square (TF 612034). Built 1810 but much altered in later 19th century. Gault brick front of three bays with panelled pilasters, central pediment and two tiers of windows; porch with round-arched entrance.

(57) Former FREE METHODIST, Bridge Street (TF 609032). 'Mount Tabor' is dated 1859. The walls are of gault brick with rendered dressings. The pedimented front has giant attached columns (capitals destroyed) flanking the central doorway, corner pilasters, and tall windows with moulded cornices.

DOWNHAM WEST

(58) Former PRIMITIVE METHODIST, Salters Lode (TF 584017). Small gault brick chapel dated 1868. (Now farm store)

EAST DEREHAM

(59) BAPTIST, High Street (TF 990131). The first chapel, built in 1784 for a newly established church, was converted to Sunday-school use when a new chapel was erected in front in 1859. The much altered rear wall of brick is part of the original building and incorporates three segmental-arched lower windows with fragments of others above. The present chapel has a rendered pedimented front of three bays with giant pilasters and two tiers of round-arched windows.

Browne (1877) 567.

Former Congregational chapel, London Road, East Dereham (60)

(60) Former CONGREGATIONAL, London Road (TF 990129). Congregational preaching commenced in 1779 and the first chapel was built in 1812; this was enlarged shortly afterwards to double its original size by a matching addition against the SE side, and superseded by the present chapel (61) in Market Place in 1874. The first chapel, subsequently converted to a Sunday-school, is of red brick with two hipped and pantiled roofs separately over the two sections. The windows throughout have pointed-arched heads with an upper range of pointed lunettes above to the front and sides. The NE end of the earliest part is of three bays with a central doorway, now converted to a window; the SE wall of the enlarged building has a central entrance between two windows and four smaller windows above.

The interior (originally 38ft by 26ft) retains no original fittings. The roof of the earlier part is supported by three king-post trusses with half trusses in the hips; a suspended ceiling has been inserted. An upper floor has been introduced to the extension.

Browne (1877) 351–5.

(61) CONGREGATIONAL, Market Place (TF 989133). 'Cowper Memorial Church' (now URC), built in 1874 to replace (60), occupies the site of a house in which William Cowper spent the last years of his life. The chapel is in the Gothic style by Edward Boardman. The gabled front is faced in Kentish rag with Bath stone dressings and has a pointed-arched traceried window above the entrance and a tower to the left which was intended to be surmounted by a spire. *Monument*: in front of chapel, recording the association of the site with William Cowper and his burial in 1800 in the parish church.

CYB (1874) 424.

EAST RUDHAM

(62) Former WESLEYAN (TF 824280). Brick with hipped pantiled roof. Three-bay E front with round-arched windows, dated 1824. Two pointed-arched pulpit windows at the W end have been blocked. Blind upper windows in long N and S sides. (Now Royal British Legion hall)

(63) Former PRIMITIVE METHODIST, Broomsthorpe Road (TF 832282). 'Ebenezer Chapel', dated 1862, has walls of red brick with gault brick dressings and a hipped roof. The front of three bays has terminal pilasters, two tiers of round-arched windows, and an oval window above the entrance.

EMNETH

(64) Former PRIMITIVE METHODIST (TF 476075). The chapel built in the mid 19th century with small later annexe alongside is now in commercial use. Superseded by chapel of 1924 on opposite side of road.

FAKENHAM

(65) BAPTIST, Swan Lane (TF 919295). The chapel, standing on a concealed site, was rebuilt in 1869.

(66) Former CONGREGATIONAL, Whitehorse Street (TF 921297). The church originally comprising both Baptists and paedobaptists was commenced in 1795. When the Baptists separated in 1819 the Independents built the present chapel. This has brick walls with a moulded eaves cornice and a hipped roof covered with dark

Former Primitive Methodist chapel, East Rudham. (63)

glazed pantiles. The W front has rusticated corner pilasters, an altered central entrance between a pair of flat-arched windows with keystones, now blocked, and three upper windows; the window over the entrance has a round-arched head with keystone and imposts. The chapel may have been enlarged to the rear; in the back wall is a large lunette replacing a pair of pulpit windows. (Now a Conservative Club)

Browne (1877) 360–1.

FELTHORPE

(67) BAPTIST (TF 163179). Low-built brick chapel with hipped roof, erected 1835 for a church founded a few years earlier. Mid 19th-century cottage attached.

FILBY

(68) FILBY CHAPEL (TG 46481298). The Presbyterian, latterly Unitarian, chapel was severely damaged by a bomb blast in 1940. Thirty years later little remained visible on the site apart from a few foundations and overgrown monuments. In 1991–2 the remains of the chapel and burial-ground were refurbished as a site of historical interest.

The first chapel was built in 1706. The lower courses of the brick walls (approximately 31¼ft by 40ft) remain up to the top of a moulded brick plinth. The front faced N and may have had two entrances with windows between but little evidence survives except for a doorway with an internally splayed jamb near the NW corner. In the late 19th century the chapel was rebuilt in a cheaper and smaller form on the eastern third of the site utilizing some of the original foundations and perhaps some of the walling. This chapel had brick walls and a hipped roof; there was a round-arched doorway with fanlight at the N end, perhaps on the site of one of the earlier entrances, and plain rectangular windows under segmental-arched heads in the other walls.

Monuments: ledger stones internally within the area of the first chapel (1) Thomas Deverson, '30 Years Collector of the Salt-Duties, Yarmouth', 1786, with oval cartouche enclosing crest of a stag's head and motto 'Have Charity', slab broken into two parts by 1971 and further damaged subsequently; (2) Henry Daliel AM, 1710/11, founder and first minister, with inscriptions in Latin and English; (3) Mary wife of John Spencer, 1770, and Mary their daughter, 1770; (4) Elizabeth (Hurry) wife of Robert Alderson, 1791; (5) Mrs Mary Hurry, 1792; (6) Robert Allen, 1794, and Margaret his widow, 1810; (7) Samuel Haw, 1799; (8) lozenge-shaped tablet reset on brick base, inscribed 'S H | 1816'.

Browne (1877) 365. Clowes (1912) 65–6. Evans (1897) 87. *Inquirer* (13 July 1991). Tooke, C., and Saul, J., *Filby Dissenters' Chapel, 1705–1940* (duplicated typescript, 1992).

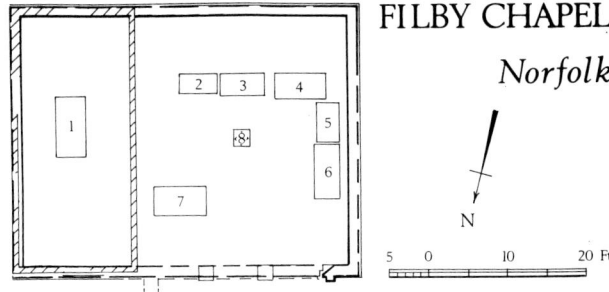

FILBY CHAPEL *Norfolk*

(69) PRIMITIVE METHODIST (TG 466134). Brick with gabled N front; dated 1886.

FINCHAM

(70) PRIMITIVE METHODIST (TF 679059). Gabled front with three windows having paired round-arched lights, dated 1878. Sunday-school in similar style, 1904, by John Whitmore of Lynn.

FLEGGBURGH

(71) WESLEYAN, Burgh St Margaret (TG 445143). Gault brick with hipped slate roof. Panelled front of three bays with round-arched doorway and tablet dated 1841. Interior refitted. *Chandelier*: brass, twelve-branch surmounted by dove, 18th-century.

WESLEYAN CHAPEL, BURGH ST MARGARET — CFS 1972

FORNCETT

(72) Former CALVINISTIC METHODIST, Forncett End (TM 142936). James Wheatley, who built the 'Tabernacle' in Norwich (156), also erected a chapel of that name in Forncett St Peter in 1754 which was registered for 'Methodists' in 1757. Both were leased to John Wesley in 1758; he preached here on 25 March 1759 and 4 January 1760 but gave up the lease in 1763. The chapel was later used by General Baptists who formed a church of the New Connexion in 1814. Baptist use ceased c.1960–70 and the building has since been used for farm storage.

The chapel (35¼ft by 23¾ft) has brick walls much renewed in 1875 and partly replacing clay lump; the roof is covered with dark glazed pantiles. The E front substantially of 1754 is of five bays with rusticated brick quoins at each end and flanking the entrance. The doorway, covered by a later porch, has a round-arched head with keystone and imposts. Two tiers of windows are separated by an inserted or altered string-course. A further building may have been attached at the S end.

Inscription: on stone tablet inserted in tympanum of doorway 'Baptist Chapel ... erected 1754 restored 1875'.

Jewson, C.B., *The Baptists in Norfolk* (1957) 88. Taylor (1818) II: 424–5. Wood (1847) 208.

The Tabernacle, FORNCETT, *Norfolk*

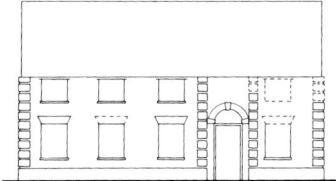

East Elevation, excluding alterations

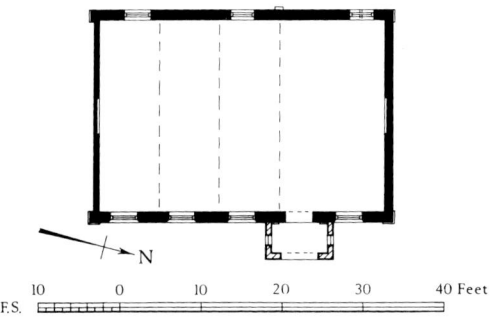

FOULSHAM

(73) BAPTIST, High Street (TG 031246). The chapel built in 1826 replacing one of 1810 has rendered brick walls and a hipped pantiled roof. Three-bay front with two tiers of sash windows. The interior has a gallery around three sides supported by iron columns. Seating comprises box-pews of plain deal with fielded-panelled doors. *Monument*: above pulpit, James Spanton, first pastor, 1828.

(74) PRIMITIVE METHODIST (TG 032248). Gabled front in red and yellow brick, dated 1871. (Proposed conversion to house 1991)

Baptist chapel, Foulsham. (73)

FOXLEY

(75) PRIMITIVE METHODIST (TG 038216). Plain three-bay brick front dated 1898, 'W. Towler, builder'. A former chapel S of parish church (TG 039217) with plain three-bay front and defaced tablet may be its predecessor.

FREETHORPE

(76) WESLEYAN, Palmer's Lane (TG 416054). Large isolated chapel half a mile W of Wickhampton church, of brick with a hipped slate roof. The W front of three bays has two tiers of windows, all except one above the doorway blocked in brickwork. Opened 1814. (Disused by 1972)

(77) PRIMITIVE METHODIST (TG 408049). Red brick with gault brick dressings. Three-bay pedimented front with central arch enclosing large lunette in tympanum; dated 1896.

FULMODESTON

(78) Former BAPTIST CHAPEL, Barney (TF 995322). Small chapel of brick with hipped roof covered with dark glazed pantiles, built c.1840. (Now Women's Institute)

(79) Former WESLEYAN or FREE METHODIST, Barney (TF 995323). Brick and pantile. Gabled front with altered tablet above entrance dated 1844. Possibly the conversion of a cottage.

GARVESTONE

(80) PRIMITIVE METHODIST (TG 018077). Red brick, yellow brick dressings to three-bay gabled front. Keystone of entrance (probably reset from earlier chapel) inscribed 'COME 1864'. Foundation stones dated 1892.

GISSING

(81) WESLEYAN, Lower Street (TM 145854). Walls of clay lump with pantiled roof. Gabled W front with central entrance, window to rear gallery over and tablet dated 1860. Closed 1972. (Reported converted to house)

GREAT DUNHAM

(82) PRIMITIVE METHODIST (TF 872150). Three-bay gabled front of knapped flint with brick dressings forming quoins around arched openings. Dated 1867, 'the land kindly granted by Mr. J. Mason'.

GREAT ELLINGHAM

(83) BAPTIST (TM 019966). The church was formed in 1699, which date is inscribed in a lunette in the front gable. Ivimey IV (1830) says 'the meeting-house was at first very small; it has since been enlarged. It is now forty-two feet long and eighteen wide, has two galleries, and will contain about three hundred persons.'

The present chapel, said to have been built in 1824, has walls of brickwork and a pantiled roof. The front wall of three bays with two tiers of windows with late 19th-century sashes has a central entrance and stone porch with two columns supporting an entablature. The interior is approximately square on plan and has a gallery around three sides supported by slender iron columns. The wide rostrum pulpit and the seating are of the late 19th century. Alongside the chapel is a separate range of stabling.

Monuments: in chapel: (1) Rev. Thomas Henry Sparham, 4½ years pastor, 1898; (2) Charles Hatcher, 38 years pastor, 1854; (3) Rev. James Cragg, 9 years pastor, 1856, with adjacent floorslab; (4) Jeremiah Colman, 1885, brass.

Browne (1877) 563–4. Ivimey IV (1830) 523.

(84) PRIMITIVE METHODIST (TM 019970). The chapel built in 1843 has thick walls, possibly of clay lump, faced with brick. Broad gabled front with gault brick dressings.

GREAT MASSINGHAM

(85) WESLEYAN (TF 799228). The small chapel of rendered brickwork dated 1827, prominently sited at a forked road junction, has an unusual polygonal plan. The W part is rectangular with N and S entrances below a gallery, but the E end has splayed sides towards the road fork and a short, possibly later chancel with a pair of pointed-arched windows.

(86) Former PRIMITIVE METHODIST (TF 798229). Three-bay gabled front dated 1870. (Converted to garage)

GREAT SNORING

(87) PRIMITIVE METHODIST (TF 947343). Broad W front of three bays in red brick with small gabled porch. The N and S walls are gabled; the former, facing the village, has dressings of yellow brick, rusticated quoins, and three graduated round-arched windows with a tablet above dated 1874. Foundation stone below window inscribed 'C. Tuthill, Builder'.

GREAT YARMOUTH

(88) THE OLD MEETING-HOUSE, Middlegate Street, now Greyfriars Way (TG 524073). The Unitarian congregation meeting in a chapel built in 1954 to replace one of 1845 destroyed by bombing traces its origins to an Independent church formed in 1644 by the subdivision of one which had embraced both Great Yarmouth and Norwich. In 1732 a disputed ministerial appointment led to the formation of a New Meeting and to the gradual adoption of a Presbyterian name and heterodox doctrines by the original society. *Plate*: prior to 1732 the plate comprised 'thirteen silver beakers, two silver tankards, one silver flagon, and seven pewter plates'; in 1732 the plate was divided between the two sections of the church, that retained by the Old Meeting included six beakers of 1638 and later, sold 1896. (*See also* monument (89))

Browne (1877) 260–2. *CHST* II (1905–6) 402–9. Clowes (1912). Evans (1897) 260–2.

(89) Former CONGREGATIONAL, Middlegate Street now Greyfriars Way (TG 524074). The seceders from the Old Meeting in 1732 acquired 'a fish-house and garden' on the E side of Middlegate and erected a new meeting-house on the site which was opened in 1733. It was described (Clowes (1912) op. cit. below) as a 'square red brick building of unmitigated ugliness, standing slightly back from the street within an iron palisaded enclosure', it had 'a pair of tall columns supporting the roof' in the traditional manner, galleries around three sides and a pulpit with broken pediment. The New Meeting-house was also known as 'Gaol Lane Chapel' for a period when the street bore that name.

The present chapel on the site of the former was built in 1870 in the Gothic style to designs by J.T. Bottle of Great Yarmouth. The walls are faced with knapped flint and Bath stone dressings. The W front is of three bays with a gabled centre having a traceried window of five lights above paired entrances and side bays with chequered gables, gallery entrances and cusped circular windows above. The interior, which has been refitted, comprises a nave of four bays with cast-iron arcades to the aisles, N and S transepts and a small apse at the E end.

At the rear is a lecture hall, dated 1879. (The church, now URC, united with Methodists at King Street in 1989 (*see* (90)); the chapel has since been converted for local government offices)

Fittings – *Monuments*: in chapel, in S transept (1) Rev. Alexander Creak, 1848, 28 years minister, signed 'T.Burgess'; (2) John Shelly,

Former Congregational chapel, Middlegate Street, Great Yarmouth. (89)

1835, signed 'Denman, 83 Regent St., London'; (3) James Hurry, 1842, and Mary his wife, 1829; externally on S and W walls of S transept (4) Robert Barrett, 1788, Rebecca his widow, 1796, and Sophia Palmer [nd] their granddaughter; (5) Ann wife of Robert Cooper Smith, 1801; (6) William Palmer, merchant, 1809; (7) Nathaniel Palmer, 1799, and Lorina his widow, 1838; (8) Mary, 1813, and Eleanor, 1814, daughters of John B. Palmer and Eleanor his wife; (9) William husband of Mary Palmer, 1802, and William Hotson Palmer, 1806; (10) Mary Corneby, 1808; (11) Richard M. Boardman, deacon, 1822, and Emma his widow, 1842; (12) Isaac Spelman, 1797, also William, 1808, and Elizabeth Spelman, 1814, grandchildren of Isaac and Margaret Spelman, and children of William and Sarah Spelman; S of chapel (13) James Hurry, 1842, and Mary his wife, 1829, ledger stone (*see also* no. (3)); also fragments of two further tablets.

Plate: the plate allotted to the New Meeting at the division of the congregation in 1732 comprised one flagon, seven beakers, three pewter plates and three candlesticks; by 1906 only the seven beakers remained, one of 1638, six of 1654 (all sold 1926).

British Weekly (27 May 1965). Browne (1877) 208–51. Clowes (1912) 72. *CHST* II (1905–6) 402–9. *CYB* (1871) 415.

(90) Former CONGREGATIONAL, King Street (TG 526074). This site was acquired by the New Meeting in 1849 and a second chapel for that church under a joint ministry was erected here in 1855.

Former Congregational chapel, King Street, Great Yarmouth. (90)

The architect, unnamed, is said (*CYB* (1857) 231) to have been responsible also for Congregational chapels at Lowestoft, Suffolk (99) and at Forest Gate, Essex (now Newham, Greater London). About 1938 the building was sold to Methodists for use as a Central Hall; it now houses the combined New Meeting (URC) and two Methodist congregations.

The chapel, in the Italian style, of gault brick with elaborate brick cornices, has a low-pitched gable to the centre bay between twin towers. The interior was redesigned in 1988–90 by Peter Codling and subdivided horizontally with the chapel at gallery level. Timber posts rise from the front of the former side galleries to support the roof structure.

CYB (1856) 255. *Methodist Recorder* (3 March 1988).

(91) BAPTIST, Crown Road (TG 527075). Park Chapel in St George's Park was built in 1863–4 for a Particular Baptist Church formed in 1861 following a disagreement over rebuilding within an older General Baptist church latterly meeting in the 'Tabernacle', Wellesley Road. The congregations reunited in 1952 at Park Chapel.

The walls are of gault brick; the gabled front of three bays has an arched centre bay rising into the pediment. The interior has galleries rounded to the rear, added 1868, with cast-iron fronts and supporting columns. (Inside subdivided 1995)

Baptist Times (6 July 1995). Browne (1877) 560.

(92) FRIENDS, 17 Howard Street South (TG 523076). In 1694 Friends acquired part of the site of a cell of the Augustinian priory of Gorleston with a building which was converted to a meeting-house. The present meeting-house incorporates in the S wall the left jamb and part of the arch of a medieval doorway. Otherwise the building dates entirely from the early 19th century and has rendered walls, a slate roof, and hung sash windows. The interior, raised above a featureless basement (converted to a room 1981), is divided into two rooms, the larger to the N, and has a gallery above the S room with a single hinged shutter opening to the principal room. In the gallery is stepped seating with fixed benches having shaped ends and open backs.

The burial-ground to the E is bounded by walls of mixed construction. There are no visible monuments.

Butler (1999) 462–3.

(93) WESLEYAN, Lowestoft Road, Gorleston (TG 526042). Gothic chapel of 1899 with its predecessor to the N dated 1866. *Pulpit*: loose in chapel, hexagonal with fielded-panelled sides, 18th-century, associated with the preaching of John Wesley; originally in a Methodist chapel of 1783 in Row 8, thence 1792 to a chapel in King Street and elsewhere.

Eastern Daily Press (11 May 1971).

(94) PRIMITIVE METHODIST TEMPLE, Priory Plain (TG 525079). The Primitive Methodist Connexion commenced its work in Great Yarmouth in 1822 and in 1829 erected the first 'Tabernacle' on this site, enlarged in 1850. The large and impressively sited chapel at the head of Priory Plain was built in 1875–6 to designs by William Freeman of Hull. The front of gault brick and stone is in three bays separated by paired Corinthian columns carrying entablature blocks; from these rise small arches supporting a frieze with altered inscription and a tall pediment. Adjacent to the left is the 'Methodist School'

Primitive Methodist Temple, Priory Plain, Great Yarmouth. (Demolished) (94)

dated 1855. (Chapel derelict 1972, since demolished for new road layout)

Patterson, A.H., *From Hayloft to Temple; The Story of Primitive Methodism in Yarmouth* (1903).

GRESSENHALL

(95) FREE METHODIST, Bittering Street (TF 960170). Early 19th-century addition to pair of cottages, now one. Low rendered walls and pantiled roof, refitted late 19th century.

GUESTWICK

(96) Former CONGREGATIONAL (TG 061272). 'Guestwick Chapel' stands in a field 200 yards N of the parish church. It was built in the late 17th century for a church founded in 1652; in 1783 the church was united with one at Briston (*see* (19)) but the chapel remained in use until *c.*1960. In 1695 a meeting-house already on the site was 'altered and rebuilt' at the insistence of a new minister and it is probable that the earliest timber-framed parts of the structure are of that date. In the 18th century the outer walls were encased in brickwork but the principal alterations were carried out in 1840 during the pastorate of Robert Drane (1824–72). In his obituary (*CYB* (1878) 313) it is stated that 'in November 1838, the old meeting-house … required complete restoration. Having with this view prepared a plan and elevation, he called a meeting of the church and congregation, at which the sum of £250 was subscribed, himself heading the list with £50. The place was reopened for public worship June 24th 1840'.

The chapel has walls of brickwork with some traces of structural timbers visible internally; the roof is covered with dark glazed pantiles. The S front, entirely of 1840, has octagonal corner buttresses surmounted by plain pinnacles; the intermediate walling has a battlemented parapet, two tiers of stone-framed windows of two lights below moulded Tudor labels. A central porch has a four-centred arched doorway and crow-stepped gable between octagonal corner buttresses with pinnacles. The N, E and W walls are of 18th-century brickwork with octagonal buttresses added to the corners in 1840; in the N wall are two stone-framed mullioned and transomed pulpit windows of 1840 replacing two earlier windows which, on internal evidence, were slightly wider and lower. The E and W walls have crow-stepped gables of 1840 replacing plain gables. In the E wall are traces of a blocked doorway and a window to the N, two gallery windows match those in the S wall. The W wall has two upper and two lower windows as before, one of the lower windows to the S being altered to a doorway, the other to the N has traces of being on the site of a former doorway.

A sketch of the exterior prior to the 1840 alterations, although said to have been drawn in 1850, shows a range of six plain two-light upper windows at the front with a sundial centrally between and two windows of five lights below with a doorway in the third bay from the left and a minor doorway close to the SE corner. The E and W walls are shown with single gables. (Marshall, P., *William Godwin* (1984) 10.)

The interior ($27\frac{1}{2}$ft by $40\frac{3}{4}$ft) was largely refitted in 1840 while retaining the general character and disposition of the earlier fittings. The roof structure, with king-post trusses of 1840, is supported by a principal E–W beam with braces, now fragmentary, from posts embedded in the end walls and from two intermediate posts; secondary N–S beams may be of a later date and some replacement or re-dressing of the beams must have occurred in the mid 19th century. Prior to the 18th century the building probably had a double roof with central valley. There is a gallery around three sides with staircases to right and left of the main entrance, a rostrum pulpit centrally against the N wall, and box-pews. The space below the W gallery has been partitioned to form a small vestry and classroom. (Chapel derelict by 1972, under conversion to house, 1994)

Fittings – *Chair*: in pulpit, 17th-century. *Communion Table*: late 17th-century. (Chair and table now at Denton, *see* (42)). *Monuments* and *Floorslabs*. *Monuments*: in chapel on W wall below gallery (1) Frances Anna wife of Rev. Robert Drane, 1855, and Robert their son, 1914, signed 'J.Stanley, Norwich', with related initialled and dated floor tiles adjacent. In burial-ground W of chapel, many 18th- and 19th-century monuments including (2) Rev. John Godwin, 1772, Ann his widow, 1809, and Richard their son, table-tomb; (3) Rev. John Sykes, 1824, in 48th year of his ministry, Frances his widow, 1841, and their children William, 1793, William, 1797, Thomas, 1803, Mary, 1807, and two infants, railed tomb; *Floorslabs*: below S gallery (1) William [ ], 1723, and Mary his widow, 1724; (2) Rev. George Mills, 1723, and Mary his widow, 1747; (3) John Armor, 1734.

Pitchpipe: mahogany, length 16in. closed, of the 19th century. *Plate*: includes a pair of shallow two-handled cups of 1658–9, one of 1683–4 with chinoiserie decoration, also one unengraved cup of 1689–90. (All now reported sold)

Anon., *Guestwick-Briston, 1652–1952* (*c.*1952) pamphlet. *CHST* XVI (1949–51) 190–203. *Norfolk Archaeology* XXI (1923) 155–74.

Guestwick Chapel. (96)

NORFOLK

HALES

(97) Former PRIMITIVE METHODIST, Briar Lane (TM 383974). Small brick chapel of 1840, converted to village hall. Successor to S (1910 by T.E. Davidson & Son) converted to house.

HARDINGHAM

(98) Former PRIMITIVE METHODIST (TG 049055). Small Gothic centenary chapel dated 1908.

HARLING

(99) Former FRIENDS, Station Road, East Harling (TL 992865). A single-cell meeting-house of 1836 was extended in 1903 when a larger meeting-house was built alongside. The original building has rendered walls of clay lump and a hipped slate roof. Outer doorways central to front and rear walls; two original windows at back. (Under conversion to house 1994) *Monuments*: in small burial-ground behind, five headstones to Everett family, 1874–1911.

Butler (1999) 441–2.

HEACHAM

(100) Former CONGREGATIONAL, High Street (TF 677373). The chapel was opened in 1832 and a church formed in the following year. In the late 19th century services were largely supported by Wesleyans who acquired the building and 'restored' it in 1891. (Disused 1994)

The original chapel has brick walls and a hipped pantiled roof. It was greatly altered in 1891 by the addition of a front gable, refenestration and an irregularly shaped extension to the side.

Browne (1877) 362–3.

HINDOLVESTON

(101) WESLEYAN (TG 038294). The chapel opened in 1845 has brick walls and a hipped pantiled roof. Front of three bays with two tiers of sash windows.

HINDRINGHAM

(102) PRIMITIVE METHODIST (TF 983360). Brick and pantile, broad rendered front with three round-arched windows, doorway lintel dated 1845.

HINGHAM

(103) CONGREGATIONAL, Chapel Street (TG 023023). Brick and slate, built 1836 but re-fronted and refenestrated 1898 by A.F. Scott. Gabled front with three cusped and traceried mullioned windows above low porch.

Browne (1877) 359.

(104) Former FRIENDS, Seamere Road (TG 032018). The meeting-house, now part of 'Lilac Farm', is believed to have been built in 1707. After closure in the early 19th century it was converted to a barn. It is a timber-framed and weather-boarded building attached to a similarly constructed but rendered cottage which is dated 'E 1671 T' (for Edwin Turk) in the end gable. The meeting-house is two bays in length and approximately square on plan but incorporates also part of a third bay of the cottage where a gallery was formed.

Butler (1999) 442.

(105) PRIMITIVE METHODIST, Bond Street (TG 022022). Brick with gabled front, octagonal corner buttresses and a window of five cusped lights above double-arched loggia entrance. Built 1900 by H. Winkworth of Ipswich.

HOLT

(106) Former WESLEYAN, 18 and 20 Albert Street (TG 077389). Built 1813, superseded by larger chapel in New Street (107) and converted to pair of two-storeyed houses. Rendered front, sides faced with pebbles and brick dressings, hipped roof.

(107) Former WESLEYAN, New Street (TG 077388). Large chapel of brick partly faced with pebbles 'built 1838, restored 1893', now the St John Hall, has a gabled front of three bays with two tiers of round-arched windows. Former burial-ground, now memorial garden, at rear.

(108) Former PRIMITIVE METHODIST, No. 8 Albert Street (TG 07753885). Red brick with pebble facing to side, blind lunette in gabled front. Built 1872. (Converted to pair of shops)

(109) FREE METHODIST, Norwich Road (TG 077387). Large, prominently sited chapel of brick and flint with polygonal end towards High Street and staircase tower at one side with octagonal turret and spire. Large plate-traceried rose window to rear. Polychromatic interior. Built 1862 by Thomas Jekyll.

Free Methodist chapel, Holt. (109)

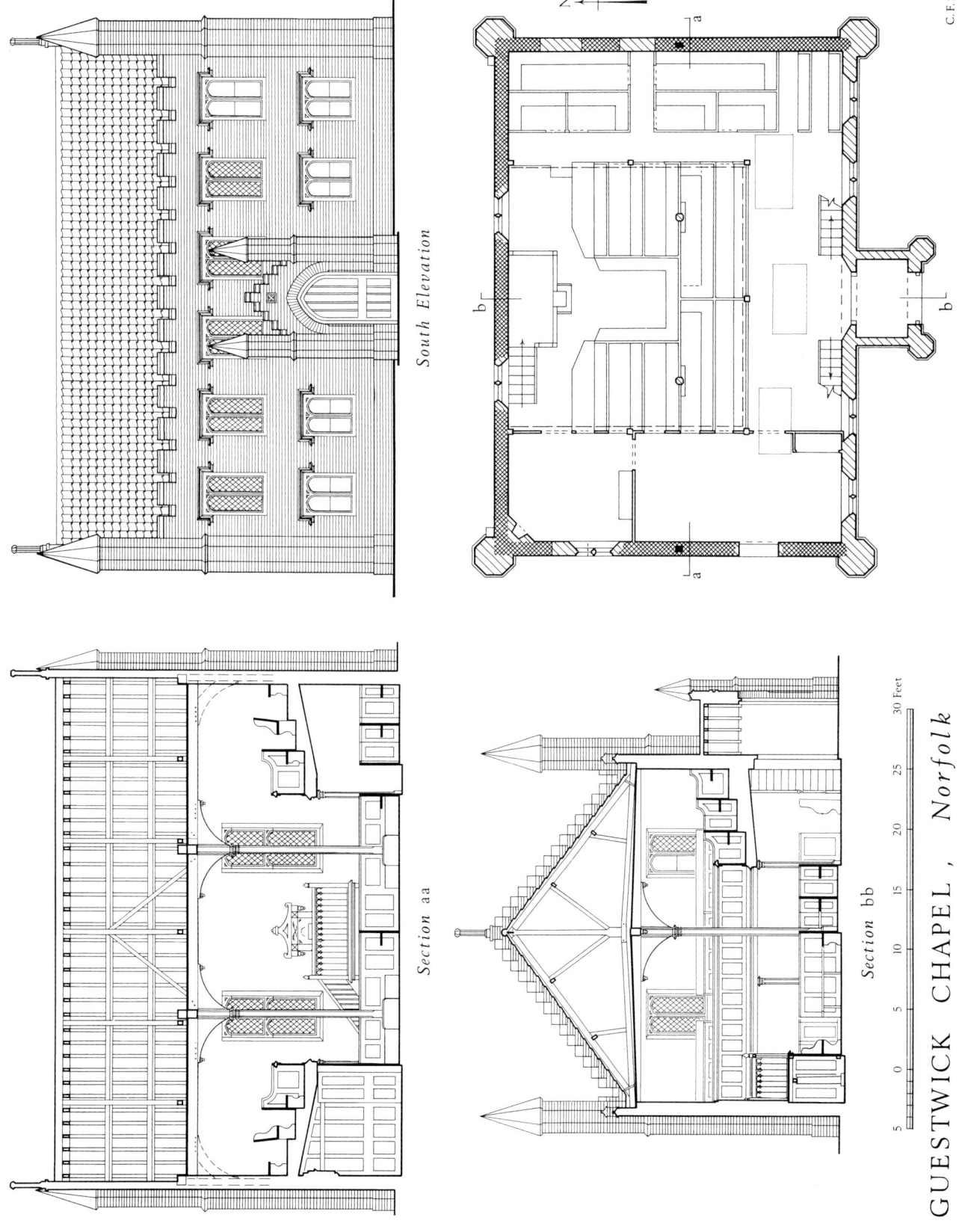

South Elevation

Section aa

Section bb

GUESTWICK CHAPEL, Norfolk

HORSFORD

(110) FREE METHODIST (TG 192163). Rendered walls, hipped pantiled roof. Two gallery windows above plain entrance. Tablet, partly defaced, dated 1866.

HORSHAM ST FAITH AND NEWTON ST FAITH

(111) WESLEYAN, Horsham St Faith (TG 217151). Brick and pantile, rendered three-bay front with pedimented porch and circular window above. Built 1822.

HUNSTANTON

(112) UNION CHAPEL, Sandringham Road (TF 673407). The chapel was built in 1870 for a mixed congregation of Baptists and Independents and placed in trust for 'Evangelical Nonconformists'. It has walls of brown stone with limestone dressings and decorative bands of tile and terracotta. At the W end is a polygonal vestibule separated from the body of the chapel by an arcade of three bays. The chapel contains some notable art-nouveau fittings given in memory of members of the Ibberson family. (URC)

Martin, R.G., *These Hundred Years: A Picture of Union Church, Hunstanton, 1870–1970* (c.1970). Virgoe, N. and Williamson, T. (eds), *Religious Dissent in East Anglia: Historical Perspectives* (1993) 120ff.

INGWORTH

(113) Former WESLEYAN REFORM (TG 193294). Brick and pantile, entrance in gabled end wall. Mid 19th-century.

ITTERINGHAM

(114) Former PRIMITIVE METHODIST, Wolterton Road (TG 147309). Built 1846, enlarged and re-fronted 1907.

KENNINGHALL

(115) Former BAPTIST, Church Street (TM 040861). The chapel built in 1807 was extended by one bay to the rear and a porch added in the later 19th century. The walls are faced with flints, knapped at the front, and have dressings of brickwork; the roof is hipped and covered with dark glazed pantiles. The front wall of three bays has two tiers of windows. The interior has a gallery around three sides with panelled front supported by square wooden posts. (Closed c.1974, now studio)

Inscription: on tablet reset in rear wall, '1807'. *Monuments*: in

Former Baptist chapel, Kenninghall. (115)

chapel (1) George Osborn, Gent., 1809. In burial-ground in front, row of nine monuments with body stones and head- and foot-stones, early 19th-century.

Browne (1877) 568.

(116) Former WESLEYAN (TM 037862). The chapel faced with red brick with yellow brick dressings has a hipped slate roof and round-arched windows. It incorporates the structure of a chapel of 1835 with walls of clay lump which was enlarged to NW and refaced *c*.1873. Small burial-ground to south. (Converted to squash court, 1978)

KING'S LYNN

(117) Former BAPTIST, Blackfriars Street (TF 621200). 'Stepney Chapel' was built in 1840–1 for a church in existence by the mid 18th century whose previous chapel had been built in 1809. The chapel, designed by James Fenton, has a pedimented front of gault brick with two entrances and groups of three narrow windows between. (Now New Life Christian Fellowship)

BM XXXIII (1841) 75, 406–7. Browne (1877) 561–3.

Stepney Chapel, Blackfriars Street, King's Lynn. (117)

(118) Former BAPTIST, Market Street (TF 620201). 'Union Chapel' built in 1859 by Robert Moffat Smith was converted for use as a museum in 1904 following the removal of the congregation to new premises in Wisbech Road in 1901. Brick with polygonal end towards the street and a square tower with stone spire.

Browne (1877) 563.

(119) Former UNITARIAN BAPTIST, Norfolk Street (TF 619203). 'Salem Chapel' was built 1811–12 for the supporters of Rev. Thomas Finch, minister of the Baptist church then meeting in the New Chapel in Broad Street, following a change in his religious sentiments. The chapel is a plain building of brick set well back on the N side of the street. The S front has a central entrance with round-arched upper window and shield-shaped tablet above inscribed 'MDCCCXI | SALEM | CHAPEL | UNITARIAN'. The interior was floored over after the chapel was closed in 1867 and converted to secular use. It had a deep gallery to the E and two windows formerly flanking the pulpit at the opposite end. The W end of the N wall incorporates an earlier gable with remains of brick tumbling. (Demolished *c*.1970)

Evans (1897) 120–1. *Monthly Repository* VI (1811) 679–80; VII (1812) 58.

Salem Chapel, King's Lynn. (Demolished) (119)

(120) FRIENDS, New Conduit Street (TF 618201). The meeting-house was registered 27 February 1775 as 'lately erected'. It had brick walls and a plain tiled roof. The broad three-bay front had a pedimented wooden porch between two wide segmental-arched windows. Two windows were set high up in the back wall above the stand. The interior (20ft by 30ft) had a stand of two stages

Former Friends' meeting-house, King's Lynn. (Demolished) (120)

extending the full width of the back wall, with two entrances flanking a raised centre and shaped ends to the front-facing benches. (Demolished in 1970)

Architectural Review XCI (April 1946) 109. Butler (1999) 443–4.

Primitive Methodist chapel, London Road, King's Lynn. (121)

(121) PRIMITIVE METHODIST, London Road (TF 621198). Brick with stone dressings; front of three bays, the centre bay with a Dutch gable and clock dial. Three round-arched doorways below arched mullioned windows with semicircular hood moulds. 1858, by J.A. Hillam.

(122) SALVATION ARMY, Wellesley Street (TF 622201). Small gable-fronted hall of 1880.

KIRBY CANE

(123) WESLEYAN, Kirby Row (TM 371927). Small brick chapel dated 1849. Gabled front with slightly splayed sides; former entrance within railed forecourt. Much enlarged to rear in 1892; Sunday-school hall added behind in 1922.

LITTLE SNORING

(124) PRIMITIVE METHODIST (TF 955323). Chapel dated 1860 with cottage attached; three-bay front to chapel but traces of blocked doorway to right of entrance indicate a re-siting of the doorway and the date tablet, perhaps the conversion of the earlier preaching-house opened in 1846.

LITTLE WALSINGHAM

(125) WESLEYAN (TF 933367). The chapel which stands at the S end of the village is set back between houses on the W side of the street. It was registered on 9 June 1794 as 'a place of Religious Worship for Protestant Dissenters'. The walls are of brickwork and the pyramidal roof is covered with pantiles. The front wall is of three bays with a central entrance having an open pediment supported by two Tuscan columns; there are two tiers of round-arched windows. The side walls have similar fenestration. The rear wall has a pair of windows flanking the pulpit.

The interior ($33\tfrac{3}{4}$ ft square) has a gallery around three sides with a panelled front; the supporting columns have mostly been replaced in cast iron but two half-pilasters remain below the back gallery. The pulpit and lower seating were replaced in the late 19th century but a full set of wood-grained box-pews remains in the gallery. Some original panelling also survives in the entrance vestibule.

Weathervane: on apex of roof, arrow with wavy tail, late 18th-century.

(126) Former PRIMITIVE METHODIST (TF 933369). Three-bay front of gault brick, sides of flint rubble. Built 1848. (Now converted to house)

Wesleyan chapel, Little Walsingham. (125)

Wesleyan chapel, Loddon. (127)

LODDON

(127) WESLEYAN, George Lane (TM 361989). The original brick chapel of 1835 remains at the rear of the present building, but much altered and converted to a school-room in 1893.

The later chapel standing to the E, built in 1893, is of red brick with sandstone dressings in a late Gothic style. The E front is gabled and divided into three bays by tall octagonal buttresses rising to ogee-topped stone cupolas and has a large five-light window above the central entrance. The interior has a single gallery at the entrance with lobby below.

(128) Former PRIMITIVE METHODIST, High Street (TM 362987). Gabled front of brick with stone dressings and three-light window with circular tracery above entrance. Porch dated 1899, foundation stones defaced. (Now youth centre)

LONG STRATTON

(129) CONGREGATIONAL, Stratton St Mary (TM 195920). A small chapel built in 1824 in Stratton St Michael was superseded by the present building in 1840–1; in 1892 a manse was built to the S and the chapel was re-fronted in a matching style. Red brick with broad gabled front and narrower centre of three bays with pediment and moulded brick details.

Browne (1877) 361–2.

Congregational chapel, Long Stratton. (129)

Former Congregational meeting-house, Mattishall. (133)

(130) WESLEYAN (TM 197930). Low three-bay brick front with round-arched openings separated by pilasters, simple pediment with ball finials at the corners; dated 1830. A rough plan accompanying the 1851 census returns shows two school-rooms below the rear gallery each side of the entrance. (Entirely refitted 1989)

Norfolk Record Society *Religious Worship in Norfolk* LXII (1998) 204.

MARTHAM

(131) BAPTIST (TG 457181). Red brick with terracotta dressings, built 1879 for church founded 1799.

Browne (1877) 561.

(132) PRIMITIVE METHODIST (TG 454180). Broad gabled front of red brick with large arch to centre bay rising into the gable filled with gault brick and enclosing three round-arched windows; built 1881 replacing a chapel of 1844 then converted to Oddfellows' Hall.

MATTISHALL

(133) Former CONGREGATIONAL (TG 030117). A nonconformist congregation in existence by the early 18th century had a meeting-house on this site, demolished *c*.1760 following the demise of the cause. About 1770 a new Independent church was established through the efforts of John Glover of Norwich who rebuilt the chapel on the original site, which is at some considerable distance from the village. This was registered on 13 July 1771 under the name of 'The Dissenters' Meeting-house'. After the opening of another chapel in the village (134) in 1857, to which the church eventually removed, the old meeting-house continued in occasional use until *c*.1955; it has since been used for farm storage.

The meeting-house is a square building of brick with a pyramidal roof covered with pantiles. It was much refitted and repaired externally in the late 19th century. Against the N side is a later annexe with lean-to roof forming an entrance vestibule and school-room; against the S wall is a small vestry and the site of an adjacent cottage, now demolished.

The E wall facing a small burial-ground is of four bays with two tiers of windows all with marginal glazing bars of the late 19th century. There is an original moulded brick eaves cornice and plinth; this cornice continues on the N side and for a short distance on the W but otherwise is of serrated brickwork. The W wall has a pair of round-arched pulpit windows with 19th-century frames. In the N wall are two upper windows, now blocked, and three openings below within the annexe, that to the E being a doorway to the meeting-house, the other two being altered and shuttered openings serving the school-room. The S wall has several blocked windows at the upper level.

The interior (32¼ft by 30¼ft) has a moulded plaster ceiling cornice. A gallery along the E side has an open iron balustraded front of the late 19th century.

Monuments: in burial-ground, of the early 19th century and later. (*See also* (134)).

Browne (1877) 351–4. *CYB* (1847) 155.

(134) CONGREGATIONAL (TG 046110). The chapel built in 1857, originally as a 'lecture hall' in connection with (133), is a simple structure of red brick with crow-stepped gables and stone-mullioned windows with square labels. The front faces W and has a small porch and the date 1857 in the gable behind. The interior was refitted in the late 19th century. (URC)

Monument: formerly preserved within the old meeting-house (133) but following closure reset externally against W wall, to John Glover (who revived the Congregational cause in Mattishall), 1774, headstone with (formerly) finely preserved decoration and added inscription at base 'NB – This Stone was put down at the Cathedral Church of NORWICH, (where the above person is Interred) but by those in Authority was not judged proper to stand,

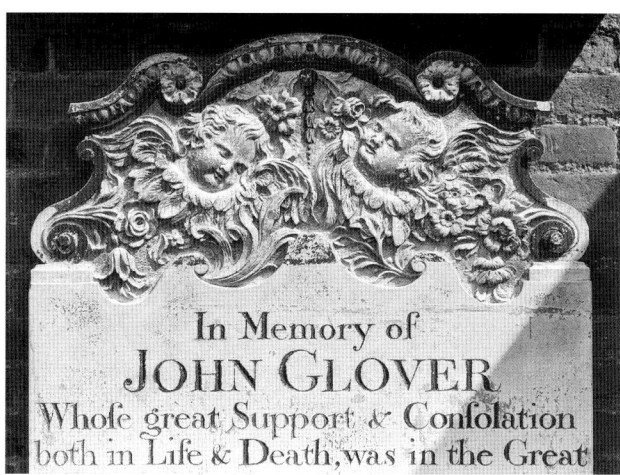

Congregational chapel, Mattishall. Monument. (134)

in consequence of which it was removed to this Place, and fixed up as a Testimony of our respect to the Deceased, and as a Declaration of our firm belief of the same Evangelical Principles expressed above'. (Stone rapidly weathering on exposure)

(135) Former FRIENDS (TG 034114). A meeting-house purchased c.1687 seems to have been rebuilt or replaced c.1700. The present building, which may be on or near the former site, is a small building of the mid 18th century. The walls are of brickwork with a serrated brick eaves cornice and the roof is hipped and pantiled; a later cottage adjoins to the south. The broad E front has a central doorway with moulded wood surround and a cornice supported by a pair of scrolled brackets; at either side is a wide segmentally arched window, that to the N with original wood frame and the remains of rectangular leaded glazing. The other three walls are blank.

The interior (20½ft by 26¼ft) retains its original fittings with a stand centrally against the W wall and two galleries at the N and S ends with partly open fronts having thin square balusters and turned newels, and separate staircases to right and left of the entrance.

Former Friends' meeting-house, Mattishall. (135)

Monument: loose externally, small Quaker headstone, to Lidi wife of Steven Gooch, 1690.

Butler (1999) 445–6.

(136) Former PRIMITIVE METHODIST, Church Plain (TG 053110). Large rectangular chapel faced with pebbles and brick dressings and with a hipped pantiled roof. Built 1856, superseded 1900. (Now converted to garage)

(137) PRIMITIVE METHODIST (TG 049112). Red and grey brick with narrow round-arched windows; Of 1900 by J. Kerridge.

METHWOLD

(138) WESLEYAN, High Street (TL 733948). Brick front, otherwise of flint with gault brick dressings. Three-bay front with giant pilasters, parapet and narrow pediment over centre dated 1831.

MULBARTON

(139) PRIMITIVE METHODIST (TG 193013). Gabled brick front with denominational name and date 1900 on large inscription panel over porch.

NEATISHEAD

(140) BAPTIST (TG 339197). The chapel of red brick with a roof covered with dark glazed pantiles was built in 1811 and extended by a wing centrally to the rear in 1857. The front is symmetrical with two round-arched pulpit windows between two doorways with open pediments. At each end are single-storey lean-to vestries, one considerably enlarged, perhaps the original stable. The interior has separate end galleries and a third gallery in the rear wing; all have plain panelled fronts supported by slender Greek Doric columns. The seating throughout is contemporary, with box-pews in the two original galleries and open-backed benches in the third; the lower pews have shaped ends.

Inscriptions: on bricks in rear wing, names and dates '1857'. *Monuments*: in chapel, on front wall (1) William Cubitt, 1814, and Martha his widow 'who survived him nearly 40 years'; (2) John Clowes, [1854?], and Ann his wife, [1851?]; (3) William Quincey Cubitt, 1872, signed 'J. Stanley, St Stephen's Norwich'; (4) William Spurgeon, first pastor, 1861, Ann his first wife, 1833, Sophia their daughter, 1816, and Elizabeth his widow, 1864; (5) John Banham, 1861, Ruth his first wife, 1824, and Mary his second wife, 1856, signed 'R.J. Perfitt, Stalham'.

Browne (1877) 555. Ivimey IV (1830) 521.

NECTON

(141) BAPTIST (TF 895093). The Particular Baptist church was formed in 1776 and the meeting-house built in 1802. Rectangular broad-fronted chapel with hipped roof, greatly altered externally by unsympathetic concrete rendering, patent tiled roof and renewal of window frames. The S front with two entrances and four windows above and between has been extended by one bay to the E to provide vestry accommodation; two windows in the N wall flank the pulpit.

The interior (20¼ft by 32ft) has a gallery around three sides, the S gallery possibly being an addition. The pulpit rostrum and lower pews date from a late 19th-century refitting.

Fittings – *Clock*: loose in gallery, by S.H. Boyce, Dereham, 19th-century. *Monuments*: in chapel, behind pulpit (1) Rev. Jonathan Carver, 36 years pastor, 1840; below E gallery (2) three children of Robert and Elizabeth Goodrick of Swaffham, 1810, 1813, 1813; below W gallery (3) Henry Perkins, 1847, and Frances his widow, 1856, signed 'Heyhoe, Lynn Road, Swaffham'; in W gallery (4) George Walker, 1882, and Ann his widow, 1890, signed 'A.S. Tucker, 147 Euston Road'; on S wall (5) George Walker, 1896; externally, in railed enclosure S of vestry (6) Richard Baker, pastor, 1859.

Browne (1877) 566.

NEW BUCKENHAM

(142) WESLEYAN (TM 086904). Big pedimented brick front with terminal pilasters, round-arched doorway and windows, and small three-bay Sunday-school alongside; both dated 1884.

NORDELPH

(143) WESLEYAN (TF 556010). Three-bay brick front with two tiers of windows, terminal pilasters with cornice. In the pedimented gable is a band inscribed 'WESLEYAN CHAPEL 1861', and a clock dial; above is a small bell-cote with one bell.

NORTH CREAKE

(144) Former PRIMITIVE METHODIST (TF 852381). Brick and pantile, gabled front with shaped stone tablet dated 1876. Sunday-school wing added 1880. (Converted to house)

NORTH ELMHAM

(145) Former CONGREGATIONAL (TF 984209). The 'Old Chapel' stands on the W side of the main road. It was opened on 12 October 1824. The brick front is of five bays separated but not terminated by brick pilasters; it was extended to the S by two further bays. The gabled N wall faced with flint pebbles has two segmentally arched pulpit windows, now blocked. (Now converted to a house)

Browne (1877) 355.

NORTH LOPHAM

(146) WESLEYAN (TM 036828). The chapel built in 1812 has a brick front, side walls faced with flint pebbles and brick dressings, and a hipped roof covered with dark glazed pantiles except for the front part, which is slated. The broad front is of three bays with two round-arched doorways and a platband between two tiers of windows.

The interior has a gallery around three sides with original seating; the lower seating and pulpit were replaced in the late 19th century.

Clock: on front of gallery, dated 1856, by Spendlove, Thetford. *Inscription*: externally, on loose tablet, 'WESLEYAN Sunday School 1835.', perhaps from demolished building alongside to left. *Monuments*: in front burial-ground, many headstones of the early 19th century and later.

Behind the chapel and extending beyond it to the right is the Wesleyan day school of 1864. The former playground at the rear is now in horticultural use and has a pair of earth closets to each side set well back from the chapel.

(147) Former PRIMITIVE METHODIST (TM 037827). Small three-bay chapel, much altered; first built 1826. (Now 'Bourne Cottage')

NORTH WALSHAM

(148) CONGREGATIONAL (TG 281304). The church claims descent from that at Bradfield (*see* Swafield (203)). A chapel was built in Vicarage Street in 1808–9 which remained in use as a Sunday-school after the erection of the present building; it was demolished c.1971. The present chapel with gabled front and Gothic windows was built in 1857–8.

Fittings – *Glass*: coloured glass window of 1870 brought from Bradfield after closure in 1967. *Monument*: loose in vestry, wall monument from Vicarage Street, to Eliza wife of Rev. James Browne, pastor, 1834, and George their son, 1828, 'buried under the pulpit'. *Plate*: from Bradfield, *see* (203).

Browne (1877) 322–3.

(149) FRIENDS, Mundesley Road (TG 285318). 'Swafield' meeting-house, so called although just outside the boundary of that parish, was built in 1772 replacing a building of 1702 on the same site. This is a square building with brick walls and a pyramidal roof covered with pantiles. The S front is of three bays with a central entrance between hung sash windows and three smaller windows above. The E and W walls have each two upper windows and the N wall is blank. A small meeting-room adjoins to the east.

The interior (28¼ft square) has a flat plaster ceiling with moulded cornice. Across the S end is a gallery with boarded front and upper rail supported by a pair of wooden columns which are repeated above. The gallery is divided by a high wooden partition (*see* p. 256) and approached by twin staircases in the front corners. The stand is continuous across the N wall. The room to the E has outer doorways to N and S, both now blocked, and wall benches around all sides.

Inscriptions: on stone in N wall below eaves, date '1772'; the same date, with initials, appears on many bricks in this wall. *Seating*: to lower floor, loose benches, some of late 18th-century date; in gallery fixed benches without backs.

Burial-ground: detached, 150 yards S of meeting-house, with brick boundary walls and gate piers to the road, contains about twelve 19th-century monuments; also one loose headstone to Elizabeth Bourn, widow, 1732.

Butler (1999) 446–8.

Wesleyan chapel, North Lopham. (146)

Friends' meeting-house, North Walsham. (149)

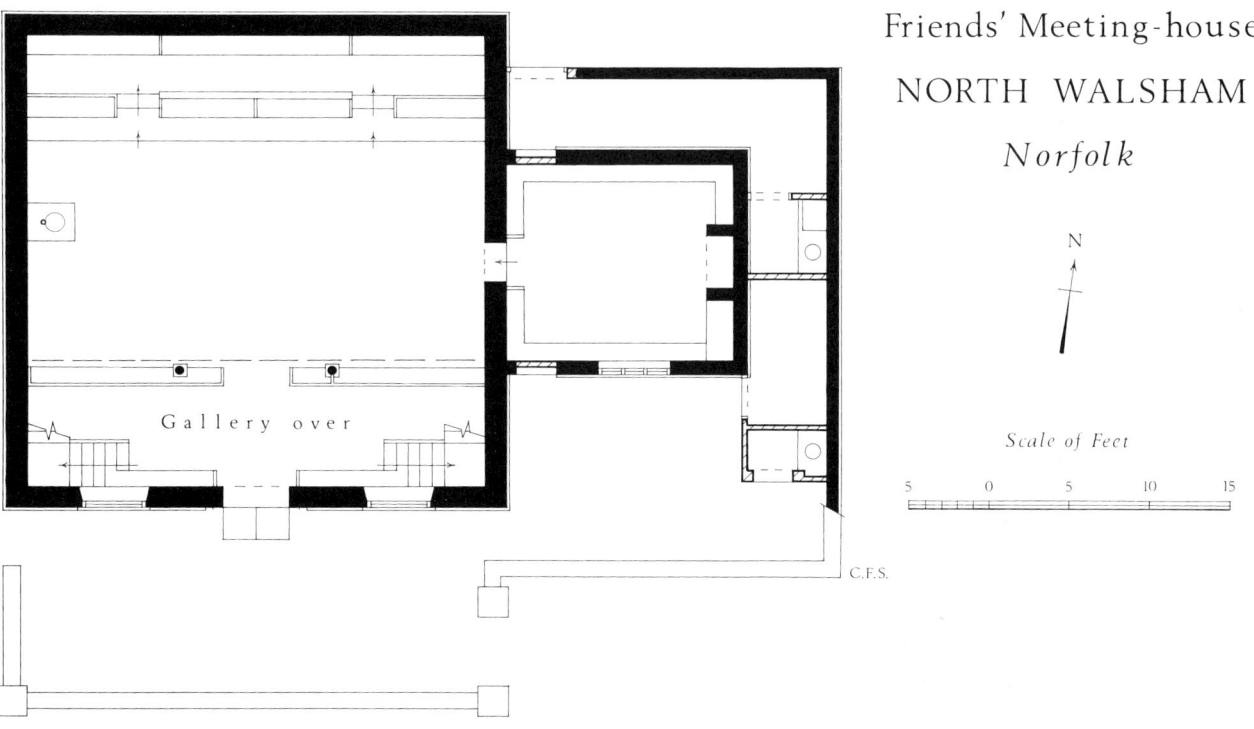

Friends' Meeting-house
NORTH WALSHAM
Norfolk

Friends' meeting-house, North Walsham. Gallery seating. (149)

NORWICH

(150) BAPTIST, St Mary's Plain (TG 22850910). The chapel of 1951–2 replaces a chapel of 1812. The congregation, in existence by 1669, originated by division from the Independent 'Old Meeting'. About 1687 they acquired the 'East Granary' or eastern cloister of Blackfriars Convent for a meeting-house. The present site was first occupied in 1744. *Plate*: includes two cups of 1746–7.

Browne (1877) 549–53. Gould, G., *et al.*, *Open Communion and the Baptists of Norwich – St Mary's Norwich Chapel Case* (1860). Jewson, C.B., *St Mary's in Four Centuries 1669–1969* (1969).

(151) Former STRICT BAPTIST, Timber Hill (TG 231083). 'Orford Hill' chapel, dated 1833, has a broad rendered front with three round-arched entrances and five plain sash windows above. (Further openings pierced in front wall on conversion to commercial use, 1993)

(152) THE OLD MEETING-HOUSE, Colegate (TG 231091). The Independent congregation originated in 1643 when a group of separatists returning from exile in Holland formed a church by dismission from the church in Rotterdam. The Society then constituted under the pastorate of William Bridge, formerly rector of St Peter's, Hungate, included members both in Norwich and Great Yarmouth. The inconvenience of this arrangement was soon apparent and in 1644 the Norwich members separated. During the Commonwealth the church met in St George's, Tombland, in which they erected an E gallery, removed 1680. By 1672 meetings were being held in the West Granary, formerly part of Blackfriars Convent and soon after 1685 a brewhouse in St Edmund's parish was converted for use as a meeting-house.

The present building, opened in 1693, stands behind houses on the N side of Colegate on 'part of the site of the Friars' great garden'. It was described by Blomefield in the mid 18th century as 'a large handsome square building with a roof flat at top and covered with lead, and the hipped part of it with tiles'. The walls are of brickwork and the hipped roof, reconstructed without the lead flat, is covered with pantiles. The S front of five bays, divided by pilasters of rubbed brick with carved stone Corinthian capitals and terminated by brick quoins, has in each bay two tiers of windows with moulded brick architraves separated by short brick bands, doorways with bracketed canopies in the end bays, and a moulded and modillioned eaves cornice which continues around the E and W end walls. In the W wall is a blocked outer doorway with segmental-arched head. The vestry against the E wall was rebuilt *c*.1862. The rear N wall has a plain eaves cornice and a platband at mid height; windows in the end bays mark the returns of the gallery while between them two tall round-arched windows with altered heads flank the pulpit – two small oval windows at the centre, inserted in the early 18th century, have been blocked internally. All the windows have hung sashes with narrow glazing bars of the late 18th century replacing cross-framed windows with leaded casements; one original window remains internally within the W wall of the vestry. A brick-built Sunday-school building SW of the meeting-house is dated 1842.

The interior (44¼ft by 64½ft) has a flat plaster ceiling. A gallery around three sides is supported by eight Roman Doric columns with an upper order rising to the ceiling having four-sided Ionic capitals varying slightly in their profiles and entablature blocks. The gallery front has bolection-moulded panels. The pulpit and seating largely date from a refitting in the mid 19th century. The roof is supported by four softwood trusses with king- and queen-posts and diagonal struts of the late 18th century.

Fittings – *Clock*: on front of S gallery, octagonal dial with bolection-moulded surround, early 18th-century. *Communion Tables*: two (1) with turned legs, top 5ft 11in. by 2ft 8in., 18th-century; (2) in deacon's vestry, refectory table on six chamfered legs, top 10ft 11in. by 2ft 7½in., late 17th-century.

Monuments and *Floorslabs*. *Monuments*: on N wall (1) John Dawson, 1756, 47 years deacon, marble tablet surmounted by obelisk bearing a crown in glory and on apron a winged cherub's head; (2) John Corey ALM, 1698, reset capstone from former table-tomb with shield-of-arms and restored Latin inscription; (3) Rev. John Boutet Innes, 1837; (4) Rev. Samuel Newton, 1810, signed 'Cushing'; (5) John Lucas, 1703, minister, and Mary his widow, 1718, reset capstone from former table-tomb, with shield-of-arms; (6) Rev. Thomas Scott, 1746, similar to (1) but with cartouche-of-arms. On E wall (7) Jeremiah Tomson, 1721, Jane his wife, 1721, and Jeremiah eldest son of James and Mary Tomson, 1721, marble tablet flanked by Corinthian columns and surmounted by urn; (8) James Tompson, 1727, and Mary (Stackhouse) his widow, 1728, with pair of Corinthian pilasters supporting a broken pediment; (9) Daniel Scott, 1804, Mary his first wife, 1771, and Mary his second wife, 1832, oval tablet between fluted pilasters; (10) John Scott, 1796, and Susannah his wife, 1773, with fluted pilasters and pediment, erected by

The Old Meeting-house, Norwich.

their sons Daniel and Thomas. On S wall (11) George Scott, 1827; (12) Elizabeth (Theobald) wife of Edward Blakey, 1824; (13) John Theobald, 1831, Mary his wife, 1828, and Thomas their grandson, 1828; (14) John Cozens, 1841, and Mary his widow, 1842, signed 'Watson'. On W wall (15) Susanna (Claydon) wife of James Walters, 1814. In gallery, on E wall (16) Thomas Theobald, 1841, and Elizabeth his widow, 1859, signed 'Watson'; on S wall (17) William Gordon Edwards, 1846, and Elizabeth his widow, 1861; (18) John Jarrold, 1852, Hannah Elizabeth his wife, 1840, and John James their eldest son, 1843.

Externally, on E wall (19) Susanna wife of Robert Ward, 1785; on S wall (20) Samuel Blunderfield, 1835, and Elizabeth his widow, 1838; (21) Hepburn John Balls, 1845; on W wall (22) Sophia Youngman, 1818; (23) John Dawson Paul, 1828, and Ann (Cole) his widow, 1834; (24) Rev. Samuel Newton, 1810, Mary his wife, 1798, and Mary Wood Newton their daughter, 1794; (25) Thomas Paul, 1787, and Anna his widow, 1821; on N wall (26) Edward Williams 'late Minister and Elder of the Baptist Congregation Lately Meeting in the Granary in the City of Norwich', 1713, reset from former table-tomb, restored 1867. In burial-ground, to N, several headstones of 18th century and later, much worn and reset; S of front, numerous ledger stones.

Floorslabs: W of pulpit (1) Mrs Prudence Browne, 1725; E of pulpit (2) Joshua Lincoln, 1742, Esther his wife, 1724, and Sarah their daughter, wife of John Allen, 1742; (3) Joseph Nicol Scott MD, 1769, with shield-of-arms; in SE vestibule (4) Joseph Brittan, 1734, *et al.*; (5) Robert Offley, 1716, Mary his wife, 1703, Mary their daughter, 1738, and Samuel Crome, her husband, 1754, with shield-of-arms; in SE vestibule (6) Elizabeth Offley, 1741, with lozenge-of-arms; (7) Maria wife of Simeon Waller, 1721; (8) Samuel Wood DD, 1767, 20 years pastor, and Mary his widow, 1788.

Organ: in W gallery, case with five sets of pipes, front decorated with dolphins and angels blowing horns, upper part of case possibly 17th-century. *Pictures*: in minister's vestry (1) portrait of Rev. John Hallett, minister 1856–78, oils; (2) interior of meeting-house, by S.A. Sewell, 1892, water-colour, showing box-pews divided by central aisle on axis of pulpit; (3) exterior of meeting-house, by John T. Cox, 1877, water-colour. In deacons' vestry (4) portrait of William Barnham, mayor 1652, MP 1658, with shield-of-arms, oils; (5) view of meeting-house from SE, lithograph by J. Gleadah after drawing by James Sillett, *c.*1800. *Pitchpipe*: in case in SE vestibule, late 18th-century. *Plate*: includes a set of six cups of 1757 and a plate of 1758. *Pulpit*: small rostrum with twin staircases, 19th-century. *Seating*: to lower floor, remade *c.*1900 incorporating material from earlier pews; chair, in case in SE vestibule, with cane seat and rounded arms, reputedly the pulpit chair of the Rev. John Cromwell, minister 1675–85, but possibly later. *Sundial*: on front

The Old Meeting-house, NORWICH · *Norfolk*

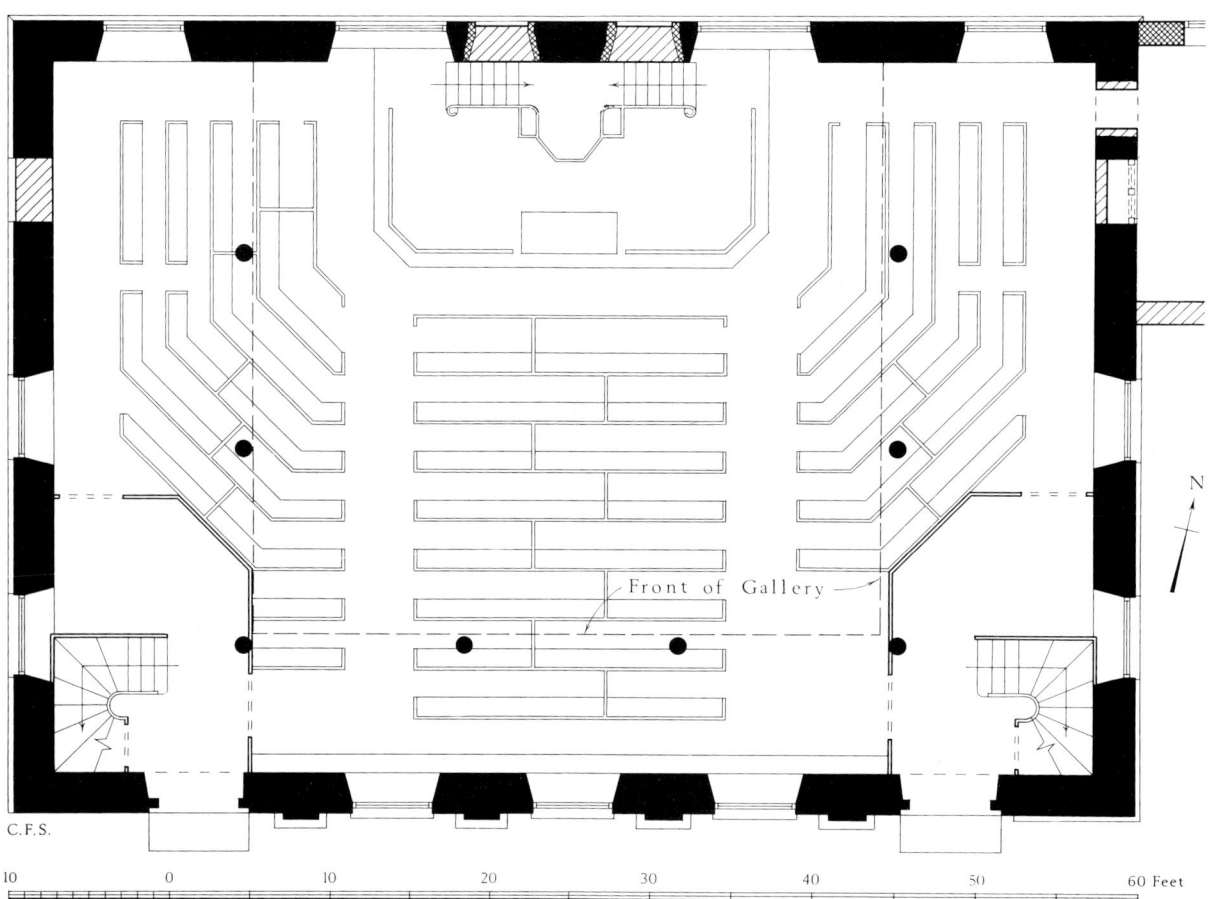

wall, rectangular dial with painted date '1693' now repainted MDCXCIII.

Blomefield, F., *History of Norfolk* II (1739) 822–5. Browne (1877) 252–74. *CYB* (1863) 339–40; (1881) 373–4. Norfolk Record Society *Miscellany* XXII (1951) 1–9.

(153) CONGREGATIONAL, Princes Street (TG 232088). The church (now URC) originated in services commenced at the Tabernacle (156) in 1817 by the Rev. John Alexander. A chapel was built in 1819 and parts of the side walls of that building are incorporated in the present structure; this was of grey brick and had a front of five bays with a three-bay pediment. The chapel was heightened, extended to the front and refitted in 1868–9 by Edward Boardman. The front is of yellow brick with four giant pilasters and an elaborately detailed pediment overall. A large school building of 1879–80 stands adjacent.

Browne (1877) 274–6. *Cong. Mag.* II (1819) 251–2. *CYB* (1869) 234, obituary of John Alexander.

(154) CONGREGATIONAL, Chapel Field (TG 227083). The chapel of 1858, by Joseph James, has walls of grey brick with Romanesque detail. The gabled front projects between two slender towers with spires. (Demolished 1972)

Browne (1877) 276–7. *CYB* (1859) 255–6; (1860) 263; (1863) 323.

(155) SURREY CHAPEL, St Crispin's Road (TG 229093). The chapel of 1976 replaces an Independent chapel of 1854 in Surrey Street. *Inscription*: reset on outer wall, tablet first erected 1931 at the Lollards' Pit, Norwich, commemorating the martyrdom of Thomas Bilney, 19 August 1531.

(156) THE TABERNACLE, Bishopsgate (TG 23730902). Calvinistic Methodism was introduced to Norwich in 1751 by James Wheatley, a Methodist preacher who earlier that year had been expelled from the Wesleyan Connexion. Wheatley's first Tabernacle was a temporary timber structure built on Timber Hill which shortly after erection suffered severely at the hands of a violent mob. The new Tabernacle in Bishopsgate was built on land acquired in 1752 and was opened by George Whitefield in August 1755. It remained the property of Wheatley who in 1758, perhaps as a result of certain alleged irregularities and a secession led by Robert Robertson, one of the assistant preachers, offered the lease of the building together with one at Forncett (72) to John Wesley. Wesley's attempts to enforce a more rigid discipline on the still largely Calvinist congregation proved impossible and he relinquished the lease in 1764. In 1775 the Tabernacle was acquired by the Countess of Huntingdon in whose connexion it remained, despite several secessions in the 19th century and a greatly depleted congregation, until its sale and demolition in 1953.

The Tabernacle, designed by Thomas Ivory, was set back on the N side of the street. The walls were of brick, probably square on plan, with two tiers of sash windows and the hipped roof was covered with pantiles. Adjacent to the chapel was a house of three storeys for the minister and first proprietor.

Seymour (1839) II: 327–52. Wearing, S.J., *Georgian Norwich, its Builders* (1926) 16–18.

(157) FRIENDS, Upper Goat Lane (TG 22800865). Prior to the erection of the first meeting-house on this site in 1679 meetings had been held in a room in St Laurence parish. The 1679 building

Friends' meeting-house, Upper Goat Lane, Norwich. (157)

was described in the minutes of Norwich monthly meeting as 40ft by 30ft externally with brick walls and four windows in the front wall and four dormer windows above; it was divided internally by 'a partition made to run with wheels to enlarge or lessen the roome as occasion requires' (Monthly Minute Book 1671–90, op. cit. below).

The present building of 1826, designed by John Thomas Patience, has brick walls with stone dressings at the front. The E front, set back in a courtyard flanked by lower wings, is of two stages: the lower stage has a central porch with four Greek Doric columns, the upper stage has three round-arched windows separated by pilasters with an entablature above.

The interior has an E vestibule; the large meeting-house beyond has an E gallery supported by four Ionic columns, two windows set high in the N and S walls and a stand at the W end with three tiers of seats. A smaller meeting-house to the W, divided from the larger by a solid wall and approached by a corridor on the S side of the building, has a S gallery supported by two columns with unusual square capitals and a low stand on the opposite side.

Butler (1999) 448–54. Norfolk Record Office, SF 53, Monthly Minute Book 1671–90.

(158) FRIENDS, Gildencroft (TG 22750933). The site was acquired about 1670 for use as a burial-ground. The meeting-house built in 1694–9 was largely demolished following severe war damage in 1942, but a fragment remains incorporated in a new building. The walls were of brickwork and the roof hipped and tiled, with a central lead flat. The S front had a wide central entrance, which remains in the surviving portion, and eight bays of cross-framed windows in two tiers with four intermediate giant pilasters.

The interior (42ft by 60ft) was drastically altered in 1892–4 on conversion for use as an adult school. The original structure appears to have been erected by agreement with 'a carpenter' who, in 1694, complained of Friends having driven a 'hard bargain'. The desire to reduce expenditure may have been responsible for a weakness in the design for in 1712 it was found necessary to strengthen the roof structure by two further pillars, in addition to the four which stood in line with the fronts of separate galleries at the E and W ends; the two added pillars being freestanding on the main axis of the entrance. The stand was centrally against the N wall.

Friends' meeting-house, Gildencroft, Norwich.
(© *Jarrolds*) (158)

The extensive burial-ground to the E is bounded by brick walls, one rebuilt 1839, with row numbers 1–20. Monuments include many uniform round-topped headstones of the 19th century and later, some with earlier dates.

Butler (1999) 453–5. Norfolk Record Office, SF 64, Monthly Meeting minutes.

(159) THE OCTAGON CHAPEL, Colegate (TG 23070907). The Presbyterian society was formed soon after 1662 under John Collinges DD, ejected vicar of St Stephen's, Norwich. In 1672 meetings appear to have been held in the 'East Granary', formerly the dorter of the Blackfriars Convent, part of which remains behind St Andrew's Hall. The present site, on the N side of Colegate, was acquired in 1686–7 and an agreement made with Thomas Sad, bricklayer, and Stephen Cooper, carpenter, for the erection of a meeting-house which was registered in 1689. The building, illustrated in a drawing of 1723 by T. Kirkpatrick, was a large rectangular structure with two parallel hipped roofs covered with pantiles, the sides were of five bays and there was a double-gabled rear wing, possibly an addition.

The Octagon Chapel, which replaced the former, was built in 1754–6 to designs by Thomas Ivory, who superseded Robert Brettingham as architect following a competition. It was visited by John Wesley in 1757, who noted in his *Journal* (23 December): 'I was shown Dr Taylor's new meeting-house, perhaps the most elegant one in all Europe. It is eight square, built of the finest brick, with sixteen sash-windows below, as many above, and eight sky lights in the dome, which indeed are purely ornamental. The inside is finished in the highest taste, and is as clean as any nobleman's saloon. The communion table is fine mahogany; the very latches of the pew doors are polished brass. How can it be thought that the old coarse gospel should find admission here?' In spite of the final comment, which may relate to the heterodox sentiments of the minister, John Taylor, which presaged the later acceptance of Unitarianism by the society, Wesley was strongly influenced by the octagonal plan, which he recommended for use in his own chapels.

The chapel is a regular octagon, with two tiers of windows, the heads segmentally arched below the gallery and round-arched above. In front of the central entrance is a wide pedimented porch with four Ionic columns. The roof, which is covered with dark glazed pantiles, has eight circular dormer windows with shaped cheeks and, at the apex, a slender finial erected in 1975 to replace one removed a century before.

The interior (60ft wide) has a domed ceiling supported by eight Corinthian columns with entablature blocks and arches above, on the line of the gallery fronts; the elaborate plaster decoration is the work of William Wilkins. The pulpit was replaced by the present rostrum in 1889 and the seating was much altered at that period although incorporating much old material. Two round-arched doorways at the rear were blocked in the 19th century and an outer entrance made to the vestry which may also be an inserted feature. The roof structure comprises a multiple collar of eight radiating parts, the ends carried by the upward extensions of the main columns and supporting a central king-post against which rest the principal rafters, which are further strengthened by queen-posts and diagonal struts.

Fittings – *Clock*: above inner doorway, signed 'Thomas Smith, Norwich' 18th-century. *Door*: see Tharston (209). *Monuments*: in chapel (1) Margaretta Dreyer, 1820, signed 'J.Bacon, London'; (2) Sarah widow of Benjamin Elden, 1763, with lozenge-of-arms; (3) Benjamin Elden, 1759, with scrolled sides and shaped top flanked by antique lamps, signed 'T.Rawlins'; (4) Sarah widow of William Petty 'silk-throwster', 1751, with lozenge-of-arms, signed 'T. Rawlins'; (5) George Coldham, 1769, with cartouche-of-arms and crest; (6) Isaac Laughton Marsh, 1834, Elizabeth his wife, 1781, and Anne Nasmith Marsh their daughter, 1841, signed 'Patent Works, Westminster'; (7) Rev. John Taylor STP, 1761, with Latin inscription, signed 'J. Bacon junr., London'; (8) John Taylor, 1826, 48 years deacon, and Susanna his wife, 1823, with shield-of-arms, signed 'S.Manning'; (9) Nathaniel Bolingbroke, 1840, Mary

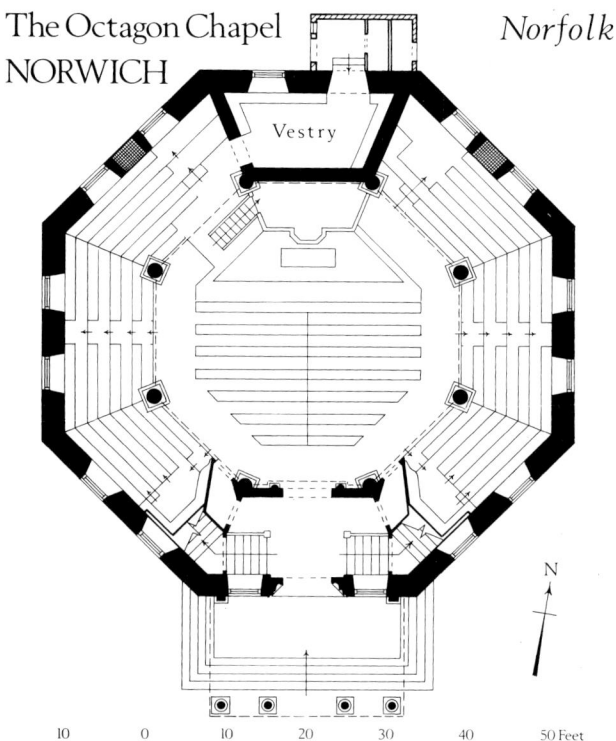

Octagon Chapel, Norwich.

his wife, 1833, and two children, Ellen, 1836, and Mary 1834; (10) Henry Reeve MD, 1814, with Latin inscription, signed 'J. Bacon junr., London'; (11) Philip Meadows Martineau, 1829, with shield-of-arms; (12) Rev. William Enfield LL.D, 1797, signed 'J. Athow'; (13) John Youngs, 1850, Lois his wife, 1845, and Kate their youngest daughter, 1833, signed 'J. Stanley'. In burial-ground W of chapel (14) Ezekiel Delight, 1797, and Sarah his widow, 1805; (15) Abraham Brook, 1792, Elizabeth his widow, 1815, and Charles their son, 1795; (16) [...]as Maltby, 1788; (17) Mary Nasmith, 1776, and Thomas Nasmith, 1781; (18) James Hay Ward, 1794; (19) Rev. W. Enfield LL.D, 1797; (20) Rev. John Hoyle, 1775, and Mary his wife, 1760; (21) G.C., 1769; (22) Rev. John Houghton, 1800, Mary his first wife, 1790, and Elizabeth his second wife, 1837.

Picture: pen drawing of former meeting-house from NE, by T. Kirkpatrick, 1723, for his *Prospect of Norwich*. *Plate*: includes four two-handled cups with covers of 1785 and six plates of 1713.

Archaeological Journal CVI (1949) 96–7. Browne (1877) 277–82. Curnock, (ed.), (1938) IV: 244. Evans (1897) 189–91. Taylor, J., and Taylor, E., *History of the Octagon Chapel, Norwich* (1848).

(160) Former PRIMITIVE METHODIST, Queens Road (TG 232078). Large chapel built 1872, of grey brick with stone dressings. Front of three bays with pedimented centre and giant pilasters flanking segmentally arched entrance with wheel-window above. (Interior gutted 1983 on conversion to office use)

(161) UNITED METHODIST, Chapel Field Road (TG 227081). Grey brick with banded rustication, gabled front of three bays formerly surmounted by urn finials, arched centre bay enclosing entrance and upper window. Foundation stones laid 1880.

(162) BLACKFRIARS' HALL (TQ 231088). The chancel of the church of the Blackfriars, rebuilt after a fire in 1413, became civic property in 1540 and the authorities allowed its use as a place of worship for 'strangers'. By the end of the 16th century it was occupied by a Dutch congregation which continued to meet occasionally until the early 20th century. The only remaining fittings are, internally on N wall (1) monument to pastor John Elison, 1639, tablet flanked by Ionic columns carrying a broken pediment; (2) brass to pastor Theophilus Ellison, 1676, son of the foregoing.

On the N side of the church, on the E and W sides of the cloisters, were the dorter and frater. These were converted to granaries in the 16th century. In the following century the former, which survives, was used as a meeting-house by the Presbyterians and subsequently by the Baptists. The frater, or W granary, demolished in 1804, was used by the Independents.

Sutermeister, Helen, *The Norwich Blackfriars* (1977).

OLD BUCKENHAM

(163) BAPTIST (TM 065917). The chapel dated 1831 on a later tablet on the front was variously altered and embellished in 1857 and in the 1880s. The walls are of brick and the roof is hipped and pantiled. The front of three bays has two later brick pilasters at the corners and formerly had two doorways which were covered by later gabled porches. The porches were removed *c.*1959, replaced by windows and a central entrance constructed. Behind the chapel is the 'Jubilee Memorial Sunday School' of 1887. The interior has a single gallery at the entrance with some original seating; other fittings date from the late 19th century. (Proposed conversion to house, 1993)

B.Hbk (1891) 149–51; (1894) 156–7. Browne (1877) 568.

(164) PRIMITIVE METHODIST (TM 060912). Red brick with yellow brick dressings; three-bay front with pedimental gable, corner pilasters and tall round-arched windows. Dated 1871.

ORMESBY ST MARGARET WITH SCRATBY

(165) Former BAPTIST, Ormesby St Margaret (TG 493150). Small chapel of red brick with yellow brick dressings. Possibly built in 1836 for a church formed in that year which now meets in the former Wesleyan chapel (*see* (166)).

(166) Former WESLEYAN, Ormesby St Margaret (TG 494151). Brick with gabled front and porch, red and yellow brick arched heads to doorway and side windows. Built 1863; now used by Baptists.

Baptist Times (16 October 1980).

OULTON

(167) OULTON CHAPEL (TG 141293). The chapel stands in a remote situation one mile W of Irmingland Hall, a property from 1644 of the Cromwellian Col. Charles Fleetwood (Browne (1877) 328). A meeting of Independents at Oulton was reported in 1669 under William Sheldrake, minister of Guestwick, and several meeting-house licences were issued in 1672. By the early 18th century an Independent congregation, then forming part of the Guestwick church, was meeting at 'Armingland' under Abraham Coveney, chaplain to the Fleetwood family. In 1724 the Oulton congregation was formed into a separate church and the present meeting-house was opened in 1731. By 1877, the cause was 'at a very low ebb' but services continued to be held until the 1970s. The meeting-house was sold to the Norfolk Historic Buildings Trust in 1989.

The chapel has walls of red brick and a double roof covered with pantiles. The front faces W and has a brick plinth and two tiers of windows in four bays, the frames replaced by hung sashes in the early 19th century. Two doorways in the end bays have segmentally arched brick heads. The N and S walls have pairs of Dutch gables and windows with segmentally arched heads and original wooden cross-frames formerly with leaded glazing. In the rear E wall are two large windows flanking the pulpit. A vestry, variously rebuilt and altered, stands against this wall. The first vestry had a gable abutting the wall between the pulpit windows, and an internal doorway, now blocked, below. This was extended to N and S and given a new roof realigned parallel to the chapel wall; a stone in the N gable is dated 1839, and two stones in the S gable have the dates 1839, 1891. (Since 1989 the vestry has been largely rebuilt to provide simple living accommodation)

The interior of the chapel (30¼ft by 40ft) has two substantial freestanding wooden posts with moulded capitals and tall square bases which support the main valley beam of the roof. A gallery around three sides, of which the W cross gallery may be an addition, has a fielded-panelled front with fluted pilasters

Oulton Chapel. Before restoration.

above the supporting columns; these last are of wood to N and S but of iron on the W side. Most of the original box-pews remain in the gallery but the lower seating dates from the late 19th century. The pulpit, centrally against the E wall, is also of this date. The chapel has a flat plaster ceiling. The roof is supported by six trusses with roughly cambered collar-beams; there are no tie-beams and the trusses do not coincide with the two principal E–W beams.

Fittings – *Monuments* and *Floorslabs*. *Monuments*: on N wall (1) William Golding, 1828, and Elizabeth his mother, 1854, with floorslab; on E wall (2) Mary (Sims) Powell, 1834, with floorslab; (3) Richard Sims, 1834; (4) Edmund Sims, 1839, and Mary his widow, 1842, with floorslab; (5) Rev. Richard Roberts, 1854, 14 years pastor, Zillah his widow, 1862, and their children Juliet Elizabeth, 1847, and George Griffith, 1853; (6) Thomas Cyrus Butteau, 1835. Externally against W wall, headstones (7) John Golding, 1868; (8) Thomas Warren, 1858, and Frances Jane his wife, 1836; (9) Henry Kiddell, 1883; S of chapel (10) Thomas Smith, deacon, 1808; (11) Thomas Sandling, 1798; *Floorslab*: in front of pulpit (1) Rev. Thomas Goldborne, 1822, 33 years pastor, stone renewed 1884.

Plate: includes a pair of pewter communion cups inscribed 'Independent Chapel, Oulton, Norfolk, May 1864'. *Pulpit*: the original back-board remains *in situ* on the wall behind the pulpit; the soffit of the former hexagonal pulpit canopy has been set below; both are inlaid with stars and geometric decoration.

Browne (1877) 328–33. *CYB* (1901) 172–3, obituary of Philip Colborne.

OVERSTRAND

(168) WESLEYAN (TG 248408). This small chapel of brick, tile and render, with roofs covered in Roman tiles, was designed by (Sir) Edwin Lutyens. It was opened in 1898. The lower stage, of brickwork with a deeply recessed entrance at the W end, is devoid of windows. Brick piers rising above the side walls carry three tie-beams which support a fully glazed clerestory with tripartite lunette windows.

The interior originally had a rostrum pulpit at the E end but this and most other original fittings have been removed.

Wesleyan chapel, Overstrand. (168)

PASTON

(169) PRIMITIVE METHODIST, Edingthorpe Green (TG 310321). Small chapel built 1830. Low brick walls with hipped pantiled roof; round-arched end entrance with fanlight, two similarly arched windows at opposite ends flank the pulpit.

QUIDENHAM

(170) PRIMITIVE METHODIST, Wilby (TM 033899). Small chapel with rendered brick walls and hipped slate roof, dated 1851. (Reported converted to house since 1973)

RAYNHAM

(171) WESLEYAN, West Raynham (TF 873253). Red brick with yellow brick dressings; gabled front. Dated 1875.

REDENHALL WITH HARLESTON

(172) CONGREGATIONAL, Harleston (TM 245832). A church for which a meeting-house was built in 1706 appears to have died out by 1773, when the building was sold to James Whiting (*see* Wortwell (237)), but afterwards 'fell for a time into the hands of the Methodists'. A new church (now URC) was formed in 1786.

The present chapel of red brick with a slate roof was built in 1819 but altered and re-fronted by Edward Boardman in 1886. The front has a three-bay centre with pediment, wide double doors, and two tiers of windows.

Browne (1877) 348–50.

REEPHAM

(173) WESLEYAN (TG 099231). Red brick with yellow brick dressings; opened 1816 but much altered in the late 19th century including the addition of a wide porch with rounded ends. *Monument*: reset externally, oval wall monument to Thomas Peck, 1840, and Ann his wife, 1826.

RINGLAND

(174) Former BAPTIST (TG 138139). Red brick with yellow brick dressings, pointed-arched windows and round-ended porch with gable above entrance. *Inscription*: loose in former school-room, tablet inscribed 'This Baptist chapel was opened for divine worship September 26th 1889'.

(175) WESLEYAN (TG 133142). Brick and slate with hipped roof, round-arched windows, and doorway with fanlight. Dated 1832.

ROCKLANDS

(176) PRIMITIVE METHODIST, Rockland St Peter (TL 990975). Brick with three-bay front and two tiers of sash windows under flat-arched heads. Dated 1859. School-room attached.

SALHOUSE

(177) BAPTIST (TG 314147). The chapel, registered in 1802 as 'A new erected House called Zion's Chapel in Salehouse', may have been altered in 1813, the date on several bricks in the front wall. Brick with hipped pantiled roof; SW front of three bays with central entrance replacing a pair of doorways in the side bays, and two tiers of sash windows. The entrance has a bracketed hood and

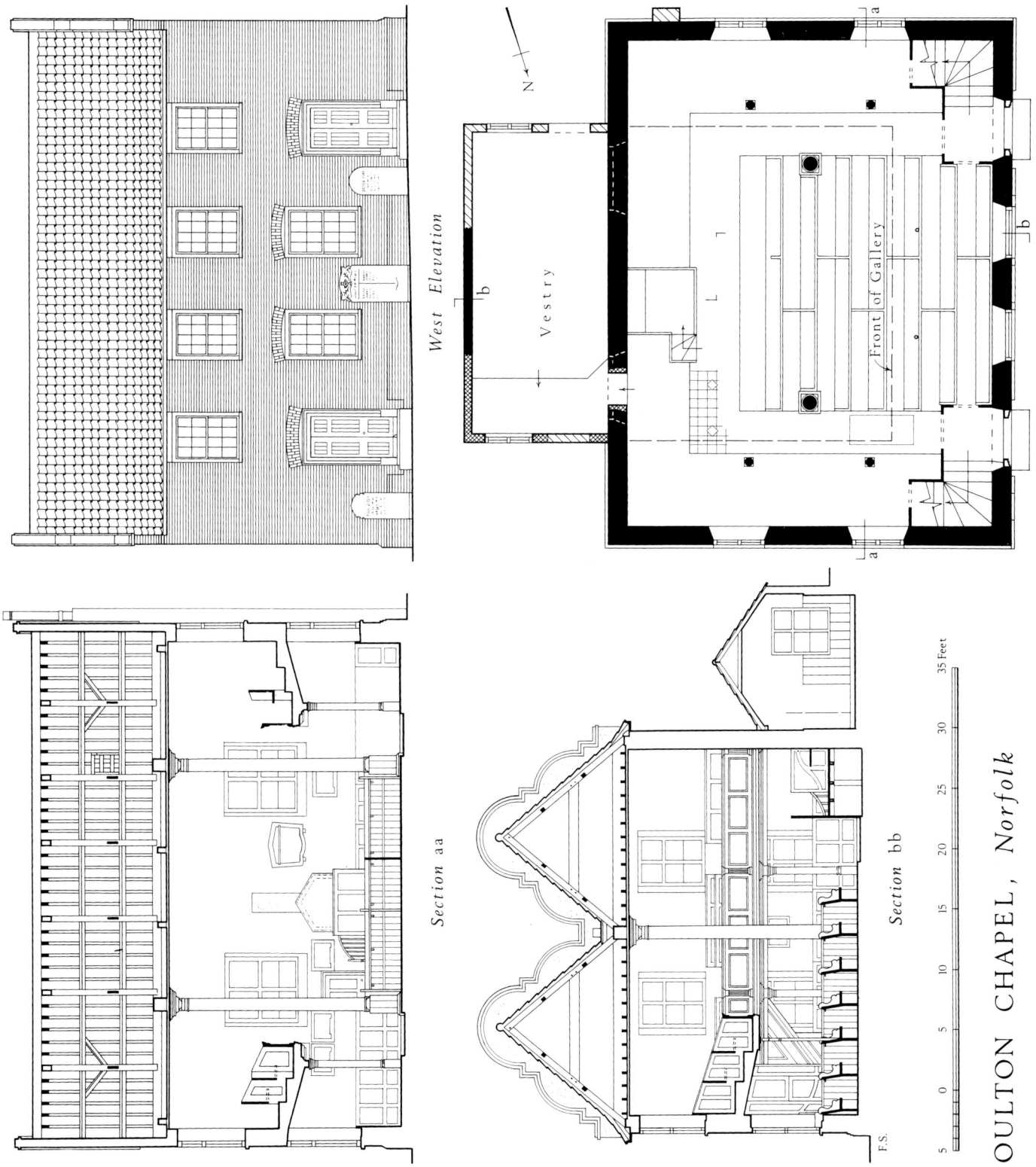

OULTON CHAPEL, Norfolk

double doors, possibly the work of 1813. Two sash windows in the rear wall flank the pulpit. The interior is square, with an early 19th-century gallery around three sides having a plain panelled front supported by wooden posts. The pulpit and lower seating are of the late 19th century. A later vestry or school-room is attached to the SE side.

Fittings – *Inscriptions*: on several bricks in front wall to right of central entrance, various initials with date '1813'. *Monuments*: externally against front wall, headstones (1) Richard son of Kitt and Mary Nickols, 1814; (2) Richard Rushmore, 1814; (3) Ebenezer son of Charles and Elizabeth Caddy, 1815. In burial-ground to SE, several 19th-century headstones, also (4) Joseph, son of H. and S. Cooper, 1829, also Esther their daughter and Sarah Cooper, [both 1829?], brick table-tomb.

Grace (August/September 1992) 17–18.

Former Baptist chapel, Shelfanger. (181)

(178) METHODIST (TG 309145). A chapel of 1775, variously described as having a rendered pedimented front, arched doorway and two round-arched sash windows, was rebuilt on the same site in 1967.

Listed Building description, 1947. Pevsner, N., *North East Norfolk and Norwich* (1962) 307.

SEDGEFORD

(179) WESLEYAN, High Street (TF 716368). Brick with hipped pantiled roof; three-bay front with two pointed-arched windows and tablet dated 1830 above central entrance.

(180) Former PRIMITIVE METHODIST (TF 709366). Built 1861. Rubble with hipped roof; front of red brick with yellow brick dressings, defaced tablet above porch. (Converted to house)

SHELFANGER

(181) Former BAPTIST (TM 106840). The church formerly meeting here and said by Browne to have been 'very high Calvinist' was formed in 1765. The chapel, largely rebuilt in 1821, has a brick front and a hipped pantiled roof. The SW front has a central entrance between tall sash windows with external shutters and two small gallery windows above with a circular tablet between dated AD 1821. The SE side wall is timber-framed and may be a survival of the earlier meeting-house; the NW wall has been rebuilt in brickwork.

The interior has a gallery around three sides with a panelled front divided by reeded pilasters. Two vestries have been formed below the SE side gallery with a passage between giving access to an outer doorway on that side. The pulpit and lower seating were replaced in the late 19th century but some earlier pews with altered backs remain in the gallery. (Reported converted to a house since 1971)

Fittings – *Baptistery*: centrally in floor. *Clock*: on gallery front, circular dial, by Davy of Kenninghall, 19th-century. *Inscriptions*: on five bricks above front entrance, in various alphabets (i) English 'W. Frost 1821'; (ii) ?Hebrew (unidentified); (iii) Greek 'P. Blomfield'; (iv) Old English 'B. Rolf 1821'; (v) Black letter 'John Jo[ll?]o'. *Monuments*: in chapel, right of entrance (1) Martha wife of John Glanfield, 1822; externally in burial-ground in front of chapel (2) Rev. Thomas Smith, 1813, and Kezia his widow, 1825, table-tomb. (The description of the funeral of Thomas Smith, first pastor, quoted by Browne from *The Universal Magazine* of January 1813, refers to the coffin being 'placed in his own waggon, preceded by his bearers, and the singers of his congregation chaunting a funeral dirge', with a wagon tilt for a pall, his children sitting around it on cornsacks, and 'the chief mourner … his own riding horse, attached by the bridle'.)

Browne (1877) 565–6.

(182) WESLEYAN (TM 108840). Small chapel with rendered walls possibly on timber frame; front rebuilt in modern brickwork. Dated 1845 but claimed (1851 census) to have been erected in 1847.

SHIPDHAM

(183) CONGREGATIONAL (TF 960074). A church formed in 1833 first occupied a Baptist chapel of 1822. This was replaced by the present building in 1881. Brick with low gabled front and circular window over entrance. (Now URC)

Browne (1877) 360.

(184) Former FREE METHODIST (TF 954072). Three-bay gabled brick front dated 1900.

SKEYTON

(185) Former WESLEYAN, Skeyton Corner (TG 254274). Small chapel of brick and pantile. Inscribed tablet above entrance with original denominational name defaced. Built 1829. (Reported converted to cottage)

SMALLBURGH

(186) Former GENERAL BAPTIST, Low Street (TG 343238). The Baptist church in Smallburgh was founded in the late 17th century by Thomas Grantham, 'a messenger of the baptized churches in Lincolnshire'. The erection of the meeting-house, now in Methodist use, is referred to in the church book of the General Baptist church at Dover, Kent, when on 17 July 1712 £1 15s. 6d. was 'collected for the church of Christ meeting at Smallbrough neere Norwich towards there building of a meeting-house'. Many members left in 1717 to form the church at Worstead (235) but the remnant continued in existence until the early 19th century when the meeting-house passed into the possession of Primitive Methodists.

The meeting-house has walls of red brick and a hipped roof covered with plain tiles but partly replaced by pantiles. The original broad SE front wall facing the road is in Flemish bond brickwork with glazed headers. At the centre is a blocked doorway with segmental-arched head between two similarly arched windows, the frames of which have been replaced by hung sashes. The rear wall has two widely spaced windows matching those in front, a small centrally placed window, now blocked, below the eaves which formerly lit the pulpit, and a small blocked opening at the SW end. In the 19th century a new doorway with rusticated surround was inserted at the SW end. The NE wall is blank except for a blocked doorway which gave access to a now demolished vestry.

The interior (20½ft by 40¼ft), entirely refitted in the late 19th century, has a rostrum pulpit at the NE end.

'Church Book of the General Baptist Church, Dover, Kent', MS in Dr Williams's Library. Jewson, C.B., *The Baptists in Norfolk* (1957) 32, 36, 50–1.

Former General Baptist chapel, Smallburgh. (186)

(187) WESLEYAN REFORM (TG 323242). Small brick chapel with round-arched entrance in gabled end wall. Built *c.*1870, schoolroom added 1939.

SOMERTON

(188) Former PRIMITIVE METHODIST, West Somerton (TG 469199). Low-built chapel of brick with hipped slate roof. Diamond-shaped inscription tablet over entrance, now defaced, *c.*1860.

Former Independent chapel, South Creake. From SE. (189)

SOUTH CREAKE

(189) Former INDEPENDENT (TF 858363). A 'building erected by Miss Ann and Martha Glover, in South Creake, called The Meeting House' was registered as a place of worship on 20 May 1779. These ladies, who 'pitying the neglected and ignorant inhabitants' built the chapel at their own cost, are said to have conducted services there themselves for some time. After their deaths the building was used by a Baptist congregation under John Temple Goggs who formed a Baptist church here in 1822. In 1835 the chapel passed to the Congregational Home Missionary Society and it remained in Congregational (latterly URC) use until *c.*1975.

The chapel has walls of brickwork with a dentil brick eaves cornice and a hipped roof covered with dark glazed pantiles. The broad SW front, largely covered by a big gabled Sunday-school wing built in 1894, has brick quoins at each end (not repeated on the NE side); there are two windows with pointed-arched heads in rubbed brick and wooden frames with intersecting tracery of three lights, and a central doorway, now internal, with pointed-arched head and double panelled doors. The rear NE wall had three windows similar to those described, but the middle window has been removed and replaced by a pair of small lancets. The SE and NW walls have each two windows as before, the arches of those to the NW being in plain brickwork; centrally between the SE windows is a doorway with pointed-arched head.

The interior (51½ft by 30½ft) was entirely refitted in the late 19th century with the pulpit at the NW end and three ranks of pews, the side pews raked. The alterations to the central window on the NE side suggest that the pulpit was at one period located in that position. The walls have a wide coved plaster cornice; the roof is ceiled at collar level and has been strengthened by two iron ties. (Disused and most seating removed 1980)

Monuments and *Floorslabs. Monuments*: in chapel on NE wall (1) John Temple Goggs, 1824, recording that 'in 1819 he obtained leave to preach in this chapel' and formed a Baptist church here on 5 April 1822 to which he was ordained pastor, white marble tablet; in burial-ground (2) Mary widow of Rev. Luke Kirby (former minister, buried at Thorne, Yorks., West Riding), 1840; (3) Thomas son of Thomas and Elizabeth Evaets, 1788; (4) Mary Lewis, 1834; (5) Jane and Bennaton Chasney, late 19th-century; (6) Thomas Evaets, 1801, and Elizabeth his wife, 17[..]; (7) Susanna wife of John Bending, 1793; (8) Mary wife of Thomas Barcham, 1791, loose fragment; *Floorslab*: in school-room, Robert Sayer, 1853, and Rebecca his daughter, 1853.

Browne (1877) 363–4.

(190) PRIMITIVE METHODIST (TF 860356). Three-bay gabled front dated 1883. (Reported converted to house)

SOUTHERY

(191) STRICT BAPTIST, Church Lane (TL 622946). Small, square brick chapel with dentil brick cornice and pyramidal roof covered with pantiles. Built 1847. Doorway with fanlight between two windows with renewed frames.

SOUTH LOPHAM

(192) Former BAPTIST, Low Common (TM 058806). The chapel, now a Brethren meeting-room, was registered in 1851. Rendered walls on brick and flint plinth. Gabled front with doorway between windows and two upper windows for intended gallery. Interior refitted in late 19th century with flat canopy above rostrum pulpit.

FORMER BAPTIST CHAPEL, SOUTH LOPHAM   CFS 1971

SOUTHREPPS

(193) Former WESLEYAN, Chapel Street (TG 257366). A Congregational church in existence by the late 17th century had a meeting-house on this site which in the early 19th century fell into the hands of Methodists who rebuilt it *c*.1854. The chapel of that date has rendered walls and a hipped pantiled roof. There is a small gallery next to the entrance. *Floorslab*: see Swafield (203). (Reported converted to house)

Browne (1877) 318–19.

(194) PRIMITIVE METHODIST, Lower Street (TG 260354). Red brick with gault brick dressings. Three-bay gabled front with rusticated round-arched openings and lean-to annexe alongside. Dated 1864.

STALHAM

(195) BAPTIST (TG 374250). The church meeting here was formed in 1653 as an Independent congregation and met originally at Ingham (1 mile NE) where a meeting-house was built in 1745 and much enlarged in 1813. The present chapel in Stalham was erected in 1884. It is of gault brick with red brick dressings; the front is gabled between terminal bays forming two short towers with round-arched doorways, tall upper windows and pyramidal roofs. *Monuments*: in chapel (1) William Howes, 1848, and Hannah his widow, 1866; (2) Obadiah Silcock, 1833, and Rebecca his widow, 1834; (3) Rev. James Venimore, 1877; (4) Henry Cooke, 1830, signed 'Logdon Yarm^O'; (5) Samuel Cooke, 1835, and Sophia his widow, 1855; (6) Richard Silcock, 1872.

Browne (1877) 554–5. Ivimey IV (1830) 521–2.

STANHOE

(196) Former WESLEYAN (TF 806370). Small chapel of brick with hipped pantiled roof. Oval date tablet of 1827 above later porch.

(197) PRIMITIVE METHODIST (TF 805371). Built 1892 replacing a chapel of 1851.

STOW BARDOLPH

(198) Former GENERAL BAPTIST, Stowbridge (TF 602073). Small brick and slate chapel concealed behind the heightened W bank of the Great Ouse. Gabled front towards river with round-arched doorway and painted inscription on blind tympanum with date 1825. Gallery at E end, low segmental-vaulted ceiling. (Derelict 1993)

Wood (1847) 226, s.v. Wiggenhall St Mary Magdalen.

(199) FREE METHODIST, Stowbridge (TF 601069). 'Bethesda Chapel', W of the bridge, is dated 1860 on a roundel in the front gable.

SURLINGHAM

(200) Former WESLEYAN (TG 317065). The chapel built as a barn in 1803 and converted to religious use in the late 19th century has brick walls and a thatched roof. The barn doors on the S side have been replaced by a pointed-arched window, opposite which on the other side a small lean-to porch has been converted to a vestry. A new entrance was made at the W end and a window inserted in the opposite wall. *Inscription*: on tablet on W wall 'T+M | 1803'. (Reported converted to house 1982)

SWAFFHAM

(201) BAPTIST, Station Road (TF 819093). Gault brick with gabled front between terminal bays rising to Italianate turrets. Foundation stone laid on 2 September 1858 by the Rev. W. Woods, pastor. Apart from the details of the tops of the turrets the design is closely similar to the Baptist chapel in Diss (47) of 1859, by W. Woods.

(202) WESLEYAN, London Street (TF 820088). The 'newly erected chapel built by Robert Goodrick in London Street' was registered in July 1813. The chapel was enlarged to the rear and re-fronted in 1875. The walls are of red brick with a yellow brick front and the roof is hipped and slated. The broad W front of three bays divided by panelled pilasters topped by short obelisks has a pediment above the centre bay.

SWAFIELD

(203) CONGREGATIONAL, Bradfield (TG 273322). The church formerly meeting here claimed to have originated in 1657. The chapel, W of Bridge Farm, rebuilt in 1872 and 'designed by the contractor Mr R.B. Lane of North Walsham' is faced with flint and stone dressings, of three bays with stepped buttresses, lancet windows and a gabled porch. The previous chapel on the site, said

Wesleyan chapel, Swaffham. (202)

by Browne to have been a converted barn, had brick walls and a thatched roof; two wooden cross-framed windows and a small doorway to the right faced the burial-ground. (Chapel closed *c.*1967, derelict 1972)

Floorslab: [Browne records a floorslab to the Rev. Charles Crowe, 1784, brought from the former chapel at Southrepps (193)]. *Inscription*: on outbuilding W of chapel, in large brick characters 'C R 1736'. *Plate*: includes a small two-handled cup of 1677, given 1737, and two pewter flagons dated 1729, 1737.

Browne (1877) 307–24.

SWANTON ABBOTT

(204) Former WESLEYAN (TG 266254). Chapel built 1829. Brick with hipped pantiled roof, S end wall with wide round-arched doorway and two tiers of windows; defaced tablet above entrance. (Now motor repair shop)

(205) WESLEYAN REFORM (TG 265255). The chapel built in 1850 has brick walls and a hipped slate roof. Original broad W front of three bays with central round-arched entrance now blocked; a lunette above the former doorway has a fanlight with intersecting glazing bars. The chapel was extended to the N and a new entrance made at the S end.

TASBURGH

(206) Former FRIENDS, Upper Tasburgh (TM 210953). A property 'purchased by Robert Jarmyn for use as a Meeting house and burial ground' was registered for use in November 1707. This building was enlarged or possibly rebuilt in 1773. A clear sign of enlargement in the N wall may indicate that a smaller building at the E end was greatly extended to the west. By the late 19th century meetings were infrequent; the building was repaired and reopened in 1926 but the meeting finally closed 1961. The premises were sold in 1961 and converted to a private house.

The walls are of brickwork and the roof is hipped and covered with pantiles. The meeting-house (externally 28ft by 51¾ft) has windows with segmental-arched heads to the lower stage and smaller windows above, all with renewed frames. A small caretaker's cottage was incorporated at the W end with a doorway, now blocked, in the S wall. The S wall has been much rebuilt although probably retaining the earlier fenestration. A straight joint and a change in the brick size in the N wall mark the line of enlargement.

Monument: loose externally, small round-topped headstone 10¼in. wide inscribed 'W:Durban | Obijt | 26 Die | 9^{bris} | 1718'. This and five other 18th-century stones uncovered in the burial-ground in 1933, but no longer visible are listed in *FHSJ* (op. cit. below).

Butler (1999) 457–8. *FHSJ* XXX (1933) 89–90. *The Wayfarer* (May 1938) Supplement.

TERRINGTON ST CLEMENT

(207) WESLEYAN, Hillgate Street (TF 547202). The chapel has a pedimented brick front of three bays with pilasters. It was built in 1844, the date on a keystone in the back wall.

TERRINGTON ST JOHN

(208) WESLEYAN, Ely Row (TF 538143). Brick with hipped pantiled roof and round-arched windows. Built 1813.

THARSTON

(209) HAPTON CHAPEL (TM 175966). An Independent congregation met in Hapton in the mid 17th century but disappeared at the Restoration. The church latterly meeting here originated in the early 18th century and seems to have been initiated by Robert Gay, brewer of Long Stratton, who fitted up a meeting-house there *c.*1700 and appointed Robert Chaplin as minister. Chaplin also commenced preaching in Hapton, where Gay owned a house and other property. After the death of Gay and his son in 1713 the work continued to be supported by his widow Elizabeth, who died in 1741 leaving the Hapton property in trust for the erection of a meeting-house for 'Presbyterians or Congregationalists' and for the support of a minister, her house becoming the manse. The meeting-house is believed to have been built in 1749–51 and timber from a disused meeting-house in New Buckenham is thought to have been used in its construction. A close association between the congregations at Hapton and at the Presbyterian (Octagon) chapel in Norwich, particularly following the death of the first minister in 1774, led to Unitarian influences amongst the trustees and congregation. Some considerable repairs were carried out *c.*1910 but by 1928 support was at a low ebb and the manse and other property were sold; by 1967 the chapel was closed and becoming seriously dilapidated. It was sold and converted to a cottage in 1977 with the loss of much of its character and internal features. The following description refers to its condition in 1967.

Hapton Chapel has rendered walls of timber-framed construction in three bays with original clay and wattle infilling on a brick plinth. The roof, gabled to E and W, may have been thatched but has been re-covered in corrugated iron [now relaid with pantiles].

The S front has a central doorway with open porch inserted *c.*1910 and three round-arched windows with wooden Y-tracery frames close below the eaves, that above the doorway being the widest and probably attenuated when the new entrance was inserted. Below the side windows alterations to the brick plinth and the infilling indicate the locations of two original entrances.

The N wall, much decayed (*see* p. 272), has two round-arched windows with renewed frames flanking the pulpit. The E and W gables have barge-boards of *c.*1910, the end walls have each two

Hapton Chapel.

lower windows and two smaller upper windows above the tie-beams, with original rectangular wood frames of two lights and leaded glazing. A small doorway at the N end of the W wall, heightened and with a renewed door, gave access from the detached former manse.

The interior (18¾ft by 31¼ft), ceiled at collar level, was entirely lined with match-boarding c.1910. It has separate galleries at the E and W ends with staircases adjacent to the original front entrances. The galleries have panelled fronts and are each supported by a single chamfered post. The floor is laid with bricks except below the two pews on the W side where it is boarded.

A small burial-ground E of the chapel was acquired in the early 19th century.

Fittings – *Door*: in S doorway, with round-arched head and six fielded panels with egg-and-dart enrichment, 1756, reused c.1910 from Octagon Chapel, Norwich (159). *Inscriptions* and *Scratchings*: on panelling of E gallery, dates '1790', '1791'. *Monuments*: in burial-ground, includes early 19th-century headstones decorated with cherubs' heads and urns in low relief, also (1) Rev. William Selby, 1856, 20 years minister, and Jane his widow, 1868; (2) Rev. James Knapton, 1902, and Martha his wife, 1872. *Plate*: includes a pair of small beakers on trumpet-shaped stems, 1670, with initials GG for George Gay. *Pulpit*: hexagonal, with plain panelled sides, moulded base and cornice, mid 18th-century. *Seating*: below W gallery, two box-pews with panelled sides, shaped ends and moulded edges to seats; below E gallery, three box-pews of lesser quality; in galleries, original seating with plain boarded backs.

Browne (1877) 283–8. Evans (1897) 100–1. Hosken (1920) 191. *Inquirer* (8 March, 5 April, 1980). Nettlefold, J.K., *Hapton Chapel* (1930). Stell, C.F., MS notes 1967. *UHST* VII (1939–42) 65.

THEMELTHORPE

(210) PRIMITIVE METHODIST (TG 056238). Small chapel with rendered walls possibly on a timber frame and pantiled roof, late 19th-century.

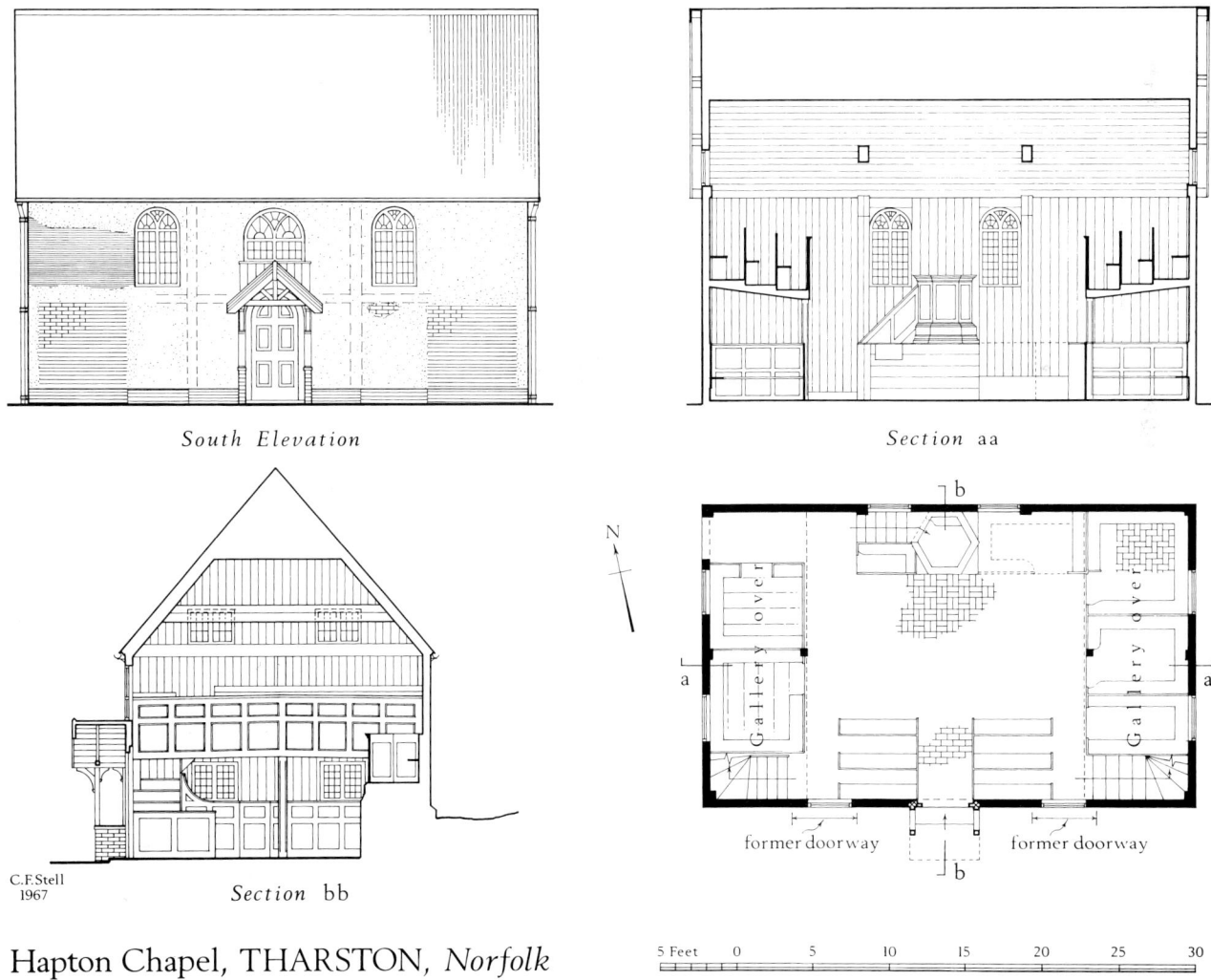

Hapton Chapel, THARSTON, *Norfolk*

Hapton Chapel: the back wall (1967). A study in dereliction.

THETFORD

(211) BAPTIST, King Street (TL 871831). Grey brick with pedimented front of three bays separated by pilasters, paired at corners; an arch over the centre bay rises into the pediment. Two round-arched doorways in outer bays. Foundation stone 1863.

(212) CONGREGATIONAL, Earles' Street (TL 872832). The chapel dated 1817 has a front of grey brick and side walls of flint with brick dressings. The roof is hipped and pantiled. The front of three bays has two round-arched doorways and two tiers of sash windows, some with altered frames. The interior has a deep gallery next to the entrance added in 1842 and now converted to an upper room; windows in the side walls make provision for further galleries never constructed. The pulpit and seating were renewed in the late 19th century. *Monuments*: in chapel (1) Susan wife of Rev. Robert Cooper, 1819; (2) Henry Brown, 1855; in burial-ground (3) Robert Fleming, 1839, 'a native of North Britain, near Dumfries'; (4) James Dunbar, 1840, inscribed as last. (URC)
Browne (1877) 358.

(213) WESLEYAN, Tanner Street (TL 870831). The chapel built in 1830 has walls of gault brick and a hipped slate roof; three-bay front with two tiers of windows, giant pilasters, and a small vestigial or altered pediment above the centre bay. Small segmental apse at rear with blocked circular window at gallery level.

THORNHAM

(214) WESLEYAN, High Street (TF 734434). The small broad-fronted chapel close to the parish church has a front of red brick with dressings of yellow brick, side walls faced with pebbles and a hipped and pantiled roof. Three-bay front with battlemented parapet rising as a crow-stepped gable at the centre. Galleried interior. Dated 1870.

TITTLESHALL

(215) Former BAPTIST (TF 892211). The chapel, much altered and refenestrated on conversion to two cottages, has rendered walls and a hipped roof covered in patent tiles. Attached to the N is the

Wesleyan chapel, Thornham. (214)

former manse, also rendered and with a hipped pantiled roof; this is of later date and is reported to cover a tablet in the N wall of the chapel inscribed 'Particular Baptist Chapel 1823'.

Ede, J., Virgoe, N., and Williamson, T., *Halls of Zion: Chapels and Meeting-Houses in Norfolk* (1994) 66.

(216) PRIMITIVE METHODIST (TF 892211). The chapel, S of (215), has a gabled front of red brick with yellow brick dressings. Foundation stone dated 1865.

TIVETSHALL ST MARGARET

(217) Former FRIENDS (TM 177876). The meeting-house 'built about 1811' (1851 census) probably on the site of an earlier one was closed in 1937. The walls are of brickwork and the roof is hipped and pantiled. The S front is symmetrical with three sash windows and two doorways. The W bay conceals an original cottage with a domestic W elevation of central entrance between two tiers of windows. In the E end wall are two windows matching those in front; the N wall is blank.

The interior of the meeting-house (30ft by 26ft), symmetrical

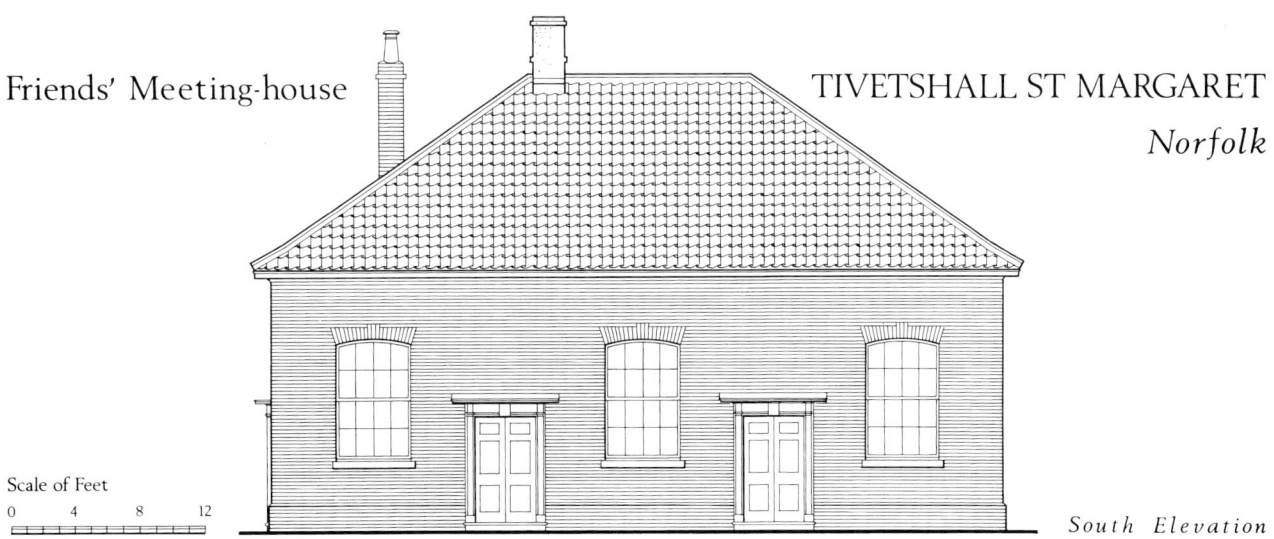

Friends' Meeting-house

TIVETSHALL ST MARGARET

Norfolk

South Elevation

about the right-hand doorway, has a stand against the N wall. The second doorway opens to a lobby within the cottage with access through to the meeting-room.

South of the meeting-house is a burial-ground with uniform round-topped headstones of the 19th century and later. Near the SW corner is a small timber-framed stable with two wood-framed windows with diamond mullions of the late 17th century. (Meeting-house reported converted to house c.1977)

Butler (1999) 458–9.

TOPCROFT

(218) Former CONGREGATIONAL, Topcroft Street (TM 265916). A chapel built 1813 was replaced in 1898 by the present building by E. Boardman & Son. Brick walls and pantiled roof; gabled front with round-arched window of five lights. The upper part of the gable is covered by a diaper of terracotta and has below a band inscribed 'DELF MEMORIAL CHURCH'. Brick-mullioned windows in the side walls. (For sale 1994)

Browne (1877) 341.

UPWELL

(219) BAPTIST, School Road (TF 497012). Red brick with gault brick front of three bays; hipped slate roof. Central entrance with rendered surround, paired pilasters and frieze dated 1844; two tiers of windows with flat-arched heads with ogee sinking and frames with marginal glazing bars. Interior with original box-pews and single gallery at entrance.

BM XXXVII (1845) 30.

Baptist chapel, Upwell. (219)

(220) WESLEYAN REFORM, Three Holes (TF 505004). Small red brick chapel dated 1850.

(221) SALVATION ARMY (TF 503027). Hall, dated 1883.

WATTON

(222) Former CONGREGATIONAL (TF 916009). Big gabled front of flint with brick dressings; short tower to left with octagonal upper stage formerly surmounted by spire. Opened 1856, bicentenary memorial Sunday-school built 1862, galleries added 1871. (Now Assembly of God)

Browne (1877) 358–9.

WELLS-NEXT-THE-SEA

(223) CONGREGATIONAL, Clubb's Lane (TF 916435). The congregation formed in 1816 built the present chapel in the following year. This is a large building of brick with a hipped pantiled roof. The W front is of three bays with two tiers of windows separated by a platband. The S wall of three wider bays with recessed centre has been extended to the E in 1826 by one further bay.

Detached to N is the Sunday-school of 1891 of brick in the Romanesque style with a big circular window in the gable.

Browne (1877) 357–8.

(224) FRIENDS, Church Street (TF 919431). The meeting-house built in 1783 replacing an earlier structure has been greatly altered and extended to the S in 1913. The original building is of brickwork on a high plinth of brick and rubble with a dentil brick eaves cornice and a hipped pantiled roof. The interior (24¼ft wide, originally about 35ft long extended to 57¾ft) has no original fittings. A shuttered partition divides the building on the line of the former S end wall. (Interior refitted and subdivided c.1993)

Butler (1999) 459–60.

(225) Former WESLEYAN (TF 918435). Methodist preaching appears to have been introduced here in the late 18th century. On 30 October 1781 John Wesley 'preached about ten in a small, neat preaching-house', possibly the house 'near the Church Marsh', 'lately fitted up' and registered in January 1780. Its successor, the former chapel on the N side of Station Road, now used as a public library, is reported (1851 census) to have been built in 1808. Although sometimes claimed to be the conversion of an existing building, this is not evident from the structure which has many characteristics of a chapel of c.1800. The walls are of brickwork with later rendering at the front and the roof is pyramidal and covered with pantiles. The S front of three bays has a central doorway with mid 19th-century surround, a small window above and two tall windows with metal frames which may have been formed by the conflation of two tiers of windows. In the W and N walls are each three upper windows only; the E wall is blank. A former Sunday-school building at the rear is dated 1888.

Former Wesleyan chapel, Wells-next-the-Sea. (225)

The interior (33¾ft square) has no original fittings but traces survive of former galleries against the E and W walls.

Inscription: on stone reset internally on E wall, 'E+G | 1759', provenance unknown.

Curnock (ed.), (1938) VI: 338–9.

(226) PRIMITIVE METHODIST, Theatre Road (TF 915437). Chapel of red brick with yellow brick dressings, gabled front with round-ended porch and three-light pointed-arched window above with cusped intersecting tracery. Foundation stones dated 1891.

A low brick building with hipped pantiled roof in Chapel Yard, formerly 'Ranters' Yard' (TF 914437), converted to a cottage and with date tablet 'W.N. 1836' on annexe has been claimed (Listed Building description) as the former chapel.

WENDLING

(227) Former PRIMITIVE METHODIST (TF 931128). Red and yellow brick with gabled front dated 1877. Foundation stones defaced. Later chapel of 1914 opposite.

WEST WALTON

(228) FREE METHODIST, Lynn Road, West Walton Highway (TF 492130). Small brick chapel with three-bay pedimented front, dated 1849.

WHINBURGH

(229) PRIMITIVE METHODIST (TG 009092). Small three-bay chapel with pedimental gable; dated 1879 on defaced tablet, foundation stones obliterated.

WIGGENHALL ST MARY MAGDALEN

(230) Former GENERAL BAPTIST, Magdalen (TF 598111). The chapel of 1840, now in secular use, is a low building of brick with a hipped slate roof. The front wall is rendered and has a small porch of 1886 between two round-arched windows; between the windows is a tablet inscribed 'GENERAL | BAPTIST | I·PORTER | Builder 1840'.

Wood (1847) 226.

WITTON

(231) PRIMITIVE METHODIST, Stonebridge (TG 340313). Red and yellow brick, gabled front of three bays with round-arched windows; finials on corners and apex of gable. Dated 1865.

WOOD DALLING

(232) Former INDEPENDENT, Red Pits (TG 098288). The chapel built for an Independent congregation in 1820–1 and formerly bearing a tablet dated 1821 was later used by a Wesleyan Reform congregation; it was sold *c.*1954 and used as a store. The walls are of brick and the roof hipped and pantiled. The broad front wall has a central entrance, enlarged for vehicle access, between two wide windows with flat-arched heads. In the rear wall are two blind or blocked windows. (Reported converted to house, 1990)

(233) PRIMITIVE METHODIST, Crabgate (TG 100275). Small wayside chapel of rendered brickwork. Opened 1860.

WOODTON

(234) PRIMITIVE METHODIST (TM 293939). The chapel of brick with a hipped slate roof has a long rectangular plan. It was built in 1836 but much altered and realigned in the later 19th century when it was given an entrance at one end. The original entrance in one of the longer sides has a wide semicircular arched head set in a slightly projecting bay with blocked window above, the bays to each side have two tiers of windows and at the extreme left-hand end is a later two-storeyed vestry wing. *Inscriptions*: on eight bricks to each side of original entrance, names and dates 1836.

WORSTEAD

(235) BAPTIST, Meeting-house Hill (TG 305283). The church meeting here was formed in 1717 by division from the General Baptist church at Smallburgh but later adopted Particular Baptist views. A meeting-house was built in 1730 and subsequently enlarged to accommodate a congregation of 500.

The present chapel 70 yards SE of the site of its predecessor, was built in 1829; it has brick walls and a hipped pantiled roof with wide boarded eaves. The front wall of three bays with two tiers of sash windows has a central round-arched entrance with fanlight and date tablet above.

The interior has galleries around three sides with plain panelled fronts supported by iron columns. The contemporary pulpit opposite the entrance is set unusually high and supported by a single bracket; there is an arched recess behind for the seat.

Surrounding the chapel is an interesting group of related buildings including school, master's house, manse and stables, caretaker's house and almshouses (Ede, J. *et al.*, *Halls of Zion: Chapels and Meeting-Houses in Norfolk* (1994) 42–3).

Fittings – *Clock*: on back gallery, signed 'Barcham, Tonbridge' mid 19th-century. *Communion Tables*: two, formerly placed together to make a table 12¾ft long, but since separated. *Monuments*: in chapel (1) Rev. Richard Clark, 1834, 20 years pastor, 'a principal contributor to the erection of this House'; (2) John Rix Blakely, 1837, 4 years pastor. *Seating*: in side galleries, a notable series of large contemporary box-pews in two ranks.

Browne (1877) 564. Ivimey IV (1830) 523–4.

Baptist chapel, Meeting-house Hill, Worstead. (235)

WORTWELL

(236) Former BAPTIST, Low Street (TM 274843). Small broad-fronted chapel of brick with a hipped pantiled roof built in 1822 for a church formed in 1819. In the latter year a meeting-house certificate, probably relevant to this congregation, was issued for 'a piece of water in Upper Sparham meadow, Alburgh, by the side of a public road from Wortwell through Alburgh in a straight direction, to be used by Baptists for performing adult Baptism'. The chapel, now used by Roman Catholics, has a modern porch at the front between two sash windows; there is one window in each of the end walls and two at the back flanking the site of the pulpit. The interior has separate end galleries.

Ivimey IV (1830) 526.

(237) CONGREGATIONAL (TM 278854). The church (now URC) originated as a section of that at Harleston (172) which had been re-commenced by James Whiting who erected the chapel at Wortwell in 1772–3. This was much altered and possibly enlarged in 1822 and partly refitted in the late 19th century. The chapel has brick walls and a hipped pantiled roof. The SE front of three bays originally had two doorways replaced by a central doorway in 1822. The rear wall has two segmental-arched upper windows and traces of two further windows below. The SW wall has two tall inserted segmental-arched windows and the remains of earlier openings. The NE wall has an inserted window at the centre and a blocked window lower down to the left. An early 19th-century vestry is attached at the N corner.

The interior has a single gallery across the SE wall, replacing two side galleries, with fielded-panelled front and supported by three later iron columns. The roof is supported by three trusses with exposed tie-beams.

Fittings – *Clock*: 'Parliament clock' with repainted octagonal dial, late 18th-century. *Monuments*: in chapel (1) Rev. John Fisher, 1832, and his brother Rev. Peter Fisher, 1834; (2) Bernard Bolingbroke Woodward, minister 1843–8, afterwards librarian in ordinary to Queen Victoria, 'the first Free Church minister to hold a court appointment', modern wooden tablet [d.1869]; in burial-ground in front of chapel (3) 'James Whiting Gent. who erected this place of worship and purchased one at Harleston and settled a handsome endowment upon them', 1787, brick table-tomb with stone panels.

Browne (1877) 348–51.

Former Baptist chapel, Low Street, Wortwell. (236)

WYMONDHAM

(238) BAPTIST (TG 111014). Red brick with squat corner tower; 1909, by A.F. Scott & Son.

(239) CONGREGATIONAL, Fairland (TG 112014). The church (now URC) originated at Wattlefield in the mid 17th century under John Money, parish lecturer and later vicar of Wymondham, ejected 1661. The meeting-house in Wymondham was first built in 1715 at the expense of Roger Gay, one of the deacons. This was greatly enlarged in 1815 and re-fronted in 1876–9. The walls are of brick and the roof is hipped and covered with pantiles. The S front, entirely of the late 19th century, is pedimented and of three bays with two tiers of windows, a central doorway, and terminal pilasters. The original front had two doorways with two cross-framed windows between and three above separated by a brick platband. The original E and W walls remain, of two bays with a platband at gallery level; the walls were extended to the N by a further two bays in 1815.

The interior ($35\frac{3}{4}$ft wide by 25ft extended to $49\frac{1}{2}$ft) has a gallery around three sides with a fielded-panelled front supported by turned wood columns with Roman Doric capitals and bases; this incorporates the basic structure of the original early 18th-century gallery. The seating and rostrum pulpit all date from a late 19th-century refitting.

Fittings – *Chair*: with arm-rests and panelled back inscribed W^{S}M, late 17th-century. *Clock*: on front of S gallery, lozenge-shaped dial with trefoil decoration in spandrels, dated 1844. *Communion Table*: with turned columnar legs, upper front rail inscribed 'E 1670 S'. *Monuments*: in chapel (1) William Jermyn, 1885, deacon; (2) Caroline (Doggett) wife of Benjamin Youngman, 1820, and Samuel their infant son, signed 'W.Hardy, Norwich'; (3) Rev. John Abbott, 1821, 10 years minister, erected by his widow. *Plate*: includes a pair of standing cups and a flagon, Sheffield plate, dated 1845.

Browne (1877) 289–94. [Scarborough, Mary], *330 Years: A Concise History of the Fairland United Reformed Church* (1982).

(240) Former FRIENDS (TG 093026). The meeting-house, remotely sited about $1\frac{1}{2}$ miles NW of the town centre, was first built in 1687 and registered in 1689 for a meeting believed to have been held previously in the mediaeval Westwade Chapel, now demolished. The original meeting-house was of timber-framed construction with a thatched roof; it was extended to the rear in 1724 and the earlier work cased in brickwork in the late 18th century; after many years of disuse it was sold in 1950 and incorporated into an adjoining house.

The original part of the building ($25\frac{3}{4}$ft by $21\frac{1}{4}$ft, extended to $30\frac{1}{4}$ft, externally) is faced in brickwork and the roof is covered at the front in pantiles. The S front has a central doorway between two tall sash windows. The E wall is gabled and has a segmental-arched upper window. The extension to the N of 1724 has walls of brickwork in Flemish bond with glazed headers and a roof of low pitch now covered in patent tiles; a small upper window in the E wall has been blocked; in the N wall are two windows with wood frames of three lights and traces of a former doorway to the E carefully blocked with old bricks.

The interior, greatly altered on conversion to domestic use, formerly had the stand against the N wall and galleries around the other three sides with a staircase in the SE corner. Two posts remained internally on the line of the former N wall and a wall plate with mortices for studs remains visible on this line.

Fittings – when the meeting-house was sold, the stand, seating, part of the gallery front, a window frame (possibly from the E side of the extension) and fragments of brick paving were removed and reused in a room at Earlham Quaker College, Richmond, Indiana, USA.

Butler (1999) 460–2. Hawkins, J., *The Quakers of Wymondham* (Wymondham Society, *c*.1985). Lidbetter (1961) 66 Fig. 20.

(241) Former WESLEYAN, White Horse Street (TG 109014). Three-bay brick front with giant rusticated pilasters and pedimental gable. Date tablet 1879, defaced.

(242) PRIMITIVE METHODIST, Town Green (TG 108018). Red and yellow brick, gabled front with narrow centre bay projecting between quadrant staircase wings. Dated 1870.

(243) PRIMITIVE METHODIST, Silfield (TM 124995). Small red brick chapel with yellow brick dressings; round-arched doorway in gabled front. Dated 1867. (Reported converted to house)

SUFFOLK

Suffolk is particularly notable for a number of architecturally and historically important early meeting-houses which have survived in a relatively unaltered state. The large timber-framed St Nicholas Street Meeting-house in Ipswich (76), built in 1700 for a Presbyterian society, now Unitarian, is a building of the highest quality. That in Churchgate Street, Bury St Edmunds (25), built by the same denomination in 1711, is of an equally prestigious status although of a contrasting construction, where it is the quality of the brickwork which has been most generally admired. At a somewhat lower social level, but exceptional for the completeness of its fittings, is the Congregational 'Old Meeting-house' at Walpole (149) which may once have been matched by other rural meeting-houses, such as Wattisfield (153), which have long since passed away. Walpole, although in origin a timber-framed house, became on its fitting-out and enlargement in the late 17th century the epitome of a meeting-house of its time. Other chapels of this period include the Congregational chapel in Whiting Street, Bury St Edmunds (28), a timber-framed building of c.1700, Long Melford (98) of 1725–6, and Wickhambrook (158) of 1734. No Baptist meeting-houses have survived from before the closing years of the 18th century.

The earliest Quaker meeting-house of importance to have remained at the time of this survey was at Woodbridge (166) of 1678, which, in spite of an unprepossessing exterior, retained fittings of an exceptionally high quality. By comparison the other early meeting-houses, at Needham Market (117) of 1704, Beccles (9) and Rattlesden (126) both of 1745, and Bury St Edmunds (30) of 1749, for example, were relatively simple or much altered in appearance.

Few chapels of the later 18th century belonging to any denomination were found. The Congregational chapel of 1750 in Rendham (127), although enlarged to the front, was of considerable interest for the completeness of its fittings, now lost or altered on conversion to a house. A chapel of later date at Wrentham (168), also built for Congregationalists, has elements of sophistication in its design which subsequent repairs and alterations have done little to enhance. Also of this period are the former Congregational chapel of 1793 in Halesworth (61) and the small former Methodist chapel in Southwold (135), both of which have been converted to houses. The only Baptist chapel to lay claim to an 18th-century date is at Grundisburgh (57) but rebuilding and enlargement have left few traces of the original structure.

Of the many chapels remaining from the early 19th century the most unusual are two Strict Baptist chapels of 1834–5 at Fressingfield (51) and Friston (52), built to an identical elongated hexagonal plan which, though internally successful, left the problems of external design rather unresolved. Other Baptist chapels of more orthodox appearance include Laxfield (95) of 1810, with an added memorial to a 16th-century Protestant martyr, Camps Road, Haverhill (66) of 1828, and Hadleigh (58) of 1830, with an arcaded front of three bays. On a larger scale is the Baptist chapel in Garland Street, Bury St Edmunds (26) of 1834, with an unusually broad front for an urban chapel. At Lakenheath the similarity in design of the former Calvinistic Independent chapel of 1815 (91) with that of the Baptists (90) built thirty years later exemplifies the continuity in village chapel design in the first half of the 19th century. Small chapels built by Baptists, Congregationalists and Methodists, generally with fronts divided into three bays, continued throughout the first half of the 19th century and beyond. One of the few to call for special mention is the former Congregational, now Baptist, chapel in Whepstead (157) of 1844, where the small chapel of local flint with brick dressings is given a quaint but picturesque appearance with buttresses, simple brick pinnacles and pointed-arched Gothic windows. A more regular use of Gothic elements is seen in the work of James Fenton at Halesworth (62) in 1836 and the former Old Independent chapel of 1843 in Haverhill (67). Fenton's alternative classically pedimented style of chapel appears in Beccles (8) and at Needham Market (116) in 1836–7.

When the Congregational meeting-house of 1720 in Tacket Street, Ipswich (77) was rebuilt in 1857–8 the architect Frederick Barnes produced a richly embellished design in the Decorated Gothic style with an unusual porch at one side between turreted staircase towers, all faced in Kentish ragstone with Caen stone dressings. A later chapel by Barnes using a similar plan was built in Stowmarket c.1863 (*CYB* (1863) 302–3) but has been rebuilt. On a more standard Gothic plan is his chapel of 1870 for the Presbyterian Church in England at Portman Road, Ipswich (89). Possibly the most ambitious chapel of the later 19th century is the Old Independent Chapel in Haverhill (67) of 1884–5 by Charles Bell, a large and lofty brick building in the Gothic style with spacious galleries and a tall tower and spire at one corner. Chapels of the early 20th century include a Congregational chapel by George and R.P. Baines in Pakefield Street, Lowestoft (100) of 1902–3, of brick with a tapered tower and spire, and the classically porticoed 'Bethesda Chapel' in Ipswich (81) of 1912–13 by Frederick G. Faunch.

Available building materials in the county were limited by the absence of suitable local building stone. Timber-framed chapels such as Nicholas Street, Ipswich (76) and the Congregational chapel in Whiting Street, Bury St Edmunds (28) appear at an early date but brickwork also makes a spectacular appearance at the latter town in 1711 in the chapel in Churchgate Street (25). In later brickwork, preference is for the lighter-coloured gault brick and so-called white facing brick as employed at Garland Street, Bury St Edmunds (26), which is a particular feature of the region. Much use is also made of flint as a facing material in conjunction with brick dressings. The most frequent covering for roofs is pantiles, either red or dark glazed, which in the earlier buildings may have been substituted for thatch of which no significant examples were found. Some use of plain tiles was also noted as well as slate, particularly in the 19th century.

ALDEBURGH

(1) UNION CHAPEL, High Street (TM 464565). The chapel, set back between adjacent buildings, was erected in 1822 for a newly formed Baptist church. The front wall of painted brickwork is of three bays with two tiers of round-arched windows. The interior has a gallery at the entrance facing a pulpit with a pedimented back-board.

Browne (1877) 586–7. Klaiber (1931) 166, 178. Price (1927) 160.

Badingham Chapel. (2)

Inscriptions: on bricks in front wall, names, initials and date 1824. *Monument*: in burial-ground, Charles Smith, 1887, pastor, and Elizabeth his wife, 1867.

BADINGHAM

(2) BADINGHAM CHAPEL (TM 326682). The tiny former Primitive Methodist chapel of brick with a hipped slate roof was built in 1836. It was sold to the Laxfield and Cransford Baptist churches in 1948. Sash windows in side walls. (Closed 1988)

BARDWELL

(3) BAPTIST, Low Street (TL 940728). Square chapel of brick with pyramidal slate roof. Front of three bays with two doorways, small gallery windows over and window between. Date tablet of 1824 formerly inscribed 'Zion Chapel'. The partly refitted interior has a rear gallery with fielded-panelled front.

BARNARDISTON

(4) PRIMITIVE METHODIST (TL 710488). Brick with hipped roof, three-bay front with pointed-arched windows. Opened 1874.

BARNINGHAM

(5) WESLEYAN (TL 968767). The chapel built in 1854 replaced one of 1811. Grey brick with gabled front, segmental-arched windows at sides. The interior, partly refitted, has a rear gallery. *Monuments*: in burial-ground, several headstones to Fison family, including (1) James Fison, 1817, late of Thetford; (2) Charlotte wife of Thomas Fison, 1846; (3) Mary Matthew wife of Thomas Fison, 1823; (4) Thomas Fison, 1861.

BARTON MILLS

(6) BAPTIST (TL 720738). The chapel, under erection in 1843 when it was severely damaged by a storm, was completed in 1844. Plain gabled brick front of three bays with centre entrance and two tiers of iron-framed windows. The interior has a rear gallery, original pulpit with shaped and panelled back-board, and contemporary box-pews. *Monuments*: in burial-ground, partly cleared or re-sited since 1971.

BM XXXVI (1844) 254–5. Browne (1877) 584–5.

BECCLES

(7) BAPTIST, Station Road (TM 423904). The 'Martyrs Memorial' chapel, built in 1860–1 to supersede a chapel of 1805, is of gault brick with a pedimented front of three bays divided by pilasters and two tiers of sash windows with marginal glazing bars. *Monument*: above entrance, to Protestant martyrs, Thomas Spicer, John Deny and Edmund Poole, burned at the stake 21 May 1556.

Browne (1877) 583.

(8) CONGREGATIONAL, Hungate (TM 423903). The chapel, now jointly URC/Methodist, was built in 1812 for a church formed in 1652 which first acquired the site in 1687. This red brick structure was re-fronted in gault brick in 1836 to a design by James Fenton. The front wall has a broad pediment over three bays and entrances in the end bays having Classical surrounds with Ionic columns *in antis*. Interior partly refitted and suspended ceiling added above gallery c.1978. Sunday-school, 1879, by E. Boardman.

Monuments: in chapel (1) Rev. Joseph Heptinstall, 1802, 29 years minister; (2) Rev. John Flower, 1881, minister 1834–73; (3) John Mayhew, 1853; (4) Rev. Isaac Sloper, 1835, 30 years pastor.

Rix, S.W., *Brief Records of the Independent Church at Beccles, Suffolk* (1837). Hosken (1920) 198–206.

(9) FRIENDS, Smallgate (TM 423904). The meeting-house built in 1745 but in use as an infant school during part of the 19th century was greatly altered in 1909 by the addition of an upper storey with a hipped pantiled roof. The original single-storeyed structure ($27\frac{3}{4}$ft by $18\frac{1}{4}$ft), which remains in part incorporated in the present building, had brick walls and a front of three bays with a central entrance.

Butler (1999) 569.

(10) WESLEYAN, Station Road (TM 424904). Grey brick with Romanesque details; gabled front with wheel-window between pyramidally capped turrets; square chapel behind with pyramid roof and ventilator at apex. Dated 1872. (Demolished 1979)

BELSTEAD

(11) CONGREGATIONAL (TM 132412). Brown brick with yellow brick dressings; three-bay front with round-arched windows. Built c.1855–60.

BILDESTON

(12) BAPTIST (TL 991495). The chapel was built in 1844 for a church formed in 1737. Brick with four-centred arched heads to doorways and windows, octagonal buttresses at front corners. Side galleries added 1867. Variously altered or repaired. *Monuments*: in burial-ground (1) John Cooper, 1762, headstone with cherubs' heads; (2) Robert Gooch, 1759, and John Cooper, 1763, similar to last; (3) Rev. John Campbell, 1849, 8 years minister; (4) William Webb, 1857, headstone with terracotta insert.

Browne (1877) 575.

BLYTHBURGH

(13) PRIMITIVE METHODIST (TM 453751). Three-bay brick front dated 1860, extended to left by one bay with small doorway and matching round-arched window. Gallery in extension.

Primitive Methodist chapel, Blythburgh. (13)

BOXFORD

(14) CONGREGATIONAL, Swan Street (TL 960407). The chapel of red brick with a hipped slated roof was built in 1823 at the expense of Robert and John Ansell. Three-bay front with two tiers of sash windows; two large pulpit windows in back wall. Gallery around three sides now covered by false ceiling. (URC)

Hosken (1920) 261–2.

BRAMFIELD

(15) CONGREGATIONAL (TM 399740). Small chapel 'erected 1841' faced with flint pebbles with gault brick dressings. Lancet windows in side walls and flanking gabled porch.

Newby (1936) 151–6.

(16) PRIMITIVE METHODIST (TM 399745). Plain rendered brick walls and gabled front. Dated 1851.

BRAMFORD

(17) WESLEYAN (TM 122467). Red brick with gault brick dressings, rusticated corner pilasters and triple-arched window below deep bracketed gable. Built 1873, by Cattermole and Eade of Ipswich.

BRANDESTON

(18) Former CONGREGATIONAL (TM 245608). Gault brick front, red brick sides and hipped slate roof. Three-bay front with two tiers of sash windows with timber lintels. Built 1838, gallery added c.1871–5. Interior gutted 1972 on conversion to secular use. *Inscription*: on brick above central doorway 'WM 1838'.

Hosken (1920) 311–12.

(19) Former FRIENDS, Friday Street (TM 242598). 'Quaker House', a 16th-century timber-framed house, possibly rebuilt or reconstructed in 1713, of three principal bays with rendered walls and a pantiled roof, was in use as a meeting-house throughout the 18th century. The meeting ceased in 1813.

Butler (1999) 570.

BRANDON

(20) BAPTIST (TL 783867). Gabled front of red brick with yellow brick quoins. Built 1854.

Browne (1877) 590.

(21) Former WESLEYAN, London Road (TL 782863). Three-bay front of knapped flint with yellow brick dressings; hipped pantiled roof. Dated 1811 on segmental band above central entrance. (Used since 1970 by Church of Christ)

BROCKLEY

(22) STRICT BAPTIST, Brockley Green (TL 824545). Plain chapel registered 1833, possibly of clay lump but refaced in brickwork, with dark pantile roof. Original rear gallery, otherwise refitted late 19th century.

BUNGAY

(23) CONGREGATIONAL, Upper Olland Street (TM 337894). The church (now jointly URC/Methodist) which originated in the mid 17th century met in a barn until 1700 when the first meeting-house was erected. This appears to have been rebuilt in 1818 but retaining the general proportions and possibly the size of the former. Extensive alterations and refitting were carried out by E. Boardman & Son c.1885 including the addition of staircase wings and an arcaded loggia across the front. (Further altered and loggia brought forward since 1972)

The chapel has a broad front of gault brick, red brick sides and a hipped pantiled roof. The interior ($40\tfrac{3}{4}$ft by 58ft) originally had a gallery around three sides but the side galleries were removed in the refitting.

Monuments: in chapel (1) Rev. John Blackie, 1840; (2) Rev. Robert Shufflebottom, 1829; on front wall inside loggia (3) Elizabeth daughter of Benjamin and Sophia De Carle, 1819. *Plate*: includes a cup of 1796.

Hosken (1920) 246–53.

Congregational chapel (URC/Methodist), Bungay. (23)

BURES ST MARY

(24) BAPTIST, High Street, Bures (TL 908342). The chapel built 1831 but possibly enlarged has a front of gault brick with five irregularly spaced giant pilasters and a pediment from which the upper cornices have been removed. The interior has a gallery around three sides and original seating. *Monuments*: externally (1) Rev. A. Anderson, 1861; (2) Rebecca Christiana wife of above, 1858.

BURY ST EDMUNDS

(25) CHURCHGATE STREET CHAPEL (TL 853641). The Presbyterian society, which had accepted Unitarianism by the early 19th century, was formed in the years following the Restoration and took out licences in 1672 to meet in the house of Samuel Moodie and at the house of John Clarke, where William Folkes, ejected minister from Sudbury, was licensed to preach. In 1690 a house in Churchgate Street was acquired with the intention of building a meeting-house on the site but instead it was converted and remained until the larger project became possible. The erection of the new chapel was ultimately agreed in March 1711 and the work completed within that year. It was registered on 29 December 1711 and formally opened by the minister, Samuel Bury, on the following day.

The chapel, one of the most elaborate of its kind, has walls of brickwork laid to English bond, minimal stone dressings and a hipped tiled roof with concealed central valley. The S front is of three bays with pilasters, plinth, moulded cornice and a panelled parapet which rises above the centre bay where it was surmounted by a pediment (removed in the early 20th century) of which only the moulded base, arched above a sundial, now survives. The central entrance has a pair of doors and a moulded brick surround with a pair of pilasters carrying a segmental broken pediment within which is a small decorative urn. Above the doorway is an oval window with radial leaded glazing and a rubbed brick surround quartered with four key-stones carved with acanthus ornament. In each of the outer bays is a single tall window with a semicircular arched head of two orders, moulded imposts and scrolled keystone; the original tripartite timber frame is arched above the central light. Below each window is a plain brick panel in a moulded stone surround.

The E and W walls are each of three bays with round-arched upper windows and segmental arches above wooden cross-framed windows to the lower stage, two of which incorporate side entrances. The N wall has two large round-arched windows with wooden frames matching those in the front wall and a pair of small oval windows inserted between which are innocent of any structural surrounds. A small external doorway allows direct access to the pulpit.

The interior of the chapel ($42\tfrac{3}{4}$ft by $46\tfrac{1}{4}$ft) has a flat plaster ceiling with moulded cornice. The roof is supported by a central timber column of circular section with high moulded base and simply moulded capital, and by two rows of three columns which also support the side galleries. The pulpit stands centrally on the N side within a shallow round-arched recess matching the surrounds of the adjacent windows. The galleries, on three sides, have

Churchgate Street Chapel, Bury St Edmunds. Before restoration.

bolection-moulded panelled fronts above a moulded lower cornice. The staircases in the SE and SW corners have turned balusters over a straight string; the ends of the S gallery are swept back as quadrants over each staircase to avoid crossing the front windows and are supported additionally by a column rising from a newel in the lower flight. The original box-pews to the lower floor were removed and screens added below the gallery fronts in the early 20th century; the screens were removed *c*.1988.

Built against the NE and NW corners are two low annexes not structurally united to the chapel but of early 18th-century date, the former being a vestry, the latter a privy. Each has a doorway in the S wall with segmental-arched head of rubbed brickwork with cut ornament on the lower edge. A square stone tablet above the vestry door, much decayed, retains no traces of any inscription. The vestry, which has a second external doorway to the W allowing access to the pulpit door through a narrow rear yard, also has an internal doorway directly into the chapel. In the W wall is a small fireplace with early 18th-century surround and against the E wall a fixed bench with shaped arm-rest at its S end.

Fittings – *Baptismal Basin*: oval bowl of veined white marble (12in. by 9in.) carved with acanthus ornament, early 18th-century. *Clock*: on front of S gallery, hexagonal dial, 18th-century. *Plate*: four large cups and four plates of 1711, part of a set, originally including two flagons, provided by the minister Rev. Samuel Bury, and given by him to the congregation when he left office. *Pulpit*: hexagonal with one bolection-moulded panel on each face, moulded cornice slightly reduced in height; on flared stem, with panelled back-board and large hexagonal canopy surmounted by urn. Spiral staircase with continuous string and twisted balusters continued in *trompe l'œil* on length of boarded dado adjacent to pulpit door. Clerk's desk at foot of stair; communion rails later. *Railings*: in front of chapel, early 19th-century. *Rainwater Heads*: two, on S wall, dated 1711. *Seating*: in gallery, original unpainted wood seats with painted numerals on doors. *Sundial*: on front wall below former pediment, circular.

Archaeological Journal CVIII (1951) 121–6. Browne (1877) 419–21. Duncan, J., 'The History of the Presbyterians in Bury St Edmunds', typescript in Dr Williams's Library (1961). Evans (1897) 38–9. *PHSJ* XII (1960–3) 100–9. *RIBA Journal* (25 August 1938) 911.

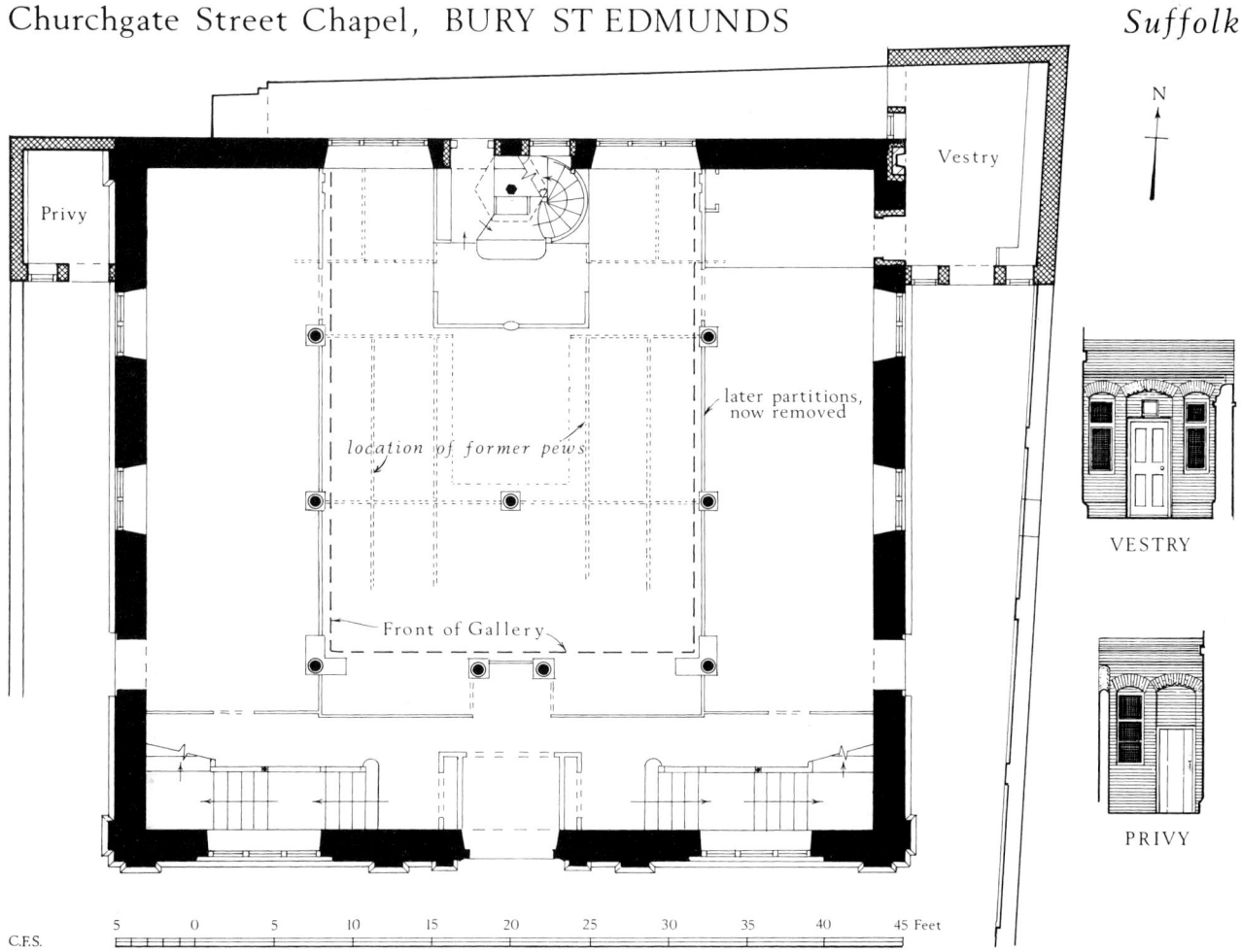

Churchgate Street Chapel, BURY ST EDMUNDS — *Suffolk*

(26) BAPTIST, Garland Street (TL 854645). The church was founded in 1800 and a meeting-house was built in that year in Nether Baxter Street. The present chapel on a new site was built in 1834 by William Steggles. The broad W front is of white brick in five bays, the three centre bays breaking forward, with two tiers of round-arched windows and entrances in the end bays; the other walls are of red brick. The interior has an original gallery around three sides with a fourth gallery added at the N end in 1842, otherwise refitted 1874–6. *Monuments*: in chapel, on E wall (1) Henry Quant, deacon, 1848, and Sarah his widow, 1863, signed 'Jackman'; (2) John Cook, 1844 and Esther his widow, 1844, marble tablet with draped urn, signed 'Wiggett'; on W wall (3) Rev. Cornelius Elven, 50 years pastor, 1873, signed 'W.T. Hale, London'; (4) Frederic Ridley, 1903; (5) Mary-Anne daughter of Rev. Cornelius Elven and wife of William Houghton, 1845, and their daughter Mary Anne, 1861, signed 'E. Wiggett'; (6) Mary Anne widow of Rev. Cornelius Elven, 1848, erected by the church and congregation.

Klaiber (1931) 24–5, 42, 70–1.

(27) Former STRICT BAPTIST, Out Westgate (TL 852637). Brick with narrow gabled front and pointed-arched doorway; dated 1840.

(28) CONGREGATIONAL, Whiting Street (TL 853639). The Independent church (now URC) was formed in 1646 and the present site was acquired in 1697. The meeting-house built *c*.1700 has rendered timber-framed walls and a hipped roof; the E end was re-fronted in 1866 in brick in the Gothic style and Sunday-schools were added to the N in 1887 by H.F. Bacon. The N and S walls have early 18th-century timber cross-framed windows. The interior, enlarged to the W in 1809 (originally approximately 50ft by 38ft), has a gallery around four sides; the seating was renewed in 1866.

Monuments: externally, to Elias Thacker and John Copping, hanged 1583 'for disseminating the principles of Independency', erected 1904; burial-ground S of chapel, stripped of monuments *c*.1970. *Pulpit*: incorporated in later rostrum, early 18th-century. *Staircases*: to gallery, 18th-century.

Grieve, A.J., and Jones, W.M., *These Three Hundred Years* (1946). Hosken (1920) 133–51. Jones, W.M., *Tercentenary Brochure* (1946).

(29) Former CONGREGATIONAL, Northgate Street (TL 85556437). The chapel built in 1828 for seceders from the foregoing was re-fronted and entirely refitted in 1866. In 1883 the church reunited with the earlier meeting and the building was later sold to Primitive Methodists. The front, by Bacon & Bell, is of brick with Italianate Gothic detail and a turret at one corner above the gallery stairs.

CYB (1867) 367. Hosken (1920) 151–2.

(30) FRIENDS, St John's Street (TL 853649). The present site, together with a house on it possibly already in use for meetings, was purchased in 1682. In 1749–50 the site was enlarged and a new meeting-house erected while retaining part of the former premises for a women's meeting-house.

The meeting-house registered in 1749 has rendered timber-framed walls and a hipped tiled roof. The broad front wall was rebuilt in white brick in the mid 19th century. The entrance is in the S wall. The interior of the principal room (44¾ft by 26¾ft) has a later gallery at the S end, now closed and the staircase removed, with

Friends' meeting-house, Bury St Edmunds. (30)

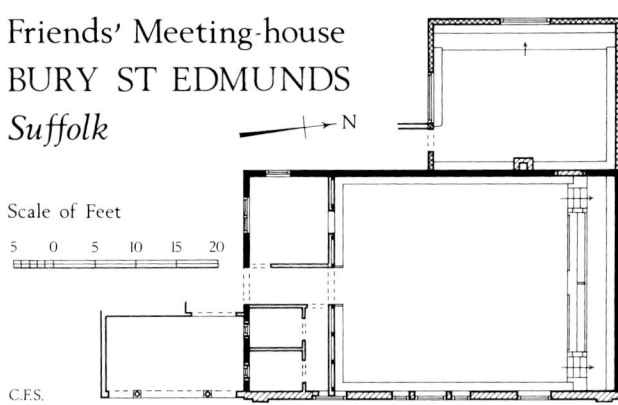

movable shutters below. The stand at the N end dates from the mid 18th century. In the W wall close to the stand is a blocked doorway communicating with the earlier timber-framed 'women's house' which projects to the west. Various extensions and alterations to the building, including a new S porch, were made *c*.1967–9.

Butler (1999) 570–1. Curtayne, B., *300 Years of Quakerism in Bury St Edmunds, Suffolk* (1982).

(31) Former WESLEYAN, St Mary's Square (TL 858638). The chapel registered for worship in 1812 was superseded by a new building in Brentgovel Street in 1878; it has since been used for commercial purposes and latterly converted to domestic use. The walls are of brick and the hipped roof is covered in dark pantiles. The S front of three bays has two tiers of round-arched windows and an altered central entrance.

BUXHALL

(32) PRIMITIVE METHODIST, Mill Green (TL 996577). Gabled brick front of three bays with round-arched openings; dated 1875.

CAVENDISH

(33) CONGREGATIONAL (TL 809465). Grey brick gabled front with graduated lancets; red brick sides. Interior with rear gallery and scissor-trussed roof. Built 1858 replacing earlier chapel. *Inscription*: tablet reset in boundary wall 'Built 1840 | Cavendish Chapel | Enlarged 1843'. (URC)

Browne (1877) 544. Hosken (1920) 310–11.

CHARSFIELD

(34) BAPTIST (TM 258563). The chapel was built in 1808 and a Strict Baptist church formed in 1809; the chapel was enlarged to the front by 9¼ft in 1846. The walls are of red brick and the roof hipped and covered with pantiles. The SW front wall of four bays has round-arched entrances in the end bays, two cross-framed windows between and four small gallery windows over. The side walls, of three bays, are similarly fenestrated. The back wall has two tall rectangular windows flanking the pulpit, one partly covered by a modern vestry.

Baptist chapel, Charsfield. (34)

The interior, now nearly square, is ceiled at collar level over the earlier part but has a flat plaster ceiling over the front extension. There is a gallery around three sides with a panelled front supported at the sides by timber columns but by cast-iron in the extension.

Baptistery: centrally in floor of original chapel, aligned at right-angles to pulpit. (An external baptistery behind the chapel is reported, now filled in) *Pulpit*: rostrum incorporating fielded panels from original pulpit (replaced since 1972).

Browne (1877) 584. *Grace* (January 1990) 19–20.

CLARE

(35) BAPTIST (TL 769455). The chapel, built in 1859 for seceders who left the Congregational church and formed a separate society in 1803, replaces an earlier building in Cavendish Lane. The side walls are of red brick. The front of gault brick is of three bays with giant pilasters and a pediment, a central doorway and two tiers of round-arched windows. The interior has a gallery around three sides with some original seating. (The original box-pews and the fittings to the lower floor were entirely removed in 1988)

Browne (1877) 509, 582–3. Hosken (1920) 243.

(36) CONGREGATIONAL, Nethergate Street (TL 769452). The congregation, now URC, derives from the work of Francis Crow, ejected vicar of Hundon. A meeting-house built in 1710 was replaced by the present chapel in 1841. This has brick walls and a hipped slate roof. The front of three bays has a central segmental-arched entrance with a blind window above and a tablet with the dates of erection and rebuilding; the adjacent bays are recessed and have round-arched upper windows. The side walls, five bays in length, have two tiers of windows. The interior has an original gallery around three sides with a fourth gallery above the vestries at the back of the pulpit. The fittings were renewed in the early 20th century. Pulpit removed *c*.1990. *Monuments*: externally (1) Samuel Ince, 1835, Ann his wife, 1831, and their children Samuel and Ann, headstone; (2) built into corner pilaster of rear bay, square floor tile inscribed 'TI | Mar 20 1829 | Aged 57 | LI | June 13 : 1834 | Aged 16'; (3) Ruth wife of Rev. R. Kemp of London, 1817, brick table-tomb, cast-iron capping with gadrooned edge.

Browne (1877) 505–10. Hosken (1920) 242–5.

COCKFIELD

(37) CONGREGATIONAL (TL 914554). Built 1841 for a branch of the Northgate Street church, Bury St Edmunds, greatly enlarged in 1860 and a school-room added in 1867. Brick with double-gabled end, barge-boards and porch between the original and later work. A second porch in the extension faces the road.

Hosken (1920) 314–15.

CONEY WESTON

(38) PRIMITIVE METHODIST (TL 956778). Red brick with yellow brick dressings, three-bay gabled front dated 1862.

COWLINGE

(39) CONGREGATIONAL, Mill Road (TL 712538). The chapel built 1835 has a brick front, side walls of flint with brick dressings, and a hipped slate roof. The front has two round-arched doorways with a wide lunette between and two upper windows. The interior has a deep gallery at the entrance with low benches for children; the lower seating comprises three ranks of unpainted box-pews with numbered doors.

Hosken (1920) 316–17.

CONGREGATIONAL CHAPEL, COWLINGE C.F.S.1971

CRANSFORD

(40) STRICT BAPTIST (TM 318648). Large chapel opened 1841, with brick walls and a gabled front of three bays having a wide central entrance and two tiers of windows. The side walls are largely unfenestrated. Interior high but without galleries; late 19th-century fittings. (Rebuilt following destruction by hurricane 16 October 1987)

Browne (1877) 589. *Grace* (December 1987) 12; (January 1990) 15.

CRATFIELD

(41) Site of CONGREGATIONAL, Bell Green (TM 311753). The chapel built in 1812 and enlarged 1837 has been demolished. It had a broad front of white brick, red brick sides and a hipped pantiled roof. *Monuments*: in burial-ground, many headstones of early 19th-century date and later, also monument to Benjamin Woolnough, 1845, Mary his wife, 1841, and Mary their daughter, 1816, erected by Elizabeth Cooper, daughter of the first, cast iron surmounted by urn.

EM NS XVI (1838) 238. Hosken (1920) 176–7. Newby (1936) 137–50.

DEBENHAM

(42) CONGREGATIONAL (TM 173634). The church (now URC) originated in the late 17th century. The present chapel was built in 1820, enlarged to the back and possibly re-fronted in 1837. The broad brick façade to the street, of three bays, is subdivided by a pair of plain pilasters carrying a simplified pediment over the centre bay; over the entrance is a triple-arched window.

The interior has a gallery around three sides with panelled front but the seating has been removed. The lower seating was renewed in 1896.

Hosken (1920) 263–8.

EARL SOHAM

(43) BAPTIST (TM 229632). Red brick sides; gabled front of gault brick with three arched bays. Tall square-headed windows with iron frames and lintels supported by ornamental consoles. *Inscription*: on tablet in front wall 'BC ERECTED 1859 J K'.

EAST BERGHOLT

(44) CONGREGATIONAL, Cemetery Lane (TM 068346). The church appears to have originated in the late 17th century as a Presbyterian society but had seriously declined by the end of the following century. The erection of the present chapel is attributed to the efforts of a new minister, Robert Roberts, appointed 1855.

The chapel of red brick with dressings of white and blue brick and a slated roof was built in 1857 to a design by Charles Forster Hayward of London. It was praised in the *Congregational Year Book* (1858) as 'an example of what a little trouble and artistic thought can make out of common-place materials'. The tall gabled front has a central doorway, three lancets above with a quatrefoil over within a pointed-arched surround, flanking lancets and an ornamental panel at the apex of the gable decorated with a cross *flory* inset in white brick. The side walls are divided into five bays with stepped buttresses.

The interior has an open roof with scissor trusses. There is a single gallery at the entrance and pitch-pine pews to the lower floor. Shuttered arches in the wall behind the pulpit open to a rear school-room cum vestry. A few early 19th-century headstones remain in the burial-ground.

Congregational chapel, East Bergholt. (44)

The Builder (2 May 1857). *CYB* (1858) 266–7; (1878) 344, obituary of Rev. R. Roberts. Hosken (1920) 269–70. Short, G.V., *East Bergholt Congregational Church, 1689–1989* (1989).

ELMSWELL

(45) WESLEYAN, School Road (TL 988638). Gabled front of red brick with white brick dressings; gabled porch, circular plate-traceried window over and corner buttresses with pinnacles. Built 1898 to replace a chapel of 1804. *Monument*: in burial-ground, Mary Anna Wright, 1837.

ERISWELL

(46) Former WESLEYAN (TL 723782). Small chapel built 1844 of knapped flint with brick dressings and a hipped pantiled roof. Above a small gabled brick porch is a stone tablet inscribed 'WESLEYs DOCTRINE'.

EYE

(47) BAPTIST, Church Street (TM 147739). The church which originated *c.*1794 registered a meeting-house in 1802 and built the first chapel on this site in 1810. The present chapel of 1868 has a gabled front of white brick divided into three bays by giant pilasters, paired at the corners, and supporting a brick entablature arched above the middle bay. There are two tiers of round-arched windows. The side walls are of red brick.

Ivimey IV (1830) 534–5.

FRAMLINGHAM

(48) THE OLD MEETING-HOUSE (TM 284635). The congregation of Independent or Presbyterian origin, but which now supports a Unitarian ministry, claims to derive from the work of Henry Sampson, ejected as rector in 1660. In 1672 Austin Plumstead, an Independent and former Fellow of Trinity College, Cambridge, was licensed to preach in the town and three houses are named as meeting-places.

The Old Meeting-house, Framlingham. (48)

The present chapel was built in 1717 on a site described on the trust deed as 'part of a garden or orchard known as Starr House Garden, now Black Horse Garden'. The walls are of red brick with dark headers in Flemish bond and the roof, of low pitch and with wide eaves, possibly replaced in the early 19th century, is hipped and slated. The S front of three bays has a platband at mid height which continues around all sides; the end bays have each a simple segmental-arched doorway with cross-framed window over, and similar windows between in the middle bay. The E and W walls had one similar window at each level but the lower window on the E side has been blocked. The N wall has two taller windows flanking the original site of the pulpit.

The interior (24½ft by 37¾ft) was drastically refitted and realigned in the late 19th century when the pulpit was re-sited at the E end and one gallery together with a possible S gallery removed.

The surviving W gallery, partly closed beneath, has a bolection-moulded panelled front supported by a pair of turned wood columns.

Fittings – *Monuments*: in chapel (1) Sarah eldest daughter of Rev. Isaac Toms and Sarah (Say) his wife, 1809, urn-shaped wooden tablet; externally on N wall (2) Thomas Barker, 1822, Elizabeth his widow, 1841, *et al.*; in burial-ground N of chapel, 19th-century headstones. *Pulpit*: replaced by late 19th-century rostrum, but retaining above it the original pediment surmounted by a carved wood dove standing on an orb.

The Christian Life (6 September – 22 November 1902) five historical articles by Alfred Amey. Evans (1897) 88–9. Hosken (1920) 301–2.

(49) Former CONGREGATIONAL, Fore Street (TM 284634). The chapel was built in 1823 to supersede a cottage converted to a meeting-house in 1819 by seceders from the Old Meeting. The front wall is of gault brick and the roof is hipped and slated with bracketed eaves. The front is of three bays with two tiers of round-arched windows and a central doorway.

Hosken (1920) 301–5.

FRAMSDEN

(50) BAPTIST, Peats Corner (TM 193607). Brick with large gabled front; round-arched window over entrance to light rear gallery. Late 19th-century fittings. Built 1833.

FRESSINGFIELD

(51) STRICT BAPTIST (TM 263774). The chapel built in 1835, of brick with a slate roof, has an elongated hexagonal plan matching that of the slightly earlier chapel at Friston (52). There is a small porch at the N end and two tiers of windows with hung sashes in the longer side walls. The roof is hipped, the hips descending to pilaster buttresses intermediately along the principal sides.

The interior has a continuous hexagonal gallery with plain front and staircases at the N end. Below the S gallery is a small vestry in front of which is the pulpit. The baptistery is placed centrally within the lower pews. (Plan p. 288)

Strict Baptist chapel, Fressingfield. (51)

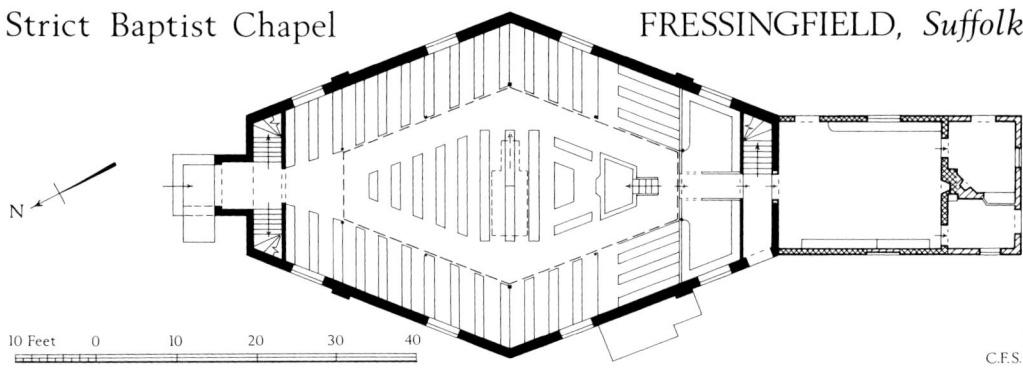

Strict Baptist Chapel — FRESSINGFIELD, *Suffolk*

Fittings – *Monuments*: in chapel (1) George Denny Spratt, 1855, 'he erected this chapel in 1835 ... and preached gratuitously for nearly twenty years'; in burial-ground (2) Mary Ann Spratt, 1840, Samuel Spratt, 1849, Mary Spratt, 1852, and George Denny Spratt, 1855. *Seating*: in gallery, original scrubbed pine seats with box-pews at the N end and open-backed benches at the sides. Lower seating and pulpit replaced 1910. (The gallery seating was totally removed and a hall to the S rebuilt larger c.1985)

FRISTON

(52) STRICT BAPTIST (TM 411601). 'The Hexagonal Chapel, Friston' was registered as a place of worship in February 1834. The walls are of red brick with flat-arched heads of yellow brick to doorways and windows and the roof is slated. The plan, an elongated hexagon, was closely followed in time and details by the chapel at Fressingfield (*see* (51)). The first pastor, William Brown, is said to have maintained himself by gaining a knowledge of land-surveying and to have 'studied architecture, and superintended several large buildings in London, among them two chapels'; his responsibility for the initial design is most likely.

The plan differs from Fressingfield in having the entrance at the S end; ancillary rooms of slightly later date are built against the NE and NW sides and incorporate gallery staircases which rise to the middle of the longer side galleries. The gallery is continuous and has a panelled front supported by octagonal posts. Behind the pulpit at the N end is a small vestry. The baptistery is central in the lower floor, beneath the communion table but is aligned N–S, at right-angles to the table-pew. (Since 1974 the window frames have been altered and much of the lower seating removed)

Fittings – *Communion Table*: trapezoidal, standing within table-pew of like shape, c.1834. *Monuments*: in chapel (1) William Brown, 1888, 54 years pastor; in burial-ground (2) Thomas Burrell [nd] and Eliza Burrell, 1836; (3) Caroline Burrell, 1843; (4) Augustus Fisher, 1851, Augustus Fisher, 1877, Mary his wife, 1875, Eliza Smith, 1854, Ellen Jane Mayes, 1852, and Charles Simon Fisher, 1885, table-tomb; (5) Leger John Henry son of Henry Thomas Pawson, Baptist minister, 1870; (6) William Brown, 1888, pastor, and Esther his wife, 1857; (7) Sarah Ann widow of Rev. William Brown, 1906, and Hannah Bridgman, 1879. *Pulpit*: rostrum with open cast-iron balustrade, late 19th-century. *Seating*: much contemporary seating remains with box-pews to the lower floor; the gallery seating is in two ranks, numbered inside the front rail.

Klaiber (1931) 79–80.

GLEMSFORD

(53) 'EBENEZER' BAPTIST CHAPEL, Egremont Street (TL 828475). Rendered walls and hipped slate roof; front with two doorways, one sash window above each, and roundel between with chapel name and date 1829. The interior has a rear gallery only and original pulpit opposite; the seating was replaced in the late 19th century. (Demolition proposed 1996)

(54) 'PROVIDENCE' BAPTIST CHAPEL (TL 829479). Red brick with yellow brick dressings; lancet windows. Rear gallery only; table-pew in front of pulpit. (Chapel derelict 1971, demolished by 1977, burial-ground remains) *Monuments*: in burial-ground, 19th-century headstones, including one to Samuel Kemp, 1874, 11 years pastor.

Strict Baptist chapel, Friston. (52)

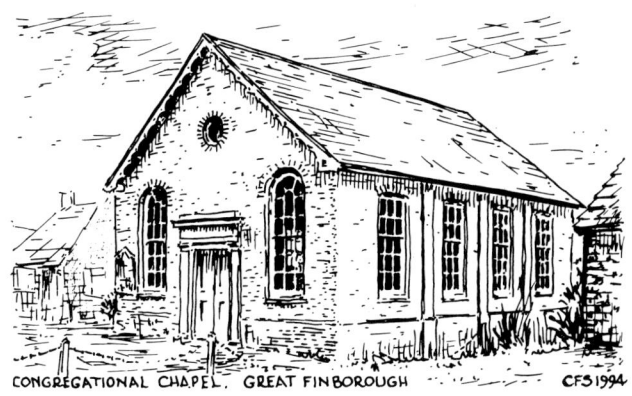

CONGREGATIONAL CHAPEL, GREAT FINBOROUGH CFS 1994

GREAT FINBOROUGH

(55) CONGREGATIONAL (TM 013574). Small chapel of grey brick with two round-arched windows in gabled front. Original rostrum pulpit, otherwise reseated. 1862, by V. Andrews of Stowmarket. (URC)

CYB (1863) 291.

GREAT THURLOW

(56) Former CONGREGATIONAL (TL 679505). The chapel built 1835, enlarged 1858, has brick walls and a hipped slate roof. The W front originally had two doorways with gallery windows over; a large vestry at the rear, possibly of 1858, obscures two original tall pulpit windows. The church closed *c*.1950. (Converted to house 1971)

Hosken (1920) 317.

GRUNDISBURGH

(57) STRICT BAPTIST (TM 227503). The chapel was built in 1798, enlarged during the pastorate of the first minister, John Thompson, and re-fronted in 1863. It is a large building (43ft by 51ft externally) of brick with a hipped pantiled roof and concealed central valley. The W front is of five bays with a central gabled porch and two tiers of sash windows; two rectangular windows in the E wall flank the pulpit. The S wall, which may be part of the original structure, is partly covered by a low vestry of the mid 19th century. The interior has a gallery around three sides, now concealed by a false ceiling rising from the gallery fronts.

Grace (October 1993) 6–7.

HADLEIGH

(58) BAPTIST, George Street (TM 028426). The chapel erected in 1830 to replace one of 1818 has walls of red brick and a hipped slate roof. The front wall is divided into three arched bays enclosing a central entrance with window above and two tiers of hung sash windows in the adjacent bays. The side walls have each a single window at mid height. The interior has a single gallery next to the entrance; the fittings were renewed in the late 19th century. (Since 1972 the front window frames have been replaced and *c*.1987 the front much obscured by further building) *Monument*: in chapel (1) Bryant Powell, 1830, and Sarah his daughter, 1826.

Browne (1877) 586. *Grace* (February 1984) 7–8.

(59) THE GREAT MEETING-HOUSE, Market Place (TM 026424). The Great Meeting, formed in the late 17th century as a Presbyterian society, became Congregational by the early 19th century (now URC). A meeting-house in Benting Street, registered in 1712, was superseded in 1832 by the present chapel. The chapel has walls of gault brick and a hipped roof covered with slates. The front wall of three bays between broad terminal pilasters has three round-arched upper windows; the central entrance, covered by a porch with two Doric columns *in antis*, was flanked by two round-arched windows in similarly arched recesses but these are now covered by a widening of the porch. The interior, which has a gallery around three sides, was entirely refitted *c*.1890.

Hosken (1920) 256–60. Sydenham, G., *The Story of Congregationalism in Hadleigh and District* (1967).

(60) PRIMITIVE METHODIST, George Street (TM 031427). Red brick, gabled front with round-arched doorway and windows. Dated 1875.

HALESWORTH

(61) Former CONGREGATIONAL, 90–91 London Road (TM 386773). The meeting-house, now a pair of cottages set well back behind the W side of the road, was built in 1793 and placed in trust for 'Calvinists and Independents'. It was superseded in 1836 by the present chapel in Quay Street (*see* (62)) and then served for a time as a Wesleyan chapel. The walls are of brickwork and the roof is hipped and covered with pantiles. The SE front has two segmental-arched end doorways, one now altered, and two wide segmental-arched windows between at two levels. The end walls had each two upper windows to light a gallery.

CYB (1851) 214–15, obituary of John Dennant. Hosken (1920) 178–80.

(62) CONGREGATIONAL, Quay Street (TM 387777). The chapel of 1836 by James Fenton, built for the congregation (now URC) from (61), has walls of gault brick to the principal sides and red brick at the rear. The front of three bays below a low gable has gabled porches with canted corners in the end bays, a window between with square head under a label and three upper windows with pointed-arched heads. The return bays at each end of the frontage project as polygonal staircase wings with stepped buttresses at the angles. The interior has four exposed roof trusses below a

Baptist chapel, Hadleigh. (58)

Congregational chapel (URC), Halesworth. (62)

polygonal ceiling. A gallery round three sides is supported by cast-iron columns; a lower choir gallery is set behind the pulpit. Most of the fittings were renewed in 1893.

Monuments: in chapel (1) Rev. John Dennant, 1851, first pastor; in small burial-ground at rear (2) William Lincolne, 1847, 30 years deacon, Mary his widow, 1848, and Mary Napier Lincolne their daughter, 1837, railed monument with ball finial. *Plate: see* Walpole (149).

EM NS XIV (1836) 304–5, 566–7. Hosken (1920) 178–80. Newby (1936) 78.

(63) PRIMITIVE METHODIST, London Road (TM 385771). Red brick with gault brick dressings; pedimented front of three bays with rusticated pilasters and arched centre bay. Dated 1877.

HARTEST

(64) Former CONGREGATIONAL, The Green (TL 834526). A 17th-century timber-framed house altered in the 18th century and converted to a pair of cottages by the beginning of the following century was fitted up as an Independent meeting-house in 1864 by the removal of an upper floor. This use ceased in 1980 and it was sold for re-conversion to a house in 1982. The walls are rendered and the roof is pantiled. The front has a gabled porch between two round-arched windows and a gabled wing to the right with a separate doorway to the chapel gallery which occupies part of the upper floor of the wing. The interior has three crown-post roof trusses with late 19th-century embellishment.

Hosken (1920) 316. Paine, C. (ed.), *Hartest, A Village History* (1984) 103–5.

HAUGHLEY

(65) CONGREGATIONAL (TM 028621). Built 1835 with walls of a light timber-framed construction but largely encased or rebuilt in brickwork in the early 20th century. The doorway in the brick gabled front incorporates original material; the rear gabled wall remains in its earlier state. (URC)

HAVERHILL

(66) STRICT BAPTIST, Camps Road, Upper Downs Slade (TL 670456). The chapel dated 1828, registered May 1829, is of brick with a hipped roof formerly covered with slates. The front has a wide central entrance with reeded pilasters between small sash windows and a lunette above. The side walls have each two arched bays enclosing windows with altered frames. One bay of two storeys was added to the back *c*.1860 to provide a vestry with

Strict Baptist chapel, Camps Road, Haverhill. (66)

second gallery over; an original rear gallery is supported by two marbled iron columns. The pulpit and seating were renewed in the late 19th century. *Clock*: signed 'Mackie, White Rose Court, Coleman Street, London'.

(67) THE OLD INDEPENDENT CHAPEL, Hamlet Road (TL 675452). A Presbyterian society originating in the late 17th century which later became Congregational (now URC) built a meeting-house in 1707. This was rebuilt in 1843 and it remains, converted to a Sunday-school, at the rear of the present chapel in Meeting Walk. It was superseded in 1884–5.

The chapel of 1843, possibly the work of James Fenton, has a front of yellow brick, red brick sides and a slate roof. The front is gabled and has five lancets, three grouped above the rebuilt central porch. In 1875 the porch, now reinstated, was replaced by a pair of porches, a small circular ventilator was added to the main gable and the chapel was extended to the rear by two bays. It has a continuous gallery of 1875 with a cast-iron open-work front.

The present chapel of 1884–5 designed by Charles Bell is a large and imposing building of red brick with Bath stone dressings in the Gothic style dominated by a tall corner tower and spire, slightly modified from the original design, and with a gabled front to the street having a traceried window of five lights and gabled porches at the corners. The sides have paired gables to the transepts. (*See* p. 292)

The interior has a high boarded ceiling with partly exposed trusses, two-bay arcades to galleried transepts and a deep rear gallery with angled corners. At the opposite end is an arched organ recess behind the pulpit and choir stalls.

Monuments: in chapel (1) William Jobson, 1833, 'first minister of Castle Camps meeting'; (2) Rev. James Bowers, 1820, 27 years pastor; (3) John Webb, 1840, and Mehetabel his widow, 1852; (4) James Webb, 1848, deacon, and Sarah his wife, 1845; (5) Joseph Nott, 1858, trustee, erected 1864; (6) Daniel Gurteen, 1856, and Grace his wife, 1840; (7) Daniel Gurteen of Chauntry House, 1893, and Caroline his wife, 1884, elaborate Gothic wall monument of marble with ogee gable over paired tablets; externally, in front of Sunday-school (8) Daniel Gurteen, 1813, and Sarah his wife, 1813; (9) Jonathan Sizer, 1827, and William his son, 1820.

CYB (1885) 351–2. Hosken (1920) 237–8.

(68) Former CONGREGATIONAL, High Street (TL 672455). A separate congregation formed by some members from the foregoing opened a meeting-house in 1836, followed by a permanent chapel in 1839, but removed in 1891 to West End (*see* (69)). The former chapel at the corner of Quakers Lane has walls of red brick, a pedimented front of three bays divided by pilasters, and round-arched upper windows. The lower part is covered by a shop front. A tablet in the pediment is dated 1839.

EM NS XIV (1836) 251. Hosken (1920) 238–41.

(69) CONGREGATIONAL, West End (TL 669458). Red brick with yellow brick and stone dressings. Gabled front with traceried window and two gabled porches. Sunday-school adjacent. Built 1891 by Charles Gray Searle & Son for the foregoing.

CYB (1892) 215.

HENSTEAD WITH HULVER STREET

(70) WESLEYAN, Hulver Street (TM 470868). Brown brick with three-bay front and pedimental gable. Pointed-arched front windows but semicircular fanlight over doorway. Dated 1840.

HEPWORTH

(71) PRIMITIVE METHODIST, The Street (TL 986746). In 1851 Primitive Methodists occupied a building adjoining a barn which had been converted to a chapel *c.*1836. The present chapel opened 1867 is part of a symmetrical timber-framed and rendered range comprising a small square chapel between two two-storeyed cottages. It has a central doorway between sash windows and a hexagonal window above. The interior is open to the roof, there is no gallery, the fittings date from the late 19th century. (Reported converted to house since 1974)

HOLBROOK

(72) WESLEYAN, The Street (TM 169366). Brick with gabled front; central doorway with segmental fanlight between two sash windows with tall round-arched window above. Rear gallery extended and two windows in side walls re-sited. Opened 1829.

HORHAM

(73) STRICT BAPTIST, Chapel Lane (TM 220715). The church was formed in 1799 as a result of the missionary preaching of Charles Farmery of Diss. The present chapel 'Built by subscription 1859'

Strict Baptist chapel, Horham. (73)

The Old Independent Chapel (URC), Hamlet Road, Haverhill.

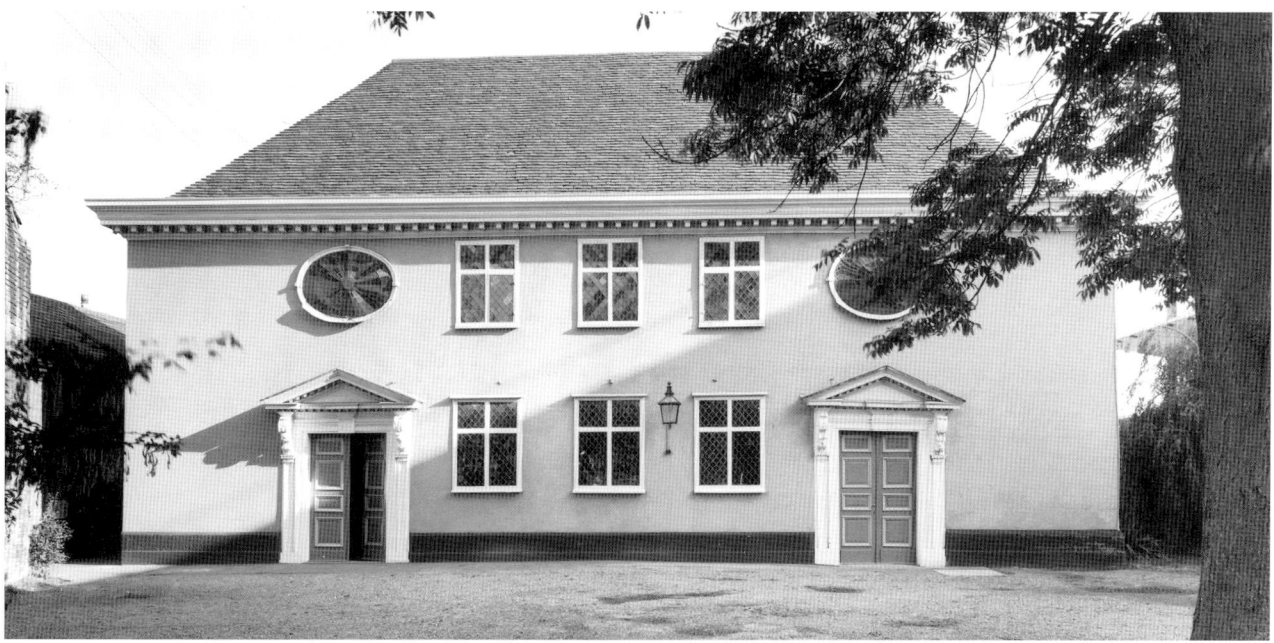

N front.

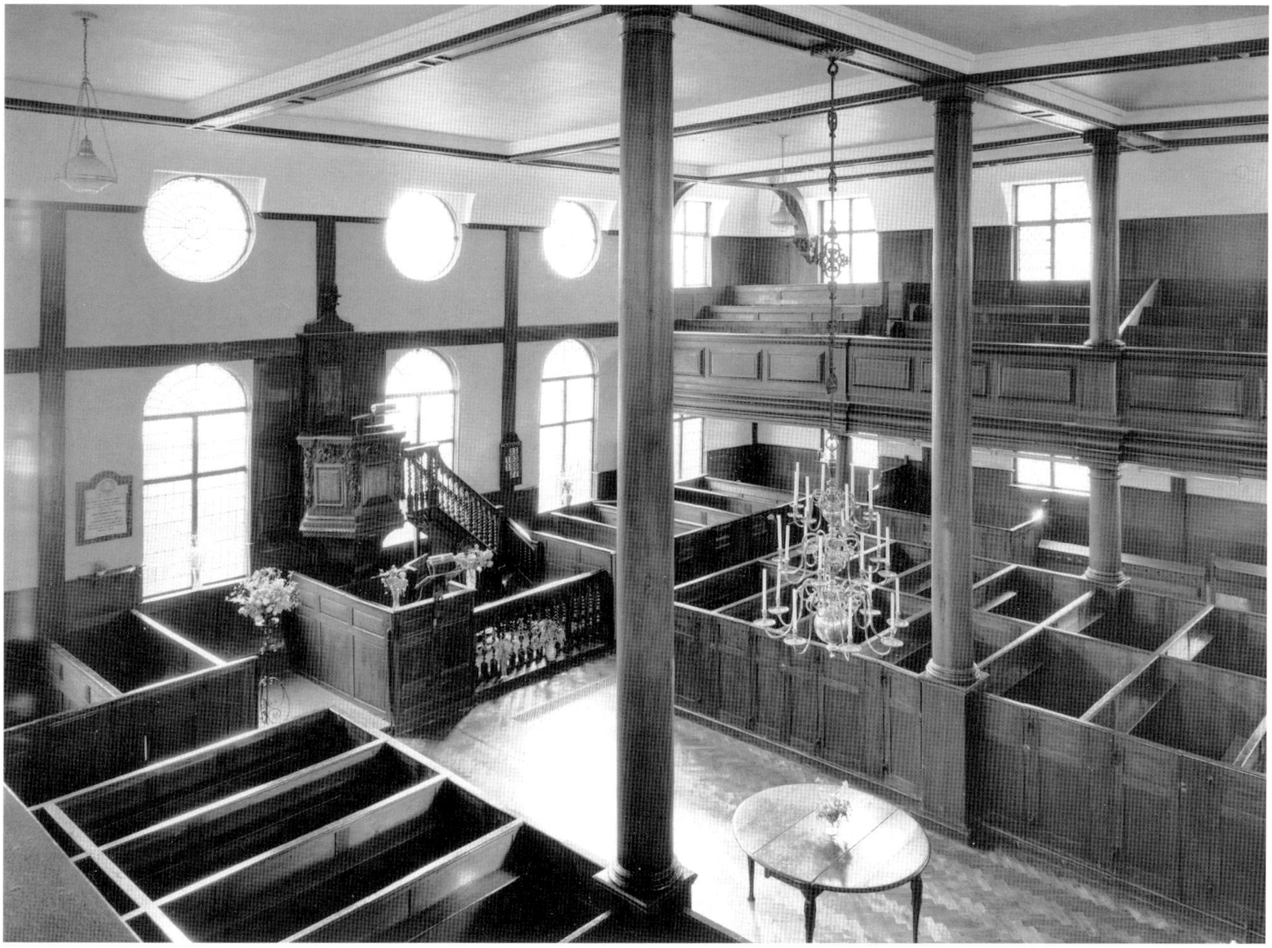

St Nicholas Street Meeting-house, Ipswich. (76)

is a large building with a gabled front of gault brick with three doorways and windows over. The other walls are of red brick. The interior has a gallery around three sides and a fourth gallery with shuttered front behind the pulpit. Extensive ancillary buildings have been added since c.1980. *Monuments*: loose in burial-ground (1) John Barnes, 1845; (2) Mary daughter of John and Mary Barnes, 1815; in front yard (3) James Goodchild, 1852, and Esther his wife, 1845.

Klaiber (1931) 63, 64, 117, 125.

HOXNE

(74) STRICT BAPTIST, Cross Street (TM 184761). The chapel opened 2 December 1834 is of brick with a gabled front divided into three arched bays each enclosing one window with altered frame, and a central doorway. A rear gallery and a vestry were added in the 1860s; the seating dates from the late 19th century.

B.Hbk (1894) 164, obituary of Charles Masterson. *BM* XXVII (1835) 74.

HUNDON

(75) CONGREGATIONAL (TL 738489). The chapel was built in 1846 for a major Evangelical secession from the parish church. The walls are of brick and the roof hipped and slated. The front, of three recessed bays between broad pilasters, has two entrances with windows above and one window in the centre bay. The interior has a gallery around three sides. Original box-pews remain to the ground floor. (Since 1972 a false ceiling has been built over the gallery, the centre rank of pews removed and a large cross erected on the front wall) (URC)

CYB (1846) 181. Hosken (1920) 315.

CONGREGATIONAL CHAPEL, HUNDON   C·F·S·1972

IPSWICH

(76) ST NICHOLAS STREET MEETING-HOUSE (TM 16154438). A meeting of Protestant dissenters embracing both Presbyterians and Independents was in existence by 1672 when Owen Stockton, formerly parish lecturer at Colchester, was licensed as a preacher at Grey Friar's House in St Nicholas Parish. In 1686 the two parties separated, the Presbyterians, who since the late 18th century have supported a Unitarian ministry, hiring a house in Silent Street, St Nicholas parish, for use as a meeting-house. The present site comprising a capital messuage the property of Thomas Bloss was acquired by the Presbyterians in 1699 and a building contract agreed with Joseph Clarke of Ipswich, 'housecarpinter', for the demolition of outbuildings on the W side of the yard behind the existing house and the erection in their place of 'a good strong and substantial house for a meeting place'.

The meeting-house is a large timber-framed structure, rendered externally, having a hipped roof with central valley open to E and W and covered with plain tiles and a moulded modillion eaves cornice around the three principal sides. The broad front wall facing N towards Friars Street across a burial-ground opened in 1806 is of five bays, with doorways in the end bays with elaborately carved pedimented surrounds and an oval window above each with narrow architrave and keystones; the intermediate bays have two tiers of cross-framed windows. The E wall facing the original approach from St Nicholas Street has a central doorway with pedimented surround and oval window above with two tiers of two cross-framed windows to each side. The W wall has four bays of windows similar to those described. The S wall of six bays has similar windows in the end bays and four bays of round-arched windows between with circular windows above.

To the E of the meeting-house is a small courtyard with a timber-framed house on the E side facing St Nicholas Street and other contemporary buildings to N and S; a brick Sunday-school dated 1881 on the W side of the yard has been demolished.

The interior (50ft by 60ft), extensively 'restored' in 1900 by R.P. Jones, has a plaster ceiling with coved border and later embellishment. The roof is supported by a row of four timber columns, two of which are freestanding and two incorporated in the fronts of the return galleries. There is a gallery around three sides with a boldly panelled front and staircases in the NE and NW corners with spirally turned balusters. Below the N gallery is a series of panelled vestries.

Fittings – *Chandelier*: brass, 24-branch in three tiers suspended from scrolled iron pendant with beast's head terminal, early 18th-century. *Clock*: on front of N gallery, repainted hexagonal dial surmounted by carved figure of winged cherub supporting an open book inscribed with musical notation and '*Glory be to God on high | God whose Glory fills the sky*', early 18th-century. *Doors and Doorcases*: in N and E walls, three, with double doors and pedimented surrounds supported by consoles carved with doves (NW), cherubs' heads (NE) and flowers and fruit (E). *Organ*: The first organ was installed in the N gallery in 1799; it was replaced in 1865, re-sited below c.1885, and replaced by the present instrument in 1900. *Plate*: includes four two-handled cups of varying styles of 1691, 1695, 1703 and 1708, and two plates of 1663 and 1682. *Pulpit*: centrally against S wall, hexagonal with elaborately carved panelled sides with marquetry inlay on ogee-shaped base and hexagonal post; bolection-moulded back-board with moulded cornice and pineapple finial; stair with spirally turned balusters. *Seating*: box-pews throughout, the lower pews reduced in height; a cleared central area may have been occupied by a communion pew and other seating.

Archaeological Journal CVIII (1951) 121–6. Evans* (1897) 114–15. Hewett, A.P., *A Short History of St Nicholas Old Meeting House now called the Unitarian Meeting House, Ipswich* (1960). Hosken (1920) 91. Notcutt, S.A., *et al.*, *Reflections on an Old Meeting House* (1976).

(77) CONGREGATIONAL, Tacket Street (TM 17054460). When the Independents separated from the Presbyterians in 1686 (*see above*)

they hired a building in Green Yard, St Peter's parish, for meetings. In 1718 a large house in Tankard Street or Tacket Street was purchased as a residence for the minister and a meeting-house built on the ground behind which was opened in 1720. That was a brick building '40ft by 45ft' with a double hipped roof of the usual form supported internally by 'two large wooden pillars'. The broad front wall was of five bays with two tiers of cross-framed windows, two pedimented doorways in the end bays and a third possibly later plain doorway at the centre; two large round-arched windows in the rear wall with smaller oval windows between closely resembled the surviving arrangement at Churchgate Street, Bury St Edmunds (25).

The old meeting-house was replaced on the same site by the present chapel (now joint URC/Baptist) in 1857–8 to satisfy the desire of a new minister, Eliezer Jones. This is an elaborate essay in the Decorated Gothic style by Frederick Barnes of Ipswich. The walls are faced with polygonal masonry and ashlar dressings. The body of the chapel is aligned E–W but the entrance is in a gabled transept on the S side; the latter comprises an open porch of three gabled arches with a circular traceried window above, flanked by octagonal staircase towers deprived in 1963 of their most distinctive feature, a pair of open turrets with spires.

The interior has a gallery around three sides carried on cast-iron columns, by E.R. & F. Turner of Ipswich, which rise to support the open trusses of the roof.

Fittings – *Brass*: in floor below pulpit, marking the grave of Rev. Thomas Milway, 1724, 3rd pastor, and Mary his widow, 1751. *Monuments*: in chapel (1) Rev. William Notcutt, 1858, 28 years pastor; (2) Rev. Charles Atkinson, 1830, 38 years minister; in burial-ground N of chapel (3) Nathaniel Byles Byles, 1847, Mary Anne his wife, 1817, and Nathaniel their eldest son, 1858; (4) [......] Notcutt, Hannah Notcutt, 1826, her sons John, 1841, and Stephen Abbot, 1847; (5) Rev. Charles Atkinson, 1830; (6) Rev. William Notcutt, 1858; (7) George Jarvis, 1730, 'Citizen of London', and later inscription to Rev. William Notcutt, 1756, and Martha his wife, 1755; (8) Rev. William Gordon DD, 1807, and Elizabeth Gordon, 1816. *Paintings*: in church hall, three portraits in oils (i) Rev. John Langston MA, first pastor 1686–1704; (ii) Rev. Benjamin Glandfield, *ob*. 1720; (iii) Rev. William Notcutt, pastor 1724–56; also (iv) water-colour drawing of S front of former meeting-house. *Plate*: includes a set of four two-handled gadrooned cups of 1701, 1704, 1729, 1729. *Pulpit*: irregular octagon with marquetry panels, on later stem, *c*.1720.

CYB (1858) 247–8; (1859) 210, obituary of Rev. W. Notcutt; (1884) 301–3, obituary of Rev. Eliezer Jones. Hosken (1920) 88–114.

St Nicholas Street Meeting-house, IPSWICH — *Suffolk*

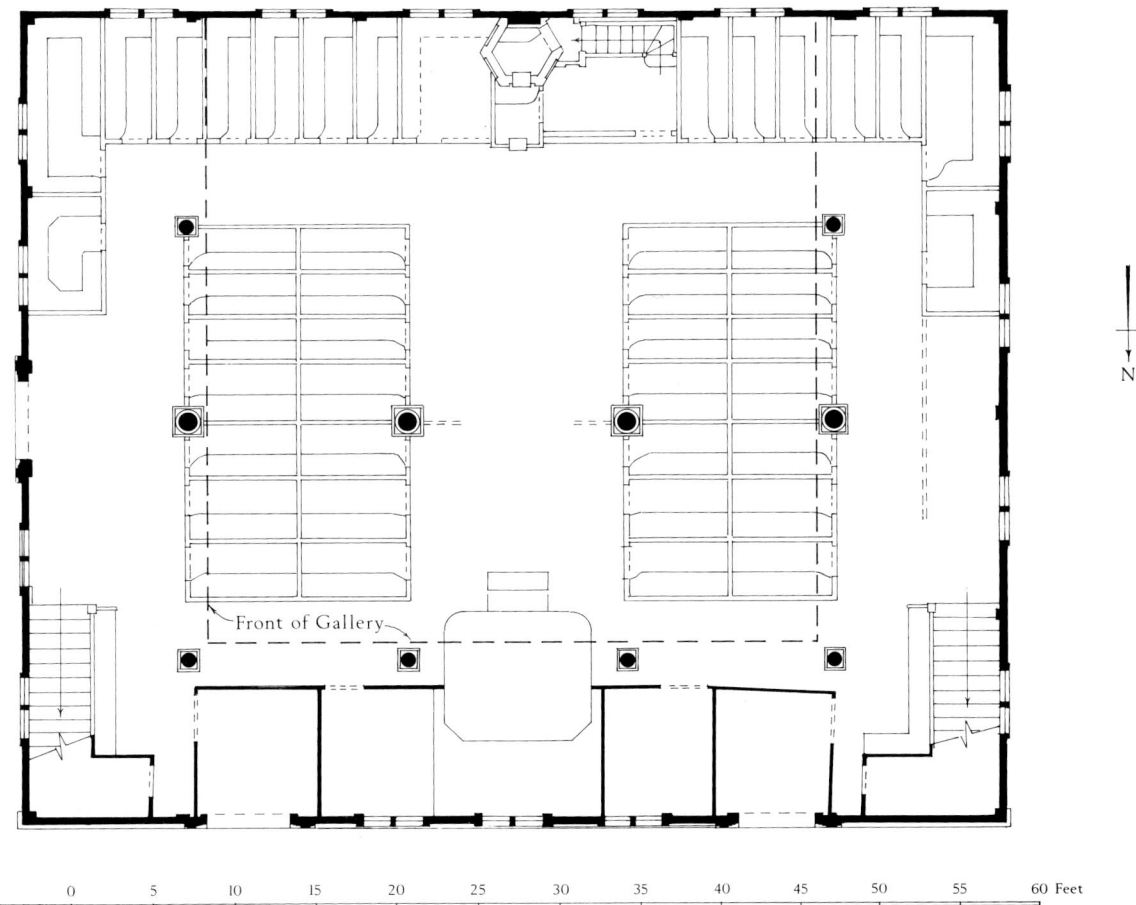

(78) Former GENERAL BAPTIST, St George's Street (TM 160449). The chapel built in 1812 passed *c*.1836 to a mixed congregation of Particular Baptists and Independents, the latter removing to a chapel in Crown Street in 1865. The building, long used for storage, has been converted for theatrical use. The walls are of brick and the roof is hipped and pantiled. The front wall of five bays has round-arched upper windows and a rebuilt central entrance. The interior, largely refitted, retains a deep S gallery. *Inscriptions*: on two tablets in front wall 'Salem Chapel | Erected 1812'.

Browne (1877) 577. Hosken (1920) 124–5. Taylor (1818) II: 446–9. Wood (1847) 208.

Former General Baptist chapel, St George's Street, Ipswich.   (78)

(79) BAPTIST, Burlington Road and London Road (TM 156448). A chapel was built in 1860–1 in Burlington Road for seceders from a Baptist church formerly meeting in Friars' Street; in 1875–6 a new 'Burlington Chapel' was built at the rear in London Road and the former converted for the Sunday-school.

The former chapel in Burlington Road is a Classical structure, possibly designed by W.P. Ribbans, of brick with rusticated quoins, a continuous modillioned eaves cornice and a pediment at the front. The front is of three bays with two segmental-arched windows and a central porch with Doric columns carrying an entablature and pediment. The present chapel facing London Road, by B. Binyon, has an Italianate front of red and gault brick with a gabled centre between staircase wings.

Browne (1877) 577–8.

(80) BAPTIST, Turret Green (TM 16324432). A chapel was built in Turret Lane in 1842 for a newly formed congregation; this was superseded in 1892 by a new chapel at the rear in Silent Street. The former chapel, now in secular use, has a front of gault brick and stone of five bays with giant pilasters and a pediment. The later chapel, of red brick in a simple Gothic style by William Eade and E. Thomas Johns, was demolished *c*.1982 and the church amalgamated with the Independent (URC) meeting in Tacket Street.

B.Hbk (1890) 368–9; (1894) 163–4 (obituary of Isaac Lord), 302. Browne (1877) 577–8.

(81) STRICT BAPTIST, Crown Street (TM 165449). The church meeting in 'Bethesda Chapel' originated in 1829 as a secession from a meeting at Stoke Green, at first occupying an existing chapel

'Bethesda Chapel', Crown Street, Ipswich.   (81)

on the present site erected *c*.1791 by Independent seceders from Tacket Street but vacated on their removal to a building in St Nicholas Street. The present chapel of 1912–13 by Frederick G. Faunch has a stone front of five bays with a three-bay portico with giant non-tapering Ionic columns of granite.

Monuments: in chapel (1) Thomas John Bedford Poock, 32 years pastor, 1879; (2) Elizabeth wife of Thomas Poock, 1858; (3) William Kern, 25 years pastor, 1903, and Anne his widow, 1903.

Browne (1877) 577. Garrard, A.E., *A Short History of 'Bethesda', Ipswich* (1924).

(82) MEETING-ROOM, High Street (TM 161450). The building now occupied by a Brethren Assembly was probably built by the Church of the New Jerusalem (Swedenborgian). Both denominations erected chapels in 1845, the former in Princes Street, the latter in High Street. The walls are of brick and the roof is hipped and slated. The W front, of white brick with red brick dressings, has an arcade of five bays enclosing tall round-arched windows. The S wall, partly obscured by a modern vestibule covering the entrance, has four narrow round-arched recesses and a wider arch between. At the N end is a small original vestry.

Brethren Meeting-room, High Street, Ipswich.   (82)

Former Congregational chapel, St Nicholas Street, Ipswich. (83)

(83) Former CONGREGATIONAL, St Nicholas Street (TM 16254440). A congregation which left Tacket Street in 1791 built their first chapel in Dairy Lane which was subsequently sold to Baptists. A new chapel, on the W side of St Nicholas Street, was built in 1828–9 and enlarged and school-rooms added in 1856. The front is of gault brick with a low gable, broad pilaster buttresses at the corners and lancet windows. The interior has a gallery of c.1840 around three sides. (Demolished 1983) *Monument*: externally [.... ?wife of] Robert Rooth, 1836, and William Henry their son, 1837.

CYB (1857) 247.

(84) CONGREGATIONAL, St Clements (TM 171441). A chapel by Cattermole and Eade was built in Fore Hamlet in 1870. This was superseded in 1887 by a new building by William Eade in Back Hamlet named the Grimwade Memorial Chapel in memory of the chairman of the Suffolk Congregational Union, who gave part of the site. This is of red brick in the Gothic style; a short tower next to the main entrance accommodates the gallery stairs. The former chapel was converted to a hall and school-rooms.

CYB (1871) 405; (1889) 222–3. Hosken (1920) 127–30.

(85) Former FRIENDS, Bank Street (TM 16454412). A small timber-framed meeting-house of four bays was built in 1700 by Joseph Clarke, probably the same person who also built the Presbyterian meeting-house in that year. In 1797–9 a larger meeting-house (60ft by 36ft) was built against the N side, of brick with a hipped slate roof, deep bracketed eaves and round-arched windows. Entrances were in the eastern bays of the N and S sides with a library room added to the E end in 1858. The stand was at the W end. After closure in 1924 the buildings were converted and extended for commercial use. No original fittings remain. (Demolished 1995)

Butler (1999) 573–5.

(86) WESLEYAN, Museum Street (TM 16054460). Gothic chapel of 1860 by Frederick Barnes superseding a chapel of 1816 (now demolished) in Old Jail Lane *alias* Market Lane. The original front to Museum Street is faced with Kentish ragstone with ashlar dressings. Gabled centre with four-light traceried window above three-bay open loggia, formerly with central pointed-arched entrance beyond; the front is flanked by separately gabled side porches enclosing stairs to the gallery. In 1959 the interior was turned around and the entrance inside the loggia rendered insignificant.

Warren, W.D., *A Century of Witness and Service 1861–1961* (1961).

(87) Former PRIMITIVE METHODIST, Clarkson Street (TM 155449). Red brick with white brick bands, circular plate-traceried window in gabled front. Of 1874 by Cattermole and Eade. (Now 'Free Church')

(88) Former PRIMITIVE METHODIST, Rope Walk (TM 168444). Red brick front of three bays divided by yellow brick pilasters; built 1839 but altered c.1896 with central doorway, arched and traceried window over and shaped gable all of that period. Sunday-school annexe dated 1896. (Now Seventh Day Adventist)

(89) Former PRESBYTERIAN, Portman Road (TM 157448). The congregation of the Presbyterian Church in England was formed in 1868 and the chapel built in 1870; since 1986 it has been occupied by the Elim Pentecostal Church. This is a prominently sited building in the Gothic style by Frederick Barnes. The walls

Former Presbyterian chapel, Portman Road, Ipswich. (89)

are faced with Kentish ragstone with ashlar dressings. The chapel comprises a nave and transepts, polygonal organ apse, and a tall corner tower with broach spire.

The interior has a rear gallery and provision for side galleries. The nave of five bays has a double hammer-beam roof. *Glass*: in main windows of transepts, *c.*1890–5, by W.G. Taylor.

LAKENHEATH

(90) BAPTIST, Mill Lane (TL 717827). Flint-faced walls, knapped at front, with gault brick dressings and hipped slate roof. Three-bay front with central entrance and two tiers of segmentally arched windows. Dated 1845. The interior has a rear gallery, original pulpit and box-pews with painted seat numbers on doors.

(91) Former CALVINISTIC INDEPENDENT, Back Street (TL 715828). 'Jehovah Jireh', so named on a tablet in the back wall dated 1815, has walls faced with flints and gault brick dressings. The E front is largely similar to (90), of three bays with segmentally arched windows; the roof is hipped and pantiled. The interior has a rear gallery with shaped front and original seating. The ceiling is coved on all sides. (Now Pentecostal, Assembly of God) *Inscriptions*: on bricks in back wall, many painted or incised initials.

(92) WESLEYAN, Back Street (TL 715829). John Wesley noted in his *Journal* in 1757 that 'One Mr Evans had lately built a large and convenient preaching-house [at Lakenheath] at his own expense'. The ruins of a chapel converted to two cottages on the S side of Anchor Lane (TL 713829) may represent that building.

The present chapel dated 1835, enlarged by one bay to the rear, has a gabled brick front; the side walls are faced with flint and gault brick dressings.

Inscription: tablet reset in side wall 'Methodist Chapel', said to be from former chapel in Anchor Lane.

Curnock (1938) IV: 245. Gill, F.C., *In the Steps of John Wesley* (1962) 124.

LAVENHAM

(93) CONGREGATIONAL (TL 916495). The church, of late 17th-century origin, previously occupied a former Baptist meeting-house in Water Street. The chapel of 1827 has brick walls and a hipped slated roof; a pedimented and stuccoed forebuilding with arched porches to each side may be of later date.

Armitage, D.M., *The Taylors of Ongar* (1939) 243. Hosken (1920) 274–5.

(94) Former PRIMITIVE METHODIST, Market Place (TL 916493). A mediaeval timber-framed building of four bays, adjacent to the guildhall, was converted to a chapel in 1861 by removing the upper floors from two bays, leaving one bay to serve as a gallery, the end bay remaining as a cottage. *Inscription*: on reset voussoir in front wall 'P | MC | 1861'.

LAXFIELD

(95) STRICT BAPTIST (TM 294724). The chapel built in 1810 for a newly formed congregation was extended to the rear in 1850 and altered internally in 1897. The walls are of red brick with a gault brick front and the hipped roof is covered with dark glazed pantiles. The broad front wall is divided into five bays, the second and fourth slightly recessed, with a continuous platband at mid-height. The recessed bays have each one round-arched doorway with fanlight and a sash window above. The middle bay has one tall round-arched window replacing windows at both levels.

The orientation of the interior was reversed in 1897, the pulpit being brought to the front below the inserted central window; a gallery extends around the other three sides.

Collecting Boxes: in chapel, inscribed with appropriate texts from Proverbs 11:25 and Deuteronomy 16:10. *Monument*: externally below centre window, John Noyes, martyred 'near this spot' 22 September 1557.

Grace (February 1996) 12–13.

Strict Baptist chapel, Laxfield. (95)

LEISTON

(96) CONGREGATIONAL, High Street (TM 445625). Red brick with gault brick dressings. Gabled front with arched heads of red and blue brick to doorway and windows. Built 1866. (URC/Methodist).

Hosken (1920) 313.

(97) FRIENDS, Waterloo Avenue (TM 443626). The first meeting-house on this site was built in 1713 but superseded in 1860 by the present building designed by William P. Ribbans of Ipswich. The walls are of red brick with gault brick window surrounds and quoins; the roof is hipped and slated. The broad E front of three bays with tall segmentally arched windows has a pedimented centre bay and a low porch covering an asymetrically placed inner doorway. The interior is divided by shutters into two principal rooms, the larger to the left having a stand at the S end.

Butler (1999) 575–6.

LONG MELFORD

(98) CONGREGATIONAL, Hall Street (TL 862454). The Presbyterian society (now URC) formed in the late 17th century seems to have adopted a Congregational polity in the following century. The meeting-house was built in 1725–6 on copyhold land leased in 1725 to Samuel Lungley who passed the building to Presbyterian trustees in 1731.

The meeting-house has walls of red brick and a hipped tiled roof with concealed double valley. The E front has a round-arched doorway at the centre between two tall similarly arched windows with altered frames, and surrounds with brick imposts and an apron below. The N and S walls are each of three bays with two tiers of wooden cross-framed windows with segmental-arched heads and aprons below; one lower window on the S has been converted to an internal doorway to the adjacent Sunday-school added 1862. The rear W wall, now covered by a later building, had two tall segmental-arched windows flanking the pulpit.

The interior (38ft square) was much altered between c.1905 and c.1917. It has a gallery of the late 19th century across the E end only, but no side galleries for which the fenestration makes allowance.

A burial-ground at the rear is bounded on the S by a serpentine wall of brickwork.

Fittings – *Monuments* and *Floorslabs*. *Monuments*: in burial-ground, 19th-century and later, including one to Elizabeth French, 1820, headstone, loose, with applied cast-iron ornament; *Floorslabs*: (1) Robert Cox, 1759, et al.; (2) Rev. David Ford, 1836, and Mary his widow, 1842. *Pulpit*: hexagonal with bolection-moulded panels on ogee base and hexagonal stem, lowered and canopy removed; staircase with spirally turned balusters, columnar newels and moulded handrail; all c.1726.

Hosken (1920) 254–5.

Congregational chapel (URC), Long Melford. (98)

LOWESTOFT

(99) CONGREGATIONAL, London Road North (TM 551934). The meeting in Lowestoft began as a section of the Yarmouth church, meeting first in a barn in Blue Anchor Lane but from 1695 in a meeting-house in High Street; this last passed to the Wesleyan Reformers on the erection of the present chapel in 1852. The chapel, claimed (*CYB* (1857) 231) to have been by the same (unnamed) architect who designed the Congregational chapels in Great Yarmouth, Norfolk (90) and Forest Gate, Essex, has a gabled W front of red and yellow brick with a short Italianate tower to the left and a lower circular stair tower to the right. The interior, variously altered in the late 19th century and in 1992–3, had a gallery round four sides but the easternmost bay has been separated.

Congregational chapel, London Road North, Lowestoft. (99)

At the rear is a Sunday-school of 1863 of brick with a front of three bays between square turrets, by W. Oldham Chambers, enlarged in 1882 by E. Boardman. (URC)

Monuments: in chapel (1) Rev. Henry Moore, 1861; (2) Rev. George Steffe Crisp, 1863.

CYB (1864) 278–9. Hosken (1920) 278–83.

(100) Former CONGREGATIONAL, Pakefield Road (TM 541911). The congregation originated with a Free Methodist mission in Kirkley which passed to Congregationalists in 1884. 'South Cliff Chapel' of 1902–3 by George and R.P. Baines is in a free Gothic style of red brick and yellow terracotta ('white Costessy work'), modified from an earlier design, with a thin tapering tower and slender spire at one corner.

CYB (1899) 153; (1903) 157. Hosken (1920) 284–7.

(101) FRIENDS, Pakefield Street (TM 540907). The small meeting-house of brick with a pantiled roof, registered 6 April 1830, was extended to the front by 7½ft in the late 19th century. Interior, subdivided by a partition on the line of the extension, has two ranks of open-backed benches.

Butler (1999) 577.

(102) Former PRIMITIVE METHODIST, St Peter's Street (TM 549938). Brick gabled front with painted dressings and defaced shaped tablet dated 1876. (Now Elim Pentecostal)

MELLIS

(103) FREE METHODIST (TM 100745). The chapel was probably built by Wesleyans c.1812 but closed by 1851 owing to the Reform agitation, later passing to the Reformers then meeting in a cottage. Flint with brick dressings and hipped pantile roof.

Broad three-bay front formerly with a central entrance, now re-sited with porch added.

Suff. Rec. Soc. XXXIX (1997) 74–5.

MELTON

(104) Former PRIMITIVE METHODIST (TM 282505). Red brick with gault brick front; three bays with pediment, round-arched doorway and tall windows. Defaced tablet over doorway with denominational name and date 1860. (Now used by 'Melton Evangelical Church')

The chapel, built in 1860, was the subject of a successful legal action by an adjacent householder, a barrister, who complained of obstruction to his right to light. As a result a local millwright moved the completed building on rollers a distance of 20ft 8in. to its present site on 18 September 1861.

Illustrated London News (5 October 1861). Kendall (1905) II: 246.

MENDLESHAM

(105) STRICT BAPTIST, Mendlesham Green (TM 094633). 'Jireh Chapel' was built in 1839, of brick with a hipped slate roof and a S front of three bays with a central entrance between two tiers of sash windows. The chapel was extended to the W in the mid 19th century and again by a lean-to section along the N side. The interior has a gallery above vestries at the W end and another on the N which serves the Sunday-school and has an arcaded front closed by shutters. *Inscription*: in porch above original doorway 'JIREH CHAPEL | Particular Baptists | Opened June 10 | 1839'.

METFIELD

(106) PRIMITIVE METHODIST (TM 294805). Red brick with yellow brick dressings. Three-bay gabled front with rusticated pilasters and arched centre bay enclosing shaped tablet dated 1866.

MIDDLETON

(107) Former WESLEYAN (TM 429678). Broad three-bay brick front and hipped pantiled roof. Two wide doorways with flat-arched heads in outer bays. Two tiers of wide rectangular windows at front; two tall pointed-arched windows with Y-tracery at rear. *Inscriptions*: in front wall, on stone tablet 'A.D.| 1828'; on brick between upper windows 'T.M. 1828'. (Conversion to house proposed 1994)

Former Primitive Methodist chapel, Melton. Relocation of chapel, 18 September 1861. (104)

MILDENHALL

(108) BAPTIST, West Row (TL 674759). Gault brick with hipped slate roof, built 1815 and extended to rear *c*.1900. Three-bay front with central entrance and two tiers of windows. Original gallery around three sides, extended and continued behind pulpit, also upper gallery with shuttered front in extension. *Monuments*: in burial-ground, with dates from 1816. *Weather Vane*: on ridge.

BM VII (1815) 483.

(109) STRICT BAPTIST, West Row (TL 670763). Small early 19th-century barn of flint with brick dressings, later lean-to added to south. Partially converted to chapel in the late 19th century.

(110) Site of FRIENDS, Holywell Row (TL 708771). An existing cottage and land were placed in trust in 1674 for use as a meeting-house and burial-ground. The former, demolished *c*.1967–8, is believed to have been a rendered timber-framed building with a pantiled roof, possibly replacing thatch; meetings ceased in 1828. The meeting-house passed into Wesleyan use before 1912 and continued to serve as a Methodist chapel until the erection of the present chapel to the NE in 1955.

The *burial-ground* is a rectangular plot bounded by gault brick walls incorporating the dates 1754 and 1771 in red brick. Several reset monuments in various styles remain of the early 18th century and later. The meeting-house stood at the N corner of the ground behind the 1897 village hall.

Butler (1999) 576.

(111) WESLEYAN, High Street (TL 710748). Gault brick with hipped slate roof; built 1829. Two tiers of sash windows to S front and E side, two storeyed annexe to left, and two taller windows with circular window over in N wall. Tall interior with gallery at S end only; otherwise refitted 1888.

Wesleyan chapel, High Street, Mildenhall. (111)

(112) WESLEYAN, Beck Row (TL 694776). The chapel dated 1829 has side walls of flint with brick dressings; it was extended to the front *c*.1860 by one bay incorporating a gallery. The front wall of gault brick is gabled and subdivided into three bays by pilasters. The interior was refitted in the late 19th century. *Monuments*: in lower school-room (1) Richard Halls 'who commenced this Sunday School in the year 1819'; in burial-ground (2) William son of William and Jane Pearmain, 1839, also William Pearmain, 1841, and Mary Amy his widow, 1848.

(113) Former WESLEYAN, West Row (TL 673761). Knapped flint with gault brick dressings and hipped roof. Central entrance between two tiers of windows. Date tablet of 1841 obscured by rendering; closed 1956, since used for storage. *Monuments*: in front burial-ground (1) Charlotte Ann daughter of George and Ann Burgess, 1846; (2) John William Ford, 1857, and Sarah his widow, 1866, brick table-tomb.

MONKS ELEIGH

(114) CONGREGATIONAL (TL 965476). A small meeting-room built in 1820 for Wesleyans but in Independent use by 1851 was superseded by the present chapel on an adjacent site in 1870. The former chapel, converted for a Sunday-school, is a long low building with a brick front but timber-framed walls to the rear and at one end. (URC) *Monument*: in Sunday-school, Thomas Steele, 1862, 8 years minister.

Hosken (1920) 260.

NAYLAND-WITH-WISSINGTON

(115) Former CONGREGATIONAL, Stoke Road, Nayland (TL 976344). A Presbyterian society, which became Congregational *c*.1738, registered a meeting-house on this site in 1690. This was replaced in 1864 by the present chapel, a tall Gothic building by Frederick Barnes. The walls are of red brick with dressings of black brick and stone. The front is gabled with two paired entrances in adjacent gabled wings. The site slopes down to the rear to allow school-rooms to be placed beneath the chapel. *Monuments*: in small burial-ground alongside chapel, include one to William Stammers, 1863, tall plinth surmounted by obelisk with claw feet.

CYB (1865) 291. Hosken (1920) 276–7.

NEEDHAM MARKET

(116) CONGREGATIONAL (TM 089550). A society, originally regarded as Presbyterian, commenced with the work of Thomas James, town preacher ejected 1662, who 'had a pretty numerous Society after his being silenc'd'. In the mid 18th century the society was subjected to Arian influences (Joseph Priestley was co-pastor 1755–8) and meetings ceased, the meeting-house serving for over 30 years as 'a playhouse of the lowest description'. The building was reopened in 1793 and the present church was then formed. (Now joint URC/Methodist)

The former meeting-house built in 1717 was of brick with a hipped tiled roof, three-bay front with a pair of doorways and two tiers of windows separated by a platband. That was superseded in 1837 by the present chapel designed by James Fenton of Chelmsford. The walls are of red brick with a gault brick front and stone dressings. The building has been variously altered, principally in 1913 by E.T. Johns and by an internal refitting in 1993.

The W front is of five bays with a pediment, the three centre bays projecting slightly and rising to a parapet within the pediment; the principal entrances are in the terminal bays between which were three windows replaced *c*.1913 by an open loggia with two Ionic columns and a stone entablature, repeated with paired pilasters around the original entrances; a trapezoidal ventilator in the pediment was also replaced by an oval window. The interior, much refitted, has a gallery around three sides.

Inscriptions: externally, on bricks in return walls of front wings, names and initials, including 'J. Quinton 1837'.

CYB (1866) 247–9, obituary of Samuel Davis. Hosken (1920) 228–36.

(117) Former FRIENDS, High Street (TM 088551). A building on this site intended for use as a meeting-house was erected by Hester Browning and conveyed to trustees in 1704; in 1752 further land was acquired and houses were later built against the street frontage with access to the rear through an archway dated 1772.

The former meeting-house, closed 1914 and latterly used for storage, dates from the early 18th century. The walls are timber-framed and rendered in pebble-dash and the roof is covered with slates. The NE front has a pair of double doors, each of two fielded panels, facing the approach from the street, and two windows to the left; the doors are covered by a short but perhaps once more extensive wooden loggia at the NW end of which is a secondary entrance to the women's meeting-house. There are four windows in the SW wall.

The interior (originally $50\frac{1}{2}$ft by 20ft) is divided into two rooms by a later boarded partition. The larger room ($36\frac{3}{4}$ft long), ceiled at collar level, was extended by one bay to the SE in the late 18th century and had a stand at the SE end marked by a rise in the match-boarded dado. The smaller room has a fireplace in the NW wall and a gallery over approached by a stair in the N corner.

Monuments: in burial-ground, uniform round-topped stones, reset, with dates from the late 18th century to 1963.

Butler (1999) 577.

NORTON

(118) BAPTIST, Woolpit Road (TL 957657). The chapel, believed to have been built in 1843, is of red brick with a pyramidal slate roof, three-bay front with central round-arched entrance and two tiers of sash windows. Rear gallery only. Re-painted inscription on blind fanlight of doorway 'Founded by S Hustler Esq of Drinkstone, Baptist Church 1834'.

Suff. Rec. Soc. XXXIX (1997) 58, item 319.

OCCOLD

(119) STRICT BAPTIST (TM 157707). The chapel was built *c*.1839 for a church formed in 1832. The walls are of red brick with yellow brick dressings and the double roof is covered with pantiles. The front comprises two gabled sections each of three bays with a central doorway between round-arched windows. The roof is supported internally by three posts on the line of the valley. There is a gallery along one side wall. (Interior gutted 1994)

Monuments: in chapel (1) Frederick William son of William and Annie Last, 1890; (2) George Sherman, 1878; (3) Mary wife of George Sherman, 1871; (4) five children of George and Mary Sherman – Charlotte, 1851, Elizabeth, 1852, Ellen-Mary, 1852, and Emma and George, infants; (5) Maria daughter of George and Mary Sherman, 1862.

OLD NEWTON WITH DAGWORTH

(120) PRIMITIVE METHODIST, Old Newton (TM 063629). Brick with gabled front. Dated 1839 but much altered in the late 19th century and refitted 1996. Porch added 1907 as a Primitive Methodist Centenary memorial.

OTLEY

(121) STRICT BAPTIST (TM 217558). The chapel built in 1800 was greatly enlarged to the front in 1837. The walls are of red brick with a gault brick front and hipped slate roof. Front of three bays with end doorways, shuttered window between and three sash windows above. Interior with gallery around three sides, partly rebuilt 1868; Sunday-school seating with superintendent's desk in cross gallery.

Browne (1877) 581–2.

PALGRAVE

(122) Site of INDEPENDENT (TM 116791). A meeting-house built in 1697, 300 yards E of Elm Vale Farm, was demolished in 1822 when the then Unitarian church removed to a new chapel in Diss, Norfolk (46). The site, which subsequently served as a burial-ground for that congregation, is a square enclosure bounded by low brick walls and high iron railings between brick piers, all of late 19th-century date, with gates on the N side. No visible trace of the former building remains.

Monuments: include (1) Timothy Garrard, 1806, and Mary his widow, 1827; (2) James Bayley, 1872, minister, and Isabella his wife, 1867; (3) Charles Frederick Biss, 1888, minister; (4) John Thomas Cooper, 1877, minister.

Browne (1877) 478–9. *UHST* VI (1935–8) 149–51.

PEASENHALL

(123) Former MEETING-HOUSE (TM 356692). A small late 18th-century garden building in the grounds of 'The Ancient House' was used from *c*.1820 as a preaching-station of the Congregational church at Rendham. It appears in the 1851 census returns as 'Independent or Congregational Schoolroom'. The simple three-bay building is of crude timber-framed construction (40ft by $9\frac{1}{2}$ft), rendered externally, on a brick plinth, with a brick SE front and a hipped thatched roof.

(124) WESLEYAN (TM 359696). The chapel was built in 1811. The walls are of brickwork and the roof is hipped and covered with dark pantiles. The front and sides are of three bays with two tiers of windows, the front originally had two round-arched doorways in the outer bays, replaced by a central porch entrance in 1893. In that year the interior, probably with a gallery around three sides and pulpit opposite the entrances, was subdivided, the galleries removed and rooms constructed in the rear third leaving the front part refitted and realigned.

RATTLESDEN

(125) STRICT BAPTIST (TL 975588). Brick with gabled ends; 'Erected 1808, Enlarged 1815, Rebuilt 1892'.

(126) Former FRIENDS, Rattlesden Road (TL 965594). The meeting-house built in 1745 was closed for regular use in 1804. In 1974 it was converted to a house, 'Quaker Cottage', with the insertion of an upper floor. The walls ($30\frac{3}{4}$ft by $18\frac{1}{2}$ft externally) are timber-framed, rendered on the outside, and the roof is tiled

Former Congregational chapel, Rendham. (127)

replacing thatch. The interior of three bays is divided into two rooms originally with a plaster ceiling at collar level. In the SE end wall is a wood-framed ovolo-moulded mullion and transom window, reset lower, which probably lit the back of the stand. The roof is supported by two trusses with V-braces above a low collar. At the rear is a two-storeyed domestic wing of similar construction which may be contemporary.

Butler (1999) 578.

RENDHAM

(127) Former CONGREGATIONAL (TM 348647). The church formerly meeting here claimed to have originated *c.*1650. By the late 17th century meetings were being held at Swefling where they continued until the erection of the present building in 1750. This was enlarged to the front in 1834 and a vestry added in 1886. (*See* p. 303)

The walls are of brick and the double roof, which has a central valley, is hipped and tiled except at the front where it is slated. The front slope of the roof was rebuilt at a lower pitch in 1834 to encompass the enlargement. The S front is of three bays with two tiers of sash windows and entrances with fanlights over in the outer bays. The E and W side walls of the original building are of two bays with two tiers of windows separated by a platband; the front extension of one bay is similarly fenestrated but without a platband. The N wall has two large round-arched windows flanking the pulpit.

The interior (originally 30ft extended to 42¼ft, by 38ft) has a gallery around three sides with a panelled front above a full entablature supported on each side by fluted Roman Doric columns; the galleries were lengthened and the columns re-sited in 1834. The original roof structure has collars and framed purlins but no ridge; a wooden girder truss was inserted on the line of the original frontage when the chapel was enlarged. (Closed 1978, converted to a house since 1986)

Fittings – *Books*: Bible with Apocrypha, printed by Robert Barker and assigns of John Bill, 1634, bound with Book of Common Prayer, by same printers, 1632. *Clock*: on front of S gallery, signed 'I.D. Bright, Saxmundham', 19th-century. *Communion Table*: repaired 1878 incorporating earlier material; wood with two legs and floor bearers and adjustable music stands added at each end, name and date 'J.Sparkes, 1878' in pencil below top. *Library*: a list of 129 books in the chapel library 'established January 1st 1833' is affixed to a cupboard in the vestry; no books remain. *Monuments* and *Floorslabs*. *Monuments*: in chapel on N wall (1) Henry Howard, 1798, oval tablet [reported removed to Saxmundham (132)]; on E wall (2) James Brewer, 1802; in burial-ground, many headstones of the late 18th century and after [many removed since 1986]; *Floorslabs*: (1) Rev. Richard Wearing [1806]; (2) Rev. William Cornell, 1760, and Margaret his widow, 1804; (3) 'H.H. 1798'. *Plate*: includes a pair of cups and two plates dated 1757 and a set of three cups and two plates dated 1840, all of Sheffield plate. *Pulpit*: centrally against N wall, hexagonal with fielded-panelled sides above a bolection-moulded base with pedimented backboard, 1750. *Seating*: complete set of box-pews of unpainted pine, *c.*1834.

Hosken (1920) 219–25. *Reform* (May 1978) 13.

RISHANGLES

(128) STRICT BAPTIST (TM 161687). The first chapel built 1841 was replaced by the present Zion Chapel in 1862. This has walls of red brick with a gabled front of gault brick and a slate roof. The front has two gabled porches with one window above each set within arched recesses. The pulpit is placed between the front entrances; at the rear is a gallery with panelled front closed above with five bays of shutters. The original seating survives with a central communion pew and flanking seats above a baptistery aligned on the longer axis of the building.

Alms Box: at rear entrance, with text from 1 Chronicles 29:9. *Communion Table*: above baptistery, 7½ft long. *Monuments*: in chapel (1) George Harris, 1901, pastor nearly 50 years; (2) Henry Ling, 1865, deacon, and Rebecca his widow, 1874; (3) Charles Keen, 1849. (Original seating destroyed and monuments expelled 1986)

BM XXXIII (1841) 570. *Grace* (February 1990) 19–21; (April 1993) 11.

NW front.

Communion pews, before removal in 1986.
Strict Baptist chapel, Rishangles. (128)

ROUGHAM

(129) STRICT BAPTIST (TL 917607). 'Bradfield Chapel' is a large chapel of brick with a gabled front of three bays divided by giant pilasters; two tiers of windows but no galleries. Dated 1850. (Rebuilt 1980)

Grace (April 1978); (May and June 1980).

RUMBURGH

(130) WESLEYAN (TM 354814). Long narrow building of three bays with pyramidal finials above clasping corner buttresses; gabled front with pointed-arched doorway and inscribed band dated 1836. Pointed-arched windows with Y-tracery frames.

ST ANDREW, ILKETSHALL

(131) WESLEYAN, Ilketshall St Andrew (TM 382875). Knapped flint with gault brick dressings and dark pantiled roof. Gabled front with ball finials (two missing), central entrance and pointed-arched windows with Y-traceried frames. Dated 1840. Gallery above entrance supported by two thin iron columns, contemporary box-pews lacking doors.

SAXMUNDHAM

(132) CONGREGATIONAL, Rendham Road (TM 383632). The congregation, formerly attached to Rendham, became independent and built the present chapel in 1850. This is of gault brick with tall lancet windows. (URC)

Hosken (1920) 226–7.

SOMERSHAM

(133) STRICT BAPTIST, Chapel Lane (TM 083488). The chapel built in 1823 for a church formed in 1815 is of brick with a hipped tiled roof. Central doorway between wide windows and a gallery window over entrance; the round-arched windows in the side walls lack voussoirs.

Strict Baptist chapel, Somersham. (133)

SOUTHWOLD

(134) CONGREGATIONAL, High Street (TM 507762). The church (now URC) formed in 1748 met first in a converted fish house. The present chapel, built in 1837, is of brick with a pedimented front of three bays with giant pilasters rendered in stucco. The central entrance is within a recessed loggia having two square piers *in antis*; in the pediment is a circular clock dial. The interior has a gallery around three sides with an organ gallery added in 1868.

EM NS XIV (1836) 113; NS XV (1837) 484–5. Hosken (1920) 166–70.

(135) Former WESLEYAN, Mill Lane (TM 50757605). The small chapel registered 1799 attached to one end of an earlier house has brick walls and a hipped pantiled roof. The S front, of two stages separated by a platband, has a central doorway between two windows with external shutters, all with round-arched heads, keystones and blind tympana, and three upper windows, the central one blocked. The W wall has three upper windows and altered openings below. In the N wall are two round-arched pulpit windows. The interior (23¾ft by 19¾ft) has a gallery around three sides with balustraded front, the S gallery possibly extended forward. (In use 1972 as builder's workshop; converted to house with extensions on W side by 1994) *Sundial*: in blocking of front window, painted metal dial with arched top, decayed inscription '[…]RO LUCEM' and date 17[9?]7.

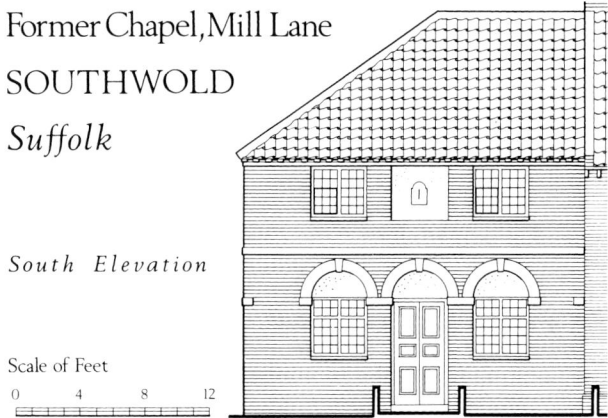

Former Chapel, Mill Lane
SOUTHWOLD
Suffolk

South Elevation

(136) WESLEYAN, East Green (TM 509763). Brick with rendered pedimented front of three bays with three round-arched upper windows; lower part covered by late 19th-century extension. Built 1835 to replace the foregoing. Galleried interior, refitted in late 19th century.

STANSFIELD

(137) CONGREGATIONAL (TL 782516). A chapel built in 1833 and successively enlarged was replaced by the present building in 1859. The front wall is of grey brick and the sides are of red brick with yellow brick dressings. The front is gabled and has two tiers of lancets between a pair of two-storeyed porches. Interior with box-pews and a gallery around three sides. Sunday-school wing behind with stables below.

CYB (1866) 281–3, obituary of John Rutter. Hosken (1920) 306–7.

Strict Baptist chapel, Stoke Ash. (138)

STOKE ASH

(138) STRICT BAPTIST (TM 114713). The chapel built for a church formed in 1805 was opened in 1846; the walls are of brick and the side walls, five bays in length, have two tiers of windows with timber lintels and labels. The front wall is gabled and has two gabled porches with windows above set in round-arched recesses, as at Rishangles (128). Tablet in gable dated 1846.

The interior has the pulpit set between the front entrances, side galleries supported by iron columns, and a cross gallery for children closed above by shutters. The pulpit and lower seating were renewed in the late 19th century.

Monuments: in chapel (1) Susan wife of John Dallison, 1841; (2) William Crisp, 1820, 14 years deacon, with later inscription on second tablet below to Mary his widow, 1824, signed 'J. Skinner, Eye'; (3) Charles Hill, 1904, 45 years pastor.

Browne (1877) 583.

STONHAM PARVA

(139) STRICT BAPTIST, Little Stonham (TM 118603). 'Bethel Chapel' built in 1816 has rendered timber-framed walls on a brick plinth. The front of three bays has a low gable with circular window, two tiers of sash windows and a central doorway. The interior, refitted in the late 19th century, has a gallery over the entrance.

Klaiber (1931) 116. Price (1927) 160.

STOWMARKET

(140) STRICT BAPTIST, Bury Street (TM 048589). 'Bethesda Chapel' built in 1813–14 for a church formed in 1795 was extended to the rear in 1836 and much altered and reoriented internally in 1890. The walls are of brickwork and the roof is hipped and covered with dark pantiles. The N front has two doorways and two upper windows, one window centrally to each stage has been carefully blocked. The side walls were originally of three bays with two tiers of sash windows.

The interior has a gallery around three sides; a return gallery at the N end was removed when the pulpit was re-sited between the entrances.

Inscriptions: names on bricks below eaves of N wall.

Monument: externally on W wall, Jabez Browne, 1819, 22 years pastor, and Mary his widow, 1820.

Browne (1877) 579–80. *EM* XXII (1814) 67.

(141) PRIMITIVE METHODIST, Regent Street (TM 049589). Gault brick with gabled front; three round-arched upper windows, lower part concealed by recent porch. Round-arched windows in side walls replace two tiers of earlier openings. Built 1836.

STRADBROKE

(142) BAPTIST (TM 233740). The chapel erected in 1841, replacing a building of 1814, is of brick with rendered dressings and a hipped slate roof. The N front, of gault brick with two tiers of windows in three bays separated by giant pilasters, closely resembles the Congregational chapel at Southwold (134) but without a pediment. The central entrance is set within an open loggia and has two square piers *in antis*. *Monuments*: in chapel (1) Rev. Thomas Goldsmith, 1842, 'founder of the Baptist Church in this place'; externally in front of chapel (2) William Darby, 1857.

BM XXXIII (1841) 570; XXXIV (1842) 191–2.

Baptist chapel, Stradbroke. (142)

SUDBURY

(143) BAPTIST, Church Street (TL 869411). Gault brick with gabled front, and pointed-arched loggia entrance with circular window over; secondary entrances in flanking staircase wings. Built 1889, by Eade and Johns.

(144) CONGREGATIONAL, School Street (TL 871412). The church (now URC) originated in 1837 as a secession from a meeting in Friars Street, which reunited here in 1956. The chapel, as built in 1839, survives only in part; it was greatly altered and much rebuilt in the later 19th century, with new galleries added in 1856, a new roof in 1858, and a major re-fronting in 1891. The front of gault brick is gabled and has a corner tower with gabled sides and octagonal wooden spirelet with louvres.

Hosken (1920) 181–9.

(145) FRIENDS, Friars Street (TL 874412). The meeting-house was built in 1804, replacing one of 1710 on the same site and an earlier meeting-place which stood in Bullocks Lane. A women's meeting-house was added at the N end in 1818. The walls are of

Baptist chapel, Sudbury. (143)

brick and the roof over the principal part is half-hipped and covered with tiles. To the S is a long and narrow burial-ground with uniform headstones. The interior retains original scrubbed pine fittings and a gallery at the N end. *Inscription*: on brick in W wall 'I·804·K'.

Butler (1999) 578–9.

TUNSTALL

(146) STRICT BAPTIST (TM 372549). The chapel built in 1808 has been twice enlarged, by widening on the N side and by an extension to the front. The walls are of brick and the roof is hipped and covered with pantiles except the N slope, which is of lower pitch and slated. The E front has two doorways with a pair of sash windows between and three small gallery windows above. The W wall has two tall windows, one in the extension, and a small upper window centrally between. The interior has been subdivided.

Redstone (1912) frontis.

UFFORD

(147) WESLEYAN (TM 294532). Small chapel of gault brick with three-bay pedimented front, plain pilasters and round-arched openings; roofed with fish-scale slating. Dated 1860.

WALDRINGFIELD

(148) STRICT BAPTIST, Waldringfield Heath (TM 267449). Chapel built 1821, of brick with rendered front and sides, and pantiled roof hipped to rear. Gabled front with altered windows, three pointed-arched windows to side wall. Interior refitted.

WALPOLE

(149) THE OLD MEETING-HOUSE (TM 373752). The Independent church which met here until 1970 was formed in 1649 by 'the saints in and about Couckley' and supported in its earliest years by several beneficed clergy who also served as pastors of the gathered church. The first of these was Samuel Habergham, rector of Heveningham in 1650; he was succeeded by John Manning who, on his becoming vicar of Sibton with Peasenhall, was followed by his brother Samuel. The latter, who until his ejection in 1660 was also rector of the combined parishes of Cookley and Walpole, remained pastor of the Independent church until after 1690. In 1672 Samuel Manning registered his house as a Congregational meeting-place and himself as 'teacher'; in the same year two houses in Cookley were registered and two other ejected ministers of the same persuasion found sanctuary there, while in Walpole a house for Presbyterian use was also registered.

The Old Meeting-house, half a mile NE of the village, incorporates three walls of a late 16th-century timber-framed house which may have served the church as a place of worship prior to the Act of Toleration. The earliest clear indication of this use, however, appears in a lease for 99 years granted on 19 August 1689 by Southwold Corporation to six representatives of the church of the 'piece of land with the house lately built on it in Walpole, compassed about [by] the highway, and containing one acre'. One possible inference from this is that as soon as toleration was in prospect the congregation provided themselves with what was, in effect, a new meeting-house while retaining for economy the basic structure of the existing building.

The meeting-house has timber-framed walls in four bays with wattle and daub infilling and external rendering; the roof is covered with plain tiles and pantiles. The broad SE front has plain doorways in the end bays with two wide windows between, each of nine lights asymmetrically divided by a vertical structural timber, and two upper windows of five lights below the eaves. The NE and SW end walls have double gables separated by a high valley parallel to the front wall. The front gables at each end belong to the original domestic structure and have below them windows of late 16th-century character, notably at the NE end where the lower window of seven lights has hollow-chamfered and beaded mullions and a timber head with external carving; the upper window at this end, of four lights with a transom, has ovolo-moulded mullions. The SW wall has been partly rebuilt in brickwork and the lower window renewed; the upper window of four lights has mullions with reeded moulding to the inner face. A further upper window, now blocked, was inserted in each end wall of the extension. The rear NW wall, which *c.*1689 was rebuilt about 8ft back from the line of the former back wall, has two tall round-arched windows flanking the pulpit and small windows at each end above and below the ends of the gallery.

The interior (28¼ft by 49¾ft) is ceiled at collar level, the valley beam being supported by three substantial timber posts of circular section with moulded capitals; the middle post rises as a single column but the other smaller posts, interrupted by the fronts of the return galleries, are treated as pairs of superimposed columns. Galleries at the NE and SW ends and a narrower cross gallery along the front wall have plain horizontally boarded fronts and are supported by square timber posts. A vestry with corner fireplace

Exterior, from east.

Pulpit.
The Old Meeting-house, Walpole.

NE end.

has been constructed below the NE gallery; an external doorway in the end wall adjacent to the fireplace has been blocked. (The chapel is now in the care of the Historic Chapels Trust)

Fittings – *Chandelier*: six slender metal branches attached to massive spherical wood core; suspended from wrought-iron bracket on central post in front of pulpit with cord of counterweight passing through the post, early 19th-century. *Clock*: on front of NE gallery, signed 'C.Seaman, Yarmouth', 19th-century. *Monuments*: in burial-ground, mid 19th-century and later. *Plate*: some or all of the following (now at Halesworth (62)) are believed to belong to this congregation, namely: three beakers of 1763, Sheffield-plate flagon of late 18th-century, and two early 18th-century pewter plates. *Pulpit*: hexagonal, possibly lowered, with large ogee canopy surmounted by ball finial, late 17th-century; stairs with thin turned balusters of later date. *Railings*: against road, wrought iron, erected *c.*1859. *Seating*: partly replaced *c.*1900 but several box-pews, some of the late 18th century, remain on lower floor including a range of five, between the front entrances, separated by high divisions, and in the gallery numerous open-backed benches.

CHST III (1907–8) 317–18. CYB (1868) 401–2. Hosken (1920) 171–5. Matthews, A.G., *Calamy Revised* (1934) 240 (S. Habergham); 336–7 (J. and S. Manning). Newby (1936) 40–63.

(150) Former PRIMITIVE METHODIST (TM 366745). Range of four early 19th-century brick cottages; two converted to chapel or built for possible conversion to cottages, with domestic windows and blocked doorways in side wall. Three-bay front to chapel.

WALSHAM-LE-WILLOWS

(151) Former WESLEYAN (TM 002713). The chapel, claimed to have been built by Wesleyans in 1844 but sold to the present Congregational church before 1885, has walls of red brick with yellow brick dressings. The front, of three bays, has a simple pediment and paired end pilasters, central doorway and porch with Roman Doric columns, and two tiers of sash windows. There are no galleries although sufficient height is allowed; original box-pews remain but without doors.

Browne (1877) 476–8. Hosken (1920) 217–18.

WASHBROOK

(152) BAPTIST, Whight's Corner (TM 122423). Red brick; three-bay gabled front with barge-boards and small porch. Late 19th-century.

WATTISFIELD

(153) CONGREGATIONAL (TM 008738). An Independent church (now URC) formed in 1654 built a meeting-house on this site in 1705–6 which survived until replaced by the present chapel in 1876–7. The former meeting-house was a large timber-framed building with a double roof and central valley, double-gabled end walls and four tall cross-framed windows in one of the longer walls, probably that occupied by the pulpit. The front wall, of four bays with doorways in the end bays had two tiers of windows. The interior was described (*CYB* 1879) as 'of the usual Nonconformist type, with galleries on three sides, and a flat ceiling supported upon four large wooden pillars'.

The present chapel, by Alfred Conder, of red brick with yellow brick dressings, has a gabled front and two tiers of paired windows in the side walls.

Browne (1877) 466–76. *CHST* III (1907–8) 251–6. *CYB* (1879) 415. Hosken (1920) 207–16.

WATTISHAM

(154) STRICT BAPTIST, Hitcham Road (TM 010520). The chapel built in 1825 stands on the site of a meeting-house erected 1763. Brick with hipped slate roof and two tiers of sash windows. Front partly concealed by later wide porch. Interior with gallery around three sides, otherwise refitted *c.*1914. Vestry with school-room over at rear.

Communion Table: in vestry, 6ft by 1ft 7in., late 18th-century.

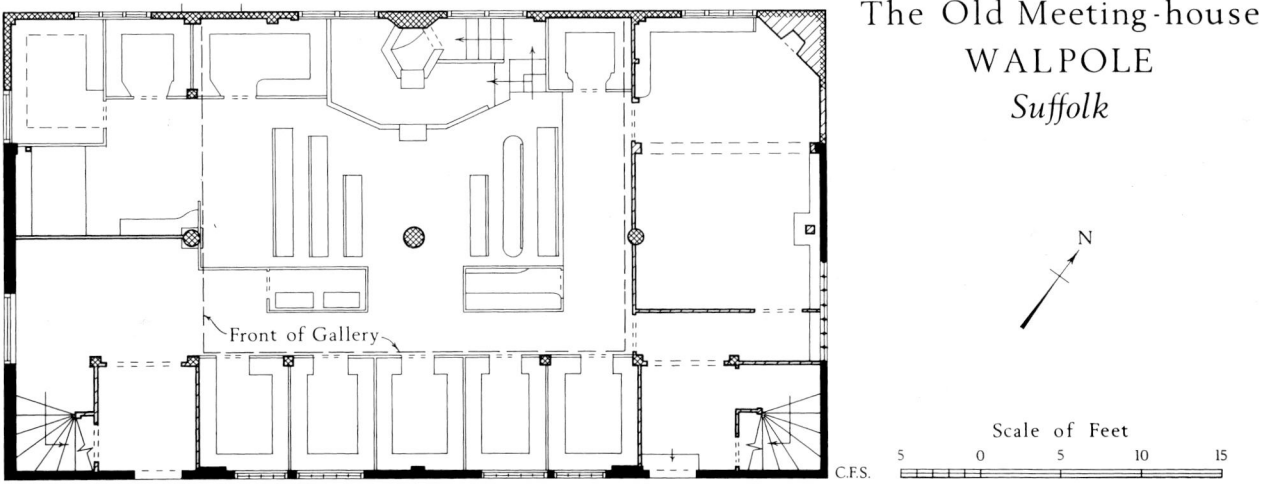

The Old Meeting-house
WALPOLE
Suffolk

Monuments: in chapel (1) John Cooper, 1881, pastor 1830–79, signed 'Simpson, Stow'kt'; (2) John Hitchcock, 1800, 38 years pastor; in burial-ground (3) Thomas Syer sen., 1770; (4) Isaac Johnson, 1769.

Browne (1877) 578–9.

WENHASTON WITH MELLS HAMLET

(155) WESLEYAN, Wenhaston (TM 422759). The chapel dated 1835 has walls faced with small flint pebbles with red brick dressings and a pantiled roof. The front is gabled and has two doorways with a window between and two above with altered frames. One bay was added to the rear in 1864. The interior, largely refitted *c*.1905, has a gallery around four sides.

WESTLETON

(156) Former PRIMITIVE METHODIST (TM 441691). Red brick with gault brick dressings; three-bay front with pilasters and simple pediment, round-arched doorway and windows. Dated 1868 on tablet above entrance. (Sold 1971)

WHEPSTEAD

(157) Former INDEPENDENT (TL 838579). The chapel, now Baptist, which became a preaching-station of Garland Street Baptist Church, Bury St Edmunds, in the late 19th century, was built in 1844. It is a small building of flint with brick dressings in a vernacular Gothic style. The gabled front is of three bays with rustic brick pinnacles at the apex and each corner; the centre bay projects slightly and has a gabled porch with diagonal buttresses and a quatrefoil window over. The side bays have each a single lancet window. The side walls are four bays in length. *Baptistery*: in chapel, constructed 1990.

Former Independent chapel (now Baptist), Whepstead.   (157)

WICKHAMBROOK

(158) CONGREGATIONAL (TL 746557). The formerly Presbyterian meeting (now URC) is claimed to have suffered from doctrinal differences in the late 18th century; it was reconstituted as a Congregational church in 1810. A barn registered in 1695 was superseded by the present meeting-house built in 1734. The walls are of brickwork and the roof, rebuilt 1889, is hipped and slated. The W front of three bays has a brick plinth and corner pilasters. Two doorways in the outer bays have segmental-arched heads and fielded-panelled doors; one window between and three above have original wooden cross-frames with later glazing. The N and S side walls of two bays had two tiers of windows as at the front, but the N wall is partly covered by a school-room of 1814. The rear E wall has two round-arched pulpit windows with original frames but diamond glazing remade 1892; a small vestry projects on this side.

The interior ($28\frac{1}{2}$ft by $34\frac{1}{4}$ft) has an original W gallery supported by two substantial wooden columns with moulded caps and bases and a moulded cornice; the upper part of the gallery front was renewed and two side galleries added *c*.1814. The chapel was much refitted in 1886–9 with a rostrum pulpit, new lower seating and an open boarded roof. (Front disfigured by large porch, and many window frames replaced, 1989)

Fittings – *Books*: New Testament, with parallel Greek and two Latin texts, 1589; also several 18th-century theological works remaining from a ministerial library, including Matthew Henry, *An Exposition of the Old and New Testaments* (5 vols, 1737) vols 1 & 5 only; *The Practical Works of the late Rev. and Pious Mr Richard Baxter* (4 vols, 1707) vols 1 & 4 only; Hon. Robert Boyle, *A Defence of Natural and Revealed Religion* (2 vols, 1739); *The Works of Joseph Boyse of Dublin* (2 vols, 1738); *The Works of John Howe* (1724) with MS inscription 1773; *The Works of Isaac Barrow* (3 vols, 1716) vol. 1 only.

Chairs: in vestry, two, one with panelled back and turned supports to arm-rests, one with tall back and woven cane panel and seat, 18th-century. *Hat-pegs*: in gallery on S and W walls only, turned wood pegs. *Monuments*: in burial-ground (1) Rev. Stephen Johnson, 1838, 24 years pastor, Sarah (Bromley) his widow, 1855, *et al.*, table-tomb; also two wooden grave-boards with iron inscription plates, late 19th-century. *Plate*: four pewter plates inscribed 'Wickhambrook Meeting', mid 18th-century. *Portrait*: Rev. Thomas Priest, minister 1726–72, pastel on paper. *Seating*: in gallery, low open-backed children's benches in side galleries, some box-pews in W gallery (all gone by 1988).

Duncan, J., *An Abridged History of Wickhambrook Congregational Church* (1969). Hosken (1920) 289–91.

(159) PRIMITIVE METHODIST, Thorns (TL 744552). 'Ebenezer Chapel' of 1850 has a big gabled front of red brick in three bays separated by tall pilasters.

WICKHAM MARKET

(160) CONGREGATIONAL, Chapel Lane (TM 303556). The chapel built in 1826 and thrice extended has walls of red brick with a gault brick front. The front wall originally of three bays separated by pilasters, with a central entrance and two tiers of windows, has been extended by one principal bay to the left, the entrance

Congregational chapel (URC), Wickhambrook. (158)

re-sited and a gallery stair built against the right-hand bay. *Monument*: externally on gallery stairs, Edward Oxborrow, 1834, *et al*.

Hosken (1920) 308–10.

WISSETT

(161) Former CONGREGATIONAL (TM 368792). Gabled front of gault brick with porch between two tall lancets; modern tablet in gable 'Erected 1841'. (Converted to house *c*.1980)

Newby (1936) 157–64.

WITHERSFIELD

(162) PRIMITIVE METHODIST (TL 657480). Red brick with yellow brick dressings; gabled front with porch and wide round-arched windows with iron frames. Dated 1893.

WITNESHAM

(163) BAPTIST, Upper Street (TM 183518). The chapel dated 1856 has brick walls; the front is gabled and the sash windows have marginal glazing and external shutters. The window heads are supported by concealed cast-iron lintels; contemporary iron guttering with lion's head masks.

WOODBRIDGE

(164) BEAUMONT CHAPEL, Chapel Street (TM 271492). The first chapel on this site was built in 1787 by Jonathan Beaumont and supplied by ministers of the Countess of Huntingdon's Connexion. The chapel was rebuilt in 1810 and a Congregational church was formed; the chapel was enlarged to the front by one bay in 1841. The building is now occupied by a Baptist church formed in 1900.

The walls are of red brick with a gault brick front. The front is gabled, of three bays between corner buttresses with pinnacles, two entrances and a tall pointed-arched window between of three lights with Y-tracery. The side walls, of five bays, are separated by stepped buttresses.

The interior has a gallery around four sides; a later organ gallery occupies the place of the original pulpit which was set between a pair of windows which remain as recesses behind the organ.

Monuments: in chapel, behind organ (1) Jonathan Beaumont, 1807, recording his erection of the chapel in 1787 and a legacy of £500 'towards supporting a Gospel ministry herein', also Diana his wife, 1799, Sarah widow of Robert Johnson of Foxhall, 1802, and later inscriptions recording the rebuilding and enlargement in 1810 and 1841; behind chapel (2) John Turner, 1813, and Elizabeth his widow, 1824; externally on front wall (3) Mary Banyard, 1822, *et al*.; (4) William Turner, 1834.

Hosken (1920) 197.

(165) CONGREGATIONAL, Quay Street (TM 273489). The church (now URC) formed in 1651 acquired the present site in 1688. The chapel, rebuilt in 1805, is of red brick with a hipped slate roof. The broad W front to the street is of six bays with two tiers of flat-arched windows; the lower windows in the penultimate bays replaced the original entrances in 1877. The present entrances are off-centre in the N and S end walls. The interior, largely refitted in 1897, has a gallery around three sides and an organ gallery on the E behind the pulpit.

Fittings – *Monuments*: externally S of chapel (1) John Bayly Tailer, 1817, and Elizabeth his wife, 1801; (2) Thomas Bridgman, 1779. *Organ*: reported made in London, 1789.

Hosken (1920) 190–7.

(166) Former FRIENDS, Turn Lane (TM 271490). The site was acquired in 1678 and a meeting-house erected; this continued in use until 1935 after which it served a variety of purposes, being in use for storage when inspected in 1972. The meeting-house has walls of red brick laid to English bond with a moulded plinth and

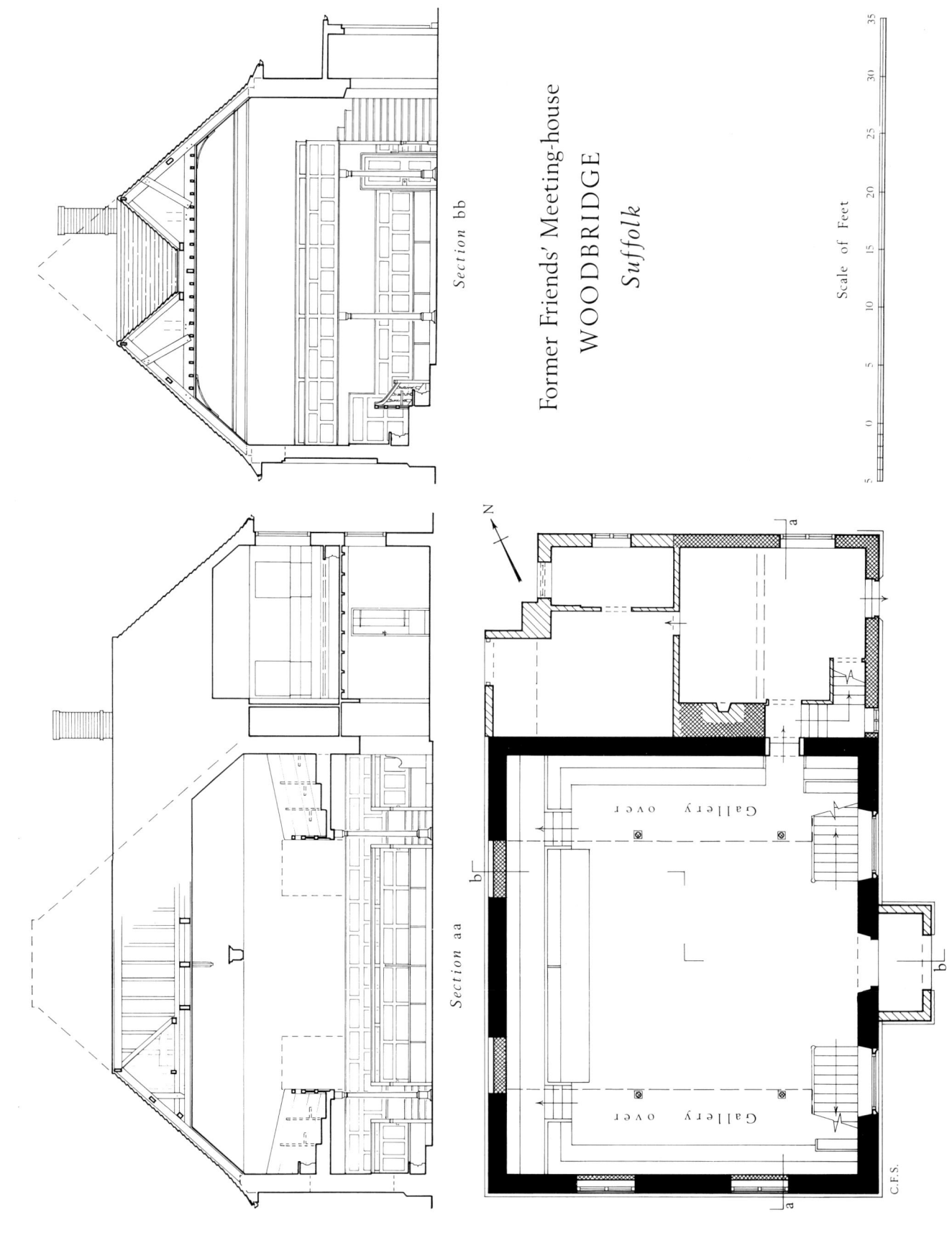

Stairs to stand.

(*Late 19th-century photograph.*)
Former Friends' meeting-house, Woodbridge.   (166)

a tiled roof with central valley but possibly originally rising to a high single ridge. Adjacent to the meeting-house on the N side is a former cottage. The front wall facing E was rendered in the late 19th century and a simple brick porch built against the central entrance; at each side of the porch is a tall sash window with wide glazing bars of the early 18th century. The W wall has two widely spaced windows, blocked at an early date. The brickwork of the S wall is decorated with lozenge diaper in dark headers; two segmental-arched windows in this wall are now blocked but retain their original wood frames. The N wall is entirely covered by later building.

The interior (30¾ft by 36½ft) is ceiled at collar level but has a substantial tie-beam on the E–W axis. The fittings, probably dating from the early 18th century, remain complete and comprise separate galleries to N and S with panelled fronts supported by turned wood columns and staircases with spirally turned balusters; the stand extends the whole length of the W wall and has two stepped entrances matching the gallery stairs. The roof structure shows signs of alteration, the tops of the principal rafters have been cut away and less substantial timbers used to construct a central valley. (Converted to house *c.*1973 with consequent loss of fittings)

The *burial-ground* N of the meeting-house, now separated from it by a wall, contains uniform headstones of the early 19th century and later to the families of Barritt, Barton, Beaumont, Brown, Morley, Muskett, Norton and Toll.

Butler (1999) 580–1.

(167) WESLEYAN, St Johns Street (TM 275493). Gault brick with gabled front and tall round-arched windows. Built 1871, by Cattermole and Eade. (All original internal character lost in total refitting)

WRENTHAM

(168) CONGREGATIONAL (TM 497827). The church (now URC) formed in the mid 17th century built a meeting-house at some distance from the village in 1710. The present chapel on a new site was built and possibly designed by John Owchin in 1778. This has brick walls and a hipped mansard roof covered with dark pantiles. The front and side walls have two tiers of round-arched windows with keystones, and an altered parapet. The broad front wall facing E is of three bays with two doorways now filled with doors of inferior character. A contemporary vestry wing projects centrally from the W wall and is flanked by widely spaced pulpit windows.

The interior (26¾ft by 39½ft) is ceiled at collar level. A gallery, deprived of its staircases, is carried around three sides on turned wood columns with larger columns at the corners.

Congregational chapel (URC), Wrentham.   (168)

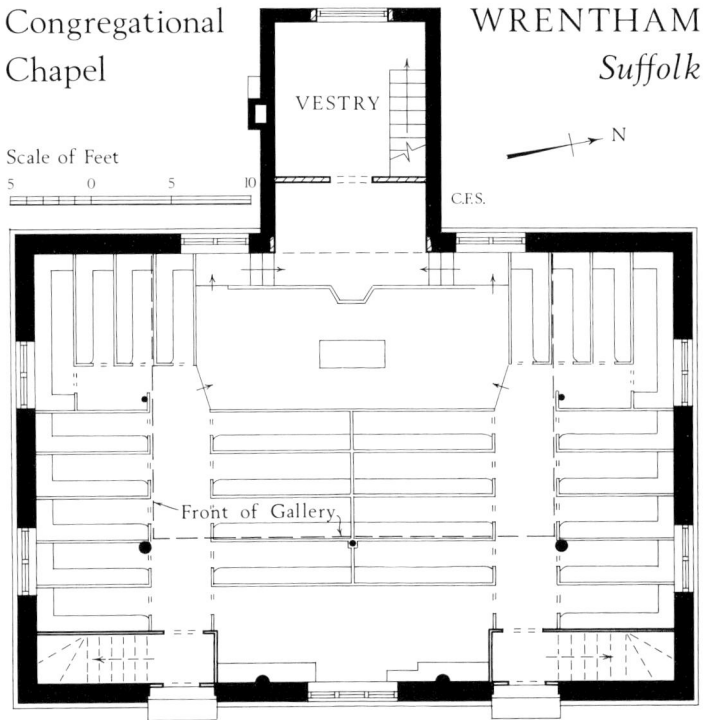

Fittings – *Baptismal Basin*: alabaster pedestal with urn decorated with acanthus leaves. *Chandelier*: eight-branch, 19th-century. *Clock*: on gallery front, signed 'William Crisp, Wrentham', late 18th-century. *Inscription*: on keystone of window in E wall, date 1778. *Monument*: in chapel, William Crisp, 1816, deacon nearly 40 years. *Plate*: includes an 18th-century pewter flagon from 'Rev Mr Townsend's Meeting, Jamaica Row, Rotherhithe Road' London. (Two cups, said to have been given to the church *c*.1650 by Francis Brewster and bearing his arms, were sold in 1970) *Miscellaneous*: MS book of 'texts preached from … at Wrentham Meeting House …' 1798–1818.

Hosken (1920) 155–65.

(169) WESLEYAN, Waterloo Road (TM 469842). Brick with pantiled roof and segmental-arched windows. 'Built 1827, renovated 1912'.

YOXFORD

(170) WESLEYAN (TM 396689). The small Gothic chapel of 1888 by William Eade stands alongside its predecessor of 1835. The latter is of red brick with gault brick dressings and a hipped roof.

(171) Former PRIMITIVE METHODIST (TM 392694). Three-bay gabled front with big round-arched windows and doorway. Dated 1856.

Fmr Primitive Methodist Chapel, Yoxford — C.F.S. 1972

SURREY

The formation of the County of London in 1888 and its subsequent enlargement deprived Surrey of those metropolitan districts, notably Southwark, in which non-conformity flourished from an early date. The remaining portion of the county is not remarkable for the number of its monuments but it is of interest for the variety of denominations represented and for several buildings of note, of which the Apostles' Chapel at Albury (1) is of outstanding architectural and denominational importance. The series of Friends' meeting-houses, at Capel (5) of 1724, Godalming (27) of 1748, Esher (19) of 1793, Guildford (31) of 1805, and Dorking (11) of 1846, is particularly instructive and includes the earliest surviving nonconformist buildings within the county.

A drawing of the former Presbyterian meeting-house of 1719 in Dorking (10), rebuilt in 1834, is indicative of the plain unembellished chapels of that period, none of which now remains, while those of the late 18th century are generally minor or fragmentary. Principal amongst these are the former Independent chapel at Tilford (53) of 1776 and the General Baptist chapel in Godalming (24) of 1789. 'Bugby's Chapel' in Epsom (17) built for Calvinistic Independents in 1779 draws attention to another denomination closely associated with Surrey. The former Congregational chapel of 1793 in Farnham (22), though much altered in subsequent use, still retains recognizable features.

The many small chapels of the early 19th century include several built for Strict Baptists but the most unusual chapel of this period, in origin and appearance, is Providence Chapel, Charlwood (6); this former guardroom from Horsham barracks, rebuilt in 1816, is a rare survival from the aftermath of the Napoleonic wars. Several chapels of the late 19th century, generally in the Gothic style, include Poulton's chapels at Redhill (44) of 1852 and Godalming (26) of 1868, the latter with an interesting polygonal Sunday-school added, and the Congregational chapel of 1864–5 at Weybridge (54) by John Tarring. From the closing years of the century a small chapel in Hindhead (34) of 1896 should be noted for its possible connection with Norman Shaw and William Lethaby, while the Wesleyan chapel at Englefield Green (15) of 1904 carries the freer use of style into the 20th century.

The principal building material throughout the county from the earliest years of chapel building is brick, with stone rarely used before the later 19th century. Plain tiles are generally used as a roof covering although slate appears frequently on later buildings and as a replacement for tiles. No significant example of timber-framed construction was observed but attention might usefully be drawn to the re-use of a timber framework when Friends built their previous meeting-house in Dorking (11), now demolished, in 1709.

ALBURY

(1) THE APOSTLES' CHAPEL (TQ 060481). Albury is of outstanding significance in the history of the Catholic Apostolic Church. Henry Drummond purchased the Albury estate in 1819 and in 1826 convened the first of a series of conferences for the study of scriptural prophecy. Some remarkable charismatic developments at Regents Square Chapel, London, in 1831 resulted in the expulsion of the minister, Edward Irving, from the Church of Scotland and the establishment of a separate 'Irvingite' congregation. Students of prophecy felt encouraged to pursue their studies with increased urgency and great reliance came to be placed on the utterances of persons regarded as having the gift of prophecy. In 1832, after his former supporter Hugh McNeile, rector of Albury, had turned against him, Drummond established a separate congregation at his own house where, as numbers increased, a stable was converted for meetings. In November of the same year the first member of a renewed apostolate was designated by prophecy; in December Drummond was similarly named as Angel (minister) of his congregation, and in the following year Albury was declared to be the divinely appointed seat of twelve latter-day apostles. Drummond became the second of the apostles in 1833 and by 1835 their number was complete. The settlement of the seat of the apostles at Albury highlighted the inadequacy of facilities for conferences and for the increasingly elaborate services of the Church, as well as the growing needs of the local congregation; this induced Drummond to erect, at his own cost, the building known as The Apostles' Chapel.

Surviving drawings dated between 1837 and 1843 show that William Wilkins was the architect responsible for the overall design, and that he was associated with W. McIntosh Brooks who

The Apostles' Chapel, Albury.

continued as sole architect after Wilkins' death in 1839; any work attributable to A.W.N. Pugin was probably confined to individual fittings. The chapel, which on the three latest drawings (1842–3) is entitled 'Cathedral Church, Albury', is in the Perpendicular Gothic style and comprises a chancel, E and S vestries, N and S transepts, nave and W tower, together with a 'chapter-house' linked by a passage to the N transept. The chapter-house was probably completed first, c.1838; the chapel was opened for worship on 4 September 1840, but work on the W tower continued for another year and on the fittings for a longer period. Additional vestries at the E end were built in 1896–7.

The walls are of brick faced externally with ironstone rubble with galleted joints which, except in the chapter-house, is interspersed with lighter blocks of yellow sandstone, a material also used for the ashlar dressings. The roofs are covered with slates. The walls have moulded plinths and battlemented parapets and are divided by stepped buttresses of two stages with crocketed pinnacles at the corners. The windows except in the chancel and vestries have cast-iron mullions and tracery painted to resemble stone.

The nave and chancel (90ft by 30ft) are undivided. The chancel, of two bays, has a circular E window with a tripartite pattern of cusped tracery and N and S windows of three lights with vertical tracery and small upper roundels in two-centred arched heads; the floor is tiled and the walls have a panelled dado. The crossing has four-centred arches with moulded jambs opening to the transepts. The nave is of three bays with windows of three lights to N and S, and a small W gallery formerly an organ loft. The roof has exposed queen-post trusses. The N and S transepts (17ft by $12\frac{1}{2}$ft) have windows of four lights in four-centred arched heads. The W tower (12ft by 13ft) is of three main stages of which the lowest serves as a porch; the W doorway has a four-centred arched head under a square label and open balustrade above; in the second stage is a large W window with four-centred arched head and small clock dial above; the upper stage has on each side a two-light belfry window with square head and label; the roof is pyramidal and surmounted by a cast-iron cross. At the E end the original S vestry has to the E a deacons' vestry, now altered, and the two later vestries E of the chancel, for visitors (N) and the Angel-in-Charge (S), are separated by a small room for the preparation of incense. The chapter-house ($24\frac{1}{2}$ft across) is octagonal and has six windows of three lights with square heads and labels, a fireplace in the E bay and a W porch; the parapet on the W side was originally surmounted by a stone cross.

Fittings – *Altar*: stone, two upright slabs and mensa, with tabernacle of cedar wood and carved oak canopy. *Bell*: in W tower, one, fixed for striking only, by Thomas Mears, London, 1841. *Clock*: in W tower, by Triggs & Son, Guildford, 1879. *Font* and *Font-cover*: octagonal; stone font with tall carved cover of wood,

The Apostles' Chapel, Albury.

with dove counterweight, suspended from bracket. *Glass*: in windows of chancel and transepts, formal painted diapers, including in N and S windows of chancel representations of the twelve scriptural Apostles and in the four upper roundels the emblems traditionally symbolic of the four evangelists, but in the Catholic Apostolic view representing 'the ministries of rule, prophecy, preaching and pastorship'. *Lectern*: brass, with trefoil base and triple stem. *Lighting*: in chancel, hanging lamp inscribed 'Vigilante et orate' and, flanking altar, two oil lamps on tall carved wood standards with tripod feet; in nave, chandelier with elaborate wrought-iron pendant. *Paintings*: in chancel, on E wall overall diaper pattern, on N and S walls the four ministerial emblems (*see* glass) and seraphim; on nave walls, biblical texts. *Piscina*: on E wall N of altar, stone corbel with leaf ornament. *Plate*: includes a pair of chalices, Birmingham 1851; flagon by Joseph and John Angel, London 1831; and two plates by Robert Garrard, one with central foot, London 1838, the other inscribed 'CATHOLIC CHURCH, ALBURY', London 1840. *Pulpit*: wood, semi-octagonal with panelled sides, on stem. *Seating*: in chancel, stalls for apostles and attendants, bench ends carved with grape ornament; in nave, oak-leaf decoration to ends of front pew, strawberry ornament to others. *Sedilia*: S side of chancel; triple seat with carved wood openwork canopy and pinnacles. *Stoup*: at W end of nave, semi-octagonal, of stone with elaborate leaf carving. *Tables*: N side of chancel, 'table of prothesis'; in chapter-house, octagonal with open central space for scribes.

Davenport, R.A., *Albury Apostles* (1970). Walmsley, R.C., and Standring, G.L., *The Years of Ferment …* (1980).

BROCKHAM

(2) BROCKHAM GREEN CHAPEL (TQ 198496). A meeting-house was built in 1783 by Christopher Abel and a Calvinistic Independent church formed in 1784; between 1803 and 1821 this became Strict and Particular Baptist. It appears from the deeds that the present building was erected on a site close to the former in 1822; the chapel was enlarged to the front in 1832 and later altered. The walls are of brick, rendered *c.*1907, and the roof is tiled. The front is gabled and has two round-arched windows with a circular window above an added porch; segmental-arched windows at side. *Monument*: against boundary wall, Thomas Biddle, minister 1858, and Lucy his wife, 1856.

Chambers I (1952) 41–4.

The Apostles' Chapel, ALBURY, *Surrey*

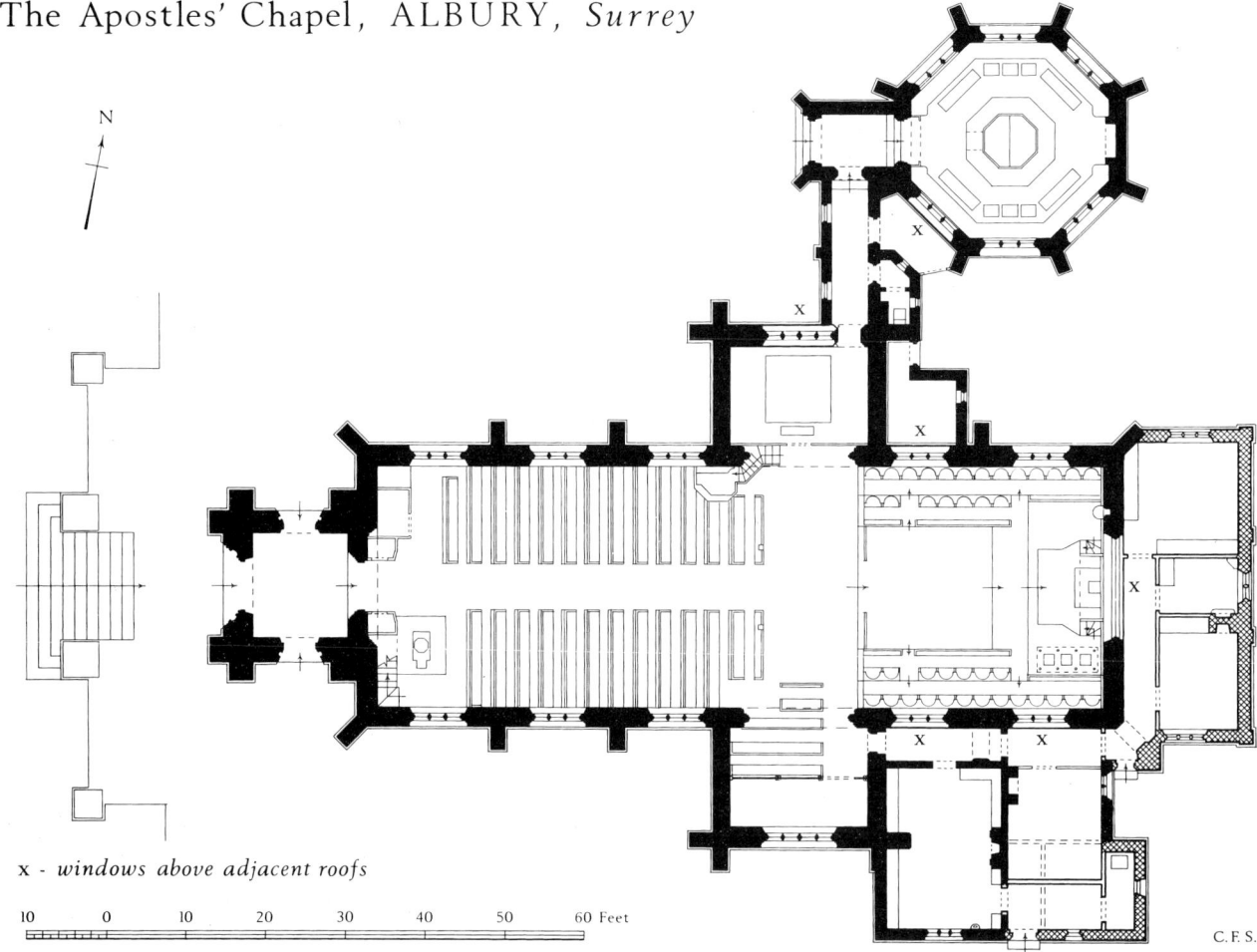

x - *windows above adjacent roofs*

BURSTOW

(3) BAPTIST, Outwood Common (TQ 327456). Built 1835 for a church formed in that year, cottage added to W at same period and chapel extended to rear in the late 19th century. Brick with hipped slate roof, three-bay S front with two storeyed cottage to left. (Closed 1979)

BAPTIST CHAPEL. OUTWOOD   CFS 1978

Fittings – *Inscriptions*: on bricks in N wall, initials 'IT', 'IN', 'EL', 'AT'. *Monuments*: in chapel (1) Rev. Thomas Green 1910; externally on S wall, (2) Eliza (Martin) wife of William Lambert, 1862, and William Martin, 1871; (3) James Martin, 1847, Amy his widow, 1849, and William son of Matthew and Sarah Martin, 1868; in burial-ground, five wooden grave-boards, late 19th-century, one retaining painted inscription to James Riley, 1869, and Elizabeth his wife. *Seat*: in chapel, with hinged back to convert to long table, mid 19th-century.

Baptist Times 11 October 1979. Chambers I (1952) 55.

(4) STRICT BAPTIST, Smallfield (TQ 319437). 'Ebenezer Chapel' was built in 1851 for supporters of Joseph Hatton, later editor of the Gospel Standard, following an unsuccessful candidature for the pastorate at Outwood. Brick with rendered gabled front and small porch. Seating comprises open-backed benches with arm-rests. *Monuments*: in burial-ground, many wooden grave-boards with square end posts and finials, dated 1860–90.

B.Hbk (1885) 150. Chambers I (1952) 53–6. Paul V (1966) 46–78.

CAPEL

(5) FRIENDS (TQ 175404). Quaker meetings were held from *c.*1655 at Pleystowe Farm, ¾ mile SSE, the home of Richard Bax, and there a burial-gound remained in use until 1849. The present meeting-house on the NW side of the main road was built in 1724. It has walls of red brick in Flemish bond with glazed headers and a tiled roof gabled NE and SW. The SE front originally had a segmental-arched doorway centrally to the principal room between two similarly arched windows; in the 19th century the doorway was re-sited to the left of the windows and one window altered. A smaller original doorway and window remain at the SW end of the front wall inside a recent porch and have a small window above. A lean-to wing was added to the SW in the later 18th

Strict Baptist chapel, Smallfield. Grave-boards. (4)

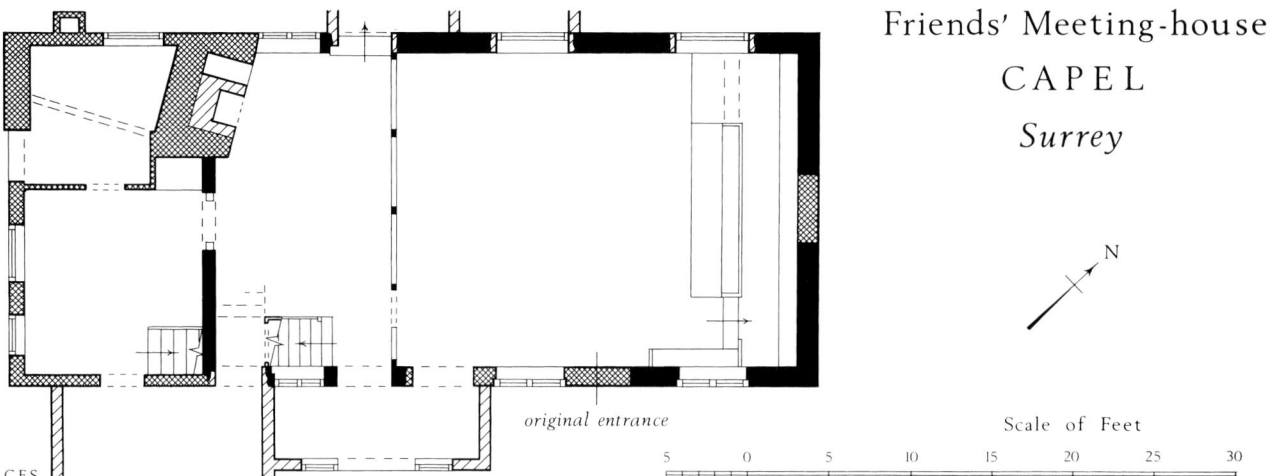

Friends' Meeting-house
CAPEL
Surrey

century and extended to the SE *c.*1903 to form a larger cottage. At the NE end is one segmental-arched window, now blocked.

The interior (36¼ft by 19½ft) is divided by a timber screen with removable shutters; the principal room has a stand at the NE end and loose benches with open backs and shaped arms. The smaller SW room has a large fireplace in one corner and a staircase with turned newel; the room above originally served as a gallery.

Coffin Stool: one, turned legs and shaped upper rails, early 18th-century.

Butler (1999) 582–3. Marsh and Marsh (1886) 1–3.

CHARLWOOD

(6) PROVIDENCE CHAPEL (TQ 246412). The Calvinistic Independent cause in Charlwood originated about 1814. A second-hand timber-framed building, the former guardroom, was acquired when the barracks at Horsham were dismantled, and this was re-erected and opened on 15 November 1816 as 'Charlwood Union Chapel'. The chapel has weather-boarded walls and a hipped slate roof. A verandah of seven bays along the SE side covers a central entrance with two windows to the right, one, formerly two, to the left, and a second doorway at the SW end; all the windows have external shutters.

The interior has two vestries at the NE end; in the space above the minister's vestry, at the E corner, two former windows are visible internally. The chapel has been partly refitted but the octagonal *pulpit* with pointed-arched back-board, at the NE end, and the *table-pew* with square splay-sided table and flanking box-pews date from the early 19th century. *Plate*: includes two pewter plates by Thomas Compton, early 19th-century.

Providence Chapel, Charlwood. (6)

Albery, W., *A Millennium of Facts in the History of Horsham and Sussex, 947–1947* (1947). Chambers I (1952) 60–1. Cleal (1908) 363–4. *The Earthen Vessel* (October 1859).

(7) Former FRIENDS, Tanyard Farm, Rectory Lane (TQ 238409). The former hall, now rear wing, of this timber-framed house was used in the 18th century as a Quaker meeting-house.

Butler (1999) 583. Harding (1976) 83.

CHERTSEY

(8) BAPTIST, Crouch Oak Lane, Addlestone (TQ 051647). Built 1872, by T. Wonnacott, replacing a chapel of 1839–40. Gabled front of yellow brick with a shallow arched recess enclosing three round-arched windows separated by stone shafts with caps and bases.

Chambers I (1952) 123.

DORKING

(9) BAPTIST, Junction Road (TQ 16324925). Three-bay gabled front with rusticated pilasters of red brick and centre bay with arch breaking into pediment. Dated 1876.

(10) CONGREGATIONAL, West Street (TQ 16354945). A Presbyterian society formed in the late 17th century under the Rev. John Wood, ejected minister of Northchapel, Sussex, and others, first met in a barn at Butter Hill. The first meeting-house on the present site was built in 1719. The latter half of the 18th century saw the ascendancy of Arian preaching coupled with a decline and eventual temporary division in the congregation. The society at the old meeting-house was re-formed as a Congregational church (now URC) at the beginning of the 19th century and the meeting-house was rebuilt in 1834.

The chapel, designed by William Hopperton assisted by William Shearburn, has brick walls with stone dressings; the pedimented S front is of three bays with rusticated quoins, one dated 3 September 1834, an original central doorway with pilastered surround and two flanking entrances replacing round-arched windows; three similarly arched windows above have altered frames. The mouldings and elaborate decoration on the pediment was greatly modified *c*.1950–60. The side walls were originally of four bays with two tiers of windows, a fifth bay was added at the rear and a Sunday-school built alongside in 1907. The interior, much altered in 1874 and later, has a gallery around three sides with open ironwork front.

Fittings – *Inscriptions*: on bricks in E wall, names and date '1834'; also reset here at side of fourth lower window from front, brick dated 1719. *Monuments*: in chapel, include (1) Rev. Alfred Dawson, 1835; (2) Mary Alexander, 1833; (3) Mrs Elizabeth Skipper, 1845; (4) Sarah wife of Rev. A. Dawson, 1828; (5) Sarah widow of Rev. John Whitehouse, 1854, and Sarah their daughter, 1844; (6) John Young, 1816, Mary his widow, 1837, and Heathfield their son, 1836; (7) Rev. Thomas Coad, 1749, marble tablet; (8) Thomas Stent, 1844; (9) Rev. John Whitehouse, 1825.

Paintings: two water-colour drawings (1) exterior of the 1719 meeting-house, four-bay front with two entrances and two tiers of windows, seating plan below; (2) two-storeyed house of four bays, captioned 'The meeting-house of the late Andrew Kippis' and signed 'J.Hasson, 1825'.

Cleal (1908) 353–63. *CYB* (1935) 253. Grantham, T.R., *Dorking Congregationalism 1662–1912* (1913).

(11) FRIENDS, South Street, Butter Hill (TQ 164492). Meetings commenced *c*.1702 and a meeting-house was built in West Street in 1709 at a cost of £161 2s. 6d. including £11 10s. 'for an old frame of a house'; Thomas Elwood received 30 shillings for 'making the writings'. The present meeting-house, built on a new site in 1846, has brick walls and a hipped slate roof. The front of five bays with sash windows has a low three-bay porch, extended at the sides, with a pair of Tuscan columns *in antis* at the entrance.

The interior is divided into two rooms of unequal size by a large pair of counterbalanced shutters set in a wide three-centred arch. At the far end of the larger room is a *stand* of two stages; *seating* comprises contemporary open-backed benches.

Butler (1999) 586–7. Marsh and Marsh (1886) 6–10.

(12) Former METHODIST, Church Street (TQ 16274940). On 23 November 1772 John Wesley opened a new preaching-house at Dorking. This has been identified with a building standing N of the 'King's Arms' in West Street which was greatly altered and converted to other uses in the early 19th century. The walls are of brick and the roof, hipped and of low pitch, is slated. The wide N front, partly obscured by later wings, retains traces of round-arched upper windows; two similar windows in the S wall probably flanked the pulpit. The interior has been entirely refitted and floors inserted. (Derelict 1971, subsequently in commercial use)

Congregational chapel (URC), Dorking. Plan and elevation of 1719 meeting-house. (10)

EFFINGHAM

(13) WESLEYAN (TQ 117537). Flint with brick dressings and slated roof. Three-bay gabled front with pointed-arched openings, dated 1854. Interior refitted *c*.1993.

Methodist Recorder (2 September 1993) 4.

EGHAM

(14) Former CONGREGATIONAL, Egham Hill (TQ 005713). Built 1851 at the cost of J. Remington Mills MP. Nave and aisles in Gothic style with rubble walls and slate roof; four-light traceried window above arched entrance. Four-bay arcades with piers alternately round and octagonal. (Now a sale room)

Cleal (1908) 294–7.

(15) WESLEYAN, Englefield Green (SU 996710). Rendered walls with brick and stone dressings in art-nouveau style with battlemented porch and corner tower, both having copper-clad domes. Opened 1904.

ELSTEAD

(16) CONGREGATIONAL (SU 910436). Rubble with brick dressings and slated roof, built 1846. Pedimented front of three bays with two stages of round-arched openings. (URC/Methodist)
Monument: in front of chapel, Rev. Edward Bromfield, 1857, nearly 17 years pastor.

EPSOM

(17) Former CALVINISTIC INDEPENDENT, Prospect Place (TQ 212610). 'Bugby's Chapel', or 'East Street Chapel', is said to have been built in 1779 by William Bugby, who had been impressed by the early preaching of William Huntington SS, together with a house alongside for his son, also William Bugby, who served as minister. Three meeting-house certificates for buildings in Epsom were taken out by 'W. Bugby' in 1777, 1778 and 1787. The 'Huntingtonian' congregation may have disbanded in the early 19th century but the chapel was still recorded in the 1851 census for Calvinistic Protestants. In 1889 the chapel was placed in the hands of a newly formed Strict Baptist church which removed in 1951 to a new chapel in Dorking Road. The former chapel then served as a synagogue but in 1994 conversion to office use was proposed.

The chapel has walls of brickwork with later rendering. The roof is hipped around four sides with a central concealed valley discharging to the W and is covered with tiles. The S front is of three bays with round-arched windows; there are two windows in the N wall and a pair of blind windows high in the E wall. On the W side a modern vestry replaces the former house. The interior ($25\frac{1}{4}$ft by $31\frac{1}{4}$ft) has no gallery or other original features. A small burial-ground, now a public garden, lies to the east.

Monuments: externally against E wall (1) Thomas Ellis, late of Gloucestershire, 1798, white marble monument with pediment, perhaps re-sited from inside chapel; (2) George Swann, 1849, Charlotte his widow, 1874, and Charlotte their daughter, 1884; (3) John Humphrey, 1866, Mary his wife, 1852, *et al*.; (4) Rev. William Bugby [ ] and Mary[?] his wife, 1787; (5) Joseph Weller, 1864, Maria his wife, 1859, and Joseph their son, [ ]; (6) James Inglefield, 1864, Ann his daughter, wife of George Snashall, 1858, and her two infant sons.

Chambers I (1952) 42–5. *CHST* XVII (1952–5) 131. White, T., and Harte, J., *Epsom: A Pictorial History* (1992) Pl. 20.

ESHER

(18) BAPTIST, Park Road (TQ 138647). Three-bay brick front with pilasters and arched centre bay rising into pediment. Built 1868 for a church previously meeting in the Friends meeting-house.

Stockwell (1909) 100–1.

(19) FRIENDS, Claremont Lane (TQ 140645). The meeting-house on the E side of the lane was built in 1793 for a meeting which had for many years been conducted in private houses. The walls are of yellow stock brick and the roof is hipped and slated. The S front is symmetrical with a central doorway having a flat canopy with shaped brackets and two tall round-arched windows to each side; the top half of the western pair of windows is blocked and superseded by a small dormer and windows in the W wall. The interior ($42\frac{3}{4}$ft by 24ft) is divided into two rooms by vertically

'Bugby's Chapel', Prospect Place, Epsom. (17)

Friends' meeting-house, Esher. (19)

sliding shutters. The larger E room has a dado of plain panelling and a stand at the E end with two splayed stepped entrances; the smaller room, or library, and a room above it intended for women's meetings, have been converted to a cottage.

Beck and Ball (1869) 315–16, 328. Butler (1999) 587–8. Haynes, R., *A Brief History of Esher Meeting of the Society of Friends* (1971).

FARNHAM

(20) STRICT BAPTIST, Bear Lane (SU 840471). Coursed rubble and slate, rendered pedimented front with porch; brick dressings to windows in side wall. Built 1852 for a church formed 1850. (Residential conversion proposed 1994)

Chambers I (1952) 71–4. *Farnham Herald* 21 August 1987.

(21) STRICT BAPTIST, Hungry Hill, Upper Hale (SU 845490). 'Bethel Chapel', of flint and brick, now rendered, and with a slated roof replaced by tiles, was built in 1834. The chapel was originally two bays in length; low vestries added to the front in 1877 were replaced by a third bay c.1970–5.

Chambers I (1952) 74–7.

(22) Former CONGREGATIONAL, East Street (SU 85254720). A new congregation formed after the dismissal in 1792 of a popular preacher at the parish church was joined by some surviving members of a Presbyterian society which traced its origins to the work of several ejected ministers in the late 17th century. A meeting-house built in East Street in 1793 was superseded in 1873 by the present Gothic chapel by T. Wonnacott, in South Street.

The former meeting-house, or 'Ebenezer Chapel', on the N side of the street, has brick walls and a hipped tiled roof, partly re-covered in slate, with a central flat area. The S front, originally of three bays with a slightly projecting centre bay, was extended to the E in the 19th century by the addition of a staircase wing; the older walling was altered to leave the two central bays projecting between the end bays. The N wall, partly rebuilt in 1898, had two windows flanking the site of the pulpit. The interior (45¼ft by 30¼ft) has been entirely refitted. The roof is supported by four queen-post trusses partly visible below an altered ceiling.

Cleal (1908) 368–75.

(23) WESLEYAN, Upper Hale (SU 843489). Flint with brick dressings and tiled roof. A round-arched recess in the gabled end wall encloses three round-arched windows set in herringbone brick infilling. Opened 1880.

GODALMING

(24) GENERAL BAPTIST, Meadrow (SU 981447). The congregation, which originated in 1783 and was for many years associated with another at Worplesdon (5½ miles N), has long been regarded as Unitarian. The meeting-house, built in 1789, was enlarged in 1821 by the addition of a cottage at the N end. In 1870 a detached school-room in the Gothic style was built next to the road and this came to be used for services until 1975 when the former building was reinstated.

The meeting-house has brick walls, rendered at the front, slate-hung at the rear, and a hipped tiled roof. The W front has a rendered plinth, quoins and a coved cornice; two tall round-arched windows to the right of a gabled 19th-century porch and one to

General Baptist chapel, Meadrow, Godalming. (24)

the left with doorway added below may be the conflation of two tiers of windows. The interior (35½ft by 22ft) is subdivided by a wall opposite the entrance leaving a square meeting-room to the S with N gallery supported by two posts which rise as columns to support the roof structure.

Baptistery: in floor, on major axis, brick-lined with four steps to the north. *Monuments*: in burial-ground to S, many headstones of the late 18th century and after.

Evans (1897) 95–6. *Inquirer* (14 August 1976). *Monthly Repository* V (1810) 458.

(25) Former CONGREGATIONAL, Mint Street (SU 96804385). The church's origins are obscure but probably lie in a Presbyterian society which existed in the late 17th century. The first meeting-house in Mint Street (formerly Harts Lane) was built in 1730 and replaced by the present building *c*.1830. After 1868 the chapel passed to the Methodists and it is now used by the Salvation Army.

The walls are of rubble with a brick front and rendered dressings. The S front of three bays with a pediment and rusticated quoins has two tiers of rectangular windows. Two round-arched windows in the N wall flank the site of the pulpit. A S gallery has been replaced by an upper room. Interior further altered pre-1994.

Cleal (1908) 400–5.

(26) Former CONGREGATIONAL, Bridge Street (SU 972441). Rubble with Bath stone dressings. Gothic, by W.F. Poulton of Reading, built 1868 for the Mint Street congregation. Gabled E front with two porches and small NE tower above the gallery staircase; octagonal turret and spire removed *c*.1969. Large polygonal Sunday-school behind, with radiating divisions to galleried school-rooms, 1884 by Welman and Street. (Closed *c*.1978, now in commercial use)

Cleal (1908) 400–5. *CYB* (1868) 331; (1883) 390–1.

(27) FRIENDS, Mill Lane (SU 967438). Godalming Friends made a collection in 1701 towards building a meeting-house but probably compromised by converting an existing structure; a lease of 1715 refers to a 'building now used for a meeting-house'. The present building was erected in 1748, which date appears on several bricks in the rear wall; a smaller annexe at the front for women's meetings was added and enlarged *c*.1772 and 1808.

The meeting-house has brick walls and a hipped tiled roof. The N front has a central entrance with flat canopy and shaped brackets between two cross-framed windows with leaded casements. The rear wall of brick, on a rubble base with galleted joints, has a central entrance and a pair of cross-framed windows; to the E is a small doorway opening to a simple rung stair between this and the adjacent cottage, giving access to the roof space.

The interior (27½ft by 26ft) has a flat plaster ceiling with moulded cornice; a single post supports a beam on the line of a former partition. The roof is double with clasped purlins and collars or V-braces.

Fittings – *Inscriptions*: on several bricks in S wall initials and date 1748; near side entrance to annexe, bricks with initials and date 1772; in meeting-house, small piece of wood inscribed 'FRIENDS MEETING HOUSE 1714'. *Monuments*: in rear burial-ground, headstones with dates from early 19th century, reset against boundary walls. *Plate*: pewter plate with initials I^SH and touch 'Baldwin', 18th-century. *Stand*: at E end, with panelled front.

Friends' meeting-house, Mill Lane, Godalming. (27)

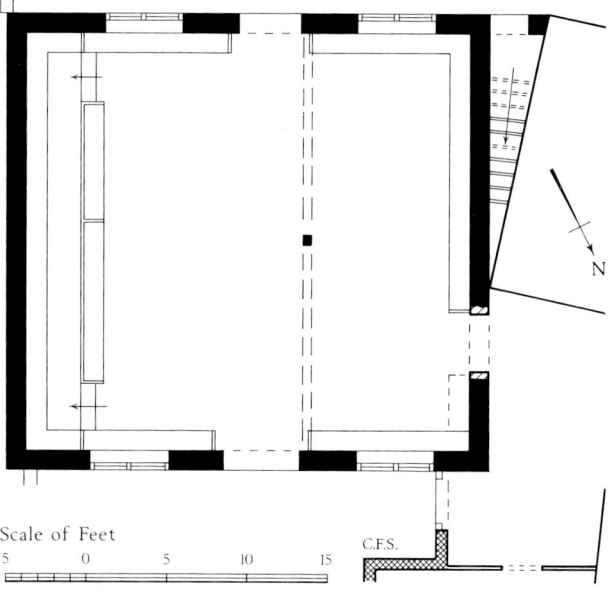

Friends' Meeting-house, Mill Lane, GODALMING *Surrey*

Butler (1999) 589–90. Marsh and Marsh (1886) 18–19. Wigfield, W.M., *A Short History of Friends' Meeting, Godalming, Surrey* [1969].

(28) FRIENDS BURIAL-GROUND, Binscombe Lane (SU 967459). The rectangular enclosure partly bounded by rubble walls, in use 1659–1790, contains no monuments. The ground was provided for the use of Friends by Thomas Patching, who suffered imprisonment in 1660 and was one of the first to be buried here. An adjacent barn, now converted to a house, is associated with the preaching of George Fox in 1655.

Butler (1999) 590. Marsh and Marsh (1886) 19, 21. Wigfield [1969] op. cit. 5–6.

(29) Former WESLEYAN, Farncombe Street (SU 97454505). Brick with lancets in gabled front; built 1842. (Closed by 1930 and since in commercial use)

GUILDFORD

(30) STRICT BAPTIST, Chertsey Street (SU 999498). 'Castle Street Memorial', red brick with stone dressings, three-bay gabled front. By W. Wray, late 19th-century. Possibly the former Primitive Methodist chapel acquired in the 1950s by the congregation formerly meeting in 'Charcoal Barn Chapel'.

Chambers I (1952) 24–9.

(31) FRIENDS, Ward Street (SU 99754968). Red brick with low-pitched hipped and slated roof, built 1805. Wide W front with two tall segmental-arched windows N of entrance, later porch, and one similar window to S divided and altered. Principal room to N with plain deal dado and stand against end wall. Bricks with initials and date 1805 at sides of doorway inside porch.

Butler (1999) 590–1. Marsh and Marsh (1886) 11–18.

Friends' meeting-house, Ward Street, Guildford. (31)

(32) UNITARIAN, Ward Street (SU 99684970). The chapel of polygonal rubble with ashlar dressings in a late Gothic style is dated 1877. Closed 1972.

Evans (1897) 96.

HASLEMERE

(33) CONGREGATIONAL, Lower Street (SU 903329). The first chapel was built in 1804 for a congregation (now URC) formed eight years before. It was extended in the early 19th century by the addition of a school-room built alongside and greatly changed in 1881–2, when a larger chapel was built to the rear and the earlier buildings converted to school use. The original chapel, which survives, had a rendered front of three bays with round-arched upper windows; the upper stage is now tile-hung and the windows altered. The present chapel by T. Roger Smith is of red brick with a vestigial polygonal turret and spire between the two parts of the building.

Cleal (1908) 410–15. Pannell, C., *The Story of the Congregational Church at Haslemere, Surrey* (1908).

Congregational chapel (URC), Haslemere. (33)

HINDHEAD AND CHURT

(34) CONGREGATIONAL, Tower Road, Hindhead (SU 885355). The chapel (now URC), originally a general-purpose hall, was built at the expense of John Grover, a prominent building contractor, and opened 9 August 1896. A combined manse and church hall were added in 1901, and the chapel was reseated and renamed the 'Free Church'. The overall design of the building has been attributed to R. Norman Shaw for whom Grover had carried out several commissions including New Scotland Yard, London.

Congregational chapel (URC), Hindhead. (34)

The chapel has walls faced with random masonry and stone dressings; the roof is tiled and has a ventilating flèche on the ridge. The N and S ends are gabled and have each a large lunette window. On the E side is a porch with segmental-arched outer doorway and three bays of mullioned windows separated by buttresses. The interior, of five bays, is ceiled at collar level. The former manse (now a private house) and the church hall stand to the N and are in a similar style to the chapel.

Fittings – *Monument*: brass to John Grover, 1913, and Sarah his widow, 1919. *Seating*: in chapel, 20 loose benches with arms and open splat backs with heart decoration and upholstered seats, said to have been designed by W.R. Lethaby.

Cleal (1908) 435–7. *CYB* (1905) 130–1.

(35) CONGREGATIONAL, Beacon Hill, Hindhead (SU 874366). John Grover, who erected (34), built two further chapels in the locality of which this was the last, completed in 1905, the second being at Hammer (*see* Linchmere, Sussex (68)). The walls are of red brick, partly rendered, with raking buttresses to the sides and timber-framing in the front gable. (URC)

Cleal (1908) 437. *CYB* (1905) 130–1.

HORLEY

(36) Former GENERAL BAPTIST, Horley Row (TQ 283441). A General Baptist church was in existence by 1712 meeting at Turners Hill, Sussex (6 miles SSE). About 1760 the church moved its meetings to a new meeting-house in Horley Row, now a house No. 3 Bakehouse Road. After 1791 meetings were transferred to Nutfield but ceased by the mid 19th century. The former meeting-house was subdivided, one half becoming a bakehouse; it is now a single dwelling of two storeys.

The walls are of brickwork to the lower floor but tile-hung above; the roof is hipped around a central valley. Two upper windows at the front and one below with segmental-arched brick head may represent original openings. The interior (about 23ft square) is divided by a later partition and inserted floors, but the E half remains to much of its original height.

BQ I (1922–3) 81; II (1924–5) 324–9. Hooper, T.R., *A Surrey and Sussex Border Church ...* (1925). Information from Mrs Jean Shelley. *UHST* I (1917–18) 191–218.

Former General Baptist chapel, Horley Row. (36)

(37) Site of STRICT BAPTIST, Lee Street (TQ 270435). A small weather-boarded chapel built in 1847 for a church which moved to a new location in 1881 has been demolished. *Monuments*: in burial-ground behind the chapel, in Mill Close, several headstones of the mid 19th century and later, including (1) Edward Miller, 1873, 27 years pastor; (2) Mary wife of Edward Miller, 1847; (3) Caroline [2nd?] wife of Edward Miller, 1897.

Chambers I (1952) 60–2, illus. facing 63.

HORSELL

(38) BAPTIST, Anthonys (TQ 015611). Small brick chapel with gabled front built 1901; 'architect and builder' F.J. Bridger.

B.Hbk (1902) 346.

(39) Former STRICT BAPTIST, Horsell Common (SU 998600). The chapel, built in 1815 for a church formed *c.*1811, has been used since 1963 by a Brethren assembly. The walls are of brick, altered and rough-cast in 1907, and the roof is tiled. The chapel was originally of two bays, with sash windows in the N and S walls, and had a hipped roof of which the structure still remains. A separately roofed vestry and upper school-room were added at the E end, and in 1907 the whole building was re-roofed and refashioned. The interior of the chapel has two windows at the E end opening from the upper school-room behind the site of the pulpit. The pulpit and pews have been removed; prior to a refitting of 1888, the pulpit was approached directly from the vestry.

Fittings – *Baptistery*: centrally in floor of chapel. *Hat-rails*: at rear, with turned wood pegs. *Inscriptions*: on bricks reset above outer doorway of porch, include initials, names 'Jas. Walker' and 'J.Grove', and date '1815'. *Monuments*: in burial-ground, of early 19th century and later, include Alfred son of Benjamin and Sarah Bensley, 1829.

Chambers I (1952) 32–9.

LINGFIELD

(40) BAPTIST, Dormans Land (TQ 405424). The first meeting-house, a small building '28ft by 16ft' built 1786, was replaced by the present chapel in 1817. The walls are of brick with a three-course platband at mid-height and the roof is tiled. The gabled S front has three upper windows, and a central entrance between two blind recesses, all with segmental-arched heads; in the gable is a tablet with the date of erection. The S gallery and subsequently the E and W galleries were added shortly after 1817. Some original benches remain in the gallery.

Chambers I (1952) 53–6. *Gospel Herald* (April 1851).

(41) STRICT BAPTIST, Lingfield (TQ 387436). 'Salem Chapel', of brick with rendered gabled front and slate roof, was built in 1836. In the burial-ground are five wooden grave-boards; dates include 1880, 1928.

Chambers I (1952) 56–7.

NORMANDY

(42) CONGREGATIONAL, Willey Green (SU 939518). The chapel built 1825 as a preaching-station for the Surrey Mission (now URC) has low walls of red brick with clasping pilaster buttresses and a hipped slate roof. Tablet above front porch inscribed 'NORMANDY CHAPEL 1825'

Cleal (1908) 393.

REIGATE

(43) STRICT BAPTIST, Redhill (TQ 279507). Stock brick with red brick dressings, dated 1858. Gabled front of three bays, raking cornice with mutules, matching porch and round-arched windows paired above entrance.

Chambers I (1952) 57–8.

(44) CONGREGATIONAL, Chapel Road, Redhill (TQ 278504). Gothic chapel by Poulton and Woodman, 1862. Redhill stone with Bath stone dressings and slate roof. Nave with polygonal apse, single aisle with four-bay arcade on paired cast-iron columns, corner tower with octagonal turret and spire. (URC)

Cleal (1908) 430–2. *CYB* (1863) 295–8.

(45) CONGREGATIONAL, High Street, Reigate (TQ 252502). A Presbyterian society of late 17th-century origin died out a century later. At the instance of the Congregationalist Thomas Wilson the old meeting-house was, in 1801, transferred to new trustees by the heir-at-law of the last surviving trustee; the latter, then imprisoned in Newgate for debt, received 20 guineas. The meeting-house, reopened in April 1801, was replaced by a new chapel in 1819 which was rebuilt in 1831 and forms the nucleus of the present building. A transeptal enlargement to the S in 1857–8 with a shallow polygonal apse and enlargement to the front in 1868–9 have entirely transformed its appearance. The front, of squared stone in the Romanesque style, has a short tower and spire at the NE corner. (Chapel demolished 1973)

Cleal (1908) 377–82.

(46) FRIENDS, Reigate (TQ 263502). The meeting-house rebuilt in 1857 replacing a much-altered building of 1688 is of red brick with stone dressings; in front is a semicircular porch with Tuscan columns. (Rebuilt 1984)

Butler (1999) 593–5. Marsh and Marsh (1886) 3–5.

(47) WESLEYAN, High Street, Reigate (TQ 251502). Gabled front of two bays, stone with Romanesque detail. Built 1884, by Frederick Boreham.

(48) MILL CHAPEL, Reigate Heath (TQ 234501). Post mill built 1765, restored 1927. Round-house in use as a chapel since 1880 by the Established Church (as Chapel of St Cross) and by others later including Baptists.

RIPLEY

(49) STRICT BAPTIST (TQ 050567). 'Ebenezer Chapel' dated 1812 has rendered walls and a slate roof, two sash windows in front and lean-to annexes with external entrances against each gabled end. Segmental-vaulted plaster ceiling. Pulpit and seating replaced c.1950 by late 19th-century seats and older pulpit from a chapel in Aylesbury, Bucks. (see *Nonconformist Chapels and Meeting-houses in Central England* (1986) 5, monument (7)). Some panels from original pulpit reset behind minister's seat; a pointed-arched recess at back probably represents the original direct approach from the vestry.

Baptistery: in front of pulpit. *Monument*: in chapel, William Meryett, 1845, 'He Erected this Chapel in the Year 1812 …'. *Pulpit*: with two tiers of fielded panelling, possibly 18th-century.

Chambers I (1952) 104–6.

SHERE

(50) CONGREGATIONAL, Holmbury St Mary (TQ 110446). 'Felday Chapel' opened 25 October 1825 has brick walls and a hipped slate roof, with two sash windows in each side wall. It was extended towards the road and refitted in the late 19th century. (Derelict 1970)

Cleal (1908) 419–21.

STAINES (formerly Middlesex)

(51) BAPTIST, Bridge Street (TQ 033716). The congregation formed in 1824 first occupied the meeting-house of a recently defunct Baptist church which stood 'at the back of Church Street'. The present chapel, opened in 1837, has a rendered pedimented front of three bays with two stages of round-arched windows.

BM XVI (1824) 83–4, 441–2; XXX (1838) 29. Whitley (1928) Nos 63, 133a.

STANWELL (formerly Middlesex)

(52) CONGREGATIONAL, Poyle (TQ 033766). Services in connection with the church at Cores End, Wooburn, Bucks. (*see Nonconformist Chapels and Meeting-houses in Central England* (1986) 30, monument (102)) were first held in a room and a separate church was formed in 1814. The present chapel, opened 12 November 1823, has brick walls and a slate roof. The front is gabled with corner buttresses of two stages and octagonal turrets; above a pointed-arched doorway is a wide rectangular window of six lights. The side walls of three bays have two-stage buttresses and tall pointed-arched windows.

Summers (1905) 58–60. VCH *Middlesex* III (1962) 49.

CONGREGATIONAL CHAPEL, POYLE

TILFORD

(53) Former CHAPEL, Tilford House (SU 870436). The chapel in the garden, formerly the stable yard, of Tilford House was built in 1776 by Elizabeth Abney, last surviving daughter of Sir Thomas Abney. It was registered 25 March 1777 for Independents under the Rev. Thomas Taylor, chaplain to Miss Abney, to whom she left the estate at her death in 1782. Whether the chapel served a regular congregation is not apparent, although it was no longer in use by 1854. It is now a garden room. The walls are of brick with a dentil eaves cornice and the roof is hipped and tiled with a central valley. The present entrance on the W between two flat-arched windows has a timber doorcase with consoles below a pediment; two similar windows occupy the N wall. A pair of round-arched windows in the E wall with intersecting glazing bars to hung sashes may have flanked the pulpit. The S wall is blank and has a minor lean-to

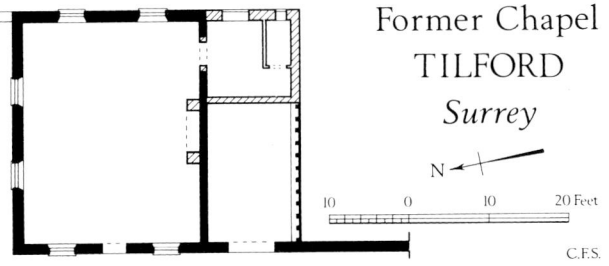

Former Chapel TILFORD Surrey

building against it. The interior (27½ft by 22ft) has a flat plaster ceiling with moulded cornice.

Inscriptions: on brick in N wall at E end 'HM 1776'; below cill of SW window '1776'.

CHST XVII (1952–5) 131. VCH *Sussex* II (1905) 593–4.

Former chapel, Tilford House, Tilford. (53)

WEYBRIDGE

(54) CONGREGATIONAL, Queens Road (TQ 082644). Gothic chapel by John Tarring, 1864–5. Random masonry with Bath stone dressings; nave and transepts with tower above side porch and tall ashlar spire rising from octagonal belfry stage. The nave roof has arched-braced trusses ceiled at collar level. (URC)

Cleal (1908) 310–14. *CYB* (1866) 308.

WITLEY

(55) CONGREGATIONAL, Milford (SU 943420). The chapel built on a new site in 1902 replaced a building of 1872. (URC)

Cleal (1908) 409–10.

WOKING

(56) STRICT BAPTIST, Westfield Road, Mayford (SU 999560). Red brick and slate with gabled SE front. Built *c.*1825 and later heightened and enlarged to the front. Two wide segmental-arched

Congregational chapel (URC), Queens Road, Weybridge. (54)

windows each side, the rear pair heightened. *Monuments*: externally on SW wall (1) James Trigg, 1838, signed 'J. Smart, Guildford'; (2) Rebecca wife of Rev. William Edwards, 1826; (3) Sarah Trigg, 1830.

Chambers I (1952) 40.

WORPLESDON

(57) CONGREGATIONAL, Perry Hill (SU 968543). Brick and tile, dated 1822. Much altered in 1896 with timber-framed front gable, porch and renewed heads to side windows. (URC)

Cleal (1908) 426–9.

SUSSEX

(East and West)

Sussex has long supported a wide range of religious denominations. While Roman Catholicism continued to find favour with some of the older landowning families in the western parts of the county, Protestant dissent received a more sympathetic reception in the east, though no part of the county was unaffected by its influence. In the city of Chichester and in the former fishing village of Brighthelmstone (Brighton) large Presbyterian congregations gathered in the early 18th century while in Lewes both Presbyterians and Independents received considerable support and Baptists, both General and Particular, as well as Quakers, also attracted appreciable numbers.

Very little remains of the 1688 Presbyterian meeting-house in Brighton (12) following various enlargements and the elegant re-fronting of *c.*1820 by Charles Busby. The chapel in Baffins Lane, Chichester (25), of 1721 is still in a recognizable state and is notable for its formerly barrel-vaulted ceiling flanked by galleried aisles together with an end pulpit, unlike more traditionally planned meeting-houses. Interestingly, its layout was copied on a smaller scale by the local General Baptists (24) in 1728. In contrast with these the formerly Presbyterian Westgate Chapel in Lewes (67), the conversion of part of an existing house, was set out in the more usual fashion with a line of posts supporting a double roof, though subdivided and reoriented in 1913.

Notable amongst the many Baptist chapels in the county is the group of General Baptist chapels most of whose congregations followed the movement towards Unitarianism which, in other parts of the country, is most evident among the older Presbyterian societies. This development amongst the General Baptists of Sussex is generally credited to Matthew Caffyn whose name is particularly associated with the church at Horsham (56); there the meeting-house of 1720–1 is of a singularly domestic appearance though variously extended and realigned internally. On a smaller scale is the meeting-house at Billingshurst (9) of 1754 with its broad three-bay frontage, a feature again found in the former chapel of 1741 in Lewes (62) and, prior to 19th-century reordering, in the contemporary chapel at Ditchling (37). The former Particular Baptist chapel of 1754 in Merchant Street, Rye (86), although converted to a house, is also notable as occupying the site of a Quaker meeting-house.

Several Quaker meeting-houses of importance remain in the county. Of the late 17th century are Ifield (33) and the former meeting-house at Steyning (93), but the most notable, if somewhat enigmatic in name, is the 'Blue Idol' at Thakeham (95), converted from an existing house in 1693. The 18th century is represented by Herstmonceux (55) of 1734, Lewes (65) of 1784 and Horsham (58) of 1786. Brighton (19) of 1805 has been much altered.

The late 18th century saw the spread of Calvinistic denominations of which the Countess of Huntingdon's Connexion is the best known. Ote Hall Chapel, Wivelsfield (108) of 1780 is of particular note and was closely associated with the countess, who had a house in the vicinity. A more fundamental form of Calvinism was that preached by William Huntington SS, who was buried behind Jireh Chapel, Lewes (64), a building of 1805–26, which is one of the most interesting nonconformist chapels in Sussex and a building of national importance. Providence Chapel, Chichester (26), of 1809 is also worthy of particular note. Closely associated with these in doctrine are the Strict and Particular Baptists whose two timber and weather-boarded chapels in Wadhurst (97, 98), both of the early 19th century, are examples of a simple but pleasing construction from which all unnecessary decoration is banished. Least well known of the denominations are the 'Cokelers' or Society of Dependents, two of whose meeting-houses appear at Loxwood (70) and Northchapel (78).

Chapels of the early 19th century include the Independent chapels at Herstmonceux (54) of 1811 and Rye (87) of 1817, the General Baptist chapel of 1810 in Northiam (79), and the strangely towered chapel of the Church of Christ in Angmering (2) of 1846. More traditional architectural elements appear in the chapels at Bosham (10) of 1837 with its simple brick pediment, the classically fronted chapel in New Road, Brighton (15), of 1820, and Arundel (3) of 1837–8 in which the Romanesque style makes a brief appearance. Italianate chapels of the later 19th century by Thomas Elworthy are found at St Leonards (47) of 1882–3, for Baptists, and Robertsbridge (89) of 1881 for Congregationalists, for whom W.F. Poulton had also built a small Gothic chapel in Seaford (90) in 1877–8. Methodist chapels, although not numerous, include one small late 18th-century chapel in Winchelsea (61) and several minor buildings of the early 19th century. With the exception of two built for Bible Christians (81, 91) all are Wesleyan foundations. Of the later period two small pedimented chapels in Hartfield (42) and Groombridge (107) are of particular note for their architectural quality while at Whatlington (103) Wesleyans attempted a more ambitious pile with tower and spire. Most notable, however, is the former chapel at Catsfield (23) of 1912 in which the attention to detail of a private donor who was both architect and builder is exemplary.

Throughout the county brickwork predominates as a walling material, usually accompanied by tiled roofs although Horsham stone slates are appropriately found on the General Baptist chapel in Horsham (56) and from an earlier period on the Friends' meeting-houses at 'Blue Idol' (95) and Ifield (33). This last is also notable for the use, or possible re-use, in the late 17th century of exceptionally fine building stone; rubble is used at a similar period at Steyning (93), clunch appears in the former chapel of 1800 at South Harting (43) and stone in small blocks at Providence Chapel, Chichester (26), of 1809. Near the coast use was made of pebbles as a facing material, notably in Brighton (12) in 1688 and in the 19th century it might be accompanied by knapped flints as at Selsey (91). Flint with brick dressings was used in the General Baptist chapel in Lewes (62) in 1741 and rough flints with flint galleting is a feature of the Congregational chapel at Yapton (113) of 1861. From the late 18th century timber-framed construction became increasingly popular: it is seen in the Friends' meeting-house at Lewes (65) and in several small chapels, many built for Calvinistic Independents, in the early 19th century. Outstanding amongst this class of building is Jireh Chapel, Lewes (64), a chapel of exceptional size in which the more prominent outer walls are hung with mathematical tiles in imitation of brickwork as are those of the nearby Friends' meeting-house.

ALFRISTON *East Sussex*

(1) CONGREGATIONAL (TQ 521031). The chapel built in 1801 for a newly formed congregation was enlarged in the 1830s by the addition of a gallery. The walls are rendered and the roof is hipped and slated. The entrance is at the narrower S end between two (blind) windows with Tudor labels; above are three pointed lunettes with wooden Y-traceried frames. Each side wall has three bays of windows matching those in the front wall. Two pointed-arched windows at the N end flank the pulpit.

The interior has a gallery around three sides with a panelled front and supported by wooden Roman Doric columns with marbled finish. The lower seating was replaced in the late 19th century but the original gallery seating remains. (URC)

Fittings – *Clock*: on gallery front, by Hooker, Lewes. *Monuments*: in chapel, on N wall (1) Elizabeth wife of Charles Brooker, 1820; (2) Ann wife of Charles Brooker, 1827; (3) Thomas Gouldsmith, 1816; (4) William, 1818, Mary Ann, 1822, and Dorcas, 1829, children of William and Mary Ann Woodhams; (5) John Bodle, 1835, and Molly his widow, 1836; on E wall (6) Elizabeth daughter of William and Elizabeth Brooker, 1820; (7) George Smith, 1814, *et al.*; (8) Charles Shelly, 1870, Charlotte his wife, 1855, and their children, painted wooden board. Externally on W wall (9) Charles Virgoe, 1804.

ANGMERING *West Sussex*

(2) ANGMERING CHAPEL, Station Road (TQ 067042). The chapel was recorded in the 1851 census as a Church of Christ, built 1846 by George Robert Paul of Portland Lodge, Worthing, and supported and superintended by him. It subsequently became a preaching-station of a Baptist church in Christchurch Road, Worthing. The chapel, of flint with red brick dressings, is unusual in having at one end a square tower of four storeys with a pyramidal roof. (Closed 1970, now private house)

ARUNDEL *West Sussex*

(3) Former CONGREGATIONAL, Tarrant Street (TQ 018070). 'Trinity Chapel' was built in 1837–8 in the Romanesque style to designs by Robert Abraham of London. The front wall faced with knapped flints with flint galleting is gabled and of three bays separated by ashlar pilaster buttresses. There are three round-arched windows at gallery level. The side walls are faced with flint and have brick dressings. The interior has a stepped gallery above the entrance but side galleries have been altered or rebuilt. Below the chapel is a large school-room. (Now an antiques market)

EM (January 1837) 30–1.

ASHBURNHAM *East Sussex*

(4) Former CONGREGATIONAL (TQ 668175). The large chapel was erected in the mid 19th century by the Earl of Ashburnham who permitted its use by dissenters. The congregation became a branch of the church meeting in Robertson Street, Hastings. In 1964 services were transferred to a former village hall.

The building is a plain rectangular structure of brick with a hipped slate roof. A porch was added and additional windows inserted in the front wall on conversion to a house.

New (1906) 37, 43–4.

BATTLE *East Sussex*

(5) Site of BAPTIST, Mount Street (TQ 747162). The ground immediately adjacent to the N of Zion Chapel (6) was occupied from 1789 by a chapel built by a then Particular Baptist church under the pastorate of William Vidler. Vidler's rapidly changing beliefs, influenced by the Universalist Elhanan Winchester, led to the church joining the General Baptist Assembly in 1803 and professing Unitarianism. The chapel, closed in 1898, then passed into secular use until suffering structural failure in 1947; it was demolished in 1958.

The chapel had brick walls and a hipped roof behind a parapet. The front was of three bays with a central round-arched entrance between segmental-arched lower windows and with three round-arched windows above. In 1971 the site was occupied by minor buildings but a few tombstones remained visible.

BM XIII (1821) 517–22. Buffard (1963) 51, 53–4. Chambers II (1954) 70–1. *Christian Freeman* (1872) 72–4. *CHST* V (1911–12) 166–7. Evans (1897) 12–13. Maguire, L.J. (ed.), *A History of the Unitarian Church at Battle, Sussex by S.C. and W.H. Burgess*, General Baptist Assembly, occasional paper No. 25 (1999). *UHST* IV (1927–30) 64–5.

(6) BAPTIST, Mount Street (TQ 747162). 'Zion Chapel' was built 1820–1 to replace a wooden meeting-house which seceders from the foregoing had erected in 1798. The chapel has brick walls, the front is rendered with three bays of windows below a pedimental gable. Above the central porch is a simple Venetian window.

BM XIII (1821) 213–14, 517–22. *See also* works cited for (5).

General Baptist chapel, Billingshurst. (9)

Baptist chapel, Mount Street, Battle. (6)

(7) WESLEYAN, Battle Hill (TQ 752154). Rendered brick walls, front with pedimental gable and finials. Dated 1826.

BECKLEY *East Sussex*

(8) WESLEYAN (TQ 851240). Brick with three bays of tall pointed-arched windows; porch between chapel and two-storeyed annexe has reset tablet dated 1840 although the 1851 census claims 1814 for the chapel.

BILLINGSHURST *West Sussex*

(9) GENERAL BAPTIST (TQ 086258). The church meeting in and about Horsham included from its earliest years a considerable number of members from Billingshurst. Local activity was further quickened from 1742 when William Evershed, a farmer and General Baptist preacher, subsequently pastor at Horsham, moved to Great Daux farm. He and William Turner conducted local meetings and in 1753 actively promoted the erection of a meeting-house. The chapel, then standing on a site of 40ft square with an 8ft-wide right of way from the road, was registered in October 1754. The congregation remained part of the Horsham church

General Baptist Chapel, BILLINGSHURST
Sussex

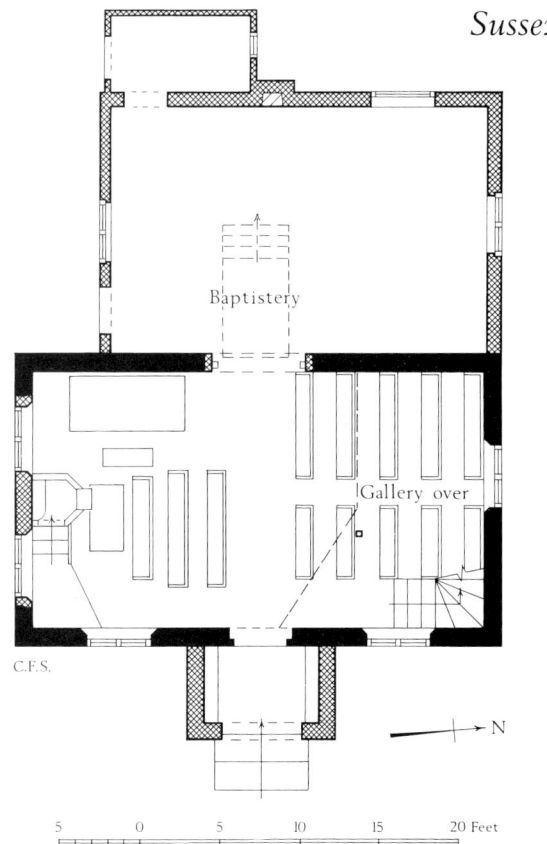

until 1818, when Billingshurst members withdrew following a decision of the parent body to insist on the strict enforcement of conditions of membership. Both churches had adopted Unitarian beliefs by the early 19th century; the last recorded baptism at Billingshurst was in 1872.

The chapel, which stands concealed on the W side of the street, is a small building of brickwork in Flemish bond with glazed headers and a tiled roof. The E front is of three bays with a central entrance, covered by an early 19th-century porch, between two segmental-arched windows with original timber frames. The N and S walls are gabled, both gables being altered or rebuilt in 1877–8 when the roof was reconstructed. A single segmental-arched window in the S wall was replaced in the early 19th century by two windows flanking the pulpit. In the N wall is an inserted window below the gallery and one in the rebuilt gable. The W wall, which has no traces of original openings, is largely covered by a brick extension; this was first added in 1825 to provide an internal baptistery and vestries but it was largely rebuilt in 1886.

The interior (16ft by 28¼ft) has been rearranged and partly refitted. The pulpit, probably initially against the W wall, was removed to the S end about 1825. A single gallery at the N end, added in the late 18th century, has a plain panelled front angled at the E end and is supported by a single post. The roof structure is of the late 19th century, ceiled at collar level, but original tie-beams remain in the gables. The W room is now approached through a wide opening from the chapel.

Fittings – *Baptistery*: below floor of W room, rendered brick with steps at W end only. *Chandelier*: brass, six branches surmounted by dove, 18th-century. *Clock*: above entrance, with shaped dial and short pendulum case, inscribed 'INKPEN [?repainted over "J. ..."] Horsham 1756'. *Coffin Stools*: two, oak, inscribed 'IK 87' for James Knight 1787, bought 1787 for 10s. *Communion Table*: oak, with turned legs, 18th-century. *Inscription*: reset internally in S wall, stone tablet inscribed 'WE WT 1754' for William Evershed and William Turner. *Library*: a substantial library of over 2,000 volumes, principally secular, housed in the W room, was dispersed or destroyed 1969.

Monuments: in chapel (1) Rev. John Jeffery, 1813, erected 1877; (2) Rev. William Evershed, 1799, and Rev. William Turner, 1772, 'the principal founders of this chapel AD 1755', erected 1878. In burial-ground, many headstones of the 18th century and later. *Plate*: includes two small two-handled cups of 1781. *Pulpit*: polygonal, with plain panelled sides, stair with thin turned balusters, round-topped back-board, early 19th-century. *Seating*: in gallery, two box-pews inscribed 'James Knight 1788'.

Archer, J., *Historical Sketch of Nonconformity in Billingshurst, Sussex* (1912) 8–9. Evans (1897) 15–16. Kensett, E., *History of the Free Christian Church, Horsham, from 1721 to 1921* (1921) passim. UHST IV (1927–30) 159–60; IX (1947–50) 160–74.

BOSHAM West Sussex

(10) CONGREGATIONAL, Bosham Lane (SU 805041). Meetings were commenced in 1812 by the Rev. John Hunt of Chichester in a converted sail-loft. The chapel was built in 1837 and the cause greatly assisted by Thomas Sainsbury, who became its pastor. The chapel has a pedimented brick front to the E of three bays;

Congregational chapel (URC), Bosham. (10)

the N wall is faced with pebbles. A detached school-room was added in 1875. (URC) (Proposed refitting and conversion of school-room, 1991)

CYB (1877) 410–11, obituary of Thomas Sainsbury.

BREDE East Sussex

(11) WESLEYAN, Broad Oak (TQ 828198). Rendered gabled front with pointed-arched windows, built 1855 replacing a chapel of 1833. *Monument*: in burial-ground, to Peter Hook, 1869, and Catharine his wife, 1845, headstone laid flat.

BRIGHTON East Sussex

(12) Former PRESBYTERIAN, Union Street (TQ 31050419). A meeting-house built in 1688 was registered as 'a house lately erected at the upper end of Ship Street, John Duke minister'. By the early 19th century the church came to be designated Congregational eventually uniting in 1904 with the church meeting in Queen Square. The meeting-house was used as a mission hall from 1905 and by Pentecostalists from 1927. Conversion to secular use was proposed in 1988.

The chapel, which stands on the N side of the street, retains some outer walling of the late 17th century but it was enlarged and re-fronted in the early 19th century, and refitted internally in 1875. The S front of c.1820, possibly designed by Charles Augustus Busby, is rendered in stucco; it has a pedimented centre of three bays with a Doric frieze and three tall windows with tapered jambs, between end entrance bays. The N wall, accessible from Ship Street Court, incorporates the original rear wall of the late 17th-century building, 49½ft in width, faced with pebbles and with red brick dressings to the corners; this has been extended to the E in brick and heightened in the late 19th century with a wide truncated gable overall.

Former Presbyterian chapel, Union Street, Brighton.   (12)

The interior (41ft by 59¾ft) as remodelled in the late 19th century has a horseshoe-shaped gallery supported by eight substantial columns which continue above to support the roof. Above the central space is a plaster semi-dome lit by windows in the N gable. Gallery staircases occupy the SE and SW corners. Below the full length of the S front of the chapel is a segmental-arched brick vault formerly approached by a wide curved stair at the E end and with traces of a few subdivisions for former burial vaults at the opposite end.

Fittings – *Inscriptions*: on tablets in S front of annexe to right (i) '16WBE88' (ii) 'BUILT ANNO DOMINI | 1688 | REPAIRED & ENLARGED | 1810' (iii) 'GLYNN VIVIAN MINERS MISSION OPENED MAY 5TH 1905.' *Monuments*: in front of chapel, memorial stone to Henry Varley, 1912, 'the great evangelist... in 1860 he built the West London Free Tabernacle which held 1700 people'; wall monuments in the chapel were removed to Queen's Square when the original church departed.

CHST V (1911–12) 103–4, 167–9. *Country Life* (14 April 1988) 138–9. PHSJ I (1914–19) 167–72.

(13) BAPTIST, Bond Street (TQ 31100430). 'Salem Chapel' on the E side of the street (formerly New Street) by Thomas Simpson, was built in 1860–1 to replace a meeting-house of 1787–8. The front of three bays with a recessed centre is faced with knapped flints and stucco dressings. (Demolished 1974)

Chambers II (1954) 19–22. Elleray (1981) 50.

(14) STRICT BAPTIST, Gloucester Road (TQ 310048). 'Galeed Chapel', built in 1868 for seceders from a Calvinistic Independent church meeting in The Tabernacle, West Street (built 1837, demolished 1965), was designed by Benjamin H. Nunn. It has a rendered pedimented front of three bays with a rusticated lower stage and pilasters between the upper windows.

Chambers II (1954) 33–6. Elleray (1981) 50. Paul II (1954) 137–217.

(15) GENERAL BAPTIST, New Road (TQ 31150437). The now Unitarian congregation originated in a secession in 1793 from the Particular Baptist church in New Street (13), joining the General Baptist Assembly in 1803. The church progressed from a small chapel in Jew Street rented in 1806, via a new building in Cavendish Street in 1812, to the present chapel by Amon Henry Wilds opened 1820. The chapel, variously described as New Road Chapel or 'Christ Church', is a plain brick structure behind a pedimented tetrastyle portico to the street with Greek Doric columns and a central doorway. The frieze, now plain, originally bore the Greek inscription ΜΟΝΩ ΘΕΩΑΙΑ ΙΗΣΟΥ ΕΡΙΣΤΟΥ ΑΟΕΑ 'To God only wise, be glory through Jesus Christ', replaced in 1905 by 'Free Christian Church'. The interior has been entirely altered.

Evans (1897) 34. Rowland, J., *The Story of Brighton Unitarian Church* (1972). UHST IV (1927–30) 287.

New Road Chapel, Brighton.   (15)

(16) CONGREGATIONAL, Queen's Square (TQ 308044). Gothic, 1854 by James and Brown, enlarged 1867. Incomplete corner tower. (Demolition proposed 1981)

(17) HANOVER CHAPEL, Queen's Road (TQ 310046). The chapel was built in 1825 for an Independent church under the Rev. James Edwards. In 1844 it was sold to a Presbyterian society. By 1972 this had amalgamated with the Congregational church at Queen's Square which, as Brighton Central Free Church (URC), converted and extended the chapel in 1985–8.

The chapel has rendered walls and a hipped slate roof. The S front, facing the remains of a large burial-ground, is of four bays. The end bays have giant pilasters and pediments and porches flanked by Roman Doric columns; between the entrances is a pair of round-arched windows with matching columns supporting inner arches. Behind the chapel is a hall dated 1866.

Monument: in burial-ground, obelisk to G.S. Walcker, 1832, 'late of Berlin and formerly of the German Spa in this town'.

CYB (1872) 317, obituary of Rev. James Edwards. *Reform* (January 1989).

(18) COUNTESS OF HUNTINGDON'S, North Street (TQ 31120419). The first chapel on this site was built in 1761, variously altered and enlarged, rebuilt 1774 and replaced in 1870 by a chapel in the Gothic style with corner tower and spire by J. Wimble of London. (Demolished 1972)

Chambers II (1954) 13–14. Elleray (1981) Pls 39–40. Seymour (1839) I: 314.

(19) FRIENDS, Ship Street/Prince Albert Street (TQ 31020415). Quakers opened a meeting-house in a converted malthouse on the N side of North Street in 1700–1. This stood at the corner of North Street and New Road, adjacent to the Chapel Royal. The present building, then known as 'Ship Street Meeting-house', was built in 1805 and the former sold and demolished. Many alterations were made during the 19th century, particularly in 1876 when the principal entrance was moved to the W end and that wall entirely refenestrated and embellished with a pediment.

The meeting-house has brick walls. The original front faces N and has a 'lobby and portico' added in 1845, now partly obscured by a later building; there are three tall segmental-arched upper windows and two similar windows on the S side. A cottage adjacent to the S is of two storeys with a third storey added. The interior comprises a single room with stand at the E end covered by a canopy added in 1817, and a gallery opposite supported by two columns with lotus capitals.

Bishop, J.G., *A Peep into the Past; Brighton in the Olden Time ...* (1892) 329–37. Butler (1999) 599–601.

(20) TRINITY CHAPEL, Ship Street (TQ 310043). The chapel, now Holy Trinity Church, was built in 1817 for Thomas Read Kemp, a nonconformist preacher, and it later passed to George Faithful who in 1825 removed with his followers to a chapel in Church Street. Trinity Chapel was sold in 1826 to become an Anglican Proprietary chapel. The building, designed by Amon Wilds, originally had a front of five bays with a three-bay pediment and a Classical turret. The interior was galleried and had a barrel vault over the central space. Alterations since 1826 have included the addition of a chancel in 1869 and re-fronting in 1885–7, but the original side walls remain as does much of the gallery structure.

Elleray (1981) 48, Pl. 42.

BURWASH *East Sussex*

(21) WESLEYAN, Burwash Weald (TQ 652232). Red brick, gabled front with lancets; dated 1843.

BUXTED *East Sussex*

(22) CALVINISTIC INDEPENDENT, Five Ash Down (TQ 477237). The chapel was built in 1784 on land given by Thomas Dicker in whose house meetings had previously been held. The original building was greatly enlarged in the late 19th century when it was given a triple-gabled W front, but part of the original brick structure, 20ft long, remains in the N wall.

Chambers II (1954) 91, 125.

CATSFIELD *East Sussex*

(23) Former WESLEYAN, Church Lane (TQ 724138). Small Gothic chapel dominated by an imposing corner tower and tall spire with elaborately detailed 13th-century-style upper windows. The chapel was designed and built in 1912 by Henry Blackman, in memory of his parents. (Converted to domestic use)

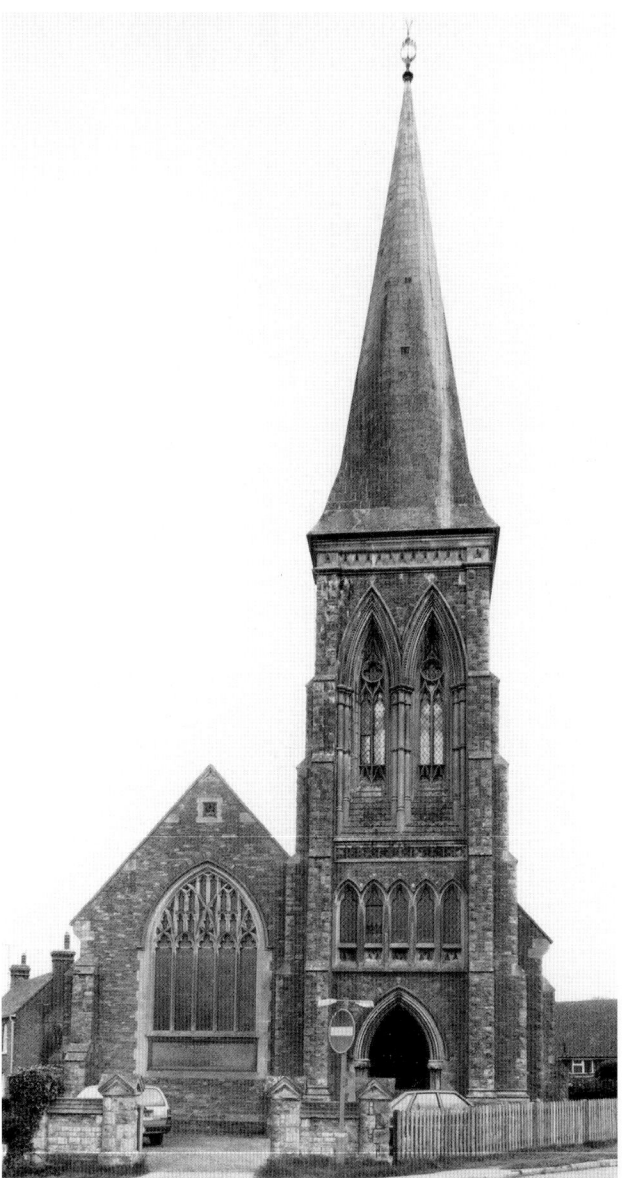

Former Wesleyan chapel, Catsfield. (23)

CHICHESTER *West Sussex*

(24) Former GENERAL BAPTIST, Eastgate (SU 865047). The Baptist church formerly meeting here is said to have originated *c*.1640 in the work of James Sicklemore, rector of Singleton, who had adopted Baptist sentiments. The present site was acquired in 1671 and the meeting-house was rebuilt in 1728. During the 18th century the church gradually accepted Unitarian doctrines but failing support led to amalgamation with the Presbyterians

at Baffins Lane in 1815. The chapel continued in occasional use, especially after the closure of Baffins Lane in 1930, but in 1940 it was reported 'closed for duration of war'; it is now a public hall.

The chapel built in 1728 has rendered walls, probably of brickwork, and a tiled roof gabled to front and rear. The NW front is concealed behind a later porch and other buildings but the original round-arched doorway remains internally, with keystone and impost blocks. Above the doorway is a tablet inscribed

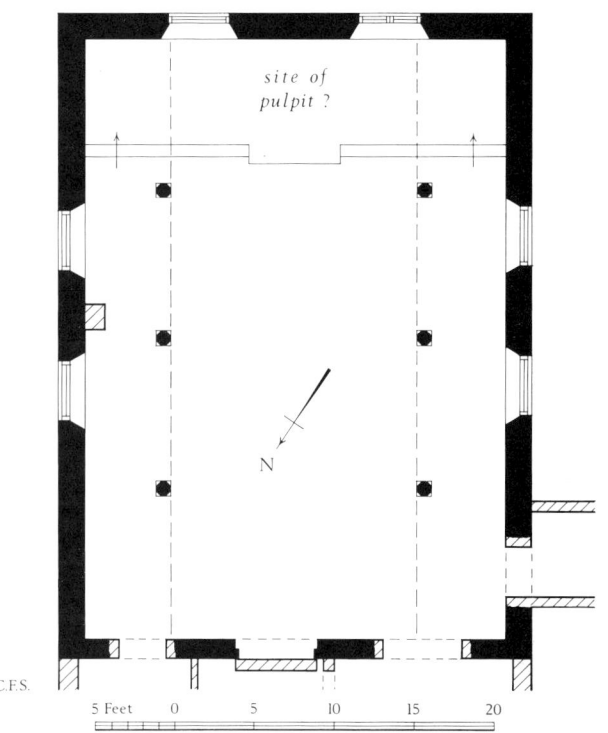

Former General Baptist chapel, Eastgate, Chichester. (24)

Former General Baptist chapel, Eastgate, Chichester. (24)

'REBUILT | ANNO.DOM | 1728'. The doorway is slightly off-centre possibly to allow for a former external vestry. The side walls have tall round-arched windows and there are two similar windows in the SE end which flanked the pulpit.

The interior (37½ft by 26¼ft), of four bays, is divided by two rows of chamfered timber posts which carry a plaster barrel vault above the central space. There are no galleries but one was recorded in 1801, possibly at the NW end.

Fittings – [*Books*: the church formerly possessed two bibles (i) 'Breeches Bible', printed by Thomas Strafford, Amsterdam, 1640 (ii) London, 1683]. *Clock*: on SW wall, with octagonal dial and long pendulum case, late 18th-century. *Monuments* and *Floorslabs*. VCH (1935) op. cit. below lists 20 18th-century floorslabs with dates from 1729 and two later wall monuments; none now visible. *Plate*: includes a pair of two-handled cups and two pairs of pewter plates, mid 18th-century.

Crosby IV (1740) 245–7. Evans (1897) 48. Ivimey II (1814) 567–9. Taylor (1818) I: 292. Thatcher, P.R., *Then and Now: Baptists in Chichester, 1648–1994* (1995). UHST V (1931–4) 327–8. VCH *Sussex* III (1935) 164.

(25) Former PRESBYTERIAN, Baffins Lane (SU 863047). The society was in existence by the late 17th century and had a meeting-house in St Pancras parish. The present site was acquired in 1721 and the meeting-house erected in that year; after the amalgamation of the Presbyterian and General Baptist congregations in 1815 under a shared Unitarian ministry, meetings appear to have been held here for a time but later transferred to Eastgate Chapel, leaving Baffins Lane out of use from 1861 to 1883. The chapel was closed and sold in 1930; it is now an auction room.

The chapel has walls of brickwork and a tiled roof with a central valley at collar level. The E front has a truncated gable covering the end of the valley, a large round-arched blind window filled with dark glazed brickwork in header bond between two smaller round-arched gallery windows, and a central doorway between lower windows. In front is a small forecourt (now covered over) and two later front wings containing the gallery stairs and closed by a screen wall with an outer doorway with segmental pediment. The side and rear walls are in English bond brickwork, the side walls have each four segmental-arched windows at gallery level only; two round-arched windows in the rear wall with intersecting wooden tracery flank the site of the pulpit.

The interior (46ft by 34½ft) has a gallery around three sides supported by timber posts which also carry the roof structure. The plaster ceiling, now removed, formed a barrel vault over the central space. The gallery fronts are of the early 19th century; some repairs to the roof including the addition of tie-beams probably date from *c*.1883.

Fittings – *Monuments*: in forecourt, Frederick William son of John and Hannah Fullager, 1821; two wall monuments, to John Fullager, 1863, pastor, and C.A. Hoddinott, 1908, minister, were removed to the General Baptist Chapel (24). *Plate*: included two two-handled cups of 1668 with ogee sides and *repoussé* decoration (sold 1930, unlocated).

Evans (1897) 47–8. UHST V (1931–4) 325–7. VCH *Sussex* III (1935) 164.

Former Presbyterian chapel, Baffins Lane, Chichester. (25)

Baffin's Hall, CHICHESTER, *Sussex*

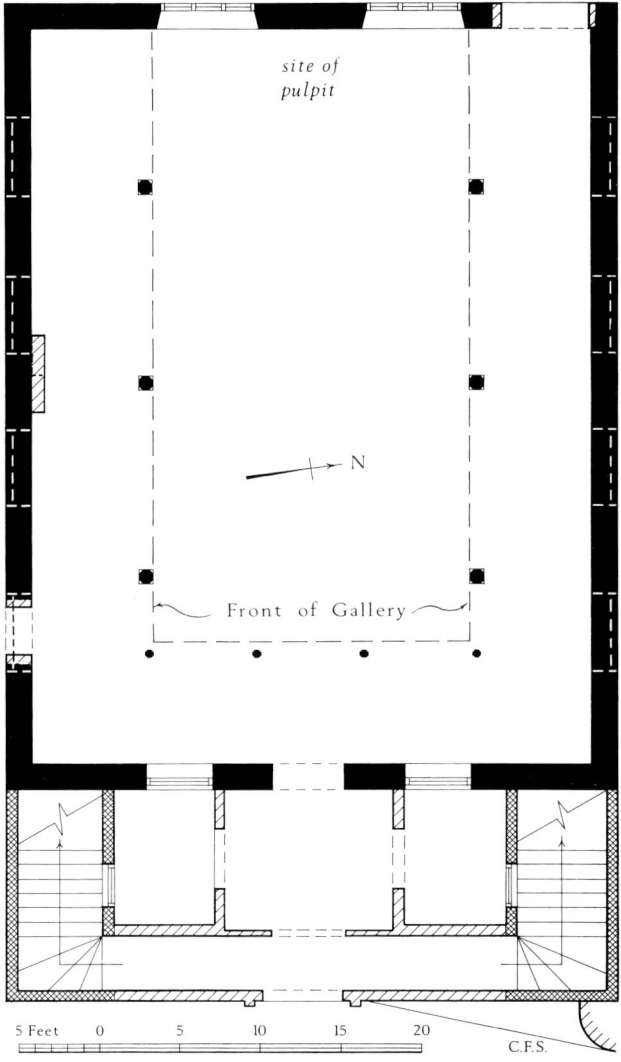

(26) PROVIDENCE CHAPEL, Chapel Street (SU 859051). The Calvinistic Independent congregation originated *c.*1803 with seceders from the Countess of Huntingdon's chapel in Chapel Street (28) who first met in a house in East Street. The present site on the W side of the street was acquired in 1808 and the chapel opened on 24 August 1809. The chapel has walls of stone with red brick dressings. The E front, of three bays with round-arched doorway and windows, has a pedimented gable with dentil brick cornices and a roundel inscribed with the name and date of erection. The side walls have windows matching those in front. At the rear is a small cottage of two storeys and basement. In front of the chapel is a forecourt, reduced in depth by road widening *c.*1973 and with iron gates erected in 1984.

The interior has a plaster ceiling with a segmental-arched barrel-vault. At the E end is a small gallery supported by a single octagonal post with moulded capital. The pulpit, table-pew and seating are all contemporary and of particular note.

Fittings – *Communion Table*: narrow rectangular table with pair of desk tops for singers, one removable when table required for communion use. *Monument*: above outer doorway, to Thomas Iveson and Richard Hook, 'martyred at Chichester 1555', erected *c.*1985. *Pulpit*: of two stages, upper stage hexagonal on flared stem, approached directly from upper vestry in cottage by short bridge with balustraded sides, clerk's desk below. *Seating*: fixed open-backed benches with arm-rests. *Table-pew*: in front of pulpit, rectangular seated enclosure with combined communion table and singer's desk at centre.

Archaeological Journal CXLII (1985) 37. Chambers II (1954) 124. Reynolds, J.S., *Providence Chapel, Chichester* (Chichester Papers, No. 19, 1961).

(27) ZION CHAPEL, Orchard Street (SU 858052). Built 1833 for Independents who left Providence Chapel in 1831 but reunited in 1878. Now used by Salvation Army. Minimal Gothic.

Reynolds (1961) op. cit. 37.

(28) COUNTESS OF HUNTINGDON'S, Chapel Street (SU 860049). The church formerly meeting here originated *c.*1770 with seceders from the Presbyterian meeting. In 1774 a meeting-house in converted premises in West Lane (now Chapel Street) was opened in the presence of the Countess of Huntingdon; it was rebuilt in 1796. From 1810, under the Rev. John Hunt, the church became Independent and the building is said to have been enlarged during his ministry. In 1893 the church removed to new premises in South Street (30) and the former chapel passed to the Established Church for use as a hall. (Demolished *c.*1947)

The chapel on the E side of the street had a brick front of five bays, two doorways in the penultimate bays with pedimented Doric doorcases between plain sash windows, the centre window blind, and round-arched upper windows with intersecting glazing bars. The interior (approximately 36ft by 45ft) had a gallery around three sides.

CYB (1857) 188, obituary of Rev. John Hunt. Reynolds (1961) op. cit. 11–15. Seymour (1839) I: 392–3. Measured drawing by H. Godwin Arnold in NMR.

(29) Former CONGREGATIONAL, St Martin's Square (SU 862049). 'Ebenezer Chapel' was converted from an existing structure in 1833 by seceders from the foregoing who reunited with that church in 1857. The building was then used for Sunday-school purposes until 1892. The gabled front wall of 1833 is rendered; it has a pointed-arched doorway between windows and a large window above. The other walls, of exposed brickwork, retain traces of two tiers of former windows.

(30) CONGREGATIONAL, South Street (SU 860046). The chapel has a gabled front of stone in a free Gothic style by E.J. Hamilton. It was built in 1892 for the church formerly meeting in Chapel Street (28). Now united with the Methodists in Southgate. (Chapel demolished)

CYB (1892) 210–11.

(31) FRIENDS, Priory Road (SU 863050). The meeting-house, of red brick dating from 1698, was rebuilt in 1967 retaining the original S and W rear walls.

Butler (1999) 601–2.

Providence Chapel, Chapel Street, Chichester.

Providence Chapel, CHICHESTER, *Sussex*

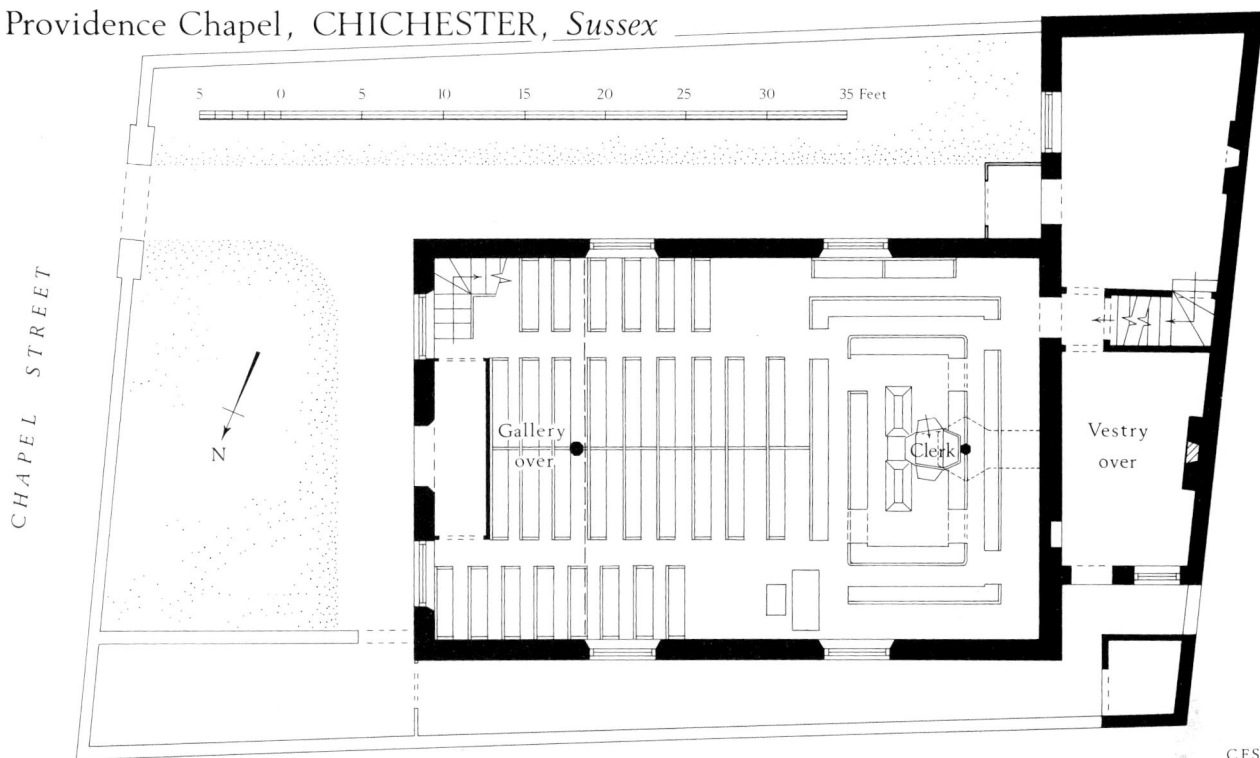

(32) WESLEYAN, Southgate (SU 861045). Wesleyan meetings began in the early 19th century and a chapel was built at East Walls in 1818, rebuilt in 1840. This was superseded in 1876–7 by the chapel on the E side of Southgate, a building in a French Gothic style by Alexander Lauder of Barnstaple. (Demolished and replaced by new chapel for joint Methodist/URC congregation, 1981–2)

Vickers, J. and Vickers, H., *Methodism in a Cathedral City* (1977).

CRAWLEY *West Sussex*

(33) FRIENDS, Langley Lane, Ifield (TQ 252379). The first meeting of Friends in Sussex is claimed to have been settled here in 1655 following a visit by George Fox and Alexander Parker. The present site was acquired in 1674 when it comprised a house, blacksmith's shop, garden and orchard. The work of erecting a meeting-house adjacent to the existing building commenced in 1675; the proposals were for a building 'with stone walls the length thereof not exceeding forty feet and the breadth not exceeding twenty four feet'.

The earliest building on the site, which now forms a cottage at the SW end of the meeting-house, dates from the 15th century and comprises a timber-framed house of three bays, the lower part of the walls rebuilt in brickwork and the upper part hung with tiles; the roof is hipped and tiled. The wider central bay originally formed an open hall into which a floor was inserted in the 17th century. The roof has plain crown-posts, a braced collar-purlin and common rafters; traces of smoke-blackening remain on the timbers.

The meeting-house, completed in 1676, has walls of squared stone (reputedly from Slaugham Place, 6 miles S) and is roofed with Horsham stone slates. A chamfered plinth extends around the three exposed sides and the SE front and central entrance are bounded by rusticated quoins. All openings have flat-arched heads of stone. Two wide windows with wooden frames flank the front entrance and have above them two truncated gables with half-hipped roofs and small windows. The rear wall repeats the fenestration of the front but is partly covered by recent extensions. Two smaller windows in the NE wall light the stand.

The interior ($35\frac{3}{4}$ft by $26\frac{3}{4}$ft) was divided into two rooms in 1822 by a screen with vertically sliding shutters. An original chamfered post supports the main timbers of the upper floor; to the S is a contemporary corner fireplace with timber lintel with a corresponding fireplace on the floor above. The stand at the NE end and the open-backed benches date from the early 19th century. The attic floor, approached from the cottage, is divided into several rooms providing additional living accommodation.

Friends' Meeting-house, Ifield CRAWLEY *Sussex*

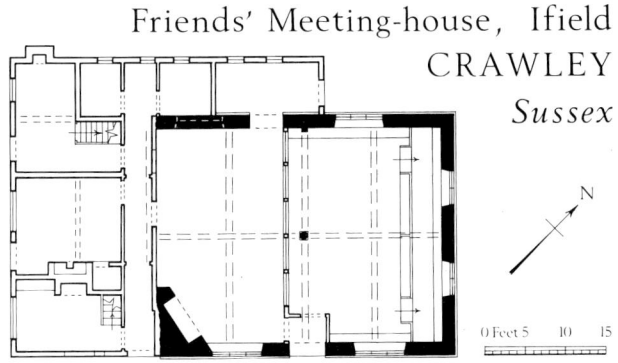

Friends' meeting-house, Ifield. (33)

Fittings – *Chair* and *Table*: oak, the former with straight panelled back and fluted supports to arms, the latter with turned legs and upper rails carved on three sides only, 17th-century, reputedly the gift of George Fox. *Door*: in NW doorway, boarded and nail-studded, late 17th-century. *Inscriptions*: on keystone of front doorway, date '1676'; on jambs to right of doorway '16 HE 84 | 16 AH 76 | 16 IK 76'.

Butler (1999) 606–7. Lidbetter (1961) Pls LIII, LIV, Fig. 37. Marsh and Marsh (1886) 26. 'B.R.', *A Short History of Ifield Meeting from 1655 to the Growth of Crawley New Town* (pamphlet, n.d. c.1960–70). Southall (1974) 29–32.

CUCKFIELD *West Sussex*

(34) Former GENERAL BAPTIST (TQ 306252). The chapel built in 1772 served a branch of the Ditchling church until c.1820. From about 1842 the chapel was used by Strict Baptists who formed a separate church in 1846 and to whom the building was eventually sold in 1905. In spite of serious financial and other problems the chapel was repaired in 1956 and much enlarged in 1968.

This is a small building of brick with rendered walls and dentil brick eaves cornices, now much extended at both ends. The original portion (26½ft by 16½ft) of three bays is ceiled at collar level and has two mid 19th-century doorways to vestries at the E end.

Monuments: in chapel on N wall (1) [Rev] Samuel Walder, 1782, Mary wife of James Walder, 1797, and John son of John and Lidia Tusler, 1805; (2) Issac, 1797, Samuel, 1798, and Rebekah, 1806, children of Thomas and Sarah Walder.

Buffard (1963) 65. Chambers II (1954) 111, Pl. facing 91. *Grace* (January 1991). Kensett (1921) 72. Maguire, L.J., *The Baptist Meeting House, Cuckfield. Trust Deeds 1772–1905*, General Baptist Assembly, occasional paper No. 3 (1988).

(35) CONGREGATIONAL (TQ 305247). Yellow brick with bands of red brick and stone dressings, gabled front with pointed-arched windows. Built 1869 by Charles G. Searle and Son replacing a chapel of 1828.

CYB (1870) 373.

DALLINGTON *East Sussex*

(36) CALVINISTIC INDEPENDENT (TQ 674196). 'Bethlehem Chapel', built 1866. Small timber-framed building with shingled walls and slate roof. Open-backed benches, hat-pegs around walls.

Chambers II (1954) 124.

DITCHLING
East Sussex

(37) GENERAL BAPTIST, The Twitten (TQ 327153). The church meeting here has been in existence since the late 17th century. By the beginning of the 18th century it had come to support the heterodox doctrines of Matthew Caffyn of Horsham and it has long accepted Unitarian beliefs. The present site, conveyed to trustees for unspecified purposes in 1740, comprised a cottage and garden; it is possible that the cottage may already have been in use as a meeting-place before the erection of the adjacent chapel.

General Baptist meeting-house, Ditchling. (37)

The chapel stands at the N end of a row of buildings aligned on a former footpath re-sited further E in the 19th century. Immediately S of the chapel is the cottage, which was extended to the S in 1808. The cottage is of two storeys with brick walls tile-hung to the upper storey, and a tiled roof. The chapel, reoriented in 1819, has brick walls laid to English bond, rendered to S and W, and a hipped tiled roof. The present front wall, which faces E, has a gabled porch of 1877 between two tall windows of which only the lower parts represent original openings. The earlier front, on the N side, has an original doorway, blocked in brickwork in 1819, between a pair of windows with wooden cross-frames, all with segmental-arched heads and in the S and E wall are each two windows of the same pattern.

The interior ($22\frac{1}{2}$ft by $33\frac{3}{4}$ft), largely refitted in 1877 and later, has an original gallery at the E end with panelled front and moulded cornice. The roof is supported by two trusses with king-posts and wavy braces.

Fittings – *Clock*: 18th-century, originally in a General Baptist chapel at Southwick, Wilts. (see *Nonconformist Chapels and Meeting-houses in South-west England* (1991) 237, monument (130)). *Communion Table*: oak, with turned legs and moulded stretchers, late 17th-century. *Monuments*: in chapel (1) Michael Marten, 1775, Elizabeth his widow, 1785, Peter their son, 1785, and five other children. Externally on N wall (2) decayed tablet, mid 18th-century; (3) Josiah Dancy, 1802, and Sarah his widow, 1813. In burial-ground S and W of chapel, several table-tombs and other monuments of 1730 and later including (4) Joseph Chatfield, 1781; (5) Samuel Thompson, 1837, tomb chest with splayed sides; a second burial-ground E of the chapel was acquired in 1821. *Seating*: in gallery, plain straight-backed pews.

Evans (1897) 72–3. Maguire, L.J., *Records of the Old Meeting House, Ditchling, Sussex* (3 vols, 1977–9).

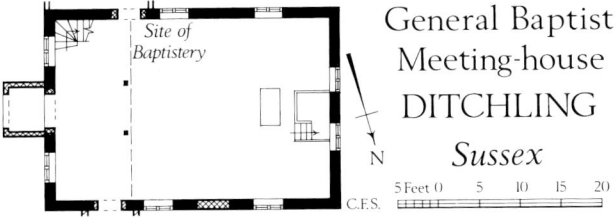

EAST GRINSTEAD
West Sussex

(38) ZION CHAPEL, West Street (TQ 394380). The chapel, of brick with a slate roof, was built in 1810 for the Countess of Huntingdon's Connexion. The original building, extended slightly to the NW, was square on plan with gabled bays centrally at two sides, each with a Venetian window below an enclosing arch, and a similar window at the SW end between two round-arched windows with intersecting glazing bars and date tablet above. (Chapel reported sold, 1980)

Zion Chapel, East Grinstead. (38)

HADLOW DOWN
East Sussex

(39) CALVINISTIC INDEPENDENT (TQ 532241). 'Providence Chapel' built in 1849 has a front of red brick of three bays with two tiers of windows below an open pediment supported by corner pilasters of brick with stone dressings. The side walls are of banded red and blue glazed brickwork. The interior is without galleries although of sufficient height to allow their insertion. (Chapel closed; damaged by storms, 1987)

Inscription: on roundel in front, name and date of chapel, and initials 'J.H. | M.' for James Hallett, minister.

Chambers II (1954) 125–6.

Providence Chapel, Hadlow Down. (39)

HAILSHAM — East Sussex

(40) STRICT BAPTIST (TQ 593093). The chapel of red brick with stone dressings was built c.1830 but greatly altered, refitted and reputedly encased in brickwork in 1909. The original early 19th-century galleries remain as does the pulpit, which incorporates a seat for the chapel clerk between two columns supporting the upper desk.

Chambers II (1954) 73–9, Pl. facing 58.

(41) STRICT BAPTIST, Magham Down (TQ 609115). 'Ebenezer Chapel' is a small building of 1846 with rendered walls. Plain open-backed benches.

Chambers II (1954) 80, Pl. facing 59.

HARTFIELD — East Sussex

(42) Former WESLEYAN (TQ 477355). Three-bay front of brick with stone dressings; round-arched doorway and windows, stone quoins and moulded pediment. Built c.1860, inscription tablet in pediment removed. (Converted to house)

HARTING — West Sussex

(43) Former MEETING-HOUSE, Mill Lane, South Harting (SU 789194). 'Rock Cottage' of clunch with brick dressings was built in 1800, probably for a newly formed Congregational church (see (44)) and converted to other use and extended after 1828. A central entrance has been blocked and moved to one side.

(44) CONGREGATIONAL, South Harting (SU 785196). Minimal Gothic, 1871 by G. Jenkins of Portsmouth, superseding and possibly on the site of a chapel of 1828 (see above). Brick with stone dressings and ventilating spirelet at apex of front gable.

CYB (1873) 426.

HASTINGS — East Sussex

(45) PARTICULAR BAPTIST, Ebenezer Street (TQ 828098). 'Ebenezer Chapel', first built in 1817 for seceders from 'Cow Lodge Chapel', Tackleway, was much enlarged in 1872, 1882 and 1886. Some brick walling remains from 1817 but this has been heightened and extended to the rear. The pedimented front, of the late 19th century, is rendered and has two tiers of sash windows and a central doorway.

Chambers II (1954) 50–2, Pl. facing 39.

(46) BAPTIST, Wellington Square (TQ 818095). The chapel, at the corner of Albert Road, was built in 1837–8. Stucco with moulded cornice and round-arched upper windows; basement rooms below.

BM XXX (1838) 214, 260–1, 539–40. Buffard (1963) 82.

(47) BAPTIST, Chapel Park Road, St Leonards (TQ 804095). Elaborate Italianate front of red brick with terracotta dressings; three bays with pedimented centre supported by paired Corinthian pilasters above wide balustraded porch. Built 1882–3, by Elworthy and Son.

B.Hbk (1885) 357–8.

Baptist chapel, Chapel Park Road, St Leonards. (47)

(48) THE TABERNACLE, Robertson Street (TQ 814094). Built 1854 for Calvinistic Independents. Gabled front of yellow brick with stone dressings; graduated lancet windows above central porch.

Chambers II (1954) 126.

(49) CONGREGATIONAL, Robertson Street (TQ 815094). The first chapel on this site, built in 1856–7, was superseded by the present building in 1884–5. This is a large neo-Classical building by Henry Ward, of stone with a wide frontage of five bays with dormers and a wider pedimented bay to the left. (URC)

CYB (1885) 252. New (1906).

(50) WESLEYAN, Cambridge Road/Robertson Street (TQ 813094). Stone with ashlar dressings, corner tower. Built 1875, by W.W. Pocock. (Demolition threatened, 1981)

Elleray (1981) 65, Pl. 135.

HEATHFIELD — East Sussex

(51) CALVINISTIC INDEPENDENT, Chapel Cross (TQ 614207). The church meeting here originated with the preaching of George Gilbert, 'the apostle of Sussex', for whom a chapel was built in 1770. The chapel was rebuilt on a larger scale in 1777 and replaced by the present building in 1809.

Calvinistic Independent chapel, Chapel Cross. (51)

The chapel stands within a large burial-ground. The S front, of brickwork in header bond, is partly rendered; it is of three bays below a gable with two tiers of sash windows with keystones and an oval window above a central porch. The rear wall on rising ground to the N has two doorways at gallery level and two pointed-arched pulpit windows between. The interior has a gallery around three sides with a panelled front and seven large box-pews to each side gallery, one at each end of the back gallery and a space between, probably the site of the singers' pew, but now reseated. The lower floor was refitted in the late 19th century.

Fittings – *Clock*: on rear gallery, signed 'Weston, Lewes'. *Monuments*: in chapel on N wall, pair of matching tablets flanking the pulpit, with kidney-shaped inscription panels, signed 'Harmer' (1) Rev. George Gilbert, 1827, 60 years pastor, and Ruth his widow, 1832, erected by their daughters; (2) Rev. John Press, 1846, 18 years co-pastor and 17 years pastor, and Rev. Joseph Ellson, 1877, 23 years pastor, dated 1878. In burial-ground to S, several headstones incorporating terracotta plaques by Jonathan Harmer (3) Elizabeth wife of John Pettit, 1820; (4) Hannah wife of Richard Goldsmith, early 19th-century; (5) Sarah wife of Jesse Smith, 1825. Also (6) 'martyrs' memorial', tall obelisk erected 1905 commemorating Richard Woodman and George Stevens of Warbleton, Margery Morris and James Morris her son, of Cade Street, Heathfield, and others, burnt to death at Lewes, 22 June 1557. *Pulpit*: hexagonal, with panelled sides and applied mouldings, early 19th-century. *Sundial*: in S gable, painted stone dial with iron gnomon, dated 1809 and inscribed 'Lat 51 Dec 26'.

Chambers II (1954) 59–60.

HELLINGLY — East Sussex

(52) ZOAR CHAPEL, Lower Dicker (TQ 568112). The Strict Baptist chapel was built in 1837 and much enlarged and altered in 1874 and 1880. The walls are of brickwork in Flemish bond with glazed headers but the N front of 1874 is rendered.

Chambers II (1954) 92–3, Pl. facing 63. Paul II (1954) 58–76, Pl. facing 72.

HENFIELD — West Sussex

(53) CONGREGATIONAL (TQ 215160). Brick and tile, built 1831–2, extended to the front c.1905 by E.J. Hamilton of Brighton.

CYB (1875) 329, obituary of George Hall; (1905) 130.

HERSTMONCEUX — East Sussex

(54) CONGREGATIONAL, Chapel Row (TQ 639121). The chapel, built in 1811 and extended to the rear by 12ft in the mid 19th century, has walls of brickwork in header bond with glazed headers and red brick dressings. The NW front of three bays has round-arched windows with intersecting glazing bars; above the slightly projecting centre bay is a small gable with oval date tablet and below is a gabled porch with three-centred arch over the doorway. The windows in the side walls are set in round-arched recesses, the windows at each end being blocked. A low Sunday-school building is attached to the NE side and beyond is a contemporary detached manse in a matching style.

The interior has a mid 19th-century gallery above the entrance with panelled front supported by two columns. Two tall columns support the roof structure on the line of extension. In 1971 the front of the original pulpit remained built into a later rostrum but all the seating had been replaced in the late 19th century. By 1994 the pulpit and the fixed seating had been removed.

Congregational Chapel, HERSTMONCEUX — Sussex

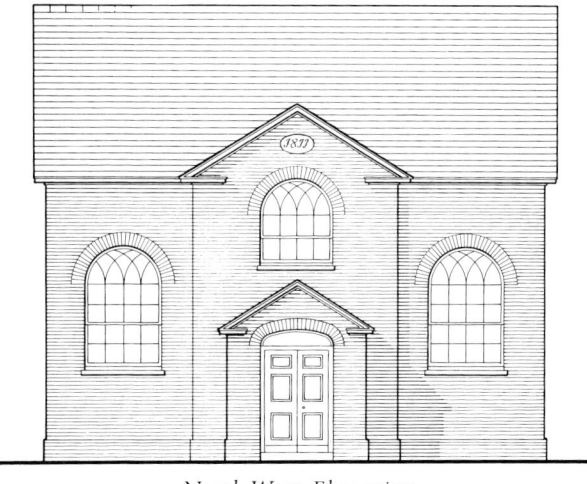

North-West Elevation

(55) FRIENDS, Gardiner Street (TQ 632127). The meeting-house, of brick with a tiled roof, was built in 1734. It originally comprised a rectangular building (28¼ft by 20ft) of a single storey of which the E end formed or became a cottage, now raised to two storeys; the meeting-house at the W end (15¾ft by 20ft) was enlarged to the N in 1897–8 with a gabled front and a central entrance. In the W wall of the original building is a blocked doorway with a stone tablet above inscribed 'B*H | 1734'.

Butler (1999) 605.

HORSHAM
West Sussex

(56) GENERAL BAPTIST, Worthing Road (TQ 169306). The congregation, now Unitarian, was in existence by 1645 with Samuel Lover as pastor. In that year a young student from Oxford, Matthew Caffyn, who had been relegated for adopting Baptist sentiments, joined the church and was soon engaged in preaching throughout the district. Caffyn was appointed one of the ministers of the church and exercised a considerable influence over many similar causes in this and the neighbouring counties. By 1686 Caffyn had begun to develop unorthodox beliefs which the General Baptist Assemby repeatedly refused to condemn. In 1696 the Assembly divided on the issue, a separate association being formed whose members only rejoined the parent body about 1734. The libertarian response of the Assembly to Caffyn's doctrinal position led to the acceptance of a rationalist and ultimately Unitarian theology in most of the older General Baptist churches, of which Matthew Caffyn's church at Horsham was amongst the first.

Little is known of the earlier meeting-places of this congregation, which drew its members from several surrounding villages, notably Billingshurst (9). The present chapel, on the W side of the road, stands on land acquired in 1720–1 and placed in trust for 'Anabaptists … maintaining the faith of General Redemption and the faith and practice of Believers' Baptism, and for such only'. In 1727 a porch was added to the front of the chapel and in 1752 a pulpit was introduced in place of a wider rostrum which had accommodated seven ministers or elders. In 1771 the need was felt for an internal baptistery which it was first intended to erect adjacent to the vestry on the W side. In the following year, however, additional land was acquired at the S end of the

General Baptist chapel, Horsham. (56)

General Baptist chapel, Horsham. (56)

meeting-house and the present baptistery and vestries were built upon it. Further land was bought in 1816 for the enlargement of the burial-ground. Various alterations were made internally during the 19th century, including the introduction of pews in 1838 presumably in place of open benches, and a drastic reorientation in 1867–72 involving the destruction of one gallery and further reseating. The present pews, introduced about 1970, were brought from Bowden Hill Chapel, Crediton, Devonshire (see *Nonconformist Chapels and Meeting-houses in South-west England* (1991) 68–71, monument (56)). In 1976 the large burial-ground S of the chapel was despoiled of most of its monuments.

The chapel has walls of brickwork and the hipped roof with concealed central valley is covered with local stone slates. The broad E front has a brick plinth above a stone levelling course and a platband between two tiers of windows. The porch was rebuilt in the late 19th century. The W wall, now covered by later building, has two semicircular-arched windows at mid height flanking the original site of the pulpit and two upper windows which lit the ends of the galleries. The N wall has a single window at the rear of the gallery and another below. The S end of the chapel, formerly fenestrated in like manner, is covered by the baptistery and vestries of 1772; these have a lean-to tiled roof with a central gable on the S side above a wide round-arched window with intersecting glazing bars.

The interior (27ft by 37ft) has a flat plaster ceiling. The roof structure is supported by two timber columns below the central valley which have moulded capitals and bases with square sub-bases. A gallery at the N end has a front of nine fielded panels supported by an octagonal post with shaped stops; a corresponding gallery at the S end has been removed. The baptistery room at the S end was converted to a chancel in 1867–72 with a semicircular-arched opening from the chapel. The room has a plaster barrel-vaulted ceiling and is flanked by two vestries or changing rooms.

Fittings – *Baptistery*: in floor at S end, brick-lined with four stone steps to S; water was supplied from a deep well in one of the adjacent rooms. *Benefaction Board*: modern tablet recording a bequest by Miss Elizabeth Gatford (1799?) of 5 guineas per annum to provide a weekly dole of bread. *Library*: numerous books, mainly secular, from the early 19th-century lending library, are inscribed 'Horsham General Baptist Book and Tract Society'. *Monuments*: in chapel (1) Thomas son of Richard and Ann Dendy, 1782, 'Student in Physic and Surgery'; (2) Walter Gatford, 1772, Mary his widow, 1784, and Elizabeth their daughter, 1799; (3) Peter Stepney, 1856; (4) Rebecca Dendy, 1836; (5) Rev. Robert Ashdowne, 1861, 30 years minister; (6) John Dendy, 1782, surgeon, and Jane his widow, 1799. Externally, on S wall (7–9) three tablets, reset, including Ann Dendy, 1777. N of porch (10) headstone, re-sited, inscribed 'IN Memory of Mr Nicholas Hayler who died April Y^e 22nd 1734 : He left this Burying Place & House & orchard adjoining to Y^e Peopel Assembling in this Place'; (11) John Dendy, 1724, surgeon, *et al.* N of chapel (12) Richard Browne, 178[.], table-tomb with fluted and gadrooned sides. *Plate*: includes a set of four two-handled cups of 1781, also a Gothic standing cup of 1840 from Bowden Hill Chapel, Devonshire (*see* above). *Seating*: in gallery, some 18th-century box-pews.

Crosby IV (1740) 328–30. Evans (1897) 105–7. Kensett (1921). Maguire, L.J. (ed.), *Records of the General Baptist Meeting House, Horsham, Sussex* (2 vols, 1981–2). Taylor (1818) I: 293. *UHST* I (1917–18) 10–22; VII (1939–42) 68–9.

(57) REHOBOTH CHAPEL, New Street (TQ 178304). The Strict Baptist chapel built in 1834 has been extended to the rear. The walls are of brickwork; the front wall is gabled, of three bays with two tiers of round-arched windows. Interior reseated in the late 19th century. *Monuments*: wall monument in chapel and headstone in rear burial-ground to Edward Mote, 1874, 26 years pastor.

Chambers II (1954) 118–20. Pl. facing 110.

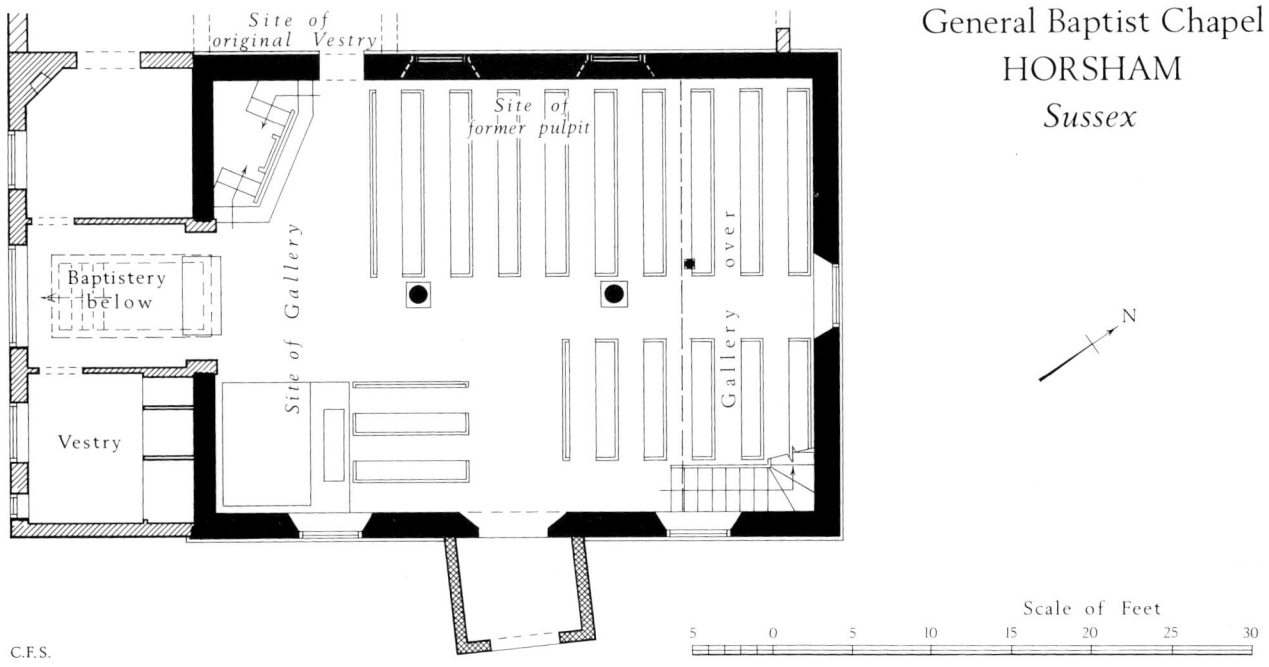

General Baptist Chapel
HORSHAM
Sussex

(58) FRIENDS, Worthing Road (TQ 168305). A meeting-house built in 1693 was superseded in 1786 by the present building on a nearby site. This has walls of red brick, laid to Flemish bond at the front but in English bond with glazed headers at the sides. The roof is hipped and tiled. The SE front has a central entrance with later porch between two round-arched windows. There is one matching window on the SW side wall. A cottage contemporary with the meeting-house adjoins the NE side.

The interior ($30\frac{1}{2}$ ft by $27\frac{1}{2}$ ft) is tall and has a flat ceiling. The walls have a horizontally boarded dado and fixed wall benches. The stand at the NW end has been partly dismantled.

Coffin Stools: two, with turned legs and moulded upper rails, early 18th-century. *Seating*: open-backed benches with turned supports to arm-rests, late 18th-century and after.

Butler (1999) 605–6. Marsh and Marsh (1886) 26–7.

HOVE   *East Sussex*

(59) BAPTIST, Holland Road (TQ 296047). The chapel of 1887 by John Wills is a large building of stone in the Gothic style. It has a tall corner tower and short spire, gabled transept and attached Sunday-school. The project was supported and financed by George Congreve, a manufacturer of cough mixture.

Baptist Times (5 May 1988). *B.Hbk* (1884) 355–6. Elleray (1981) 68, Pl. 153.

ICKLESHAM   *East Sussex*

(60) WESLEYAN, Icklesham (TQ 877164). Small brick chapel of 1843 with two pointed-arched windows facing the road. Entrance in gable end covered by modern annexe.

(61) METHODIST, Winchelsea (TQ 903174). The chapel of brick with a tiled mansard roof is attached to the back of an earlier house. The chapel was built in 1785 and may be the 'New erected house called Evens's Chapel' registered for dissenters in October 1786. The W front has a segmental-arched doorway between two windows with altered frames; there are two sash windows in the E wall. The interior ($20\frac{3}{4}$ ft by 27ft) has an original pulpit immediately opposite the entrance and an early 19th-century gallery at the N end with plain benches without backs. The tie-beam of one roof truss comes behind the gallery front. *Pulpit*: square with fielded-panelled sides, backboard with two arched panels and moulded cornice, late 18th-century.

Dolbey (1964) 97–8. *WHSP* XIII (1921–2) 135–8.

Baptist chapel, Holland Road, Hove.   (59)

Methodist chapel, Winchelsea.   (61)

LEWES
East Sussex

(62) Former GENERAL BAPTIST, Eastport Lane (TQ 414098). The congregation formerly meeting here may have been in existence by the late 17th century in connection with the Ditchling church. By the early 19th century, in common with similar congregations in the county, this had accepted a Unitarian theology and in 1825 it united with the society meeting in Westgate chapel (67). The chapel subsequently served a variety of users including the Salvation Army. (Converted to private house since 1972)

Former GENERAL BAPTIST MEETING-HOUSE, LEWES   CFS 1972

The chapel, built in 1741, has walls of flint with red brick dressings; the roof is hipped and covered with tiles. The broad N front facing the lane has a modern porch covering the entrance, between two segmental-arched windows having original sashes with wide softwood glazing bars and formerly with external shutters; to the right is a small window inserted to light a later gallery. The S wall is similarly fenestrated and has an inserted doorway. The W wall is blank except for a later chimney-stack; the E wall has been partly rebuilt to allow the insertion of a flue but traces remain of two tall windows which may have flanked the pulpit.

The interior ($27\frac{1}{4}$ft by $17\frac{3}{4}$ft) retains no original fittings. At the W end, below the site of the gallery, is a small fireplace, and another at the opposite end with circular paterae of the early 19th century.

Inscriptions: externally above original entrance, stone tablet inscribed 'The First Stone | Laid May Y^e 14 | 1741'; on a square panel of bricks in rear wall:

IS 1741; MH 1741; AC; AH 1741; MC; H; H 1741; HH 1741
Monuments: Keeble (1934) op. cit. below records 'at the rear is the old burying ground with its interesting gravestones and quaint inscriptions'; in 1972 this was entirely covered with concrete although a few early 19th-century headstones had been reset at the W end.

Horsfield I (1824) 304–5. Keeble, E.B., *'These Hundred and Fifty Years': The Story of Lewes Baptists, Third Jubilee – 1784–1934* (1934) 2.

(63) BAPTIST, Eastgate Street (TQ 417104). The Particular Baptist meeting was commenced in 1784 by Joseph Middleton formerly minister at the Countess of Huntingdon's chapel. Services were first held in the former Friends' meeting-house of 1752, which was purchased; from 1785 this was replaced by a timber-framed chapel in Foundry Lane which had a broad front of three bays. The first chapel on the present site was built or converted in 1819 and superseded by the existing building in 1843.

The chapel, of flint with dressings of yellow brick and stone, with Romanesque detail, has a gabled front and corner tower. The top of the tower was rebuilt in 1915.

Monument: externally on front wall, Rev. John Daymond Ellis, 1845, 10 years missionary in India.

BM XXXV (1843) 371, 583–4. *B.Hbk* (1879) 161, obituary of W.K. Armstrong. Chambers II (1954) 43. Horsfield I (1824) 305–6. Keeble (1934) op. cit.

(64) JIREH CHAPEL, Malling Street (TQ 421104). The origin of the society of Calvinistic Independents in Lewes is to be found in the Countess of Huntingdon's chapel at The Cliffe, built in 1775 (closed *c.*1879 and since demolished). Following the withdrawal in 1784 of the minister, Joseph Middleton, to form a Baptist congregation a former student from the Countess's college at Trevecca, Jenkin Jenkins, was appointed to the charge. In 1792 Jenkins became acquainted with William Huntington, then exercising a popular if eccentric ministry in London at Providence Chapel, Titchfield Street, and adopted his more radical Calvinistic position. In 1805 the trustees of the Cliffe chapel felt obliged to remove Jenkins who, with his supporters, immediately commenced the erection of Jireh Chapel on a site about 200 yards NW of the former. The new chapel, opened by William Huntington on 7 July 1805, was greatly enlarged in 1826 by extension to the front, and refitted internally including the refashioning of the galleries and the provision of a more elaborate ceiling. The formal organization of the church dates from 1821.

Jireh chapel is an exceptionally complete and unspoilt example of early 19th-century chapel architecture. Built by the adherents of an attractive and uncompromising preacher, and enlarged after his death for an even larger auditory, it combines the simplicity of scrubbed pitch-pine pews, dominant pulpit and clerk's desk with the colonnaded side galleries and vaulted nave of more sophisticated buildings. A severely plain exterior contrasts strongly with the architectural quality within.

The funeral of William Huntington SS in 1813 presented a like contrast. Huntington was buried without religious ceremony in a plain tomb behind the chapel and he wrote his own flamboyant epitaph, which is inscribed upon it. The simple burial was preceded by an elaborate and lengthy funeral procession from Tunbridge Wells; the hearse and six was followed by seven mourning coaches including his own carriage painted with the initials 'W.H.,S.S.' and many other private carriages and horsemen. Huntington explained his use of the initials 'SS': 'As I cannot get a D.D. for want of cash neither can I get an M.A. for want of learning, therefore I am compelled to fly for refuge to S.S., by which I mean "Sinner Saved".' The initials 'W.A.', which appear on a tablet in the front wall after the name of Jenkin Jenkins, recall Huntington's habit of referring to the latter as the 'Welsh Ambassador'.

The chapel stands E of the town on a site much exposed by road development in recent years. The walls are of timber-framed construction on a brick base and are covered on the N and E sides

Exterior, before alteration to forecourt.

Jireh Chapel, Lewes.

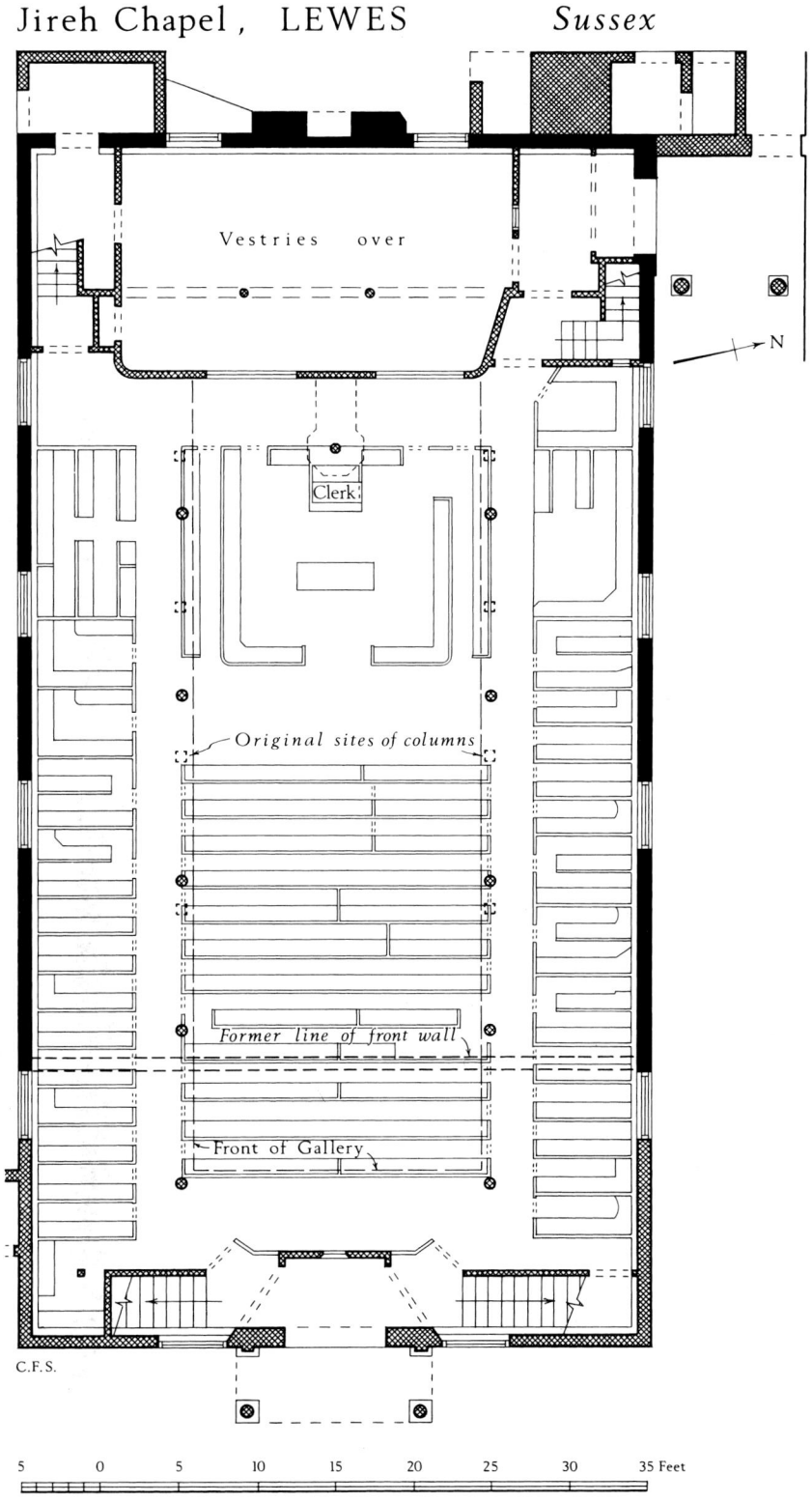

Jireh Chapel, LEWES *Sussex*

by mathematical tiles, on the S by slate-hanging and on the W by plain tiles; the roof is slated. The windows throughout are in two tiers with plain hung sashes. The E front of 1826 is of three bays with a central porch having two Tuscan columns formerly carrying a pedimented roof. In the gable is a small circular window with reset date tablet above. The N and S walls have four bays of windows; the line of enlargement to the front is marked by a joint in the brick plinth. The W end has a substantial brick chimney-stack at the centre; minor offices formerly adjacent have been demolished. A Sunday-school of 1874, N of the chapel (demolished c.1990), was linked to it by a pedimented porch with two columns which previously stood in front of the adjacent chapel doorway. The chapel was severely damaged by a storm in 1987, works of repair and rehabilitation were completed in 1996.

The interior (originally 59ft by 38½ft, extended to the front by 18ft) remains largely at it was left in 1826. The walls have a boarded dado and rails with hat-pegs. There is a gallery around four sides with plain panelled front supported on N and S by colonnades of five timber columns with moulded capitals which continue above as slender columns with enriched capitals supporting the roof structure. The pulpit at the W end, with clerk's desk and railed communion area below, is approached directly from the W gallery. Gallery staircases are placed in all four corners of the chapel (the SW staircase was removed c.1980). At the W end on the lower floor is a large vestry with shutters opening to the chapel; above it are two smaller vestries, the minister's vestry to the N having a fireplace with a basket hob-grate of the early 19th century. The ceiling of the chapel has a plaster barrel-vault between the colonnades and a flat ceiling over the side galleries; the vault is pierced by two domical recesses for light fittings. The roof is supported by four original trusses, three of which have been altered for the insertion of the vault, and two later trusses with scissor braces.

Fittings – *Clock*: on front of S gallery, with circular brass dial, signed 'Harben, Lewes', early 19th-century (stolen c.1980). *Inscription*: in E gable, reset stone tablet inscribed 'JIREH CHAPEL | erected | by J. JENKINS W.A. | with the | Voluntary Contributions | of the CITIZENS of ZION | ANNO DOMI: MDCCCV'. *Library*: in upper N vestry, small lending library of miscellaneous volumes, 19th-century.

Monument: in yard W of chapel, over vault, large, plain stone tomb with coped top inscribed to: Rev. Jenkin Jenkins, 1810, pastor; William Huntington, 1813; Thomas Hooper, 1830, Mary his widow, 1833, and Mary their daughter, 1810; Thomas Marchant, 1832, and Ann his widow, 1847; Rev. John Vinall, 1860, 45 years minister, Ann his first wife, 1823, Benjamin their son, 1856, and Anna, 1851, second wife of John Vinall. Huntington's memorial is inscribed:

> Here lies the Coal Heaver who departed this life July 1 1813 in the 69th year of his age beloved of his God but abhored of men. The Omniscient Judge at the Grand Assize shall ratify and confirm this to the confusion of many thousands for England and its Metropolis shall know that there hath been a prophet among them. W.H.S.S. Dictated by himself a few days previous to his death.

Painting: in minister's vestry, portrait in oils of the Rev. William Huntington, 1774–1813; also two portraits of Huntington and Jenkin Jenkins, engraved by James Fittler after paintings by R. Bowyer and J.F. Burrell. *Pitchpipe*: mahogany, early 19th-century. *Plate*: pair of pewter cups and flagon, early 19th-century (stolen c.1980). *Pulpit*: octagonal with reeded-panelled sides and flared base on octagonal stem, bridge access from W gallery; plain-panelled clerk's desk in front. *Seating*: below side galleries, numbered box-pews, sides 3ft 9in. high; in central space backless benches with added backs, and open-backed benches, converted to box-pews; in gallery, box-pews.

Chambers II (1954) 43–4, 127. *EM* XIII (1805) 476; XXI (1813) 316. North, J.E., *A History of Jireh Chapel, Lewes* (1996). Stell, C.F., *The World of Interiors* (January 1988) 124–7. Wright (1909) 98, 212–14, 270–2.

(65) FRIENDS, Friars Walk (TQ 418101). A meeting-house in Puddlewharf was acquired in 1675 and rebuilt in 1752. In 1784 this was sold to Particular Baptists and the present building erected on a new site. This is partly of timber construction on a brick base and faced in front with mathematical tiles; the roof is covered with slates. The front wall faces SE and has a wide pedimented porch of the mid 19th century covering a pair of doorways. To the right are two windows to the principal room with three-centred arched heads and hung sashes. An earlier or intended entrance appears to have been sited between these windows, of which some evidence remains in the plinth. To the left of the porch is a third window, formerly a doorway, and another window above to an upper room. The SW end wall is gabled and partly tile-hung, with a brick chimney-stack and two tiers of windows to the left. The NW rear wall is partly covered by later building. A cottage built 1801 attached to the NE has stone steps leading to a former upper school-room. Beyond the meeting-house is a coach-house with an iron-framed lunette window in the gable wall facing the burial-ground.

The interior of the meeting-house (43½ft average length by 20ft) comprises a large meeting-room with coved ceiling cornice and a smaller room to the SW with a room above having an original fireplace. The larger room formerly had a line of shutters near the

Friends' meeting-house, Lewes. (65)

SW end separating the room from a through passage with a gallery over. Fragments of the stand remain at the NE end.

Monuments: in burial-ground, uniform headstones of the 19th century and later with some earlier dates including (1) John Rickman, 1789; (2) Elizabeth Rickman, 1795.

Butler (1999) 607–9.

(66) Former WESLEYAN, Railway Street (TQ 416101). Brick with four-light plate-traceried window in front gable. Built 1867, adjacent Sunday-school 1874. (Now in commercial use)

(67) WESTGATE CHAPEL (TQ 413099). The congregation meeting here originated in two societies gathered by two local rectors, Edward Newton of St Mary, Westout, with St John's, Southover, and Walter Postlethwaite of St Michael's, Lewes, ejected respectively in 1662 and 1660. The society gathered by Edward Newton, which was Presbyterian, fitted up a meeting-house *c.*1687 in Crown Lane (Market Lane). The other society was Congregational. In 1695 Thomas Barnard was appointed assistant minister to the flourishing Presbyterian society whose need for larger premises resulted in the purchase by Barnard of a house on the present site, adjacent to the West Gate. He converted this building to a meeting-house, retaining it as his own personal property until 1719 when it was placed in trust. Barnard's action was considered precipitate and was opposed by Newton whose supporters continued to use the Lower Meeting-house in Crown Lane, subsequently removing to Watergate Lane, until 1759 when they reunited with the seceders at Westgate. Barnard's faction at the Upper Meeting (Westgate Chapel) constituted the major part of the Presbyterian society, although after separation they were designated Independent. Meanwhile Postlethwaite's Congregationalists continued to meet separately under a pastoral succession of three further ejected ministers until, in 1711, they united with Barnard's society under a joint pastorate. The reunion of the two sections of the Presbyterian society in 1759 was followed in 1825 by a further accession of members from the General Baptist church in Eastport Lane (62), which like the Westgate society had by then become Unitarian.

The chapel incorporates part of the structure of the house purchased by Barnard in 1695, another portion of which to the N became the Bull Inn (now Bull House). The house was built *c.*1595 for George Goring of Danny. Several late 16th-century features including a blocked doorway and traces of windows remain in the E wall facing Bull Lane. Conversion to a meeting-house *c.*1700 involved some rebuilding including the addition of a range parallel to and N of the existing S range, resulting in a typical double-pile structure with two parallel roofs supported by a pair of timber posts. Major repairs were carried out in 1843 when most of the S wall was rebuilt, a third post introduced below the roof, some windows renewed and the interior generally refitted. In 1913 the chapel was further altered by R.P. Jones when it was subdivided along the line of posts, the S half remaining as a chapel, but again

Westgate Chapel, Lewes. Interior before 1913.

refitted and realigned E instead of S, the N half becoming a meeting-room and common entrance.

The N wall facing towards High Street is partly covered by Bull House and is approached through a narrow courtyard. The E wall facing Bull Lane, partly of flint with stone dressings, retains one doorway with four-centred arched head and a blocked window to its left with brick jambs, both of 16th-century date. The left-hand half of this wall is gabled and represents one end of the original house; of that period, one three-light mullioned attic window remains with a large mullioned and transomed window below and traces of blocked windows to the basement. The right-hand half of this elevation has a hipped roof; the wall sets back at mid-height and is tile-hung, with a large wooden mullioned and transomed window probably of 1843 but matching the other in its general proportions. The S wall, much rebuilt in 1843, has two stone mullioned and transomed windows with iron lattice frames, and a lean-to vestry.

The interior (40ft by 52ft) now comprises a chapel to the S and meeting-room to the N separated by a wall incorporating the two original timber posts of the meeting-house and a third of cast iron added in 1843. The pulpit originally against the S wall was altered in 1843 to front a recess in the wall probably approached directly from the external vestry but subsequently lowered.

Fittings – *Books*: in vestry, substantial ministerial library of the early 19th century. *Clock*: in N room, circular dial and kidney-shaped pendulum case, signed 'Notman, Lewes', late 18th-century. *Font*: octagonal Gothic column, mid 19th-century. *Hatchment*: in chapel, with arms of Francis, 5th Lord Napier, of Corsica Hall, Ringmer, Sussex, 1773, impaling those of his first and second wives. *Monuments*: in chapel (1) Thomas Walker Horsfield FSA, minister 1817–27, erected 1927; (2) to several ejected ministers, erected 1927. *Pulpit*: polygonal with bolection-moulded panels, 18th-century, on modern base; hexagonal canopy with inlaid star on soffit, reused inverted in table top, c.1700.

CHST V (1911–12) 175–7. Connell, J.M., *The Story of an Old Meeting House* (1916). Evans (1897) 130–1. Horsfield I (1824) 302–4. UHST I (1917–18) 177–90; VII (1939–42) 187.

LINCHMERE *West Sussex*

(68) INDEPENDENT, Hammer (SU 875322). One of three chapels (*see* also Hindhead and Churt, Surrey (34, 35)) erected at the expense of John Grover, a builder, for Congregationalists. The chapel opened in 1903 stands on a sloping site and has rooms beneath. Red brick with large lunette windows in gabled ends. Bricks in weathering of buttresses stamped 'Grover, Haslemere'.

Cleal (1908) 437. *CYB* (1905) 130.

LITTLEHAMPTON *West Sussex*

(69) FRIENDS, Church Street (TQ 031021). The meeting-house occupies the former premises of a 'penny school' built 1836, subsequently used by the Brethren and acquired by Friends in 1965. The walls are faced with cobbles and have dressings of red brick. The building comprised a school-room with two pointed-arched windows in the S wall and a doorway to the left, together with a master's house attached as a wing at the E end.

Butler (1999) 610.

LOXWOOD *West Sussex*

(70) 'EMMANUEL FELLOWSHIP', Spy Lane (TQ 041319). The principal chapel of the Society of Dependents or 'Cokelers', built c.1862, is a small building in red Flemish bond brickwork with dark glazed headers. The front is gabled with a small porch and a circular window in the gable. The original chapel, three bays in length, has been twice extended to the rear. The former rear wall has been replaced by a shuttered partition. To the S of the chapel is a former shelter for horses or vehicles, now enclosed.

At the rear is a large burial-ground with stones indicating grave alignments but without any monuments.

Scott (1949) 81–8.

MIDHURST *West Sussex*

(71) Former BAPTIST, Bepton Road (SU 882212). The chapel opened on 12 September 1833 has been greatly altered for use as a Masonic hall. The walls are of brickwork with a rendered pedimented front formerly having a circular window above the entrance. *Monuments*: in burial-ground, have mostly been lifted and stacked.

BM XXV (1833) 518.

NEWHAVEN *East Sussex*

(72) Former BAPTIST CHAPEL, South Road (TQ 446012). Rendered front of three bays with pointed-arched windows and vestigial buttresses. Foundation stones dated ?1865. Architect W.S. Parnacott. (Now a boys' club)

Buffard (1963) 119–20.

(73) Former CONGREGATIONAL, Meeching Rise (TQ 445012). The first chapel built in 1797 was superseded in 1865–6 by the present building designed by Horatio N. Goulty of Brighton. This has a rendered pedimented front of three bays with a central arched entrance and arched recesses in the flanking bays with small circular windows above. Closed c.1950. (Derelict and interior gutted 1971)

CYB (1866) 332; (1890) 203–4, obituary of Rev. John Williams.

(74) Former WESLEYAN, Chapel Street (TQ 447013). Gabled brick front with circular window over entrance. Foundation stones laid on 24 May 1893, one by W. Wilmer Pocock. Architect Charles Bell. Closed 1970.

NEWICK *East Sussex*

(75) ZION CHAPEL (TQ 411214). Strict Baptist chapel built 1834, of brick with gabled front, original porch dated 1834 between two tall round-arched windows.

Chambers II (1954) 109–10.

NINFIELD *East Sussex*

(76) NAZARINE CHAPEL (TQ 707125). The Calvinistic Independent chapel, built in 1831 at the cost of George Davey, is a small timber-framed building in part rendered and in part tile-hung. The interior has a segmental barrel-vaulted ceiling. The pulpit at the W end is a plain box with shaped back-board of the early 19th century and has a communion pew in front. The walls are lined with a double row of hat-pegs. The chapel was repaired and probably reseated in 1878.

Chambers II (1954) 128. Paul II (1954) 48–57.

(77) Former WESLEYAN, Russell's Green (TQ 701113). Small building of brick with hipped slate roof; originally of two bays, dated 1832 on defaced tablet, and extended by one bay in the later 19th century. A later chapel that stood to the NE suffered wartime damage and has been demolished.

NORTHCHAPEL *West Sussex*

(78) Former DEPENDENTS, Petworth Road (SU 951292). The chapel set back on the W side of the road has stone walls with brick dressings and a slate roof. It is four bays in length and has a gabled front with a small circular window above a brick porch. Date tablet in rear wall inscribed 'MAY 29 W+T 1972'. (Closed *c.*1988, now used for storage)

Scott (1949) 81–8.

Former Dependents' chapel, Northchapel.   (78)

NORTHIAM *East Sussex*

(79) GENERAL BAPTIST, Dixter Road (TQ 824250). The congregation gathered in or about 1796 owes its origin to the influence of William Vidler, minister at Battle, whose religious outlook it adopted. The first Baptist meeting-house on this site was a timber-framed building registered in 1795. An attempt to enlarge this in 1810 by raising the whole structure by 3ft resulted in its collapse and the erection of its successor. This is a small building of brick with a tiled mansard roof half-hipped at each end. The broad front faces SE, and has a round-arched doorway at the centre with tablet above dated 1810 between two windows, each of three graduated lancets. Two windows in the NW wall have wooden frames with mullions and transoms.

General Baptist chapel, Northiam.   (79)

The interior (39½ft by 19ft) has no gallery, the walls have a dado of early 19th-century fielded panels with moulded capping. Pews and pulpit date from a late 19th-century refitting.

Monuments: in small burial-ground to NE (1) 'Elliss' wife of William Hanson, 1812, with oval terracotta inset by Harmer; (2) William Hanson, 1868, and Mary his second wife, 1868. (*see also* Packer (1988) op. cit. below.)

Monthly Repository V (1810) 569. Packer, B., *Planted by Vidler: Northiam Unitarian Chapel, A History* (1988).

(80) Former WESLEYAN, Dixter Road (TQ 825249). Rendered pedimented front of three bays with round-arched doorway and windows; tile-hung sides, extended to rear. Small oval tablet above entrance inscribed 'Wesleyan Chapel'. Opened 1814. (Closed since 1974 and converted to commercial use; front openings replaced by shop front)

PETT *East Sussex*

(81) MOUNT CALVARY (TQ 870140). Small, brick Bible Christian chapel of 1848 with three-bay gabled front, much extended to one side in 1956. *Monument*: in burial-ground, to Delias wife of Richard Dowm, Bible Christian minister, daughter of James and Delias Woodcock of St Martins, Isles of Scilly, 1864, and Emily her daughter, 1864.

PETWORTH *West Sussex*

(82) EBENEZER CHAPEL, Park Road (SU 976217). The Calvinistic Independent chapel, now Strict Baptist, was built in 1887 for a congregation derived from an earlier cause which had met in a chapel in Golden Square. Red brick, three-bay gabled front.

Chambers II (1954) 121.

(83) Former CONGREGATIONAL, East Street (SU 978218). The Congregational church recorded in its return to the 1851 religious census that their chapel built in 1819 had been lost to them in 1849 and meetings were being held in 'a very small place'. The former chapel in East Street, dated 1819, has a front of yellow brick with a former pedimental gable, now heightened, and three round-arched upper windows. The lower part is obscured by an extension reusing an original doorway with rusticated stone surround and pediment. Tablet in front gable flanked by scrolls and inscribed with date 1819. Original railings in front with crescent finials.

Vickers (ed.) (1989) 128.

SUSSEX 354

(84) CONGREGATIONAL, Golden Square (SU 977216). Random rubble and tile in Gothic style with corner turret having octagonal wooden upper stage and spire. Built *c*.1860 with Sunday-school added 1889. (URC)

POYNINGS *West Sussex*

(85) ZION CHAPEL (TQ 262120). Strict Baptist chapel, brick and flint, partly rendered, with plain pedimented front dated 1843.
Chambers II (1954) 40.

RYE *East Sussex*

(86) Former BAPTIST, Mermaid Street (TQ 91952025). 'Quakers' House', on the S side of the street, stands on the site of a Friends' meeting-house built in 1700. In 1753 the meeting-house, described as being in a 'very dilapidated condition and past hope of repair', was sold to a newly formed body of Particular Baptists. It was then demolished and replaced by the present building, opened 1754, which remained in use until a new chapel was erected in Cinque Ports Street in 1909, the former chapel being converted to a private house with the addition of floors and dormer windows in the roof.

The walls are of brickwork and the roof is tiled to the rear but covered with slates in front. The front wall (29½ft wide) is of three bays with two tiers of segmentally arched windows and hung sashes separated by a platband. The wide central entrance, approached by a double flight of steps from the street, has double doors and is covered by a flat canopy on shaped brackets. The back wall has two segmentally arched windows at mid-height flanking the site of the pulpit and a small gabled projection between which may have served as a vestry.

Butler (1999) 610. Chambers II (1954) 54–5. Ivimey IV (1830) 538–9.

(87) Former INDEPENDENT, Watchbell Street (TQ 92052020). Seceders from the Baptist church, with their minister Thomas Purdy, set up a separate meeting in his house in 1813. The chapel, built after Purdy's death in 1817, has brick walls and a hipped tiled roof. The front is of three bays, partly masked by an earlier building, with two tiers of round-arched windows separated by a stone platband, and a central entrance with fanlight. The chapel yard in front is entered between a pair of brick gate piers with stone caps and ball finials. (Closed before 1949; now in secular use)

Chambers II (1954) 55. *CYB* (1874) 338–9, obituary of W.D. Jenkyn.

FORMER INDEPENDENT CHAPEL, RYE — C.F.S. 1971

SALEHURST *East Sussex*

(88) STRICT BAPTIST CHAPEL, High Street, Robertsbridge (TQ 738237). Gabled brick front with central entrance and two pointed-arched windows with Y-tracery in wood frames; tile hanging at side. Tablet in front gable inscribed 'Bethel 1842'.
Chambers II (1954) 88–9.

(89) CONGREGATIONAL, High Street, Robertsbridge (TQ 738236). Front of brick with terracotta dressings. Three principal bays with central pediment flanked by balustrade with urns. Round-arched windows, paired above entrance. Built 1881, by Thomas Elworthy. (URC)

SEAFORD *East Sussex*

(90) CONGREGATIONAL, Clinton Place (TV 483992). Simple Gothic chapel of 1877–8 by W.F. Poulton. Flint with ashlar dressings, lancet windows and corner turret rising from a pair of buttresses with an octagonal timber upper stage and shingled spirelet. Interior partly refitted. Roof supported by partly exposed trusses with columnar king-posts, queen-posts and paired collars. (URC)

Monument: in chapel, to Rev. James Ransom Cooper, 1867, 7 years pastor. *Ventilators*: by Shillito and Shorland.

CYB (1878) 422–3; (1887) 201–3, obituary of Edwin Green.

Former Baptist chapel, Mermaid Street, Rye. (86)

SELSEY — West Sussex

(91) BIBLE CHRISTIAN, High Street (SZ 854935). Walls faced in front with knapped flint and at sides with pebbles; gault brick dressings. Gabled front and plain lancet windows; dated 1867.

SLAUGHAM — West Sussex

(92) ZOAR CHAPEL, Handcross (TQ 262299). Strict Baptist, built 1887 to replace a timber-framed chapel of 1782. Red brick with white brick dressings.

Chambers II (1954) 6–9.

STEYNING — West Sussex

(93) Former FRIENDS, Horsham Road (TQ 174116). The meeting-house, now 'Penn's House', was an existing timber-framed building purchased and converted by Quakers in 1678. It comprises a meeting-house to the S and a cottage to the north. The former (15¾ft by 27ft) is of three bays of which the E wall retains elements of the original timber-framing. The W wall facing the road is now of rubble with brick dressings and has a blocked doorway near the S end. The S wall is of late 17th-century brickwork. The roof over the former meeting-house is supported by two trusses with tie-beams and collars, that over the cottage has common rafters with collars to each pair.

The building passed into use as a Methodist school about 1843 and was later sold for conversion to cottages.

Butler (1999) 610–11.

(94) Former CHAPEL, Jarvis Lane (TQ 179111). The meeting-house now used by Plymouth Brethren is probably Trinity Chapel referred to in the 1851 census returns as erected in 1835 by the Countess of Huntingdon's Connexion which passed into Wesleyan

Former Friends meeting-house, Steyning. CFS.1971

use in 1841. It has a rendered front of three bays with a pediment and two round-arched windows.

Vickers (ed.) (1989) 114.

THAKEHAM — West Sussex

(95) FRIENDS, 'BLUE IDOL' (TQ 107232). A meeting held until 1682 at the house of John Snashold was then transferred to the houses of William Penn and John Shaw. Penn had been living at Warminghurst on the estate of his wife Gulielma since 1677 where he remained until 1696, though absent in America from 1682 to 1684. Shaw had property at Shipley and it was as the 'Shipley meeting' that in 1691 a more permanent meeting-house was sought. Shaw accordingly offered the tenement known as 'Little Slatter', 2½ miles W of Shipley, for conversion to a meeting-house and the work appears to have been completed by 1693. The Thakeham meeting, as it was eventually called, suffered a marked decline in

Friends' meeting-house, 'Blue Idol', Thakeham. (95)

membership in the following century and from 1791 until 1874 only very occasional meetings were held. It is thought that the name 'Blue Idol' (i.e. 'Idle' meaning 'empty house') dates from this period. A more regular use of the building was then resumed and the adjacent cottage, which forms an integral part of the building, was variously altered or enlarged to provide accommodation for visitors. An additional wing was built at the N end in 1934–5.

The meeting-house stands on a secluded site on the E side of a lane ¼ mile E of Balls Green. The walls are timber-framed with rendered infilling clad on the S in painted weather-boarding; the roof is covered with Horsham slates. The building dates from the 16th century and comprises the original house of two storeys with a brick chimney-stack at the N end, and a cross wing at the S end of two storeys and attic of which the two principal storeys were conflated on conversion to a meeting-house. The W wall of this wing has a tall central window of *c.*1691. The entrance is in the S wall with a small window over and a dormer window in the roof. A brick chimney-breast projects to the right of the entrance.

The interior of the S wing (approximately 17ft by 28ft), now the meeting-house, which is of three bays, was converted by the removal of the timbers of the first floor in the centre and W bays leaving the upper floor of the E bay to serve as a gallery. The gallery has a plain panelled front; the mortices for the former floor joists remain visible in the beam below. The stand is irregularly sited in the NW corner of the room facing the entrance.

Fittings – *Ephemera*: printed proclamation 'Prohibiting all unlawful, and seditious Meetings and Conventicles under pretence of Religious Worship' dated 10 January 1660/1, concerning 'Anabaptists and Quakers and Fifth-Monarchy Men'. *Seating*: one open-backed bench with arms and turned supports, late 18th-century; others later. *Stand*: with boarded back and plain balustraded front, 19th-century.

Butler (1999) 611–13. Lidbetter (1961) Fig. 27, Pls XXXIX, XL. Marsh and Marsh (1886) 30–9. P[ierce], J.H., *Thakeham Meeting House and the Blue Idol Guest House* (1981).

UCKFIELD *East Sussex*

(96) BAPTIST (TQ 476218). The first chapel was built in 1788–9 for Strict Baptist seceders from an Independent meeting at Five Ash Down (22). This was replaced in 1874 by the present chapel of brick with round-arched windows and wavy barge-boards above the gable-end entrance.

Chambers II (1954) 95.

WADHURST *East Sussex*

(97) REHOBOTH CHAPEL, Pell Green (TQ 645332). The chapel built in 1824 for a Strict Baptist church formed in 1818 was enlarged in 1828, 1831 and 1841. The walls are timber-framed and weather-boarded and the roof is slated. The chapel was originally of three bays with a central doorway in the longer S wall facing the street between a pair of round-arched windows with hung sashes and external shutters (since removed). It was extended to the W by a further bay with a matching window and smaller doorway and subsequently a lean-to kitchen was built against the W end. The chapel was also enlarged to the rear with an irregularly shaped extension to take it to the site boundary. An earlier cottage adjoins to the east.

The interior (originally 19½ft by 32ft) now has a gallery around three sides supported by nine timber columns with moulded caps and bases; five iron columns rise above the supports of the N gallery to carry the roof on the line of the rear extension. The roof has two king-post trusses over the original structure and a third on the line of the W extension. Below the floor of the chapel are seven brick-lined and vaulted burial vaults. The most notable feature of the interior is the wealth of memorial inscriptions on the walls. (Conversion to house proposed 1986)

Fittings – *Monuments*: in chapel, on S wall (1) Jane Crundwell, 1846, and her sons William, 1857, and Stephen, 1868, stone tablet; (2) Edward Sears Shoesmith, 1862, painted metal sheet with arched top; (3) Ebenezer John Kemp, 1844, Martha (Siggs), 1846, his mother, first wife of Henry Kemp, also Rhoda (Russel), 1853, second wife of Henry Kemp, painted board; (4) Absalom Hawkins, 1865, and Harriet his wife, 1865, painted board; (5) Mary wife of Edward Sears Shoesmith, 1836, William their son, 1838, and Martha their daughter, 1855, painted board; (6) William Crouch, 1861, 45 years pastor, and Elizabeth his widow, 1871, stone tablet; (7) William Winslow, 1904, 42 years pastor, and Harriet his wife, 1889, stone tablet; (8) William Crowhurst, 1850, painted board; (9) Henry Dunk, 1841, painted board. In gallery, in NW corner (10) Mary Ann wife of William Wicker, 1840, Frances their daughter, 1838, John their son, 1857, and John his son, 1926, 40 years Baptist minister in Kent and elsewhere, signed 'Penfold, Ticehurst', painted panel. In NW corner of lean-to extension (11) Mary Ielding, 1835, servant to Samuel Hobden, and Martha Unicomb, 1837, her niece, headstone.

Pulpit: polygonal front with applied mouldings to panels, round-topped back-board, stair to W with plain balusters, early 19th-century. *Seating*: in gallery, early or mid 19th-century, some seats with boarded backs and shaped ends; lower seating renewed in late 19th century.

Chambers II (1954) 84–5, Pl. facing 59. Paul II (1954) 43–7.

(98) Former STRICT BAPTIST, Shover's Green (TQ 653305). The chapel was built in 1816–17. The walls are timber-framed and hung with tiles probably replacing weather-boarding, and the roof is hipped and slated. The NE front is of three bays with round-arched windows and external shutters and has a doorway between the left-hand pair of windows, an inserted doorway to the right and a lean-to vestry against the NW end. Two windows in the rear wall flank the pulpit. (Now converted to a house)

Monuments: in front burial-ground (1) James Jones of Wadhurst, 1888, 45 years pastor; (2) Elizabeth wife of Henry Rogers, 1836.

Chambers II (1954) 81–4, Pl. facing 59. Paul II (1954) 34–43, Pl. facing 40.

(99) WESLEYAN (TQ 642317). Red brick with yellow brick dressings, gabled front of three bays, arched at centre. Dated 1874.

WALDRON *East Sussex*

(100) Former CALVINISTIC INDEPENDENT, Little London (TQ 570198). Small brick chapel built 1879, closed 1979. (Now 'Chapel House')

Chambers II (1954) 128.

WARBLETON *East Sussex*

(101) EBENEZER CHAPEL, Bodle Street Green (TQ 649149). Built 1835 for Calvinistic Independents who formed a Strict Baptist church in 1864. Rendered timber-framed walls, formerly

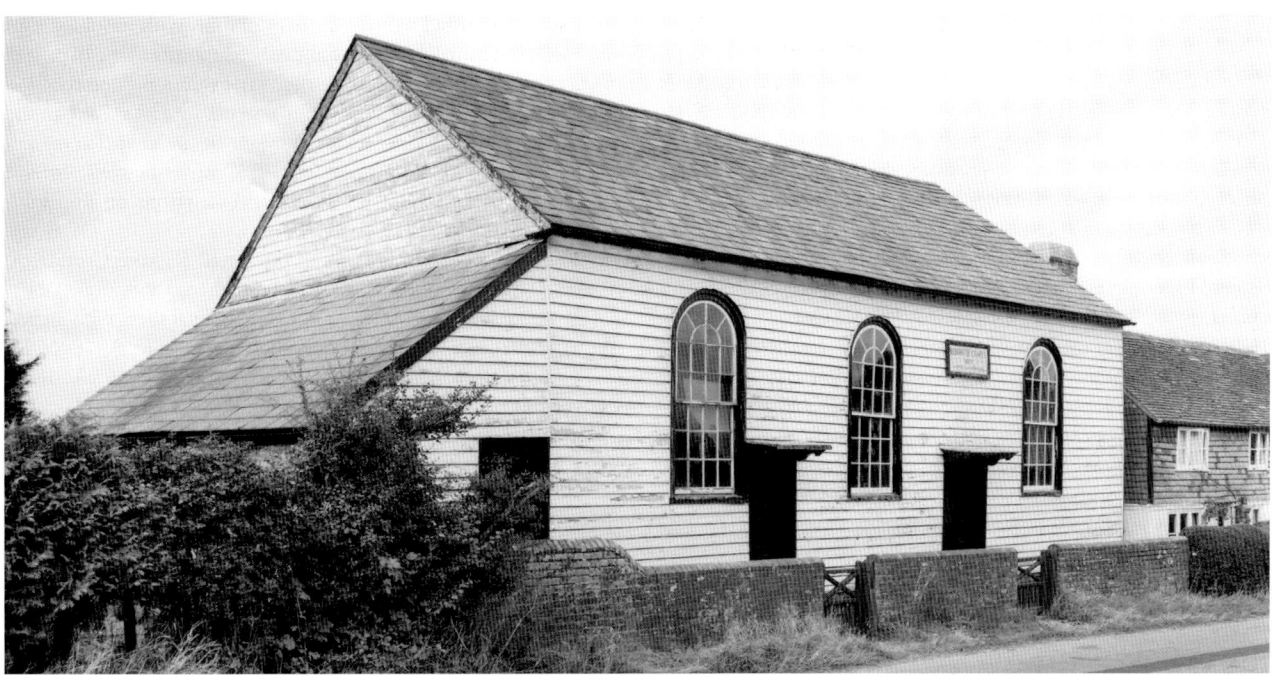

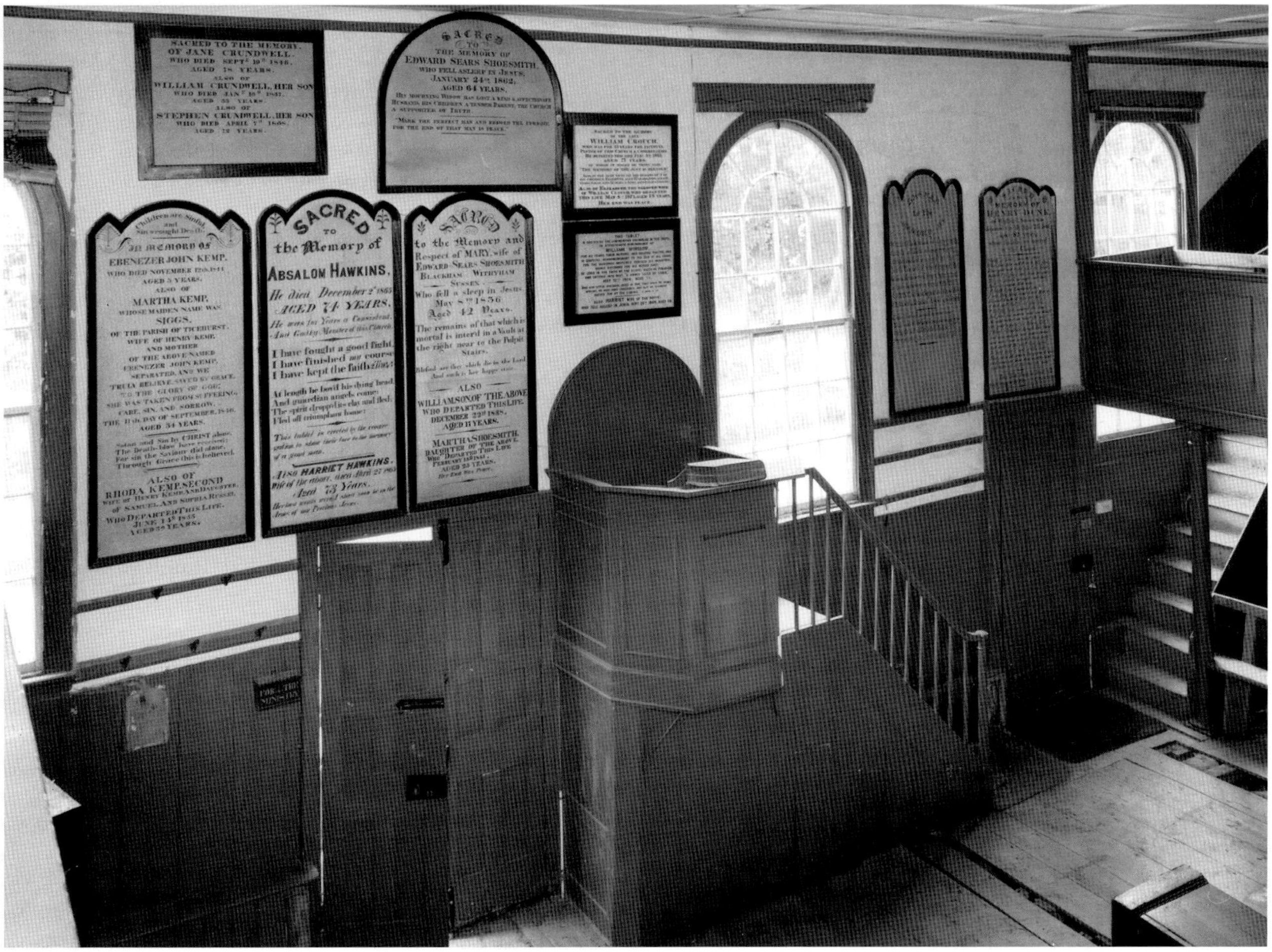

Rehoboth Chapel, Pell Green, Wadhurst. (97)

weather-boarded. The W front has a low porch, gallery window over and date tablet in gable.

Chambers II (1954) 64–6, Pl. facing 43. Paul II (1954) 54–5, Pl. facing 57.

WEST HOATHLY *West Sussex*

(102) COUNTESS OF HUNTINGDON'S (TQ 365330). Timber-framed and weather-boarded chapel of 1824, brick school-room with gabled front added to left 1904.

WHATLINGTON *East Sussex*

(103) Former WESLEYAN (TQ 763194). Tall chapel with rendered walls, pointed-arched windows and tower and spire above entrance. School-rooms below. Built 1872. (Now in commercial use)

WILLINGDON *East Sussex*

(104) Former STRICT BAPTIST, Wannock Lane (TQ 582033). Small chapel built *c.*1851 with rendered walls and two sash windows in gabled front. Railings with fleur-de-lis finials and gate standards incorporating bootscrapers.

Chambers II (1954) 80.

WISBOROUGH GREEN *West Sussex*

(105) ZOAR CHAPEL (TQ 048259). The Calvinistic Independent chapel built in 1753 appears to have been rebuilt in 1820. It is a plain building of brick with a gabled front and an entrance between two pairs of windows, the upper ones with round-arched heads. The interior has a gallery above the entrance and pulpit opposite between two windows in the back wall. The roof is supported by two queen-post trusses.

Fittings – *Inscriptions*: on two tablets in front wall 'EW│1753', 'Enlarged│1820'; on curved wooden overthrow to gates 'Zoar Chapel 1753'. *Monuments*: in burial-ground alongside chapel, several late 18th-century headstones carved with symbols of mortality, including Mary widow of William Nettlefold and daughter of late Edmund Weston Sen., 1759.

CHST XX (1965–70) 361–3.

WITHYHAM *East Sussex*

(106) STRICT BAPTIST, Forest Fold (TQ 510325). Services commenced in 1832 in a barn on the present site; this was partly rebuilt and enlarged and eventually substantially replaced in 1897. The walls are of stone and incorporate masonry of the early 19th century; the front of 1897 is gabled and has a central porch. *Monuments*: in chapel (1) John Saxby, 1867, 14 years pastor, Jane his wife, 1857, and two daughters; (2) George Doggett, late of Withyham, 'who introduced the Gospel to this neighbourhood in 1832', and P. Dickerson [pastor of Little Alie Street chapel, London], who formed the church in 1844; (3) Ebenezer Littleton, 1920, 52 years pastor, and Mary his wife, 1896.

Chambers II (1954) 97–101, Pl. facing 71. Delves, S., *A History of the Rise, Progress and Present Position of Forest Fold Baptist Chapel, Crowborough* (1932).

(107) Former WESLEYAN, Groombridge (TQ 531373). Elaborately rusticated and pedimented brick front of three bays with round-arched doorway and windows with rendered quoins. Dated 1857. (Now RC Church of St Pius V)

Former Wesleyan chapel, Groombridge. (107)

WIVELSFIELD *East Sussex*

(108) OTE HALL CHAPEL (TQ 342204). The Independent chapel was built in 1780 through the initiative of the Countess of Huntingdon who had taken a lease of Great Ote Hall and commenced services there in 1778. The walls are of glazed brickwork with red brick dressings and the roof is hipped and tiled. The broad W front is of three bays with a central entrance, now blocked, between two windows, all with round-arched heads. There are two similar windows in the E wall. The entrance was re-sited at the N end in the late 19th century.

Ote Hall Chapel, Wivelsfield. (108)

A contemporary manse adjacent to the S end was demolished and replaced in 1956 by a hall. The interior (37ft by 25ft) has been reseated; it has a plaster ceiling with original moulded plaster cornice.

Fittings – *Chandeliers*: pair, late 19th-century. *Inscription*: on roof tile from former manse 'James Davey | Carpenter Ditchling | 1789'. *Pulpit*: at S end, three sides of late 18th-century pulpit with moulded cornice and base, incorporated in later rostrum.

Seymour (1839) I: 133, 316–17.

(109) BETHEL CHAPEL (TQ 339199). The Strict Baptist church formed in 1763 originated with several members from the General Baptist meeting in Ditchling who had been influenced by the preaching of George Whitefield. The present site was conveyed to trustees in 1779 and the chapel opened in the following year. The chapel of brick with hipped tiled roofs has been much altered and enlarged. The original building appears to have been a simple rectangle, the N half of the present chapel, with a cottage attached to the W; the chapel was enlarged to the S by 18½ft in the early 19th century and the cottage or manse also greatly extended. The N front has a wide arched doorway to the chapel with gallery windows above; to the right of the doorway are traces of an earlier entrance. The interior (now 35¼ft by 22½ft) has a moulded plaster cornice. There is a gallery at the N end with a plain panelled front and open-backed benches.

Fittings – *Clock*: on front of gallery, signed 'Tho. Harben, Lewes'. *Monument*: in burial-ground, to Henry Booker, pastor, 1799, and Sarah his wife, 1779. *Painting*: portrait in oils on wood of Henry Booker 'first preacher of the Gospel at Bethel Chapel, Wivelsfield, Sussex, 1780, died 22 May 1799 aged 69'. *Pulpit*: polygonal with applied mouldings, early 19th-century. *Seating*: lower seats replaced by later 19th-century seats from former Ebenezer Chapel, Brighton.

Chambers II (1954) 15–19, Pl. facing 11.

Former Wesleyan chapel, Bedford Row, Worthing. (112)

WORTHING *West Sussex*

(110) WORTHING TABERNACLE, Chapel Road (TQ 148029). Evangelical Free Church, big gabled front with wheel tracery in main window between thin octagonal turrets. Built 1897–1908, by James E. Lund.

(111) Former WESLEYAN, Marine Place (TQ 150025). Three-bay front faced with pebbles and brick dressings. Pedimental gable with lunette above two round-arched windows. Built 1822 and superseded in 1840. (Now in commercial use)

(112) Former WESLEYAN, Bedford Row (TQ 150026). Built 1840 to replace (111). Greek Classical stuccoed front by Charles Hide, of three bays with pediment and tall windows with tapered jambs; pedimented window above entrance. Closed *c*.1900. (Now in commercial use)

YAPTON *West Sussex*

(113) Former CONGREGATIONAL (SU 976033). The chapel, built 1861, and adjacent Sunday-school at right-angles to it have walls of flint with flint galleting and ashlar dressings. The chapel, now gutted internally, has a gabled N front and porch; the school, of three bays, has a gabled centre. (Now Evangelical Free Church)

ABBREVIATIONS

NMR	National Monuments Record
RC	Roman Catholic
RCHME	Royal Commission on the Historical Monuments of England
URC	United Reformed Church

BIBLIOGRAPHICAL SOURCES
other than those fully titled in the text

AMST	*Transactions of the Ancient Monuments Society* (New Series, from 1952).
Aspland, R.B. 1850	*Memoir of the Life, Works and Correspondence of the Rev. Robert Aspland, of Hackney.*
Barker, J.T. 1860	*Congregationalism in Lincolnshire.*
Beck, W. and Ball, T.F. 1869	*The London Friends' Meetings . . . .*
Belden, A.D. (c.1930)	*George Whitefield – The Awakener.*
Betjeman, J. 1952	*First and Last Loves.*
Beyer, W. 1931	*The Seven Churches in London . . . .*
B.Hbk	*The Baptist Handbook* (Baptist Union of GB and Ireland, from 1861).
Black, K.M. 1906	*The Scots Churches in England.*
Blaxhill, E.A. 1948	*The Nonconformist Churches of Colchester.*
BM	*The Baptist Magazine* (from 1809).
Bolam, C.G. 1962	*Three Hundred Years, 1662–1962: The Story of the Churches forming the North Midland Presbyterian and Unitarian Association.*
Bourne, C. (ed.) 1993	*The Dunstable Methodist Circuit: One Hundred and Fifty Years of Witness, 1843–1993.*
Bourne, F.W. 1905	*The Bible Christians: Their Origin and History (1815–1900).*
BQ	*The Baptist Quarterly* (from 1922). Incorporating *Trans. Baptist Hist. Soc.*
Briggs, M.S. 1946	*Puritan Architecture and its Future.*
Browne, J. 1877	*History of Congregationalism and Memorials of the Churches in Norfolk and Suffolk.*
Buffard, F. 1963	*Kent and Sussex Baptist Associations.*
Butler, D.M. 1999	*The Quaker Meeting Houses of Britain* (2 vols).
Calamy, E. 1713	*An Abridgement of Mr Calamy's History of his Life and Times* (2nd edn, 2 vols).
Chambers, R.F.	*The Strict Baptist Chapels of England*:
1952	I: *The Chapels of Surrey and Hampshire.*
1954	II: *The Chapels of Sussex.*
1956	III: *The Chapels of Kent.*
1963	IV: *The Chapels of the Industrial Midlands.*
CHST	*Transactions of the Congregational Historical Society* (21 vols, 1901–72).
Cleal, E.E. 1908	*The Story of Congregationalism in Surrey.*
Clowes, J.E. 1912	*Chronicles of the Old Congregational Church at Great Yarmouth, 1642–1858.*
Coleman, T. 1853	*Memorials of the Independent Churches in Northamptonshire.*
Cong. Mag.	*The London Christian Instructor, or Congregational Magazine* (from 1818).
Crosby, T. 1738–40	*The History of the English Baptists . . .* (4 vols).
Curnock, N. (ed.) 1938	*The Journal of the Rev. John Wesley, A.M. . . .* (8 vols: 1909–16, reprinted 1938).
CYB	*The Congregational Year Book* (Congregational Union of England and Wales, 1846–1972).
Dixon, R.W. 1887	*A Century of Village Nonconformity at Bluntisham, Hunts, 1787–1887.*

Dolbey, G.W. 1964	*The Architectural Expression of Methodism: The First Hundred Years.*
Durley, T. 1910	*Centenary Annals of . . . Wesleyan Methodism in Aylesbury and the Surrounding Villages.*
Elleray, D.R. 1981	*The Victorian Churches of Sussex.*
EM	*The Evangelical Magazine* (1793–1904).
England, J. 1888	*Moravian Chapels and Preaching Houses . . . Lancashire, Cheshire, The Midlands and Scotland.*
Evans, G.E. 1897	*Vestiges of Protestant Dissent.*
Evans List	*Dissenting Congregations in England and Wales.* MS in Dr. Williams's Library compiled by John Evans, 1715–29.
FHSJ	*Journal of the Friends Historical Society* (from 1903).
Gardner, R. 1851	*History, Gazetteer and Directory of Cambridgeshire . . . .*
Hadfield, G. 1825	*The Manchester Socinian Controversy . . . .*
Hague, G. and Hague, J. 1986	*The Unitarian Heritage: An Architectural Survey of Chapels and Churches in the Unitarian Tradition in the British Isles.*
Harding, J.M. 1976	*Four Centuries of Charlwood Houses.*
Hindmarsh, R. 1861	*Rise and Progress of the New Jerusalem Church.*
Hine, R.L. 1929	*The History of Hitchin* (2 vols).
Homan, R. 1984	*The Victorian Churches of Kent.*
Horsfield, T.W. 1824–7	*The History and Antiquities of Lewes and its Vicinity* (2 vols).
Hosken, T.J. 1920	*History of Congregationalism and Memorials of the Churches of our Order in Suffolk.*
Ivimey, J. 1811–30	*A History of the English Baptists* (4 vols).
Jarvis, L.D. 1953	*The Free Church History of Uxbridge . . . .*
Jobson, F.J. 1850	*Chapel and School Architecture . . . .*
Kendall, H.B. 1905	*The Origin and History of the Primitive Methodist Church* (2 vols).
Kensett, E. 1921	*History of the Free Christian Church, Horsham, from 1721 to 1921.*
Klaiber, A.J. 1931	*The Story of the Suffolk Baptists.*
Leary, W. and Vickers, J. 1984	*A Methodist Guide to Lincolnshire and East Anglia.*
Lester, G. 1890	*Grimsby Methodism (1743–1889) and The Wesleys in Lincolnshire.*
Lidbetter, H. 1961	*The Friends' Meeting House.*
Lindley, K. 1969	*Chapels and Meeting Houses.*
Lock, J. 1919	*The History of Grove Chapel, Camberwell.*
Mackelvie, W. 1873	*Annals and Statistics of the United Presbyterian Church.*
Marsh, T.W. and Marsh, A.W. 1886	*Some Records of the Early Friends in Surrey and Sussex . . . .*
Mearns, A. 1882, 1883	*Guide to the Congregational Churches of London.*
Miller, A.C. 1924	*Eythorne, the Story of a Village Baptist Church.*
Murch, J. 1835	*A History of the Presbyterian and General Baptist Churches in the West of England.*
New, C. 1906	*Robertson Street Congregational Church, Hastings, Jubilee Year, 1906.*
Newby, J.W. 1936	*A History of Independency . . . in Halesworth and District.*
Nicholson, C. and Spooner, C. (c.1910)	*Recent English Ecclesiastical Architecture.*
Page, G.E. 1953	*Some Baptist Churches in the Bedford Area.*
Palmer, S. 1802–3	*The Nonconformist's Memorial* (2nd edn, 3 vols).
Paul, S.F.	*Further History of the Gospel Standard Baptists*:
1951	I: *Some London Churches.*
1954	II: *Some Sussex Churches.*
1958	III: *Some Midland and Eastern Churches.*
1966	V: *Some Surrey and Kent Churches.*
PHSJ	*Journal of the Presbyterian Historical Society of England* (14 vols, 1914–72).
Price, S.J. 1927	*A Popular History of the Baptist Building Fund.*
Redstone, V.B. 1912	*Records of Protestant Dissenters in Suffolk.*
Richards, J.M. (ed.) 1942	*The Bombed Buildings of Britain.*
Robinson, D. (ed.) 1997	*The 1851 Religious Census: Surrey.*
Ruston, A.R. 1979	*Unitarianism in Hertfordshire.*

Scott, H. 1949	*Secret Sussex: Some Unknown Places and People of Sussex.*
[Seymour, A.C.H.] 1839	*The Life and Times of Selina, Countess of Huntingdon* (2 vols).
Showler, K. 1970	*A Review of the History of the Society of Friends in Kent, 1655–1966.*
Sorrell, M. 1979	*The Peculiar People.*
Southall, K.H. 1974	*Our Quaker Heritage: Early Meeting Houses Built Prior to 1720 and in use Today.*
Stockwell, A.H. (*c.*1909)	*The Baptist Churches of Surrey.*
Strange, C.H. 1949	*Nonconformity in Tunbridge Wells.*
Stuart, J. 1907	*Beechen Grove Baptist Church, Watford.*
Summers, W.H. 1905	*History of the Congregational Churches in the Berks., South Oxon. and South Bucks. Association.*
Tarrant, W.G. 1900	*London Unitarians and the Churches where they worship.*
Taylor, A. 1818	*The History of the English General Baptists* (2 vols).
Temple, P. 1992	*Islington Chapels: An Architectural Guide to Nonconformist and Roman Catholic Places of Worship in the London Borough of Islington.*
Timpson, T. 1859	*Church History of Kent.*
UHST	*Transactions of the Unitarian Historical Society* (from 1917).
URCHSJ	*The Journal of the United Reformed Church History Society* (from 1973).
Urwick, W. 1884	*Nonconformity in Hertfordshire . . . .*
VCH	Victoria History of the Counties of England.
Vickers, J.A. (ed.)1989	*The Religious Census of Sussex, 1851* (Sussex Record Society, vol. 75).
Watts, D. 1978	*A History of the Hertfordshire Baptists.*
White, W.M. 1971	*Six Weeks Meeting 1671–1971: Three Hundred Years of Quaker Responsibility.*
Whitley, W.T. 1928	*The Baptists of London, 1612–1928 . . . .*
Whitten, W. 1897	*Quaker Pictures* (2nd series, revised).
WHSP	*Proceedings of the Wesley Historical Society* (from 1897).
Wilson, W. 1808–14	*History and Antiquities of Dissenting Churches and Meeting Houses in London, Westminster and Southwark* (4 vols).
Witard, D. 1962	*Bibles in Barrels: A History of Essex Baptists.*
Wood, J.H. 1847	*A Condensed History of the General Baptists of the New Connexion.*
Wright, T. 1909	*The Life of William Huntington S.S..*

INDEX

NOTES: Personal names are indexed under the heading 'surnames' and also under headings such as 'artists and engravers', 'benefactors', 'ministers, preachers, etc.'. The index reflects the coverage of the book in emphasising buildings and fittings dating from before 1800. Pre-1974 county names are used in the index.

Abbess Beauchamp and Berners Roding, Essex, Abbess Roding, 47a, 48a
Abbots Langley, Herts., 128a
Abingdon, Berks., 35b, 127b, 138b
Abney Park Cemetery, Gr. London, 88b, 118b
Aby with Greenfield, Lincs., 195a
Ackworth, Yorks., W. Riding, 82a
Acle, Norfolk, 230a
Acton, Gr. London, 80a
Addlestone, Surrey, 321a
Agapemonites, 86b–88a
Ailsworth, Hunts., 149a
Albury, Surrey, xvib, xix, 315a–318b
Aldbury, Herts., 128a
Aldeburgh, Suffolk, 279a
Alford, Lincs., 194a, 195a–b
Alfriston, Sussex, 330a
Alkborough, Lincs., 195b
alms boxes, 304b; *see also* collecting boxes
almshouses: 18th-cent., 182a; 19th-cent., 157a
Althorpe, Lincs., 212b
Alvingham, Lincs., 195b
Ampthill, Beds., 1a, 2a–b
Anerley, Gr. London, 69b, 74a
Angmering, Sussex, 329b, 330a
Appledore, Kent, 162a
architects, surveyors and builders:
Abraham, Robert, 122a, 330b; Aiken, Edward, 85a; Akehurst, Rev. S.H., 24b; Anderson, J. MacVicar, 31b; Andrews, V., 289a; Anscombe, Arthur, 133a; Arnold, Thomas, 72b; Ashley, Henry, 84a; Avern, Edward, 89a; Bacon, H.F., 284a; Bacon and Bell, 284a; Baines, George, 70b, 72a, 72b, 222a; Baines, George, and Son, 14a, 21a, 26b, 35b, 69b, 81b, 89b, 127b, 136a, 141a, 180a; Baines, George and Reginald Palmer, 14b, 29a, 70b, 89b, 90a, 106a, 278b, 299b; Balfour (*see also* Pite and Balfour); Balfour, Eustace (Balfour and Turner), 126b; Banks, T. Lewis, 47b, 58a, 111a; Barker, J.T., 80a; Barnes, Frederick, 47b, 51b, 56b, 66b, 278b, 295a, 297b, 301b; Barnett and Birch, 104b; Beaumont, J.W. and R.F., 74a; Beaumont, P., 60a; Bedells (*see* Lander and Bedells); Bell (*see also* Bacon and Bell); Bell, Charles, 47b, 64a, 70b, 88b, 111b, 116b, 179b, 185b, 204a, 222a, 224a, 278b, 291a, 352b; Bell, G., Withers and Meredith, 210a; Bell and Meredith, 148a; Bickerdike (*see* Paull and Bickerdike); Bidwell, Wilson, 141a; Biggs, William, 62a; Binyon, B., 296a; Birch (*see* Barnett and Birch); Blackman, Henry, 334b; Bland, S.K., 110a, 114a; Blunt, John, 15b; Blyth, John, 99b; Boardman, Edward, 229b, 239a, 259a, 264b, 280a, 299b; Boardman, Edward, and Son, 274a, 281a; Bonella and Paull, 69a, 97a; Boney, W.H., 90a; Boreham, Frederick, 327a; Botterill, W., 195b; Bottle, J.T., 242b; Bower (*see* Drewe and Bower); Brandon, J.R., 69a, 77a; Brettingham, Robert, 260a; Bridger, F.J., 326a; Brock (*see* Habershon and Brock); Brooks, W. McIntosh, 315b–316a; Brown (*see also* Innocent, C.J., and Brown; James and Brown); Brown, John, 127b, 147a–b; Brown, William, 288a; Brydon, J.M., 88b; Busby, Charles Augustus, 329a, 332b; Caley, H.M., 185b; Carvell, Jasper, 63a; Cattermole and Eade, 280b, 297a, 297b, 313b; Chambers, W. Oldham, 299b; Chapman, J. Wallis, 69a, 80b, 88b, 110b, 127b, 139a, 147b; Church, W.D., 69a, 80a, 113b, 117b, 129a; Clark, J., 89b; Clarke, J., 10b; Clarke, Joseph, 294b, 297a; Clarke, T. Chatfeild, 88a, 101a, 111a; Clarke, T. Chatfeild, and Son(s), 86a, 104a; Codling, Peter, 243b; Collis, John, 50b; Concrete Building Company, 74a; Conder, Alfred, 122a, 309b; Cooper, Stephen, 260a; Cowell, J., 35a; Cowell, Jasper, 63a; Cozens, T.G., 192b; Crisholm, R., 102b; Crosby, Thomas, 51a; Cubitt, James, 26b, 31a, 69a, 88b, 97b, 108a, 125b; Daglish (*see* Kennedy and Daglish); Dance, George, 99b; Darbyshire, H.A., 85b; Davidson, T.E., and Son, 246a; Davies, John, 112b, 127b, 138b; Davies, Morgan H., 35b; Dawkes, Stephen Whitfield, 139b; Dawkins, Albert, 119b; Dawson, C.J., 70a; Dearn, Thomas D.W., 169b, 170a–b; Devey, George, 180a; Dixon, W. Allen, 62b; Donaldson, T.L., 82a; Drewe and Bower, 182b; Eade (*see also* Cattermole and Eade); Eade, William, 296a, 297a, 314b; Eade and Johns, 306b; Elworthy, Thomas, 329b, 354b; Elworthy and Son, 342b; Evans, Daniel, 77b; Faunch, Frederick G., 279a, 296b; Fawkner (*see* Habershon, W.G., and Fawkner); Fenton, James, 26b, 32a, 38b, 47b, 48a, 48b, 50a, 54a, 58a, 67a, 67b, 94b, 161b, 192b, 198a, 215a, 229b, 249a, 278b, 280a, 289b, 291a, 301b; Finch Hill and Paraire, 95b; Fleming-Williams (*see* Mummery and Fleming-Williams); Freeman, Richard, and Sons, 33b; Freeman, William, 243b; Fuller, Henry, 81b, 83b; Gardner, Joseph, 172b, 175b, 176b, 177a; Gersdorf, Sigismund, 103b; Gibbon, Thomas, 56b; Gibson, John, 68b, 74b; Glover, Morton M., 83b; Glover and Salter, 127b, 143a; Goodall, A.H., 89a; Gordon and Gunton, 26b, 31b, 116b, 198b, 204b; Gosling, Edward C., 50a, 101b; Goulty, Horatio N., 352b; Gribble, Charles R., 119a; Grover, John, 325b, 352a; Gunton (*see also* Gordon and Gunton); Gunton, Josiah, 33b, 38b, 41b; Habershon, W.G. and E., 69a, 71a, 96b; Habershon, W.G., and Fawkner, 102b; Habershon, W.G., and Pite, 72a, 121a, 156a, 222a; Habershon and Brock, 84b, 141a; Haig, Axel, 126b; Hamilton, E.J., 62b, 337b, 343b; Hanley, W.J.E., 74a; Hannell and Robb, 42b; Hardy (*see* Bellamy and Hardy); Haughton, S.W., 175a; Hawkes, G.F., 178b; Hawkins, Percival W., 88b; Hayes (*see* Searle and Hayes; Searle, Son and Hayes); Hayward, Charles Forster, 286a; Henman, Charles, junr., 80a; Hide, Charles, 359b; Higgs, William, 105b; Hill (*see* Finch Hill and Paraire); Hillam, J.A., 250b; Hinds, G.M., 184a; Hobbs (*see* Tait and Hobbs); Hodge, Henry, 96a; Hoole, E., 62b; Hopperton, William, 321b; Horder, P. Morley, 69b, 72b, 89b, 118b, 132a; Horsford, James, 4a; Howgate and Keith, 112a; Huckvale, W., 145a; Hutchinson, R., 42b; Ibberson, H.G., 127b, 132a; Inman, W.S., 84a; Innocent, C.J., and Brown, 198b; Ivimey, John, 74b; Ivory, Thomas, 259a, 260a; Jackson (*see* Wing and Jackson); James, Joseph, 112b, 127b, 135b, 259a; James and Brown, 333b; Jardine, H.S., 43b; Jekyll, Thomas, 246b; Jenkins, G., 342b; Jenkins, William, 125a, 127b, 143b, 161b, 167a, 184b; Jobson, F.J., 26b, 33b, 161b, 162b; Johns (*see also* Eade and Johns); Johns, E. Thomas, 296a, 301b; Johnson, ____, 119a; Johnson, John, 78a, 111a; Jones, Charles, 80b; Jones, R.P., 26b, 294b, 351b; Keen, Arthur, 74b; Keith (*see* Howgate and Keith); Kennedy and Daglish, 223b; Kerridge, J., 253b; Kewell, Henry,

architects, surveyors and builders (*cont.*) 184b; King, W.R., 162a; Knightley, Thomas E., 81a, 118a; Lambert, A.E., 82a, 218a; Lanchester and Rickards, 122a, 125b; Lander and Bedells, 82b, 89b, 98a; Lane, R.B., 268b; Lauder, Alexander, 103a, 339a; Lawrence, Frederick, 69b; Lethaby, W.R., 315b, 325b; Lewin, Stephen, 198b; Lockwood, H.F. (Lockwood and Mawson), 69b; Lund, James E., 359b; Lutyens, Sir Edwin, 69b, 70b, 229b, 264a; McKilliam and Proctor, 90a; McKissack, J., 110a; Mason, ____, 202a; Mawson (*see* Lockwood and Mawson); Mercer, F.T., 24b; Meredith (*see* Bell, G., Withers and Meredith; Bell and Meredith; Withers and Meredith); Metallic Paving Company, 70a; Millard, Daniel, 3b; Moore, ____, 53a; Moore, S.H., 39b; Morris, Joseph, 69a, 88a; Mould, J.D. and S.D., 15b; Mumford, William, 80a; Mummery and Fleming-Williams, 90a; Murrell, H.F., 74b; Myers (*see* Spalding, Spalding and Myers); Neale, J., 13a, 135a; North, C. McJ., 118a; Nunn, Benjamin H., 333b; Oakley, Sir George, 131a; Owchin, John, 313b; Paget (*see* Seely and Paget); Paine, Edward J., 159a; Paraire (*see* Finch Hill and Paraire); Parnacott, W.S., 352b; Patience, John Thomas, 229a, 259b; Paul, George Robert, 330a; Paull (*see also* Bonella and Paull); Paull and Bickerdike, 106a; Peachey, William, 29b; Peacock, James, 99b; Pearson, ____, 141b; Pearson, J.L., 69a, 121b; Pearson, W.J., 14b; Peckover, Algernon, 46b; Pertwee, Charles, 47b, 51a, 56a, 56b, 71b; Phelps, A.J., 104b; Pilkington, Thomas, 200a; Pite (*see also* Habershon, W.G., and Pite); Pite and Balfour, 79b; Plumbe, Rowland, 77a; Pocock, W.F., 102b; Pocock, W.W., 15a, 99b, 114b, 161b, 172a, 342b; Porter, I., 275a; Pouget, Francis, 110a; Poulton, W.F., 53a, 69a, 95b, 123a, 161b, 162a, 324a, 354b; Poulton and Woodman, 127b, 130b, 143b, 161b, 179a, 182a, 187b, 188a, 315b, 326b; Proctor (*see* McKilliam and Proctor); Pugin, A.W.N., 316a; Ranger, W., 92a; Ransome (patent siliceous stone), 96a; Reed, Thomas, 172b; Reeve, R. Dalby, 182b; Rennie, John, 115a; Rhodes (*see* Sulman and Rhodes); Ribbans, William P., 296a, 298b; Rickards (*see* Lanchester and Rickards); Robb (*see* Hannell and Robb); Robins, J.G., 35b; Roper, D.R., 113a; Rowan, W.G., 110a; Rowntree, Fred, 71a, 77b; Sad, Thomas, 260a; Sadd, John, 51a; Salter (*see* Glover and Salter); Sampson, George, 101a; Scaping, Herbert G., 210a; Scott, A.F., 235a, 246a; Scott, A.F., and Son, 230a, 277a; Scott, W. Gillbee, 74b; Searle, Charles Gray, 77a, 95a, 96b, 121b; Searle, Charles Gray, and Son, 82a, 96a, 291b, 340b; Searle and Hayes, 50a, 114b; Searle, Son and Hayes, 61b; Searle, Son and Yelf, 71b; Sears, J.E., 71a; Seely and Paget, 69b; Shaw, R. Norman, 315b, 325b; Shearburn, William, 321b; Simpson, Thomas, 333b; Smith, J. Roger, 78a; Smith, Robert Moffat, 156a, 249a; Smith, T. Roger, 325b; Smith, Thomas, and Son, 127b, 136b; Smithies, John W., 94a; Spalding, Spalding and Myers, 90b; Speed, E., 108a; Stapleton, J.G., 119b; Steggles, William, 284a; Stevens, T., 91b; Stibbs, Thomas, 116b; Stiff, J., and Sons, 105b; Stocking, F.W., 88b; Stone, T. and W., 101a; Street (*see* Welman and Street); Sturdy, Francis, 111a; Sulman, John, 74a, 92a; Sulman and Rhodes, 189b; Sutton, R.C. and E.R., 205b; Syme, W.H., 147b; Tait, James, 151a, 195a, 208b; Tait and Hobbs, 175b; Tarring, John, 14b, 54a, 69a, 78b, 80b, 102a, 117b, 118b, 149b, 155b, 157a, 161b, 184a, 187a, 315b, 328a; Tarring, John, and Son, 81a; Taylor (*see* Wimble and Taylor); Thompson, T. Brownlow, 197b; Thurbin, William, 92a; Towler, W., 241a; Townsend, C. Harrison, 69b, 111b; Trimen, Andrew, 102a; Turner (*see* Balfour and Turner); Tuthill, C., 241b; Usher, John, 3b, 11b, 20a; Wallace, W., 113a; Wallen, William, and Son, 85b; Ward, Henry, 342b; Ward, J.T., 225a; Waterhouse, Alfred, 69a, 77b, 125a; Webb, Sir Aston, 126a; Weir, James, 119b, 125a; Welman and Street, 324a; Wheeler, F., 108a; Whitaker, E.M., 111a; Whitmore, John, 240a; Wilds, Amon, 334a; Wilds, Amon Henry, 333b; Wilkins, William, 315b–316a; Willem, J., 70b; Wills, John, 164a, 346b; Wills, John, and Son(s), 90b, 222a, 226a; Wilson, James, 104b, 106b, 183a; Wimble, J., 334a; Wimble and Taylor, 185b; Wing and Jackson, 3a; Winkworth, H., 246b; Winter, J., 53a; Withers (*see also* Bell, G., Withers and Meredith); Withers and Meredith, 110b; Wonnacott, T., 321a, 323a; Woodland, W., 184a; Woodman (*see* Poulton and Woodman); Woods, W., 236b, 268b; Woodthorpe, Edmund, 89a; Worthington, Thomas, 69a, 78a; Wray, W., 325b; Yelf (*see* Searle, Son and Yelf)

Ardeley, Herts., 128a
Ardleigh, Essex, 48a
Artillery Lane, Tower Hamlets, Gr. London, 69a, 117a–b
artists and engravers: Baddeley, M., 131a; Bowyer, R., 350b; Burrell, Francis, 170a; Burrell, J.F., 350b; Cox, John T., 258b; Fittler, James, 350b; Gleadah, J., 258b; Godby, J., 170a; Grange, J.A., 146a; Hasson, J., 321b; Jackson, H., 150a; Kirkpatrick, T., 260a, 262a; Sewell, S.A., 258b; Sillett, James, 258b; Tabor, E., 50a; *see also* glass-makers and designers
Arundel, Sussex, 329b, 330b
Ash, Kent, 162a
Ash-cum-Ridley, Kent, Ash Green, 162a

Ashburnham, Sussex, 330b
Ashford, Kent, 161b, 162a–b
Ashwell, Herts., 128a–b
Aslackby and Laughton, Lincs., 196a
Aspley Guise, Beds., 2b
Aswardby, Lincs., 196a
Attleborough, Norfolk, 230a
Authorpe, Lincs., 196a
Aveley, Essex, 66a
Axholme, Isle of, Lincs., 194a, 203b, 204a
Aylesbury, Bucks., 327a
Aylesford, Kent, 161b, 162b
Aylsham, Norfolk, 229b, 230a

Bacton, Norfolk, 229b, 230b
Badingham, Suffolk, 279a
Baldock, Herts., xvb, 127a, 127b, 128b–129a
Balls Green, Essex, 56a
Bangor, Carnarvons., 125a
Banham, Norfolk, 230b
Bannister Green, Essex, 54a–b
baptismal basins: 17th-cent., 125a, 213b; 18th-cent., 55a, 283a–b; 19th-cent., 86a–b; undated, 314a; *see also* fontlets
Baptist chapels, dating from before 1800 *see* chapels and meeting-houses
baptisteries: 19th-cent., 22a, 24a, 44b; 20th-cent., 170a, 310a; undated, 57b, 154a, 169b, 234b, 266b, 285a, 324a, 326b, 327a, 332a, 345b
baptisteries, external: 18th-cent., 168a; 19th-cent., 210a; undated, 285a
Bardney, Lincs., 196a
Bardney Dairies, Lincs., 196a
Bardwell, Suffolk, 279a–b
Barfrestone, Kent, 174a
Barham, Kent, 163a
Barking, Gr. London, 70a
Barkston, Lincs., 196a
Barkway, Herts., 129a
Barley, Herts., 129a–b
Barlings, Lincs., 196b
Barnardiston, Suffolk, 279b
Barnet, Gr. London, 70b–71a, 101b; *see also* Hampstead Garden Suburb; Hendon
Barnetby le Wold, Lincs., 196b
Barney, Norfolk, 241a
Barningham, Suffolk, 279b
Barnstaple, Devon, 339a
Barrington, Cambs., 26b, 27a, 35a
Barrow upon Humber, Lincs., xvia, 194b, 196b
Barton-le-Clay, Beds., 2b
Barton-upon-Humber, Lincs., 197a
Barton Mills, Suffolk, 280a
Bassingbourn, Cambs., xva, 26a, 26b, 27b–28a
Bassingham, Lincs., 197a
Bath, Som., 38a, 104b, 131b
Bathside, Essex, 57b
Battle, Sussex, 330b–331a, 353a
Baumber, Lincs., 197a
Bawdeswell, Norfolk, 230b–231a

Bayswater, Gr. London, Queensway, 69b, 125b–126a
beakers *see* plate
Beccles, Suffolk, 235b, 278a, 278b, 280a
Beck Row, Suffolk, 301a
Beckenham, Gr. London, 74a
Beckley, Sussex, 331a
Bedford, Beds., 1a, 2b–4a, 4b, 7a, 139a; architects, surveyors and builders, 3a, 3b, 4a, 11b; Bunyan Museum, 115a; clockmakers, 9a, 20a; House of Industry, 18b; sculptors and monumental masons, 4a, 9a, 12a, 24b
Bedmond, Herts., 128a
Beeston with Bittering, Norfolk, 231a
Beetley, Norfolk, 231a
Belchford, Lincs., 197b
bellfounders: Mears, Thomas, 316b; Mears and Stainbank, 33b
bells, 19th-cent., 33b, 316b
Belstead, Suffolk, 280a
Belton, Lincs., 197b
Belvedere, Gr. London, 71b–72a
Bendish, Herts., 140b, 141a
benefaction boards and tablets: 19th-cent., 118b; 20th-cent., 131a, 345b; undated, 20a
benefactors: Abel, Christopher, 318b; Abney, Elizabeth, 327b; Ackroyd, William, 10a; Andrews, ___, 99b; Angell, Benjamin and Sarah, 95a; Ansell, Robert and John, 280b; Ashburnham, Earl of, 330b; Atlee, John, 91b; Ayscough (Hyscoghe), Hugh, 209a, 210a; Bailey, Sarah, 55a; Baldock, John, 227b; Barnard, John, 233b; Barnard, Thomas, 351a–b; Battams, James/Margaret, 11a; Beaumont, Jonathan, 311a, 311b; Beckley, James, 132a; Bedford, Duke of, 3a; Brackenbury, Robert Carr, 194b, 220a, 225a; Brett, John, 143b; Brewster, Francis, 314a; Brown, Potto, 154b; Browning, Hester, 302a; Bugby, William, 322a; Burge, George, 179b; Burtt, Joseph, 225a; Bury, Samuel, 283b; Chambers, Waddelow, 32b; Chaplin family, 34b; Chapman, John, 112a; Chivers, Stephen, 35b; Congreve, George, 346b; Coulson, Isaac, 40a; Culmer family, 164a–b; Curtis, William, 20a; Davey, George, 352b; Davis, Richard, 132a; de la Pierre, Peter, 165b; de Merveilleux, John George, 224a; Dent, David, 217b; Dicker, Thomas, 334a; Disney family, 213a, 214b; Docwra, Alice, 31a; Drake, Elizabeth, 83a–b; Drawbridge, William, 178a; Drummond, Henry, 315a–b; Dutton, Ann(e), 153a, 153b; Elsdale, Samuel, 103a; Evans, ___, 298a; Fenowillet, Peter, 79a–b; Fines, Henry and Jane, 213b; Fleming, John, 111a; Fletcher, Alexander, 50a; Fordham, George, 141b; Fordham, H., 143b; Foster family, 141a; Frankling (later Grieves), Elizabeth, 231b; Garrod, John, 53a; Gatford, Elizabeth, 345b; Gay, Elizabeth, 269b; Gay, George, 271b; Gay, Robert, 269b; Gay, Roger, 277a; Glover, Ann and Martha, 267b; Glover, John, 252a, 252b–253a; Goodrick, Robert, 268b; Goodwin, Mrs John, 164b; Grieves, Elizabeth, 231b; Grover, John, 325a, 352a; Hancock, Thomas, 34b; Hastings, Selina *see* Huntingdon, Countess of; Hawkins, Susanna, 13a; Hayler, Nicholas, 345b; Higgs family, 105b; Honeywood, Ralph, 77b; Hook family, 188b; How, B., 150a; Huntingdon, Countess of, 185a, 185b, 259a, 329a, 337b, 358b; Hustler, S., 302a; Hyscoghe, Hugh (*see* Ayscough); Jarmyn, Robert, 269a; Johnson, I.C., 177b; Knowles, Ellen, 133a; Lungley, Samuel, 298b; Lycett, Sir Francis, 70b, 90a; Maberly, William, 84a; Manchester, Duchess of, 126b; Mardling, John, 11b; Mason, J., 241a; Meryett, William, 327a; Metcalfe, Charles James, 19b; Mills, J. Remington, 322a; Morley, Samuel, 180a; Norman, William, 36a; Oakley, John, 81b; Owchin, John, 313b; Palmer, Samuel, 101a; Parker, Elizabeth, 103a; Patching, Thomas, 324b; Paul, George Robert, 330a; Payne, John, 74b; Peacock, John, 157b; Peto, Sir Morton, 74b, 77a; Phillips, Ann, 131a; Puget, J.H., 71b; Reckitt, Julia, 141a; Robinson, Thomas, 200b; Robinson, William, 217b; Russell, John, 4a; Sanford, John, 67b; Sanford, Mary Ann, 67b; Sanford, Thomas, 67b; Smith, Humphrey, 55a; Spratt, George Denny, 288a; Storr, William, 219a; Stringer, Joan, 119b; Swannell, Joseph, 11b; Taverner, Samuel, 172a, 172b; Tayler, Lady, 180b; Taylor, John, 29a; Tilden, James, 188b; Toomer, Samuel, 193b; Treen, Frances, 225a; Tyler, John, 175a; Walker, Francis, 4a; Wellard, John, 170b; Whitbread, Samuel, 2b; Whiting, James, 264b, 276a, 276b; Willoughby, Stephen, 207a; Wilson, Thomas, 98b, 122a, 327a; Worley, Mrs, 143a; Yoakley, Michael, 182b; Zinzendorf, Count, 103b, 104a
Benwick, Cambs., 28a
Berkhamsted, Herts., 127a, 129b–130a, 144b
Bermondsey, Gr. London, 113b, 116b; Horsleydown, 108b, 113b
Bessels Green, Kent, xvb, 161a, 167b–168b, 175b
Besthorpe, Norfolk, 231a
Bethersden, Kent, 163a
Bethnal Green, Gr. London, 117b
Bexley, Gr. London, 71b–72b
Bexleyheath, Gr. London, 72a–b
Bible Christians, 178a–b, 190a, 353b, 355a
Bicker, Lincs., 197b
Biddenden, Kent, 163a
Biggleswade, Beds., 1b, 4a, 22a
Bildeston, Suffolk, 280a–b
Billericay, Essex, 48a–b
Billinghay, Lincs., 197b
Billingshurst, Sussex, xvib, 329a, 331a–332a, 344a
Billington, Beds., 4b

Bilsby, Lincs., 197b
Binbrook, Lincs., 197b
Binham, Norfolk, 231b
Birchington, Kent, 182b
Birmingham, Warws., 178b, 318a
Bishop's Stortford, Herts., xvb, 127b, 130a–131a
Bittering Street, Norfolk, 244a
Blackheath, Gr. London, 110a
Blakeney, Norfolk, 231b
Bloomsbury Baptist Chapel, Gr. London, 68b, 74b–75b
'Blue Idol', Thakenden, Sussex, xvib, 329b, 330a, 355b–356a
Bluetown, Sheerness, Kent, 161a, 187a–b
Blunham, Beds., 1a, 4b
Bluntisham, Hunts., 149a–150a, 150b, 156b
Blythburgh, Suffolk, 280b
Blyton, Lincs., 197b
Bocking, Essex, 48b, 51a
Bocking End, Essex, xva, 47a, 48b–50a
Bodle Street Green, Sussex, 356b–358a
Bolingbroke, Lincs., 198a
Bolnhurst and Keysoe, Beds., 1a, 1b, 4b–7b, 18b
Bonby, Lincs., 198a
books and libraries, 41b–42a, 83a, 138a, 141a, 153b, 172b, 190b, 304a, 310b, 332a, 336a, 345b, 350a, 352a
bootscrapers, 20a, 25b, 27b, 32b, 41b, 150b, 155a, 178b
Boreham, Essex, 58b
Borough Green, Kent, 163a
Bosham, Sussex, 329b, 332a–b
Boston, Lincs., xvia, 194b, 198a–199b
Bottisham, Cambs., 28b, 41b–42a
Boughton Malherbe, Kent, 163a–b
Boughton under Blean, Kent, Boughton Street, 163b
Bounds Cross, Lashenden, Kent, 163a
Bourne, Lincs., 199b–200a, 223a
Bovingdon, Herts., 132b
Box Lane, Boxmoor, Herts., 127a, 133a–135a
Boxford, Suffolk, 280b
Boxmoor, Herts., 135a–b; Box Lane, 127a, 133a–135a
Boyden Gate, Kent, 168b
Brabourne Lees, Kent, 163b, 188b
Bradbourne, Kent, 168a
Bradenham, Norfolk, 231b
Bradfield, Essex, Bradfield Heath, 48b
Bradfield, Norfolk, 254b, 268b–269a
Bradfield, Suffolk, 304b
Bradford, Yorks., W. Riding, 31b
Bradley, Lincs., 200b
Braintree and Bocking, Essex, 47a, 48b–50a
Bramfield, Suffolk, 280b
Bramford, Suffolk, 280b
Brandeston, Suffolk, 280b–281a
Brandon, Suffolk, 281a
Brant Broughton and Stragglethorpe, Lincs., xvia, 194a, 200b–201b

Brasted, Kent, 164a
Braughing, Herts., xvb, 127a, 131a–b
Breachwood Green, Herts., 127b, 140b–141a
Brede, Sussex, 332b
Bredgar, Kent, 162b, 164a
Brenchley, Kent, 164a
Brent, Gr. London, 72b
Brentford, Gr. London, 94a–b
Brentwood, Essex, 50a
Brewood, Staffs., 132a
Bridgham, Norfolk, 231b
Brigflatts, Yorks., W. Riding, 127b, 141a
Brigg, Lincs., 202a, 207b–208a
Brightlingsea, Essex, 47b, 50a
Brighton, Sussex, 104a, 170b, 329a, 329b, 330b, 332b–334a, 359a; architects, surveyors and builders, 343b, 352b
Brigsley, Lincs., 201b
Bristol, Glos., 13a, 74b, 135a
Briston, Norfolk, 229b, 231b–232a, 244a
Brixton, Gr. London, 105b–106a
Broad Oak, Sussex, 332b
Broadhembury, Devon, 77a
Broadstairs, Kent, 161a, 164a–165a
Brockham, Surrey, 318b
Brockley, Suffolk, Brockley Green, 281a
Bromley, Gr. London, 72b–74a; *see also* Anerley; Penge
Brook End, Keysoe, Beds., 1a, 4b–7a
Brooke, Norfolk, 232a
Broughton, Hunts., 150a
Broughton, Lincs., 201b
bugles, 18b
builders *see* architects, surveyors and builders
Bungay, Suffolk, 281a
Bunhill Fields, Gr. London, 101b–102a
Buntingford, Herts., 127a, 131b, 157a
Bunwell, Norfolk, 232b
Bures St Mary, Suffolk, 281b
Burgh le Marsh, Lincs., 202a, 209a
Burgh St Margaret, Norfolk, 240a
Burgh St Peter, Norfolk, 232b
Burham, Kent, 165a
burial-grounds, detached: Friends, 102a, 113b, 167a, 202a, 227b, 254b, 324b; Huguenot, 119b–121a; other, 26a, 40a, 88b, 101b–102a, 113b
Burnham on Crouch, Essex, 50a
Burnham Green, Herts., 132b
Burnham Market, Norfolk, 232b
Burslem, Staffs., 77a
Burstow, Surrey, 319a–b
Burton upon Stather, Lincs., 202a
Burwash, Sussex, 334a
Burwell, Cambs., 26a, 26b, 28b–29a
Burwell, Lincs., 202a
Bury St Edmunds, Suffolk, xvia, xix, 278a, 278b, 279a, 279b, 281b–284b, 285b, 310a
Bushey, Herts., 132b
Butterwick, Lincs., 204a
Buxhall, Suffolk, 284b
Buxted, Sussex, 334a

Buxton Heath, Norfolk, 232b
Buxton with Lammas, Norfolk, 232b–233a

Cade Street, Sussex, 343a
Cadney, Lincs., 202a
Caister-on-Sea, Norfolk, 233b
Caistor, Lincs., 194b, 202a–b
Caledonian Road, Islington, Gr. London, 101a
Camberwell, Gr. London, 113a–b, 116a
Cambridge, Cambs., xva, 26a, 26b, 29a–31b; clockmakers, 34b, 42a; sculptors and monumental masons, 34b, 38a, 40b, 44b, 131b
Camden, Gr. London, 74a–79b; Dr Williams's Library, 104a; *see also* Bloomsbury Baptist Chapel; Catholic Apostolic church, Gordon Square; Hampstead; Kentish Town; Seven Dials
Camden Road, Islington, Gr. London, 95a–b, 101b
Canterbury, Kent, 161a, 161b, 165a, 165a–167b
Capel, Surrey, 315a, 319b–320b
Cardington, Beds., 7b
Carleton Rode, Norfolk, 229b, 233b
Carlton and Chellington, Beds., xva, 1a, 7b–9a
Carrington, Lincs., 202b
Castle Acre, Norfolk, 234a
Castle Hedingham, Essex, 50a–b
Castor, Hunts., 150a
Catfield, Norfolk, 234a
Catholic Apostolic church: Apostles Chapel, Albury, Surrey, xvib, xix, 315a–318b; Gordon Square, Gr. London, xva, 69a, 76a–b, 77a; Maida Avenue, Paddington, Gr. London, xvb, 69a, 121b–122a
Catsfield, Sussex, 330a, 334b
Catterick, Yorks., N. Riding, 104a
Catworth, Hunts., 150a
Cavendish, Suffolk, 284b
Cawston, Norfolk, 234a
Caxton, Cambs., 31b
Caythorpe, Lincs., 202b
cemeteries, detached *see* burial-grounds
Chadwell Street, Islington, Gr. London, 99a
chairs: 17th-cent., 29a, 38a, 138b, 168a, 235b, 244b, 258b, 277a, 340a; 18th-cent., 3b, 310b
Chalgrave, Beds., 9b
chalices *see* plate
chandeliers: 18th-cent., 64b, 126b, 168a, 217b, 240a, 294b, 332a; 19th-cent., 309a, 314a, 359a; undated, 318a
Chapel Cross, Sussex, xvib, 343a
Chapel Hill, Lincs., 203b
Chapel St Leonards, Lincs., 202b
chapels and meeting-houses, dating from before 1800
BAPTIST
converted premises: houses and cottages, 161a, 162b, 168b–169b, 188a; monastic buildings, 256a, 262a
17th-cent., 161a, 172a

18th-cent.: *1700–50*, 1a, 22b–24b, 47a, 61a–b, 68a, 108a–110a, 149a, 153a–b, 161a, 165a–b, 167b–168a, 178b–179a, 194a, 195b, 209a–210a, 229a, 267a, 329a, 330a, 330b, 334b–336a, 341a–b, 344a–345b, 347a; *1750–1800*, 1a, 4b, 7b–9a, 10a, 15b, 47a, 48a, 57a–b, 58a–b, 60b–61a, 61a–b, 91b–92a, 127a, 144b–145a, 149a, 149b, 151a–153a, 154a–b, 161a, 165a, 168a–b, 176a–b, 194a, 208a, 212a, 217a–b, 222b–223a, 229b, 234a–b, 238b, 278a, 289a, 323b–324a, 326a, 329a, 331a–332a, 354a–b, 359a
CONGREGATIONAL OR INDEPENDENT
converted premises: barns, 19b, 127a, 131a; houses, 278a, 307b–309a; monastic buildings, 256a–b, 262a
17th-cent., 127a, 133a–135a, 229a, 256a–259a
18th-cent.: *1700–50*, 1a, 4b–7a, 26a, 26b, 34b–35a, 39b–40a, 47a, 47b, 48b–50a, 51a–b, 55b, 58b–59b, 61a, 112a, 229a, 244a–245b, 247a–b, 262b–264a, 265a–b, 277a–b, 278a, 279a, 284a, 287a–b, 298b–299a; *c. 1750*, 117a–b, 278a, 303a–b, 304a; *1750–1800*, 1a, 3b, 26a, 26b, 27b–28a, 29a, 31a, 32b, 33b–34a, 47a, 53b, 54b–55a, 64a–65b, 92b, 93a–b, 94a–b, 106b–108a, 110b–111a, 112a–b, 115b, 117b, 127a, 131a, 141b, 146a–147a, 161a, 184a, 187a–b, 194b, 195a, 196b, 208a–b, 229a, 231b–232a, 252a–b, 267a–268a, 276a–b, 278a, 289b, 315a, 322a–b, 323a–b, 327a–328a, 329b, 334a, 358b–359a
COUNTESS OF HUNTINGDON'S CONNEXION
18th-cent., 47b, 55a, 161a, 162b, 170b–171a, 175b
FRIENDS, SOCIETY OF
converted premises: houses, 281a, 321a, 329a, 330a, 355b–356a; monastic buildings, 243b; other, 56a, 329a, 330a, 355a
17th-cent., 47a, 47b, 63b–64b, 71b, 127a, 136b–138b, 149a, 157b–158b, 194a, 214a–b, 215b–216a, 229a, 259b–260a, 277a–b, 278a, 311b–313b, 329a, 330a, 339a–340b
18th-cent.: *1700–50*, 26a, 42a–43a, 47a, 53a, 127a, 136b, 194a, 200b–201b, 205b–206b, 229a, 232b–233a, 236b–238b, 238a–b, 246a, 269a–b, 278a, 280a, 284a–b, 297a, 302a, 302b–304a, 315a, 319b–320b, 324a–b, 329b, 343b; *c.1750*, 127a, 128b, 229a, 253a–b; *1750–1800*, 1a, 2a, 13a–b, 15a, 26a, 31a, 32a, 62a–b, 68b, 81b–82a, 94b–95a, 105a, 119b, 161a, 184a–b, 227a, 229a, 249b–250a, 254b–256a, 274b, 297a, 315a, 322b–323a, 329b, 330b, 346a–b, 350b–351a

HUGUENOT
  18th-cent., 68a–b, 79a–b, 116b–117a
INDEPENDENT *see* CONGREGATIONAL OR INDEPENDENT
LUTHERAN
  18th-cent., 68b, 118a–b
METHODIST
  converted premises: buttercross, 202a
  18th-cent.: *1750–1800*, 11a, 68b, 99b–101a, 161a, 165a, 194b, 206b–207a, 219a–b, 220a–b, 221a–b, 229a, 229b, 230a, 240b, 250b, 278a, 305b, 321b, 329b, 346b
MORAVIAN
  18th-cent., 103b–104a
PRESBYTERIAN
  converted premises: houses, 329a, 351a–352a; monastic buildings, 194b, 212b–213b, 260a, 262a; other, 104b
  17th-cent., 127a, 142a–b, 329a, 330b, 332b–333a
  18th-cent.: *1700–50*, 68a, 85b–86b, 89a–b, 92a–b, 161a, 162a, 180b–181b, 184b, 186a–b, 190a–b, 191a–b, 194a–b, 214b–215a, 278a, 279a, 281b–283b, 287a–b, 293a–b, 294a–b, 295a–b, 310b, 311a–b, 329a, 336a–337b; *c. 1750*, 229a, 269b–271b, 272a–b; *1750–1800*, 85a, 229a, 260a–262a
QUAKER *see* FRIENDS, SOCIETY OF
UNITARIAN
  18th-cent., 101b
OTHER
  converted premises: monastic buildings, 262a; other, 43b–44a
  17th-cent., 153a
  18th-cent., 115a–b, 118a, 118b–119a
Charing Cross Road, Westminster, Gr. London, 125b
Charlwood, Surrey, xvib, 315b, 320a–321a
Charsfield, Suffolk, 285a
Chatham, Kent, 167b
Chatteris, Cambs., 26a, 26b, 31b–32a
Chelmsford, Essex, 47a–b, 50b; architects, surveyors and builders, 47b, 50b, 51a, 67a, 67b, 94b, 192b, 301b
Chelsea, Gr. London, 102a–104b; *see also* Crosby Hall
Chenies, Bucks., 132a
Chertsey, Surrey, 321a
Chesham, Bucks., 129b–130a
Chesterton, Cambs., 29b
Chevening, Kent, 167b–168b; Bessels Green, xvb, 161a, 167b–168b, 175b
Chichester, Sussex, xvib, 329a, 329b, 330a, 332a, 334b–339b
Chignall Smealy, Essex, 50b
Chigwell, Essex, 50b
Chipperfield, Herts., 132a, 132b
Chipping Ongar, Essex, 51a
Chipstead, Kent, 168b
Chishill, Cambs., 39b

Chislet, Kent, 168b
Chittering, Cambs., 43a
Chorleywood, Herts., 127b, 132a–b
Chrishall, Essex, 51a
Christ Church, Westminster Bridge Road, Lambeth, Gr. London, 106a–b, 107a–b
christening bowls *see* baptismal basins
Christian Mission *see* Salvation Army
City Temple, Gr. London, 68a, 68b, 69a–70a
Clacton-on-Sea, Essex, 98b
Clapton, Gr. London, xva, 83b–84a
Clare, Suffolk, 285a–b
Clavering, Essex, 51a
Claxby, Lincs., 202b
Claxton, Norfolk, 229b, 234a–b
Claypole, Lincs., 202b
Cleethorpes, Lincs., 202b, 203a
Clerkenwell, Gr. London, 98b–99a
Cley next the Sea, Norfolk, 234b
Clifton, Beds., xva, 1b, 9b–10a
clockmakers: Andrews, William, 27b; Ballard, 169b; Barcham, 275b; Bartlett, 180b; Billinghurst, William, 78a; Boyce, S.H., 254a; Bright, I.D., 304a; Cavit, E., 9a; Clare, 20a; Covington, William, 24b; Crisp, William, 314a; Davy, 266b; Fordham, Thomas, 64b; Galer, John, 143b; Harben, 350a; Harben, Thomas, 359a; Hooker, 330a; Inkpen, 332a; Inskip, 21a; Kefford, Thomas, 40a, 153a–b; Knight, 57a; Lickert, H., 42a; Linsell, 131b; Mackie, 291a; Notman, 352a; Peacock, 155b; Pepper, James, 22a; Pinchbeck, Edward, 133b; Sainsbury, H., 33b; Seaman, C., 309a; Simmons, E.L., 138b; Smith, 170a; Smith, Thomas, 260b; Spendlove, 254b; Thatcher, George, 190b; Triggs and Son, 316b; Weston, 343a; Wilson, Thomas, 34b
clocks: 18th-cent., 9a, 22a, 24b, 40a, 64b, 78a, 79b, 133b, 153a–b, 168a, 190b, 256b, 260b, 276b, 283b, 294b, 314a, 332a, 336a, 341a, 352a; 19th-cent., 20a, 27b, 33b, 34b, 38a, 138b, 143b, 180b, 234a, 254a, 254b, 266b, 275b, 277a, 304a, 309a, 316b, 350a; undated, 21a, 42a, 57a, 131b, 155b, 169b, 170a, 291a, 330a, 343a, 359a
Cockfield, Suffolk, 285b
coffin stools, 18th-cent., 320a, 332a, 346b
Coggeshall, Essex, 47b, 51a–b
Cokelers (Society of Dependents), 352b, 353a
Colby, Norfolk, 234b
Colchester, Essex, 47a, 47b, 51b–53a, 294a
Coleman Green, Herts., 140b
collecting boxes: undated, 298b; *see also* alms boxes
collecting shovels: 18th-cent., 20a–b; 19th-cent., 22a, 150a, 210a; undated, 170a, 220b, 223a
Colmworth, Beds., 10a, 18b
Colney Heath, Herts., 132b
Coltishall, Norfolk, 234b–235a
Comberton, Cambs., 32a

communion cups *see* plate
communion tables: 17th-cent., 3a, 213a, 235b, 244b, 256b, 277a, 341b; 18th-cent., 18b, 20b, 48b, 99b, 133b, 143a, 154a–b, 168a, 256b, 309b, 332a; 19th-cent., 21a, 163a, 288b, 304a; undated, 9a, 42a, 169b, 275b, 304b, 337b
Coney Weston, Suffolk, 285b
Congregational chapels, dating from before 1800 *see* chapels and meeting-houses
Coningsby, Lincs., 202b–203a
Conisholme, Lincs., 203a
Cookley, Suffolk, 307b
Cores End, Bucks., 327b
Corpusty, Norfolk, 235a
Costessey, Norfolk, 235a
Cottenham, Cambs., 26a, 32a–b, 40a
Cottered, Herts., 132b
Cotton End, Beds., 10b–11a
Countess of Huntingdon's Connexion, chapels, dating from before 1800 *see* chapels and meeting-houses
Coveney, Cambs., 32b
Coventry, Warws., 22a
Cowlinge, Suffolk, 285b
Coxheath, Kent, 162b, 180b
Crabgate, Norfolk, 275a
Cranbrook, Kent, xvb, 161a–b, 162b, 168b–170b, 171a–b; clockmakers, 169b, 170a, 190b
Cranfield, Beds., 1a, 10a
Cransford, Suffolk, 279a, 285b–286a
Cratfield, Suffolk, 286a
Craven Chapel, Gr. London, 122a
Crawley, Sussex, Ifield, xvib, 329a, 330a, 339a–340b
Crawley End, Essex, 51a
Crediton, Devon, Bowden Hill Chapel, 345a, 345b
Creed and Decalogue, tables of *see* tables of Lord's Prayer, Creed and Decalogue
Crewkerne, Som., 110a
Cromer, Norfolk, 235a–b
Crosby Hall, Gr. London, 68a, 104a–b
Crowland, Lincs., 203b
Crowle, Lincs., 203b
Crown Court, Westminster, Gr. London, 126b
Croydon, Cambs., 153a
Croydon, Gr. London, 69a, 79b–80a; Spurgeon's College, 53a
Cuckfield, Sussex, 340a–b
cups *see* love-feast cups; plate
Curzon Street, Westminster, Gr. London, 122a

Dallington, Sussex, 340b
Dalston, Gr. London, 84a–85a
Danny, Sussex, 351b
Dargate, Kent, 179b
Dartford, Kent, xvb, 161a, 161b, 162b, 170b–172a; architects, surveyors and builders, 175b
Datchworth, Herts., 131a, 132b, 144a

Deal, Kent, 161a, 172a–b
Dean and Shelton, Beds., 10a
Debenham, Suffolk, 286a
Decalogue, tables of *see* tables of Lord's Prayer, Creed and Decalogue
Deeping St James, Lincs., 194b, 203b
'Denmark Place Chapel', Gr. London, 105a
Denton, Norfolk, xvia, 229b, 235b, 237a–b
Deopham, Norfolk, 235b
Dependents, Society of (Cokelers), 352b, 353a
Deptford, Gr. London, 68a, 108a–110a
Derby, Derbys., 164a
Derringstone, Kent, 163a
Dersingham, Norfolk, 236a
Diss, Norfolk, xvia, 229a, 229b, 236a–238a, 268b, 291b, 302b
Ditchling, Sussex, 329a, 340a, 341a–b, 359a
Docking, Norfolk, 238a
Doddington, Cambs., 32b
Doddington, Kent, 172b
Dogdyke, Lincs., 203b
Dogsthorpe, Hunts., 156b
Dorking, Surrey, 315a, 315b, 321a–b
Dormans Land, Surrey, 326b
Dover, Kent, xvb, 110a, 161a, 172b–175a, 267a
Downham, Cambs., 32b
Downham Market, Norfolk, 238a–b
Downham West, Norfolk, 238b
Dowsdale Bar, Lincs., 228a
drawings *see* paintings and drawings
Drinkstone, Suffolk, 302a
Dulwich, Gr. London, 69a, 113b
Dunholme, Lincs., 203b
Dunstable, Beds., 10b, 25a
Dunston, Lincs., 204a
Dunton, Beds., 10b
Duxford, Cambs., 26a, 26b, 32b–33a
Dyke, Lincs., 200a

Ealing, Gr. London, 69a, 80a–b
Ealing Green, Gr. London, 80b
Earith, Hunts., 149a, 149b, 150b
Earl Soham, Suffolk, 286a
Earls Colne, Essex, xva, 47a, 53a
East Barkwith, Lincs., 204a
East Bergholt, Suffolk, 286a–b
East Bradenham, Norfolk, 231b
East Dereham, Norfolk, 229b, 238b–239a, 254a
East Finchley, Gr. London, 70b
East Green, Suffolk, 305b
East Grinstead, Sussex, 175a, 341b
East Harling, Norfolk, 246a
East Kirkby, Lincs., 204a
East Peckham, Kent, 175a
East Rudham, Norfolk, 239a
Eastcastle Street, Westminster, Gr. London, 120a–b, 121a–b
Eastcotts, Beds., 10b–11a
Eastoft, Lincs., 204a
Eastrea, Cambs., 43b

Eastry, Kent, 175a
Eastville, Lincs., 204a
Eaton Bray, Beds., 11a
Eaton Socon, Hunts., 149b, 150b, 151a–b
Edenbridge, Kent, 175a
Edingthorpe Green, Norfolk, 264b
Effingham, Surrey, 322a
Egerton, Kent, 175a
Eggington, Beds., 11a
Egham, Surrey, Englefield Green, 315b, 322a
Elham, Kent, 175a–b
Ellington, Hunts., 150b
Elmstead Market, Essex, 53b
Elmswell, Suffolk, 286b
Elstead, Surrey, 322a
Elstow, Beds., 11a
Elsworth, Cambs., 33a
Eltisley, Cambs., 33a
Elton, Hunts., 150b
Ely, Cambs., 33a–b, 35b
Emneth, Norfolk, 239a
Enfield, Gr. London, 69a, 81a–82a; *see also* Winchmore Hill
Enfield Wash, Gr. London, 81a
Englefield Green, Surrey, 315b, 322a
engravers *see* artists and engravers
Epping, Essex, 47a, 53b
Epping Upland, Essex, Epping Long Green, 54a
Epsom, Surrey, 315a, 322a–b
Epworth, Lincs., 194a, 194b, 203b, 204a–b
Eriswell, Suffolk, 286b
Esher, Surrey, xvib, 315a, 322b–323a
Everton, Hunts., 18a, 26a, 32b, 128a, 149a
Exeter, Devon, 110a
Eye, Suffolk, 286a, 306a
Eynsford, Kent, 170b, 175b
Eythorne, Kent, 161a, 175a, 175b

Fakenham, Norfolk, 239a–b
Farnham, Surrey, 315a, 323a–b
Faversham, Kent, 161a, 175b–176a
Fawler, Oxon., 64b
Felday, Surrey, 327a
Felden, Herts., 133b
Felmersham, Beds., 11a–b
Felsted, Essex, xva, 47b, 54a–b
Felthorpe, Norfolk, 239b
Fenstanton, Hunts., 151a, 160a
Filby, Norfolk, 239b–240a
Fincham, Norfolk, 240a
Finchingfield, Essex, 54b–55a
Finchley, Gr. London, 70b
Firsby, Lincs., 204b
Fiskerton, Lincs., 204b
fittings *see* alms boxes; baptismal basins; bells; benefaction boards and tablets; books and libraries; bootscrapers; chairs; chandeliers; clocks; coffin stools; collecting boxes; collecting shovels; communion tables; fontlets; fonts; glass; hat rails and pegs; hatchments; lecterns; light fittings; love-feast cups; models; mounting steps; musical instruments; notice boards; organs; paintings and drawings; pitchpipes; plate; pulpits; railings and gates; rainwater heads; reredoses; royal arms; sculpture; stoves; sundials; tables; tables of Lord's Prayer, Creed and Decalogue; weathervanes
Five Ash Down, Sussex, 334a
flagons *see* plate
Flaunden, Herts., 132b
Fleet, Lincs., 205a, 207a, 207b, 211b, 216a–b, 223a, 226a
Fleggburgh, Norfolk, 240a
Folkestone, Kent, 176a–177a, 188b; architects, surveyors and builders, 172b, 175b
Folkingham, Lincs., 205a
fontlets: 19th-cent., 131a, 184a; undated, 219a; *see also* baptismal basins
fonts: 19th-cent., 190b, 352a; 20th-cent., 78a, 104a; undated, 126b, 316b–318a; *see also* fontlets
Fordham, Cambs., 26b, 33b
Fordham, Essex, 47b, 55a
Forest Gate, Gr. London, 110b, 111a, 243b, 299a
Forncett, Norfolk, 229b, 240b, 259a
Foulsham, Norfolk, 240b–241a
Fowlmere, Cambs., 26a, 26b, 33b–34a
Foxearth, Essex, 55b
Foxhall, Suffolk, 311b
Foxley, Norfolk, 241a
Framlingham, Suffolk, xvia, 287a–b
Framsden, Suffolk, 287b
Freethorpe, Norfolk, 241a
Fressingfield, Suffolk, xvia, 278b, 287b–288b
Friday Street, Suffolk, 281a
Friends, Society of, meeting-houses, dating from before 1800 *see* chapels and meeting-houses
Frinton and Walton, Essex, 56a
Friskney, Lincs., 205a–b
Friston, Suffolk, xvia, 278b, 288a–b
Frithgate, Kent, 182b
Frittenden, Kent, 161b, 177a–b
Fulbeck, Lincs., 205b
Fulbourn, Cambs., 34a–b
Fulham, Gr. London, 88b–89a
Fulmodeston, Norfolk, 241a
Fulstow, Lincs., 205b
Furlong Road, Islington, Gr. London, 101a

Gaddesden Row, Herts., 133a
Gainsborough, Lincs., 194a, 194b, 205b–207a
Gamlingay, Cambs., 26a, 26b, 34b–35a
'Garner Chapel', Gr. London, 105a–b
Garvestone, Norfolk, 241a
gates *see* railings and gates
Gedney, Lincs., 205a, 207a–b
Gedney Hill, Lincs., 207b
Gelston, Lincs., 212b
Gillingham, Kent, 161b–162a, 177b
Gissing, Norfolk, 229b, 241a
Glanford Brigg, Lincs. *see* Brigg

Glasgow, Scotland, 223b
glass: 19th-cent., 66b, 78a, 88a, 99b, 125a, 129b, 133b, 147a, 178a, 183a, 193b, 254b, 298a; 20th-cent., 11a, 172b; undated, 57a, 318a; *see also* love-feast cups
glass-makers and designers: Britten and Gilson, 88a; Burne-Jones, Sir Edward, 78a; Chance, 147a; Crane, Walter, 88a; Hardman, 78a; Hartley, 66b; Hemming, A.O., 99b; Holiday, Henry, 78a; Sparrow, J.S., 88a; Taylor, W.G., 298a; Wilson and Hammond, 78a
Glemsford, Suffolk, 288b
Glentham, Lincs., 208a
Godalming, Surrey, xvib, 315a, 315b, 323b–324b
Godmanchester, Hunts., 155a–b
Golders Green, Gr. London, 70b
Goldington, Beds., 2b
Gorleston, Norfolk, 243b
Gosberton, Lincs., 194a, 208a
Goudhurst, Kent, 177b
Goxhill, Lincs., 208a
Grafton Square, Lambeth, Gr. London, 105b
Grafty Green, Kent, 163a–b
Grainthorpe, Lincs., 208a
Grantchester, Cambs., 35a
Grantham, Lincs., 208a–b
Gravesend, Kent, 177b
Great Baddow, Essex, 56a
Great Bardfield, Essex, 56a
Great Bentley, Essex, 47b, 56a
Great Bromley, Essex, 56a
Great Chesterford, Essex, 56b
Great Clacton, Essex, 56b
Great Dunham, Norfolk, 241a
Great Dunmow, Essex, 47b, 56b
Great Ellingham, Norfolk, 241b
Great Eversden, Cambs., 35a
Great Finborough, Suffolk, 289a
Great Gaddesden, Herts., 133a
Great Gidding, Hunts., xvb, xix, 149a, 151a–153a
Great Gonerby, Lincs., 208b
Great Gransden, Hunts., xvb, 149a, 153a–b
Great Limber, Lincs., 208b
Great Massingham, Norfolk, 241b
Great Oakley, Essex, 56b
Great Shelford, Cambs., 35a–b
Great Snoring, Norfolk, 241b
Great Staughton, Hunts., 153b, 154a
Great Steeping, Lincs. *see* Monksthorpe
Great Sturton, Lincs., 210a
Great Thurlow, Suffolk, 289a
Great Totham, Essex, 56b
Great Wakering, Essex, 56b
Great Wilbraham, Cambs., 35b
Great Yarmouth, Norfolk, 229a, 229b, 240a, 242a–244a, 299a; clockmakers, 309a; sculptors and monumental masons, 268b
Greenhithe, Kent *see* Swanscombe
Greenwich, Gr. London, 82a–83b
Gressenhall, Norfolk, 244a

Grimsby, Lincs., 210a
Groombridge, Sussex, 329b, 358a
Grundisburgh, Suffolk, 278a, 289a
Guestwick, Norfolk, xvia, xix, 229a, 231b, 235b, 244a–245a, 247a–b, 262b
Guilden Morden, Cambs., 35b
Guildford, Surrey, 315a, 316b, 325a, 328b
Guyhirn, Cambs., 46b

Hackney, Gr. London, 83b–88b; *see also* Newington Green; Stamford Hill; Stoke Newington
Haconby, Lincs., 195a, 210a–b, 223a
Haddenham, Cambs., 35b
Hadham, Herts., 131b; *see also* Much Hadham
Hadleigh, Suffolk, 278b, 289a–b
Hadlow, Kent, 178a
Hadlow Down, Sussex, 341b–342a
Hagworthingham, Lincs., 211a
Hail Weston, Hunts., 13b, 149b, 154a–b
Hailsham, Sussex, 342a
Hales, Norfolk, 246a
Halesworth, Suffolk, xvib, 278a, 278b, 289b–290b
Halstead, Essex, 47a, 47b, 56b–57a
Halton Holegate, Lincs., 211a
Hammer, Sussex, 352a
Hammeringham, Lincs., 211a
Hammersmith, Gr. London, 88b–89a
Hampstead, Gr. London, 77a–b; *see also* Rosslyn Hill Chapel
Hampstead Garden Suburb, Gr. London, xva, 69b, 70b–71a
Hanbury Street, Tower Hamlets, Gr. London, 118a
Handcross, Sussex, 355a
Hapton, Norfolk, 229a, 269b–271b, 272a–b
Harcourt Street, Westminster, Gr. London, 126b
Hardingham, Norfolk, 246a
Harecourt Chapel, Gr. London, 69b, 96a–b
Harefield, Gr. London, 91b
Haringey, Gr. London, 78a, 89a–90a; *see also* Highgate
Harlesden, Gr. London, 72b
Harleston, Norfolk, 229b, 264b, 276a, 276b
Harling, Norfolk, 246a
Harlington, Gr. London, 91b–92a
Harlow, Essex, xva, 47a, 57a–b
Harpenden, Herts., 133a
Harrold, Beds., 11b, 24b
Harrow, Gr. London, 90a–91a
Harston, Cambs., 35b
Hartest, Suffolk, 290a–b
Hartfield, Sussex, 329b, 342a
Harting, Sussex, 330a, 342a
Hartlip, Kent, 161b, 178a–b
Harwich, Essex, 57b–58a
Haslemere, Surrey, 325a–b, 352a
Haslingfield, Cambs., 35b
Hastings, Sussex, 330b, 342a–b; St Leonards, 329b, 342b

hat rails and pegs, 310b, 326b
hatchments, 18th-cent., 83a–b, 352a
Hatcliffe, Lincs., 211a
Hatfield Broad Oak, Essex, Hatfield Heath, 47b, 58a
Haughley, Suffolk, 290b
Haven Bank, Lincs., 227b
Haven Green, Ealing, Gr. London, 69a, 80a–b
Haverhill, Suffolk, 278b, 290b–291b, 292a–b
Havering, Gr. London, 91a–b
Hawkhurst, Kent, 178a
Hawkinge, Kent, 178b
Haxey, Lincs., 211a
Haynes, Beds., 11b
Heacham, Norfolk, 246a
Headcorn, Kent, 161a, 178b–179a
Heapham, Lincs., 211a
Heath and Reach, Beds., 12a
Heathfield, Sussex, xvib, 343a
Heckington, Lincs., 211a–b
Heighington, Lincs., 211b
Hellingly, Sussex, 343a
Helpringham, Lincs., 211b
Hemel Hempstead, Herts., 127a, 127b, 133a–136a, 147b
Hemingby, Lincs., 211b
Hendon, Gr. London, 69a, 71a
Henfield, Sussex, 343b
Henstead with Hulver Street, Suffolk, 291b
Hepworth, Suffolk, 291b
heraldry *see* hatchments; royal arms
Herne Bay, Kent, 161b, 179a–b
Hernhill, Kent, 179b
Herstmonceux, Sussex, 329b, 343b
Hertford, Herts., xvb, xix, 99b, 127a, 127b, 136a–138b; sculptors and monumental masons, 131b
Heveningham, Suffolk, 307b
Heybridge Basin, Essex, 60a
High Barnet, Gr. London, 101b
High Easter, Essex, 58a
High Green, Norfolk, 232a
High Halden, Kent, 188b
High Wycombe, Bucks., 94b
Highbury Crescent, Islington, Gr. London, 101b
Highbury Grove, Islington, Gr. London, 101b
Highgate, Gr. London, 68a, 78a, 89a–b, 90a
Hill Green, Essex, 51a
Hillingdon, Gr. London, 91b–94a; *see also* Uxbridge
Hinde Street, Westminster, Gr. London, 125a–b
Hindhead and Churt, Surrey, 315b, 325b
Hindolveston, Norfolk, 246a
Hindringham, Norfolk, 246a
Hingham, Norfolk, 246a–b
Hinxworth, Herts., 4a
Histon, Cambs., 26b, 35b
Hitchin, Herts., xvb, 127b, 138b–140a
Hockliffe, Beds., 12a, 24b
Hoddesdon, Herts., xvb, 127a, 140a

Hogsthorpe, Lincs., 211b
Holbeach, Lincs., 205a, 211b–212a
Holbrook, Suffolk, 291b
Holmbury St Mary, Surrey, 327a
Holt, Norfolk, 229b, 246b
Holywell-cum-Needingworth, Hunts., 154b
Holywell Row, Suffolk, 301a
Hope Street Chapel, Gr. London, 117b
'Horbury Chapel', Gr. London, 69a, 102a
Horham, Suffolk, 66a, 291b–294a
Horkstow, Lincs., 212a
Horley, Surrey, 326a
Horncastle, Lincs., 194a, 212a
Horsell, Surrey, 326a–b
Horsford, Norfolk, 248a
Horsham, Sussex, xvib, 320b, 329a, 329b, 330a, 331a, 331b, 341a, 344a–346b; clockmakers, 332a
Horsham St Faith and Newton St Faith, Norfolk, 248a
Horsington, Lincs., 212b
Horsleydown, Bermondsey, Gr. London, 108b, 113b
Horsmonden, Kent, 180a
Hough-on-the-Hill, Lincs., 212b
Hougham Without, Kent, 180a
Houghton Conquest, Beds., 12a
Houghton Regis, Beds., 1b, 12a–b
Houghton and Wyton, Hunts., 149a, 154b–155a
Hounslow, Gr. London, 94a–95a; see also Isleworth
Hove, Sussex, 346a, 346b
Howsham, Lincs., 202a
Hoxne, Suffolk, 294a
Hoxton, Gr. London, 85b, 223b
Huddersfield, Yorks., W. Riding, 149a
Huguenot chapels, dating from before 1800 see chapels and meeting-houses
Hull, Yorks., E. Riding, 195b, 243b
Hulver Street, Suffolk, 291b
Humberston, Lincs., 212b
Hundleby, Lincs., 212b
Hundon, Suffolk, 285a, 294a
Hunstanton, Norfolk, 248a–b
Huntingdon, Hunts., 149a, 149b, 155b
Hunton Bridge, Herts., 128a
Huttoft, Lincs., 212b
Hythe, Kent, 176a, 180a

Ickleford, Herts., 140a
Icklesham, Sussex, 346b; Winchelsea, 329b, 346b
Ickleton, Cambs., 36a
Ifield, Sussex, xvib, 329a, 330a, 339a–340b
Ightham, Kent, 180a
Ilketshall St Andrew, Suffolk, 305a
Immingham, Lincs., 196b
Independent chapels, dating from before 1800 see chapels and meeting-houses
Ingatestone and Fryerning, Essex, 58a
Ingham, Lincs., 212b

Ingham, Norfolk, 268a
Ingress Vale, Kent, 189b
Ingworth, Norfolk, 248b
insurance plaques, 232a
Ipswich, Suffolk, xvib, 60b, 278b, 279a, 294a–298a; architects, surveyors and builders, 47b, 51b, 66b, 246b, 280b, 294a, 295a, 298b; St Nicholas Street Meeting-house, xvib, xix, 278a, 279a, 293a–b, 294a–b, 295a–b; sculptors and monumental masons, 60b
Irby in the Marsh, Lincs., 212b
Irmingland, Norfolk, 262b
ironfounders: Brown and Green Ltd, 14b; Munro, A., 135a; Shillito and Shortland, 354b; Tidcombe, G., and Son, 148a; Turner, E.R. and F., 295b; Watts, 131a
Isle of Dogs, Gr. London, West Ferry Road, 69b, 117b–118a
Isleham, Cambs., 26b, 36a–b, 40b
Isleworth, Gr. London, xva, 68b, 94b–95a
Islington, Gr. London, 68a, 69a, 95a–102a; Finsbury Chapel, 48b, 50a; see also Harecourt Chapel; Offord Road; Pentonville Road; Tollington Park; Union Chapel; Upper Street; Wesley's Chapel
Itteringham, Norfolk, 248b

Jamaica Row, Rotherhithe Road, Southwark, Gr. London, 314a
Junction Road, Islington, Gr. London, 95b

Keadby with Althorpe, Lincs., 212b
Keelby, Lincs., 212b
Kelvedon, Essex, 47a, 58a
Kenninghall, Norfolk, 229b, 248b–249a, 266b
Kensington and Chelsea, Gr. London, 102a–104b; West London Free Tabernacle, 333a; see also Crosby Hall; 'Horbury Chapel'
Kensworth, Beds. (formerly Herts.), 10b, 13b, 142b
Kentish Town, Gr. London, 69a, 78b, 79a, 190b
'Kenyon Baptist Chapel', Gr. London, 105b
Kettering, Northants., 223a
Keysoe, Beds., 1a, 1b, 4b–7b
Kilburn, Gr. London, 72b
Killingholme, Lincs. see South Killingholme
Kimbolton, Hunts., 155b
Kimpton, Herts., 140a
King's Cross, Gr. London, 79a
King's Cross Road, Islington, Gr. London, 95b
Kings Langley, Herts., 127a, 140b
King's Lynn, Norfolk, 229b, 240a, 249a–250b
King's Walden, Herts., 127b, 140b–141a
King's Weigh House Chapel, Westminster, Gr. London, xvb, 69a, 123b–125a
'Kingsgate Chapel', Camden, Gr. London, 74a–b
Kingston, Cambs., 26b, 36b
Kingston upon Hull, Yorks., E. Riding, 195b, 243b
Kingston upon Thames, Gr. London, 68b, 104b–105a

Kirby Cane, Norfolk, 250b
Kirkley, Suffolk, 299b
Kirkstead, Lincs., 194b, 212b–213b
Kirton (in Holland), Lincs., 213b
Kirton Holme, Lincs., 213b
Kirton in Lindsey, Lincs., 213b–214a
Knotting and Souldrop, Beds., 12b

Lakenheath, Suffolk, 278b, 298a
Lamas, Norfolk, 232b–233a
Lamberhurst, Kent, 180a
Lambeth, Gr. London, 105a–108a; see also Riggindale Road
Landbeach, Cambs., 36b
Langford, Beds., 13b
Langham, Essex, 58a–b
Langworth, Lincs., 196b
Lashenden, Kent, 163a
Lavenham, Suffolk, 298a
Laxfield, Suffolk, 278b, 279a, 298a–b
Layer Breton, Essex, 58b, 59a–b
Leadenham, Lincs., 214a
lecterns: 19th-cent., 88a; undated, 318a
Lee Street, Surrey, 326a
Legbourne, Lincs., 214a
Legsby, Lincs., 214a
Leicester, Leics., 35a, 195a
Leigh, Kent, 180a
Leighton Buzzard, Beds., 1a, 12a, 13a–b
Leighton-Linslade, Beds., 13a–b; see also Leighton Buzzard
Leiston, Suffolk, 298b
Lenham, Kent, 180a
Leominster, Herefs., 50b
Letchworth, Herts., 127b, 141a
Leverton, Lincs., 214a
Lewes, Sussex, xvib, xix, 329a, 329b, 330b, 343a, 347a–352a; clockmakers, 330a, 343a, 350a, 352a, 359a
Lewisham, Gr. London, 108a–110a; see also Deptford
Leyton, Gr. London, 68a, 118b
libraries see books and libraries
light fittings: 19th-cent., 98a, 133b, 143a; undated, 104a, 318a; see also chandeliers
Linchmere, Sussex, 352a
Lincoln, Lincs., xvia, 194a–b, 195a, 195b, 214b–216a
Lingfield, Surrey, 326b
Linslade, Beds., 13a
Linton, Cambs., xva, 26a, 36b–38a, 127a, 157a
Lissington, Lincs., 216a
Little Baddow, Essex, xva, 47a, 58b–59b
Little Clacton, Essex, 47b, 59b
Little Coggeshall, Essex, 51a
Little Hale, Lincs., 216a
Little London, Sussex, 356b
Little Shelford, Cambs., 38b
Little Shelton, Beds., 15b
Little Snoring, Norfolk, 250b
Little Staughton, Beds., 13b
Little Stonham, Suffolk, 306a

Little Walsingham, Norfolk, xvia, 229a, 250b–251b
Little Waltham, Essex, 59b–60a
Littlehampton, Sussex, 352a
Littleport, Cambs., 38a–b
'Locks Field Meeting House', Gr. London, 115b
Loddon, Norfolk, 251b
Lode, Cambs., 38b
London
  architects, surveyors and builders, 38b, 53a, 54a, 56b, 63a, 74a, 185b, 286a, 330b, 334a
  bellfounders, 316b
  City of London, county of, 68a; City Temple, Holborn Viaduct, 68a, 68b, 69a–70a; Crosby Hall, 68a, 104a–b; former chapels and meeting-houses, 68a, 68b, 69a–b, 84b, 88a, 90b, 95b, 96a, 101a, 101b–102a, 103b, 118b, 123b–125a
  clockmakers, 33b, 78a, 133b, 138b, 291a
  Greater London *see* Barking; Barnet; Bexley; Brent; Bromley; Camden; Croydon; Ealing; Enfield; Greenwich; Hackney; Haringey; Harrow; Havering; Hillingdon; Hounslow; Islington; Kensington and Chelsea; Kingston upon Thames; Lambeth; Lewisham; Newham; Richmond upon Thames; Southwark; Tower Hamlets; Wandsworth; Westminster
  organ builders, 41b, 311b
  persons of, monuments/inscriptions in other counties, 48b, 129b, 132a, 285b, 295b, 358a
  plate made at, 318a
  sculptors and monumental masons, 35b, 61a, 86b, 103a, 110a, 243a, 254a, 260b, 262a, 284a
  Victoria and Albert Museum, 84b–85a
Long Marston, Herts., 144b
Long Melford, Suffolk, xvib, 278a, 298b–299a
Long Stratton, Norfolk, 251b–252a, 269b
Long Sutton, Lincs., 194b, 216a–b
Loose, Kent, Coxheath, 162b, 180b
Lord's Prayer, Creed and Decalogue, tables of, 101a, 118b
Louth, Lincs., 194b, 216b–217a; sculptors and monumental masons, 217b
love-feast cups, glass, 19th-cent., 225a
Low Burnham, Lincs., 211a
Low Common, Norfolk, 268a
Low Street, Norfolk, 276a
Lower Dicker, Sussex, 343a
Lower Tooting, Gr. London, 119a
Lowestoft, Suffolk, 243b, 278b, 299a–b
Loxwood, Sussex, 329b, 352b
Lusby, Lincs., 217a
Lutheran chapels, dating from before 1800 *see* chapels and meeting-houses
Luton, Beds., 1b, 12a, 13b–15b
Lutton, Lincs., 205a, 216b, 217a

Maberley Chapel, Gr. London, 84a–b

Magdalen, Norfolk, 275a
Magham Down, Sussex, 342a
Maidstone, Kent, 161a, 161b, 180b–182a
Maldon, Essex, 47b, 51a, 60a
Maltby le Marsh, Lincs., 194a, 217a–b
Manby, Lincs., 217b
Manchester, Lancs., 15b, 69b
Manningtree, Essex, 47b, 60a–b
Mansford Street, Tower Hamlets, Gr. London, 117b
March, Cambs., 38b–39a
Mareham on the Hill, Lincs., 217b
Margate, Kent, 161b, 182a–b
Market Rasen, Lincs., 195a, 218a
Marston Moretaine, Beds., 15b
Martham, Norfolk, 252a
Martin, Lincs., 218a
Marton, Lincs., 218a
Matfield Green, Kent, 164a
Mattishall, Norfolk, 229a, 252a–253b
Maulden, Beds., 1a, 2a, 15b
Mayflower memorials, 48a
Mayford, Surrey, 328a–b
Meadrow, Surrey, 323b–324a
Meeting-house Hill, Worstead, Norfolk, 229b, 267a, 275b
meeting-houses, dating from before 1800 *see* chapels and meeting-houses
Melbourn, Cambs., xva, 26a, 26b, 39a–40a
Melchbourne and Yielden, Beds., 15b
Meldreth, Cambs., 39b, 40a
Mellis, Suffolk, 299b–300a
Melton, Suffolk, 300a
Mendlesham, Suffolk, 300a–b
Meopham, Kent, 182b
Mersham, Kent, 182b
Merton, Gr. London, Raynes Park, 69b, 110b
Messingham, Lincs., 218a
Metfield, Suffolk, 300b
Metheringham, Lincs., 218a
Methodist chapels, dating from before 1800 *see* chapels and meeting-houses
Methwold, Norfolk, 253b
Middlesex (now Gr. London), 68a
Middleton, Suffolk, 300b
Midhurst, Sussex, 352b
Mildenhall, Suffolk, 301a–b
Mile Town, Sheerness, Kent, 187a
Milford, Surrey, 328b
Mill End, Essex, 65b
Mill End, Herts., 141b
Mill Green, Suffolk, 284b
Mill Hill, Gr. London, 71b
Milton, Cambs., 40a
Milton Ernest, Beds., 16a
Milton Regis, Kent, 143b, 161b, 187b–188a
ministers, preachers, etc.: Abbott, John, 277a; Akehurst, S.H., 24b; Alexander, John, 259a; Allen, William, 29b; Allon, Henry, 97b; Anderson, A., 281b; Andrews, Edward, 115b; Angus, John, 131a; Ashdowne, Robert, 345b; Asplan, William, 150a;

Aspland, Robert, 43b, 85a; Atkinson, Charles, 295b; Bain, John, 57b; Baker, Richard, 254a; Ball, Nathaniel, 39b; Bampton, W., 225b; Barnard, Thomas, 351a–b; Barnes, Robert, 91b; Barnes, William, 131a; Bartholomew, Henry, 164a; Bass, James, 57a; Bates, William, 85a; Bayley, James, 302b; Beeman, Isaac, 169b; Berridge, John, 18a, 26a, 27b, 32b, 128a, 149a; Biddle, Thomas, 318b; Billio, ____, 85a; Billio, Joseph, 60a; Billio, Robert, 63a, 131a; Biss, Charles Frederick, 302b; Bissill, John, 225b; Blackburn, John, 55a; Blackie, John, 281a; Blaine, Henry, 145b; Blakely, John Rix, 275b; Boardman, Richard M., 243a; Bocking, Daniel, 131a; Boodger, Thomas, 44a, 44b; Booker, Henry, 359a; Booth, William, 84a, 106b; Bottle, Henry, 160b; Bowers, James, 291a; Brackenbury, Robert Carr, 194b, 220a, 225a; Bradbury, Thomas, 113a; Bradshaw, Matthew, 94b; Bradshaw, Nathaniel, 44a; Bridge, William, 256a; Briggs, John, 168a; Briggs, Thomas Barker Wawne, 110a, 174a; Brinkley, William, 39b; Bromfield, Edward, 322a; Brook, John, 165a; Brown, Edward, 224b; Brown, William, 288a, 288b; Browne, Jabez, 306b; Browne, James, 254b; Bugby, William, 322a, 322b; Bull, Samuel, 28a; Bunker, Thomas, 12b; Bunyan, John, 1a, 2b, 3a, 7a, 34b, 102a, 131a, 138b, 139a, 141a; Burgess, Daniel, 96b; Burgess, William, 223a; Burls, Robert, 60a; Burnet, John, 113b; Burton, Edward, 22a; Bury, Samuel, 281b, 283b; Caffyn, Matthew, 329a, 341a, 344a; Calamy, Edmund, 115a; Campbell, John, 280b; Cantlow, W.W., 36a; Cappel, Louis, 118b; Carey, William, 135a; Carlier, Egbert A., 110a; Carter, John, 48b; Carver, Jonathan, 254a; Carver, William, 40a; Cawthorn, Joseph, 224a–b; Cecil, Richard, 25a, 51a; Cennick, John, 19a, 104a; Chaplin, Robert, 269b; Chaplin, William, 131a; Chessher, Lawrence, 10b; Clack, W., 141b; Clarabut, Daniel, 145b; Clark, Johnathan, 179a; Clark, Richard, 275b; Clayton, John, 69a; Clement, John, 145b; Coad, Thomas, 321b; Cole, Baxter, 50b; Coles, William, 15b; Colgate, Stephen, 168a; Collinges, John, 260a; Compton, George, 35b; Cooper, James Ransom, 354b; Cooper, John, 310a; Cooper, John Thomas, 302b; Cooper, Robert, 273a; Corkran, Charles Loftus, 117b; Cornell, William, 304a; Couling, S., 132a; Coupland, John, 179a; Covell, Francis, 80a; Coveney, Abraham, 262b; Cragg, James, 241b; Craig, Thomas, 48b; Cramp, Thomas, 165a; Creak, Alexander, 242a; Crisp, George Steffe, 299b; Crisp, William (Stoke Ash), 306b; Crisp, William (Wrentham), 314a; Cromwell, John, 258b; Cromwell, Thomas, 86b; Crooks, George, 223a; Crouch, William, 356b;

ministers, preachers, etc. (*cont.*)
Crow, Francis, 285a; Crowe, Charles, 269a; Crump, John, 180b; Cullen, John Edward, 33b; Daliel, Henry, 240a; Davies, J. Ossian, 122a; Davies, Mosses, 64b; Dawson, Alfred, 321b; Dawson, John, 256b; Dennant, John, 290a; Dickerson, P., 358a; Doggett, George, 358a; Donne, John, 4b–7a; Dowm, Richard, 353b; Drane, Robert, 244a, 244b; Drew, Thomas, 184a; Drummond, Henry, 315a–b; Duke, John, 332b; Dunkley, John, 213a; Dutton, Benjamin, 153a; Edwards, Henry, 43a; Edwards, James, 333b; Edwards, William, 328b; Elison, John, 262a; Elliot, Richard, 141a; Ellis, John Daymond, 347b; Ellison, Theophilus, 262a; Ellson, Joseph, 343a; Elridge, Samuel, 106a; Elven, Cornelius, 284a; Emery, John, 13b; Emery, Richard, 20b; Enfield, William, 262a; Evans, Benjamin James, 35b; Evans, Daniel, 77b; Evershed, William, 331a–b, 332a; Faithful, George, 334a; Farmery, Charles, 291b; Farrar, Abraham Eccles, 125a; Fawcett, Joseph, 118b; Feary, Coxe, 149a–b, 150a; Fernie, John, 132a; Field, Joseph (Diss), 236b; Field, Joseph (Halstead), 57a; Finch, Thomas, 249b; Fisher, John, 276b; Fisher, Peter, 276b; Fletcher, Alexander, 48b, 50a; Fletcher, J.E., 110a; Flood, James, 39b; Flower, John, 280a; Folkes, William, 281b; Ford, David, 299a; Fordham, Samuel, 31b; Foreman, John, 29b; Forster, Stephen, 60a; Foskett, Louis R., 145b; Fox, George, 102a, 324b, 339a, 340a; Freeland, John, 126b; Freeman, George, 132a; Fullager, John, 336b; Fuller, Andrew, 40b; Galland, Thomas, 217a; Gamble, Robert, 33b; Gamby, John, 22a; Gascoigne, Michael Castle, 110a; Gaulter, John, 103a; Gifford, Andrew, 74b; Gifford, John, 2b; Gilbert, George, 343a; Gisburne, John, 36a, 41b; Glandfield, Benjamin, 295b; Glover, Richard, 145a; Godwin, John, 244b; Godwin, Thomas, 155a; Goggs, John Temple, 267b; Goldborne, Thomas, 264a; Goldsmith, Thomas, 306b; Goodwin, Thomas, 69a; Gordon, William, 295b; Grantham, Thomas, 267a; Green, Samuel, 150a; Green, Thomas, 319a; Greenwood, Abraham, 196b, 223a; Gridley, Richard, 147a; Groom, John Alfred, 98b; Gwennap, Joseph, 61b; Habergham, Samuel, 307b; Haigh, John, 24b; Hallett, James, 341b; Hallett, John, 258b; Hannath, John, 223a; Harris, A.M., 180b; Harris, George, 304b; Harris, John (Fordham), 55a; Harris, John (St Albans), 143b; Harrison, Benjamin, 213b; Harvey, Matthew, 66a; Hatcher, Charles, 241b; Hatton, Joseph, 319b; Hay, John, 51a; Hayter, Benjamin, 58a; Henry, Matthew, 85a; Heptinstall, Joseph, 280b; Herrick, Joseph, 52a; Hickman, Edward, 235b; Higgs, William, 105b; Hill, Charles, 306a; Hill, John, 212a; Hill, Rowland, 115a; Hill, Thomas, 57b; Hillier, D., 132a; Hitchcock, John, 310a; Hobson, Samuel, 15b; Hocking, Joseph, 111b; Hoddinott, C.A., 336b; Hodgkins, Benjamin, 40b; Holcroft, Francis, 26a, 40a, 153a; Holden, Robert, 228b; Holloway, John, 11a; Holman, William, 57a; Holmes, Nathaniel, 235b; Hopkins, Thomas, 38a; Horsfield, Thomas Walker, 352a; Houghton, John, 262a; Howard, John, 55b; Hoyle, John, 262a; Hull, Thomas, 9a; Hunt, John, 332a; 337b; Huntington, William, 92b, 112a, 169b, 170a, 170b, 208a, 322a, 329b, 347b, 350a; Hupton, Job, 234b; Hurrion, John, 235b; Hurrion, Samuel, 235b; Innes, John Boutet, 256b; Irish, David, 156b, 160a; Irons, Joseph, 113a; Irving, Edward, 77a, 315a; Jackson, Thomas, 108a; James, Joseph, 13a; James, Thomas, 301b; Jay, James, 113a; Jeffery, John, 332a; Jeffery, William, 167b; Jenkins, Jenkin, 347b, 350a, 350b; Jenkins, William, 125a; Jenkyn, ____, 184a; Jermyn, William, 277a; Jezreel, J.J., 177b; Jobson, F.J., 26b, 33b; Jobson, William, 291a; Johnson, Stephen, 310b; Jollie, Timothy, 69a; Jones, Eliezer, 295b; Jones, James, 356b; Jones, William, 11b; Keen, C.T., 230a; Kemp, John, 163a; Kemp, R., 285b; Kemp, Samuel, 288b; Kemp, Thomas Read, 334a; Kemp, William, 64b; Kern, William, 296b; Kewell, Henry, 184b; Keymer, Timothy, 153b; Kiddall, James, 217b; Kilham, Alexander, 204b; Kilpin, William, 11a; Kinghorn, Joseph, 230a; Kingsford, Samuel, 165b; Kirby, Luke, 267b; Kittson, Joseph, 28a; Knapton, James, 271b; Landels, William, 77a; Langston, John, 295b; Larkin, John, 51a; Latchford, John, 98b; Lee, Samuel, 85b; Lee, Thomas, 40b; Lepine, John de, 126a; Lincolne, William, 290a; Lindsey, Theophilus, 104a; Ling, Henry, 304b; Littleton, Ebenezer, 358a; Lorkin, John, 51a; Love, Edward, 179a; Lover, Samuel, 344a; Lucas, John, 256b; Macgregor, George Douglas, 122a; McNeile, Hugh, 315a; Manning, John (Spaldwick), 159b; Manning, John (Walpole), 307b; Manning, Samuel, 307b; Mark, John Jonas, 54a; Marten, Benjamin, 172b, 174a; Marten, John, 174a; Martin, Samuel, 123a, 123b; Martyn, John Henry, 16a–b; Martyn, John King, 18a; Matthews, Timothy Richard, 4a, 18b; Mayo, Richard, 104b; Merchant, William, 34a; Middleton, Joseph, 347a, 347b; Miles, Joel, 7b; Miller, Edward, 326a; Mills, George, 244b; Milnes, James, 186b; Milway, Thomas, 295b; Mitchell, ____, 177a; Money, John, 277a; Moon, William, 110a; Moore, Henry, 299b; Moores, William, 141a; Morell, Stephen, 59b; Morell, Thomas, 59b; Mote, Edward, 345b; Mountain, James, 185b; Munsey, Ellis, 44b; Nevile, John, 175b; Newton, Edward, 351a; Newton, Samuel, 256b, 258a; Nichols, George, 38a; Norman, George, 41a; Norris, Joseph, 153a; North, Richard Gridley, 147a, 147b; Notcutt, ____, 63a; Notcutt, William (d. 1756), 295b; Notcutt, William (d. 1858), 295b; Nottage, John, 57b; Oakes, John, 58b; Oakshett, James, 180a; Oddy, Joseph, 26a, 32a, 40a; Orchard, W.E., 125a; Osland, Henry, 26a, 40a; Oswald, Thomas, 126b; Owen, John, 51a, 51b; Page, James, 145a; Pain, John, 212a; Parker, Alexander, 339a; Parker, Joseph, 69b; Parry, William, 59b; Pawson, Henry Thomas, 288b; Pearce, George, 147b; Penn, William, 138a; Perry, Richard, 57b; Phillips, George Bull, 11b; Philpot, J.C., 224a; Pilkington, James, 61a; Plumstead, Austin, 287a; Pocock, Thomas John Bedford, 296b; Poole, Henry, 216a–b; Pooley, Samuel, 122a; Pope, Richard, 113a; Postlethwaite, Walter, 351a, 351b; Press, John, 343a; Price, Richard, 86b; Priest, Thomas, 310b; Priestley, Joseph, 301b; Prince, H.J., 86b, 88a; Prudden, George, 40b; Purdy, Thomas, 354b; Pyall, Robert, 179a; Quant, Henry, 284a; Rathband, William, 89a; Rees, John, 145b; Relley, James, 104b; Reynolds, John, 36a; Richardson, John (London), 69a; Richardson, John (Stamford), 224b; Roberts, Griffith, 228b; Roberts, Richard, 264a; Roberts, Robert, 286a; Robertson, Robert, 259a; Robinson, John, 205b; Rock, Josiah, 213a; Roff, Robert, 29a; Rogers, Jacob, 3b; Rootham, John, 44b; Sainsbury, Thomas, 332a; St Clair, George, 215a; Sames (Sams), John, 51a; Sampson, Henry, 287a; Sanders, Joseph, 31a; Saxby, John, 358a; Scandrett, William, 155a; Scott, John, 125a; Scott, Joseph, 31b; Scott, Thomas, 256b; Sears, Septimus, 10a; Selby, William, 271b; Sheldrake, William, 262b; Shepherd, Thomas, 48b; Sherman, James, 115a; Shrubsole, William, 187a, 187b; Shufflebottom, Robert, 281a; Sicklemore, James, 334b; Simmons, John Edmund, 150a; Skinner, Joseph, 163b; Slack, William, 41b; Slater, Martin, 33b; Sloper, Isaac, 280a; Smith, Charles, 279b; Smith, Thomas (Oulton), 264a; Smith, Thomas (Shelfanger), 266b; Smyth-Piggott, J.H., 88a; Spanton, James, 240b; Sparham, Thomas Henry, 241b; Spratt, George Denny, 288a; Spurgeon, C.H., 36a, 43a, 47a, 53a, 68b, 114b, 175b; Spurgeon, William, 253b; Squier, John Omer, 110a; Stalham, John, 64a; Stanger, John, 168a, 168b, 175b; Stanley, Thomas, 125a; Starkie (Starkey), James, 85b; Starr, Comfort, 186a; Steane, Edward, 132a; Steele, Thomas, 301b; Steevens, Thomas, 51b; Stephens, Edward, 65b; Stittle, John, 29b, 31a; Stockton, Owen, 294a; Stonehouse,

George, 104a, 169b; Stratten, James, 122a;
Such, Joseph, 24b; Sutton, James, 131b;
Sykes, John, 231b, 244b; Taverner, Samuel,
172a, 172b; Tay, Thomas, 22a; Taylor, Dan,
198a, 225b; Taylor, Isaac, 51a; Taylor, John,
213a, 260a, 260b; Taylor, Thomas, 327b;
Temple, Ebenezer, 61a; Thackray, William,
2b; Thodey, Samuel, 31a; Thomas, David,
106b; Thompson, John, 289a; Tite, William,
18b; Toms, Isaac, 287b; Toomer, Samuel
Elgar, 192b, 193b; Toplady, Augustus
Montague, 77a; Towne, Thomas, 141b;
Townsend, George, 184a; Tryon, Frederick,
203b; Turner, William, 331b, 332a; Tyler,
Herbert, 144a; Upton, William, 143a;
Urwick, William, 143b; Utting, Henry,
234a, 234b; Vane, Matthew, 188a; Varley,
Henry, 333a; Venimore, James, 268b; Venn,
Henry, 149a; Vidler, William, 117a, 198b,
330b, 353a; Vinall, John, 350a; Vorley,
Charles, 9a; Wake, Thomas, 13a; Wakeham,
Thomas, 222b; Walder, Samuel, 340b;
Waller, William Finch, 164a; Warburton,
John, 22a; Ward, John Charles, 40b; Ward,
William, 236b; Waschel, Gustavus Anthony,
118b; Watts, Isaac, 50b, 88b; Wearing,
Richard, 304a; Webb, James, 291a; Webb,
Thomas, 42a; Wesley, John, 4a, 18a, 79a,
99b, 165a, 167a, 185b, 187a, 194b, 203a,
204a, 220a, 240b, 243b, 259a, 260a, 274b,
298a, 321b; Wesley, Samuel, 194a; Wheatley,
James, 240b, 259a; Whitefield, George, 77a,
82b, 95b, 185b, 187a, 259a, 359a;
Whitehead, Thomas, 133b; Whitehouse,
John, 321b; Wicker, John, 356b; Wickes,
Thomas, 235b; Wilderspin, Charles, 42a;
Williams, David, 89a; Williams, Edward,
258a; Wilmshurst, Simon, 60a; Wilson, John,
180a; Wilson, Thomas, 180b; Winchester,
Elhanan, 117a, 330b; Winslow, William,
356b; Wood, John, 321b; Wood, Samuel,
258b; Wood, Thomas, 141a; Woods, W.,
268b; Woodward, Bernard Bolingbroke,
276b; Woodward, William Henry, 131a;
Wooster, J.C., 24b; Worthington, Hugh,
101b; Wright, Isaac Morley, 122a; Wright,
John, 57b; Wright, Richard, 198b, 228b;
Young, John, 146a
Minster, Kent, 182b
Minting, Lincs., 218b
models of chapels and meeting-houses, 19th-
cent., 51b, 92a, 92b
Money Bridge, Lincs. *see* Pinchbeck
Monks Eleigh, Suffolk, 301b
Monksthorpe, Lincs., xvia, xix, 194a, 195b,
209a–210a
Monmouth Road, Westminster, Gr. London,
126b
monumental masons *see* sculptors and
monumental masons
Moravian chapels, dating from before 1800 *see*
chapels and meeting-houses

Mortlake, Gr. London, 112a
Morton, Lincs., 218b
Moulton, Lincs., 218b
Moulton Seas End, Lincs., 218b
mounting steps, 19th-cent., 201a
Much Hadham, Herts., 141a; *see also* Hadham
Mulbarton, Norfolk, 253b
Murrow, Cambs., 46b
musical instruments: bugles, 18b; *see also*
organs; pitchpipes
Muswell Hill, Gr. London, 89b, 90a

Nayland-with-Wissington, Suffolk, 301b
Nazeing, Essex, 57a
Neatishead, Norfolk, 229b, 253b
Necton, Norfolk, 229b, 253b–254a
Needham Market, Suffolk, 278a, 278b,
301b–302a
Needingworth, Hunts., 154b
Nene Terrace, Lincs., 203b
Nettleden with Potten End, Herts., 141a
Nettleton, Lincs., 219a
New Barnet, Gr. London, 71b
New Bolingbroke, Lincs., 202b
New Buckenham, Norfolk, 254a, 269b
New Church (Swedenborgian), 50a, 69b, 74a,
101b, 188b, 296b
New Leake, Lincs., 219a
New Mill, Herts., 127a, 145a, 145b–146a
New York, Lincs., 228a
Newark, Hunts., 156b
Newham, Gr. London, 110b–111a, 243b
Newhaven, Sussex, 352b
Newick, Sussex, 352b
Newington Butts, Gr. London, Metropolitan
Tabernacle, 68b, 114a–b
Newington Green, Gr. London, xva, 68a,
85b–86b
Ninfield, Sussex, 352b–353a
Nordelph, Norfolk, 254a
Normanby by Spital, Lincs., 219a
Normandy, Surrey, 326b
North Creake, Norfolk, 254a
North Elmham, Norfolk, 254a
North Finchley, Gr. London, 71b
North Kyme, Lincs., 219a
North Lopham, Norfolk, 254a–b
North Scarle, Lincs., 194b, 219a–b
North Thoresby, Lincs., 219b
North Walsham, Norfolk, xvia, 229a,
254b–256a, 268b
Northampton Tabernacle, Islington, Gr.
London, 99b
Northchapel, Sussex, 321a, 329b, 353a
Northiam, Sussex, 329b, 353a–b
Northlands, Lincs., 220b
Northolme Chapel, Lincs. *see* Wainfleet St
Thomas
Norton, Suffolk, 302a
Norwich, Norfolk, xvia, xix, 229a, 229b,
230a, 252a, 252b, 256a–262a, 269b;
clockmakers, 260b; sculptors and

monumental masons, 244b, 253b, 277a
notice boards: 19th-cent., 133b–135a, 135b;
undated, 98b
Nutfield, Surrey, 326a

Oakington, Cambs., 26a, 40a–b
Occold, Suffolk, 302a
Offord Road, Islington, Gr. London, 69b,
98a–b
Old Bolingbroke, Lincs., 198a
Old Buckenham, Norfolk, 262a–b
Old Newton with Dagworth, Suffolk, 302a–b
Old Weston, Hunts., 156a
Olney, Bucks., 9a
organ builders: Bryson Bros and Ellis, 41b;
Hill, William, 31b; Schmidt, Gerard, 4a;
Willis, Henry ('Father'), 80a, 98a, 102a,
123b; Willis, Henry, & Sons, 88a
organs: 17th-cent., 258b; 18th-cent., 4a, 311b;
19th-cent., 31b, 80a, 88a, 98a, 102a, 123b;
20th-cent., 41b, 294b
Ormesby St Margaret with Scratby, Norfolk,
262b
Orton Waterville, Hunts., 156a
Osgodby, Lincs., 219b
Otley, Suffolk, 302b
Oulton, Norfolk, xvia, xix, 229a, 262b–264a,
265a–b
Outwood Common, Surrey, 319a–b
Over, Cambs., 40b
Overstrand, Norfolk, 229b, 264a
Owston Ferry, Lincs., 219b
Oxford, Oxon., Manchester College, 104a

Paddington, Gr. London, 122a; Catholic
Apostolic church, Maida Avenue, xvb, 69a,
121b–122a
paintings and drawings: 17th-cent., 258b;
17th/18th-cent., 126a; 18th-cent., 126b,
170a, 262a, 295b, 310b; 19th-cent., 38a, 50a,
60a, 131a, 146a, 170a–b, 174a, 216a, 258b,
321b, 350a–b; undated, 60a, 62a, 150a, 318a,
321b, 359a
Palgrave, Suffolk, 236a, 302b
Palmers Green, Gr. London, 81b, 82a
Parliament Court Chapel, Gr. London, 68a–b,
117a
Parson Drove, Cambs., 40b
Partney, Lincs., 219b
Paston, Norfolk, 264b
Peasenhall, Suffolk, 302b, 307b
Peckham, Gr. London, 68b, 113b, 114a
Peculiar People, 47b, 61a, 64a, 66a, 66b
Pegsdon, Beds., 21b
Pell Green, Wadhurst, Sussex, xvib, 329b,
356a–b, 357a–b
Penge, Gr. London, 69b, 72b–73b
Pentonville Road, Islington, Gr. London, 69b,
96a, 98b
Perry Green, Herts., 140a
Pertenhall, Beds., xva, 1b, 7a, 16a–18a
Peterborough, 149b, 156a–b

Pett, Sussex, 353b
Petworth, Sussex, 353b–354a
Pidley cum Fenton, Hunts., 156b
'Pilgrim Fathers, Church of the', Gr. London, 68a, 114b–115a
Pinchbeck, Lincs., Money Bridge, 194b, 219b–220a
Pinner, Gr. London, 90b
pitchpipes: 18th-cent., 258b; 19th-cent., 42b, 244b, 350b
plate
  17th-cent.: beakers, 115a, 213b, 242a, 243a, 271b; cups, 31a, 78a, 79a–b, 85a, 125a, 190b, 205b, 244b, 269a, 294b, 336b; plates, 294b; other, 213b
  18th-cent.: beakers, 52a, 92b, 115a, 309a; cups, 4b, 31a, 36a, 43a, 48a, 52a, 57b, 59b, 74b, 78a, 86b, 92b, 101a, 110a, 119a, 125a, 168a, 186b, 205b, 256a, 258b, 262a, 281a, 283b, 294b, 295b, 304a, 332a, 336a, 345b; flagons, 74b, 78a, 269a, 309a, 314a; plates, 78a, 85a, 92a, 92b, 101a, 110a, 115a, 125a, 135a, 186a, 235b, 258b, 262a, 283b, 304a, 309a, 310b, 324a, 336a
  19th-cent.: chalices, 318a; cups, 29a, 31a, 34a, 36a, 43a, 70b, 83a, 132a, 174b, 264a, 277a, 304a, 345b, 350b; flagons, 132a, 174b, 277a, 318a, 350b; plates, 174b, 304a, 318a, 320b; other, 126b
  undated: beakers, 96b; cups, 20b; plates, 20b, 96b, 132a; other, 170b
Pointon and Sempringham, Lincs., 220a
Ponders End, Gr. London, 81b
poor-boxes see alms boxes
Portsmouth, Hants., 342a
Potsgrove, Beds., 18a
Potten End, Herts., 141a
Potter Street, Essex, xva, 47a, 57a–b
Potterhanworth, Lincs., 220a
Potter's Forstal, Kent, 175a
Potton, Beds., 18a–b
Pound Green, Cambs., 35b
Pound Hill, Frittenden, Kent, 161b, 177a–b
Poyle, Surrey, 327b
Poynings, Sussex, 354a
preachers see ministers, preachers, etc.
Presbyterian chapels, dating from before 1800 see chapels and meeting-houses
Preston, Herts., 141a
Preston, Kent, 193b
Prior Fen, Cambs., 42b
Puckeridge, Herts., 144a
pulpits: 17th-cent., 141a, 213a, 309a; 18th-cent., 9a, 50b, 243b, 264a, 271b, 283b, 284a, 287b, 294b, 295b, 299a, 304a, 327b, 346b, 352a, 359a; 19th-cent., 20a, 22a, 44b, 98a, 112b, 131b, 135a, 155b, 174b, 184a, 235b, 258b, 288b, 332a, 343b, 356b, 359a; 20th-cent., 104a; undated, 99b, 115a, 118b, 126b, 129b, 141b, 153a, 163a, 170b, 180b, 190b, 285a, 318a, 337b, 350b
Putney, Gr. London, 119a, 119b

Quaker meeting-houses, dating from before 1800 see chapels and meeting-houses
Quidenham, Norfolk, 264b

Radwell, Beds., 11a–b
railings and gates: 18th-cent., 94a; 19th-cent., 98b, 129a, 139a, 150b, 283b, 309a; undated, 14b
rainwater heads, 18th-cent., 283b
Raithby, Lincs., xvia, 194b, 220a–b, 221a–b
Ramsey, Hunts., 28a, 156b–157a, 160a
Ramsgate, Kent, xvb, 161b, 164b, 183a–184a
Rattlesden, Suffolk, 278a, 302b–304a
Ravensden, Beds., 18b
Rawstorne Street, Islington, Gr. London, 96b
Rayleigh, Essex, 60b–61a
Raynes Park, Gr. London, 69b, 110b
Raynham, Norfolk, 264b
Reading, Berks., 115a; architects, surveyors and builders, 123a, 130b, 143b, 162a, 324a
Red Hill, Herts., 143b
Red Pits, Norfolk, 275a
Redbourn, Herts., 141a–b
Redbridge, Gr. London, 111a–112a; see also Woodford Green
Redenhall with Harleston, Norfolk, 264b
Redhill, Surrey, 315b, 326b
Reepham, Norfolk, 264b
Regent's Park, Gr. London, 77a
Reigate, Surrey, 326b–327a; Redhill, 315b, 326b
Rendham, Suffolk, 278a, 302b, 303a–b, 304a, 305a
reredoses: 17th-cent., 84b–85a; 18th-cent., 101a; 20th-cent., 104a
Richmond, Indiana, USA, Earlham Quaker College, 277b
Richmond upon Thames, Gr. London, 112a–113a
Rickmansworth, Herts., 141b
Ridgmont, Beds., 19a
Riggindale Road, Lambeth, Gr. London, 69b, 108a
Ringland, Norfolk, 264b
Ringmer, Sussex, 352a
Ripley, Surrey, 327a
Riseley, Beds., 19a–b
Rishangles, Suffolk, 304b, 306a
Robertsbridge, Sussex, 329b, 354b
Rochester, Kent, 161a, 161b, 184a–b
Rochford, Essex, 61a
Rocklands, Norfolk, Rockland St Peter, 264b
Roe Green, Herts., 143b
Romford, Gr. London, 91a
Rosslyn Hill Chapel, Gr. London, 69a, 77b–78a, 104a
Rougham, Suffolk, 304b
Roxeth, Gr. London, 91a
Roxton, Beds., xva, 1b, 19b–20a
royal arms: 17th/18th-cent., 126a; 18th-cent., 118b, 126b; 19th-cent., 83b
Royal Tunbridge Wells, Kent, xvb, 161a, 161b, 184b–185b, 347b
Roydon, Essex, 61a
Royston, Herts., 39b, 141b–142a; clockmakers, 27b, 40a, 153b
Ruckinge, Kent, 185b
Rumburgh, Suffolk, 305a
Russell's Green, Sussex, 353a
Rye, Sussex, 329a, 329b, 354a–b

Saffron Walden, Essex, 47a, 61a–62b, 174a
St Albans, Herts., 127a, 127b, 142a–143b, 144a–b
St Andrew, Ilketshall, Suffolk, 305a
St George's German Lutheran Church, Gr. London, 68b, 118a–b
St Ives, Hunts., 127a, 149a, 149b, 157a–158b; sculptors and monumental masons, 35b, 40b
St John's Wood, Gr. London, 68b, 121a, 122a
St Leonards, Sussex, 329b, 342b
St Martins, Isles of Scilly, Cornwall, 353b
St Neots, Hunts., 19b, 159a, 160a
St Nicholas at Wade, Kent, 185b–186a
St Peters, Kent, 165a
Salehurst, Sussex, Robertsbridge, 329b, 354b
Salhouse, Norfolk, 264b–266a
Salters Lode, Norfolk, 238b
Saltfleet, Lincs., 222a
Saltfleetby St Peter, Lincs., 220b
Salvation Army (Christian Mission), 80a
Sandemanians, 101a–b
Sandhurst, Kent, 186a
Sandon, Herts., 143b
Sandwich, Kent, 161a, 186a–187a
Saracen's Head, Lincs., 228a
Sarratt, Herts., 143b
Saundby, Notts., 213a
Sawbridgeworth, Herts., 127b, 143b–144a
Sawtry, Hunts., 159a
Saxmundham, Suffolk, 304a, 305a
Scamblesby, Lincs., 220b
schools, day, Wesleyan, 254b
Scothern, Lincs., 220b
Scotter, Lincs., 220b
sculptors and monumental masons: Andrews, James, 9a; Athow, J., 262a; Backhouse, 60b; Bacon, J., 260b; Bacon, J., junr., 260b, 262a; Baily, E.H., 88b; Biggs, 38a; Biggs, J.P., 38a, 131b; Brown, R., 86b; Burgess, T., 242b; Cannam, 40b; Clark, J., 110a; Clayton, 34b; Clothier, 86b; Cushing, 256b; Cusworth, 103a; Denman, 243a; Dottridge, 125a; Doulton, 117b; Drew, C., 24b; Fuller, 35b; Gilbert, 44b, 131b; Hale, W.T., 284a; Hardy, W., 277a; Harmer, 343a, 353b; Harmer, Jonathan, 343a; Haselgrove, W., 38a; Haselgrove, William, 40b; Hatchard, E., 103a; Heyhoe, 254a; Hide, 35b; Hull and Pollard, 35a; Jackman, 284a; Jones, Ronald Potter, 78a, 104a; Levet, G., 41a; Logdon, 268b; Manning, S., 260b; Marsh, T., 61a; Miller, 9a; Peck, D., 131b; Peck, David, 131b; Penfold, 356b; Perfitt, R.J., 253b;

Pollard (*see* Hull and Pollard); Prior, 4a, 24b; Rawlins, T., 260b; Seager, B., 22a; Simpson, 310a; Skinner, J., 306a; Slight and Smith, 198b; Smart, J., 328b; Smith (*see also* Slight and Smith); Smith, B., 110a; Stanley, J., 244b, 253b, 262a; Stark, 217b; Swinton, 38a; Thrupp, Frederick, 3a; Tomson, 44b; Tomson, F. and T., 44b; Tucker, A.S., 254a; Watson, 258a; Wiggett, 284b; Wiggett, E., 284a; Wiles, 44b; Wing, 12a; Wood, Enoch, 77a; Woolvine, 35b; Yeatman and Sons, 110a
sculpture: 18th-cent., 92b; 19th-cent., 38a, 104a, 123b, 180b; 20th-cent., 126a; undated, 77a
Seaford, Sussex, 329b, 354b
Sedgeford, Norfolk, 266a
Selsey, Sussex, 330b, 355a
Seven Dials, Gr. London, 68b, 79a–b
Sevenoaks, Kent, 161b, 187a
Sevenoaks Weald, Kent, 187a
Shallows, Kent, 165a
Sharnbrook, Beds., 1b, 20a–b
Sheerness, Kent, 161a, 187a–b
Sheffield, Yorks., W. Riding, 198b
Shefford, Beds., 21a
Shelfanger, Norfolk, 266a–b
Shenley, Herts., 144a
Shere, Surrey, 327a
Shillington, Beds., 21a–b
Shipdham, Norfolk, 266b
Shipley, Sussex, 355b
Shoreditch, Gr. London, 108b
Shorne, Kent, 187b
Shover's Green, Wadhurst, Sussex, 329b, 356b
Sibsey, Lincs., 220b
Sibton with Peasenhall, Suffolk, 307b
Sidcup, Gr. London, 72b
Sidmouth, Devon, 110a
Silfield, Norfolk, 277b
Singleton, Sussex, 334b
Sittingbourne and Milton, Kent, 187b–188a; *see also* Milton Regis
Skegness, Lincs., 222a
Skeyton, Norfolk, 266b
Skidbrooke with Saltfleet Haven, Lincs., 222a
Skillington, Lincs., 222a
Slaugham, Sussex, 339a, 355a
Sleaford, Lincs., 222a
Sleapshyde, Herts., 132b
Smallburgh, Norfolk, 229a, 267a, 275b
Smallfield, Surrey, 319b
Smarden, Kent, 161a, 188a–b
Smeeth, Kent, 188b
Snitterby, Lincs., 222b
Snodland, Kent, 161b, 188b
Soham, Cambs., 26b, 40b–41b, 141b
Soho, Gr. London, 74b, 126a–b
Somersham, Hunts., 149b, 156b, 159a–b
Somersham, Suffolk, 305a
Somerton, Norfolk, 267a
Souldrop, Beds., 12b, 20b
South Cockerington, Lincs., 222b

South Creake, Norfolk, 229a–b, 267b–268a
South Croydon, Gr. London, 80a
South Ferriby, Lincs., 222b
South Hackney, Gr. London, 85b
South Harting, Sussex, 330a, 342a
South Kelsey, Lincs., 222b
South Killingholme, Lincs., xvia, 194a, 222b–223a
South Lopham, Norfolk, 268a
South Ockendon, Essex, 66a
South Weald, Essex, 89a
South Willingham, Lincs., 223a
Southend-on-Sea, Essex, 62b, 63a
Southery, Norfolk, 268a
Southill, Beds., xva, 1a, 1b, 21b–22a
Southminster, Essex, 62b
Southrepps, Norfolk, 268a, 269a
Southrey, Lincs., 196a
Southwark, Gr. London, 43a, 68b, 113a–116b; *see also* Dulwich; Jamaica Row; Newington Butts; Peckham; 'Pilgrim Fathers, Church of the'; Surrey Chapel
Southwick, Wilts., 341a
Southwold, Suffolk, 235b, 278a, 305b, 306b, 307b
Spalding, Lincs., 199b, 205a, 208a, 223a–b
Spaldwick, Hunts., 159b
Spaxton, Som., 86b
'Spencer Place Chapel', Gr. London, 95b
Spilsby, Lincs., 223b–224a
Spitalfields, Gr. London, Fournier Street, 68a, 116b–117a
Staines, Surrey, 327a–b
Stalham, Norfolk, 253b, 268a–b
Stamford, Lincs., 194a, 194b, 224a–225a
Stamford Hill, Gr. London: sculptors and monumental masons, 103a; 'The Ark of the Covenant', Rookwood Road, xva, xix, 69a, 86b–88a
Stamford Street Chapel, Gr. London, 68b, 115a
Stanbridge, Beds., 22b
Standon, Herts., 144a
Stanground South, Hunts., 149b, 159b
Stanhoe, Norfolk, 268b
Stansfield, Suffolk, 305b
Stansted Mountfitchet, Essex, 63a
Stanwell, Surrey, 327b
Staplehurst, Kent, 188a, 189a
Stebbing, Essex, 47a, 47b, 63a–64b
Steeple, Essex, 64a
Steeple Bumpstead, Essex, 47b, 64a
Steeple Morden, Cambs., 41b
Stevington, Beds., xva, 1a, 22b–24b
Steyning, Sussex, 329a, 330a, 355a–b
Stilton, Hunts., 159b–160a
Stockwell Green, Gr. London, 106b–108a
Stoke Ash, Suffolk, 306a
Stoke Newington, Gr. London, 68a, 88a–b; Abney Park Cemetery, 88b, 118b
Stone-cum-Ebony, Kent, xvb, 161b, 189a
Stonebridge, Norfolk, 275a

Stonesby, Leics., 222a
Stonham Parva, Suffolk, 306a
Stotfold, Beds., 24b
Stourmouth, Kent, 193b
stoves, 19th-cent., 22a
Stow, Lincs., 225a
Stow Bardolph, Norfolk, 268b
Stowbridge, Norfolk, 268b
Stowmarket, Suffolk, 278b, 289a, 306a–b, 310a
Stradbroke, Suffolk, 306b
Stratford, Gr. London, 110b–111a
Stratton St Mary, Norfolk, 251b
Stratton St Michael, Norfolk, 251b
Streatham, Gr. London, 108a
Stretham, Cambs., 41b
Strood, Kent, 184a
Sturton by Stow, Lincs., 225a–b
Sudbury, Suffolk, 281b, 306b–307a
sundials: 17th-cent., 258b–259a; 18th-cent., 117a, 305b; 19th-cent., 201a, 343a; undated, 33b, 283b
Surbiton, Gr. London, 104b
Surlingham, Norfolk, 268b
surnames: Abbott, 199a, 277a; Abel, 318b; Abney, 88b, 327b; Abraham, 25a, 122a, 330b; Ackroyd, 10a; Adams, 147a; Aiken, 85a; Akehurst, 24b; Alderson, 240a; Alexander, 259a, 321b; Allen, 29b, 232a, 240a, 258b; Allon, 97b; Anderson, 31b, 205a, 281b; Andrews, 9a, 27b, 99b, 115b, 289a; Angel, 318a; Angell, 95a; Angus, 131a; Anscombe, 133a; Ansell, 164a, 280b; Archdeacon, 172b; Armor, 244b; Armstrong, 223a; Arnold, 35a, 72b; Asa, 57a; Ashburnham, 330b; Ashdowne, 345b; Ashley, 84a, 210a; Ashton, 35b; Asplan, 150a; Aspland, 43b, 85a; Athow, 262a; Atkinson, 295b; Atlee, 91b; Austin, 133b; Avern, 89a; Ayscough, 209a, 210a; Backhouse, 60b; Bacon, 260b, 262a, 284a; Baddeley, 131a; Bailey, 55a; Baily, 88b; Bain, 57b; Bainbridge, 116b; Baines, 14a, 14b, 21a, 26b, 29a, 35b, 69b, 70b, 72a, 72b, 81b, 89b, 90a, 106a, 127b, 136a, 141a, 180a, 222a, 278b, 299b; Baker, 31b, 254a; Baldock, 227b; Baldwin, 324a; Balfour, 79b, 126b; Ball, 39b; Ballard, 169b; Balls, 258a; Bampton, 225b; Banham, 253b; Banks, 47b, 58a, 111a; Banyard, 311b; Barbauld, 86b; Barcham, 268a, 275b; Barclay, 82a; Barker, 80a, 287b, 304a; Barnard, 233b, 351a–b; Barnes, 47b, 51b, 56b, 66b, 91b, 131a, 278b, 294a, 295a, 297a, 297b, 301b; Barnett, 104b; Barnham, 258b; Barrett, 243a; Barringer, 22a; Barritt, 313b; Barrow, 310b; Barston, 208b; Bartholomew, 164a; Bartle, 41a; Bartlett, 180b; Barton, 313b; Bass, 57a; Bates, 85a; Battams, 11a; Bax, 319b; Baxter, 164b, 310b; Bayes, 19b; Bayley, 138a, 182b, 302b; Beadel, 67b; Beadle, 147b; Beaumont, 60a, 74a, 139a, 311a, 311b, 313b; Beckley, 132a; Beckman, 118b; Bedells, 82b, 89b,

surnames (*cont.*)

98a; Bedford, 3a, 215a; Beeman, 169b, 170a; Bell, 47b, 64a, 70b, 88b, 111b, 116a, 148a, 179b, 185b, 204a, 210a, 220a, 222a, 224a, 278b, 284a, 291a, 352b; Bellamy, 195a, 215a, 216a; Bellin, 50b; Bending, 268a; Bennel, 2b; Bennell, 2b; Bennett, 15b, 141a; Bensley, 326b; Benson, 58a; Benton, 29b; Berridge, 18a, 26a, 27b, 32b, 128a, 149a; Besse, 138a; Bickerdike, 106a; Biddall, 35b; Biddle, 318b; Bidwell, 141a; Biggs, 38a, 62a, 131b, 132a; Bill, 304a; Billing, 35b; Billinghurst, 78a; Billio, 60a, 63a, 85a, 131a; Bilney, 259a; Binfield, 198b; Binyon, 296a; Birch, 104b; Bird, 144a; Biss, 302b; Bissill, 225b; Blackburn, 55a; Blackie, 281a; Blackman, 57b, 334b; Blackwell, 135a; Blaine, 145b; Blakely, 275b; Blakey, 258a; Bland, 110a, 114a; Blomfield, 266b; Bloomfield, 113a; Bloss, 294a; Blunderfield, 258a; Blunt, 15b; Blyth, 64b, 99b; Boardman, 229b, 239a, 243a, 259a, 264b, 274a, 280a, 281a, 299b; Bocking, 131a; Bodle, 330a; Bolingbroke, 260b–262a; Bonella, 69a, 97a; Boney, 90a; Boodger, 44a, 44b; Booker, 359a; Boosey, 48b; Booth, 84a, 106b; Boreham, 327a; Botterill, 195b; Bottle, 160b, 242b; Bourn, 254b; Bower, 182b; Bowers, 291b; Bowyer, 350b; Boyce, 254a; Boyle, 310b; Boyse, 310b; Brackenbury, 194b, 220a, 225a; Bradbury, 113a; Bradshaw, 44a, 94b, 110a; Brandon, 69a, 77a; Bransby, 233a; Brent, 110a; Brett, 143b; Brettingham, 260a; Brewer, 304a; Brewster, 314a; Brice, 150b; Bridge, 256a; Bridger, 326a; Bridgman, 288b, 311b; Briggs, 110a, 168a, 174a; Bright, 304a; Brightwell, 38a; Brinkley, 39b; Brittan, 258b; Britten, 88a; Brock, 84b, 141a; Brockway, 53a; Bromfield, 322a; Bromley, 310b; Brook, 165a, 262a; Brooke, 123b; Brooker, 330a; Brooks, 13a, 315b–316a; Brown, 2b, 14b, 57a, 86b, 127b, 147a–b, 154b, 198b, 224b, 273a, 288a, 288b, 313b, 333b; Browne, 48a, 254a, 258a, 306b, 345b; Browning, 24b, 115b, 302a; Brydon, 88b; Bryson, 41b; Buck, 83a; Buckenham, 66a; Budgin, 179a; Bugby, 322a, 322b; Bull, 28a; Bunker, 12b; Bunyan, 1a, 2b, 3a, 7a, 34b, 102a, 131a, 138b, 139a, 141a; Burge, 179b; Burgess, 96b, 223a, 242b, 301b; Burls, 60a; Burne-Jones, 78a; Burnet, 113b; Burrell, 170a, 288b, 350b; Burton, 22a; Burtt, 225a; Bury, 281b, 283b; Busby, 329a, 332b; Butcher, 145b; Butteau, 264a; Byles, 295b; Caddy, 266a; Caffyn, 329a, 341a, 344a; Calamy, 115b; Calder, 125a; Caley, 185b; Campbell, 280b; Campion, 24b; Cannam, 40b; Cannon, 223a; Cantlow, 36a; Cappel, 118b; Carey, 135a; Carlier, 110a; Carr, 164a; Carslake, 110a; Carter, 48b, 113a, 144a; Carvell, 63a; Carver, 40a, 254a; Catteel, 40b; Cattermole, 280b, 297a, 297b, 313b; Cavit, 9a; Cawthorn, 224a–b; Cecil, 25a, 51a; Cennick, 19a, 104a; Chambers, 32b, 110a, 299b; Chance, 147a; Chaplin, 34b, 131a, 269b; Chapman, 69a, 80b, 88b, 110b, 112a, 127b, 139a, 147b; Chasney, 267b; Chatterton, 198a; Chessher, 10b; Chitty, 174a; Chivers, 35b; Christy, 128a; Church, 69a, 80a, 113b, 117b, 129a, 135b; Circhen, 238a–b; Clack, 141b; Clarabut, 145b; Clare, 20a; Clark, 89b, 110a, 179a, 275b; Clarke, 10b, 64b, 86a, 88a, 101a, 104a, 111a, 125a, 281b, 294b, 297a, 341a; Claydon, 258a; Clayton, 34b, 69a; Clement, 145b; Clements, 147b; Clifford, 177b; Clothier, 86b; Clowes, 253b; Coad, 321b; Codling, 243b; Coldham, 260b; Cole, 11b, 12a, 50b, 131b, 258a; Coleman, 175a; Coles, 15b; Colgate, 168a; Collier, 34b; Collinges, 260a; Collins, 238a; Collis, 50b; Colman, 241b; Compton, 35b, 320b; Conder, 122a, 309b; Congreve, 346b; Connebee, 33b; Connold, 230a; Conquest, 4a; Cook, 284a; Cooke, 268b; Cooper, 260a, 266a, 273a, 280a, 280b, 286a, 302b, 310a, 354b; Copping, 284a; Corderoy, 125a, 125a–b; Corey, 256b; Corkran, 117b; Corneby, 243a; Cornell, 304a; Costa, da, 119a; Couling, 132a; Coulson, 40a; Coupland, 179a; Cousins, 64b; Covell, 80c; Coveney, 262b; Covington, 24b; Cowell, 35a, 63a; Cowper, 179a, 239a; Cox, 145b, 258b, 299a; Cozens, 192b, 258a; Cragg, 241b; Craig, 48b; Cramp, 165a; Crane, 88a; Creak, 242b; Cream, 29b; Crisholm, 102b; Crisp, 299b, 306a, 314a; Croke, 110a; Crome, 258b; Cromwell, 86b, 149a, 157b, 258b; Crook, 138a; Crooks, 223a; Cropley, 29a; Crosby, 51a, 104a; Crouch, 356b; Crow, 12b, 285a; Crowe, 269a; Crowhurst, 356b; Crown, 50b; Crump, 180a; Crundwell, 356b; Cubitt, 26b, 31a, 69a, 88b, 97b, 108a, 125b, 253b; Cullen, 33b; Culmer, 164a–b; Curtis, 19b, 20a; Cushing, 256b; Cusworth, 103a; da Costa, 119a; Daglish, 223b; Daking, 131a; Daliel, 240a; Dallison, 306a; Dams, 64b; Dance, 99b; Dancy, 341b; Daniel, 83a; Darby, 306b; Darbyshire, 85b; Davey, 352b, 359a; Davidson, 246a; Davies, 35b, 64b, 112a, 122a, 127b, 138b; Davis, 132a; Davy, 266a; Dawkes, 139b; Dawkins, 119b; Dawson, 70a, 256b, 321b; Day, 63a; De Carle, 281a; de la Pierre, 165b; de Merveilleux, 224a; Dearn, 169a, 170a–b; Delight, 262a; Dendy, 345b; Denman, 243a; Dennant, 290a; Dent, 217b; Deny, 280a; Devereux, 235b; Deverson, 240a; Devey, 180a; Dicker, 334a; Dickerson, 358a; Disney, 213a, 214b; Dixon, 62b; Docwra, 31a; Doggett, 277a, 358a; Donaldson, 82a; Donne, 4b–7a; Dottridge, 125a; Doulton, 117b; Dowm, 353b; Downes, 138a; Doyle, 238b; Drake, 83a–b; Drane, 244a, 244b; Drawbridge, 178a; Drew, 24b, 184a; Drewe, 182b; Dreyer, 260b; Drummond, 315a–b; Duke, 332b; Dunbar, 273a; Dunk, 356b; Dunkley, 213a; Durban, 269b; Dutton, 153a, 153b; Dyer, 175a; Eade, 280b, 296a, 297a, 297b, 306b, 313b, 314b; Ebbetts, 230a; Edwards, 43a, 258a, 328b, 333b; Eedis, 61b; Elden, 260b; Elgar, 193b; Elison, 262a; Elliot, 141a; Ellis, 41b, 322b, 347b; Ellison, 213a, 262a; Ellson, 343a; Elridge, 106a; Elsdale, 103a; Elven, 284a; Elwood, 321b; Elworthy, 329b, 342b, 354b; Emery, 13b, 20b; Enfield, 262a; Evaets, 267b; Evans, 35b, 77b, 298a; Evens, 346b; Everett, 246a; Evershed, 331a–b, 332a; Everson, 225b; Ewen, 205a; Faithful, 334a; Farmery, 291b; Farrar, 125a; Faulkner, 94b; Faunch, 279a, 296b; Fawcett, 118b; Fawkner, 102b; Feary, 149a–b, 150a; Fen, 44b; Fenowillet, 79a–b; Fensom, 24b; Fenton, 26b, 32a, 38b, 47b, 48a, 48b, 50a, 54a, 58a, 67a, 67b, 94b, 161b, 192b, 198a, 215a, 229b, 249a, 278b, 280a, 289b, 291a, 301b; Fernie, 132a; Field, 57a, 236b; Fiennes-Clinton, 213a; Finch, 95b, 249b; Fines, 213a–b, 213b; Fisher, 138a, 276b, 288b; Fison, 279b; Fittler, 350b; Flack, 29b; Fleetwood, 262b; Fleming, 111a, 273a; Fleming-Williams, 90a; Fletcher, 48b, 50a, 110a; Flood, 39b; Flower, 280a; Folkes, 281b; Ford, 299a, 301b; Fordham, 31b, 41a, 64b, 141b, 143b; Foreman, 29b, 175b; Forster, 60a; Foskett, 139a, 145b; Foster, 29a, 131a, 141a; Fothergill, 82a; Fowler, 12a, 12b, 223a; Fox, 102a, 324b, 339a, 340a; Frankling, 231b; Freeland, 126b; Freeman, 33b, 132a, 243b; French, 299a; Frost, 266b; Fulcher, 233a; Fulks, 145b; Fullager, 336b; Fuller, 35b, 40b, 81b, 83b, 168a, 233a; Galer, 143b; Galland, 217a; Gamble, 33b; Gamby, 22a; Gardner, 172b, 175b, 176b, 177a; Garneth, 145b; Garrard, 302b, 318a; Garrett, 117b; Garrod, 53a; Gascoigne, 110a; Gatford, 345b; Gaulter, 103a; Gay, 269b, 271b, 277a; Gersdorf, 103b; Gibbon, 56b; Gibson, 68b, 74b; Gifford, 2b, 40b, 74b; Gilbert, 44b, 131b, 343a; Giles, 234b; Gill, 102a; Gilson, 88b; Gisburne, 36a, 41b; Glandfield, 295b; Glanfield, 266b; Gleadah, 258b; Glover, 83b, 127b, 143a, 145a, 252a, 252b–253a, 267b; Godby, 170a; Goddard, 238a; Godfrey, 25a; Godwin, 155a, 244b; Goggs, 267b; Goldborne, 264a; Golding, 264a; Goldsmith, 232a, 306b, 343a; Gooch, 253b, 280b; Goodall, 89b; Goodchild, 294a; Goodman, 154b; Goodrick, 254a, 268b; Goodwin, 69a, 164b, 165a; Gordon, 26b, 31b, 116b, 198b, 204b, 295b; Goring, 351b; Gosling, 50a, 101b; Gouldsmith, 330a; Goulty, 352b; Grange, 146a; Granger, 64b; Grantham, 267a; Gray, 94b; Green, 14b, 150a, 319a; Greenwood, 196b, 223a; Gribble, 119a; Gridley, 147a; Grieves, 231b;

Griffith, 264a; Grimwade, 297a; Groom, 98b; Grove, 326b; Grover, 325b, 352a; Gunton, 26b, 31b, 33b, 38b, 41b, 116b, 198b, 204b; Gurteen, 291a; Gwennap, 61b; Habergham, 307b; Habershon, 69a, 71a, 72a, 84b, 96b, 102b, 121a, 141a, 156a, 222a; Hague, 188b; Haig, 126b; Haigh, 24b; Hale, 284a; Hall, 119a; Hallett, 258b, 341b; Halls, 301a; Hamilton, 62b, 337b, 343b; Hammond, 78a; Hanbury, 164a; Hancock, 34b; Hanley, 74a; Hannath, 223a; Hannell, 42b; Hanson, 353b; Harben, 350a, 359a; Harberd, 133b; Hardman, 78a; Hardy, 195a, 215a, 216a, 277a; Harford, 233a; Harmer, 343a, 353b; Harpam, 209b, 210a; Harradence, 147a; Harris, 12b, 50b, 55a, 143b, 180b, 304b; Harrison, 213b; Hartley, 66b; Harvey, 4a, 33b, 66a, 230a; Haselgrove, 38a, 40b; Hasson, 321b; Hastings *see* Huntingdon (Countess of); Hatchard, 103a; Hatcher, 241b; Hatton, 319b; Haughton, 175a; Haw, 240a; Hawkes, 178b; Hawkins, 13a, 88b, 356b; Hay, 51a; Hayes, 39b, 50a, 61b, 114b; Hayler, 345b; Hayter, 58a; Hayward, 286a; Hemming, 99b; Hempstead, 29b; Henman, 80a; Henry, 85a, 310b; Heptinstall, 280a; Herrick, 52a; Heward, 51b; Heyhoe, 254a; Hickman, 235b; Hide, 35b, 359b; Higgs, 105b; Hill, 31b, 57b, 95b, 115a, 133b, 212a, 232a, 306a; Hillam, 250b; Hillier, 132a; Hilton, 146a; Hindes, 29b; Hinds, 184a; Hine, 129a; Hitchcock, 60b, 310a; Hoare, 82a; Hobbs, 175b; Hobden, 356b; Hobson, 15b, 135a; Hocking, 111b; Hoddinott, 336b; Hodge, 96a; Hodgkins, 40b; Hodsoll, 175b; Holbert, 115b; Holcroft, 26a, 40a, 153a; Holden, 228b; Holiday, 78a; Holloway, 11a; Holman, 57b; Holmes, 235b; Honeywood, 77b; Hook, 188b, 332b, 337b; Hooker, 330a; Hoole, 62b; Hooper, 350a; Hopkins, 38a; Hopperton, 321b; Horder, 69b, 72b, 89b, 118b, 132a; Horsfield, 352a; Horsford, 4a; Horton, 163b; Houghton, 262a, 284a; How, 150a; Howard, 55b, 304a; Howard (John), 3b; Howe, 310b; Howell, 238a; Howes, 268a; Howgate, 112a; Hoyle, 262a; Hubbert, 198b; Huckvale, 145a; Hudnal, 10b; Hull, 9a, 35a; Humphrey, 322b; Hunnilove, 3a; Hunt, 33b, 119a, 332a, 337b; Huntingdon (Countess of), 185a, 185b, 259a, 329b, 337b, 358b; Huntington, 92b, 112a, 169b, 170a, 170b, 208b, 322a, 329b, 347b, 350a; Hupton, 234b; Hurrion, 235b; Hurry, 240a, 243a; Hurst, 165a; Hursthouse, 205b; Hustler, 302a; Hutchinson, 42b; Hyscoghe, 209b, 210a; Ibberson, 127b, 132a, 248a; Ielding, 356b; Igglesden, 174a, 179a; Ince, 285b; Inglefield, 322b; Inkpen, 332a; Inman, 84a; Innes, 256b; Innocent, 198b; Inskip, 21a; Irish, 156b, 160a; Irons, 113a; Irving, 77a, 315a; Iveson, 337b; Ivimey, 74b; Ivory, 259a, 260a;

Jackman, 284a; Jackson, 3a, 38a, 108a, 150a; James, 13a, 112b, 113b, 127b, 135b, 259a, 301b, 333b; Jardine, 43b; Jarmyn, 269a; Jarrold, 258a; Jarvis, 295b; Jay, 113a; Jeffery, 167b, 332a; Jekyll, 246b; Jenkins, 125a, 127b, 143b, 161b, 167a, 184b, 342a, 347b, 350a, 350b; Jenkyn, 184a; Jermyn, 277a; Jezreel, 177b; Jobson, 26b, 33b, 161b, 162b, 291a; Johns, 296a, 301b, 306b; Johnson, 78a, 111a, 119a, 125a, 175a–b, 177b, 310a, 310b, 311b; Johnston, 122a; Jollie, 69a; Jollo, 266b; Jones, 11b, 26b, 59b, 78a, 80b, 104a, 110a, 294b, 295a, 351b, 356b; Jordan, 132a; Judd, 131a; Keen, 74b, 230a, 304b; Kefford, 40a, 153a–b; Keith, 112a; Kemp, 64b, 163a, 285b, 288b, 334a, 356b; Kenhelmin, 188a; Kennedy, 223b; Kern, 296b; Kerridge, 253b; Kewell, 184b; Keymer, 153b; Kiddall, 217b; Kiddell, 264a; Kilham, 204b; Kilpin, 11a; King, 33b, 59b, 94b, 162a, 168a; Kinghorn, 230a; Kingsford, 110a, 165b; Kippis, 215a, 321b; Kirby, 233a, 267b; Kirbyshire, 128a; Kirkpatrick, 260a, 262a; Kitchin, 174a–b; Kittson, 28a; Knapton, 271b; Knight, 57a, 174b, 332a; Knightley, 81a, 118a; Knowles, 133a; Knowlton, 133b; Koestritz, 104a; Kruse, 103a; Lamb, 212a; Lambert, 82a, 218a, 319a; Lanchester, 122a, 125b; Landels, 77a; Lander, 82b, 89b, 98a; Lane, 268b; Langerman, 48a; Langston, 295b; Larkin, 51a; Last, 302a; Latchford, 98b; Lauder, 103a, 339a; Lawrence, 69b, 145b, 220a; Leach, 51b, 233a; Lee, 40b, 85b, 205a; Legerton, 67a; Lepine, 126a; Lethaby, 315b, 325b; Levatt, 145a; Lever, 11b; Levet, 41a; Lewin, 198b; Lewis, 143a, 267b; Lickert, 42a; Lidbetter, 185b; Lilley, 29a; Lincoln, 258a–b; Lincolne, 290a; Lindsey, 104a; Ling, 304b; Linsell, 131b; Little, 57b; Littleton, 358a; Livingstone, 51a; Lockwood, 69b; Logdon, 268b; Lorkin, 51a; Love, 179a; Lover, 344a; Lucas, 256b; Lund, 359b; Lungley, 298b; Lutyens, 69b, 70b, 229b, 264a; Lycett, 70b, 90a; Maberly, 84a; Macgregor, 122a; Mackie, 291a; McKilliam, 90a; McKissack, 110a; McNeile, 315a; Maling, 38a; Maltby, 262a; Manchester (Duchess of), 126b; Manning, 159b, 260b, 307b; Manser, 140a; Marchant, 163b, 350a; Mardling, 11b; Mark, 54a; Marsh, 61a, 174a, 260b; Marten, 172b, 174a, 341b; Martin, 48a, 123a, 123b, 319a; Martineau, 262a; Martyn, 16a–b, 18a; Mason, 202a, 223a, 241a; Matthews, 4a, 18b; Mawson, 69b; Mayes, 288b; Mayhew, 280a; Mayo, 104b; Mead, 70a; Mears, 33b, 316b; Mercer, 24b; Merchant, 34a; Meredith, 110b, 148a, 210a; Meryett, 327a; Metcalfe, 19b; Meyer, 118b; Middleton, 347a, 347b; Miles, 7b; Millard, 3b; Miller, 9a, 29a, 326a; Mills, 244b, 322a; Milnes, 186b; Milton, 138a; Milway, 295b; Minter, 174a; Mitchell, 177a; Money, 277a;

Montague, 133b; Montgomery, 94b; Moodie, 281b; Moon, 110a; Moore, 39b, 53a, 213a, 299b; Moores, 141a; Morell, 59b; Morley, 180a, 313b; Morris, 69a, 88a, 131b, 343a; Mortimer, 99b; Mote, 345b; Mould, 15b; Mountain, 185b; Mumford, 80a, 108a, 131b; Mummery, 90a; Munro, 135a; Munsey, 44b; Murrell, 74b; Muskett, 313b; Myers, 90b; Napier, 352a; Nash, 40a; Nasmith, 262a; Neale, 13a, 135a; Nettlefold, 358a; Nevile, 175b; Newman, 138a; Newton, 133a, 256b, 258a, 351b; Nicholls, 51a; Nichols, 38a, 234b; Nickols, 266a; Norman, 36a, 41a, 58a; Norris, 153a; North, 118a, 147a, 147b; Norton, 313b; Notcutt, 63b, 295b; Notman, 352a; Nott, 291a; Nottage, 57b; Noyes, 298b; Nunn, 333b; Oakes, 58b; Oakley, 81b, 131a; Oakshett, 180a; Ockendon, 110a; Oddy, 26a, 32a, 40a; Offley, 258b; Oliver, 133b; Orchard, 125a; Osborn, 249a; Osland, 26a, 40a; Oswald, 126b; Owchin, 313b; Owen, 51a, 51b; Owers, 41b; Oxborrow, 311a; Page, 145a, 175b; Paget, 69b; Pain, 212a; Paine, 25a, 35a, 159a; Palmer, 101a, 243a; Paraire, 95b; Parker, 69b, 103a, 235b, 339a; Parnacott, 352b; Parry, 59b; Patching, 324b; Patience, 229a, 259b; Paul, 258a, 330a; Paull, 69a, 97a, 106a; Pawson, 288b; Payne, 74b; Peachey, 29b; Peacock, 99b, 113b, 155b, 157b; Pear, 174b; Pearce, 147b; Pearmain, 301a; Pearson, 14b, 69a, 121b, 141b; Peck, 131b, 264b; Peckover, 46b; Pedder, 230a; Peggram, 131b; Penfold, 356b; Penn, 138a, 355b; Pepper, 22a; Perfitt, 253b; Perkins, 254a; Perry, 57b; Pertwee, 47b, 51a, 56a, 56b, 71b; Pestell, 230b; Peto, 74b, 77a; Pettingell, 132a; Pettit, 343a; Petty, 260b; Phelps, 104b; Phillips, 11b, 131a; Philpot, 224a; Philpotts, 174b; Pierse, 113b; Pilkington, 61b, 200a; Pinchbeck, 133b; Pite, 72a, 79b, 121a, 156a, 222a; Pitty, 128a; Plumbe, 77a; Plumstead, 287a; Pocock, 15a, 99b, 102b, 114b, 161b, 172a, 296b, 342b, 352b; Pollard, 35a; Poole, 216a–b, 280a; Pooley, 122a; Pope, 113a; Porter, 275a; Postlethwaite, 351a, 351b; Potto, 135a; Pouget, 110a; Poulton, 53a, 69a, 95b, 123a, 127b, 130b, 143b, 161b, 162a, 179a, 182a, 187b, 188a, 315b, 324a, 326b, 354b; Powell, 264a, 289a; Power, 48a; Press, 343a; Price, 86b; Priest, 310b; Priestley, 301b; Prime, 28a; Prince, 86b, 88a, 94b; Prior, 4a, 24b; Pritchard, 86b; Proctor, 90a; Prudden, 40b; Puget, 71b; Pugin, 316b; Purdy, 354b; Pyall, 179a; Quant, 284a; Quinton, 302a; Ranger, 92a; Ransome, 96a; Rathband, 89a; Rawlins, 260b; Razafy, 119a; Read, 44b; Reckitt, 141a; Reed, 172b; Rees, 145b; Reeve, 182b, 262a; Relley, 104b; Rennie, 115a; Reynolds, 36a, 215a; Rhodes, 189b; Ribbans, 296a, 298b; Richardson, 28a, 69a, 224b; Rickards,

surnames (cont.)
122a, 125b; Rickman, 119b, 351a; Ridley, 54a, 284a; Riley, 319a; Rippon, 102a, 153a; Ripshire, 128a; Riste, 36a; Rix, 235b; Robb, 42b; Roberts, 228b, 230a, 264a, 286a; Robertson, 259a; Robins, 35b, 232a; Robinson, 200b, 205b, 217b, 235b; Rock, 213a; Roff, 29a; Rogers, 3b, 86b, 356b; Rolf, 266b; Rolls, 38a; Rooth, 297a; Rootham, 44b; Roper, 113a; Rose, 35b; Rowan, 110a; Rowlatt, 150b; Rowntree, 71a, 77b; Royson, 172b; Rushmore, 266a; Ruskin, 115b; Russel, 356b; Russell, 4a, 260a; Sadd, 51a; Sainsbury, 33b, 332a; St Clair, 215a; Salter, 127b, 143a; Sames (Sams), 51a; Sampson, 101a, 287a; Sanders, 31a; Sandling, 264a; Sanford, 67b; Savage, 15b; Savell, 129b; Savidge, 113b; Savill, 50b; Saxby, 358a; Say, 287b; Sayer, 268a; Scandrett, 155a; Scaping, 210a; Schmidt, 4a; Scott, 31b, 74b, 125a, 230a, 235a, 246a, 256b–258a, 256b, 258a, 258b, 277a; Scroggs, 12b; Seager, 22a; Seamur, 233a; Sear, 35b; Searle, 50a, 61b, 71b, 77a, 82a, 95a, 96a, 96b, 114b, 121b, 291b, 340b; Sears, 10a, 71a; Seely, 69b; Selby, 271b; Sewell, 233a, 258b; Shamley, 153a; Sharpe, 86b; Shaw, 315b, 325b, 355b; Shearburn, 321b; Sheffield, 24b; Sheldrake, 262b; Shelly, 242b, 330a; Shepherd, 48b; Sherman, 115a, 302a; Shillito, 354b; Shoesmith, 356b; Shorland, 354b; Shrubsole, 187a, 187b; Shufflebottom, 281a; Sicklemore, 334b; Sieveking, 118b; Siggs, 356b; Silcock, 268b; Sillett, 258b; Simmons, 150a; Simpson, 310a, 333a; Sims, 264a; Sizer, 291a; Skilleter, 153b; Skinner, 163b, 306a; Skipper, 321b; Slack, 41b; Slater, 33b; Slator, 228a; Slaughter, 174b; Slight, 198b; Sloper, 280a; Smart, 328b; Smeeton, 213b; Smith, 29a, 33b, 55a, 78a, 110a, 127b, 136b, 156a, 174a, 198b, 223a, 243a, 249a, 264a, 266b, 279b, 288b, 325b, 330a, 343a; Smithies, 94a; Smyth-Piggott, 88a; Smythies, 233a; Snashall, 322b; Snashold, 355b; Southon, 177b; Spalding, 90b; Spanton, 240b; Sparham, 241b; Sparkes, 304a; Sparrow, 88a; Speed, 108a; Spelman, 243a; Spencer, 240a; Spicer, 280a; Spratt, 288a; Spring, 208a; Spurgeon, 36a, 43a, 47a, 53a, 68b, 114b, 175b, 253b; Squier, 110a; Squire, 174a; Stackhouse, 256b; Staden, 215a; Stainbank, 33b; Stalham, 64a; Stammers, 301b; Stanger, 168a, 168b, 175b; Stanley, 125a, 244b, 253b, 262a; Stapleton, 119b; Stark, 217b; Starkie (Starkey), 85b; Starr, 186a; Steane, 132a; Steele, 301b; Steevens, 51b; Steggles, 284a; Stent, 321b; Stephens, 29a, 65b; Stepney, 345b; Stevens, 44b, 91b, 147a, 343a; Stibbs, 116b; Stiff, 105b; Stittle, 29b, 31a; Stocking, 88b; Stockton, 294a; Stone, 101a; Stonehouse, 104a, 169b; Storr, 219a; Story, 138a, 139a; Strafford, 336a; Strange, 12b; Stratten, 122a; Street, 324a; Stringer, 119b; Sturdy, 111a; Such, 24b; Sulman, 74a, 92a, 189b; Sutton, 4b, 131b, 145b, 205b; Swann, 322b; Swannell, 11b; Swinton, 38a; Syer, 310a; Sykes, 231b, 244b; Syme, 147b; Tabor, 50a; Tailer, 311b; Tait, 151a, 175b, 195a, 208b; Tapp, 86b; Tarring, 14b, 54a, 69a, 78a, 80b, 81a, 102a, 117b, 118b, 149b, 155b, 157a, 161b, 184a, 187a, 315b, 328a; Taverner, 172a, 172b; Tay, 22a; Tayler, 180b; Taylor, 29a, 38a, 51a, 56b, 132a, 185b, 198a, 213a, 225b, 260a, 260b, 298a, 327b; Tebbit, 43a; Temple, 61a; Thacker, 284a; Thackray, 2b; Theobald, 258a; Thodey, 31a; Thomas, 106b; Thompson, 197b, 235b, 289a, 341b; Thorne, 128b; Thorogood, 48a; Thrupp, 3a; Thurbin, 92a; Tidcombe, 148a; Tiffin, 174a; Tilden, 188b; Tite, 18b; Toll, 313b; Tompson, 256b; Toms, 208b, 287b; Tomson, 44b, 256b; Toomer, 192b, 193b; Toplady, 77a; Towler, 241a; Towne, 141b; Townsend, 69b, 111b, 184a; Treen, 225b; Trigg, 328b; Trimen, 102a; Tryon, 203b; Tucker, 254a; Turk, 246a; Turner, 126b, 295b, 311b, 331b, 332a; Tusler, 340b; Tuthill, 241b; Tyler, 144a, 175a; Tyndall, 101b; Unicomb, 356b; Unwin, 51b; Upton, 143a; Urwick, 143b; Usher, 3b, 11b, 20a; Utting, 234a, 234b; Uwins, 61a; Vane, 188a; Varley, 333a; Venimore, 268b; Venn, 149a; Vidler, 117a, 198b, 330b, 353a; Vinall, 350a; Vintner, 31b; Virgoe, 330a; Vivian, 333a; Vorley, 9a; Wake, 13a; Wakeham, 222b; Walcker, 334a; Walder, 340b; Walker, 4a, 254a, 326b; Wallace, 113a; Wallen, 85b; Waller, 164a, 258b; Wallinger, 132a; Walmsley, 94b, 217b; Walters, 133a, 258a; Warboys, 128b; Warburton, 22a; Ward, 20b, 40b, 140a, 154b, 225a, 236b, 258a, 262a, 342b; Warren, 264a; Warter, 213a; Waschel, 118b; Waterhouse, 69a, 77a, 125a; Waters, 42b; Watkins, 94b; Watson, 258a; Watts, 43a, 50b, 88b, 131a; Wearing, 304a; Webb, 42a, 126b, 280b, 291a; Webster, 131a; Weir, 119b, 125b; Wellard, 170b; Weller, 322b; Wells, 164a; Welman, 324a; Wesley, 102a, 194a; Wesley (John), 4a, 18a, 79a, 99b, 165a, 167a, 185b, 187a, 194b, 203a, 204a, 220a, 240b, 243b, 259a, 260a, 274b, 298a, 321b; Westbrook, 113b; Weston, 232a, 358a; Wheatley, 240b, 259a; Wheeler, 108a; Whitaker, 111a; Whitbread, 2b; Whitefield, 77a, 82b, 95b, 185b, 187a, 259a, 359a; Whitehead, 133b; Whitehouse, 321b; Whiting, 264b, 276a, 276b; Whitmore, 240a; Wicker, 356b; Wickes, 235b; Wiggett, 284a; Wilderspin, 42a; Wilds, 333b, 334a; Wiles, 44b; Wilkins, 260b, 315b–316a; Willem, 70b; Williams, 89a, 102a, 258a; Willis, 24b, 80a, 88a, 98a, 102a, 123b; Willoughby, 207a; Wills, 90b, 164a, 222a, 226a, 346b; Willsdon, 64b; Willshier, 64b; Wilmshurst, 60a; Wilson, 78a, 94b, 98b, 104b, 106b, 115b, 122a, 129b, 180a, 180b, 183a, 327a; Wimble, 185b, 334a; Winchester, 117a, 330b; Wing, 3a, 12a; Winkworth, 246b; Winslow, 356b; Winter, 53b; Wire, 147a; Withers, 110b, 210a; Wonnacott, 321a, 323a; Wood, 77a, 141a, 179a, 258b, 321b; Woodcock, 353b; Woodham, 40a; Woodhams, 330a; Woodland, 184a; Woodman, 127b, 130b, 143b, 161b, 179a, 182a, 187b, 188a, 315b, 326b, 343a; Woods, 236b, 268b; Woodthorpe, 89a; Woodward, 131a, 276b; Woolnough, 286a; Woolvine, 35b; Worley, 143a; Worsley, 94b; Worthington, 69a, 78a; Wray, 325a; Wright, 11b, 51b, 233a, 286b; Wybroe, 29b; Yeatman, 110a; Yelf, 71b; Yeomans, 110a; Yoakley, 182a; Young, 321b; Youngman, 258a, 277a; Youngs, 262a; Zinzendorf, 103b, 104a

Surrey Chapel, Gr. London, 69b, 115a–b
surveyors *see* architects, surveyors and builders
Sutherland Chapel, Gr. London, 116a
Sutterton, Lincs., 225b
Sutton, Cambs., 26a, 41b
Sutton, Gr. London, 116b
Sutton-at-Hone, Kent, 175b, 189a
Sutton St James, Lincs., 226a
Sutton on Sea, Lincs., 226a
Sutton Valence, Kent, 189a–b
Swaby, Lincs., 226a
Swaffham, Norfolk, 229b, 236b, 254a, 268b, 269a
Swaffham Prior, Cambs., 26b, 41b–42b
Swafield, Norfolk, 254b; Bradfield, 254b, 268b–269a
Swanscombe, Kent, 189b; Greenhithe, 161b, 177b, 189b
Swanton Abbott, Norfolk, 269a
Swavesey, Cambs., 26a, 42b–43a, 157b
Swedenborgians *see* New Church
Swefling, Suffolk, 304a
Swineshead, Lincs., 226a
Swingfield Minnis, Kent, 190a

tables: 17th-cent., 340a; 19th-cent., 3b, 4b, 21a; undated, 318b; *see also* communion tables
tables of Lord's Prayer, Creed and Decalogue, 101a, 118b
Tasburgh, Norfolk, 269a–b
Tatternhoe, Bucks., 10b
Tattershall, Lincs., 202b, 226a
Tattershall Bridge, Lincs., 197b
Tealby, Lincs., 226a–b
Tebworth, Beds., 9b
Tempsford, Beds., 24b
Tenterden, Kent, xvb, 161a, 162a, 190a–b, 191a–b
Terling, Essex, xva, 47a, 64a–65b
Terrington St Clement, Norfolk, 269b
Terrington St John, Norfolk, 269b
Tetworth, Hunts. *see* Everton

Teversham, Cambs., 43a
Teynham, Kent, 190b
Thakeham, Sussex, 'Blue Idol', xvib, 329b, 330a, 355b–356a
Tharston, Norfolk see Hapton
Thaxted, Essex, 63a, 65b–66a
Thealby, Lincs., 202a
Theddlethorpe St Helen, Lincs., 226b
Themelthorpe, Norfolk, 271b
Therfield, Herts., 144a
Thetford, Norfolk, 254b, 273a, 279b
Thimbleby, Lincs., 226b
Thorn, Beds., 12a–b
Thorne, Yorks., W. Riding, 267b
Thornham, Norfolk, 273a
Thornton Curtis, Lincs., 226b
Thorpe on the Hill, Lincs., 226b
Thorpe-le-Soken, Essex, 66a
Three Holes, Norfolk, 274a
Thundersley, Essex, 66a
Thurleigh, Beds., 24b
Thurrock, Essex, 66a
Ticehurst, Sussex, 356b
Tilford, Surrey, 315a, 327b–328a
Tillingham, Essex, 47b, 66b
Tilsworth, Beds., 24b
Timberland, Lincs., 226b
Tiptree, Essex, 66b
Tittleshall, Norfolk, 273a–b
Tivetshall St Margaret, Norfolk, 273b–274a
Toddington, Beds., 12a, 24b–25a
Tollington Park, Gr. London, 68a, 96b–97a
Tonbridge, Kent, 190b, 275b
Topcroft, Norfolk, 274a
Toseland, Hunts., 160a
Totham, Essex, 56b
Tottenham, Gr. London, 89b, 90a
Tottenham Court Road Chapel, Gr. London, 77a
Totternhoe, Beds., 25a
Tower Hamlets, Gr. London, 69a, 116b–118b; Little Alie Street Chapel, 358a; see also Parliament Court Chapel; St George's German Lutheran Church; Spitalfields; West Ferry Road
Toynton All Saints, Lincs., 226b
Toynton St Peter, Lincs., 227a
Trevecca College, Talgarth, Brecons., 219b, 347b
Tring, Herts., 127a, 130a, 144b–146a
Tunbridge Wells, Kent see Royal Tunbridge Wells
Tunstall, Suffolk, 307a
Turners Hill, Sussex, 326a
Turvey, Beds., 25a
Two Waters, Herts., 136a
Tydd St Giles, Cambs., 226a

Uckfield, Sussex, 356a
Ufford, Suffolk, 307a
Union Chapel, Islington, Gr. London, xvb, 69a, 97b–98a

Unitarian chapels, dating from before 1800 see chapels and meeting-houses
Universalists, 198b–199a
Up Hill, Kent, 178b
Upminster, Gr. London, 91a–b
Upper Dean, Beds., 10a
Upper Hale, Surrey, 323a, 323b
Upper Street, Islington, Gr. London, 69a, 96a–b, 97a, 101a
Upper Tasburgh, Norfolk, 269a–b
Upton, Lincs., 227a
Upwell, Cambs., 43a
Upwell, Norfolk, 274a
Uxbridge, Gr. London, 68a, 68b, 92a–b, 93a–b

Waddingham, Lincs., 227a
Wadhurst, Sussex, xvib, 329b, 356a–b, 357a–b
Wainfleet All Saints, Lincs., 227a
Wainfleet Bank, Lincs., 227a
Wainfleet St Mary, Lincs., 227a, 227b
Wainfleet St Thomas, Lincs., Northolme Chapel, 194a, 198a
Walcot near Billinghay, Lincs., 227b
Waldringfield, Suffolk, 307a
Waldron, Sussex, 356b
Walesby, Lincs., 213a
Walkern, Herts., 146a
Walpole, Suffolk, frontispiece, xvib, xix, 278a, 307b–309a
Walsham-le-Willows, Suffolk, 309a–b
Waltham Forest, Gr. London, 118b–119a; see also Leyton
Waltham Holy Cross, Essex, Waltham Abbey, 66b
Walthamstow, Gr. London, 118b–119a
Walton on the Naze, Essex, 56a
Walworth, Gr. London, 115b
Wandsworth, Gr. London, 68b, 119a–121a
Wanstead, Gr. London, 111a–b
Wapping, Gr. London, 126b
Warbleton, Sussex, 343a, 356b–358a
Warboys, Hunts., 149a, 156b, 160a
Ware, Herts., 127a, 127b, 146a–147b
Wareside, Herts., 147b
Warminghurst, Sussex, 355b
Washbrook, Suffolk, 309b
Waterbeach, Cambs., 43a
Watford, Herts., 127b, 147b–148a
Wattisfield, Suffolk, 278a, 309b
Wattisham, Suffolk, 309b–310a
Watton, Norfolk, 274a
Wealdstone, Gr. London, 90b, 91a
weathervanes: 18th-cent., 250b; undated, 301a
Welbourn, Lincs., 227b
Welby, Lincs., 227b
Wellingore, Lincs., 227b
Wells-next-the-Sea, Norfolk, 274b–275a
Welton, Lincs., 227b
Welwyn, Herts., 148a–b
Wendling, Norfolk, 275a
Wenhaston with Mells Hamlet, Suffolk, 310a
Werrington, Hunts., 156b

Wesley's Chapel, Gr. London, xvb, 68b, 99b–101a; Wesley's house, 79a, 99b
West Butterwick, Lincs., 227b–228a
West Croydon, Gr. London, 69a, 80a
West Drayton, Gr. London, 92b–94a
West Ferry Road, Tower Hamlets, Gr. London, 69b, 117b–118a
West Hampstead, Gr. London, 79b
West Hoathly, Sussex, 358a
West Hougham, Kent, 180a
West Malling, Kent, 192a
West Mersea, Essex, 66b–67a
West Norwood, Gr. London, 108a, 110a
West Raynham, Norfolk, 264b
West Row, Suffolk, 301a, 301b
West Somerton, Norfolk, 267a
West Walton, Norfolk, 275a
West Wratting, Cambs., 26b, 43a–b
Westbourne Grove, Westminster, Gr. London, 121b
Westerham, Kent, 192a
Westleton, Suffolk, 310a
Westminster, City of, Gr. London, 68a, 121a–126b; King's Weigh House Chapel, xvb, 69a, 123b–125a; Providence Chapel, Titchfield Street, 170b, 347b; Westminster Central Hall, 125b; Westminster Chapel, xvb, 69a, 122b, 123a–b, 127b, 131a; see also Bayswater; Paddington; St John's Wood
Weston Colville, Cambs., Weston Green, 43a
Westoning, Beds., 25a
Westwoodside, Lincs., 211a
Wethersfield, Essex, 67a
Weybridge, Surrey, 315b, 328a
Whaplode, Lincs., 228a
Whaplode Drove, Lincs., 228a
Whatlington, Sussex, 329b–330a, 358a
Wheathampstead, Herts., 148b
Whepstead, Suffolk, xvib, 278b, 310a
Whight's Corner, Suffolk, 309b
Whinburgh, Norfolk, 275a
White Roothing, Essex, White Roding, 67a
Whitefield Tabernacle, Gr. London, 90a, 95b–96a
Whitstable, Kent, 192a–b
Whittlesey, Cambs., 43b
Whittlesford, Cambs., 43b
Wicken, Cambs., 43b–44a
Wickham Bishops, Essex, 63a, 131a
Wickham Market, Suffolk, 310b–311a
Wickhambrook, Suffolk, xvib, 278a, 310b, 311a–b
Widford, Herts., 148b
Wiggenhall St Mary Magdalen, Norfolk, 275a
Wilby, Norfolk, 264b
Wilden, Beds., 25b
Wildmore, Lincs., 228a
Willey Green, Surrey, 326b
Willingdon, Sussex, 358a
Willingham, Cambs., 26a, 40a, 44a–46a
Willoughton, Lincs., 228a
Wilshamstead, Beds., 25b

Wilstone, Herts., 144b
Winchelsea, Sussex, 329b, 346b
Winchmore Hill, Gr. London, xva, 68b, 81b–82a
Wingham, Kent, xvb, 161b, 192b–193b
Winwick, Hunts., 151a, 160a–b
Wisbech, Cambs., 46a–b
Wisbech St Mary, Cambs., 46b
Wisborough Green, Sussex, 358a
Wissett, Suffolk, 311a
Wistow, Hunts., 160b
Witchford, Cambs., 46b
Witham, Essex, 47b, 67a–b
Withersfield, Suffolk, 311a
Withyham, Sussex, 358a; Groombridge, 329b, 358a
Witley, Surrey, 328a
Witnesham, Suffolk, 311a
Witton, Norfolk, 275a
Wivelsfield, Sussex, 329b, 358b–359a
Wivenhoe, Essex, 47b, 67b
Woburn, Beds., 12a, 25b
Woking, Surrey, 328a–b
Wooburn, Bucks., 327b
Wood Dalling, Norfolk, 275a
Wood End, Ardeley, Herts., 128a
Wood End, Hemel Hempstead, Herts., 136a
Wood End, Pertenhall, Beds., xva, 1b, 16a–18a
Wood Green, Gr. London, 89b–90a
Woodbridge, Suffolk, 98b, 278a, 311a–313b
Woodbridge Chapel, Gr. London, 98b
Woodford, Gr. London, 111b
Woodford Green, Gr. London, 69b, 111b–112a
Woodhall Spa, Lincs., 228a–b
Woodham Ferrers, Essex, 67b
Woodhurst, Hunts., 150a
Woodton, Norfolk, 275b
Woolwich, Gr. London, 82b–83b
Wootton, Beds., 25b
Worlaby, Lincs., 228b
Worplesdon, Surrey, 323b, 328b
Worstead, Norfolk, 229b, 267a, 275b
Worthing, Sussex, 330a, 359b
Wortwell, Norfolk, 276a–b
Wrangle, Lincs., 228b
Wrentham, Suffolk, xvib, 278a, 313b–314b
Wye, Kent, 193b
Wymondham, Norfolk, 229a, 277a–b

Yapton, Sussex, 330b, 359b
Yarburgh, Lincs., 228b
Yaxley, Hunts., 160b
Yelling, Hunts., 149a, 149b, 160b
Yielden, Beds., 15b
York, 29b
Yoxford, Suffolk, 314b